THE PSYCHIATRIC

PERSUASION

THE PSYCHIATRIC PERSUASION

KNOWLEDGE, GENDER, AND POWER IN MODERN AMERICA

Elizabeth Lunbeck

PRINCETON UNIVERSITY PRESS

PRINCETON, NEW JERSEY

COPYRIGHT © 1994 BY PRINCETON UNIVERSITY PRESS
PUBLISHED BY PRINCETON UNIVERSITY PRESS, 41 WILLIAM STREET,
PRINCETON, NEW JERSEY 08540
IN THE UNITED KINGDOM: PRINCETON UNIVERSITY PRESS, CHICHESTER, WEST SUSSEX

ALL PATIENTS' NAMES AND IDENTIFYING CHARACTERISTICS
HAVE BEEN ALTERED.

LIBRARY OF CONGRESS CATALOGING-IN-PUBLICATION DATA
LUNBECK, ELIZABETH.
THE PSYCHIATRIC PERSUASION : KNOWLEDGE, GENDER, AND
POWER IN MODERN AMERICA / ELIZABETH LUNBECK.
P.   CM.
INCLUDES BIBLIOGRAPHICAL REFERENCES AND INDEX.
ISBN 0-691-04804-5 (CL)
ISBN 0-691-02584-3 (PBK.)
1. PSYCHIATRY—UNITED STATES—PHILOSOPHY—HISTORY.
2. BOSTON STATE HOSPITAL. PSYCHOPATHIC DEPT.—HISTORY.
3. PSYCHOANALYSIS AND CULTURE—UNITED STATES.   I. TITLE.
[DNLM: 1. PERSUASIVE COMMUNICATION.   2. GENDER IDENTITY.   BF
637.P4 L961p 1994]
RC437.5.L89 1994
616.89'00973—dc20
DNLM/DLC
FOR LIBRARY OF CONGRESS   93-43818

THIS BOOK HAS BEEN COMPOSED IN ADOBE SABON

PRINCETON UNIVERSITY PRESS BOOKS ARE PRINTED
ON ACID-FREE PAPER AND MEET THE GUIDELINES FOR
PERMANENCE AND DURABILITY OF THE COMMITTEE ON
PRODUCTION GUIDELINES FOR BOOK LONGEVITY
OF THE COUNCIL ON LIBRARY RESOURCES

PRINTED IN THE UNITED STATES OF AMERICA
BY PRINCETON ACADEMIC PRESS

THIRD PRINTING, AND FIRST PAPERBACK PRINTING, 1995

3   5   7   9   10   8   6   4

For Gary

CONTENTS

ELEVEN

ILLUSTRATIONS

FIGURES

PLATES

Following page 182

TABLES

ACKNOWLEDGMENTS

THE COUNSEL and support of many friends and colleagues helped me write this book. I wish to thank Peter Brown, Laura Engelstein, Gerald Geison, Gerald Grob, Daniel Rodgers, my advisors, Barbara G. Rosenkrantz and Stephan Thernstrom, and my editor, Lauren Osborne, all of whom wrestled with major portions of the manuscript and offered me astute advice. I am also grateful to John Carson, Lorraine Daston, Michael Donnelly, Arthur Goldhammer, Dirk Hartog, Christopher Lasch, Arno Mayer, and Charles Rosenberg for reading and commenting on chapters falling within their own areas of interest and expertise. Eve Niedergang, Kevin Downing, John Giggie, and Paul Kramer assisted in the final stages of research and writing. In addition, I have benefited from Joel Perlmann's advice on quantitative issues, from Jane Lincoln Taylor's informed and meticulous editing, and from the many small kindnesses extended to me by the staff of Princeton's history department.

Several friendships were particularly important to the development of this project. Bonnie Smith read many drafts, provided sage advice on intellectual and practical issues, and cheered me at critical junctures. Stephanie Engel spent countless hours discussing psychiatry with me, offering me the benefit of her insider's perspective. Peter Mandler argued through many of the book's points with me, reined in my rhetoric, and, most important, appreciated my ambitions. Finally, I owe much to the intellectual generosity and exacting vision of John W. Cell, who introduced me as an undergraduate to the historian's craft.

A number of institutions supported my research and writing. I benefited greatly from a postdoctoral fellowship at the Rutgers-Princeton Program in Mental Health Research, under the direction of David Mechanic. The University of Rochester graciously granted and helped fund a year's leave. The Charles Warren Center, Harvard University; the National Library of Medicine; and Princeton University gave me generous financial support and time to write. I thank them all.

I could not have undertaken this project without the cooperation of Miles F. Shore, who kindly granted me access to the Boston Psychopathic Hospital's patient records and smoothed the book's transit through the hospital and state bureaucracy. Richard J. Wolfe, curator of rare books and manuscripts at the Countway Library of Medicine, Boston, has been extraordinarily helpful in locating documents, manuscripts, and photographs; he and his staff made my visits to Countway productive and pleasurable. Dan De Hainaut assisted me in choosing photographs at the

Massachusetts Mental Health Center. The employees of the State Records Center, formerly located at Metropolitan State Hospital, provided welcome companionship through the years I spent immersed in Psychopathic Hospital records.

My greatest debts are familial. The unwavering support of my parents has been critical to my development as a historian. The demands and delights of daily life with my sons Danny and Sam have kept me firmly planted in the present. Their father, Gary Gerstle, has lived with this book from its inception. His contributions to it have been both dramatic and subtle, too varied for me to specify adequately. His love has enriched my life beyond measure.

THE PSYCHIATRIC
PERSUASION

INTRODUCTION

W E'VE GONE PSYCHIATRIC," an astute cultural critic commented in 1930, referring to the public's growing habit of assessing human behavior along what he suggested were characteristically psychiatric lines—in terms of deviations, maladjustments, and maladaptations vis-à-vis the normal.[1] Adding variations, deficits, assets, and liabilities to this catalogue of concepts, other contemporary students of the psychiatric persuasion elaborated on the metric mode of thinking that informed such concepts. Within psychiatry, they explained, the normal was no longer sharply distinguished from the abnormal. Rather, the same mechanisms of mind and habits of personality, the same sorts of deficits and capacities—compounded, to be sure, in different measure— were thought to yield both the normal character and the psychopathic deviant as well as a range of types in between. Psychiatrists were less interested in insanity than in normality and its variations. Who was normal, who abnormal—this was what drew their interest and guided their practice.

In the early years of the twentieth century, as these after-the-fact appraisals suggest, American psychiatry was fundamentally transformed from a discipline concerned primarily with insanity to one equally concerned with normality, as focused on normal persons and their problems as on the recognized insane. Late-nineteenth-century alienists, as psychiatrists' disciplinary forebears called themselves, practiced what many of them agreed was a marginal specialty in large, custodial asylums, isolated from the nation's centers of population and from medicine's main currents. Aligning themselves with science and the forces of progress, a number of early-twentieth-century psychiatrists envisioned greater possibilities for their specialty and set out to remake it. They established new kinds of institutions, modeled on hospitals, not asylums. They successfully lobbied for new laws that would yield patients who were not insane but nearly normal. And, most significant, they laid new conceptual foundations for their specialty, delineating a realm of everyday concerns—sex, marriage, womanhood and manhood; work, ambition, worldly failure; habits, desires, inclinations—as properly psychiatric and bringing them within their purview. In practice and in print, they created a new psychiatry, one that is the predecessor of psychiatry as we know it today, a discipline that deals as much with everyday problems as with established mental diseases. They brought psychiatry and psychiatric thinking from the asylum into the cultural mainstream, where it has remained.

This book examines the process by which psychiatrists in the early twentieth century effected this momentous shift in their discipline's foundations and fortunes. Focusing on one institution, the Boston Psychopathic Hospital, it chronicles the evolution of psychiatric thought and practice during this period of disciplinary reorganization. Like the psychiatric science it reconstructs, a science that took shape in practice, it is based in large part on patients' case records, records that for the first time documented what the French philosopher of the human sciences Michel Foucault has called "the everyday individuality of everybody."[2] Pressing the Psychopathic Hospital's rich archive into historical service, it explores the nature of the psychiatric encounter from the perspective of both patient and psychiatrist. It analyzes psychiatry's knowledge problem—the elusiveness of certainty that so frustrated psychiatrists— as well as the categories they fashioned to address it. And it follows psychiatrists and their female colleagues, the psychiatric social workers, into the realm of the everyday, showing how they turned the issues with which others presented them— sexual delinquency and aggression, marital relations, men's characters, women's desires—into the stuff of their science.

In this book, I locate the sources of psychiatry's cultural authority not in institutions but in the discipline's conceptual apparatuses. Many critics of psychiatry have located its power in its institutional manifestations— asylums, hospitals, prisons—even as they have proposed (and have somewhat paradoxically demonstrated) that psychiatry in its formal guise has been and remains marginal and open to attack, that its position in the medical hierarchy has been and remains embarrassingly low, and that its science and practices have been and remain open to charges of fraudulence.[3] I propose here that the discipline's authority instead be located in the spread of a psychiatric perspective that has little to do with psychiatrists' institutional power. Employing a rough metric of the normal, this perspective would constantly assess individuals' normality in any number of dimensions (behavioral, sexual, characterological), arraying them on a spectrum ranging from the abnormal to the normal. Committed to a program of bringing their specialty's insights to bear on every human endeavor, early-twentieth-century psychiatrists mined both the descriptive dimension of the normal (which referred to what is most common) and the evaluative one (which referred to what ought to be), attending to life's routine aspects and issuing judgments concerning them.

The disciplinary trajectory I trace also differs from those common in the sociological and historical literature of psychiatry. Reconstructing a process of discipline formation that was full of contingencies, unexpected outcomes, and puzzling encounters that have dropped from psychiatry's official memory, I not only attend little to the neat narratives of social control favored by the discipline's critics but also barely register the more flattering genealogies of disciplinary authority that either highlight founding figures and movements—Sigmund Freud, George Beard, mental hygiene—or gesture toward what one commentator has called "grand cultural affinities," like the well-documented triumph of the therapeutic. Aspects of all are to varying degrees significant, but none can account for psychiatry's turn-of-the-century epistemological transformation.[4] My focus is local and intensive. I examine a psychiatric stance that did not result from a coherently articulated strategy but took its shape in programs—psychiatrists' statements about and reflections on their discipline, its aims and meanings—and in practice, in the day-to-day management of patients and of the institution in which they were confined.[5]

Early-twentieth-century psychiatrists worked within a disciplinary perspective in the making. Discipline, as both a mode of power and a congeries of procedures for producing knowledge, figures centrally in my account, for the psychiatric program I reconstruct gravitated less toward social control than toward the point at which knowledge and power fostered the conditions conducive to the realization of both. Power without knowledge was illusory, a principle voiced by one psychiatrist in his candid admission that locking up bothersome persons they could not classify was "a practical solution of convenience" but "not a solution of the problem." It simply meant, he continued, that "we are not able to solve this problem."[6] Disciplinary power, as conceived of by Foucault, is not fixed and easily identified, like the juridical power that he argues it largely displaces, but is dispersed throughout the social body; this was the conception of power that Psychopathic Hospital psychiatrists both promoted and exploited as they redefined the conventions governing commitment and confinement. Centering on the norm and trading in normalizing judgments, disciplinary thinking classifies individuals hierarchically in terms of their capacities in relation to one another, a project in which psychiatrists eagerly joined. And disciplinary techniques, most importantly the examination, bring individuals into the domain of science, constituting them as cases while subjecting them to disciplinary surveillance. Psychiatrists both employed and theorized the procedure, an unequal but productive encounter that produced new forms of knowledge, offering the inquisitor access to previously unexamined aspects of everyday life. Psychiatric knowledge thus took shape in the hospital, in a complex field of power relations, but, I suggest, it is not reducible to those relations; psychiatrists served knowledge as much as—in many circumstances, more than—power. That their disciplinary project did not create docile, normalized subjects would not have surprised them, for their aim was rather to nurture proclivities for self-scrutiny, a project in which generations of practitioners would join.[7]

Gender, largely ignored by Foucault, also figures importantly in my account of psychiatry's transformation. Gender conflict, real and rhetorical, shaped day-to-day practice and colored psychiatrists' and social workers' reflections upon it. It was encoded in the categories that ordered their observations, sometimes overtly (as in the category of the hypersexual) and sometimes silently (as in the category of manic-depressive insanity). Finally, the project of everyday life—which invariably led to some aspect of sex—saw practitioners of both specialties confronting gender in an unusually direct and sometimes unsettling way. The manifest story here traces the repudiation of the Victorian gender synthesis, with a reorganized, recognizably modern system of practices, prescriptions, and representations taking its place. This is the story of the advent of sexual modernity, a modernity that many have suggested psychiatry enabled, even promoted. Examined in its particulars, however, the transformation appears less thorough, the modernity more equivocal than psychiatrists promised. This was at least in part because both they and social workers brought to the project notions, drawn from their own experience, of men's and women's natures and rights that they unreflectingly incorporated into the roughly specified norms they produced. The territory they covered was fraught with gender tension; it would be hard to overstate the centrality of gender to the practice of a specialty that its own most prominent spokesmen could characterize variously as "an exigent mistress, never satisfied" and "the Cinderella of medicine," or about which they could complain—most weirdly of all—that others thought it "a pin-up girl."[8] Still, the workings of gender in psychiatric and social work practice were complex. Women as well as men could put the interests of their professions ahead of what might appear in retrospect to have been their more immediate gender interests.

A word on my stance toward psychiatrists and their project. Although this book is loosely organized around a Foucauldian notion of discipline, I have not adopted the antipsychiatry perspective with which his work is often associated. My interest has been to trace, not to condemn, the consolidation of a recognizably modern psychiatric point of view in early-twentieth-century institutional practice. This stated, it is worth noting that psychiatrists have figured among their discipline's harshest critics. The psychiatrists examined here tended to denigrate their forebears as they went about establishing their own claims to truth; their disciplinary descendants would in turn consign them and their practices to psychiatry's prescientific past.[9] Psychiatrists' sense of history was at once heightened and foreshortened. They were constantly chronicling their discipline's progress; they were united in their conviction that its Dark Ages were just behind them. Aware of his colleagues' tendency to judge their forebears harshly, one prominent practitioner speculated in 1921 "that one hundred years from now a speaker, reviewing the progress of psychiatry, will see a great deal to

criticize in our present day organization." He continued: "In his enlightenment he may wonder that we could be blind to certain things," but then he
reminded his readers that they were themselves participants in the process
of disciplinary self-scrutiny that would eventually bring history's harsh
judgments upon them.[10] The historian no more than the psychiatrist, it
seems to me, should claim to speak from a position of final enlightenment.
Psychiatry's truths are still emerging.

PART ONE
FROM INSANITY TO NORMALITY

ONE

PSYCHIATRY BETWEEN OLD AND NEW

IN JUNE 1912, the Boston Psychopathic Hospital formally opened its doors, signifying to the city's reform-minded psychiatrists that their profession had come of age. An imposing, four-story brick building modeled on the German psychiatrist Emil Kraepelin's Munich-based clinic, the hospital represented in concrete form all that was new in psychiatry. It was, in the estimation of its proponents, closer in conception, design, and operation to the general hospital than to the isolated, overcrowded, and scientifically backward asylum. An urban institution, located on the outer edges of the Harvard Medical School's complex of buildings and hospitals, it was easily accessible from all the city's districts, a short streetcar ride from its center. Relatively small, it accommodated just over one hundred patients but had on its staff approximately twenty physicians and nearly as many medical interns, significantly more than asylums housing many more patients. Its purpose and province scientific, it was intended more for the observation and examination of patients than for their long-term incarceration, more for the treatment of those afflicted by acute and potentially curable mental diseases than for that of those recognized to be insane. The hospital presented psychiatrists with a novel arrangement of material and intellectual resources—from its laboratories and proximity to libraries and lecture halls to the "nearly normal" patients it attracted—which they assiduously pressed into service as they went about remaking their discipline.

Commentators of all persuasions have noted that at the turn of the century psychiatry was somehow transformed, agreeing that the discipline that had in the nineteenth century been visible only at the margins—in the asylum—had by the second decade of the twentieth century established itself at the center of social and cultural life. Psychopathic Hospital psychiatrists were instrumental in effecting this shift in their discipline's fortunes, employing maneuvers that freed them from the abnormal and bizarre and brought them up against what was normal. In published papers, professional addresses, and, most important, in day-to-day practice, they fashioned a psychiatry of normality—of life's routine aspects—that would become dominant within the American branch of the profession by the 1920s. Their attempts to remake their specialty had local accents and national resonances; the psychiatry of the twenties, which was as concerned with mental health as with disease, as focused on "social maladjustment and even unhappiness" as on insanity, was a discipline forged in many crucibles.[1] Prominent psychiatrists in other cities—San Francisco, Baltimore, New York, Ann Arbor—were taking the profession in the same direction, establishing similar institutions, setting similar policies, and publishing articles that advocated similar perspectives. Still, Boston was, by many accounts, the nation's psychiatric capital throughout the first twenty years of the century, the Psychopathic Hospital the newest star in its firmament of illustrious privately and publicly funded institutions that were routinely classed under the rubric "charitable."[2]

Known as "the paradise of charities," the city could boast of a distinguished lineage in the realm of public welfare.[3] From Charles Dickens's pleasing appraisal of its institutions—in 1842, he visited the Perkins Institute and the Institution for the Insane—as "as nearly perfect, as the most considerate wisdom, benevolence, and humanity, can make them";[4] through the proud catalogue that appeared in the city's official history, published in 1880, of its 177 voluntary organizations, a broadly construed category encompassing universities, hospitals, relief societies, and homes for needy individuals of all sorts;[5] to, in the new century, the proliferation of organizations and institutions testifying to the "quickening" of the citizenry's social conscience:[6] All offered proper Bostonians occasion to reflect on their city's superiority. Massachusetts had early taken the lead in providing for the care of the insane at public expense, in 1833 establishing an institution—the Worcester State Lunatic Hospital—that would serve as a prototype for many other state asylums; it had also established, in 1863, the first state board of charities, a centralizing move quickly emulated by other states.[7] By the century's end, twenty-nine public and private institutions, clustered in the state's more populous eastern half, held nearly ten thousand inmates; by 1919, Massachusetts had attained the dubious distinction of having the highest psychiatric-institution admission rate in the nation.[8] In any account of American psychiatry's progress, Boston and Massachusetts figured prominently.

The Post-Victorian City

Turn-of-the-century Boston was a city rich in contrasts. A compact, tightly packed metropolis of five hundred thousand, its prosperous neighborhoods were as elegant and its poor neighborhoods as squalid as any to be found in the nation. The disparity between the grand, bow-fronted brownstones that lined the broad avenues of the recently settled Back Bay, enclave of the city's Yankee elite, and the tenement houses, crowded with recent Italian, Irish, and Jewish immigrants, that abutted the crooked, narrow streets and alleys of the North End testified graphically to the class and racial divisions that marked the city's political and social life. In the political arena, the last years of the nineteenth century saw Yankee patricians and working-class Irish pols incongruously yet powerfully allied in this best-governed of cities, but the new century witnessed the demise of Yankee leadership and the ascendancy of a factional, corrupt, and patronage-ridden Irish machine. Socially, the city was home to the legendary Brahmin aristocracy, of all the nation's urban elites possibly the most persistent, politically engaged, professionally active, and intellectually distinguished. Yet Boston was increasingly a city of immigrants. A small army of alarmist investigators pored over state and national census figures, and gleaned from them confirmation of what any city dweller knew—that a third of the city's populace was foreign-born, and another third was of foreign extraction. As these harbingers of doom never tired of reminding their readers, three of the four faces a stroller would likely encounter on a sojourn through the city would be recognizably foreign.[9]

Prompted by civic pride or xenophobia, fired by muckraking zeal or reformist sentiments, a number of turn-of-the-century Bostonians took stock of their city and its place in the nation. A few wrote celebratory histories, chronicling the city's distinctive and distinguished past, and closed them soberly with examinations of the city's rapidly changing racial mix and its baleful political consequences.[10] Others walked the streets and studied the inhabitants of the city's slum neighborhoods, some issuing calls for economic and social justice and others producing precisely rendered accounts of daily life in the city's poorest quarters.[11] Industrious social scientists culled statistics from a flood of government reports, creatively partitioning and recombining them in such a way that tramping, crime, delinquency, drunkenness, and insanity—vices long associated with the urban poor—appeared dangerously on the increase. As they surveyed the state of their city and society, whether lamenting with a bitterly nostalgic backward glance the passing of civilization as they knew it—like the weary Henry Adams—or looking ahead to see in it signs of the divisive and leveling modernity that was sure to come, these diverse commentators could agree only that the moment was one of crisis.[12]

A city of distinctive neighborhoods, Boston still retained "its old-time town feeling."[13] The horizons of many of its inhabitants were bound by the several streets they traversed each day as they went to work and to market. Yet the signs of modernity were everywhere apparent. On the streets, the new noises of the automobile mingled with the familiar pounding clatter of the iron-shod horse. Electric trolleys carried passengers, for five cents, at twice the speed of the horse-drawn cars they were gradually replacing. Incandescent mantles lit streets that first lanterns, then the naked flames of gas lights, had once illuminated. And, in the homes of the moderately well-to-do, telephones were beginning to appear.[14]

The smells and sounds of the city changed as its infrastructure and economy assumed more recognizably modern shape. New ordinances silenced the late-nineteenth-century peddlers' street cries—"Wild duck, wild duck," "Any old rags or bottles," "Fresh mackerel," "Sixteen bananas for a quarter"—as well as the hand organ and the street band. "The delectable music of the flute, violin and harp which played trios in front of grog-shops is not heard," noted one observer with a touch of nostalgia, lamenting that the shriek of the streetcar's wheels was drowning out the twitter of the sparrow, and that the stench of burning gasoline and oil was supplanting the sweet smell of horse manure.[15] Still, the harsh jangling of glass milk bottles continued to rouse the wealthy from their slumbers just as the bell-like noises of tin milk cans had in the eighties and nineties.[16] Cows could still be seen grazing in the pastures of South Boston.[17] And the pungent odors of leather and hides from the city's hundreds of shoemaking factories, the sweet smells of chocolate from its Dorchester-based candy factories, and the aroma of roasting coffee from its downtown district filled the air as they had for years.[18]

The city was, and remained, extraordinarily dirty. Residents of its poorest districts pitched trash onto filthy streets.[19] Some of the wealthy piled their rubbish helter-skelter in dark alleys.[20] Children dropped banana peels and orange rinds on public ways already littered with ashes and papers. Malodorous, open-topped garbage carts plied the city's fashionable thoroughfares and dingy alleys alike. Manure—on streets and in stables—bred flies that disturbed the sensibilities of some and threatened the health of all. Insects swarmed and cats crawled over foodstuffs in the city's poorer markets. Ignoring spittoons, tobacco-chewing men spat everywhere—on floors, streets, even the velvet carpets of railroad cars. Smoke belched from factories, settling over the metropolis like a dirty cloud, blackening clothing and dirtying buildings inside and out.[21] "Filth of all kinds is continually tracked and blown into our homes and carried in on our clothing," complained the fastidious ladies of the Women's Municipal League in the midst of their relentless campaign against dirt.[22]

The ladies lived apart from the worst of the city's filth in the fashionable Beacon Hill and Back Bay districts, on streets and avenues—Marlborough, Commonwealth, Hereford, Clarendon—graced with names meant to evoke associations with aristocratic England. Beacon Hill had been home to the elite since the early nineteenth century, when Brahmin real estate speculators had developed it, erecting family mansions that stand to this day.[23] Between the late 1850s and 1880, the city, in conjunction with private investors, had filled in the Back Bay, a muddy marsh turned cesspool, and wealthy Bostonians quickly abandoned the old South End for the new area's fine residences, churches, and public institutions.[24] There stood the Boston Public Library and the Museum of Fine Arts, monuments to Brahmin gentility and class stewardship.[25] Worries that the festering muck on which the Back Bay was built would adversely affect the health of its new citizens proved groundless. On every measure—infant mortality, deaths due to diphtheria, consumption, and typhoid fever—they ranked among the city's healthiest, although this was likely due as much, one self-satisfied observer noted, "to the character of the population" as to the spacious conditions in which they lived and the sunshine that brightened the district like few others.[26]

The city's South End, like the Back Bay, was built on landfill, and it, too, had been planned as a fashionable quarter for the affluent. By midcentury, developers were building narrow, high-stooped, "swell-front" brick town-houses on orderly, uniform grids of streets modeled on those of Georgian London, and for twenty years or so, until the 1870s, the city's wealthy made the South End their home. After the panic of 1873, however, commercial establishments began to encroach on the area's exclusively residential character and developers began to line the area's main avenues with tenements that attracted the city's Irish and Jewish poor. By the turn of the century, the appurtenances of the well-to-do—the "liveried coachmen and white-capped nursemaids airing their charges" of one sociologist's memory—were long gone, the rich having fled the area "like rats."[27] Once-elegant private homes were turned into lodging houses whose exteriors still betokened gentility; even the most alert passersby might have taken them for the homes of the moderately rich.[28] Elsewhere the signs of decline were more evident. In the area's meanest precincts, families crowded into miserable two- and three-room tenement flats in which, as Mary Antin would later write in a lyrical memoir of her passage through Boston's slums, they slept "two to four in a bed, in windowless bedrooms."[29] The life of the ghetto was to be found on the streets. There, shawl-clad older women bustled from one pushcart to another as they did their marketing; tastefully dressed young working women paraded about, displaying their finery; young children played tag and older children tempted fate by stepping in front of oncoming trolleys; and "thirsty souls" passed, seeking the solace of drink in the district's many saloons.[30] Between the Back Bay and the South End, adjacent districts, there was little commerce. The genteel serenity of the former was worlds apart from the insistent clamor of the latter. As a girl, Antin had admired her Back Bay schoolmates, but from a distance. "Innocent of envy," she had yet "discovered something inimitable in the way the Back Bay girls carried themselves."[31]

The city's North and West Ends were, if anything, further from the imagined common life of the metropolis than was the South End. The South End's theaters, churches, and public institutions drew a diverse crowd, and many of the area's residents walked to work in the shops and offices of the city's central business district. The North and West Ends, by contrast, were isolated, almost foreign territory.[32] One Yankee neatly disposed of the North End, the city's oldest residential quarter, with the observation that it offered "but little that is interesting at present."[33] "Invaded" (as the immoderate usage of the day had it) by successive waves of foreign immigrants—first Irish, then Jewish and Italian—who had displaced its original "Anglo-Saxon" inhabitants, the area and its buildings, our Yankee sniffed, had taken on "something of the seedy and degraded air of those who inhabit them."[34] By any measure, the area was extremely poor. Its mostly Italian and Jewish inhabitants occupied cramped quarters in dark, ramshackle, poorly ventilated tenements that faced onto narrow alleys and courts. Its death rate was the city's highest; scarlet fever, diphtheria, croup, pneumonia, and whooping cough killed a disproportionate number of its residents. Stillbirths were common.[35] Families scrambled to make ends meet. Fully half of the Italian men worked for low wages as laborers, and a number of the Jewish men ran dingy basement shops. Women worked in the garment trades for meager sums—three to five dollars a week. The area's lodging houses drew a "floating population" of homeless men begging on street corners, journeymen traveling in search of employment, and sailors on shore leave, who could be seen lounging about the district's many saloons or loafing in its squares.[36]

Yet even those who portrayed the area as a classic slum could not help amassing evidence that throws light on a world of prosaic comings and goings, of delights and diversions beyond their dour comprehension. The streets of the North End and the neighboring West End, which housed a mélange of immigrants as well as a substantial settlement of African-Americans, were alive with activity day and night, summer and winter. Pushcarts piled high with artfully arranged displays of fruits, vegetables, fishes, and crabs crowded busy streets and sidewalks. Jewish merchants hawked their wares, enticing customers with promises of "Fresh bagels" and "Fish! Fresh fish." Old women, knitting needles in hand, sat on doorsteps, trading gossip with neighbors. Men gathered in large numbers to do the same by day; nights they spent drinking and gaming in saloons. Gangs of boys congregated in doorways to shoot craps, and their elders passed the hours playing "Pinnacle" (pinochle) and games of chance. Girls met their lovers in coal bins, woodsheds, and dark alleys. Cheap hotels and kitchen barrooms in private houses catered to illicit lovers. Brothels, evangelical missions, marionette shows, burlesque queens, and saloons in the background, the young cheerfully went about their business, oblivious to the street's many corruptions, a West-Ender would later recall. The constant bustle of activity meant the streets were safe at any hour.[37]

In their more sanguine moments proper Bostonians could dismiss the inhabitants of the North and West Ends as so many strange, poverty-stricken immigrants. The place seemed more of the Old World than the New; the foreign voices, costumes, and quaint habits of its newly arrived residents roused from the most charitable of visitors visions of exotic foreign lands. Such immigrants were, in the estimation of those who considered themselves their social betters, at least properly domestic. They married (but separated perhaps too readily); they delighted in their children (but had perhaps too many); they carefully supervised their daughters (in this the Italians seemed especially given to excess); and they went as families to churches and synagogues, theaters and art galleries. In all, they were respectful of patriarchy. Her poverty aside, the Portuguese wife might have been a Back Bay matron, entertaining her lady friends with a glass of wine and a homemade cake. "In the simpler round of domestic life," noted an approving student of their mores, "the people are to a surprising degree without reproach."[38]

The same could not be said for the native-born, "American" inhabitants of the city's South and West End lodging-house districts. If the mores of the immigrants, in spirit if not in practice, harkened back to an earlier age, those of the lodger class presaged the future. Young and single, they appeared at every turn to spurn the conventions of domesticity. Some fifteen hundred women ran lodging houses in Boston in 1900, having signed leases on the abandoned homes of the rich, still crammed with their former owners' plush furniture and tapestries, to try their luck at what seemed a tolerable, even pleasant way of making a living. Half of these landladies, as they were known, were widowed, and among them were many whose circumstances had once been better: wives of sea captains, newspaper editors, shoe manufacturers.[39] Their lodgers—seventeen to twenty in a house— were newcomers, men and women who had left the farms and towns of New England for the city's seemingly boundless opportunities. Among the men were well-educated physicians and dentists, respectable clerks and salesmen, students and librarians, skilled machinists and carpenters, and black waiters, cooks, and barbers. They lived beside their female counterparts, who worked as stenographers, bookkeepers, saleswomen, and waitresses, eking meager livings out of wages that amounted to perhaps half of what the men could earn.[40]

The mores of this *population nomade* held a weird fascination for those who investigated their purportedly promiscuous comings and goings.[41] The lodgers' daily trek to the downtown district's offices and shops left the streets deserted. They returned in the evening to take their meals not in homes but in the cafés and basement dining rooms that were thickly clustered on the district's main thoroughfares. The streets then came alive as the lodgers stepped out, making the rounds of the South End's many hotel barrooms, illegal speakeasies, poolrooms, theaters, and dance halls in the company of chance acquaintances and new lovers. "Pleasure seekers fill the sidewalks . . . the hurdy-gurdy jingles merrily; and the street is changed for a time into a sort of fair," noted one observer with disdain, for all he, and a host of others, could see in this lively tableau were "the fascinations of vice."[42]

Condemnations of metropolitan vice had long been staples of the reformer's critical apparatus: lurid sketches of the drunk's depredations; gruesome accounts of quarrelers turned murderers; sensational evocations of thieves and gamblers who would prey on the unsuspecting. In the lodging-house district, however, intemperance was rare, murders were few, and gambling, while not unknown, was largely confined to "playing for drinks in pool rooms."[43] The melodramatic conventions that earlier observers had fashioned in their confrontations with the Victorian city were of little use when it came to describing the peculiar moral landscape of the South End, for by all accounts its inhabitants came from good families and worked at respectable occupations for regular, if not entirely adequate, wages. Their failings were not of character, ambition, or education; in these they were commonly considered far superior to the city's tenement dwellers. Yet, several sociologists observed, while the latter cultivated the simple but enduring joys of family life, women and men of the lodger class, fashioning themselves pseudo-bohemians, refused to marry and evinced little desire to reproduce. To lodgers, the city was not a site of moral and physical danger but "a veritable elysium of opportunity"—of chance meetings, temporary alliances, artificial excitements, and "free-and-easy relations" between the sexes—that they enthusiastically exploited. Annoyed and puzzled by the district's promiscuous mixing of the good with the bad, observers wavered between, on the one hand, somewhat improbably characterizing all its women as predatory prostitutes (and the occasional man as a roué) and, on the other, from a less gendered perspective, seeing both the women and the men as harbingers of the coming triumph of selfish individuality over responsibility to home and family.[44]

In the sociologists' appraisals of the district's inhabitants and their mores one can glimpse the more general history of decline that contemporaries were piecing together in the first two decades of the new century. Adumbrated in countless popular and social scientific books and articles, this history told of the intensifying crisis of the family—the rising divorce rate, the falling birthrate, the lowering of moral standards—that attended the demise of the traditional, highly regulated, and morally cohesive nineteenth-century neighborhood. The disintegrative forces of industry, "the purveyors of recreation," feminism—all were loosening the bonds of family and tradition, setting (and here gender enters the story) women adrift. Commentators chided men for favoring the ephemeral pleasures of illicit unions and material goods over marriage's many burdens, but they focused most of their attention—their investigations, interventions, and condemnations—on women and their newly troubled relation to the home. The single, wage-earning young woman—the kind of woman who lived in Boston's South End—bore most of the opprobrium heaped on her gender, regardless of age and class. An object of reformers' concern and pity in the nineteenth century, she had become, in the turn-of-the-century sociological literature, a hardbitten prostitute who preyed on innocent country lads. Sophisticated, self-seeking, and promiscuous, she was an emblem of fragmented, anomic modernity, a frightening embodiment of the "moral uncertainty" of the times.[45]

Inscribed in the city's official histories is a differently inflected account of woman's fortunes, one that celebrates what the sociologists so roundly condemned. The woman of 1880, as featured in the celebratory *Memorial History of Boston*, is narrowly drawn, a prosperous Yankee matron. "Exemplary in her conduct as a wife and mother," she was reserved in manner, pure in morals, subdued in dress, and orderly in housekeeping. Her home "a radiating centre of goodness and happiness," she exemplified Boston womanhood, an identity on which women outside the familial nexus— "old maids," working women, "lost women"—could make only a feeble claim.[46] From the perspective of 1930, this was a quaintly admiring characterization of the city's women, appropriate for a time that saw women "tightly shut in by their circumstances." In a volume marking the city's tercentenary, Frances G. Curtis, a Radcliffe-educated single woman active in reform and political affairs, celebrated Boston women's "racy individuality" and their new immersion in "the hurly-burly of life." She trumpeted their accomplishments in the public sphere—in education, religion, the arts, municipal politics, medicine, social work, and the law—and noted their entry into all manner of paid occupations, from manufacturing to the new fields created by the invention of the typewriter and telephone. No longer satisfied to "live idly," waiting for a husband to appear, Curtis's exemplary woman was the "independent girl in her own apartment, working hard at her chosen job, . . . answerable only to her push-button and calling tube." Free to choose her "own mode of life," she inhabited a landscape of personal opportunity, not, like her predecessors, moral danger.[47]

The sociologists' narrative of apocalyptic decline was part of a broader response to the breakup of the Victorian gender synthesis. Articulated in the first two decades of the century, it told of the chaos that attended woman's movement away from the home to which Victorianism had confined her, in ideology if not in fact. Curtis's tale of heady emancipation belongs to a later period, a time of accommodation in which a new gender synthesis had already taken shape. This synthesis granted women limited equality, provided they played by men's rules—that they must be sexy and flirtatious before marriage, sexy and faithful after. Although differing in emphasis, the accounts of both sociologist and feminist were linear; neither

captured the tumult—the contingencies, contradictions, and ambiva-
lences—that marked the waning of Victorianism and the birth of modernity. Between decline at the one explanatory extreme and emancipation at
the other, however, it is possible to sketch the contours of a fractious,
decades-long, and societywide reorganization of personal identities and
gender relations, in which a number of psychiatrists were central players,
that left few aspects of everyday experience untouched. This reorganization consigned the *Memorial History*'s Yankee matron to the distant past,
freeing her daughters from the home's narrow confines while at the same
time subjecting them to new forms of regulation and control. This reorganization also brought a constellation of related concerns—sexual mores,
marriage, the family—under sustained scrutiny, subtly transforming them
in ways that the "epic register" of crisis favored by historians of the period
cannot convey.[48]

The Psychiatrist as "Philosopher of the Social Life"

Boston Psychopathic Hospital psychiatrists, like their reform-minded contemporaries, warned of crisis as they surveyed the city and its increasingly
diverse and unruly inhabitants.[49] Eager to secure formal institutional and
political power, a number of them outlined an ambitious program that
addressed a range of issues already defined as pressing—immigration, poverty, crime, delinquency, drunkenness—and demonstrated how each was
amenable to psychiatric intervention. Well versed in the developing idiom
of progressivism, they spoke of science, expertise, efficiency, adjustment,
and control—vigorous terms resonant with purpose and power. In retrospect, they appear the perfect progressives, their program squaring neatly
with, and sometimes providing exemplary instances for, narratives chronicling the rise of this or that—of experts, of social control, of the therapeutic ethos, of the welfare state. Indeed, their collective extramural endeavors, in the just-emerging fields of eugenics, juvenile delinquency, psychological testing, public health, military psychiatry, and criminology, might
have amounted to a textbook of progressive reform. Elmer Ernest Southard, Herman Adler, Lawson G. Lowrey, Abraham Myerson, Alfred P.
Noyes, Harry C. Solomon, A. Warren Stearns, Douglas A. Thom, and the
psychologist Robert M. Yerkes: these practitioners, associated with the
hospital in its first decade, were widely acknowledged as leaders and inno-
vators within the profession, locally and—some of them—nationally.

Although recognized by their contemporaries for their research, institutional leadership, and contributions to various reform efforts, these psychiatrists formulated a disciplinary agenda around everyday concerns that has
proven of more enduring significance than their explicitly reform-oriented

program. Largely hidden from historical view, this agenda, elaborated on in the course of the twentieth century, has secured their profession what cultural authority it enjoys today. It did not result from a coherently articulated strategy, but took shape piecemeal, in print and in day-to-day practice.[50] Discussing and diagnosing patients, formulating and enforcing regulations and policies, in chance and structured interactions among themselves and with other members of institutional staffs, psychiatrists collectively envisioned, and realized, new possibilities for themselves and their specialty, articulating a psychiatric program of the everyday. Their interest in life's normal, routine aspects distinguished them, as they told it, from their do-nothing disciplinary forebears, who had shown themselves content to superintend the insane in large institutions, attracting public censure for their efforts and condemning their discipline to marginal status. Psychopathic Hospital psychiatrists, by contrast, imagined themselves men of action, bringing their disciplinary perspective to bear on "practically the entire human world." From the public arena of politics to the privacy of domestic life; in disciplines as diverse as sociology, economics, and ethics; in pursuits ranging from social work to education: to all, the psychiatrist would preach his "gospel about mind," illuminating what had been shrouded in darkness. The difficulty facing the ambitious psychiatrist, as Southard—the first director and intellectual impresario of the hospital—so bluntly put it, was that "the chronic insane form a comparatively small group of unfortunates."[51] Turn-of-the-century psychiatrists' singular achievement lay in surmounting this limitation, in envisioning a psychiatry of the everyday and in fashioning the conceptual tools necessary to realize it.

A keenly felt sense of professional inferiority underwrote their ambitions. "American psychiatry has lagged," Southard charged in 1913, arguing that the German-speaking countries, their workers imbued with a scientific spirit sustained by a network of state-supported universities, clinics, and laboratories, were leading the world in the production of "new tests, new methods, and new laboratory ideas." Alzheimer, Bleuler, Freud, Jung, Kraepelin, Nissl, Wernicke, and Ziehen: the Germans' eminence in psychiatry, Southard reported, was altogether unrivaled. American psychiatry, by contrast, had achieved what he called a "perfected custodial state." The large asylums—in Massachusetts each housing between five hundred and one thousand patients—for which nineteenth-century reformers had campaigned were now widely condemned as understaffed and overcrowded, institutions in which persons were not treated but, rather, subjected to unfair restraint. The science to which his profession could lay claim, Southard charged, was underdeveloped and derivative, its truths mere "elaborations of the obvious" and its bent over-somatic and "unduly neurologized."[52]

Southard maintained that were American psychiatry to excel, it would not do so solely in the realm of science as practiced by the Germans, in laboratories and institutes divorced from hospitals and patients. It would follow a different course, achieving distinction by means of a "medico-social" synthesis. It would define laboratory problems and seek solutions on the wards—in patients, the psychiatric investigator's "living material"—and explore not only the structure of the nervous system but such defining human capacities as sense, intellect, emotion, and will. At the same time, it would bring the particularly American "spirit of sociology" to bear on matters that had been considered medical. Southard identified the local makings of such a synthesis, emphasizing that Boston's scientific establishment—its universities, laboratories, and institutions—was becoming more closely aligned with the "highly coordinated" Bavarians, Prussians, and Swiss, and singling out the establishment of a social service department at the Massachusetts General Hospital as emblematic of psychiatry's more sociologically informed future. Signaling a break with his profession's past, Southard argued that psychiatrists had attended too little to the "*intrinsic normality*" of the structures—the brain, the nervous system—that produced mental diseases, and proclaimed that it was altogether possible that the causes of mental disease lay not in the nervous system but elsewhere in the body, even "conceivably in the environment at large."[53]

The displacement of asylum by hospital, eagerly promoted by Southard and his colleagues, was part of the larger disciplinary transition that practitioners of the new psychiatry managed to effect. Throughout the first decade of the new century, as what became known as "the hospital ideal" —the notion that asylums should be staffed and operated like hospitals— gained adherents throughout the profession, institutions statewide, termed insane hospitals or insane asylums, were redesignated state hospitals. Thus, the Worcester Insane Asylum became Worcester State Hospital, and the Boston Insane Hospital was renamed Boston State Hospital. Although dismissed as a "great fad" by some, the hospital ideal—and, more specifically, the psychopathic hospital ideal—took firm hold in the psychiatrist's lexicon, a term he could invoke, in print and in discussions at professional conferences, to signal his alignment with the forces of progress.[54] In this same period, the locus of psychiatric practice began to shift, from the large institutions in which nearly all late-nineteenth-century alienists had practiced, to hospitals (like the Psychopathic Hospital) and outpatient clinics, and later to private practice.[55] In the Psychopathic Hospital's first decade, the leading psychiatrists on its staff saw themselves practicing in what Southard called an intermediary field that was neither wholly public, which he and others associated with custodial care of the insane, nor wholly private, associated in his mind with the neurologist's office-based practice.

It was a sort of practice that contemporaries found difficult to classify. Reflecting on Boston Psychopathic Hospital practice, the prominent psychiatrist Adolf Meyer had this to say: "Never was there more psychiatry with so little psychiatry in the ordinary sense of study of mental disease as seen in life."[56]

More psychiatry, but not in the ordinary sense—a perceptive, if awkwardly expressed, characterization of what Southard and his colleagues were up to. They situated themselves on the intermediary field of the social, a largely untheorized interpretive ground, where the issues of personal identity and gender relations with which contemporaries were so concerned could be legitimately addressed. In the course of the nineteenth century, "the social," in the hands of various reform-minded investigators, had come to encompass a range of issues identified as social problems: poverty, the working-class family, the morals of the poor. In retrospect it is clear that the rubric encompassed not only problems but a range of discourses concerning, as Michael Donnelly has pointed out, "the formation of 'character'" and "the exercise of moral influence . . . by one party over another," concerns central to the management of social relations among all of society's actors, not only those identified as difficult.[57] But few, if any, in the nineteenth century articulated this explicitly. Early-twentieth-century psychiatrists did, one proposing, in a characteristic formulation, that "the general problem of human personality has come to be one of the important issues of social organization."[58] General problems, applicable to all, not merely the insane—these were what drew the new psychiatrist's interest. This reconfiguring of the social to encompass the morals and management of everyone was among the new psychiatry's signal conceptual achievements.

Sigmund Freud's new science of psychoanalysis in many respects was, like institutional psychiatrists' new psychiatry, a discipline of the everyday. It highlighted the significance of life's routine aspects, and it blurred the distinction between the normal and the abnormal that had characterized so much nineteenth-century thinking about the human population. Freud's visit to Clark University in 1909 introduced him to the American psychiatric community, but it is important to underscore how little professional currency psychoanalysis enjoyed before 1915 or so. To be sure, in the early teens a few self-trained practitioners of the new technique set themselves up in private practice in Boston, but their efforts were marginal to the large-scale institutional practice of psychiatry in the city.[59] In addition, although many Psychopathic Hospital psychiatrists were familiar, to some degree, with the main outlines of Freud's developing project, discussing it spiritedly (if only sporadically) in their staff meetings and referring to it in passing in their published papers, their stance was largely skeptical, even dismissive; not until the end of the decade was psychoanalysis established enough to command the institutional psychiatrists' grudging respect. Southard, for example, complained of what he characterized as the theory's overly teleological bent, arguing that the Freudian established "syntheses vitually from the start," ingeniously and paradoxically unifying facts and events, a view to which his colleagues apparently gave their assent.[60]

It was not only intellectual style, however, that distinguished the institutional psychiatrist from the Freudian, for each entertained a radically different model of the mind. In the psychiatrist's largely untheorized conception, the mind's topography was flat, its workings unproblematically evident in behavior. The Freudian, by contrast, conceived of the mind in terms of mechanisms and drives, and proposed that a portion or a function of the mind—the unconscious—was in normal circumstances altogether inaccessible, beyond individuals' conscious control. In addition, despite their common focus on the normal (an "ideal fiction" in Freud's characterization),[61] the psychiatrist and the Freudian conceived of it in divergent ways. As Juliet Mitchell has pointed out, the structure and content of Freud's *Three Essays on the Theory of Sexuality*, published in 1905, "erodes any idea of normative sexuality,"[62] a concept that psychiatrists did not question but rather promoted. That mainstream American psychiatry would warm to psychoanalysis in the twenties, fashioning it into a peculiarly American dynamic psychiatry, should not obscure how independent were the trajectories both disciplines pursued in the decade preceding their merger.[63] The lineage of the psychiatry that would come to be organized around the normal was far more complex than psychiatrists, who commonly traced it directly back to Freud, would remember.[64]

The city offered early-twentieth-century psychiatrists a vast reservoir of material with which to work. The diversity of its inhabitants; the issues it presented for the moralist's and the sociologist's analysis; the impetus it gave to the loosening of traditions—psychiatrists, eager to participate in the reorganization of everyday experience, seized on all it had to offer. Examining and observing the many "nearly normal" patients who passed through the hospital, the many "variations of character" and "accidents of life" to which their practice gave them access, psychiatrists pieced together a new science of the everyday.[65] This science took several forms. Much of it was codified in books and articles, professional and popular, thus constituting the formally defined psychiatric corpus. Some of it took the form of statements, made to patients or among colleagues, that formed a less well defined but still important tradition within psychiatry, a tradition that was passed down informally from mentor to student, from patient to relatives and friends. It has come down to us in the form of a discipline that deals as much with normative arrangements, including gender arrangements, in everyday life as with recognized mental disease.

TWO

PROFESSING GENDER

A PROFESSION is a brotherhood."[1] So ventured Abraham Flexner, perhaps the best-known turn-of-the-century spokesman for the professions, brandishing the masculinism that powerfully but invisibly shaped the professional ethos.[2] This ethos was avowedly democratic. Repudiating the "gratuitous and arbitrary distinctions" on which aristocratic institutions were premised, it professed to honor only those distinctions conferred by merit and achievement and to respect only those truths derived from science. Its declared stance was disinterested, altruistically oriented toward service and the common good.

That this high-minded rhetoric masked the professional's more self-interested claims is, by now, an unexceptionable critique. Several decades of sociological revisionism, together with a revival of popular distrust toward professional prerogatives, monopolistic practices, and fees, has conditioned even the most naïve of observers to question the professional's presentation of self.[3] Yet our own fin de siècle cynicism should not obscure how powerfully this newly enunciated ethos of service in the name of science worked its effects on contemporaries. It was the creation of a new cohort of first-generation university-educated men (and a smattering of women) from similar backgrounds, mostly small-town Protestants from the old middle class, who were imbued with a common sense of purpose but who were scattered among occupations diverse enough that they, in Robert Wiebe's felicitous phrase, constituted a class—the so-called new middle class—"only by courtesy of the historian's afterthought."[4] But these men and women—doctors, lawyers, engineers, economists, and teachers among them—articulated a common mythology of origins, aspirations, and purpose that appealed simultaneously to altruism and truth, a potent mix in a culture enamored of experts but disdainful of privilege. Their mythology took the shape of an ethos of occupation and station that was doubly compelling for all its unacknowledged contradictions. This, the professional's ethos, allowed its exponents to rail against privilege while enhancing their own prerogatives; to profess deference to science while venturing far beyond its bounds; to imagine themselves free of the baleful burdens of inheritance while intensifying (in, for example, their elaboration of racialist doctrines) the same burden for those they considered their social inferiors. It endowed worldly ambitions with higher meaning and offered identities that claimed to transcend the partisan particularities—of

birth, wealth, ethnicity—that characterized the communities its bearers
had left behind. Central to the new middle class's sense of self, it illustrates what an acute observer of the nation's upper class has suggested is
the allure, when it comes to self-fashioning, of merit and class in combination.[5]

The professional ethos thus claimed to abjure all invidious social distinctions, but in fact incorporated them, expressed them, and created new
ones.[6] Flexner's blunt invocation of the bonds of manhood notwithstanding, no distinctions would prove more paradoxically pervasive and elusive
than those arising from sexual difference, for these were everywhere apparent but rarely registered, rendered invisible by their commonness. The
masculinism on which the professional ethos was structured found only
fleeting expression in Flexner's singular dictum, which was in any case
uttered less tendentiously than its equation of professionalism and masculine camaraderie suggests. But for its "invidious implications," Flexner
averred, he might have invoked caste to denote the professional's "class
consciousness," his manifest subject. Yet it is significant that Flexner delivered his precept in the course of a lecture explaining to social workers—
most of them women—why social work was not, could not be, a profession. Appealing to professional ideology, he made his case on the high
ground of science and skill, arguing that social workers had little of either.
That Flexner could imagine "brotherhood" free of invidious implications,
in an arena as highly charged with gender tension as this, only underscores
how imperceptible yet significant gender was in the avowedly meritocratic
world of the professions.

This chapter explores the resonances of Flexner's dictum as it addresses
his question anew. In asking why social work was not, and could not be, a
profession, it charts the workings of gender in the disciplines of psychiatry
and social work, looking at how it shaped their practices and representations.[7] It suggests that the impact of gender transcended the rather straightforward and politically apprehensible issue of access—the numbers of
women in this or that profession—to work its effects more insidiously in
the realm of representation, where, mirroring everyday gender relations, it
was disguised by its apparent naturalness. And it looks at how difficult it
was for social workers to disrupt this naturalness, to gain a hearing for
their tentatively expressed belief that gender was *the* gratuitous distinction
around which the professional ethos was structured.

Brotherhood of Psychiatrists

Medicine, the paradigmatic profession that has most successfully defended
its privileges, knowledge base, and monopolistic control, established itself

at the top of the professional hierarchy in the early years of the twentieth century and has remained there since. Nineteeth-century medicine was weak, divided by sectarian claims, rife with cranks; its status was middling, somewhere beneath that of the law; its practitioners were a motley lot, encompassing on the one hand a genteel, college-educated, European-trained elite and on the other men (and some women) in far greater numbers whose skills were informally acquired through the unregulated means of apprenticeship and short medical courses. By the first decade of the twentieth century, the measures that would ensure medicine's transformation and eventual dominance were already taking effect. Educational reformers, their eyes trained on the German universities' laboratories and scientific curricula, raised admission standards and lengthened courses at the nation's premier institutions, restricting access to the desired superior class of individuals. Others argued for the reinstitution of licensing, limiting competition and driving irregular practitioners from the field. Its ranks cleansed of the undereducated and the unorthodox, medicine was well positioned to assert its dominance, and to benefit from the science to which a growing body of discoveries—in bacteriology and immunology, for example, which isolated the causative agents of disease—attested, a science that physicians consolidated into a powerful ideology of medical efficacy and mastery. In a culture fascinated with the power of science, and in which science (in the form of electricity, for example) was transforming life in visible and fundamental ways, doctors successfully established themselves as its omniscient exemplars.[8]

The specialty of psychiatry had existed, from its origins in the 1820s and 1830s, somewhat apart from the rest of medicine. Its practitioners—"alienists," as they were known—labored in asylums, concerned largely with issues of institutional management; its science was an amalgam of moral and religious speculations that no medical school deigned to teach; its punitive practices brought it repeatedly under the scrutiny of an outraged public. When medicine, late in the nineteenth century, began to embrace science, psychiatry's status became even more marginal. The development of the scientifically identified specialty of neurology from physicians' Civil War experience with gunshot wounds further highlighted the alienists' marginality.[9] In 1894, the eminent neurologist S. Weir Mitchell berated his psychiatric colleagues, in an address before their professional organization, the American Medico-Psychological Association, for, among other things, their isolation from medicine's main institutional and scientific currents and their lack of inquiring spirit. That his listeners merely concurred was a measure of their demoralization.[10]

Distancing themselves from their specialty's past, which they rejected as feeble and ineffectual, characterized by a do-nothing outlook, a number of young psychiatrists set out to remake themselves and their discipline. In

1919, in his presidential address to the American Medico-Psychological Association, Southard briefly invoked the figure of the inconsequential alienist, his interests narrowly focused on insanity, before asking his listeners to "rejoice" that as psychiatrists they were better fitted "than perhaps any other men" to diagnose the ills of modern society, that "their analytic powers, their ingrained optimism, and their tried strength of purpose" were demanded not only in "the narrow circles of frank disease" but in education, in the sphere of morals, in jurisprudence, and above all in economics and industry.[11] This was strong stuff, a prescription for psychiatry's future as much as a description of its present, but Southard's words would have rung true to those of his listeners who considered themselves in the profession's vanguard. Among them were his Psychopathic Hospital colleagues, a group of men (and a very few women) who were collectively and determinedly forging a new professional persona for the psychiatrist as a worldly man of science. These practitioners were educated at elite colleges and universities and top-rank medical schools: Harvard, Columbia, Pennsylvania, Tufts. Most of them had trained as pathologists, some as neurologists; all thought of themselves, in contrast to their disciplinary predecessors, as physician-scientists more than administrator-superintendents. They were young—Southard was thirty-six when he assumed the hospital's directorship, and many of his colleagues were younger—and their origins were diverse. Three of the hospital's most prominent physicians—Herman Adler, Lawson G. Lowrey, and Harry C. Solomon— were themselves sons of physicians.[12] Two were from small towns; the rest were raised in cities, although only Adler—the son of a prominent physician, the nephew of Felix Adler, and the grandson of a noted Talmudic scholar—was a member of an urban elite.[13] Adler, Abraham Myerson, and Solomon were Jews, which distinguishes this group of professionals from the predominantly small-town Protestant cohorts that have drawn historians' interest.[14]

The professional outlook these psychiatrists articulated, bred of elite scientific training and of the intensities and frustrations of everyday practice, was likely representative of a broader new-middle-class sensibility. It structured the autobiographical leavings of several of them, tales of ascent in which the old middle-class virtues of industriousness and self-interested pursuit of private gain, shorn of their crass, worldly associations, played a part—turned, now, toward higher, disinterested ends. The resentments of privilege, which these men from modest backgrounds had experienced in sometimes acutely painful ways, resounded through their narratives with a revealing self-consciousness. The prerogatives of gender that their professional endeavors intensified were, by contrast, so seemingly natural, so much a part of the professional's estate, that they found only stray expression. The professional man's ethos thus spun a story about class while quietly encoding a program of gender.

Southard grasped the spirit of this ethos but struggled with its application. "It becomes increasingly difficult," he wrote to his parents, two years shy of a Harvard professorship, "to figure out the technique of becoming a great man." A bit unsettled by the vulgarity of Southard's ambition, his biographer hastened to clothe it in the professional garb of science, explaining that Southard sought prestige only so that his "real work" might be protected from the rabble's uninformed interference.[15] By any measure, however, Southard's ambitions were grandiose, expansive enough to account for his ability to surmount the privations of working-class life in South Boston where he had been born in 1876. With an arch, studied adroitness, his fragmentary autobiography tells the story of his life, one of grim determination enlivened by elements of the picaresque. As he tells it, he was born in the midst of "the still very wretched Irish," a liability he felt rather keenly. The family, Protestants, lived for several years in a small, two-family house on a narrow side street in South Boston's most thickly settled area, in his memory "not far above the level of the slums." Southard's father ran a small but moderately successful draying business that brought him into daily contact with the poverty-stricken neighbors with whom, by all accounts, he enjoyed good relations. Business was good enough that he was able to move the family into a substantial townhouse (still in South Boston) shortly after Ernest was born.[16]

Southard shrouded the early years of his life in a haze of populist good feeling. The boy of his autobiography roamed the district in the company of Irish friends, playing in vacant lots, scaling the neighborhood's imposing dirt hills, spying on Catholic orphans at play in their institution's barren yard, and delighting his mates with colorful tales of his own invention, narrated as they walked long miles to the bathing beach, the Boston Public Library, and Franklin Park. The scourge of religious and racial prejudice, however, came inevitably to blight this youthful, remembered paradise of boyish escapades, and Southard gradually drew apart from his Irish friends. He learned that they were papists, their minds filled with the teachings of devious Jesuits, and that he was of honorable Yankee stock. Although the etiquette of the streets held it improper to inquire into another's religion, it was hardly necessary to do so. The South Boston of Southard's youth was, he recalled, "full of the sharpest demarcations between Protestant and Catholic, Yankee and Irishman."

Southard was sent to local schools from the age of five and to the Boston Latin School when he was nine. There his education was for the first time guided by men, his biographer carefully noted, not, as in the primary grades, women. "And they were real men," he emphasized, not bothering to explain what he meant. A fellow Latin School alumnus, the biographer did, however, provide short sketches of these masters, a weird bunch— "large, stout, mellifluous"; "stout, chunky, and irritable"; "greying, scholarly, and alert"; one of them "lame and rather put upon by his students";

another a "surreptitious writer of popular novels"—who had etched
something "lasting and distinctive" on the memory that he could not,
for the passage of time, specify but that his context makes clear had
something to do with the boy's admission to the exclusive company of
men.[17] First in the long line of the professional man's mentors, these
teachers signaled the entry of gender into Southard's life tale, where it
would become invisibly intertwined with his more manifest narrative,
structured around class.

At the Latin School, Southard, immersed in the city's larger landscape of
class, was forced to adjust not only his gender consciousness but also his
social imagination. As his relations with his Irish neighbors became a
matter more of choice than of necessity, they assumed the shape of a sentimental, defensive kinship that united both parties in opposition to Boston's
Brahmin caste, "those 'successful' adventurers and their children who
occupied a portion of Beacon Hill and the Back Bay land especially 'made'
for them." Yet Southard's *Bildung*, an educational odyssey through the
city's once wholly patrician institutions, stirred in him a desire to master
the knowledge and culture that the patriciate guarded as its own. He
combed his ancestry for evidence of a bookish strain, which he duly found
and dated to the Revolutionary War, to account for his ascent and the continuing poverty of his Irish neighbors. And, first at the Latin School, lately
abandoned by the elite in favor of private boarding schools situated in
small New England towns, then at Harvard College, which, under the aegis
of its progressive Brahmin president, Charles W. Eliot, was being transformed from a provincial, upper-class college into one of the nation's
premier universities, Southard immersed himself in the classical curricu-
lum, excelling in ancient and modern languages and philosophy, subjects
whose lack of utility fitted them for both gentlemen scholars and striving
intellectuals.[18]

"I want to emerge superior to various classmates who were of 'society' in
college," Southard wrote, curiously but frankly admitting that his ambition was fueled, in part, by class resentment. He had entered Harvard "a fat
boy, rather greasy and unkempt," clearly, a classmate would later recall,
"from a South Boston working man's family."[19] A bit uncomfortable at
first, an outsider because of his origins, Southard flourished at Harvard,
studying philosophy with Josiah Royce and psychology with William
James and indulging his passion for chess, which brought him distinction
and the admiration of his fellows. However speculative his interests, Southard was enough the workingman's son to follow a worldly course. Early on
he announced his intention of becoming a doctor and, in 1897, entered
Harvard Medical School, where he trained as a pathologist. There, too,
resentment surfaced; he professed disgust at the "hereditary dominance"
in certain of the school's departments by "Bunker Hill scions." At the same

time he continued to cultivate his self-conscious intellectuality, augmenting his medical studies with forays into philosophy and psychology. A regular member of Royce's famous seminar, Southard bridged Harvard's two worlds as successfully as anyone.[20]

Within the decade, Southard was traveling in the most rarefied and convivial intellectual circles. While still single, he ventured out nearly every night—to the symphony or the theater, to Cambridge for dinner, to a club. He was a member of the Wicht Club and the Shop Club. The Wicht was an association of self-styled geniuses that counted among its members some ten or so Harvard philosophers and psychologists whose monthly gatherings in hotels or (Southard's biographer again) "at some 'Dago' restaurant" featured informal talks, "drinking and frivolity." Wives— "Wichtinnen"—were excluded from this masculine conclave but invited to the group's annual meeting. Most notably, Southard gained admittance to Boston's venerable St. Botolph Club, citadel of intellectual Brahminism.[21]

By 1914, when Southard began to sketch the outlines of his autobiography, he had scaled Boston's ladder of class. Still "secretly ashamed" of his origins, he began to recast them as assiduously as any arriviste.[22] Diligently he constructed a distinguished ancestry for himself, shuffling some two hundred index cards, consulting genealogists at Oxford, poring over directories at the British Museum. In the end he was proud to count among his forebears Aldens, Bradfords, Peabodys, and Standishes—members of the colonial elite of Massachusetts. What he called his "ancestor worship" provided him with the security of an aristocratic lineage, however spurious, that served as a backdrop against which he could comfortably play out the tensions between his meritocratic and his more aristocratic leanings. On the one hand, he could claim to value social position achieved through education far more highly than that conferred by birth, and, invoking paternal authority, point to his father's decrying of ancestry and his disdain for Anglomania. And he could stress that his humble origins had awakened his desire to serve, dating it to his youthful proximity to South Boston's lunatic asylum, fleeting friendships with the blind boys from the Perkins Institute, and several visits to the nearby house of correction, where he glimpsed "mute, pallid men sewing overalls of a drab rough material," a vision of misery that, he wrote in 1914, sustained him still. On the other hand, invoking scientific authority, he could claim to dismiss the "plain man's view" that family did not count, maintaining that it "suppressed a germ of eugenical reasoning," and fashion himself a member of a new aristocracy, worthier than that of the Brahmins, an aristocracy of seekers after truth, of "people who want to dig out novelty."[23]

Southard wrestled with the same conflict between the professions' patently meritocratic ethos and their exclusionary, "aristocratic" practices that Flexner had identified but could not resolve.[24] Southard did not so much resolve as dissolve the tension. He embraced the professional's identity as a respectable alternative to the patrician persona he could never have assumed and professed to disdain, while at the same time cultivating the patrician strain within it. His distaste for the imperatives of the workaday world, voiced in his lament that his father had been compelled to "lead a competitive business life" when, had he been a physician, he "could have lived quietly on a salary," was expressive of a sensibility more characteristic of the genteel patrician, to whom money is absolutely necessary but invisible, than of the professional, who, many sociologists have shown, is tainted by the marketplace even as he claims to be above it.[25] Southard's trust that his father, a migrant from rural Maine with a meager formal education, would have chosen to pursue professional rather than business endeavors is a measure not only of how fertile a ground the past provides for the play of imaginative fancy but also of the younger Southard's solipsism.

We know far less of the other psychiatrists than of Southard, who was particularly interested in establishing his patrimony. Yet it is clear that two of them, Harry C. Solomon and Abraham Myerson, were equally conversant in the vocabulary of professionalism. Their professionalism was a bit scrappier—as Jews, for example, they could hardly claim Yankee ancestries—but it was shot through with the same antiaristocratic sentiments as that of Southard. Solomon was born in Nebraska, raised in pleasant middle-class circumstances in Los Angeles, and educated at Berkeley. He headed east to enroll in Harvard's medical school in 1910, the same year that Flexner issued his report calling for the reorganization of American medical education. To Solomon, Harvard was Mecca, for it had, he enthusiastically recalled, "all the laboratory facilities, the full-time scientists, the fine clinic facilities, [and the] high educational standards" that Flexner had proposed American medical schools should adopt. University reform brought new blood to the faculty, in Solomon's estimation a distinguished but inbred patriciate of Bigelows, Shattucks, Warrens, and Jacksons who had "all descended from the same stock." Men of science, several trained at Johns Hopkins, with "names not indigenous to New England"—Cushing, Cannon, Folin, even a Karsner and a Rosenau—joined this Brahmin-dominated faculty, generating opposition but also a stimulating ferment in which the young Solomon was able to fashion an identity for himself as more than anything else a scientist.[26]

Myerson was an immigrant, born in the ghetto village of Yanova, Lithuania, in 1881, the son of a decidedly agnostic, socialist teacher who had been educated as a rabbi. Family lore had it that the elder Myerson had made his way to the United States after he had been threatened with exile by a czarist inspector who found several banned books in his small library. He sent for his wife and children in 1886, a year later, and within a few years the family had moved to the South End, where Myerson *père* went into business as a junk dealer. Abraham Myerson was given to depicting his youth on South Boston's streets "as a series of amazing adventures and heroic events," his own son recalled. He traveled in the company of gangs, bested neighborhood bullies, and claimed to have nearly joined the circus. (Solomon, too, told of such escapades; in one, he returned home, bloodied and crying, from a boxing match with boys from the neighborhood's wild crowd, whereupon, he recalled, his father told him "if he caught me crying again he'd give me something to really cry about" and instructed him to "hit the guy back.") Myerson's childhood was marked by grinding poverty. He labored in his brother's shop, cutting pipe, for seven years after he was graduated from high school. He never attended college, and, after a year at Columbia University's medical school, he was forced back to manual labor.[27]

Myerson, like Solomon, identified as a man of science. Resolutely anti-Victorian, he delighted in upsetting pious conventionalities in its name. His writings on the tyrannies of domesticity, which appeared in professional journals and popular books and magazines, are incisive, witty, and analytically sophisticated.[28] And, although he was an early advocate of sterilization for eugenic purposes, as an immigrant Jew he was alert to the eugenicists' racist assumptions and intentions. He became a vigorous and clever opponent of eugenics, suggesting, for example, in a dry, scholarly caricature of the eugenicists' modus operandi, replete with genealogical charts dating to the seventeenth century, that manic-depressive insanity was rife among members of Boston's Brahmin caste. Had the forebears of the state's chief justices and governors, its poets, philosophers, and psychologists, whose families were tainted by insanity, been sterilized, as eugenicists were proposing the defective should be, "the 'Who's Who' of American development," he suggested, would look entirely different. Disingenuously claiming he had no ax to grind, Myerson hinted that the James and Holmes families were among those he had in mind.[29] Ostensibly an attack on bad science, Myerson's investigation was also a thinly veiled swipe at the pretensions of patrician ancestor worship.

No one on the hospital's staff was more self-consciously a man of science than the Harvard-trained psychologist Robert Yerkes. The son of a Presbyterian farmer, Yerkes was born in rural Pennsylvania, he wrote, "in the midst of a beautiful agricultural country, inhabited by intelligent, self-respecting, law-abiding, prosperous folk." His vocational hero worship stirred by his physician-cousin's ministrations to the sick, Yerkes decided he would, as "an alleviator of human suffering," devote his life to service. After seven years in the local ungraded public school, where he worked hard, motivated by "ambition and social prestige," he left home to attend Ursinus College. There he encountered Darwinism, which challenged his strongly held religious convictions, and he embarked on a journey from religion to science, from the farm to the university, that thousands of other middle-class men would follow. He enrolled at Harvard, where he intended to prepare for medical studies. Instead he decided on a career in psychology, completing a Ph.D. degree under Hugo Münsterberg in 1902. Although Yerkes was primarily an animal psychologist, he was among the first enthusiasts of mental testing in the United States. At the Psychopathic Hospital, where he served as psychologist until 1917, he developed a point scale for measuring human intelligence. His conception of vocation as "work for which one is well fitted by nature and acquisition," through which one could render service and "utilize one's special abilities to the utmost," nicely expresses both the professional's concern with service and the psychologist's concern that it be efficiently employed.[30]

If it appears that Southard, Solomon, Myerson, and Yerkes adopted the scientist's persona effortlessly, this is in part because they, and others of their generation, were instrumental in shaping it. Each structured his life's tale as a rather uncomplicated ascent, with scarcely a backward glance, from the common lot of poverty (Southard and Myerson) or innocence (Solomon and Yerkes), through the medium of science, to a realm of knowledge and power in which he moved confidently—addressing scientific congresses, running institutions, advising government officials, making policy. Whatever privations, awkwardnesses, or resentments these men felt along the way—and there were many—assumed the form of sentimental set pieces in their narratives. As they told it, science was the great leveler, blotting out the invidious distinctions of place and class that had constrained them. Science, as they experienced it, was democratic, bringing Solomon, whose family scrimped to send him to medical school, into the company of a scion of the Brahmin Forbes family, the workingman's son Southard into easy consort with Jacksons and Cabots, and the farm boy Yerkes into the company of Harvard luminaries. The scientist, as they imagined him, abjured distinctions founded on anything but truth.

These men never directly addressed the gender of the scientist; they simply assumed he was a man. They represented science as male, sentiment as female, and wrote a genealogy of gender into their profession's history, portraying it, in language shot through with muscular masculinism, as the triumph of aggressive resolve over Victorian timidity. This progression presented them with a paradox, for much of the knowledge they would claim as their own fell under a broad rubric we might term "domestic." Marital relations, temperamental difficulties, delicate moral issues, quirks of personality, the child's bad habits, the man's disappointed ambitions— these, the stuff of psychiatrists' ambitious reach, fell within woman's traditional purview; all were culturally "feminine." There was thus an edge to psychiatrists' ridiculing of their nineteeth-century predecessors as "a pussy-footed race" and their contrasting them unfavorably to the modern psychiatrist who boldly proclaimed his expertise, refusing to "hide his light under a bushel." As a favored formulation—borrowed from the masculine theater of war—had it, psychiatry was "taking its stand in the front line trenches."[31]

The social practices of science underwrote psychiatrists' aggressive masculinism. From the moment they entered medical training, if not before, psychiatrists traveled in a world of masculine satisfactions, a self-sufficient world of male peers with whom they spent long hours and of authoritative male mentors who inspired intense loyalties. Although only some were bachelors, many lived as though they were, spending evenings and even nights at the hospital. As a medical student, for example, Solomon lived alone in a rooming house in the Back Bay and, in his last year, at the Psychopathic Hospital, from which he and his companions set off on regular Saturday-night forays into Boston's notorious Scollay Square, the putative site of many a young girl's ruin. After he was married, like some of his peers, to a woman with a career of her own, he would return to the hospital in the evenings to work with Southard.[32] "Girls"—but not wives—could provide the psychiatrist welcome company; Karl A. Menninger told of going with Southard to a professional meeting in New York, where the two were to enjoy a pleasant luncheon with "a girl he wanted me to meet" who "was going to bring a friend of hers for me." Southard's extramarital interests were well enough known among his colleagues to prompt one's memory of their collective collusion in protecting his wife "from the facts."[33] The more cosmopolitan of the hospital's staff, among them Southard and Yerkes, were regularly in and out of Cambridge's stately mansions, attending evening seminars hosted by Harvard's brightest stars, meeting with their fellows in exclusive clubs, and attending private dinners.[34] "It was my good fortune," Yerkes wrote, "to be intimately associated with men of genius in scholarship and in the art of living." Yerkes' tribute to fraternal fellowship was echoed on a baser level in an eminent colleague of Meyerson's regular admonition to the latter's son to "K Y P I Y P," a cryptic directive the boy later discovered meant "keep your pecker in your pants."[35] If the meaning of this remained obscure, its gendered specificity was abundantly clear.

"Velvet-Gloved" Social Workers

As a low-status specialty, psychiatry was somewhat more open to women than were the more venerable medical specialties.[36] Yet although the hospital attracted a number of women to its staff, none was able to rise to a position of visibility and importance. Women psychiatrists tended to stay at the hospital for short stints, and when they left, to move on to positions in the public sector. After three years at the Psychopathic Hospital, for example, Harriet Gervais became a medical inspector for the New York City schools; Esther Woodward worked for the Westchester County, New York, Committee on the Socially Unadjusted; and Anna Wellington, who had served as the hospital's executive assistant in a high but largely administrative post, was employed by the Red Cross in Paris. Several others, like Geneva Tryon and Cornelia Schorer, assumed posts as hospital psychiatrists. These women physicians all labored in a realm that was associated more with well-established traditions of womanly service than with manly science, and their endeavors attracted little negative comment. By contrast, the hospital's male psychiatrists counted the pathologists Annie Taft and Myrtelle Canavan among their small elite, granting them informal status as honorary men. This was no doubt because Taft and Canavan were skilled practitioners of an inarguably scientific specialty. Isolated in the laboratory, they never came in contact with patients, nurses, or social workers; they could hardly be associated with service. Solomon, for example, judged Taft "an excellent neuropathologist, a meticulous worker." But if Taft's mind and craft were male, her body was still female. She was, Solomon confessed, one of the most beautiful women he had ever seen. "I used to kid her all the time. Why the hell didn't she get married? How in the world could she avoid it?"[37]

The poignancy of Taft's reply that she had remained a maiden lady because she did not come in contact with the right sort of people, that those who wanted her were no good and that she did not dare risk showing interest in the ones she wanted, was not lost on Solomon, who was still haunted by it some sixty years later. His aggressive kidding was in part a mark of his acceptance of her as a colleague, evidence she was admitted to the laboratory's rough company of men. But it was also a somewhat cruel expression of his anxiety about her presence, for, as her measured reply indicates, the kidding was entirely one-sided.

Despite the substantial presence of women practitioners, psychiatry was a man's field. Women psychiatrists were either relegated to the profession's lower echelons or nervously tolerated, at what appears to have been great personal cost, at its highest ranks. The hospital's battle over the gender of profession—a battle with larger resonances—would be waged not among psychiatrists but between them and social workers, all of whom were female.

From the start, social work was woman's work, an apparently natural extension of properly feminine domestic duties into the public sphere. In the nineteenth century, the social worker's progenitrix, the "friendly visitor," had distributed relief to the worthy poor while attempting at the same time to reform their characters and habits. "Sympathy, tact, patience,

cheer"—it was not by accident that the exemplary visitor's personal qualities were those associated with proper womanhood, for, as Christine Stansell has suggested in her study of nineteeth-century New York, the city's
charitable bourgeois women articulated a vision of their own particular
virtues as they confronted, on their missions into working-class neighborhoods, the deficiencies of their less fortunate sisters.[38] From the twentieth-
century social worker's perspective, the friendly visitor was but the public
face of the proper woman, an uncontested representation of feminine moral
rectitude.

Early in the new century, paid, college-educated social workers began to
voice their professional aspirations and to challenge the comforting conflation of woman's specially virtuous character and her special fitness for
social service that had lent ideological legitimacy to their predecessors'
transgressive endeavors beyond woman's sphere. This generation of social
workers was not associated, like the visitors, with the charitable organizations that functioned in a genteel realm animated by the distinctions
of class and family, a realm in which a woman might enjoy an honored,
special status as Lady Bountiful by virtue of her benevolent deeds. Rather,
these workers were employed in the intensely hierarchical and authoritarian world of the hospital and the specialized clinic, where the anomalies
of their status—women, but not nurses; skilled, but at what?—quickly
surfaced. Prompted to position themselves in the hierarchy, these workers
rejected their predecessors' association with sentimental notions of womanly service, and instead asserted that they were professionals, something
like the physicians at whose behest they had first entered the medical
domain.[39]

Social workers' ambitions brought them squarely up against the prerogatives of psychiatrists, whose own professional dominance required
social workers' subordination.[40] This was in part because psychiatry and
social work, for all their differences, shared a newly defined body of expertise and technique. One body of knowledge could support but one profession; the professions that have most successfully persuaded a larger public
of their legitimacy, like medicine and the law, have done so in large part by
laying claim to knowledge they have defined as specialized and esoteric,
theirs alone. The early-twentieth-century psychiatrists who expanded their
discipline's reach, fashioning themselves not merely physicians but arbiters
of social norms, asserting their expertise in matters far beyond the established medical realm of disease, and, most problematically, meddling in the
domestic domain, which was hedged about with feminine associations,
strayed on to new disciplinary territory, part of which women—in the
guise of friendly visitors—had been covering for decades. Much of the
knowledge psychiatrists proclaimed "psychiatric," then, was not medical
but social, not esoteric but common, not scientific but domestic—risky

ground from which to advance claims for special expertise. Psychiatrists appear to have been somewhat aware of this difficulty, although Southard's repeatedly voiced admission that "alienists [had] long been social workers in their fashion" was the closest any of them came to acknowledging it.[41]

Such affirmations of common purpose, however, were at best magnanimous gestures that obscured the tenacity with which psychiatrists held on to their superiority, which was in any case formidable. It was deceptively natural, merely mirroring what many accepted as society's necessary hierarchy of gender; it was formally organized, protected by an impressive arsenal of degrees, educational institutions, and licensing bodies; and it was enhanced by a venerable history (although, as social workers pointed out, not so venerable as psychiatrists liked to imagine). Yet psychiatrists would be compelled to create it anew in their wrangling with social workers, for the confrontation threatened to expose how much of the apparent inevitability of their domination was premised on their prerogatives as men. Psychiatrists warded off this threatened unmasking by simple but vigorous assertion. Their argument was straightforward: Psychiatry was science, and science was masculine; social work was sentiment, and sentiment was feminine. Forced, by their own ambitions, to abjure hierarchical claims vis-à-vis social workers based primarily on expertise, psychiatrists simply redefined as "scientific" that to which the term referred.

The play of gender in the psychiatrists' argument lays bare the latent masculinism of the professional ethos. What psychiatrists believed, but had to argue on other grounds, was that because social workers were women they could not be professionals. Social workers contested this in word and deed, focusing attention away from psychiatrists' absolutist stance and turning the dispute into an occasion for negotiating the terms on which women would be admitted to the professional world. When psychiatrists felt their control slipping, they could resort to condescension and bullying. This suggests that they sometimes imagined themselves, if only fleetingly, the equals of social workers, like them members of a profession in the making. Only appreciation of the historical moment can account for the psychiatrists' spirited and sometimes nasty engagement in a dispute they were sure to win.

Psychiatrists waged their professional battles on two fronts. In print and at conferences, they were constantly attacking the superintendents, "institution men," and sundry other conservatives who were, to their minds, impeding psychiatry's progress. Something of the intensity of this conflict can be gleaned from Southard's rather incidental remarks, in the midst of an important professional address, that luckily those "incorrigible practical men who will see nothing in theory"—the theory to which he subscribed—"are fast dying out."[42] On a daily basis, however, psychiatrists saw little of these men; their differences with them were a matter for the world beyond the hospital. This was not the case with respect to their dispute with social workers. For the most part decorous, it was negotiated in the pages of professional journals and constrained by both parties' interest in day-to-day cooperation.[43] But it was also protracted and immediate, negotiated in the hospital's halls and conference rooms. Intergroup relations could turn rancorous. Pointing out that he had "made many friends amongst the social workers," Southard, for example, warned his fellow physicians that they should anticipate that their own "well-known spiritual pride" would clash with the "new as yet uncertainly founded pride of the social workers," ruling out "the best cooperation for some time to come."[44] Southard saw to it that his portent would be fulfilled. Psychiatrists, he made clear, would brook no rivals.

Paradoxically, however, social service was integral to Southard's vision of psychiatry's newly enlarged realm of expertise, and for this reason he intermittently suspended his concerns. Shortly after the hospital opened, he appointed Mary C. Jarrett, a social worker of proven mettle, to the position of chief of the social service, and granted her the space and resources to develop the department as she desired, with the proviso—which he admitted was a prejudice—that the department's endeavors were to be "dominated" by physicians.[45] Jarrett, in her mid-thirties, hailed from a middle-class Baltimore background. She was graduated from Woman's College of Baltimore (later Goucher College), had taught for several years, and had, most recently, worked for the Boston Children's Aid Society.[46] Following a week's consultation with experts in various cities and several months' study of the dimensions of her charge, Jarrett opened the department, which, Southard's intentions notwithstanding, would be chronically short of staff and resources. In 1914, with Southard's blessing, she organized a six-month apprenticeship program at the hospital that trained six to seven students at a time. The course several years later would provide the foundation for the Smith College Training School for Social Work, of which she was the first associate director. Colleagues testified that Jarrett and Southard worked together well. They collaborated on several important projects and wrote *The Kingdom of Evils*, a casebook of psychiatric social work that bears the mark of Southard's weirdly eccentric genius and Jarrett's methodical good sense.[47]

Despite their productive partnership, Jarrett and Southard sparred regularly over the social worker's standing in the professional hierarchy. Confident one moment, defensive the next, Southard tirelessly reiterated his position—the same as Flexner's: social work was not, could not be, a profession. He specified the ideal social worker's qualities: "sympathy and firmness, adaptability and steadfastness, quick insight and profound commonsense, modesty and knowledge of the world." Of course, Southard allowed, "people in general ought to have these qualities too," but that only underscored his point. For the social worker of his imagining was on the one hand perfectly ordinary, a person "every man of the world" would recognize as fitted to the task, and on the other so absolutely ineffable he could only propose that—"Alas!"—such a person was born, not made; *nascitur, non fit.*[48]

Although Southard tried to avoid invidiously gendered argument, his prose betrayed that, to his mind, the social worker could only be a woman. Few would have proposed that sympathy, firmness, and adaptability would fit a man for anything in particular, let alone for medicine; conversely, few would have recoiled from specifying the qualities the profession demanded —a scientific intelligence foremost among them. However, if Southard here seemed in danger of succumbing to sentiment in the contemplation of feminine virtue so selflessly deployed, he could drop the gallant's pose and sternly address the ladies. He warned them not to rush precipitously into professionalization. He expressed his pleasure that they had the "grace" not to claim their endeavors were scientific, and that they rightly eschewed all "stuff and nonsense about any so-called social *science.*" But, he chided social workers, their recently adopted "muscular posture" and group consciousness were exposing them to the deserved derision of "physicians, judges, men of the world." How much better if they could strike an attitude of "humble pride or proud humility" toward physicians, "their acknowledged leaders." In any case, Southard maintained, the social worker's sense of superiority to nurses was wholly unwarranted. The former were "apt to be of a finer grain and a more finished higher education" than the latter, but "a girl might become either." If social work was a profession, then so too was nursing, Southard suggested, knowing full well no judgment would rankle the social worker more.[49] In Southard's hands, the "velvet glove" of social work would pose no threat to the physician's prerogatives.[50]

Jarrett rose to the challenge, asserting that the social worker was not a nurse but the physician's equal, "the type of woman who under other circumstances might have studied medicine." She boldly proposed a program for the professionalization of her discipline. She admitted that social work was still an obscure field, too often ignorantly identified with nursing, neighborliness, or a missionary impulse. And she allowed that the social worker's "expertness" was of a sort different from that practitioners of the older professions possessed, amounting at bottom to "a kind of well-developed common sense" that seemed paltry indeed when measured against the physician's or the lawyer's well-defined store of knowledge. Jarrett argued that "the official discomfort of inferior status"—a mannered phrase that held any number of slights—would be eased only if social workers were to reject the do-gooding, philanthropic ethos that invited many parties' condescension and, instead, to signal their professional aspirations by adopting a scientific stance.[51] Controlled experimentation carried out by accomplished workers would yield the "defined and systematized principles" and "communicable technique" that would enable the field to advance beyond dependence "upon personal qualities in the social worker."[52]

Science, Jarrett subtly suggested, was not so wholly masculine a preserve as men imagined and experienced it. Further, she hinted subversively, social work at present was at the stage where medicine had been only one hundred years previously, lacking in doctrine and method. Efforts directed at building up the field's woefully deficient fund of detailed and "exact" scientific knowledge—studies, for example, of the casework different sorts of agencies carried out—would both sustain its professional claims, in much the same way that medicine in the nineteenth century had turned science to its benefit, and provide teachers of social work something concrete to convey to their students. As Jarrett admitted privately, teachers of social work had little in the way of "formulated technique or systemized knowledge" to teach. Lacking this, they were forced to rely on intuition.[53]

If "intuition" verged perilously close to popular conceptions of woman's true nature, Jarrett was well aware of the difficulty. Both she and her critics knew that because social work lacked any of the attributes of a profession, its standing would ultimately turn on the character of its practitioners.[54] Psychiatrists opportunistically homed in on this, suggesting that the notion of a woman's profession was absurd, even paradoxical: for one, women did not have advanced degrees; further, they did not need them anyway, for was it not true that the social worker was born, not made? Jarrett, addressing the same conundrum from a different angle, proposed that high-grade but degreeless social workers "should be accorded a rank unmerited by professional training," a stance she must have known was untenable.[55]

Jarrett's strenuous scientism could be read as a measure of naïveté, of the newcomer's trust that establishing the formal attributes of professionalism—the specialized expertise, the credentials—would secure full professional status for her endeavors. But it could also be evaluated as part of a strategy meant to tease the social worker out of the woman in which men reflexively embedded her. Myerson's conflation of the "type of woman" social work needed and "good, solid, young womanhood" was typical, illustrative of the psychiatrist's inability to envision the social worker, in vague but gender-specific terms, as anything but the best sort of woman— his wife, his sister, his daughter.[56] Jarrett, by contrast, argued that social work needed persons of high caliber with expertise in social matters, "capacity for independent judgment, analytical ability, personal power."[57] The social worker of Jarrett's imagining was endowed with the same abilities as the man of science.

Jarrett was well aware, however, that the social worker entered the professional arena burdened by her womanhood. Jarrett counseled her students in the politics of deference—to psychiatrists, to clients, to knowledge. They were not to discuss psychoanalysis in front of psychiatrists, for that, a student recalled, "amounted to threatening their professional stature." They must appear innocent of worldly knowledge, for, recalled another, clients would wonder why "ladies who look so much like ladies know so much." They were to appear theoretically unsophisticated, to advance their claims only tentatively. And, to avoid what the social worker Maida H. Solomon in her notes called "any lady bountiful class clash," they were forbidden to wear "fancy or provocative clothes" and told, if they had automobiles, to park them out of patients' sight when visiting them at their homes.[58] Deference, innocence, modesty—all would allow the social worker to pose as a proper woman even as, day to day, she challenged the category's strictures. Strategic dissembling—the "playing dumb" to which smart women have traditionally resorted to outfox men—would allow her to assure those unsettled by her public presence of her essential womanliness. In urging this tack, Jarrett was far more canny a strategist than has been recognized.

Rhetoric aside, psychiatrists reconciled themselves to, and even encouraged, social workers' ambitions. Southard, Myerson, and Lowrey were among the thirty-odd specialists—psychiatrists, asylum superintendents, social workers—who traveled, in the exceptionally hot summer of 1918, to remote, bucolic Smith College to deliver lectures on psychiatric social work to seventy women. By the summer's end, Southard was marveling at the maturity and zeal of his students and, relieved that none manifested "the peculiarities of the professional uplifter or reformer," he generously granted that there was indeed "room in the world" for the social worker.[59] Another instructor agreed, emphasizing that social work needed to rule out the "uplifters" and "energetic social reformer[s]," the embarrassingly ardent women whose good intentions were no substitute for the scientific method serious social work demanded.[60] Myerson chimed in a bit more bluntly, warning that the overemotional woman and the "Prude" should stay away from social work. As he explained, flaunting his modernity, "in psychiatry one meets sex not only naked but often perverted as well," and "squeamishness to *Fact*" was "the essence of Prudery."[61] Southard, for his part, ventured that the women had betrayed not a trace of "evil reaction or discomfort" when presented with psychiatry's facts.[62]

The trajectory from sentiment to science, from feminine frailty to masculine fortitude, that these men sketched for social work was precisely the one Jarrett herself proposed. Psychiatrists would explain that it was the wartime emergency—the specter of too many thousands of debilitated soldiers for psychiatrists to handle alone—that prompted their change of heart. They would clearly need help dealing with the soldiers, and, although the question arose, a woman physician wrote with a heavily ironic touch, whether wisdom lay in admitting women "into the sacred precincts of the temple of psychiatric thought," in the interest of the common good the men were willing to give their assent.[63] Yet they made it clear that the women—or "aides," as they insisted on referring to them—were not to be trained in diagnosis, the psychiatrist's most jealously guarded prerogative, but in sociology, psychology, history taking, mental testing: topics whose very range would ensure that social workers would remain generalists, professional laymen, in Southard's gender-inverted oxymoron.[64]

But social workers set their sights higher. In the twenties they would abandon the diffusely social perspective that psychiatrists encouraged them to adopt, a perspective that had the social worker still visiting, going from hospital to home, casting her as a "useful intermediary" and a "universal solvent."[65] Social workers instead began to fashion themselves psychotherapists, focusing not on social meliorism but on patients' inner lives.[66] "We see case-work about to pass into a psychological phase," Jarrett predicted in 1918. "It is clear that environment prevails at present. It is becoming evident that personality will become the leading interest in the future."[67] Adoption of psychotherapy as technique gave psychiatric social workers the theoretically consistent and scientifically derived conception of casework they had sought for some twenty years. The allure of psychiatric technique, however, would prove paradoxical. It would encourage social workers to delineate a properly professional identity to replace vague conceptions of them as "dealers in morals" and "moral advisors." But it would also ensure they would forever remain subordinate to psychiatrists. One science, one technique, can support but one profession, and psychiatrists, for historical reasons and because they were men, were able to make that theirs.

But this is to get ahead of our story. For the moment, professionalism offered more immediate rewards. It allowed the social worker to appropriate the professional's universalist claims for herself, temporarily to transcend the limitations of her gender, and perhaps to move a bit more confidently on terrain that was male: to attend and deliver lectures, to read and write journal articles, to obtain and confer, in colleges, institutions, and professional organizations, the emblems of professional status. Day-to-day immersion in the bracing rough-and-tumble of the professional world presented many challenges and disappointments to social workers, but it also afforded them satisfactions—a measure of power and mastery, in their relations with patients if not with psychiatrists—that lives of genteel visiting and volunteer charitable endeavors would not have yielded. Comporting themselves as professionals, social workers could also alleviate some of the fatigue that Jarrett admitted plagued them. Authority flowed from the social worker who imagined herself possessed of real knowledge and technique, enabling her to command the respect of patients and, if it was not forthcoming, to administer occasionally a satisfying "small dose of reproof" to the recalcitrant. Authority would substitute for indignation. The social worker confident of her position and craft could handle the annoyingly uncooperative housewives, persistent liars, and delinquent girls who constituted her practice more expeditiously than one strained by overwork and vexed by lack of knowledge. Abandon the pieties of woman's sphere, Jarrett advised her fellow workers: "to be scientific is not to be less humane; to be thoughtful is not to be unfeeling."[68] What Jarrett clearly meant was that to be either did not disqualify one as a woman.

Still, adoption of the professional's persona did not come naturally to women, especially those with children. What was for men a wholly self-affirming identity was for women a matter of constant negotiation, careful planning, and conscious strategizing. With four children, a psychiatrist spouse, and a career to occupy her, Maida Solomon had little choice but to plan the most prosaic aspects of her family's daily regimen. For example, she drew up a detailed schedule for the German nurse she employed, listing hour by hour her assigned chores, from the early-morning dressing and feeding of the children, through the midmorning sweeping and laundry and the early-afternoon naps and walks to the store, to the serving of supper and the washing of the dishes. Solomon and her husband decided before marriage that they would both pursue careers, and that the children would be spaced to allow them to do so. She credited his steady cooperation and their daily communication, as well as her "devoted domestic help," with making it possible for her to juggle career, marriage, and motherhood. Still, she was the one who set aside her lunch hours to pick up her children from school, she was the one who went to the parent-teacher meetings, she was the one who set aside time to read to her children and to play tennis with them, and she was the one who, when two of her children were hospitalized for four days, moved in with her typewriter.[69] With no models to guide her, Solomon forged her professional identity not only in the hospital but in the home and in the space that lay between the two.

"Is social work really a profession?" Jarrett observed that in any gathering of social workers the question was sure to arise.[70] The answer must be yes, and no. Yes, formally, for social work did establish the schools, the licensing, the technique and knowledge that any aspiring profession must. No, in practice, for social work never would establish the dominance, and with it the autonomy and authority, that any aspiring profession desires. As women's work—work done by women, as well as work associated with "woman"—social work was condemned to semiprofessional status at best.

The professional's distinctive occupational authority was underwritten on the one hand by his authority in the larger culture (his class, race, and gender) and, on the other, by his successful association of his endeavors with science and objectivity ("manly" knowledge). Social workers were doubly handicapped; the "professional sisterhood" resonates feebly.

Psychiatrists made clear how monstrously unnatural was the woman who would question their prerogatives. The social worker was no woman, Southard suggested; she could be an unfeeling, hectoring brute. She too readily suggested that patients belonged in institutions; she was "apt to rush into premature conclusions"; and she took delight in devising "stiff legislation."[71] Myerson elaborated on this characterization in a morality tale that contrasted a pretty, feminine, and pregnant "Miss Seventeen," endowed with "a strong, attractive female body," with a plain, sturdy, and celibate forty-year-old social worker—so familiar, so pitiable she needed no Bunyanesque sobriquet. The social worker's "organism, made and oriented for pregnancy," had prepared some four hundred times "to receive a sperm" but was barren still. She had brought the girl, whom everyone thought abnormal, to psychiatric attention. Yet, Myerson continued, no one thought the social worker, pleasant and intelligent but "completely biologically maladapted," anything but normal. "What a fool I am!"—the social worker's final, anguished cry resounds through the women's colleges and schools of social work, a stark reminder of biology's imperatives and a lesson in the folly of transgression.[72] Myerson's tale, its point made at the social worker's expense, is one measure of how much was at stake when women made gender trouble.

THREE

THE PSYCHIATRY OF EVERYDAY LIFE

THE PRACTICING PSYCHIATRIST, maintained one of them, was forever running up against problems having to do with "every day matters of conduct and behavior," subjects on which the discipline offered little guidance. No one had established or even explored the "psychology of every day life," he complained, and the consequence was that no one could say with certainty what was normal.[1] Nineteenth-century alienists, this psychiatrist's disciplinary predecessors, had constituted "the insane" as a category of persons properly subject to their control and had defined "the abnormal" as a domain of medical expertise. The ubiquitous, overcrowded asylum testified to their achievement. But what this psychiatrist suggested and others put more bluntly was that the insane alone, however expansively defined, could not sustain psychiatrists' ambitious professional program. If what Southard termed "the psychiatric point of view" was to achieve the dominance he thought it merited, psychiatrists would have to demonstrate its usefulness in matters far beyond the rather narrow, easily marginalized sphere of disease. They would have to establish a psychiatry of the prosaic and routine to supplement the established psychiatry of the abnormal, a psychiatry, Southard proposed, "to aid the common man and woman to deeper, practical insights into everyday questions."[2]

Twentieth-century psychiatrists would establish their discipline's cultural dominance by pursuing, just as Southard suggested, a strategy of producing and compiling knowledge of the everyday. This strategy took shape as psychiatrists confronted, questioned, and puzzled over the hundreds of individuals who came under their scrutiny suffering not from the symptoms of insanity as both parties understood it—hallucinations, delusions, markedly disordered thinking—but from difficulties that appeared rooted in everyday life, difficulties that might have plagued anyone: poor marital relations, temperamental oddities, failed ambitions, heightened sensitivities, a proclivity for lying, a nervous disposition. In the course of observing and extracting testimony from such patients, psychiatrists fashioned a psychiatry of the everyday, a psychiatry that took as its object what one practitioner called life's "normal activities" and what Southard and Jarrett suggested was the character structure of "normal human beings."[3] This psychiatry, not the psychiatry of serious mental maladies, is the predecessor of the discipline that today enjoys a measure of cultural authority.

And this psychiatry, not the other, is the foundation on which rests the discipline's normalizing imperative, its claim to authority regarding, in Foucault's formulation, "the mental normalisation of individuals."[4]

Commentators have observed that in the early years of the twentieth century American psychiatry was fundamentally transformed, noting that the discipline that had in the nineteenth century been narrowly focused on insanity was, by the second decade of the twentieth, staking its disciplinary claim to "the normal"—both normal persons and normal, everyday problems.[5] This chapter suggests that the sources of psychiatry's widely noted dominance lie neither in its long-overdue embrace of science, as those writing from within the discipline have argued, nor in its enduring commitment to social control, as many critics of psychiatry have proposed, but here, in psychiatrists' delineation of a realm of everyday concerns—sex, marriage, womanhood, and manhood; work, ambition, worldly failure; habits, desires, inclinations—as properly psychiatric.[6] Further, it suggests that any normalizing power the discipline enjoys today is premised not on psychiatrists' authority over insanity, for most are willing to cede them that, but on their turn-of-the-century forebears' bold appropriation of day-to-day life and their subtle weaving of a psychiatric point of view into its many aspects.

Foundations for a New Psychiatry

Although psychiatric diagnoses from the start rested, at least in part, on popular understandings of what was abnormal, constituting "normality" as a site for the play of psychiatric scrutiny was not a matter of simply specifying that to which abnormality had long been silently opposed. It was, rather, a discrete project, one in which psychiatrists would be challenged to fashion the conceptual tools necessary to construe the normal as an object that science could apprehend. To be sure, practices that would give rise to what Foucault has called "normalizing judgments," implicitly quantitative judgments that assessed persons in relation not to a fixed standard (the law, for example) but to each other and that defined difference not absolutely but "in relation to all other differences," were current in the nineteenth century, central to the rise of the human sciences and to the exercise of discipline in prisons, schools, the military, and asylums. Within the psychiatric domain, however, hierarchical rankings or scaled assessments of individuals in terms of their behavior or natures— normalizing appraisals, by Foucault's account—were a feature more of the twentieth than of the nineteenth century; they were not a natural corollary of normalizing practices but the result of psychiatrists' efforts to establish new foundations for their discipline.[7] Further, the concept of the normal has both a descriptive dimension (what is most common) and an evaluative one (what ought to be), and the normalizing judgments that Foucault argues constituted the regime of the norm were primarily expressive of the latter. Early-twentieth-century psychiatrists attended to *both* dimensions of the normal, like their colleagues in other fields issuing normalizing judgments but also—what is obscured in Foucault's account—defining life's common, routine aspects as within their science's domain.[8]

Psychiatrists' project of delineating the concepts that would enable them to bring life into science took shape somewhat fitfully and not always intentionally as they set about remaking their discipline, attempting to align themselves with medicine and science. Determined to inhabit the scientist's persona, psychiatrists regularly engaged in the ritualistic slaying of their forebears as they unburdened themselves of a disciplinary heritage that they argued was embarrassing, informed by superstition, and unscientific, tainted by association with its poorly trained practitioners, the alienist-administrators. Presiding over what they imagined was psychiatry's rebirth, they cast the moment as one of disciplinary discontinuity, playing down what they owed to their predecessors. In envisioning their discipline not as an elaboration of the old in a newly scientific idiom but as entirely new, psychiatrists were emboldened by several critical but discrete and unreplicated findings and developments in syphilology (the study of syphilis) and mental testing. They fashioned these findings into what were to their minds indisputably scientific foundations for their specialty, and referred to them to sustain their claims to authority over not only the insane but, as Southard somewhat grandiosely put it, "practically the entire human world."[9]

Constituting a science that would take the whole human world as its object presented psychiatrists with a paradox. On the one hand, it brought them closer to the scientific domain. The two paradigms they formulated around the somewhat unlikely partners of syphilology and mental testing, paradigms they used to analyze the vast, unordered ensemble of phenomena that made up "life," were cast in the language of science.[10] Psychiatrists formulated the first, a disease paradigm, around syphilis, amid a series of striking developments that were unraveling its mysteries. A disease to which physicians had long attributed a distinctive etiology, course, and outcome, syphilis afflicted, by various estimates, between 10 and 25 percent of those who came under psychiatric scrutiny. Psychiatrists borrowed the second, a metric paradigm, from the early psychometricians, the psychologists at the turn of the century whose attempts to measure men's (and some women's) mental capacities resulted in the first mental tests. Psychiatrists quickly adopted the tests to identify the feebleminded and, although soon abandoning them, incorporated the metric thinking of which they were expressive into their own.

Yet in putting together a psychiatry of everyday life, psychiatrists were pulled away from science's conventions—its abstruse, specialized language, its carefully controlled field of operations—and drawn closer to what was common, the property not of the scientist but of anyone. A number of the practices they wanted to submit to psychiatric scrutiny in the interest of establishing "new facts" and, in turn, a new science were the focus of popular interest and spirited public debate—sex in particular, but also such concerns as women's nature and the tenor of relations between the sexes. And some of the practices they scrutinized had long belonged to the domestic domain. Character training, emotional control, the making of responsible citizens—all belonged to the sphere of social reproduction over which middle-class women asserted control as they were being shut out of public life in the second and third decades of the nineteenth century.[11]

Reflecting on his specialty's "attitude to the normal," Abraham Myerson observed that when the psychiatrist limited himself to mental diseases, he could claim an authority few would dispute, but "where he steps into everyday life, he must prepare for buffets and incredulity."[12] The account that follows, which shows how psychiatrists in search of science somewhat inadvertently identified the conceptual apparatuses with which to approach normality, reproduces something of the contingency of the whole endeavor. In form, therefore, it is not linear; it replicates some of the twists and turns that Myerson said the psychiatrist would inevitably meet.

Syphilis and Sexual Scrutiny

Syphilis first appeared in epidemic proportions in late-fifteenth-century Europe. Almost immediately, astrologers, noting the disease's distinctive genital origins, attributed its appearance to celestial effects, specifically "the conjunction of Saturn and Jupiter in the third aspect of Scorpio," the sign believed to rule the genitals. Early on, syphilis was burdened with the associations of sinfulness that it bears to this day, and, correspondingly, syphilology was compounded of religious, ethical, and medical observations.[13] Early in the nineteenth century, the French physician A. L. J. Bayle described a disease state—characterized by impaired locomotion and speech, partial paralysis, delusions of grandeur, and eventual dementia— that another Frenchman, L. F. Calmeil, termed "general paralysis of the insane" or "general paresis." For nearly a century, researchers debated its possible syphilitic origins; these were definitively established between 1905 and 1913, when the causative agent of syphilis—the spirochete *treponema pallidum*—was discovered and then identified post-mortem in the brain tissue of persons who had suffered from general paralysis. With the development of the Wassermann diagnostic test for syphilitic infection in 1906 and the discovery of an effective treatment for the disease in the drug Salvarsan in 1909, psychiatrists claimed to see one of the most common of mental afflictions shed its mystical associations and assume instead the shape of a medical problem.[14]

It would be hard to overstate the impact of these findings on psychiatrists, who already considered general paralysis the most scientifically interesting form of brain disease.[15] "Syphilis is in a sense the making of psychiatry," Southard predicted in a refrain that many others would echo.[16] Almost immediately, psychiatrists assembled these findings into a paradigm of disease caused by an identifiable agent and amenable to a specific chemotherapeutic antidote—the "paradigm of general paresis," to which they were certain other mental disorders would conform. At a stroke, the realm of psychiatric ignorance was reduced by perhaps one-quarter, and latter-day practitioners would establish their own modernity as they marveled at the "astonishing statements"—linking the disease to sexual excess—that, they argued, therapeutic ignorance had forced from even the most respected physicians.[17] To be sure, the tradition that had from the start termed syphilis the "carnal scourge" would prove remarkably durable, but many psychiatrists self-consciously abjured it. In this vein, Southard maintained that he had found it pointless to preach against "sex indulgence."[18] Bringing general paresis into medicine proper offered satisfactions that dispensing simple moralisms could not. It underwrote the psychiatrist's claim to scientific status, allowing him to turn the tables on the physicians who considered psychiatry apart from medicine proper, proving to those who for years had contemptuously dismissed syphilitic patients and their symptoms—headaches, nervousness, fatigue, failing memory—as merely neurasthenic that there was indeed something real (that is, organic) afflicting them.[19] Just as important, it allowed the psychiatrist to imagine that he was being scientifically neutral while stripping sex—which, if no longer the exciting cause, was still implicated in the disease—of its many higher meanings and constituting it as a simple "fact," equivalent to any other.[20]

Psychiatrists would repeatedly maintain that they were merely heeding science's dictates in treating sex straightforwardly. But, as their own elaboration of the syphilis complex makes clear, this was itself a highly polemical stance. Apprehending the truth of sex—making it a fact—was no simple matter. Psychiatrists would first have to pry testimony regarding sex from the discreet silence in which, they argued, Victorian convention shrouded it before they could subject it to their dispassionate scrutiny. Arguing that science made such scrutiny absolutely necessary, they boldly posed questions about sex that embarrassed, ruffled, and annoyed patients. Because science had provided both a reliable diagnostic test and an efficacious treatment for this highly infectious disease, which could, psychiatrists emphasized, unknowingly be transmitted to the innocent because of its capacity to lie dormant and unrecognized for many years, it was imperative that all cases be identified, persuaded to submit to a therapeutic regimen, and rendered at least temporarily chaste—or so the reasoning went. Thus, they argued, it was necessary for the syphilitic to divulge the initial source of infection (whether conjugal or promiscuous) as well as others with whom he or she was currently having sexual relations.[21]

Psychiatrists and social workers were well aware that this sort of testimony went against the grain of public opinion. Maida Solomon related the story of her encounter with an editor of a leading newspaper who, claiming he was catering to a wide and easily offended public, refused to use the word "syphilis" in his paper's columns. Solomon proposed that the public was enlightened enough "to at least read the word." She and other social workers and psychiatrists who dealt with syphilitic patients sketched an ethics of disclosure that was meant to induce patients to speak while at the same time protecting their privacy. This approach promised patients that, in return for speaking frankly, their cases would be handled on a scientific, not a moral, basis. Maintaining that syphilis was neither a moral disease nor a stigma, Solomon stressed that social workers did not "probe into the method of contraction." She and her purportedly enlightened public knew that inquiries in that direction were likely to yield evidence of premarital or extramarital sexual activity—a wife's affair or, more likely, a husband's forays into the demimonde. Aware, perhaps, that they were on treacherous territory in taking on the well-established tradition of the "medical secret," which many contemporary physicians invoked as justification for not informing wives of their husbands' venereal infections (the secret "was in the interest of the social order," a prominent specialist wrote in 1904), social workers attempted to honor the gender dimension the secret encoded.[22] Solomon emphasized that social workers were prepared to quell wives' well-founded suspicions of their husbands by reassuring them "that quite probably the spouse contracted the disease before marriage," even though in most cases this was either impossible to ascertain or patently untrue. "No family upheavals nor any undue unhappiness have ever resulted from our handling of several hundred cases in this manner," Solomon somewhat improbably maintained.[23] Lying in the service of truth, social workers proffered small fictions to one party in the hope of extracting scientifically important facts from the other.

This ethics of disclosure, which pressed confession into the service of science, was premised on a principle of disinterested inducement that was insufficiently coercive for the task at hand. It was thus more tenable as a precept than as a strategy. Inducing the recalcitrant to speak of sex often involved a sort of detective work that no one could argue protected the privacy of the individual in question, as the exemplary case of one David Collins, a forty-five-year-old, out-of-work, hard-drinking paretic machinist, makes clear. Their ingenuity and persuasiveness pushed to the limit by Collins's obtuseness, the social workers felt it necessary to question his wife, his priest, his previous employers, the neighborhood storekeeper, his daughter's teacher, his landlord, a previous landlady, and a neighbor, all of whom supplied valuable but unspecified data regarding his domestic relations, his employment history, and his taste for drink.[24] Judging Collins's particularly difficult case a success, Southard and Jarrett invoked "the modern point of view," which held that syphilitic persons were "hardly entitled to so much privacy as that which normal persons enjoy," to account for the social workers' investigatory ardor. From this it was only a short step to arguing, as they did, that the recalcitrant should be "pertinaciously pursued."[25]

Southard and Jarrett portrayed themselves as helplessly beholden to the modern point of view, which willed them to inquire indiscreetly and in the process to offend the public's sensibilities. But they did not simply inherit this modern stance; they were instrumental in shaping it. Casting modernity—which they associated with allegiance to science, frankness, and a generally pragmatic stance—as the enlightened antithesis to Victorianism, psychiatrists employed it as a platform from which to launch their more general attack on propriety and privacy as outmoded remnants from the prescientific past, an attack that, if suggested by the imperatives of syphilis, went far beyond its bounds. Syphilis offered psychiatrists and social workers a tantalizing but perfectly legitimate entrée into the domestic realm, and, as such, underwrote their conviction that in the future science would exempt no human activity, however intimate, from expert scrutiny.

For the moment, psychiatrists and social workers anchored their assault firmly to syphilis. But they employed a succession of domestic images that suggested just how broadly based it would become. From their matter-of-fact, policelike dictum that "the house of a syphilitic is not his castle,"[26] through their cryptic but suggestive judgment that "the most appealing difficulties" associated with syphilis "lodge within the bosom of the family,"[27] to their recording of their mildly prurient delight that in the course of treatment Collins's wife had reported that the two had become "like sweethearts again"[28]—these images captured the range of satisfactions to be derived from dealing with syphilis. For all their professed distinterestedness, psychiatrists and social workers could not help being moved by the momentousness of a science that necessitated such intimate inquiries. Maida Solomon hinted at this in her reflection that part of the appeal of working with syphilitics lay in the opportunity it presented to deal "with human nature stripped of the conventions of society," without, she proposed, subterfuge or guile. "It is always absorbing to see one's fellow citizens as they *are*," she explained, expressing with untutored directness the rarely voiced conviction that governed psychiatrists' day-to-day practice—that science would bring them closer to life itself.[29]

No human endeavor was more enticing in this regard than sex, which psychiatrists, working within a well-established Western tradition that privileged it with a special claim on truth, envisioned as especially laden with meaning but unnecessarily elusive, hedged about with the prohibitions of civilization. Apprehending it straightforwardly as a fact was thus a defiant strategy, one meant in part to signal psychiatrists' and social workers' unflinching modernity. Their pose of frankness is nowhere more evident than in Jarrett's presentation of the case of Harold Gordon, an affable forty-five-year-old syphilitic steamfitter, into which crept not a trace of opprobrium. Dispensing with decorum, the various workers who treated the case reported that Gordon was currently "having sex relations" two to three times a week with the widow Driscoll, who, although she claimed to be "without passion," was as a result pregnant and contemplating an abortion. Social workers quickly determined that Gordon's domestic arrangements were complex. He and Bessie Driscoll, who supported herself by doing housework, had not married on her account—she admitted to knowing better, but claimed she cared nothing for her reputation. Her two prosperous brothers, who helped with the rent, wanted nothing to do with Gordon; they knew he was syphilitic and were disgusted that the two had been having sex. A further complication was that Driscoll had taken a dislike to Gordon's mother, calling her "an indifferent, old-fashioned Yankee, who cares more for the dollar than for anything else." And Gordon's family thought Driscoll was "a drag on them," and wished they were rid of her. Illicit sex, petty jealousies and resentments, quarrels over money— Gordon's case offered ample opportunities for dispensing morally tinged advice. Yet throughout, interviewing one party after another, social workers treated the case with equanimity, as one that turned on the making of practical arrangements—escorting Driscoll to the gynecological clinic, setting up employment interviews—and nothing more. In the end, Gordon and Driscoll, prompted by social workers, decided to marry, but this, too, the social workers presented as a practical matter having as much to do with the whereabouts of the eleven dollars they had advanced to the couple to cover costs as with any higher meanings.[30]

Sex, as social workers constructed it in Gordon's case, was what Southard termed a "real problem," a concrete, practical thing of known (or knowable) dimensions and quality that demanded neither philosophical nor divine wisdom to resolve. It was not inherently so; the vagaries of sexual desire, Southard suggested, resisted neat apprehension.[31] But syphilology had helped make it possible for psychiatrists to conceptualize sex as a discrete, nonpsychological issue, and to imagine that in implementing a policelike investigatory strategy they were acting in the name of science, not morality. Syphilolgy brought psychiatry into medicine by means of the disease paradigm to which it conformed. Just as important, however, it gave psychiatrists license to bring sex into psychiatry.

Syphilology and all it suggested figured centrally, but somewhat differently, in social workers' day-to-day practice and in their sense of professionalism. The social worker dealing with syphilitic patients could imagine herself as much a scientist as any physician, for in researching obscure issues and tracking down obscure points she was party to what Maida Solomon called "the thrill of adventure," even if her work yielded only negative results—a luxury few women could enjoy. In addition, the social worker dealing with syphilis stood on medicine's firm ground rather than, like her predecessors, on morality's shifting sands; so placed, she could act authoritatively, making her forays into private lives and homes with relative impunity. Most important, she could mobilize the science of syphilology to enhance her professional persona, distinguishing herself from her "humanitarian" predecessors as she substituted scientifically neutral assessments for the judgments of the dissolute they had proffered. Disciplining her professional self in the interest of discipline formation, the social worker so engaged displayed the fortitude desirable in one who would discipline another.[32]

Mental Tests: Capturing the Normal

The development of mental tests, of which the Binet test was the prototype, provided psychiatrists with a means to ground nebulous notions of normality and its obverse, pathology, in something concrete—in this case a grade, meant as a measure of innate intelligence.[33] The earliest mental tests resulted from a series of examinations that the French psychologist Alfred Binet conducted on Parisian schoolchildren in the early years of the century. Presenting them with a series of practical tasks, Binet assessed their performance according to a scale graded by age, and assigned a mental age to each child.[34] American psychologists and psychiatrists were quick to discern the tests' significance, asserting that they satisfied any number of scientific criteria. Early on, even before he had seen Binet's landmark work, the enthusiast of testing Lewis M. Terman proposed that mental tests would yield empirical results (or data, as they would be termed today) that would in time replace the "interesting stories" told about children as a basis on which to classify them.[35] Premised on the principle of measurement, which was to many minds the sine qua non of any science, the tests, he suggested, would turn "every-day experience" into something concrete.[36]

In short, what he and many others grasped was that the tests offered a way to bridge the chasm that separated life—the thoughts, feelings, and actions of individuals that the psychologist's domain encompassed—from science.

The investigation of cases of syphilis promised to do the same. But mental tests, which from the start were structured so that they transformed rough notions of normality (normality, that is, as most would define it)[37] into numbers, promised to reinstate the nexus of normality and pathology that syphilis, when treated straightforwardly as a disease like any other, threatened to jettison from the medical realm. The tests effected the transformation from life, with its roughly specified notions of normality, to science, which honored exactness, by means of an alchemy that many critics have charged was (and remains) fraudulent. I will examine this shortly. For the moment, let the novelty of the testing enterprise be registered. As an expression of a metric mode of thinking, testing furnished psychiatrists with a means to achieve the specificity that by their own account their science so embarrassingly lacked. As they saw it, because testing produced numbers that documented, finally and inarguably, what many had known for centuries was the variability of human mental endowments, it was proof somehow that other human capabilities could be measured and thus brought within the scientific domain. The science of human nature that some philosophers, John Stuart Mill among them, had declared impossible and others had been endeavoring to produce could at last be realized.

"The happy inspiration of Binet"—so Southard summed up the tests' significance. The tests made it possible, he proposed, for psychiatrists to pursue a new line of attack in their quest for knowledge of human character; they were in his estimation "the most important achievement in our field aside from the discovery of the importance of syphilis."[38] The metric principle to which they testified would in time possibly yield not only "more measures of things" but also, he trusted, "more things to measure." It would, that is, prove applicable not only to intelligence but also to other aspects of character—feelings, emotions, sentiments. Southard was well aware that physicians would only reluctantly assimilate the statistical constructs integral to the Binet method. The psychologist's "so-called norms," "beautiful new bell-curve," "metric argument"—these would remain foreign to the psychiatric mind, which he argued was resolutely individualistic, not statistical, in orientation.[39] Indeed, for the most part psychiatrists treated the Binet grade as an absolute, a dichotomous measure that indicated simply whether the individual in question was feebleminded or not. Endowing the condition it presumed to measure with an appealing and practical concreteness, it functioned much like the Wassermann test, which indicated the presence of syphilitic infection in the blood.

Psychiatrists did not invent the category of mental defect, for observers had long classified purportedly defective individuals as either idiots (those with the least intelligence) or imbeciles (persons possessed of middling subnormal intelligence). Feeblemindedness, which in its narrow usage denoted the defective with the most intelligence—the newly named "morons" or, as Southard termed them, the "higher subnormals"—and more inclusively referred to all defective persons, had its modern conceptual origins in the discourses of defectiveness woven together in the nineteenth century: craniometry, criminal anthropology, phrenology. But feeblemindedness in either sense assumed specificity only by virtue of the test of which it was a referent; it was, in other words, a discrete condition distinguishable from normality only because mental tests labeled it as such. Southard granted that the tests could not identify the highest of the subnormals "with perfect accuracy," and allowed that no one could rightfully claim to sort the mass of substandard persons into the normal and the definitely subnormal. Indeed, he admitted that it was "a shock to the layman's mind" to find "persons of but slightly substandard mentality termed feebleminded."[40] But the tests' virtues outweighed their shortcomings, and psychiatrists employed them enthusiastically, rarely pausing to question their validity. The tests made it easy to dispose of some otherwise complex cases, for once it was determined that an individual was feebleminded, that person's case was as good as closed for psychiatrists' purposes. They were happy either to hand the feebleminded over to various authorities—state social workers, parole officers, and the like—or to release them to the care of family or friends.[41]

The case of twenty-year-old Rosa Giordani, a recently married immigrant from the Azores who was feebleminded by the tests' reckoning, shows how, with the aid of a poor Binet score, even the most contested of cases could be handily resolved. Giordani's case might have turned on the domestic disagreements that figured so conspicuously in it had she not fared poorly on the tests, for psychiatrists at first thought her normal, intelligent, and agreeable. Domestic discord structured the case from the start. Giordani's Italian-born husband, Luigi, who brought her to the hospital claiming she was crazy, opened his audience with the admitting physician by pulling a notebook from his pocket, saying, in lawyerly fashion, "I kept a good record of this case and I'll read to you from my notes." The record he had so carefully compiled was damning indeed. His wife had left his home and was boarding with a Portuguese family in Cambridge; she was, he maintained, careless, in fact filthy, a poor housekeeper who had most recently burned her dress and underwear by sitting on the edge of the stove while cooking; and, speaking eugenically, he pointed out that her father was "a drunkard and her mother was queer" and thus he was "afraid to bring up a family" with her. Rosa Giordani, who said she had entered the hospital willingly, was able to answer each of her husband's charges calmly and convincingly. She explained that she had moved out because of her mother-in-law, who had scolded her about her cleaning and "threatened her with a knife," adding that the woman had locked her out of the house and had deposited her belongings on the front steps; she had burned her dress just a little while standing too close to the stove on a cold day as she prepared macaroni; and she admitted that her father was a quarrelsome drunkard who scared his own children. After questioning her extensively, psychiatrists concluded that Rosa Giordani's complaints were not in the least delusional, that her thought processes were quick and accurate, and that she showed insight concerning the events that had brought her under their scrutiny. Only her poor test score grounded this small drama, in which a husband's filial piety, ethnic loyalty—"She is Portuguese and I am Italian," Luigi Giordani emphasized—and heightened awareness of a man's conjugal rights was set against a wife's cheerful but somewhat ad hoc determination to secure for herself a square deal. It is likely that the case otherwise would have been resolved, like so many others, only after extensive social work investigations aimed at determining which party's tale was true, which false.[42]

As useful as it was in identifying the defective, the Binet test, and the statistical reasoning on which it purported to rest, was even more significant because it gave psychiatrists license to explore the normal that they so desperately wanted to bring under psychiatric scrutiny. Psychiatrists would find it far easier to delineate the abnormal than the normal, and for all their talk of the latter, they would continue to equate it with, one psychometrician observed, "the usual run of things."[43] But normality, in any of its slightly different guises, insistently arose in any consideration of the tests. This was in part because the tests, which comprised tasks (like counting coins) a person might encounter in day-to-day life,[44] could be administered not only to those thought intellectually deficient but to everyone—normal persons who might in fact be abnormal, an argument psychiatrists often made in alarmist tones.[45] More abstractly, the logic on which mental testing quickly came to be premised was not only numerical but probabilistic, for many of the tests subsequent to Binet's were constructed to yield results that could be arrayed on the so-called normal curve—the now-familiar bell curve or Gaussian distribution. Once the Binet score, a "mental age," had been transformed into an "intelligence quotient" or IQ (by dividing it by the test-taker's chronological age)[46] and then, by Terman, standardized on the scale that set the mean score at 100, any single score situated its bearer in relation to all those who had been and would be tested—in relation to the norm.[47]

The normal was a curious quantity, an evaluative concept (signifying that which is ideal, which ought to be) that passed as a statistical outcome (the average or, alternatively, most common result).[48] As any number of critics have suggested, the tests codified the term's useful ambiguity. However, the tests did not entirely invent that ambiguity, for the normative thinking current in everyday social exchanges rested on a similar conflation of meanings. Relatives of some of the individuals psychiatrists deemed feebleminded described them variously as "queer," "different," "eccentric," and "peculiar"—all, like "normal," assessments that assumed meaning only in reference to the not-queer and not-different, the common and expected. The tests, in effect, set these evaluative categories on a scale that presumed to measure the distance between, say, "eccentric" and normal, a distance that relatives could convey only inexactly, by citing instances of strange behavior. Further, the tests' codification of the ambiguity of the normal was not so easily achieved. Results produced by the mass testing of nearly two million World War I army recruits under the direction of Robert M. Yerkes suggested that the ideal and the average might differ considerably, for they showed that the "normal" (that is, average or most common) American was "abnormal," a moron of subnormal intelligence—a finding that generated mostly alarmed but also some amused commentary.[49] Mental testing, then, first underscored the dual nature of the normal that everyday usage encoded before psychologists set out to eliminate it, adjusting the tests' scales so that statistically pleasing results would always be produced.

The self-validating nature of the tests—and here the issue of fraudulent alchemy arises—has been neither fully addressed nor surmounted: they were constructed to produce normally distributed scores, and their doing so was interpreted as a measure of their validity.[50] In addition, critics have long charged that the tests, which presumed to measure the quantity known as "general intelligence," in fact created it. In the early twenties, the psychologist Edwin G. Boring maintained that intelligence could be defined only as "what the tests test," a proposition that would still be hard to fault.[51] In common parlance, intelligence was composed of a number of disparate qualities, expressed in varying, not wholly comparable, ways— "high marks in Greek Syntax," say, or "the capacity of men to command troops or to administer provinces."[52] The psychologist-architects of mental tests addressed this knotty problem with simple assertions and complex statistics, with the result that once "general intelligence" was assigned a number, placed on a scale, analyzed, and standardized, few outside the profession bothered to ask to what, precisely, it referred.

Yet however faulty we might think it, the work of the early psychometricians—Binet, Yerkes, Terman—did provide one solution to a problem that had troubled statisticians for some thirty years: How could the elusive, amorphous, and various components of intelligence be rendered in measurable form? The English gentleman-scientist Francis Galton, who devoted his life to establishing the immutable laws of heredity (and who coined the term *eugenics*), had wrestled with this problem in his early

(1869) work, *Hereditary Genius*, which argued that men's talents and abilities flowed along family lines. (Something of how Galton thought women's talents could be assessed can be gleaned from his "beauty map" investigations, which he carried out in a "semi-jocular" spirit. In pre-Freudian innocence, Galton wrote that as he walked city streets, using a "needle mounted as a pricker, wherewith to prick holes, unseen, in a piece of [cross-shaped] paper" that would serve as a record of his observations, he unobtrusively gathered "beauty data, classifying the girls I passed . . . as attractive, indifferent, or repellent." The girls of London scored highest.)[53] Galton proposed that men could be sorted into fourteen categories, arrayed on a scale that would group the most eminent at one end, the "vast abundance of mediocrity in the middle," and the abject idiots at the other end. The ranks of the scale Galton had in mind corresponded, he asserted, to equivalent quantities of ability. But because he had no way of measuring the abilities and mental capacities he scaled, the validity of the scale was based wholly on his assertion that such qualities were distributed in the population much like men's stature, a quality that was readily susceptible to measurement. Premised on questionable reasoning by analogy, the metric scale for intelligence has proven no less durable for being so.[54]

If Galton laid the statistical foundation on which rested the convention of fitting mental capacity, a nonmetric quantity at best, onto a metric scale,[55] it remained for Binet and his followers to provide a means by which to translate that quantity into numerical form. The alchemy that brought life into science—that, as Terman put it, proved that "psychology and life are not prime to each other"—was thus a two-step process.[56] Once it was completed, psychiatrists saw that the tests offered them an entirely new way of apprehending the world, a conceptual template they could lay over the bewildering mosaic of human activity that would enable them to order and assess facets of life that had resisted apprehension. Psychiatrists and social workers grappled with ways of putting this metric template to specific use beyond the realm of intelligence. Early on, for example, social workers devised a scale for measuring the "level of efficiency" at which individuals conducted their affairs. A formidably level "line of highest possible efficiency" topped the chart; on the x-axis, they plotted time, and on the y-axis, the "standard of living based on conduct" (fig. 3.1). This chart succinctly summarized a patient's efficiency trajectory, showing, in our example, that Margaret Hadley's efficiency was lowest when she was admitted to the hospital and slightly higher upon discharge, after which, under social work supervision, it slowly rose, only to fall again and to reach a new low when she and her husband quarreled. By the end, the chart had Hadley operating at near-highest efficiency, graphically underscoring the value of social work intervention.

Social workers experimented with other charts, all variations on the

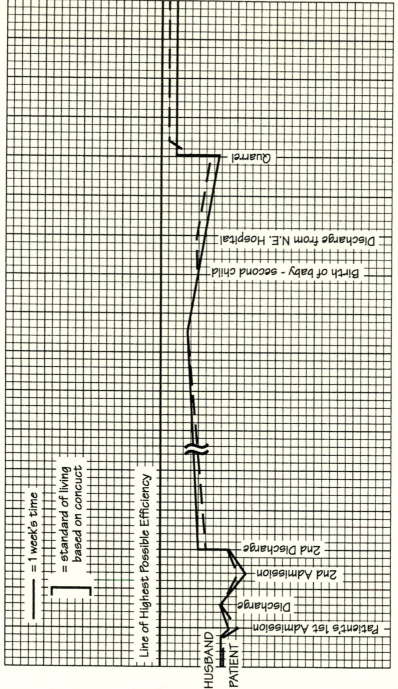

Fig. 3.1. Efficiency graph, prepared by social workers in the case of Margaret Hadley, charting her "standard of living based on conduct" over an eight-month period (case 2747, 1914).

efficiency graph, but their metric impulses quickly fizzled. Such charts took time to construct and it is likely that overextended social workers found them more burdensome than helpful. More important, the charts lacked the critical transformative capacity that made the Binet tests so compelling. In contrast to mental tests, which appeared to convert the ill-defined quantity "intelligence" into an easily interpreted number at a single stroke, social workers' charts worked no alchemy. They merely recorded, on a misleading scale, rough appraisals of individuals' "efficiency," a quantity even more amorphous than intelligence. Quickly abandoned, the charts were one measure of how difficult it would prove to replicate the metric principle exemplified by the Binet tests.[57]

In this respect the metric principle differed little from the disease paradigm that syphilis brought into psychiatric thinking, for the latter, too, proved frustratingly elusive. Psychiatrists would dissect hundreds of brains and identify pathological signs with stunning precision postmortem, but they would be unable to determine a relationship between their findings and any observed behaviors or diseases. Yet this, like social workers' metric imaginings, mattered little, for the two models would powerfully shape psychiatric thinking. The lineaments of the disease model were familiar in medicine but new to psychiatry, eagerly incorporated by psychiatrists once syphilology established the model's pertinence. The outlines of the metric model were altogether new, and therefore doubly strange to psychiatrists, who embraced the tests while resisting the logic on which they were premised. Yet, somewhat unwittingly, psychiatrists gradually grafted the metric model onto the more clearly delineated disease model, setting the parameters of a new psychiatry that would, like the old, deal handily with recognized diseases—dementia praecox, manic-depressive insanity—while at the same time asserting its authority over the entire range of human behaviors, from the abnormal to the highly prized normal.

From Feeblemindedness to Psychopathy

Psychiatrists construed the disease and metric models, syphilis and feeblemindedness, as indisputably scientific foundations for a psychiatry they asserted was altogether new. Constantly invoking the authority of science, with which they claimed their discipline was now allied, they outlined an ambitious professional program aimed at securing them the formal institutional and political power that had eluded their predecessors' grasp. This program, like the science on which it was premised, had several dimensions. One was manifestly directed at securing psychiatrists a broad, respected role in the public sphere; another was focused more diffusely on a domestic sphere they argued was private. Of the two, psychiatrists' public program was the more coherent but also the more bound by their period's particular conventions, and thus more ephemeral. Articulated with confidence and expressed in often wildly exaggerated claims, this program still was the means by which psychiatrists effected the transition from a psychiatry of insanity to a psychiatry that took the whole of the human endeavor for its subject. What they achieved in this sphere is perhaps more difficult to appreciate but just as significant as what they accomplished in the domestic realm.

Psychiatrists entered the public sphere aggressively promoting an agenda of defect and difference that they provocatively cast as a wholesale assault on the egalitarian heritage of the Enlightenment.[58] Proposing to identify defect where others saw soundness, difference where ideologues saw sameness, psychiatrists staked their claim to the uncharted territory that they argued lay between frank manifestations of disease on the one hand and indisputable normality on the other. They maintained that expert scrutiny of this territory would yield any number of dangerously but (to the layperson) imperceptibly abnormal individuals, the magnitude of whose assembled defects would, Southard ventured, put the "quite unfounded" and "superficially inspiring" but characteristically American belief that "all men are born free and equal" to well-deserved rest.[59] As they saw it, the science of Alfred Binet would prove Thomas Jefferson's optimistically egalitarian vision obsolete.

Psychiatrists were hardly alone in charting egalitarianism's demise. Nor were they alone in linking it to the ascent of difference. The progressive visionary Herbert Croly, for one, warned that differences—"of interest, of intellectual outlook, of moral and technical standards, and of manner of life"—were displacing what was in his estimation instinctive but, for a number of reasons, outmoded American homogeneity.[60] Other, more alarmist commentators brandished the differences he assessed equivocally as evidence that the nation was facing a crisis of unprecedented proportions. To be sure, the last two decades of the nineteenth century had brought depression and financial panic, labor organization and unrest, rural and urban unemployment, political corruption and rebellion under the banner of populism; a range of observers was claiming to see strife supplant stability. It would take a peculiar sensibility, however, by turns wildly expansive and narrowly focused, to weave these disparate events into a powerfully cataclysmic vision while at the same time tracing them to a single, racial cause. Favoring simplicity over complexity, this was the sensibility that would successfully reduce the whole of the social problem to a problem of difference, focusing anxious attention on the ever more numerous and visible stranger within. Crime, pauperism, feeblemindedness, insanity, and, most important, immigration—the incantation became familiar and trite, its explanatory power enhanced as it resonated through nativist propaganda, reformers' investigations, and government reports.

Psychiatrists were alert to the possibilities opened by an ideological atmosphere as highly charged as this, and they did little to unsettle the popular litany of evils. They could somewhat opportunistically adopt the idiom of progressivism and, proffering a weakly environmentalist vision, endorse the civic reformer's stance that human nature was more shaped by than the shaper of circumstances. But their vision was tellingly inexact. Environment is "evidently a factor in producing mental disease" and mental disease is "evidently a factor in producing social disorder"—so went one characteristic formulation.[61] Psychiatrists bristled in contemplation of the environmentalists' excesses, their faith that social forces, not individual drives and endowments, molded behavior, and their conviction that planning healthy environments—housing, parks, playgrounds—would produce better citizens.[62] Maintaining that science, especially the science of intelligence, was proving that persons were at birth and throughout life unequally endowed, psychiatrists argued that environmental approaches to social problems, which rested on a belief in human perfectibility, were at worst naïvely misguided, at best merely beyond the psychiatrist's ken. Thus, Southard could allow that environmentalist "group views of men" were fine for others—for sociologists, judges, probation officers, and teachers. And he could frame the issue as a matter of occupational temperament, submitting that the physician was a "born individualist," and thus concerned less with establishing the "fitness of the environment" than with a "toning-down of the 'undesirable citizen.' "[63]

For the most part, however, psychiatrists framed the issue as a matter not of temperament but of truth. This truth was by their telling a sober affair, its axioms derived in large part from the eugenic science with which many cast their lot. Eugenics, a popular movement devoted to the betterment of the "human breed," had its roots in the attempts made by late-nineteenth-century scientists and propagandists, their interest stimulated by the theory of natural selection, to demonstrate the inheritability of such "traits" as immorality and pauperism. The rediscovery of Gregor Mendel's studies of inheritance in 1900 gave them the apparatus necessary to chart heredity's workings, and with inspired ardor the eugenically minded drafted elaborate genealogies of defectiveness, tracing the threads of criminality, pauperism, insanity, and, especially, feeblemindedness through the generations. The menace of the feebleminded their leitmotiv (and the title of a popular tract), eugenicists nurtured and at the same time exploited the popular perception that the once-pure American racial stock was deteriorating, tracing this to the immutable dictates of heredity. Studies in feeblemindedness might discomfit egalitarians, but their objections, and those of other "foolish persons," scoffed Southard, sure that truth was on his side, were senseless protests against the imperatives of measurement that would inevitably prevail.[64]

Psychiatrists maintained that measurement was proving all men, not just the foreign-born, different. For too long, Southard grumbled, philosophers and social statisticians had sought the "average man," the Quetelean fiction expressive of the postrevolutionary age's inclination toward moderation and the *juste milieu*.[65] The mean (or average) that for the nineteenth-century Belgian statistician Adolphe Quetelet represented all that was best in a society was, Southard proposed, a repository of mediocrity, the average man a "Humpty-Dumpty type" that science would soon shatter. "The whole brood of humdrummers" that looked for identities rather than differences was "bound to degenerate and die out," he went on, for "individualization is the war cry."[66]

Southard imagined himself engaged in a battle of social philosophies in which the pragmatism of the new century would vanquish the idealism of the old. This battle, played out over the figure of the "undesirable," was joined by many psychiatrists and psychologists, who declaimed as authoritatively as Southard on the shortcomings of the feebleminded, the psychopathic, the eccentric, and the otherwise deviant—the nation's population of undesirables—and the social consequences thereof. All summoned up evidence of difference to argue for the naturalness of inequality. One cautioned, for example, that the time had come "to abandon certain idealistic conceptions" and to accept that "capacity is not equally distributed."[67] "How can there be such a thing as social equality with this wide range of mental capacity?" asked another.[68] "Science leaves no ground for the denial of human inequality," the psychologist Yerkes insisted, adding that, however inspiring, democratic notions of "human equality and freedom" were fundamentally misleading. Classes in a democracy merely reflected the unequal distribution of men's "bodily and mental characteristics."[69] And so the indictments piled up, the feebleminded—their condition in Southard's estimation "one of the saddest features of the world"—the occasion for psychiatrists' styling themselves pragmatic philosophers of the body politic.[70]

But feeblemindedness would quickly prove too circumscribed a condition for psychiatrists' purposes.[71] Even as psychiatrists, in the guise of social critics, imagined themselves dispensing it freely as a diagnosis, designating this person and that group defective, they were enumerating its many limitations as a category. Feeblemindedness was too easily identified; a psychologist, or, for that matter, nearly anyone with a bit of training, could assign a grade in thirty minutes' time. Further, psychiatrists complained, the intellectual deficit that it encompassed was too narrow a measure of a person's character. Psychometric methods were powerless to identify significant deviations from normality, for example those displayed by the smart but inferior persons, familiar to everyone, who for lack of ambition or judgment failed at all they undertook.[72] Most important, the individual's subjective emotions and feelings were of no consequence in a determination of feeblemindedness. The exactness that drew psychiatrists to the category would also vex them, for it offered only the narrowest of arenas in which to ply their metric wares.[73]

With psychopathy, a newly invented category that encompassed a broad range of defects, psychiatrists addressed all the deficiencies of feeblemindedness. They employed the term and its most common American variant, "psychopathic personality," much the way they employed "feeblemindedness," to diagnose the abnormality that they argued passed everywhere as normality. Psychopathy at its simplest rendered a range of behaviors beyond the mental tests' measure—eccentricities, peculiarities, oddities, quirks—as signs of innate defect and brought them within the psychiatrist's purview. As a category it was far more malleable than feeblemindedness, and this, in part, is what sustained psychiatrists' interest in it. Feeblemindedness connoted precision and, as measured by the tests, referred to a discrete deficiency of intellectual capacity concerning the parameters of which there was little controversy. Psychopathy was, by contrast, usefully but dangerously indeterminate, a rubric that comfortably encompassed incarcerated criminals and dissipated high-livers, promiscuous girls and lazy men, deficiencies so various, so numerous, and, in the end, so elusive that some wondered whether it referred to anything at all.[74]

The tale psychiatrists spun around psychopathy can be briefly told. The nation's cities, they asserted, were home to an ever-increasing number of defective persons whom science was classing psychopathic. Unstable, irritable, impulsive, and otherwise unreliable, these individuals often appeared merely odd or weird to the laity, who tended to tolerate them as eccentric rather than to condemn them as defective. But defective they were, as much so as the recognized insane. Vagabonds and tramps, criminals and delinquents, prostitutes and sex perverts, labor leaders and fanatic reformers, revolutionaries and anarchists, poets and musicians, traveling salesmen and professional baseball players were prominent in their ranks. In one editorialist's estimation "iconoclasts incarnate," psychopaths recklessly flouted convention.[75] They lacked common decency and civic consciousness, and were unable to comport themselves in accordance with community standards. They refused to take life seriously. They were, from one perspective, fun-loving individuals whose attraction to what several psychiatrists primly dismissed as "the play side of life" made them incapable of observing society's "rules of conduct."[76] The metropolis, thick with seductions, offered them fertile territory on which to pursue their antisocial aims. Cranks at best, criminals at worst, psychopaths constituted a menace that for society's sake was best shut away in institutions or put to work on agricultural colonies.[77]

By 1915 or so, psychiatrists had placed psychopathy at the center of their social agenda, regularly chronicling the depredations of exemplary psychopaths in support of their contention that what appeared to the lay person to be social issues were in fact properly psychiatric concerns.[78] Southard succinctly voiced the main tenets of this perspective, which for example locates the cause of poverty not in bad institutions or in simple lack of money but in the character defects of the poor, in his suggestion that the problems of many social misfits were intrapsychic, intrapersonal, and the result of alterations in personality—that is, rooted in psychopathy. Once delineated as a condition, psychopathy quickly displaced feeblemindedness as the ground from which psychiatrists would choose to speak in the national discourse about defectiveness. Repeatedly cautioning that the public had to be apprised of the psychopathic menace if, as one authority bluntly put it, "the psychiatrists' contributions to social problems are to attain their full pragmatic value," psychiatrists shamelessly mined the term's polemical possibilities, spinning around it a scenario concerned with defectiveness and its control.[79] They were not above claiming knowledge they did not possess. In one notable instance from 1915, for example, the prominent psychiatrist Thomas W. Salmon attempted to persuade Congress that the ranks of undesirables—idiots, imbeciles, insane persons—excluded by law under the provisions of various immigration bills should be augmented by the addition of "constitutional psychopathic inferiors." The term, he argued, had "a definite meaning in that branch of medical science which devotes itself to diseases of the mind," a claim that quick perusal of any psychiatric journal would have proved false. Salmon went on to concede that it was "quite impossible, even with the most careful examination," to recognize the condition, but he turned this to his profession's advantage: the term's elusiveness would guarantee psychiatrists a role in identifying it.[80]

Psychiatrists could produce long lists of psychopathic types, a familiar litany of misfits—ne'er-do-wells and prostitutes, tramps and petty criminals. And they could produce lists of psychopathic symptoms, citing irritability, suggestibility, instability, inconsistency, egotism, weakness of will, pathological levity and affectivity, among other traits, as indicative of psychopathy, exempting only the purely intellectual aspects of character. But they were hard-pressed to define psychopathy itself. From the start, they vacillated between conceiving of it as, on the one hand, a discrete disease and, on the other, a diffusely defined abnormality that anyone might manifest. The earliest of the German psychiatrists who, from the 1880s on, outlined the concept in its modern form conceived of it as both. They split over whether it was "constitutional" (inborn) or acquired or even temporary, and over whether it was at bottom a weakness of the brain or simply bad behavior. They all agreed, however, that psychopathy, whatever it was, flourished in the space that lay between psychic health at one extreme and mental disease at the other.[81]

Many of the American psychiatrists who embraced the term early in the new century simply exploited its indeterminacy. They set its parameters broadly, branding all purported psychopaths with the qualities displayed by the worst. By their telling, only the vagaries of circumstance, not the firmament of character, set the psychopathic man serving out his sentence at Sing Sing apart from the psychopathic woman who preyed on unsuspecting men in cafés and hotel bars. Many psychiatrists indiscriminately conferred a diagnosis of psychopathic personality on anyone they thought strange or offensive, and argued that such individuals were best shut away from civilization. So many persons were potentially involved that the psychoanalyst A. A. Brill was moved to remark wryly that, if psychiatrists were to be believed, "at least 50 per cent of the population will have to be segregated and the rest will have to attend to them."[82]

But psychiatrists also wrestled with psychopathy's indeterminacy, for the category's protean nature—its capacity to shelter such diverse types—also meant it was in constant danger of unraveling altogether. Even as they declared that psychopaths suffered from an inborn, untreatable, and damningly antisocial condition, psychiatrists admitted among themselves that psychopathic personality was not, as one suggested, "a well-defined entity," but a "rag-bag" or wastebasket.[83] Southard conceded that "the well-established entity that the psychiatric world has agreed upon amounts to us saying [someone] is an odd person."[84] In many cases, one of his colleagues maintained, psychopathic personality "really does not mean anything except that [the patient] is not normal."[85] And one psychiatrist, venturing that practitioners "could not hope to find psychopaths of copybook clearness . . . except in text-books," came close to conceding that the category did not in fact exist, a stance Southard underlined with his suggestion that every psychopath might be sui generis.[86] Psychiatrists chided themselves for employing so imprecise a term. As one plaintively ventured at the conclusion of an address on psychopathic inferiority in which the speaker had offered an elaborate nosology of psychopathic types, "we are made fun of, in a way, by our colleagues for our overtechnicality."[87]

Psychiatrists never settled on a satisfactory definition of psychopathy. This was largely because, as an unstable epistemological amalgam of the disease and metric paradigms, psychopathy represented an altogether new type of category, one that was especially abhorrent, Southard ventured, to the "old-time alienist," tied as he was to a narrow, legalistic vision of insanity.[88] The enduring significance of psychopathy lies in that, as a singularly expansive, malleable, and unstable rubric, it provided psychiatrists a framework, contested but (within the psychiatric domain) legitimate nonetheless, within which to fashion a new psychiatry from aspects of the old. Around psychopathy, psychiatrists cast the lineaments of the so-called personality disorders—the inadequate personality, the borderline personality, the sociopathic personality—that figure so prominently in psychiatric nosologies today.[89] And around psychopathy they articulated what would come to be recognized as a characteristically psychiatric perspective on the relation between the normal and the abnormal, the mentally healthy and the ill—that they were arrayed on a continuum, inexactly and unstably demarcated, the abnormal but a variation on the normal, as one psychiatrist proposed, "in degree rather than kind."[90] In elaborating the concept of psychopathy, psychiatrists abandoned the sharp distinctions between insanity and sanity that characterized much psychiatric thinking and embraced instead (later, perhaps, than their confreres in other disciplines) the language of normalization—of deviations, grades, and scales; of "assets and liabilities"—that Foucault has argued is characteristic within the disciplines.[91]

Drawing on the much-debated but well-established concept of moral insanity, a disorder, in the words of the first English-speaking physician to delineate it, of the feelings and affections that sometimes left the intellectual faculties unimpaired,[92] psychiatrists at first had tried to constitute psychopathy along the lines it suggested, as a disease. But this quickly proved impossible. Precise delineation of the etiology, clinical picture, and prognosis associated with the disorder—all elements integral to the disease concept—turned out to be frustratingly elusive. In the end, psychiatrists could only specify what psychopathy was—and they were sure it was something—by reference to what it was not, and that was normality. The metric template they had constructed around the mental tests offered them a conceptual apparatus within which to talk about, apprehend, and assess the normality that was even less well defined in contrast to psychopathy than to feeblemindedness. Psychiatrists transposed it onto the field of the personality, an entity they began to define at the same time, bringing both the personality and metric thinking concurrently into psychiatric thought proper.

Around psychopathy, then, psychiatrists began to constitute "personality" in its modern form, as at once a possession, something a person "has" or displays, and an object of analysis. Raymond Williams tells us that the term, which in its earliest usages denoted merely "the quality of being a person and not a thing," only began to assume meanings familiar to us in the eighteenth century, when writers used it to refer to persons' individuality and distinctiveness; slightly later, it began to resonate with the associations of liveliness and spiritedness that it still carries.[93] But personality only came into common usage at the turn of the century, when it supplanted character as a designation for individuals' natures. The shift in usage had significant implications. Character offered the Victorian Americans who constantly invoked it, Warren Susman has argued, a program "for both mastery and development of the self." Associated with such high-minded notions as duty, work, honor, integrity, and above all, Susman writes, manhood,[94] character was not only a quality but also an imperative, dictating for men a life of hard work and sparse enjoyments consonant with the producer-oriented society in which it was current.

Personality shouldered a lighter moral load. It spoke to a different, less exalted constellation of values, and perhaps for that reason it was, in contrast to character, a quality women as well as men could evince.[95] From the start, in the hundreds of early-twentieth-century manuals that explained how personality could be created, the term was associated with such adjectives as fascinating, stunning, magnetic, masterful, and dominant.[96] Character connoted something intrinsic to the self, but personality was less a stable quality than a pose one could assume and discard as the occasion demanded. As a strategy of self-presentation, it was well suited to the emerging culture of mass consumption in which it was articulated.

Early-twentieth-century psychiatry's focus on the personality, adumbrated first around psychopathy, was an important means by which the discipline effected the shift from the necessarily limited psychiatry of the abnormal to a psychiatry of normality. The symptom—which was what drew the alienist's attention—was relatively rare, exhibited by a disturbed few. In contrast, the personality, which by the mid-twenties would displace the symptom as the discipline's unit of analysis, offered psychiatrists a dramatically broadened investigatory field, for, as they saw it, both its ubiquity (everyone had one) and its separability from the core of the self (its malleability) invited their intervention. "Only the total personality," a psychiatrist would write in the forties, reflecting on his specialty's abandonment of the symptom, "is the legitimate object of the psychiatric therapeutic attempt."[97] The term's turn-of-the-century usage anticipated and facilitated the discipline's adoption of the psychiatry of adjustment, a psychiatry applicable to everyone.

The ascendency of "personality" in psychiatric thought testifies to the democratization of the psychiatric vision. Character, in Victorian thought, presumed a degree of respectability, of participation in the wider world of work and politics, to which only a portion of the male population could reasonably aspire.[98] Personality, by contrast, entered the language free of the implicit and restrictive provisos with which character was burdened. Anyone could have a personality; indeed, as psychiatrists sometimes appear to have seen it, the problem was that everyone *did* have a personality, one typically styled with a measure of devotion to the self that they judged unseemly.[99] True to their taste for the abnormal and distinctive, psychiatrists could not help but pathologize personality in the process of apprehending it, asserting, for example, that the fascination, charm, and personal magnetism so trumpeted by the purveyors of popular advice were the qualities indicative of psychopathy at its most objectionable. Yet, in bringing under analysis constellations of ignoble qualities that anyone—women as well as men, the dissolute as well as the respectable—could display, psychiatrists conferred on such persons the dignity of being freestanding individuals in possession of what Williams has called an "estimable" existence that had not formerly been theirs.[100]

Psychiatrists could hardly speak of psychopathy without invoking metric thinking, for the condition's referents were altogether comparative, its symptoms slight variations on traits displayed by anyone: excessive irritability, pathological selfishness. In this it differed substantially from the other classifications psychiatrists employed. The others were either premised on something concrete (like feeblemindedness, which took as its referent a test and a number) or were shorthand for constellations of symptoms that psychiatrists could describe and that many laypersons found undeniably peculiar (like the most serious of diagnoses). Only with respect to psychopathy did psychiatrists conceive of symptoms as quantities, amounts, or exaggerations, premising diagnoses on too little of one thing—honesty, reliability, emotional control, loyalty—and too much of another.[101] And only in psychopathy could they argue that behavior indicative of the condition did not "differ strikingly from normal human behavior,"[102] or, in a similar vein, that persons branded by it "lie exceedingly near to what we conceive as the normal."[103] Psychiatrists pathologized the normal, a quantity as ill defined as the psychopathy to which it was juxtaposed, in the process of attempting to apprehend it, just as they pathologized the personality. They attended little to its precise delineation, and they bandied it about, proffering damning pronouncements, like one's hyperbolic assertion that "a vast majority of the human race might properly be called *constitutionally inferior*" (another variant of psychopathic), and that "the *normal* man [was] very rare indeed," representing "a standard of perfection not yet having been attained by any one."[104] The patently paradoxical notion that the normal was rare, now a staple of psychiatric thought as popularly understood, found repeated expression as psychiatrists sketched the contours of psychopathy.[105] Like the assessments issued in the wake of mass intelligence testing, it conflated the ideal and the average, the normative and statistical dimensions of normal. A mélange of concepts central to the metric model underwrote it. Thus, in reference to psychopathy, psychiatrists consistently arrayed the personalities they assessed on a continuum. They proposed, for example, that psychopathy represented a "borderland condition" or that it encompassed "borderline phenomena";[106] that the normal and abnormal were shaded together much like "colours of the spectrum";[107] and that "the demarcation between normal and psychopath [was] gradual and, in a sense, arbitrary."[108]

The scale that statements like these implicitly invoked appeared in con-

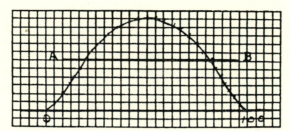

Fig. 3.2. The normal distribution in the realm
of psychopathy.

crete form only once in the vast literature of psychopathy, in the guise of a
bell curve bisected horizontally by a "normal line" that divided the population between the normals and the psychopaths (fig. 3.2). This curve,
unlike the one on which it was modeled, the curve that represented the
distribution of intelligence in the population, conveyed little information
and required a complex and confusing explanation. Psychopathy represented a mix of qualities too diverse to fit on a single scale and too elusive to
be simply measured, as feeblemindedness could be—and in this lay much
of its appeal. In the realm of psychopathy, psychiatrists more easily replicated the spirit than the particulars of the metric model. They were happy
to trade the psychologist's norms, which, from the perspective of the medical mind, traded in an illusory objectivity, for the psychiatric imperative to
probe the individual's subjectivity to the full.[109]

From Domestic to Scientific
Knowledge

If, in the realm of psychopathy, psychiatrists mined the normative, evaluative dimension of the normal, in their program for the domestic sphere they
exploited its complementary statistical dimension, gathering facts about
what was common and routine. Psychiatrists' program for reform of the
private sphere took shape even less deliberately than their public program,
which, after all, was structured at least in part around well-established
notions of defect current in the wider culture. To be sure, as they pursued
their agenda of exposing and reorganizing what they and many others
argued Victorians had so carefully shielded, psychiatrists entered an ongoing, fractious discussion—joined by medical reformers, social scientists,
popular writers, and cultural radicals—of the "crisis of the family." Yet
they did not so much construct as happen upon the domestic dimension of

their overall program. It was not theory but practice that suggested the home might be a rich source of knowledge for their discipline. Emboldened by science (in particular the science of syphilology), fired by "panoptic ambitions," and confronted with patients who appeared to deviate little from the normal, psychiatrists quickly realized that the particulars of what Southard in another context called "the filigree psychic interior of many a personal situation" were theirs for the asking.[110] Whereas nineteenth-century inquisitors of the sexual had constructed their science by concentrating on, as Foucault has argued, "aberrations, perversions, exceptional oddities, pathological abatements, and morbid aggravations," early-twentieth-century psychiatrists would constitute theirs in confrontations with slight deviations from normality, "as they practically occur in everyday life."[111] Extracting testimony from patients regarding their domestic affairs, feelings, habits, and concerns, psychiatrists gained access, in Foucault's words, "to the bodies of individuals, to their acts, attitudes and modes of everyday behavior,"[112] practices and ideologies whose apparent naturalness and universality obscured their potential significance in the domain of the human sciences.[113] In investigating, recording, and analyzing such everyday practices, in teasing them out of what Myerson called the "warp and woof of organized human life,"[114] psychiatrists endowed them with a sociology and even a weak history, at the same time constituting them as objects science could apprehend.

Fashioning themselves iconoclastic moderns, psychiatrists mounted a vigorous attack on what they argued were the hypocrisies of Victorianism. Where Victorianism traded in tantalizing but tyrannical secrecies, especially concerning sex and the body, they would promote an honest stance toward life. Where Victorianism traded in rigid, sharply dichotomized notions of men's and women's natures, notions that psychiatrists held unfairly encumbered women, they would argue for a vision of the sexes as more similar than not. And where Victorianism traded in pious conventionalities, uttered in muted, embarrassed tones, they would loudly proclaim the truth, however indiscreet. To be sure, as Foucault has persuasively argued, the Victorians were constantly and everywhere "talking sex" in the guise of repression, creating and classifying sexualities in a prohibitionary mode that incited as much as it dampened desire. Psychiatrists' commitment to honest talk about sex, from this perspective, was less a critique of their forebears than a continuation of their project in a defiantly announced different register. Recognition of the continuities that underlay the psychiatrists' project should not, however, obscure what did distinguish them from their predecessors. Trading euphemism for frankness, silence for plain speaking, psychiatrists advocated not the preservation but the intense scrutiny of the home, not its necessity but its contingency, not its warmth but its many oppressions.[115] In the name of modernity, they advanced—first in their dealings with individual patients, later in published writings—a sharp critique of the domestic sphere and of the gender arrangements that sustained it.[116]

The psychiatrists' critique was avowedly gender-neutral, even faintly feminist. They maintained that the home was not the space of tranquility and romance that its proponents imagined it to be, but an institution shot through with the same inequalities that animated the larger society from which it was supposedly apart. Within its sentimentalized confines, they suggested, men and women indulged in tyrannies large and small. Men saw to it that women were confined at home, sentenced to lives of drudgery while they fled daily into the world of work and male sociability. Women, in turn, resorted to tearful complaining and worse, igniting quarrels over money and sex in skewed reproach to men's derelictions, quarrels that blighted marriage for both husband and wife. "The home which unites them also separates them," Myerson, the most ardent of psychiatric chroniclers of the battle of the sexes, observed of the married pair, adding that of the two, the man had "by far the easier time of it as compared with his wife, just as man in general is better treated by life than woman."[117] He, unlike his mate, sentimentalized the home in song and verse, but, Myerson added dryly, "the woman lives there," in a misery few men could comprehend, engaged in constant "warfare with dust, dirt and disorder."[118]

Myerson proposed that feminism would go far in upsetting the balance of the sexes' relations and rights. In its name women were demanding the rights that were any man's by birth: to vote, to labor outside the home, to control reproduction.[119] Dissatisfied with the lot men had assigned them, women who could were spurning it, choosing to pursue professional careers, while others were quietly rebelling within marriage, attempting to tame their men by nurturing in them a taste for things domestic. Men in consequence were witnessing a curtailment of their rights, a development Myerson and his colleagues judged salutary. The man who would simply "cut loose" from marriage and its strictures, indulge his whims, and land himself and his mate in divorce court was common but, Myerson suggested, outmoded. Women were seeing to it that the days when a man could forsake the home for his club, his fishing expedition, or the "free and easy masculine barbarism" of the smoking room were numbered.[120]

Myerson and his colleagues were more strategic than consistent in their advocacy of a feminist perspective. They could speak from within feminism when faced with a particularly masculinist man, using it punitively to challenge his assumptions regarding his prerogatives. But they could also regroup to defend their own sex against what they perceived as women's nagging demands. Moderation was their guiding principle. If women were to declare men in need of reform, then it was only fair that men could find fault with women and their ways. As psychiatrists saw it, artful guile characterized women's mode of engagement with the world as aptly as brash straightforwardness characterized that of men. Women who claimed equality with men, Myerson suggested, should style themselves neither coquettes nor weaklings but, rather, persons whose honesty, directness, and transparency fitted them for full participation in the world's affairs.

That this was an apt characterization of the social worker, the woman on whose professional persona Myerson and his fellows intermittently heaped such obloquies, suggests that psychiatrists' professed neutrality on the question of gender collided, in practice, with a set of reflexively conventional convictions. Myerson could, on the one hand, celebrate the modern woman's newfound freedom, what we might call her assumption of a civic personality, and on the other spin unthinkingly nasty tales featuring the social worker who worked by his side.[121] Psychiatrists flaunted their modernity in assessing the home and its effects on women and men so harshly, proposing that only a thorough reorganization of the domestic sphere would suffice to remedy its worst effects, but in their confrontations with patients they were only inconsistently as iconoclastic as they liked to imagine themselves. In practice, they subjected the home to only uneven scrutiny, imagining it at times as an abstract, almost atavistic, domain, a distraction from the issues at hand. As physicians, their proclaimed interest was in the individual, not the family.[122] Social workers' stance vis-à-vis the home was decidedly more conventional than that of the psychiatrists. In contrast to psychiatrists, who questioned patients individually, in the hospital, social workers visited patients in their homes. It was the social worker, not the psychiatrist, who regularly talked to and corresponded with families, somehow convincing, for example, the syphilitic's wife and children to submit to treatment.[123] And it was the social worker who ventured uninvited into the homes of patients, who took over management of families' household economies, and who attempted to orchestrate their emotional lives, all of which gave her a palpable sense of the family's reality that psychiatrists, ensconced in the hospital, did not share. "Be it ever so normal, / There's no place like home"—so went a ditty popular among students of social work attending the summer course at Smith College.[124] The disparity between the psychiatric and social work outlooks is evident in the contrast between this and Southard's statement that "it is pretty hard to uncover an absolutely normal and perfectly adjusted family."[125]

Psychiatrists and social workers formulated their science of the everyday through a process of iteration, in the words of Southard and Jarrett "inductively building up the facts," construing the bodies and testimony of their subjects as sources of disciplinary knowledge.[126] Sex, marital rights and wrongs, men's culturally sanctioned boorishness, women's crafty recourse to tears, everyday issues and concerns—in their confrontations with patients psychiatrists homed in on all of this, isolating it from the familial context that rendered it invisible. Exposing to science's unforgiving view what the home, by Victorian convention, shrouded in secrecy, psychiatrists and social workers located themselves on the terrain of the social, a "sphere of influence" that lay between what was conventionally deemed public, under the auspices of organized government, and what was considered private. Maintaining that the "usual distinction" between public and private was useful but "no longer able to serve our best purposes," Southard and Jarrett proposed that the private sphere be drastically narrowed to encompass, in effect, only the home. There, persons could revel in privacy, and they could enjoy the "warmth and intimacy" that was theirs by right. As Southard and Jarrett envisioned it, the private, domestic sphere was a free space, "not yet reduced to rigid rules and regulations," that would compensate individuals for accepting the increasing restraint to which they would find themselves subject in the public realm.[127]

Yet, even as psychiatrists and social workers proposed that the private sphere be protected, they imposed on it the rules and regulations, the scrutiny and oversight, of which they argued it was to be free. Many of the concerns most critically important to the general welfare were not identified as public, Southard argued, and thus not subject to formal, governmental regulation—syphilis proving exemplary in this regard. Psychiatrists, he proposed, beholden only to science, were well suited to assume control over concerns that were neither wholly public nor private; few disputed this claim. More ambiguous was the situation of the social worker, who might conclude that a particular family would be best served by an "invasion of individual rights" or by an assessment of the case that saw "the interests of [the] individual running counter to his desires." Social workers found themselves so situated, in what Southard and Jarrett termed "a position of danger," as a matter not of chance but of course; intervening where they were not wanted, and inviting thereby charges of causing unnecessary difficulties, was the substance of much of social work practice.[128] In the end, rejecting not only Victorianism but also the liberal tradition, to which the autonomous, rights-bearing self was integral, psychiatrists and social workers maintained that no sphere of human activity was exempt from their potential oversight and control.

To propose, as various historians and sociologists have, that psychiatrists either "invaded" a once-private domestic domain or wrested control of it from the clergy is to misconstrue a far more complex process.[129] The first claim is premised on a dimly delineated portrait of the Victorian family as—in the characterization of Christopher Lasch—a .haven that protected its members from the heartless world around them. A "stronghold

of . . . private rights," the family from Lasch's perspective neatly conformed in practice to the picture its most vocal adherents drew, a smoothly
functioning unit in which the interests of one—the patriarch—were the
interests of all.[130] There is, however, ample evidence to support an alternative interpretation of the family as an institution both internally differenti-
ated and coercive. Men's and women's interests within poor, working, and
middle-class families often diverged. Obscured by the bourgeois ideology
of complementarity, this divergence was structural, not situational, in all
sorts of families, created and sustained by men's easy access to public space
and their adoption of public personae and women's confinement, in ideology if not in fact, to the home.[131] Further, the tasks necessary to produce
adults capable of functioning properly in a modern society demanded of
the mother, who from the early years of the nineteenth century was increasingly entrusted with them, a strict adherence to discipline and a constant
administration of control over the bodies of her young—what Mary Ryan
has called "routine and intense maternal vigilance."[132]

The often-advanced claim that psychiatrists became the secular priests
of the modern age, dislodging the clergy from their once-secure position as
moral advisors to all and sundry, relies on a narrowly formal construction
of the discipline's genealogy. In this view, individuals who in the nineteenth
century might have confided in their pastors were by the twentieth seeking
out the psychiatrists, psychologists, and social workers who had successfully medicalized the moral realm and established, at the same time,
their professional hegemony.[133] But there is much to suggest that men and
women poured out their woes not only to the clergy but also to friends,
neighbors, relatives, and work mates and, correspondingly, that management of what appears in historical light private could take highly visible
public forms, orchestrated in many cases by women.[134] One might just as
well term the everyday knowledge psychiatrists compiled "domestic"—
knowledge concerning character training and affect control, necessary to
the socialization of individuals and their emergence from the home—and
chronicle psychiatrists' engagement with it, an engagement that resulted in
its codification in a form consonant with science's demands. Domestic
knowledge was hardly new, but its appearance in the domain of science was.

Psychiatrists would consistently conflate the evaluative and descriptive
dimensions of the normal, ensuring that the science of the everyday that
they pieced together from observations of patients and testimony extracted
from them would not only describe but also prescribe what was normal—
that it would be, in short, a normative science. The psychiatric "regime of
the norm" that Foucault, among others, has cast as paradigmatic of the
guise in which power in its modern, dispersed, and fragmentary form
appears is less a natural effect of the discipline than a discrete project, one

that psychiatrists could only envision and realize once they had settled on a means of apprehending the normal aspects of life. This accomplished, psychiatrists could publicly abjure the juridical functions that they argued had engaged their predecessors' energies and interests. Southard knew that the laity looked on the psychiatrist with suspicion, as an ogre bent on ensnaring harmless individuals in his "institutional net," an image he was prepared to counter.[135] In the ogre's place twentieth-century psychiatrists would put the practitioner less focused on the insane than on the world, one to whom "advanced thinkers" would willingly cede the authority to pronounce upon questions ranging from the domestic to the political.[136] Under the cover of what one astute critic has termed "nobler or simply blander intentionalites" (specifically, to understand, to cure), psychiatrists would define and oversee a kind of power more contingent but also far more expansive than what their forebears had, a power that not only enforced norms but also, more insidiously and more interestingly, established "the normality of normativeness itself."[137]

PART TWO

INSTITUTIONAL PRACTICES

FOUR

PATHWAYS TO PSYCHIATRIC SCRUTINY

G RAY OR DRAB difficulties," Southard ventured, formed the "stock-in-life of a number of 'normal enough' persons" for whom psychiatric attention would prove efficacious.[1] The spousal quarrels, financial problems, legal entanglements, and symptoms indicative of mild neurosis—worrying, dizziness, inability to sleep—that plagued such persons, making them fit candidates for psychiatric oversight, Southard was here suggesting, were not extraordinary but ordinary, tribulations part and parcel of what was for many the dreary business of making it from one day to the next. Southard readily conceded that such difficulties, taken together, might appear only marginally medical or psychiatric. Yet to him and his colleagues this was less a problem than a challenge. Locating the precipitants of psychiatric problems in what he referred to as "everyday facts" and, correspondingly, establishing the ordinariness of the psychiatric encounter were among the chief aims of Southard's and his colleagues' professional project, a project that would highlight what was prosaic and routine while downplaying what was strange and exceptional.

Turn-of-the-century psychiatrists attempted to appropriate the realm of everyday practices for their science. Asserting their authority over such practices was difficult enough, but realizing it would prove more difficult still. However convinced they were of their specialty's centrality to the world's affairs, large and small, their patients—the stuff of their science— were for the most part unwilling and elusive subjects, persons turned patients not of their own but of someone else's will. In popular estimation, psychiatrists realized, psychiatry was associated with the institutionalized insane—the dangerous, demented, or inexplicably strange—and psychiatrists, their keepers, were seen as little more than policemen manqué. Were psychiatry ever to achieve the dominance they argued it merited, psychiatrists knew they would have to make psychiatry and the institutions in which it was practiced palatable, even attractive, to a broader range of persons.

To this end, psychiatrists advanced an ambitious program of institutional reform intended to signal their profession's break with its ignoble past. The issue of commitment—what Southard carefully referred to as the "intake of patients"—was at the center of this program, for on no other issue did they feel the past's burdens so keenly.[2] From around 1860, commitment, a legal proceeding that provided for the involuntary detention of individuals found insane, had sparked passionate and politically resonant condemnations of a medico-legal system that deprived persons of their constitutional liberties. Turn-of-the-century psychiatrists maintained that as long as forcible commitment remained the means by which most persons became patients or, more precisely, asylum inmates, psychiatrists would be inextricably and unfavorably linked in public estimation to the asylum. As in the past, only the recognizably insane, not the nearly normal, would come under their scrutiny. Mindful of the harrowing tales circulated by the "complaining families" of ex-patients, the relatives and friends of those who were not insane but needed treatment would continue to be deterred from seeking it.[3] Existing commitment procedures highlighted what psychiatrists argued was the admittedly popular but outmoded and medically irrelevant distinction between the sane and the insane. Such procedures, which, psychiatrists argued, brought a legal attitude to bear on what were properly medical matters, made it all the more difficult for them to remake their professional selves, to slough off the punitive persona bequeathed them by their predecessors and to assume instead the mantle of science.

Nationwide, psychiatrists campaigned successfully for the passage of laws that brought commitment from the legal into the medical arena, transforming it, in their estimation, from a highly charged question of law into a straightforward question of medical judgment. Under the so-called voluntary and temporary statutes, a mélange of laws enacted in some twenty-nine states, mostly in the second decade of the new century, commitment was made procedurally simpler and, at the same time, redefined.[4] Patients were no longer to be committed but *admitted*, psychiatrists explained; what one characterized as the "opportunity for care and treatment" was under the laws' provisions made available to all.[5] In consequence, Southard observed, psychiatrists now had access to a stratum of society, composed of the sane but not entirely normal, that had eluded their predecessors' institutional net. With what he and others referred to as the "stigma" of insanity diminishing, individuals who never would have been committed to asylums were finding their way to the Psychopathic Hospital and institutions like it.[6]

The many pathways that patients followed to psychiatric scrutiny in early-twentieth-century Boston can be put in five broad categories: 8 percent of all patients entered the hospital voluntarily; 43 percent were committed by their families; 26 percent were brought to the institution by the police; 12 percent were committed or sent by courts for observation to determine their mental states; and 11 percent were transferred from other hospitals because they were thought to be insane.[7] This chapter, which examines these pathways and the patients who traveled them, is loosely organized around the paradigm of the police, a paradigm that psychiatrists rejected but that patients and those who committed them constantly invoked. Analyzing policing in different modes, it looks first at self-policing, the largely unattainable ideal against which psychiatrists measured the progress of their program; second at the various sorts of intrafamilial policing that were responsible for bringing the largest group of patients to their attention; and third at the actual police and the circumscribed role they played in the work of psychiatric policing. Foucault's dictum that "power is tolerable only on condition that it mask a substantial part of itself" is particularly apt in this context, for the police, who animate the collective fantasies of many of those subject to—as well as those who are students of—psychiatric control, usefully provide, in the words of the critic D. A. Miller, "a representation of the containment of power."[8] Historically it has proven far more palatable to blame the police for unjustly incarcerating the innocent than to imagine that the power that delivers them up to the authorities might be distributed throughout the social body, exercised by many and sustained by the troubled relations of everyday life.

Willing Subjects

Voluntary patients, the relatively few persons who entered institutions of their own will, were central players in early-twentieth-century psychiatrists' efforts to redefine the means and meanings of psychiatric commitment. Since 1881 individuals had been able to enter mental institutions voluntarily in Massachusetts, and statewide approximately 100 did so each year. In 1905, the law was amended to allow for the public support of voluntary patients, and their numbers began to increase steadily, by some 30 to 50 yearly. In 1913, over 600 persons were classed as voluntary patients; 440 of these were admitted to the Psychopathic Hospital, which had opened the previous year.[9] Cheered by the increase, psychiatrists suggested that nothing else would so confound the popular association of psychiatry with the dreaded asylum. That persons would willingly seek institutional care was compelling testimony to its essential benignity, even efficacy.

By 1924, twenty-eight states, following the early lead of Massachusetts, had made provisions for the voluntary admission of persons to mental institutions.[10] Through the first two decades of the century, psychiatrists nationwide argued the case for such provisions on narrowly and, to their minds, unimpeachably medical grounds. Asserting that early identification and treatment of mental disorders resulted in more favorable outcomes, they maintained that the usual route of admission to an institution— a court hearing in which the person had to be declared legally insane— deterred prospective patients and stood in the way of medical progress.[11]

They argued that the mildly and incipiently ill might more easily be persuaded to sign what was known as a voluntary paper than to entangle themselves and their families in what one authority characterized as the "legal red tape" of court commitment.[12] Families' reputations would be spared and individuals' diseases would be treated more efficaciously. As important, the prospect of patients voluntarily "flocking to their doors" would enable psychiatrists to take pride in their professional identity as men of science, not custodians of the hopelessly insane.[13]

Psychiatrists were united in their conviction that existing laws allowed lawyers and judges too great a say in what were properly medical decisions, an intolerable insult to their own sense of professionalism. Yet even as they censured what one historian would later call the "disgraceful legal attitude" that informed commitment procedures, psychiatrists were careful to disavow mere partisanship.[14] Rather, they situated the issue at the center of a teleological tale that chronicled the inevitable triumph of enlightenment over ignorance, of progress over backwardness, of humanity over barbarism, even of "actual facts" over "wild traditions."[15] Medical control of commitment, as psychiatrists would have it, was not a narrowly professional issue, but *the* measure of civilization's advance. Southard invoked the matrix of progress when speaking of voluntary admissions, underscoring the advanced character of the Massachusetts legislature with gentle reproofs to the benighted "law-makers of less civilized communities."[16] In the estimation of another prominent psychiatrist, courts were atavistic, for, as he explained, they "retained the superstitions and the ignorance of the folk soul longer than any other profession."[17] To another proponent of reform, the issue of voluntary admissions was at once a simple matter of access, of passing "constructive legislation" to remove the many legal barriers that frightened potential patients away, and one of several sure signs of psychiatry's evolution toward modernity.[18] Yet another commentator, complaining that legalities too often prevented psychiatrists—but not physicians—from administering medically necessary and proper care, argued that the "old safeguards" intended to protect innocent persons from the machinations of "scheming relatives" were dispensable, and predicted they would shortly be swept aside.[19] The choice the public faced, as members of the Massachusetts State Board of Insanity framed it for legislators in 1908, was between "legal formalities to protect personal liberties" on the one hand and modernity ("enlightened" treatment) on the other, which was no choice at all.[20]

The legal mechanisms that psychiatrists contemptuously dismissed were, however, not mere formalities but the substance of a well-established Anglo-American legal principle—recognized first in the Magna Carta and later in the fifth and fourteenth amendments to the Constitution—that protected persons from deprivation of liberty without due process.[21] Admission to the many asylums founded in the first half of the nineteenth century was largely unregulated, a matter of negotiation between hospital superintendents and those who wished to see someone treated or incarcerated.[22] In the estimation of psychiatric reformers, these were their discipline's halcyon years, a time when physician-alienists had worked free of legal oversight, the welfare of patients their only concern. Mechanisms instituted in the wake of several scandals, publicized by individuals claiming to have been sane yet committed by relatives or others in collusion with alienists, brought this putative golden age to an end. The well-publicized three-year ordeal of Elizabeth Packard, a woman committed to the Illinois State Hospital by her husband in 1860 under the provisions of a remarkable statute that provided for the commitment of married women "at the request of the husband . . . without the evidence of insanity required in other cases," exerted a particularly strong hold on the public imagination.[23] By the 1860s and 1870s, legislatures across the country were making moves toward state oversight of the insane, establishing boards of charity (as in Massachusetts) or commissions in lunacy (as in New York), and formalizing commitment procedures, mandating variously that persons had to be declared insane by (as in Massachusetts from 1862 on) "two reputable physicians," judges, or even, in Packard's home state of Illinois, juries, before they could be consigned to asylums.[24] Although hospital superintendents decried these laws from the start, predicting they would lead to unnecessary "trouble, annoyance and expense" for patients' friends, the numbers of those willing to suffer the annoyance and able to negotiate the maze of regulations was sufficient to lead to a tripling of the population of persons institutionalized for insanity in the years from 1880 to 1904.[25]

Commitment laws, the "old safeguards," were thus neither so venerable nor so superfluous as early-twentieth-century reformers imagined them.[26] Intended primarily to protect the rights of the sane (for no one was contesting the confinement of the patently insane), the laws, as psychiatrists somewhat solipsistically saw them, served less to shield the innocent than to reaffirm their own subordinate status in the public realm. Voluntary patients figured so importantly in the story they spun of their discipline's progress in part because such patients subverted the neat alignment of accused innocents on the one side and accusing, scheming relatives on the other on which the commitment mechanisms they found so unpalatable were premised. Given that commitment, defined by one psychiatrist as "enforced detention under legal authority in an institution,"[27] necessarily deprived individuals of their liberty, "voluntary" commitment was satisfyingly oxymoronic, a useful support for psychiatrists' contention that existing commitment procedures were mired in needless legalisms. The voluntary patient thus offered them the tantalizing possibility of abandoning the juridical functions that they claimed distracted attention from psychiatry's scientific attainments.

Psychiatrists' suggestion that "mere persuasion" would yield them more patients than the old commitment laws ever had was predicated on the ubiquity of subjects possessing a complex and enlightened sense of self.[28] As envisioned by psychiatrists, voluntary patients were self-interested enough to diagnose their own difficulties, yet disinterested enough to submit to the inducements of others. "Acutely conscious of the fact that [they were] not normal," they were easily induced to seek treatment.[29] Engaged in constant, exacting self-supervision, they were, although nominally free, their own keepers. Like psychiatrists, they conceived of freedom not negatively, as the absence of restraint, but positively, as the right of access to treatment. Psychiatrists' nineteenth-century predecessors had exercised the power of confinement over their subjects, power that was highly visible and, as the states' drawing up of commitment laws would prove, vulnerable to attack. Around the voluntary subject psychiatrists adumbrated their vision of a less visible but just as effective mode of power, the exercise of which would be nearly automatic, carried out by those subjected to its strictures. When Southard hailed the increasing number of persons who, realizing that their difficulties were psychopathic, voluntarily sought institutional care, he was speaking from within what Foucault has characterized as the disciplinary regime, a regime in which power is invisible, resident in neither a single individual nor a single profession but dispersed "throughout the whole social body."[30] Were all persons as willing to police themselves as was the model voluntary patient, hospitals and institutions would fill up spontaneously and psychiatrists could relegate the policelike aspects of their craft firmly to the past.

Like all voluntary patients, James Flynn, an unmarried forty-year-old native of Fall River who approached the Psychopathic Hospital for advice about his mental state in January 1916, exercised his freedom in relinquishing it. A reader of electric meters, Flynn was a man of good appearance who had, some eight years before, fallen into a state of mind he termed abnormal. Every person and every event, he told the psychiatrist who admitted him to the Psychopathic Hospital, every picture and moving picture had an "allegoric" meaning to him, and he had begun to feel himself the victim of a plot perpetrated "by the Catholics, both political parties and the Odd Fellows." Within several years, he was hearing faint voices, "as if through a telephone," which said derogatory things about him, inducing a state of nervousness so marked that he had given up his trade. Realizing that his mind was troubled and fully aware that psychiatrists might doubt his sanity, Flynn signed a voluntary admission paper and entered the hospital for a week's stay.

Flynn's directness impressed the psychiatrists, and they assessed him with exceptional gentleness. He was, they noted, pleasant and agreeable, and gave the impression of being intelligent and well-informed, perhaps, they added, "moreso than his education and employment would lead one to expect." Flynn told the psychiatrists he knew his hallucinations were "queer," but that he also could not "doubt the evidence of his own senses," asserting that the voices had to be "due to something like wireless telephony." Flynn's ability to scrutinize himself from without, as abnormal, while at the same time telling of experiencing sensations so real he could not discount them, was almost unique among patients, and evidence of a degree of insight psychiatrists prized highly. In willingly putting himself in their hands and admitting to what he realized were bizarre notions, Flynn exhibited both the enlightened self-interest and the inclination for possibly damaging self-disclosure displayed by the voluntary patient of psychiatrists' most sanguine imaginings. Flynn was the sort of patient Southard had in mind when he invited the public to see in the swelling numbers of voluntary admissions signs of civilization's advance.[31]

Yet although approximately 17 percent of the Psychopathic Hospital's patients were admitted under the provisions of the voluntary statute through the first decade of its operation, slightly less than half of these—8 percent of all admissions—were in any sense truly voluntary. Instances in which family members either persuaded reluctant individuals to enter the hospital "voluntarily" or notified police and had them haul recalcitrant relatives to the hospital, all the while maintaining the fiction of free choice, made up the other 9 percent of all cases that were classed as voluntary. That psychiatrists, mindful of what Southard might have termed the propaganda value of large numbers of willing subjects, were perhaps overly eager to classify equivocal cases as voluntary can partly account for these figures. Indeed, Southard matter-of-factly declared that hospital psychiatrists "have had fully in mind to get all patients registered under the voluntary law so far as possible." Although he maintained that he and his colleagues carefully respected the letter of the law, insisting that voluntary patients be fully cognizant of their status, it is clear some had little idea of what they were in for.[32] One woman who signed a voluntary paper, for example, wrote that she had "not the remotest idea that it was a hospital" when she entered the institution, as the general practitioner from whom she had sought advice and who had arranged for her admission, she insisted, "did not tell me so."[33] Another woman wrote that she had come "as a voluntary patient but did not understand the nature of this institution."[34] Few voluntary patients were so well informed as was Flynn, who had spent several months in a state hospital six years before his sojourn in the Psychopathic Hospital.

The problem with the voluntary law lay not so much in its administration, in the latitude it allowed for the exercise of persuasion that shaded into coercion, but in its central, paradoxical premise—that individuals could be of sound enough mind to consent, in terms the legal system could recognize, to the loss of their liberty but of unsound enough mind to need psychiatric treatment.[35] Constrained on the one hand by the law's provision that, as Adolf Meyer noted, "no man shall deed away his liberty" and on the other by their desire to eschew the forcible commitments that had brought their predecessors under public scrutiny, psychiatrists subjected the issue to nervous debate in their writings while resolving it bluntly in practice.[36] Consent, once granted, was difficult to revoke, and persons turned patients found their options limited by the peculiarly hermetic logic of the psychiatric worldview. Just how roundabout this logic could be is evident in psychiatrists' reasoning that voluntary patients who did not understand their right to be released from the institution within three to seven days of giving notice should not be released (a step that would have honored the spirit of the law) but committed outright, their lack of comprehension interpreted as a symptom of illness.[37] Conversely, voluntary patients astute enough to comprehend their situations were, in psychiatrists' estimation, all too likely to give notice of their intention to leave the institution before it was in their interest to do so.[38] They, too, could be committed outright, as was Patrick Bailey, a fifty-year-old Irish stonemason who was one of the unfortunate third of all those who entered the hospital as a voluntary patient who left it committed to an asylum. Three days into his week-long hospital stay, Bailey wrote to the psychiatrists that as he had "come in here voluntarily I did not think I would be detained against my will." He had entered the hospital thinking psychiatrists would give him some "medicine to be taken outside the institution," and added that from experience he knew he "would be much better outside and at work." Adopting (but getting a bit wrong) a legalistic tone meant to convey his seriousness, Bailey wrote that he trusted psychiatrists would release him "consistent with law and the usages of the institution." Bailey, however, was sadly misinformed, for his commitment to Taunton State Hospital was unexpected but altogether consistent with the law.[39] "I don't want to detain you against your will," Meyer would tell patients who insisted on leaving his clinic before he thought advisable; "you have your own choice, either to stay voluntarily or to go on commitment to another institution."[40] As many would discover, behind the "open door" of voluntary admissions lay a maze.[41]

The paradigmatic voluntary patient, however useful in theory, was too singular a figure on which to stake the wholesale reworking of the commitment process that psychiatrists had in mind. Too few individuals were both resolute enough to seek treatment and compliant enough not to chafe at its restrictions. Too few could sustain the fiction that they were free as they signed papers ensuring they were not.[42] And too few were capable of the sort of self-governance in the interest of the general welfare on which the voluntary laws were premised. The Foucauldian vision of society as a self-regulated panopticon that psychiatrists elaborated around the voluntary issue was altogether utopian. If they were to navigate between the Scylla of frustratingly elusive consent and the Charybdis of forcible detention, psychiatrists would need to craft broadly applicable laws that demanded of their subjects less finely calibrated measures of will and self-interest than the voluntary statutes did.

The so-called temporary care laws, enacted first in Massachusetts and adopted, as of 1921, by fourteen other states, met this criterion exactly. Like the voluntary laws, the temporary care laws circumvented what Southard called "the old judicial procedure," the court hearing with its necessary proof of insanity that so rankled psychiatrists' professional sensibilities.[43] Under the provisions of the Massachusetts law of 1911, for example, any of a variety of persons—physicians in the community, members of the board of health, police officers—could request that a hospital superintendent care for someone appearing mentally deranged or insane, who could then be "temporarily" committed for up to ten (later thirty) days. The voluntary laws called on individuals to police themselves. The temporary laws, which made of everyone a police officer, did away with consent, the most problematic of the suppositions that informed the voluntary laws, while at the same time sustaining the diffuse distribution of power that they were intended to effect. The laws made it possible for one person to have another committed expeditiously, without engaging a lawyer and without going to court but by simply (as was most often the case) approaching a physician in the community who, if he thought the person in question was in need of treatment, signed the necessary papers. The suspected mentally ill person, whether willing or not, was then confined for a period ranging from ten to thirty days or more.

Psychiatrists contended that the temporary laws did not—indeed, could not—endanger individual liberties. Their contention was premised on a subject with as paradoxically enlightened a conception of her rights as the voluntary subject, a subject prepared to risk her "rights as an individual" in order to enhance her "cause *as patient*."[44] Temporary patients, as psychiatrists construed them, were not, like voluntary patients, altogether model disciplinary subjects. Although they welcomed the scrutiny of others, they did not engage in self-scrutiny. And, although they complied with psychiatrists' directives, they did not seek out their supervision. Persuasion and inducement were for them insufficient incentives. Yet they, like voluntary patients, identified liberty not with the absence of restraint but with the freedom to participate in society subject to psychiatrists' active regulation, regulation intended to ensure that all would conduct their lives within the parameters of normality. Presumably they would have appreciated the remarkable logic of Southard's suggestion to one woman, who had been temporarily committed but found "not insane" and who felt shamed by the matter, that she should consider herself "perhaps better off than various persons in the community who have not yet received the diagnosis of 'Not Insane.'"[45]

More than half of all persons who passed through the Psychopathic

Hospital in its first decade of operation were admitted under the provisions of the various temporary care laws, and it is likely that few of them would have appreciated the subtleties in which psychiatrists traded. In practice, this mattered little, for once the laws' operations were routinized, the coerciveness of commitment that psychiatrists argued was neutralized by its temporariness inevitably came to the fore. Many of those committed under the temporary laws' provisions were angry and dismayed, and some argued that such a means of detention was unlawful. Establishing that such detention was not only lawful but, in many instances, salutary was central to psychiatrists' goal of shedding their punitive professional selves, and they thus felt compelled constantly to explain their position. The principle of quarantine, they insisted, had long been enforced in the realm of public health "without violating constitutional rights of the individual." Drawing a parallel between infectious diseases, which everyone agreed should be the occasion for the exercise of policelike powers, and mental disturbances, they argued that quarantine of the former provided a precedent for the latter, in order to guard "the sovereign citizen against himself in obvious need."[46]

This was hardly the obvious and unexceptionable proposition psychiatrists assumed it to be, and perhaps for that reason they made it over and over. They also maintained that improper commitments, which it was thought would result once lawyers were excluded from the process, were impossible both procedurally, for hospital superintendents could turn away any prospective temporary patient (although in fact they rarely, if ever, did so), and logically. As Southard explained, it was obvious that the temporarily committed patient found not insane but "sane" "must possess the feeling that he has been given a fair chance to prove the suspicion of mental derangement (entertained by his relatives or by experts) right or wrong."[47] From the psychiatrist's perspective, persons' rights were not endangered but enhanced by the change of venue from court to clinic.

Rarely was the issue of commitment as dispassionately adjudicated as psychiatrists assumed, yet they at times appeared genuinely unable to fathom that anyone might have approached it otherwise. They tangled at some length over the question of wrongful commitment with a patient named Bessie Thomas, a recently married fifty-six-year-old woman whose husband had her committed to the hospital as a temporary patient in the summer of 1919. Thomas maintained that her husband had done so to get control of her money, and she told psychiatrists that she suspected they were holding her, a sane person, unjustly. Incredulous, a psychiatrist challenged her, "Do you think that physicians would keep you in a hospital for the insane for the rest of your life if you were not insane, just because your husband wanted it?" Yes, she replied, "because it takes your husband and the doctor to get you out." The psychiatrist pressed further: "If you are perfectly well mentally you think the physicians would keep you in an institution for the insane?" She parried, "If my uncle came after me this morning, would you people let me go?" Accusing her of dodging the question but doing the same himself, the psychiatrist restated his original question two more times, but Thomas stood her ground. Although in the end, following five weeks of confinement, psychiatrists judged her "not insane," they noted that her statements were indicative of "very marked defects in judgment" while allowing that "a great many people have that idea."[48]

Thomas's case had about it elements of unseemly spectacle reminiscent of those that had characterized the most notorious of the nineteenth-century cases of wrongful commitment, and it is possible that this may account for the psychiatrists' obtuseness. Mislaid, possibly filched, bank-books; a duplicitous sister-in-law; a bluff, verbally abusive husband (who announced to his hospitalized wife that "the gates of hell were not hot enough" for her); a proudly independent woman railroaded into an asylum by her greedy husband: as psychiatrists pieced it together, Thomas's story turned on the machinations of the scheming relatives who, they argued, were altogether out of the picture under the new commitment laws. Psychiatrists had to believe that Bessie Thomas's story was wrong—that she was not wronged but paranoid or senile—if they were to believe that their own story of psychiatry's progress was right.[49]

Psychiatrists tussled with other patients who, like Thomas, refused to play by their new rules. They found those who persisted in talking of rights especially irksome. In gaining control of commitment processes, psychiatrists claimed to be freeing prospective patients from the law's narrow confines and the courts' close atmosphere, to be bringing into the hospital's bracing milieu what had been hidden occasions for shame. As a little-noted consequence of these high-minded intentions, however, patients were denied any ground on which to protest unwanted confinement. Talk of rights was comprehensible only within a legal framework. To the psychiatric mind a patient's appeal to the law was at best an annoying distraction, at worst a sign of disease—of the "litigation psychosis" of the pathologically querulous.[50]

Just how perplexing this could be is evident in psychiatrists' exchanges with Blanche Philpott, a genteel, never-married eighty-year-old retired real estate agent who was conversant with the language of rights. Her detention, in September 1914, was by all accounts a mistake. Responding to a neighbor's complaint of loud screaming in the middle of the night, police had entered a house in which Philpott was visiting, had accused her of being drunk, and had taken her to a station house. There, after some confusion concerning her identity, the sergeant on duty had decided that as Philpott was "probably an escaped lunatic," she should be temporarily committed to the Psychopathic Hospital for observation. While confined, Philpott addressed several letters to psychiatrists demanding her discharge, "according to law," pointing out that she had never had a court hearing. Southard admitted to his colleagues that Philpott was harmless—she explained that her friend's "superstitious and illiterate" Italian neighbors, afraid of ghosts, had done the screaming—and that her commitment was "a horrible mistake." But when she mounted the same argument, citing the statutory law she had studied in her support, he took exception. He first defended "the poor policemen," as they were "only performing their duty." He pointed out that she could "be kept here forever," and, when she objected, blurted out, "Do you presume to sit here and tell me how I can keep patients?" Her commitment, he maintained, "might be morally wrong but not legally." Then, acting the injured party, he accused her of "pointing revolvers at us" ("Revolvers? I have no revolvers," she shot back), of proposing to "fix" him with the aid of lawyers and powerful friends, and of planning "to get redress," all of which she disavowed, claiming only to want her liberty.

Southard ended this discussion by trading on his power over Philpott, whom he dismissed as "a poor, harmless litigant." The matter would be settled, he proclaimed, "on psychiatric grounds—not legal." Philpott had plenty to say about the legalities of the case, as indeed would anyone who had the wherewithal to examine the law. But she could say nothing at all about the science of it. Southard's move left her defenseless, feebly asking to hear psychiatrists' reports and to be informed of her diagnosis.[51]

With her talk of laws, courts, and rights, Philpott, like Bessie Thomas, conjured up the old commitment scenario that psychiatrists claimed was outdated as a result of their efforts. It quickly became clear that this, not her supposed screams or her purported drunkenness, was the ground on which psychiatrists held her for ten days, puzzling all the while over the possibility that her questioning of their procedures and her impugning of motives constituted evidence of insanity.[52] Deeming her "hardly normal" but not committable, psychiatrists released Philpott, much to the relief of the female friends who had visited her in the hospital.

The contempt for the law that psychiatrists displayed in Philpott's case grew in part from their conviction that legal niceties stood in the way of psychiatry's progress. Psychiatrists were convinced of the benignity of their interventions, and they believed that enlightened men, agreeing with them on this, would overlook their stretching the law to its limits in the interest of delivering treatment. It is likely that psychiatrists' contempt was intensified in this instance because their antagonist was a woman. Men and women alike invoked their rights as freeborn American citizens in protesting undeserved confinement, but psychiatrists treated the women who did so particularly harshly, undercutting their arguments about rights by re-

treating to the higher ground of science.[53] Was there something presump-
tuous about a woman who would invoke the matrix of rights, as if hers
were the same as a man's, when it was unclear what rights women had? As
thirty-nine-year-old Lucy Parsons pointed out, complaining, in 1916, of
having fared poorly "under man made laws and in man run institutions,"
members of her sex had not even secured the franchise, by any criterion a
fundamental measure of citizenship. Was there something unseemly about
a woman who would dare to use the law to challenge men's authority?
Philpott knew which statute said what and used her knowledge to charge
psychiatrists with misinterpretation and worse. Parsons, for her part, was
resourceful enough to obtain and circulate marked-up copies of what she
called the "Temporary (Elastic) Law" and smart enough to discern that it
was "not American." Or was it simply that, as Parsons aphoristically put it,
"no man likes a clever woman unless she is useing [sic] that cleverness for
his benefit or gain," which these women most decidedly were not?[54]

Psychiatrists' maneuvers in the case of the magazine writer Bernice Mansfield underscore the suggestion that the everyday relations of gender informed their commitment practices. Suffering from heat exhaustion, Mansfield entered a local general hospital in late September 1914. She obtained
little relief there—the temperature was well over 90 degrees—and decided
she would sail to Provincetown the next day. But the institution's head
physician, acting, it appears, on the word of a head nurse, decided that
Mansfield was mentally disturbed (she had, she admitted, moaned several
times as she had lain, motionless, on a chair on the hospital terrace, and the
nurse had told her she was "a perfect nuisance"), and had summoned an
automobile that took her forcibly to the Psychopathic Hospital, to which
she was temporarily committed. Psychiatrists there quickly determined
that Mansfield was not deranged but sick and began to treat her as such,
plying her with the raw eggs and malted milks she desired. But they refused
to release her, even though, she claimed, one told her "they considered such
a method of sending a patient there a great mistake."

Mansfield consulted a lawyer when she finally was, after seven days, set
free. The lax procedures that allowed the observations of a nurse to be
transformed into a judgment of insanity, however temporary, galled her.
The formalities and safeguards she argued would have prevented such
an infringement of her "human and constitutional rights" were precisely
those psychiatric reformers had been arguing were unnecessary. Her lawyer, in a politely firm letter to Southard, argued that even those safeguards
against unwarranted detention that the law still provided for were, in this
case, blatantly contravened. Once declared sane, the patient should have
been released forthwith. Southard, in response, transformed the question
of proper procedure, which the lawyer had construed in legal terms, into a
matter of medicine. First voicing his agreement with the lawyer's inter-

pretation of the law, he acknowledged that its provision for the immediate release of a sane patient was "exceedingly explicit." But a diagnosis was rarely rendered within the short period Mansfield had claimed hers was; indeed, Southard wrote, "it would probably be scientifically accurate to say that although the patient may not be legally insane at this time, she is a victim of mental difficulty which does not fall far short of legal insanity." She was, he claimed, a psychoneurotic.

Southard's claim was at best a misrepresentation intended to put an end to a potentially embarrassing chain of events, for no Psychopathic Hospital patient eventually determined to be psychoneurotic—the least serious of diagnoses—was ever in serious danger of being labeled insane. Mansfield had threatened to publicize her tale and to seek legal redress. Southard, by his own account fearing that "she would fall into the hands of lawyers who would endeavor to make something of her condition," had refused to surrender the papers under which she had been committed. He apologized to the lawyer for this, but went on to emphasize that the decision to release her had been narrow and that her age was "not wholly in her favor." Closing the matter, he wrote, "I am sorry to say that I think the patient's very attitude in the present situation is at least partly to be interpreted as a symptom of her condition."[55]

Gender was no doubt at work in this case. Mansfield's indignation and talk of rights—her "symptom"—was, from Southard's perspective, altogether unwarranted, coming as it did from one in a position of dependence. He was prepared to protect her from scheming lawyers by infringing on her legal rights, which, he assumed, she was in no condition to exercise. Still, aspects of this and other cases resist a simple gender reading. Psychiatrists' contempt for women cannot fully account for their refusal to entertain rights-based arguments, which came from men as well as women. Their refusal was at bottom a corollary of their enmeshment within a disciplinary paradigm, according to the conventions of which talk of rights—linked as it was to their discipline's sorry history—was inadmissible. Consider, for example, Mansfield's lawyer's suggestion to Southard that "in the interest of [his] peace of mind" he carefully reexamine the law to avoid further trouble, in light of "the public suspicion—even of the State Institutions— that persons are illegally restrained." Suspicion, illegalities, restraint—to psychiatrists these were terms resonant with punitive associations that belonged to their discipline's past. They were all but incomprehensible from the perspective psychiatrists were laboring to maintain.

. And labor they did. Southard crossed the country and traveled, by steamer, to Europe to explicate and promote what he referred to as the psychopathic hospital idea. He and his colleagues lobbied the legislature, delivered public lectures, and wrote hundreds of papers on behalf of psychiatry's "new point of view."[56] In the new psychiatry there was little place for the antinomies between sane and insane, freedom and confinement, rights and their lack, that had characterized the old. In the new psychiatry, harmonious cooperation among patients, families, psychiatrists, and governmental bodies would supplant the adversarial relations that had set one against another, generating suspicion and distrust, in the old. In psychiatrists' vision, power would not be exercised from the top down, but distributed widely among society's actors. Relations of domination would give way to relations of truth. Psychiatrists' vision gravitated less toward social control than toward the point at which knowledge and power fostered the conditions conducive to the realization of both. Southard's observation that temporary patients represented "entirely new subjects for study" was advanced from precisely this point.[57]

Psychiatrists claimed to prefer the sane to the insane as subjects, for there was not much to be learned from the latter. They were happy to hand control of them to others—asylum superintendents, even the state and its mechanisms of commitment.[58] And they complained that the police, the courts, and others were sending them "a good many" inappropriate cases.[59] Yet, however much psychiatrists repudiated the juridical role their predecessors had played, the problem of the police, figurative and actual, pressed insistently against their vision of their practices as unobjectionable. Some patients raised it directly, in protests similar to that of one man who contended that involuntary detention interfered with his "rights as an American citizen and [his] liberty."[60] Psychiatrists tried to circumvent it, but in proposals such as one that would authorize institutions "to control the person of a patient" but not "remove his self-respect," they only underscored the impossibility of doing so.[61] Only Meyer confronted the matter directly, maintaining that commitment laws were an issue of police power broadly construed.[62]

The difficulty here was that although psychiatrists claimed to be uninterested in acting as police, the temporary commitment laws that they advocated did not do away with policing but, rather, allowed a range of persons—disgruntled husbands, frightened wives, exasperated mothers, annoyed neighbors—to play the officer's part. The new laws in place, psychiatrists oversaw a system in which the power to police was neither singular, vested in government officials, nor uniform, a matter of law. The power to police took multiple forms. It was evident, faintly, in the induced introspection of the voluntary patient; less subtly in the strained compliance of the temporary patient committed by no-longer-scheming but nonetheless partial relatives; not at all subtly in the anguished protests of abusive men committed by women they claimed to love. Woven into the relations of everyday life, police power of this diffuse sort was sustained not by the police (although they were sometimes implicated) but by the prosaic passions, antagonisms, and drab difficulties that ran through the lives of just about everyone.[64]

Familial Regulation

That anyone could play the officer's part is nowhere more evident than in the cases of those persons who were committed by members of their own families. Close relations were responsible for committing 43 percent of all patients to the hospital. Men made up 42 percent of this group, women 58 percent. Half of them were single, divorced, or widowed; 36 percent were married. Relatives' motives for committing their own varied. Many argued that the individual in question was somehow strange—peculiar or abnormal—and had recently changed. Of these patients, 30 percent were reportedly plagued by delusions, 23 percent were unable to work, and 18 percent had threatened or attempted suicide. Fears of poison and electricity plagued some; depression, crying spells, and inability to sleep others. The strangeness that provoked family members' concern could become intolerable. Out-of-work, irrational husbands who sat motionless by the fire; wives, claiming to hear voices, who passed the days in prayer; once-responsible brothers who refused to work; elderly mothers who could not sleep for fear someone would kill them: individuals like these elicited a mix of emotions, ranging from puzzlement and concern to disgust and anger, in those closest to them. Some families sought "compulsion and law," others a more therapeutic approach.[64] In some cases it took a spectacular outburst of violence to induce someone to commit another; in others the annoyance occasioned by long-tolerated eccentricities sufficed. Whatever led families to commit their own, that they did so is evidence that the family did not necessarily shelter its members from society's oppressions, one of its manifest purposes. Rather, family-initiated commitments suggest that the domination, management, and regulation of individuals that many have assumed were functions of the state were also carried out by—indeed, are constitutive of—the family. As D. A. Miller has astutely observed, "only by assuming the burden of an immense internal regulation" could the family sustain its representation in liberal discourse as a "free, private, and individual domain."[65]

Examining the mix of factors that prompted families to commit their own, which varied from case to case, one can glimpse the workings of the intrafamily regulation that routine circumstances hid from view. Although many families confronted difficulties of the sort that impelled some to seek psychiatric intervention, only those who did so have left us an archive of their troubles. Members of some families simply endured, others were left mired in resignation, and still others followed paths that are largely lost to the historian. The character and intensity of each family's internal regulation and, correspondingly, of the likelihood that one of its members would seek outside intervention when that regulation foundered, was shaped by the vagaries of temperament and disposition, about which the historian can have little, in general terms, to say. However, neighborhood conditions, cultural traditions, and material circumstances also shaped families' regulatory styles, in systematic ways that bear examination.

With respect to behavioral oddities, the city was at once more forgiving and more exacting than the small town or rural area. Individuals, especially men, could travel through the city's many public spaces in relative anonymity, but at home and in their own neighborhoods they were subjected to relentless scrutiny. Small apartments in crowded districts could hold some secrets, but much that men and women might have preferred to keep private spilled over into the streets, where it became the property of all, as the unsolicited testimony concerning the domestic life of one patient—"All who live in this neighborhood cannot help but see and hear how things go"—makes clear.[66] Some persons were known around their neighborhoods simply as strange or queer. As the family doctor of one middle-class, middle-aged woman committed by her siblings said of her, "It is a matter of common opinion and knowledge in the neighborhood that [she] is eccentric."[67] A man might be known to beat his wife, as was one man for whom a neighbor had "no use," or to drink to excess, or, in more general terms, to be "a good man," "the best in the neighborhood" on account of his ability and willingness to provide, the most salient dimension of his public persona.[68] A woman was most often known by her sexual morals and the quality of her housekeeping, the most salient aspects of hers. Many were quick to remark on one's low wage and another's squalid front parlor, to censure deviations from their community's norms of deportment and behavior, and to listen in on what spilled out. "The neighbors are complaining," wrote Louise Warner, a Roxbury resident, explaining her decision to consult authorities concerning her paretic husband's raving, swearing, and physical abuse.

A number of women, Louise Warner among them, attempted to manage their mates in the interest of preserving an elusive familial decorum. Warner humored and protected her husband in many small ways, for example by persuading the landlord, who was threatening to confront her husband about the noise, not to visit their apartment.[69] "I have learned to manage him as I would an insane man—by strategy," wrote another woman in a long statement that detailed her husband's many "abnormal traits."[70] Another told psychiatrists that she had "not handled her husband correctly."[71] In the cases that came to psychiatrists' attention, management of this sort, difficult to sustain, had clearly broken down. When it did, those (women, in most cases) who assumed responsibility for it appear to have welcomed the neighborly oversight—the intrusive inquiries, the harsh judgments—that their previous efforts had been intended to deflect. In a moment of crisis, such oversight could strengthen wavering resolve, reminding someone that it was imperative to have a close relative committed, a step that to many constituted a violation of the family's integrity.

Although families from all of Boston's racial and ethnic groups took the steps that resulted in commitment, particular ethnic traditions consistently shaped the manner in which they did so. In most instances, family members moved toward institutionalization hesitantly and with trepidation, approaching a physician in the community who arranged for either temporary commitment (79 percent of all family-initiated cases) or voluntary admission (17 percent of such cases) to the hospital.[72] Some instigated more formal proceedings, petitioning to have their relative committed for observation as an insane person. Of all Boston's ethnic groups, Jews equivocated the most on the decision to commit.[73] Known for their persistence in searching for expert medical advice, Jews typically consulted many physicians before deciding to send a family member to the hospital. Southard and Jarrett applauded the Jews' "excellent habit (from a mental hygiene point of view) of very speedily resorting to physicians for their ills"; they might just as well have noted that Jews mistrusted much of the advice physicians dispensed.[74] The sons of Russian-born Stella Meyer, for example, a fifty-two-year-old woman who was convinced that someone was trying to kill her and that she would soon die from heart disease, took her to the family physician and, unsatisfied, to a dozen specialists before bringing her to the hospital, from which they promptly removed her against psychiatrists' advice.[75] A student of immigrant Jewish mores would later observe that families did everything they could to avoid placing their own in institutions, keeping their disturbed members at home until their behavior became intolerable. This was so even in families bound together only by a culturally enforced sense of duty, not affection.[76] The travails of the Eastman family, immigrants from Russia with a troubled seventeen-year-old son, provide a case in point. By his mother's account, the boy, Samuel, was "talking about telepathy a great deal," refusing to go outside for fear of being laughed at, and accusing a neighboring dentist of making his tooth ache. She was frantic about his condition, she told social workers, so desperate that she was ready to call the police and have them forcibly take him to the hospital. Yet when it came to committing him for observation, she equivocated, finally agreeing to do so only under the provisions of the voluntary statute. Once he was in the hospital, she hounded social workers (as they told it) "to tell the doctor this and that, and to do this and that" for her son, and she removed him against psychiatrists' advice six days later, announcing that she would care for him at home and that her sister (the boy's aunt, with whom she shared a home) would "if necessary help support him." Still, the aunt thought him lazy, her husband judged him spoiled, a boy who should have been "turned out of the house and made to stay out," and the mother, the picture of selfless maternal solicitude, admitted that she could not bear to have him around the house any longer. Half a year later, however, there he was, listless and working irregularly, to the great annoyance of his mother and aunt.[77]

The Eastman family achieved its putative freedom at the price of an emotionally freighted, ambivalent self-regulation. Among Boston's Irish, such regulation was carried out more straightforwardly. Less distrustful of the state, the Irish were of all Boston's racial and ethnic groups the most adept at working the system for their own ends and the most inclined to take their disputes and troubles to court. Molly Ryan, for example, whose husband had successfully petitioned physicians at City Hall to have her committed after a domestic set-to, accounted for her husband's action by explaining to psychiatrists that "his people always had their folks put into insane asylums."[78] And the poor, widowed mother of Dennis Farrell, who deemed her single, thirty-three-year-old drinking son "an Obstinate Mule" who had "acted very unwisely," showed no hesitation in entreating political figures—Irish, of course—to smooth his transit through various institutions. From the mayor's secretary she obtained a letter, most likely unnecessary, instructing physicians at the City Hospital to admit her son and, she wrote when his health dramatically declined, she "immediately got in touch with our Senator to have him sent to Rutland Sanitarium."[79] Indeed, under pressure from families, state senators of Irish extraction monitored the passage of a number of their own through various institutions; the patients were informally known as "political pressure cases."[80] To consign a family member to an asylum was for Jews "the ultimate shame"; to the Irish it was a pragmatic step that signified how much they felt the state's mechanisms of authority were theirs to control.[81] Jewish physicians were prominent at the Psychopathic (a "Jewish Bug-House," in one patient's characterization), distinguishing it from the asylums that were likely seen, by Jews and Irish alike, as agencies of the Irish-dominated commonwealth. It is possible that family physicians were able to persuade Jews to commit their own to the Psychopathic Hospital with assurances that they would be examined by a Dr. Solomon, Adler, or Myerson; at least one patient was heartened by Myerson's presence, although he judged the doctor a "nervous young man."[82] The Irish who did commit their own showed little ambivalence about doing so, for many were secure in the conviction that they could remove them from psychiatrists' control at any time.

Material circumstances, too, shaped families' styles of self-regulation, although somewhat less consistently than cultural traditions. Some of those with the means to do so consulted one private physician after another and made elaborate arrangements to care for a mentally disturbed relative at home, going so far as to hire private attendants or to establish a residence for him or her with a "friend" in constant attendance.[83] In many less-advantaged families, women dutifully assumed the role of unpaid attendants, sacrificing their already circumscribed autonomy to look after their nervous, depressed, and delusional relatives. The women who did so made clear that this was no light undertaking, emotionally or materially. The sister of twenty-nine-year-old Albert Andrews, for example, a printer with paranoid ideas, spent her days carefully monitoring his mental state, consulting psychiatrists only when he seemed to be "losing control of himself rapidly." Even though he kept telling her "he cannot live this way much longer," she backed away from involuntarily committing him, worrying all the while that he would harm himself, hoping that he would decide to enter the institution, and chastising herself for not handling the situation better.[84] The concerns of Catherine Jordan's niece were more concrete. She and her husband, she explained, were "a young Couple" who could not afford to keep the fifty-nine-year-old Jordan, who slept all day and walked about all night. "Her nerves are so bad," the young woman wrote, "she just keeps me watching her and I cannot do it."[85] Many poor families were pushed to the brink of desperation by the loss of the depressed or disturbed person's wage—or unpaid household labor when that person was a woman—together with the added burden of caring for him or her. The fears of one elderly father that he would soon be facing the poorhouse because of his daughter Helen Gale's inability to care for herself and her children were similar to those voiced by others in economically marginal circumstances.[86] This man had hoped that Gale would help support him as he grew older, but for more than four years he had instead been supporting her. Members of Dennis Farrell's family—his mother and two brothers, all three disabled by rheumatism—expressed similar fears in a more rancorous tone. Farrell, the Irishman with political friends, worked as an elevator operator in a city building, earning fifteen dollars a week until fired for drinking six months before his family committed him. Without his wages, they were reduced to eating two meals a day. "We cant get the Proper food here as we are in dire needs," one brother wrote, "and them meals are very meager if I was to tell you what we have been living [on] for the Past week you wouldn't believe it." This brother termed Farrell "the Weakling of the family . . . the Cause of all our Adversity," a spineless character who refused "to do our biding." Although other families were as desperate, few admitted to as much bitterness, suggesting that factors other than their straitened circumstances determined how poor families handled difficult members.[87]

In many of the families that brought one of their members to psychiatric attention, behavioral and moral regulation was relatively imperceptible and ostensibly benign, carried out with the interests of the disturbed person foremost in mind. This was so in Helen Gale's family, which, although nearing its financial and emotional limits, sheltered her for years. Familial regulation took on a more malign cast in cases, like Farrell's, that relatives could and did construe as instances of the patient's willful repudiation of social and behavioral norms. The twenty-year-old bellboy, in his stepfather's estimation "a terrible boy to get along with," whose family "never could make anything of him"; the just-married, footloose twenty-two-year-old whose husband vowed he would "do no more chasing after her and bringing her home," proclaiming that he did not "intend to pay any more bills she runs"; the young man deemed eccentric and "considerable of a 'Rolling Stone'" by his mother, who was "rather tired of answering letters concerning him and his peculiar characteristics": in cases like these, family members had no trouble framing the issue as one of failed regulation.[88] The way in which a family defined and addressed issues that psychiatrists argued were psychiatric was shaped as much by its own particular emotional configuration as it was by cultural traditions and material circumstances. Some families were harsh and unforgiving, turning out their own while proclaiming variously that their patience was exhausted, that they no longer cared to be mixed up in the patient's difficulties, or that, as the aunts of one woman put it, the patient deserved "long and severe punishment."[89] Other families were more forgiving of behavioral quirks and annoyances, maintaining that harmless but eccentric persons should be cared for at home. "She dont boder no one," a woman wrote in this vein of her fifty-year-old Catholic aunt. "When she get nerves she scolds only to herself and no one hear her so she dont hurt no one."[90] Although neighborhood conditions, cultural traditions, and material circumstances influenced families' regulatory styles, and although, of these, cultural expectations most decisively governed patterns of familial commitment, in the end there is no accounting for why what was tolerable to one constituted the acme of annoyance to another.

Of all family-initiated commitments, those in which wives, claiming abuse, committed their husbands were emotionally the most charged. Although relatively few in number, such commitments dramatically brought to the fore, in exaggerated form, the inequalities that structured all families, peaceable and violent alike. In the terms of the liberal political theory that historically has governed much of our thinking about the family, these inequalities were conceived of as natural and were thus left largely unexamined. The family itself was envisioned as a "rightless realm," an arena in which women toiled and men enjoyed not rights but extralegal, "private" prerogatives—from sexual access to their wives to a hot meal each night—that were bestowed by custom and won by love, obligations moderated only by fierce spousal negotiation.[91] The otherwise resourceless women who engaged legal and psychiatric means to challenge and even subvert their husbands' "right" violently to abuse them forced an examination of the balance of power that governed relations in their families. Some of their men recognized this. Telling psychiatrists that he had been a "good husband," a thirty-four-year-old Italian barber who was committed at his wife's behest—he had given her a black eye and had threatened her with a razor—complained that lately she had "seemed to try to boss me or overpower me and that isn't right, I ought to have all the power, I'm to command."[92]

Psychiatrists were eager to right the marital balance of power that gave rise to such immoderate assertions of masculine prerogative. Inviting the men who had been committed by their wives to expound on the terms that governed their marriages, psychiatrists heard one man complain that he had "a sort of independent girl for a wife," another argue that what he expected was to have "always the woman behind the man," and still another, whose wife had summoned the police to remove him from their home, lightheartedly explain that he did not "know the term abuse—probably I was too good for her."[93] Various men who were accused of abusing their wives—of hitting, slapping, punching, and kicking them—told psychiatrists of feeling that their positions vis-à-vis their wives were weaker than they should have been, that their own control was slipping, and that their wives were to blame for any violence that occurred. Sentiments like these drew psychiatrists' censure, for they were indicative of marital arrangements that psychiatrists, as moderns, considered outmoded. Indeed, as Myerson saw it, a woman's expectation that she should *not* be beaten was entirely new, a sign of modernity.[94]

Still, for all their impatience with such men and their attempts to exonerate themselves ("I haven't done half as much as other men done," protested one),[95] psychiatrists did not frame domestic violence as an issue in its own right. They listened to women and men speak of it, but they rarely commented on it. In their analyses, it was buried among the drab difficulties—poverty, unemployment, bad temper—that they argued colored the lives of most persons. In their handling of cases, they were content, quite uncharacteristically, to leave its adjudication to the courts.

Psychiatrists' indifference to the professional possibilities of defining abuse as a psychiatric issue is anomalous in light of other aspects of their program. Even as they did not or could not formulate it in psychiatric terms, they were eagerly defining all sorts of other ills and failings as psychiatric problems or symptoms of disease. Further, they were committed to a thorough reorganization of the domestic sphere, to bringing under scrutiny the family secrets that Victorianism had shielded from view. Finally, they complained volubly of the legal system's mishandling of cases that involved even the most "indefinite mental symptoms," arguing that they were themselves better equipped than lawyers and judges to determine the disposition thereof.[96] From each of these perspectives, domestic violence appears to have been well suited to psychiatrists' purposes. It was certainly indicative of some sort of failing; it was evidence that the domestic sphere demanded scrutiny; it was, as a legal offense, often mishandled. Yet, for the most part, psychiatrists simply could not, or would not, see the violence to which women attested and men often admitted. This was in part because of its very ordinariness. Yet even when psychiatrists did take note of violence, they did not privilege it, treating it instead as a symptom of something else—marital dissension, a wife's extravagance, a husband's drinking.

The dimensions of psychiatrists' inability to conceive of domestic violence as a problem in its own right are evident in their handling of the case of Richard Byrne, a solidly middle-class man whose wife Nellie petitioned the Probate Court of Suffolk County in March 1913 to have him committed as an insane person. Nellie Byrne told the court that for three months her thirty-four-year-old husband, a wastepaper dealer of Irish descent, had been in a frenzy. He had been drinking hard for seven days; he had issued a threat, which he later dismissed as a "foolish remark," that he would smash all their furniture; and, after an argument about the quality of the coffee she had prepared, he had promised to "fix" her with an ax. According to his wife, Byrne had been a drinker since boyhood and became "crazy drunk" about once a week. When drunk he was often violent: in a drunken rage he once had "divested himself of his waistcoat, tor[n] his panama hat and commenced to spar with his wife"; recently, declaring he would kill her, he had struck his wife with a hurling club; and he regularly accused her of gallivanting about and of entertaining men in their home, and continually threatened to throw things in her face. He was extremely excitable, she told psychiatrists: "One moment I am the best girl that ever lived, and the next thing: get to hell with your damn kids, I don't give a damn."[97]

Nellie Byrne was no stranger to the workings of the law. She had summoned police to arrest her husband for drunkenness, assault, and disturbing the peace three times before, and she had engaged a lawyer to draw up a provisional separation agreement. Her decision to petition the court was, in several respects, merely the logical next step in an escalating series of actions she had taken against her husband. She had taken the first of these measures hastily, in response to an immediate crisis. Richard Byrne had come home drunk one night, and she took the children to her mother's house, found a policeman, and returned home to confront her husband. On another occasion, a passerby heard her screaming, entered the house, rescued her, and summoned the police. But improvised measures like these quickly gave way to moves requiring far more forethought. When Byrne was arrested for disturbing the peace on his wife's complaint, both parties engaged lawyers who, before the case could come to trial, conferred and drew up an agreement that both signed. Petitioning the court to apprehend her husband as an insane person was much the same sort of step.

Byrne had never served any time in jail. Psychiatrists noted caustically that he had repeatedly promised judges he would never drink, only to "abuse his wife the moment they left the courtroom." At first, it appeared he would fare as well under psychiatric scrutiny as he had in the hands of the law. The court physicians who examined him quickly determined—largely, it appears, on the basis of his upright, respectable appearance—that there was "nothing the matter" with him and that he ought to be let go, and psychiatrists at first concurred. They could find "nothing abnormal" about him at all, except, they noted, that he was suspicious of his wife and that "he has threatened to kill her recently." Herman Adler explained to his colleagues that Byrne felt "he would rather get a crack at [his wife] than keep the peace"—he had "money enough to pay all these fines" the courts had levied—but Adler went on to report that he had just that morning informed Byrne's wife that psychiatrists could not find anything wrong with the man.

It was a strange outlook that could discern nothing abnormal in a man who, by his admission, threatened to kill his wife and to take an ax to the family piano. Although psychiatrists could not settle on a psychiatric alternative to the legal view that held Byrne was not a criminal because he had not "done anything," a contestable interpretation, their prolonged attempt to make the case turn on his character—discernible in his actions and threats, but separate from them—suggests they were not entirely comfortable with the narrow construction the law put on such a case.[98] One inexperienced doctor wanted to give the case back to the court, saying he thought it was "a case for alienists to settle." The others preferred to settle the issue among themselves, but they could agree on little. Was he insane? Was he defective, delinquent, or "of the criminal type"? Only one's suggestion that the patient was "lacking something" offered psychiatrists a way out of the legal thinking that held that such determinations were to be made by a judge. "Lack of something" was the sort of determination in which metrically minded psychiatrists claimed to specialize. But what Richard Byrne lacked was unclear. Moral sensibility? Good sense? Psychiatrists could agree it was "something" but were puzzled because, as Warren Stearns put it, "outside of this difficulty with his wife he does not seem to have any trouble."

Psychiatrists' obtuseness regarding a man who some predicted would one day "take an ax to his wife" can be accounted for in part by the fact that Byrne was a respectable middle-class merchant whose business, owned by his father, was worth a good deal. Psychiatrists treated the middle-class man's character as unproblematic, a simple extension of his social position, so once the discussion turned to the issue of character, only Nellie Byrne's was available for inspection. The portrait they painted was not pretty. They argued that Nellie Byrne, formerly a lowly stenographer, had likely been "dazzled" by Byrne and his wealth; her interruption of marital relations—Byrne admitted the pair had not "had any connection" for about eight weeks—was significant, a sign that she was, one psychiatrist guessed, "tired of a man who is unable to improve on conditions." The wife, added another, was not a good woman, "and the fact that he married this particular individual may have mortified his career more or less." In the end, then, psychiatrists were able to consider Byrne's career but not his abusiveness, which they repeatedly minimized as his "difficulty with his wife," as an issue worthy of their attention. That Byrne admitted to everything of which his wife had accused him makes this all the more striking.[99]

Women brought domestic violence to psychiatric attention by a variety of routes, challenging—sometimes directly, other times indirectly—the common assessment of it as ordinary and inevitable.[100] Those who summoned police to handle abusive husbands did so straightforwardly. Some of these men were undoubtedly let go, but police apprehended others and decided to commit a subset of those to the hospital for observation. Margaret Fitzpatrick, for example, had for seven years repeatedly called the police to her South Boston home and had gone to court several times. She told police that her forty-three-year-old husband Michael, a bookkeeper, was constantly threatening to kill her and their children, predicting "when he reads in the Papers about tragedies 'that there will be a tragedy in this house greater than that.'" Although Fitzpatrick claimed the police had said to him, "you are all right," they in fact took him to headquarters and committed him as an insane person forthwith.[101]

Under psychiatric scrutiny Fitzpatrick fared as well as Byrne had. Even though Margaret Fitzpatrick insisted she was "afraid all the time that he will do us injury," psychiatrists wondered whether the examining physicians had been overly influenced by reports of Fitzpatrick's threats to kill his wife. "There are threats and threats, of course," Southard pointed out. Myerson thought him not insane, just "an irascible individual." The social worker, a Miss Chapman, volunteered that she had interviewed the wife and found her "very unreliable," adding that the family's priest told her the same thing.

Psychiatrists found Fitzpatrick not insane but alcoholic and released him, an outcome Margaret Fitzpatrick and the city physician who signed the original commitment paper deemed "a crime." Within a month, she was writing to Jarrett that she had already approached the police station and was living "in hopes before many hours he'll be safe under lock and key at the hospital." In their handling of this case psychiatrists had turned the threatened violence that, from a legal standpoint, lay at the center of the case into a character defect, a sign of irascibility. They also brought in the woman's character when reference to the man's alone could not explain the situation.

Few of the women whose actions culminated in their husbands' commitment, whether they had approached the court directly or whether, like Margaret Fitzpatrick, they had called police who then committed the men, cited violence as a factor without linking it to drink. In doing so, these women drew on a venerable, popular, and in part feminist temperance tradition that linked drink to domestic violence as well as on their own experience, in which violence was only one of the consequences of a man's drinking. Women found it easier to assign blame, to approach authorities, and to make sense of unraveling the familial bonds that bad relations and violence had already strained in cases where a man's drinking was at issue. The woman who wrote to social workers after she had committed her husband that in her opinion "what he needs most is hard work and plenty of it,"[102] and the like-minded woman who wrote to her incarcerated husband, a heavy drinker, that she hoped "they have knocked something into your block at the Hospital,"[103] had no trouble assigning blame. By contrast, the ravings and random violence of men who did not drink was puzzling, perhaps doubly terrifying because apparently independent of any stimulus. Louise Warner wrote to a psychiatrist concerning her syphilitic thirty-three-year-old husband, an irregularly employed machinist, that she did not like "him hitting me he might kill me dead his hands are so hard." His "constant swearing and cutting up here is very bad he seem to loose his head altogether . . . he talks and raves so loud," she continued, the neighbors "think we are all getting killed with him shouting so loud and the children crying." Yet she had not given up on him, like many of the wives of drinkers had, and expressed her hope that it was "nothing worse than that he needs a good rest."[104]

With drink—a psychiatric issue of long standing—in the picture, as it was in perhaps three-quarters of these cases, psychiatrists could focus on it rather than the abuse. Still, their inability or failure to apprehend domestic violence as a psychiatric issue in its own right had deeper roots, instructive in several ways. It is illustrative of how critically important categories were in psychiatrists' project of bringing everyday life into science. These categories were neither natural nor inevitable, although in retrospect they appear to have been both; once specified, they guided psychiatrists' observations of everyday life, enabling them more systematically to construe some issues— but not violence—as psychiatric. Psychiatrists' lack of attention to violence is indicative also of the limits of their program to reform the private sphere, to break down the distinction between public and private, and to argue for the subordination of the individual's "natural rights" when it was in society's interest to do so.[105] Using syphilis as an entrée, psychiatrists boldly

asserted their intention to examine and regulate nominally private concerns. In practice, they probed into patients' sexual, marital, and emotional
secrets, confident that in doing so they were serving science. But they stopped
at the threshold when it came to domestic violence, in effect treating it—as
it was treated in the liberal tradition they otherwise rejected—as a private
matter between two individuals, a consequence of a man's drinking or a
comprehensible response to a domineering woman's nagging demands.
Relating the story of his treatment of a particularly "meek fellow," a
"wreck" of a man, Myerson told of finally understanding, upon meeting
the man's wife, the source of his difficulty. A veritable Xanthippe, the
woman's "tongue hardly rested from the moment she got in to the time she
went out." For the man, the choice was clear: a broken spirit on the one
hand, "wife desertion or wife beating" on the other. Myerson was not
suggesting that the man beat his chattering wife; rather he prescribed "two
months' rest—away from his family" for him.[106] But the casual manner in
which he invoked wife-beating is illustrative of how "natural" and thus
invisible domestic violence could seem.

Psychiatry and the Police

The police were responsible for the commitment of a quarter of all Psychopathic Hospital patients. Many historians have seen police apprehensions
of the suspected insane as evidence of a generalized impulse, on the part of
bourgeois society, to control the behavior of deviant individuals—the
poor, the unemployed, the foreign-born—and to purge the body politic of
their offensive presence. Behavioral policing, however, was a function of the
family as much as of any other institution. When it came to questions of
public order and decorum, the police did not act simply as agents of the
state. In some circumstances, they served community interests, removing
persons whom "the general opinion" had already deemed bothersome or
demented. In other cases, they served families' interests, hauling away
suicidal individuals and abusive men. The police undoubtedly plucked
some harmlessly eccentric individuals off the street, but, in general, the
straightforward alignment of the powerful against the oppressed, to which
police commitments apparently attested, obscured complex series of events
in which police involvement was either invited or merely a fortuitous
capstone to a career of entanglements with authorities.

"ROW IN TAXI DRAWS CROWD: South End Merchant Now in Psychopathic Hospital"—so read the headline to the newspaper account of the
twenty-five-year-old businessman Abraham Patelsky's harrowing public
seizure, the beginning of a narrative of social control that contemporaries
and later commentators alike have seen as paradigmatic of the stories those

unfortunate enough to have forcibly landed under psychiatric scrutiny might have told. Patelsky was a Russian-born Jew, the owner of a small department store. His travails began the morning of 30 April 1913, when his physician, Dr. Silas Ayer, called on him at his store and asked him to go for an auto ride. Patelsky agreed to go, and they picked up another doctor, Francis Mahoney, before proceeding to City Hall, where Patelsky was to undergo the mental examination for which, he would learn, his brother, claiming that Patelsky was talking strangely, had arranged. Realizing that he had been hoodwinked, Patelsky was by this point too agitated to undergo a proper examination, and the city examiner arranged for him to be transferred directly to the Psychopathic Hospital. But Patelsky would have none of this. A strong young man of stocky build, he struggled with the two police officers who tried to force him into a taxicab and, as the newspapers reported the next day, "sounds of breaking glass, loud outcries and protests" drew the attention of more than a thousand people in the crowded city center. Patelsky, his face and hands bleeding from broken glass, had given "the officers a lively tussle."

Doctors Ayer and Mahoney petitioned successfully to have Patelsky committed to the hospital. They wrote that he entertained delusions of grandeur and persecution, noting, at his brother's insistence, that he was convinced his relatives were trying to cheat him out of his property. They noted further that Patelsky was excited, adducing as evidence that he had assaulted the officers who had seized him and had broken the windows of the carriage that brought him to the hospital. Patelsky has ideas of persecution, they recorded; he thinks "that everybody is working against his interest," an interpretation of events that appears to have been less a delusion than "the Truth" that Patelsky was certain would be his salvation. Despite his measured protests and, later, threats of legal action, Patelsky was held for over a month in the Psychopathic Hospital and then committed to an asylum proper.[107]

The police figured centrally, one of them by name, in the newspaper account of Patelsky's seizure, underwriting the widely shared opinion that power was theirs to wield. They "secured and bound" him as he shouted and kicked, while his brother, who had arranged for his seizure in the first place and who supplied information critical to its continuance, merely "accompanied" him to the hospital. Neither the state nor the police were wholly responsible for Patelsky's misfortunes, although both were participants, which suggests that even in this paradigmatic case the narrative of social control may obscure as much as it illuminates.[108]

Eighty percent of persons brought to the hospital by the police were either arrested or apprehended for observation on account of their public behavior.[109] Wandering about aimlessly, causing a disturbance, yelling and screaming, stumbling as if drunk, noisily threatening suicide: such disturbances of public order, if witnessed by a patrolman, could result in commitment. The patrolman's witnessing was more often invited than random, however, for in many cases he was summoned by neighbors, passersby, or busybodies. The officer who came upon the fifty-year-old Irishman Charles Connelly, who was "creating a scene" in front of his South Boston home, "surrounded by a crowd," did not note whether he had been summoned, but Connelly was known in the neighborhood (as social workers would later learn) as a nuisance and a drunk, and this suggests that his neighbors may have used the disturbance as a pretext for exercising some rough justice, delivering up to the police a man who had offended everyone with his swearing and drunken insults.[110] There is no question that someone summoned the police in Bernard Winston's case, for the officer who brought him to the hospital said that he had been told (by whom, it is not clear) "that the patient had been acting strangely for over a month and that something should be done." An unemployed middle-aged man who lived by himself, Winston was picked up outside a restaurant while waiting, as he told psychiatrists, "for the cook to get some grub ready." His offense was against public decorum; approached by the officer, he started to climb the side of the building, yelling, "You let me alone. I'm an American citizen." He complained it was "getting so a feller can't stand on the street."[111]

Or sleep in his bed. In March 1917, a patrolman who happened to be in Edward McBurney's Roxbury neighborhood decided, on the spot, to arrest him, aware that his wife had taken out a warrant against him because of his drinking and abuse. Finding the door locked, the patrolman had a young boy climb in the window to let him in. It is hardly surprising that McBurney felt "everybody [was] after him," or that some of the men who were arrested at their wives' request castigated the police who apprehended them by calling them "women."[112] One elderly man, who claimed his wife had "hatched a charge of non-support" against him, jested to psychiatrists that the courts who had deprived him of his "natural rights" were presided over "by a lot of old women in men's clothes";[113] and Richard Byrne a bit disingenuously told them that he "didn't think a woman could get a police officer to come to her house for nothing."[114] In fact, the police were not always so eager to arrest men on women's account; one asked Alice McGinley several times if she were sure she wanted him to haul away her drunken husband before agreeing to do so, telling the man he "did not like to take him."[115] Characterizing as women those who would regulate their behavior and curtail their rights was one way to overcome the shock of arrest. One man, who told psychiatrists that he had seen "the whole thing in a flash"—"there was a crowd in the street and the patrol was waiting there and there were two police officers there"—called this the sense of "This is for me."[116]

The police brought approximately 470 persons to the hospital each year,

TABLE 4.1
Arrests in Boston

	1910	1915	1920
Total arrests	71,201	96,476	58,817
Percent male	91	91	93
Percent foreign-born	46	43	36
Percent nonresident	40	38	32
Arrests for drunkenness[a]	48,000	65,000	22,000
Percent male	91	92	94
Selected "nuisance" arrests[b]			
Idle and disorderly persons	220	280	180
Profane and obscene persons	190	200	270
Suspicious persons	2,050	800	2,100
Tramps and vagrants	290	290	120

Source: Police Commissioner for the City of Boston, *Annual Reports,* 5 (1911), 10 (1916), and (1921).
[a] To nearest 1,000.
[b] To nearest 10.

many of them at the behest of others.[117] Their work with the insane formed only a small portion of all police business, for each year they made tens of thousands of arrests: approximately fifty thousand in 1905; seventy thousand in 1910; one hundred thousand in 1915; and sixty thousand in 1920 (table 4.1). Arrests for drunkenness constituted two-thirds of these (a proportion that fell dramatically in 1920, after Prohibition). By contrast, nuisance arrests—arrests for persons designated as idle and disorderly, as tramps and vagrants, as suspicious, profane, or obscene—constituted between 2 and 5 percent of all arrests; those brought to the hospital formed a subset of these.[118] In the period covered by table 4.1, the police were granted greater latitude in their handling of persons they thought insane. Before the hospital opened, only the dangerously insane could be apprehended without a warrant; the patrolman's right to restrain an apparently insane person was "no greater than that of any private person," for, as police regulations read, "insanity in itself is neither a crime nor a just ground for arrest."[119] With the passage of the Police Law in 1910, the category of persons subject to police apprehension was broadened to include all those suffering from "delirium, mania, mental confusion, delusions or hallucinations." The suspected insane were no longer to be locked up in the city prison, jails, or police stations, but briefly examined and taken to the Psychopathic Hospital.[120]

Considered as a group, without regard for the circumstances and behavior that initially sparked police attention, police patients differed from the

Boston population from which they were drawn; their gender, class back-grounds, and ethnic identities were all related to the pathways they traveled to the institution. Male patients were twice as likely as female patients to have been brought by the police. Among the men who ended up as patients, Jews were the least likely to have done so on account of the police, Italians the most likely; among all police patients, the Irish were overrepresented relative to their prominence in Boston's population and WASPs—native-born white Protestants, the offspring of native-born parents—were under-represented. Further, across all ethnic groups, working-class men were nearly twice as likely as men of the middle class to have fallen into police hands.[121] Still, considered in the context of police work, such patients, so few in number, were of little consequence.

In psychiatrists' thinking, the police were relegated to the past but polic-ing was not. From the perspective they were attempting to maintain, the police were an anachronism, an embarrassing survival from their disci-pline's past. The police conjured up visions of force, of the prisons and lock-ups to which many still likened the modern psychopathic hospital, despite psychiatrists' efforts to drive home the differences between the penal and psychiatric outlooks. Psychiatrists entertained their own visions of a more efficacious mode of policing, one in which the actual police would play no part—whether it was a program of combing through records in preparation for seeking in the community those amenable to treatment, or actually sending "psychopathic ward authorities . . . out into the commu-nity" to locate persons whom others had reported in need of attention. Southard exhorted his colleagues to consider the latter procedure, which a New York City ordinance had recently made legal, "for possible imitation in Massachusetts."[122] In the meantime, psychiatrists in Boston would have to satisfy themselves with a more metaphorical mode of policing, leaving the actual seizure of persons to the men in blue.

Some 17,000 persons became patients at the Psychopathic Hospital from the time it opened in 1912 through 1922. In every respect they were a diverse lot. They came from Boston and its surrounding cities and towns—Brookline, Cambridge, Somerville, Chelsea, Revere, and Lynn. Nearly half of them had lived in Massachusetts from birth; the rest had emigrated to the state from near (Newfoundland and Nova Scotia, New York and New Jersey) and far (Ireland, Italy, Russia, Syria, Armenia, and China). They represented a range of racial and ethnic groups: Yankee, Canadian, Irish, Jewish, and, to a lesser extent, Italian and African-American. Among those who became patients were nurses, artists, farmers, peddlers, stenogra-phers, clerks, machinists, teamsters, soldiers, and students. They came from material circumstances ranging from comfortable to wretched, with most falling somewhere between.

This population of patients was remarkably heterogeneous, yet it closely mirrored the Boston population from which it was drawn on a number of critical race, class, and gender-related measures. Its racial and ethnic composition was remarkably similar to that of the city. Members of the middle class were represented in it proportional to their percentage citywide. And it encompassed equal numbers of women and men. The ways in which patients differed from nonpatients—inclination, disposition, emotional state, the vagaries of circumstance—are not quantifiable; they are recoverable only in the individual case histories. In addition, the alignments of power, persuasion, and interest that brought them under psychiatric scrutiny were not at all uniform, varying instead with individuals' material and emotional resources.

Hospital psychiatrists were certain that among their patients were many who, but for the ease and informality of commitment under the provisions of the temporary laws, would never have come into their care.[123] In this they were undoubtedly right, for the surprisingly broad spectrum of patients the hospital drew set it apart from the state hospitals, or asylums, that, by the turn of the century, were housing ever-larger numbers of elderly and long-term, chronic patients.[124] Psychiatrists especially prized what Southard referred to as the "higher type" of patient, the patient whose social position and near-normality elevated him or her above the mass of lower types with which psychiatrists' predecessors had perforce been content. That their hospital was, as Southard put it, tapping "society in a new stratum" was not only integral to psychiatrists' vision of themselves and their institution but also likely true.[125] The self-described "nervous" Chicago resident who, after reading a news article extolling the institution's virtues, had the financial and emotional means to quit his job, travel to Boston, and voluntarily sign himself into the institution was perhaps peculiarly resolute but not unique.

Yet the institution and its patient population were not altogether so singular as their proponents maintained. Like the asylums from which psychiatrists labored to distinguish it, the hospital took in the poor, the elderly, and the seriously disturbed. Serving as the institution of first resort for Bostonians, it received nearly all of the city's residents who were institutionalized on suspicion of mental disorder. Families, the police, and courts—those who usually petitioned for commitment of the insane—were encouraged, and in the case of the police mandated, temporarily to commit suspected insane persons to it rather than to seek regular court commitments. For these reasons, it is likely that the hospital's patient population was more similar to those of other urban carceral institutions than psychiatrists liked to imagine.[126]

The Psychopathic Hospital patient population might best be characterized as transitional, sharing some characteristics with asylum popula-

tions but, especially in its concentration of higher types, presaging psychiatry's extrainstitutional future. The locus of self-proclaimed advanced
psychiatric practice remained institutional through the twenties at least.
But it would shift, first to the outpatient clinics established in large numbers in the 1910s, later to office-based practice. Like the Psychopathic
Hospital, both attracted a broader range of persons than state hospitals
ever had.[127]

FIVE

CLASSIFICATION

ASSUMING the attitude he thought proper to one of his station, which he characterized as "brainless," Richard Clarke, a sixty-four-year-old Irish clerk who had just been subjected to the intense form of psychiatric scrutiny known as the staff meeting, addressed his observations on the whole procedure to the governor of Massachusetts in a crisp, flowing hand. The circumstances were melancholy, he wrote. The psychiatrists, though expert—"Brainy . . . Diagnosers of Symptoms"—had shown questionable goodwill; the chief examiner had merely done his job, alert to the "interests of his employers and to the continuance of his salary." Examination was, Clarke submitted, a social necessity, "culminating in the delinquents incarceration and confinement," but in his case it had been less than thorough because, as he put it, the "real reason" for his only tentative submission to the ordeal had never been heard. "Oh dear, what a dreadful calamity if men were incapable of being pronounced Lunatics," Clarke concluded. "The consequences are too utterly utter to contemplate."[1]

Here we have the several dimensions of diagnosis put succinctly and with what psychiatrists in other circumstances might have seen as legendary Irish wit. The melancholy born of recognition that a life had gone astray; the psychiatric imperative to classify, rooted not in lofty humanitarian but in base professional motives; and the whole procedure's quality as event, even spectacle, in which the Brainy (including "Ladies"—the social workers Clarke would have seen at his examination) confronted and passed judgment on the Brainless, an event to which the patient's submission was demanded but in this case not fully yielded—all were evident in Clarke's brief but pithy analysis. In it, the succession of historians' approaches to the psychiatric sensibility was neatly recapitulated: from a whiggish humanitarianism, through a focus on professionalization, culminating in a playful skepticism that he underscored with his observation that diagnosis was at once absurd but absolutely necessary—"too utterly utter to contemplate."

That the psychiatrist harbors a peculiar affinity for the diagnostic endeavor would become, in the course of the twentieth century, a staple of psychiatric self-criticism as well as of popular declamation. To psychiatry's critics as well as to some psychiatrists themselves, who routinely denigrated their forebears while staking their own claims to truth, it seemed that two thousand years of classificatory enthusiasm, from the ancient Greeks to the modern Germans, had generated one grand nosology after another and an arcane vocabulary of Latinate neologisms but precious little else—primitive, even punitive, treatments and no cures. The historian could all too easily fashion the classificatory endeavors of Southard and his colleagues into a chapter in this well-established history of psychiatric sophistry. Southard delighted in drawing up elaborate taxonomies, in coining linguistic hybrids, and in debating with his philosopher colleagues—Josiah Royce, Charles Saunders Pierce, Roscoe Pound—the meanings of diagnosis.[2] His and his colleagues' hospital practice consisted, for the most part, in observing and assessing patients as a prelude to sorting and classifying them; they did, or so it seemed, little else. Indeed, the generation of dynamic psychiatrists that followed them would make precisely this charge. Through the thirties and forties, such leaders of the profession as William A. White and Karl Menninger would dismiss their elders' diagnostic schemes and enthusiasms as relics of the golden era of "descriptive psychiatry," as the unfortunate culmination of their profession's well-known classificatory mania.[3]

There is, however, a different story to be told about early-twentieth-century psychiatry. To tell it this episode must be extracted from the standard historical narratives in which it has been embedded, both from those of the dynamic psychiatrists, who saw in it the last vestiges of a nosological tradition soon to expire, and from those of the profession's antipsychiatric critics, who cast its practitioners as duplicitous scientists manqué. A curiously presentist distinction between classification and science informs both sorts of narratives, as if the two endeavors stood in eternal, fixed opposition, as if the first were sterile and static while the second were "true," capable of producing results—treatments, efficacious cures. From the Enlightenment through much of the nineteenth century, however, the science of psychiatry, and even much of medicine, was classification *tout court*. Only the landmark discoveries of the late nineteenth century—in bacteriology, for example, the establishment of the germ theory of disease—would sever these endeavors in professional and popular estimation, elevating science into a loftier domain and leaving behind classification as an avocation of the small-minded.[4]

The different story, then, seeks neither to describe the relationship between psychiatry and this popular notion of science as true and efficacious, nor to contest the point at which psychiatry could rightfully claim the mantle of science. Rather, it treats this episode in psychiatry's history as a critical moment in the profession's constitution of itself qua profession. It looks at psychiatrists as they gather their disciplinary knowledge, carefully coaxing it out of the very subjects under their control. The story looks at the discipline of psychiatry both as knowledge or science and as social practice.[5]

"The Obscurity and the Delights of Psychiatric Diagnosis!"

Diagnosis was so integral a part of psychiatric practice that in its everyday guise it appeared natural and necessary.[6] Few questioned the psychiatrist's prerogative to observe, analyze, and classify the behavior and symptoms of his patients. Indeed, the lay public—friends and families, the police, representatives of the courts and various social agencies—expected psychiatrists would determine whether the individual in question was sane or insane, responsible or sick, capable of self-care or in need of supervision. Patients themselves, though they might disagree with the outcomes, demanded that psychiatrists render judgments concerning their sanity. And psychiatrists, for their part, worked on the presumption that arriving at diagnoses was the sine qua non of practice. Who would question that diagnoses were critical? They grouped patients' symptoms into useful categories and provided hypotheses that accounted for their illnesses and predicted their prognoses. From these perspectives diagnosis was unremarkable.

Psychiatrists daily treated the diagnostic categories they employed (dementia praecox, manic-depressive insanity) and their characteristic symptoms (hallucinations, delusions) as natural and real, problematic in their particulars but not in relation to what they were meant to signify. Yet a spectrum of difficulties, ranging from the relatively empirical (this category or that?) to the ontological (did the category itself exist?), some of them acknowledged and acrimoniously debated, others wholly unheeded, disrupted the apparent naturalness of the diagnostic enterprise. For the most part, psychiatrists adopted a straightforward stance toward diagnosis, one conditioned by training and reinforced by the exigencies of practice. This stance, however, which altogether ignored the more philosophical questions that undercut the certainties of diagnosis, was an expression of a contested professional ideology and, as such, had to be constantly argued for. Among themselves psychiatrists could at times admit to knowing embarrassingly little about the mental maladies, but to a larger—and in their estimation, largely ignorant—public, they presented a unified, resolutely authoritative front. Their shuttling between these two positions was an expression not of duplicity but of the tension between knowledge, tantalizingly close but ultimately elusive, and its frustrating lack, a tension that animated the entire discipline of psychiatry.

Was psychiatry science or art? The advances associated with syphilology never far from their minds, practitioners at the Boston Psychopathic Hospital boldly proclaimed it was the former. However elusive the paradigm of general paresis would prove, the medical model of disease it underwrote attained a hegemonic position within psychiatric thought, even though it remained unreplicated. It provided one solution to the discipline's knowledge problem, allowing practitioners to order their observations as if disease—with its attendant etiology, course, and outcome—underlay what they could see.

This mode of thinking, however compelling to the medical mind, did not go unchallenged. As early as 1904, the prominent psychiatrist Adolf Meyer was questioning "why general paralysis, and not some less uniformly working disease process, should be the paradigm of psychiatry."[7] The question was apt but largely unaddressed until the twenties, for many psychiatrists' enthusiasm for the controversial speculations and systems of Emil Kraepelin reinforced, for some time, medical thinking in psychiatry. Kraepelin grouped together the symptoms and clinical pictures that he observed were characteristic of mental disorders into categories, discrete disease entities to which he appended distinct etiologies, courses, and outcomes. His isolation of two distinct disorders, dementia praecox and manic-depressive insanity, from the nosological morass that encompassed the functional (that is, nonorganic) psychoses, at first controversial but quickly adopted by American psychiatrists, was perhaps the most arresting (and enduring—the distinction is critical in psychiatric theory today) of his many bold reorderings of the old psychiatry.[8] Hypothesizing that distinct morbid processes, symptomatologies, and prognoses characterized the two disorders, the first of which culminated in inevitable deterioration, the second in cycles of acute attack and remission, Kraepelin in a stroke offered psychiatrists a structure through which to address the major psychoses, which by many estimates afflicted over half of all psychiatric patients.[9]

Kraepelin has fared alternately well and poorly in psychiatric thought. Standard histories of the discipline proclaim him the "father of modern psychiatry," no small honor in a tradition so conscious of its origins and so protective of its patrilineage. As his advocates would have it, it was Kraepelin who brought forth order and method from psychiatry's crippling nosological confusion. Turning his gaze from the microscope, under which the old-time organicist would hope to identify, in fastidiously prepared sections of patients' brain tissue, the signal lesions of disease, Kraepelin focused on what was visible to the naked eye, the patient's symptoms and behaviors, and on that to which the patient could attest: feelings and emotions, disorders of perception and of will.[10] Although he ascribed "morbid processes" to different varieties of illness, that they could not be identified did not unduly color his observations; his simple yet elegant distinction between manic-depressive insanity and dementia praecox, for example, was based almost solely on acute observation.[11] Kraepelin, from this approving perspective, brought the methods of clinical medicine to the psychiatric wasteland.

The assessment of the dynamic psychiatrists was less favorable. From their perspective, Kraepelin, who, with Teutonic resolve and thoroughness, churned out one massive tome after another (his inaptly titled *Short Textbook* of 1887 amounted to 540 pages, and the eighth edition of his no-longer-short *Textbook* came to more than 3,000), represented the unfortunate culmination of the nineteenth-century nosological mania to which their profession—especially its German branch—had succumbed. To the dynamicists' minds, the German tradition, encompassing such admittedly brilliant students of neuroanatomy as Wilhelm Griesinger (often linked with his maxim "mental diseases are brain diseases"), Theodor Meynert, Theodor Ziehen, Carl Wernicke, and Kraepelin, had fostered a misguided organicism, a belief in the existence of disease entities and their correspondence to lesions in the brain, that impeded the progress of psychiatry and the recognition of new "facts."[12] As they constructed their own myth of origin, dynamic psychiatrists portrayed Kraepelin and the Kraepelinian endeavor as static, the antithesis of their own dynamic project. "Scientific" study of the human personality was showing, dynamic psychiatrists argued, that mental disease was most emphatically not brain disease but, rather, the product of defective life adjustment.

Dynamic psychiatrists would spurn diagnosis in favor of attention to the "whole person" and his or her fit to the environment. Focus on disease entities—schizophrenia, for example—split the patient into too many parts, they argued, and made the disease, not the patient, the object of attention. Disease should be thought of, in Menninger's words, as a disturbance of the total economics of the personality rather than as something alien to the patient.[13] Dynamic psychiatrists would dismiss progressive psychiatry as the golden age of "descriptive psychiatry," and condemnations of Kraepelin would figure prominently in their dismissals of what they considered sterile nosological pursuits. As dynamic psychiatrists embraced their version of Freud and constructed personality as a series of adjustments between internal and external relations, they claimed that their elders, among them Southard and his colleagues, had squandered their considerable talents in pursuit of the chimerical disease entities whose existence they were repudiating.

Rather than choosing sides in a debate that divides psychiatry to this day,[14] I see early-twentieth-century psychiatrists, like other physicians, as practitioners of a rapidly but unevenly evolving clinical science, with the qualification that their science, unlike medicine, lacked the critical capacity to inscribe itself on the body.[15] Psychiatrists had few signs with which to identify disease; they had to be content to work with the ephemera commonly known as symptoms. The symptom, unlike the sign, could not be apprehended without at least minimal cooperation from the patient; there was nothing fixed or concrete about it.[16] That syphilitic infection could be established so handily, that its signs were so reliably pathognomic, and that it could be treated so straightforwardly (although not necessarily efficaciously) only underscored how imperfectly medical the rest of the psychiatric domain remained. The enduring uncertainty of psychiatric knowledge has undoubtedly affected the rapidity with which nosological fashions wax and wane, spawning heated debates such as that which has contested Kraepelin's claim to truth.

Psychiatrists' province was the mind—not the brain, for the latter would have presupposed a coherent neuroanatomy—and this, from time to time, brought them up against problems of the sort that engaged professional philosophers. Indeed, the question of whether disease entities (as in Kraepelinian psychiatry) or only infinitely various individuals (as in dynamic psychiatry) existed split psychiatrists into warring camps from the mid-teens on. Speaking as a philosopher, Southard maintained that he saw in the dynamicists' assertion that no two persons were alike "an extraordinary overdevelopment in application of the principle of identity of indiscernibles" that bespoke a discomfort in the world of logic equal to that of "those who are forever generalizing." The psychiatrist of necessity situated himself between particular and universal claims, and Southard, who had little patience for unitarians who would deny that disease entities existed, could only finesse the issue, proclaiming he had "no objection to any entity whatever, provided there is a good argument in the general psychiatric mind for its existence."[17]

On the vexing question of diagnosis, Southard reiterated that his intentions were wholly pragmatic, as if to disarm critics who would accuse him of metaphysical malfeasance. "The true aim of diagnosis," he asserted, was "the pragmatic aim of showing what is best to do."[18] This established, he maintained that there was no point quibbling over the meanings of such commonplace but undefined terms as "entity, diagnosis, symptom, symptom-complex, syndrome, and the like."[19] The psychiatrist was best off getting on with the job, and to this end, Southard proposed a utilitarian diagnostic scheme that grouped more than one hundred disease entities into eleven broad categories. This was the diagnostic scheme used at the Psychopathic Hospital. From the medical certainties of the disorders associated with syphilitic infection at the one extreme, to the dubiously expansive category of the psychopathies at the other, the diagnostic spectrum spanned psychiatric knowledge. This array of neatly bounded categories, each of which was meant to denote a distinct disease entity, bespoke a confidence in their discipline's scientific stature from which psychiatrists, humbled by the frustrations of practice, would sometimes retreat. Yet

TABLE 5.1
Diagnoses

Diagnostic Group	Diagnoses Included	Percent of All Patients in Group[a]
Dementia praecox	Catatonic, paranoid, hebephrenic forms; paranoia; "unclassified" paranoid conditions	26
Manic-depressive insanity	Manic, depressive, mixed forms; involutional insanity	11
Alcoholic disorders	Delirium tremens, acute alcoholic psychoses, chronic alcoholism, drug addiction	10
Syphilitic disorders	General paralysis, neurosyphilis, cerebral syphilis	8
Other psychoses	Psychoses with brain tumors, postinfectious psychoses, puerperal psychoses	8
Feeblemindedness	Moronism, imbecility, idiocy, mental defectiveness, subnormal mentality	9
Senile psychoses		5
Psychopathic personality		5
Epilepsy		3
Psychoneurosis		4
"Sane"		4

[a]$N = 1,105$; 25 patients not diagnosed.

the categories were useful, for they imparted an appealing concreteness to the classificatory task. Each category carried with it a prescribed future for the one who would bear it, providing a rationale for the whole endeavor. "What boots the most ingenious diagnosis," Southard asked, "if therapeutic results are not obtained?"[20]

One-quarter—26 percent—of all patients received the diagnosis of dementia praecox (table 5.1). Psychiatrists found 11 percent manic-depressive, 10 percent alcoholic, and 8 percent suffering from the effects of syphilis. Feeblemindedness accounted for 9 percent of all admissions, psychoneuroses for 4 percent and psychopathic personality for 5 percent. Psychiatrists judged 4 percent of all patients "sane." Although patients' gender and racial and ethnic identities (but not their class backgrounds) were related to the diagnoses they received, diagnosis was not a simple proxy for either (table 5.2); the relationships among diagnosis, gender, and race were intricate.

TABLE 5.2
Hospital Population, Classified by Gender, Ethnicity, and Diagnosis (percent)

	Alcohol	Dementia Praecox	Manic-Depressive	Syphilis	Other[a]	Sane[a]	(N)
Men							(454)
Irish[b]	28	30	5	10	21	6[c]	(121)
Jewish	8	40	10	12	15	15	(40)
WASP	12	20	16	16	16	20	(50)
Other native-born	19	35	7	16	12	12	(121)
Canadian, U.K.-born	14	16	7	35	26	2	(43)
Other foreign-born	13	41	8	17	12	10	(78)
Women							(436)
Irish	8	41	15	4	21	10	(137)
Jewish	—	33	27	3	3	33	(33)
WASP	5	26	25	2	18	25	(61)
Other native-born	5	26	13	5	10	41	(104)
Canadian, U.K.-born	9	30	24	4	17	17	(54)
Other foreign-born	4	40	19	—	26	11	(47)

Note: All three of the bivariate relationships shown in this three-variable table were found to be statistically significant when tested simultaneously in a log-linear analysis. (See Appendix on log-linear techniques.)

[a] "Other" includes senile patients and those with other symptomatic psychoses. "Sane" includes patients diagnosed with neurosis or psychopathic personality, and sane patients. The number of unclassified, epileptic, and feebleminded patients is relatively small; they have been excluded from analysis.

[b] See Appendix for explanation of ethnic categories.

[c] Row percentages sum to 100 (excluding errors due to rounding).

Classifying Patients: Race

Although psychiatrists' gender thinking was complex, in day-to-day practice they treated gender straightforwardly, as a natural marker of identity. Their approach to race—an unstable amalgam of national origins, religion, and color—was uneven and, on the surface, more complicated. On the one hand, they could treat race as they treated gender, as a visible marker of identity. From this perspective, race was simply what one saw when observing another; there was not much to say about it. On the other hand, it was critical to their sense of themselves as scientists that they keep abreast of trends in racial thinking and that their handling of race be as scientific—as orderly, consistent, and predictable—as possible.

Psychiatrists' racial thinking is best appreciated in the context of contemporary race thought. The early-twentieth-century discipline of psychiatry, in its public guise, was shot through with racial concerns. To contemporaries, nothing about insanity was more certain than that it was dangerously on the increase, a corollary of unrestricted, largely European, immigration. Several decades' worth of investigation undertaken to establish that insane foreigners outnumbered their American counterparts smoothed the way for widespread acceptance of the necessary relation between immigration and insanity, which were, by the 1920s, yoked alliteratively together in nativist propaganda, government reports, psychiatrists' professional literature, and public debate. From the 1880s through the 1910s, with mounting urgency, hospital superintendents and psychiatrists nationwide busied themselves compiling, analyzing, and publishing figures culled from public asylums that purported to show the foreign-born disproportionately represented therein. These single-minded investigators classified patients along racial lines in various ways while altogether ignoring other measures of identity and circumstance. Some simply divided institutional populations between the foreign-born and the native-born; others classed them by nation of birth; still others devised more ambitious schemes, analyzing patients by discrete racial groups. However partitioned, the figures invariably appeared to document the preponderance of the foreign-born and "racially inferior" among the insane, irrefutable evidence, in the words of one prominent psychiatrist, that "the off-scourings of all Europe" were hastening to American shores.[21]

After the turn of the century, these off-scourings came increasingly from southern and eastern Europe. The Germans, British, Irish, and Scandinavians who had formed the bulk of the nineteenth-century immigrant stream were outnumbered, from 1900 until the outbreak of World War I, more than three to one by dark-skinned Italians, Jews, Russians, and Slavs.[22] Contemporary thinking on race evolved apace. Currents of nativism that since the 1880s had cast foreigners, irrespective of their particular national origins, as a grave but generalized threat to the survival of American ways hardened into a scientifically respectable racism that divided the peoples of Europe into distinct races on the basis of physiological and temperamental differences. A mix of what John Higham has called race-thinkers—patrician nativists who had long celebrated the nation's Anglo-Saxon heritage; eugenicists whose science warned of its inevitable demise—laid the intellectual groundwork for acceptance of new racial taxonomies that discriminated not only between old immigrants, the northern Europeans who purportedly had absorbed the Anglo-Saxons' taste for democracy, and the new immigrants who, it was asserted, were racially inclined toward violence and anarchy, but also, in one popular scheme, among the Teutonic or Nordic, Alpine, Mediterranean, and Jewish races. Patrician sentiment and eugenic science proved compelling in combination. The former's concern with racial purity and the latter's with defect set the terms of the public debate that preceded passage of the Immigration Restriction Act of 1924, in which the specter of America as an asylum writ large held a somewhat morbid fascination for legislators who voted to erect stiff barriers against the entry of nearly every category of the non-Anglo-Saxon foreign-born, sane and insane alike. So conflated were foreignness and defectiveness by the second decade of the century that warnings that the "social inadequacy" and "racial degeneracy" of the newly arrived Jews, Italians, Russians, and Poles were turning the nation that had once provided political asylum for oppressed but "high minded and splendidly equipped" patriots into "a custodial asylum for degenerates" occasioned little dissent.[23]

Eager to keep apace of racial thinking, Psychopathic Hospital psychiatrists carefully recorded the constitutive elements of patients' racial identities—color, religion, nation of origin—on elaborate printed admissions blanks while interviewing new arrivals. Yet in quick succession they adopted, abandoned, revised, and finally ignored these blanks, for their attempts to capture ever more precisely dimensions of identity that corresponded to popular perceptions and everyday usage—"what everybody knew"—while respecting science's demand for regularity and system yielded not a system but a useless classificatory hodgepodge. Part of the difficulty they faced was that the determinants of racial identity in both popular perception and scientific taxonomies varied across racial groups. Religion, for example, was the critical determinant in classing a person Jewish (or "Hebrew"); color was critical in classing someone a Negro; national ancestry was critical in a determination of Irishness. Just as problematic, these determinants were in many cases not determinative but confusing and even contradictory. Was the second-generation Protestant man of German ancestry racially a German, an American, white, or all or none of these? Did it matter? For science yes, but day-to-day no, at least until the war, for such a man was likely a German in some circumstances and an American in others, depending on the context and his own self-presentation. As instances like this suggest and as the futility of the psychiatrists' classificatory endeavors would make clear, the concept of race resisted neat theorization: it could not be consistently grounded in its constituent elements. Further, race thinking, which traded in singular and fixed identities, could not accommodate the shifting salience of different dimensions of individuals' identities, in their own perception and in that of others.

Unusable and most often ignored, the psychiatrists' short-lived racial taxonomies merit brief attention, if only as a measure of the epistemological confusion surrounding the category of race. The vicissitudes of their race thinking can be traced in the admissions blanks, the bureaucratic leavings of daily practice. Forms in use through the hospital's first year of operation were designed to allow psychiatrists to record the nativity, complexion, and religion, but not the race, of patients. Intended to encourage precision through iteration, the forms instead yielded some untenable anomalies. For example, psychiatrists noted that Abraham Patelsky, committed to the institution in April 1913, was a Russian-born, dark-complected man, religiously a Hebrew. Two months later they noted that Martin Geary, a native of Quincy, just south of the city, was dark as well, but they did not record his religion. The categories accurately if indirectly captured Patelsky's race, for it and his religion were equivalent; he identified as a Jew, and was likely identified as such by others. The same categories, alone and in combination, however, failed altogether to convey Geary's Irishness (both of his parents were natives of Ireland), which was, from the psychiatrists' perspective, and likely his own as well, the most salient aspect of his ethnic or racial identity. The purported swarthiness of both was of little consequence, for it served only as a somewhat misleading proxy for their foreignness; whereas Patelsky was a recent immigrant, Geary had lived in the area his whole life. More problematic, what was to distinguish their dark complexions from that of a Negro?[24]

In the summer of 1913, the psychiatrists adopted new admissions blanks that allowed them to record patients' races directly instead of obliquely, and they gradually phased out those that had them registering, with spurious precision, racially meaningless nuances in skin tone. For some three years thereafter, they treated race as a dichotomous measure, classifying patients as either white or Negro (or Colored or Black), and a few as Chinese.[25] Those of Irish ancestry who were categorized as dark under the old system were now admitted to the ranks of the white race, as were sundry persons of Lithuanian, Greek, and Russian-Jewish descent. The problem with the old forms was that they produced too many distinctions. By 1916 it was clear that the new produced too few, for by its conventions nearly everyone was racially white.

Yet another form was devised, by whom it is unclear, one that invited psychiatrists to make note of a patient's birthplace, color, race, and religion.[26] This they dutifully did for at least another year, with, again, somewhat improbable results. In making use of this new taxonomy, psychiatrists treated color, not race, as a dichotomous measure, deeming patients either white or black (and a few yellow or olive). At the same time, they partitioned race into a profusion of discrete categories: American, Canadian, English, Irish, German, Austrian, Russian, Turkish, Syrian, and so on—but not Jewish or Negro. These new racial categories were in practice simple signifiers of nationality, and psychiatrists were at first absolutely consistent in using them to denote nothing more. Thus, in their hands, the German, Russian, and Austrian races encompassed both Jew and non-Jew, the American race both black and white. Admirably ecumenical, perhaps, these categories were in practice useless, even misleading, for they highlighted distinctions that were of no significance to psychiatrists, like that between English and Canadian, while obliterating distinctions that were in their estimation critical.[27] Psychiatrists appear to have realized this, for beginning in early 1917, they sporadically stopped filling in the blank for race, an uncharacteristic move for those so bureaucratically inclined and so alert to the ramifications of the category. It may be that they deemed the information it conveyed superfluous, which in many cases it was. It is more likely, however, that their bid for consistency had them classifying too many Jews of Russian ancestry as Russian and too many native-born persons of Irish ancestry, with Irish names and Irish afflictions, as American. This system, which grounded race in nationality, yielded not only useless but, from their perspective, wrong information.

That psychiatrists could not theorize race consistently did not stop them, however, from recognizing it when they saw it. They classified the fifty-year-old baker David Goldberg, a man of the Hebrew religion, as racially an Austrian, but several days later commented on his "racial characteristics," specifically his tendency to overwork, which had resulted in "fatigue neurosis," which they agreed was a typically Jewish affliction. They then discussed whether he was "normal" or simply "normal for his race," which all assumed to be Jewish, not, as the form they had filled out indicated, Austrian.[28] Similarly, they failed to record the race of Charles Cudahy, a sixty-one-year-old coal passer who was, along with both of his parents, native to Boston, but considered him *echt* Irish. "He is an Irishman and has the humorous way," Southard, assessing his behavior, told his colleagues. "It is his racial character, and he gives me a slap every time he speaks."[29] And they registered Marion Fuller's race as American, but concluded she was a "pretty high type of negro girl," certainly "above the general average of her race," by which they meant the Negro, not the American.[30] As is clear from these examples, psychiatrists might strive for scientific consistency, but their thinking on race was at bottom reflexively prosaic.

Envisaged in everyday terms as it was in discussions like these, race mattered to psychiatrists because it accounted for peculiarities that were otherwise attributable only to pathology. They could trade easily in racial stereotypes drawn from their culture and from a burgeoning professional literature that advanced a fragmentary psychology of the races in which, for the most part, racist and xenophobic commonplaces were simply reconfigured in the language and form of science. Not surprisingly, the Irish in this classification of racial traits were given to alcoholism, Jews tended toward nervousness, Italians were sluggish and backward, and Negroes were feebleminded.

Psychiatrists were alert to racial variations in temperament, but they did not diagnose patients straightforwardly along racial or ethnic lines. More often than not, when they drew on racial psychology they did so to brand individuals not abnormal but *normal*, invoking race to account for and render inconsequential otherwise damaging behaviors. Thus, they judged the baker Goldberg's nervousness as racial but of little diagnostic significance. Saying he was "in sympathy with the man," one psychiatrist maintained he had "seen many of his race showing the same instability and emotional tone," before he and his colleagues went on to diagnose him not, say, manic-depressive, but alcoholic. They could not settle on a diagnosis in Cudahy's case, even though they quizzed him concerning his taste for drink and ascertained that he imbibed heavily. Likewise, they registered Fuller as "not insane" while commenting on the many delinquencies that, had she been white, would have marked her as psychopathic. In these and other instances, psychiatrists measured patients' behavior favorably against the roughly specified racial norms of custom and science, and thus rendered less serious diagnoses.[31] Associated with danger and difference, race carried more weight in the realm of public propaganda than in the day-to-day practice of psychiatry.

Diagnostic Classifications

Psychiatrists employed the diagnoses of neurosyphilis, dementia praecox, and manic-depressive insanity to classify nearly half of all Psychopathic Hospital patients. In what follows, these diagnoses are affixed to persons, treated as relatively unproblematic and real, just as psychiatrists treated them in day-to-day practice.[32]

Neurosyphilis: The psychiatrist, Southard argued, should first either establish or rule out the presence of syphilitic infection in a patient thought to be suffering from mental disease. Although neurosyphilis was among "the most protean of diseases," and although its symptomatic manifestations were often confused with those of other diseases, it was, among all the mental disorders, the most reliably established by the simple Wassermann test to which psychiatrists subjected samples of almost all patients' blood.[33] Charles Cosgrove, a thirty-eight-year-old Irish Catholic locomotive engineer, was typical of patients, overwhelmingly male, classed under the rubric of neurosyphilis.[34] Cosgrove had been studying hard, he told psychiatrists, and had developed a "rather large scheme" for extending railway service that he had anxiously put before his employer. A little wrought up and nervous as a result of his labors, he entered the hospital on the advice of his own doctor. Hospital psychiatrists judged him confused, euphoric, disoriented, and restless, and noted that his speech was defective and his memory failing.

Cosgrove displayed many of the symptoms associated with general paresis. These symptoms, however, could indicate any number of disorders. Only Cosgrove's positive reaction on the Wassermann test confirmed the presence of the syphilitic infection that his symptoms suggested and showed he was not suffering from dementia praecox, the manifestations of which were similar to and often mistaken for those of general paresis. Though the prognosis for general paresis was poor—physicians had long judged the condition fatal—psychiatrists at the Psychopathic Hospital treated the syphilitic psychoses, including the less serious neurosyphilis, with Salvarsan and neosalvarsan. When injected intravenously, Salvarsan, an arsenic compound discovered by the German immunologist Paul Ehrlich in 1909, resulted in negative Wassermann reactions and sometimes in the remission of symptoms. Psychiatrists injected Cosgrove with various arsenic compounds over the course of his three-month stay in the hospital. He complained the treatments caused his "left fore arm to swell" and caused "steady pain," but his florid symptoms diminished somewhat and he was, psychiatrists judged, strong enough to return home to his wife and small children.[35]

Cosgrove was well aware that he was suffering from the effects of syphilitic infection. He reported that the condition had been suspected at least ten years before. Like others diagnosed similarly, he was physically weak. He offered no objections to the diagnosis, which psychiatrists presented to him with as little elaboration as they would have any straightforwardly medical condition. Perhaps seeing in their patient an upright family man, a man who owned his own home and spoke of missing his children terribly, they never attempted to ascertain the source of his initial infection, nor did they locate his painful treatments within a moral nexus.

Dementia praecox: Two weeks before she was committed to the hospital, twenty-five-year-old Catherine O'Connor, complaining she was discontented, left her parents' home to live on her own and work in a shoe factory. In the estimation of an older married sister, O'Connor had always been "a good living girl," but she had been acting strangely for several years. She had given up steady work, coming home, her sister reported, "one time saying she was sick and was going to die that she had heart disease and a weak mind." She wouldn't "eat a square meal like the rest of us she wants sweet stuff and *candy* all the time and that is what she has been living on this summer." Most of the time she stayed at home, consumed by the fear "that her mind will always be growing weaker."

O'Connor's sister thought her a victim of an overactive imagination. "She is making herself sick imagining she is sick," the sister wrote in frustration to psychiatrists, advising them to "tell her there is nothing the matter with her and send her home." But to the psychiatrist, O'Connor was as distinct a case of dementia praecox as could be found. Her withdrawal from normal activities, her fear of death, and her delusional belief she had heart disease were symptomatic of the disorder; further, her youthfulness squared with the early onset psychiatrists associated with dementia praecox.[36]

Kraepelin first set the contours of dementia praecox as a distinct disease in the sixth edition of his textbook, published in 1899.[37] Progressive and inevitable deterioration (dementia) and early onset (praecox) characterized it. Its gloomy prognosis distinguished it from the other major endogenous psychosis (that is, a psychosis that seemed to arise apart from any external causes), manic-depressive insanity, a disorder that Kraepelin also identified. Psychiatrists did not know the etiology of dementia praecox, but their working assumption was that the brains of praecox patients exhibited "demonstrable microscopic cortex changes" as well as "gross anatomical anomalies" that did not necessarily result in but were a necessary precondition for the disorder.[38] Southard, for example, admitted that "personally" he felt dementia praecox patients "as against psychoneurosis and manic-depressive insanity are apt to show stigmata externally, that is, small size or queer ear, and inside to see a small heart and such things."[39]

But few patients exhibited external stigmata, and internal signs could only be diagnosed postmortem. Psychiatrists thus had to diagnose dementia praecox on the basis of patients' behaviors and symptoms. Delusions (false beliefs) and hallucinations (false perceptions) were the symptoms most commonly associated with this disorder. One patient's delusion that a Catholic priest had allowed people to "get within different parts of [his] body" to transact business was typical of many dementia praecox patients' fantastic beliefs. "While in that condition my brains have been opened to public view in such a way," the thirty-four-year-old fireman explained, "as to advertise business peoples' wares, for which those said people seemed to appreciate very much."[40] Relatives noted that patients had recently changed in many of these cases, and psychiatrists deemed these patients indifferent and apathetic and noted that many exhibited mannerisms.

Southard advocated modification of the Kraepelinian term dementia praecox, with its "*horrible*" connotation and unnecessarily "evil prognosis,"[41] and adoption of a term the Swiss psychiatrist Eugen Bleuler had introduced in 1911, schizophrenia. Schizophrenia, Southard held, better captured the "split-mindedness" that was the essential feature of the disease. Kraepelin had grouped together a variety of clinical pictures in dementia praecox because they seemed to result in similar states of dementia, but Southard held that evidence for dementia praecox as an entity was shaky. The Kraepelinian assumption that one disease process underlay all forms of dementia praecox, whether paranoid or catatonic, and that deterioration inevitably resulted, was to his mind unfounded. Southard contrasted this to the "tremendous clinical variety" and "great variations in curability" he observed. Although Kraepelin did not remain wedded to the unity and inevitable deterioration of dementia praecox—late in his life he allowed that a certain number of patients recovered permanently and that the disease did not always have an early onset—the association of his name with dementia praecox as an ossified entity stood fast.[42]

The diagnosis schizophrenia, first used at the Psychopathic Hospital in 1919, directed attention to the psychological processes that underlay the disorder.[43] Psychiatrists argued, for example, that the language used by Harry Musavi, a thirty-one-year-old Syrian printer who had been in the United States for five years and who was brought to the hospital after he told a police officer he was afraid he might kill himself—as he put it, "my lunacy may develop an uncontrollable temper"—indicated schizophrenic thought processes. Under observation, for example, Musavi admitted to suffering from auditory hallucinations—voices from behind the ceiling of his room, alternately encouraging and threatening, kept him awake at night—and told psychiatrists he was unable to concentrate or to control his temper. He unwittingly insulted people and had lost his last job through what he called "incidental disrespectfulness" toward his boss. At times he thought of himself as insane, "owing to the works of nonsensical and illiterate habits," and he suffered from "scattered brainities," which he explained were "irresponsible states of most mentalities." Southard pressed him on the voices, trying to determine whether they were true auditory hallucinations. Were they not just brainities? Perhaps they came from within himself? "Suppose I say to you, as a doctor, that the voices are manufactured inside your brain?" Musavi could not accept this, arguing, "Something itself is making these voices. There is something in the air," verifying thereby the presence of hallucinations.

Despite his symptoms and worries, Musavi wrote that he was enjoying himself in the hospital. Under the care of "humanitarian and brotherly fellow workers," he felt he was getting better, and would "come off with better health and vigor." From his room he enjoyed "watching some of our female employees playing their favorite tennis ball, over the velvety greens, full of youths and red blood corpuscles upon their cheeks," and he especially admired the "group of finely educated and nursery graduated young lady workers, all are self contented and honest type of women whose presence are such blessings." Psychiatrists were struck by Musavi's peculiar usages, and argued they were "not entirely because of any language difficulty." They pointed to his neologisms—"brainities," for example—and rhyming, flowery vocabulary as symptoms. Together with his hallucinations, delusions, and mannerisms, these symptoms indicated a diagnosis of dementia praecox or schizophrenia, terms psychiatrists would use interchangeably through the twenties.[44]

Manic-depressive insanity: Two weeks before her mother and father brought her to the hospital, Dorothy Elwood, a thirty-two-year-old shop clerk, cried out in the middle of the night for her fiancé William, who had just broken his engagement to her and disappeared. William was calling her, she yelled, he was dying and being doped. Her family quieted Elwood down, but observed that from that night she was unusually excited and talked continually of William, against whom they felt very bitter. The day before admission Elwood had chased a woman who looked like William's mother from the shop where she worked. The same night she insisted she was going to die and bequeathed all her possessions to her mother. Concerned that Elwood was not "just right," her parents brought her to the hospital, where she laughed loudly and thrashed about wildly. "Profane" and "indecent," she swore and cursed, and, psychiatrists noted, showed "marked flight of ideas," shrieking, "Mary Pickford was dancing—I am going to be a nurse—This is the one that is full of jokes, and we took it out of her—This room is a stable, it is fit for pigs." She then cried out "Harry K. Thaw" for a full minute.[45]

Elwood continued to talk so rapidly that psychiatrists could not understand her. They quickly decided she was suffering from manic-depressive insanity. The flight of ideas, exalted mood, and pressure of activity Elwood demonstrated constituted the essential symptoms found in the manic phase of the disorder. A depressive state, characterized by "sad or anxious moodiness and also sluggishness of thought and action," would inevitably follow, and although slight "psychic weakness" might develop, Elwood's case, according to Kraepelinian psychiatry, would result in neither profound dementia nor deterioration. Indeed, long periods of relatively normal mental states might separate attacks.

The habits of thought evident in these exemplary cases were those psychiatrists employed in daily practice: cases, disease entities, and symptoms were real and concrete, "facts" from which the psychiatrist built his science. But at least some psychiatrists knew these habits of thought obscured issues that would ensure that psychiatry's claim to science would be problematic. Even as psychiatrists built up new categories, they tore them down, only to reassert their realness. I turn now to that process, examining the case and how it was constituted, and then, in a discussion of the gendering of psychosis, I examine the psychiatrists' admission that diagnosis could be more interpretation than science.

Individuals and Cases

Foucault's shrewd analysis of the multiform nature of the "case" historicizes a rarely scrutinized but critical psychiatric conceit: that cases—the psychiatrist's atom, his unit of analysis—describe individuals. Its referents unstable, "the case" could denote a person (the "real" individual, as in "the cases are for the most part still alive . . . and willing to tell their stories");[46] a person's life, rendered by psychiatrists in narrative form (as in the cases—stories—that made up the newly ubiquitous psychiatric "casebook"); an exemplary manifestation of a disease or pathology (as in, for example, "A Case of Ambulatory Automatism");[47] or, most commonly, all three at once. In psychiatrists' everyday practice the term's ambiguity was unproblematic, allowing them a useful economy of expression that was, at the same time, a measure of how natural a construct the case had become. Behind their elliptical thinking and mode of expression, however, lay a history that Foucault has suggestively illuminated.

"For a long time ordinary individuality—the everyday individuality of everybody—remained below the threshold of description," Foucault observed. Only the powerful enjoyed the privilege of being "looked at, observed, described in detail, followed from day to day by an uninterrupted writing," of having their individuality inscribed into a chronicle or history that attested, in turn, to their power. The late-eighteenth-century triumph of the clinical disciplines—medicine, psychiatry, criminology—democratized individuality, Foucault argued, "lower[ing] the threshold of describable individuality" as practitioners instituted a series of procedures (the examination, the anamnesis) and techniques (the file) that brought the particularities of individuals into the discourse of science, constituting them as "cases" while subjecting them to disciplinary surveillance. Ordinary "real lives," like aristocratic lives, could find written expression, but, for the heroic lives of kings and exploits of popular bandits, psychiatry—Foucault's paradigmatic discipline—would substitute the dour, grim, "carefully collated life" of the mental patient. The individuality of the ordinary person and the case as both heuristic fiction and palpable construct thus made a joint debut, making possible the proliferation of the human sciences and the ascent of the disciplinary regimes.[48]

The case assumed a new form in the early years of the century. Nineteenth-century asylum superintendents, for the most part, recorded information concerning patients in large, bound casebooks. Each patient typically was allotted a single page in these books; physicians recorded histories and clinical notes on it, turning to another page—far back in the book or in another volume altogether—when the first was filled.[49] The result, from the perspective of psychiatrists, was a confusing jumble that ill served science. They argued that better classification of patients required better methods of record keeping, and they abandoned the unwieldy casebook, adopting in its place the expandable file.[50] The file was superior in several respects. It readily accommodated the rapidly growing number of documents —laboratory reports, medical notes, transcripts of examinations, social service reports—that psychiatrists and social workers were producing. More significant, the file better suited what psychiatrists argued was the newly inductive nature of their specialty, for it, unlike the casebook, encouraged practitioners to record everything—especially "what had hitherto remained unrecorded." Indeed, the imperative to record, rather than simply to rely on memory, was critical to the new psychiatrist's self-definition, and it was taken as a sign of progress that records were now, as one psychiatrist explained in 1910, "complete in every detail."[51]

New technologies made this proliferation of documentation possible. By 1910, physicians in several of the state's institutions were using dictating machines in the compilation of patient records, and, although some worried that the process encouraged verbosity, most agreed that greater efficiency resulted. "The long grind of penmanship" to which the young physician historically had been subjected was no more; highly skilled and relatively well paid stenographers could now produce reams of neatly typed records.[52] Not only efficiency but also what one historian has called "an unexpected tyranny of volume" ensued.[53] In 1915, Southard reported that the Psychopathic Hospital's staff of eight stenographers was, in their transcriptions, "143 case records behind, or in terms of phonograph cylinders, 161 cylinders behind."[54]

Through all this the nature of the relationship between the individual and the case remained murky. The great Aristotelian problem—whether there could be a science of the individual—perhaps demanded, Foucault observed, great solutions, but none was forthcoming.[55] For the most part psychiatrists, pragmatically rather than philosophically inclined and fully engaged by the demands of everyday practice, ignored this as they did so many other imponderables. Southard, however, attacked the conundrum head-on in a series of unpublished notes and papers, perhaps realizing that it lay at the critical juncture where medical craft could claim to be medical science, a juncture that psychiatry, were it to duplicate medicine's ascent, would have to negotiate skillfully. "The familiar paradox of the 'Aristotelian system,'" he noted, "is that while true being is individual what science knows is universal."[56] The physician as practitioner deals with the individual, with "true being."[57] "The case is his unit of interest," Southard argued, and his stance was resolutely unscientific to the point where he believed "there are no rules, save a few thumb rules, for this his 'case.'"[58]

Yet it was only from "case system" psychiatry, Southard maintained, that "in the Aristotelian manner . . . knowledge of the formal or general features of psychiatry" could be derived and a science of psychiatry established.[59] In practice, ideally, inductive logic prevailed, but as Southard himself admitted, it was common for young physicians "not to see the woods for the trees, not to observe disease principles in the rush of individual patients."[60] For a few years it had seemed as though psychiatry, like medicine, would lay claim to a fully scientific status. The establishment of the paradigm of general paresis had laid down, Southard observed, the general lines of a tantalizing correlation between disorders of mental function and brain disorders.[61] But the paradigm remained unreplicated, and by the mid-teens Southard was questioning whether the model had led psychiatrists and even physicians astray. "My dope is, look for effects and don't go back to causes unless you are absolutely forced to do so," he wrote in confidence to a colleague, proposing that the futile etiological search, which had "in the small group of the infectious diseases . . . so brilliantly lighted up a part of the last century" and had provided the outlines for the biomedical paradigm of disease, be left to "the teutonizing pathologists."[62] Psychiatry would have to construct its science from the examination of "actual tangible men and women."[63]

But even this modest empirical project posed difficulties. The complex individuality of persons that the physician might attempt to convey through the medium of the case defied both apprehension and description. In his practice, Southard maintained, the physician confronted the body in its materiality, its "thingness," and thus could feel confident he was dealing with an individual but when it came to describing that body, necessarily he abandoned the individual and resorted to a theoretically antithetical sort of statistical thinking. In attempting to present infinitely peculiar individuals in their "empiric greatness," he argued, physicians habitually employed such categories as constitution, behavior, character, temperament, and "the architecture of the body" as convenient abstractions that made perception and then communication possible but at the same time submerged the very individuality they were meant to convey. As a physician, Southard submitted he had to feel there was "something real" to these categories, but as a philosopher he felt it necessary to refrain from specifying of what precisely their "positive base" consisted.[64]

The modern sensibility, Southard ventured, would choose to deal in "facts" over cases, for while cases were always cases *of* something, facts could stand alone. Or could they? Just as those who dealt in cases, however sincere, "must infallibly have already a scheme, entity, principle, or beginning of a collection into which to fit these," those who dealt in facts, Southard hypothesized, pace Kant and Comte, filtered their observations through theory.[65] The case, in which the facts of psychiatry were embedded, was thus a heuristic fiction that was at the same time real, and although physicians might proclaim they were done with cases and now, as moderns, concerned with "facts," the psychiatrist was hard-pressed to get beyond them.[66]

The Examination and the Constitution of the Case

From the moment they entered the hospital, patients were subjected to a regimen of relentless, if uneven, scrutiny. From the initial assessment made in the admitting office, to which thirty minutes, on average, were devoted, through the physical examination (twenty minutes), the neurological examination (fifteen minutes), the mental examination (one hour), the X-ray examination (forty-five minutes), the psychological examination (two and one-half hours), and assorted other examinations and tests, culminating in the highly ritualized staff meeting (one hour), patients were subjected to the "principle of compulsory visibility" that Foucault has seen at the heart of the disciplinary enterprise.[67] Psychiatrists, psychologists, social workers, nurses, attendants, and other patients—all observed, measured, assessed, and classified the new patient. The file grew thick with the various anamnesic, psychological, laboratory, and clinical reports, and the individual, endowed now with a history, a diagnosis, and an imputed future, took the shape of a case.

No one has explicated the phenomenon of the "perpetual examination" more deftly than Foucault. Its techniques—"its rituals, its methods, its characters and their roles, its play of questions and answers"—and its power relations made it possible, he argues, "to extract and constitute knowledge" at the same time. Bringing together the "ceremony of power and the form of the experiment," the examination robbed patients of their subjectivity while it offered them up as objects for the physician's pleasure. The disciplinary domain was no longer solely textual, restricted to "the tradition of the author-authorities," but constantly animated afresh by the bodies, minds, symptoms, and stories of the patients "perpetually offered for examination."[68]

It was thus a far more contingent domain than it appeared. If examination was, as Foucault suggests, a "space of domination," it was also, in psychiatry, a space where that domination could be subverted by willful or simply uncooperative patients. In psychiatry, more than in any of the other branches of clinical medicine, patients were empowered by the relative invisibility of their symptoms. Psychiatrists could, to be sure, establish the presence of syphilitic infection with laboratory tests, but to arrive at many other diagnoses with comfortable certainty psychiatrists depended on the cooperation of those they would classify. What patients *did* was easily ascertained, and in some cases sufficient. But what patients felt, thought, believed, heard, saw—this, on which diagnosis could turn, they might choose not to divulge or they might find themselves incapable of expressing.

The regimen of interrogatory rituals signaled to patients from the moment they arrived that cooperation was necessary, normal, and natural. What on the outside had been unspoken and private was on the inside, under the psychiatrists' gaze, to be attested to and made visible, to be spoken and divulged. But psychiatrists had to argue for this reversal of everyday proprieties, and when the mere presence of the mechanisms meant to sustain it failed to convince patients of its necessity, they resorted to bullying and hectoring.

Agnes Moran, a twenty-seven-year-old single woman of Irish descent who lived with her widowed mother and who entered the hospital voluntarily in a nervous condition, captured the singularity of the interrogatory experience in a neatly penned twenty-page chronicle of her hospital stay.[69] Deeply unsettled by the "questions of a personal character" psychiatrists put to her from the start, she attempted to master her escalating embarrassment and fear through a precise recording of both the routine and the extraordinary—from the exact times at which meals were served to the details of her admittedly hysterical response to the physical examination. Moran portrayed herself as, at times, bored: " 'Very monotonous to say the least,' " she wrote after setting down that once again she had eaten supper, bathed, and retired, the quotation marks suggestive of an attempt at irony. But moments of confusion and of sheer terror punctuate her account, disrupting her pose of indifference and imparting to her story a confessional flavor. "Just the same thing over and over," then, alternates with reflections on her childhood propensity to faint, scream, and sequester herself when confronted with a medical procedure.[70]

Moran was questioned by this doctor and that, in private and in the annoying presence of other patients, on subjects ranging from her school studies ("most of which I had forgotten," she dutifully recorded) to her most personal affairs. She was asked by—unbeknownst to her—a psychologist "many absurd questions" and challenged to put puzzles together and to tell stories about various pictures. Having survived "a great many experiments or tests, some of which seemed absurd" (a favorite malediction), she was then summoned to appear before the entire hospital staff—some ten to fifteen psychiatrists, psychologists, social workers, occasional visitors, and a stenographer who recorded the entire proceeding. This was the staff meeting, the most formal but also the least predictable of examinations. The procedure's manifest purpose was simple: psychiatrists and other staff would convene daily to examine and then collectively and correctly diagnose especially interesting or difficult cases—approximately 10 percent of all patients. In practice it was sometimes that and no more. But psychiatrists were not always so disinterested. Exhibiting, refining, and challenging their own diagnostic expertise was as important as aiding patients, and these aims tempered their altruism, transforming the staff meeting into a charged arena in which patients confronted their powerlessness and psychiatrists the limits of their science.[71]

"Our own doctor read off everything we ever told him, how we came out in all the tests and in fact every single thing you have said or done is read off before these doctors and they pass their views as to your sanity," Moran recalled. Patients sat in the middle of a large room facing the staff—

"Dr. Southard (the Alienist) stands staring you right in the eyes," Moran noted—who often opened the examination by asking patients straightforward questions such as when they had last worked or how they had ended up in the hospital. Patients had already answered these questions over the course of several days' examinations, and psychiatrists thus could anticipate their replies. In a routine staff meeting the intention was not so much to unearth new stories, explanations, and symptoms, but rather to elicit anew from patients, this time before a score of professionals, that to which they had already privately confessed and attested.

The interrogation of George Henderson, a forty-year-old native-born Protestant salesman, proceeded as if it had been rehearsed. Dr. Stearns prefaced his questioning with the mildly damning observation that some friends of Henderson (who was not yet in the room) had told him he was a neurasthenic, which, the psychiatrist wryly noted, "had pleased his feelings." The real diagnosis would be much more severe, and Stearns posed questions that would quickly make that clear. He asked Henderson what symptoms he had exhibited. "I have had depression and irritability and suspicions—exhausted condition," replied the patient, who knew better than most what qualified as a symptom. Stearns continued, certain of the reply: "You have also had hallucinations?" The patient assented. Auditory? Visual? Yes on both counts. "What is it you speak of as 'vibrations'?" Stearns asked. "I imagined I had vibrations transmitted to me from some persons. I could hear them calling me all sorts of names if I did not bend to their will. They willed me to do certain things," replied Henderson, who, under Stearns's direction, went on to explain that he felt he had to obey their commands, to admit that he had lost his own personality, and to utter some quite damning nonsense about seeing brain images in which "past and present seemed to come all together," which the psychiatrist did not even bother to dissect. Henderson made it easy for psychiatrists. He described his hallucinations as calmly as the indigestion and "low vitality" to which he later turned, not realizing that the former marked him as a victim not of neurasthenia but of dementia praecox, the most serious of the mental maladies, while the latter were of absolutely no consequence.[72]

Psychiatrist and patient worked toward the same end in this examination. Calmly and dispassionately, Henderson answered Stearns's questions and, even when invited to comment on anything, offered only that the place was "all right" and went on in a lively manner about the efficiency of the help. He showed no desire to argue a contrary case or to present a scenario different from that which he and Stearns quickly constructed in tandem.

But more often than not, psychiatrist and patient worked at cross-purposes, and in these instances the tenor of the examination was hardly so equable. Psychiatrists, for example, expected patients would be willing and able to speak plainly of their histories, habits, symptoms, thoughts, and feelings, and that a patient's failure to do so indicated either defect, as in cases of feeblemindedness, or a contemptible willfulness that invited punishment. Frustrated by patients whose replies to their questions seemed insufficiently revealing, psychiatrists could judge them punitively, as they did one woman, "either crazy or very foolish."[73] Thus, psychiatrists opined that a twenty-two-year-old woman's fear of tests was "indicative of her own knowledge of her own inferiority." Argued one: "Every time a test comes her way she feels she is meeting her fate," a response he admitted was common but that he still judged "abnormal." Another faulted her for answering "in the fashion she expected people would want her to," and characterized her as a "prig" for doing so.[74] And, to a nineteen-year-old woman who refused to answer his queries, Dr. Lowrey threateningly burst out, "You know exactly what will happen to you if you don't talk. Do you want to go to an institution for the rest of your life? Why don't you talk? No normal person would behave like you do, and that is what institutions are for—abnormal people."[75] The imperative to disclose could hardly have been more clearly stated.

Although the capacity and inclination for full disclosure that psychiatrists assumed the average individual possessed and on which the success of the examination depended came naturally to some patients, to others, many of them women, nothing was more perplexing. The conventions of day-to-day life demanded that a woman be discreet about her affairs—her loves, her passions, her desires, her past—and in return they shielded her from unwanted inquiries and advances. Indeed, a demure modesty was among the most salient marks of proper womanhood. Some women drew the boundaries of the private self tightly, reserving to themselves only their deepest feelings. Florence Edwards, a forty-two-year-old teacher who had been troubled by suicidal impulses, expounded at length and "perfectly truthfully" upon her fears and disappointments, her habits and preferences, her mental upsets and their corporeal manifestations—a "death like clutch," a constriction "right through the abdominal region." She faltered only when psychiatrists began to home in on her loneliness. Yes, she had many, many friends, but she did feel rather alone in the world. Had she ever any love affairs? No, she admitted, "I am one of the unique women." Had she ever thought of marrying? No, she had given it up when she was young, in high school. "Then you intended to marry at that age?" the examining psychiatrist asked. "Oh no," she countered, "I mean as young as that I decided that was not the life for me." How had she decided that? Edwards began to explain but then burst out, "How close into the heart of a person you drive in this inquiry," and went on to explain that she was not suggesting psychiatrists had no right to do so, and to answer the question by confessing she had never felt that she, "for lack of physical beauty, should want to give myself to any man."[76]

Edwards was well versed in the language of self-disclosure. Prior to entering the hospital, she had consulted with a number of physicians about her depression and exhaustion, and had told her tale many times. Further, as a single, college-educated working woman, a teacher of "industrial economic history," she had likely already dispensed with the self-protecting reserve of proper womanhood; she traveled in a man's world and her self was as open to view as that of any man. Edwards was in this respect more modern than many women. Yet how she bridled when psychiatrists pushed too far!

For many other women the private self was more expansive, encompassing not only thoughts and feelings, history and past, but proclivities and preferences—even the readily observable habits of daily life. To divulge any part of this self to psychiatrists, nearly all of them men, in a public arena was, for these women, to transgress a cardinal precept of womanhood. Embarrassment overwhelmed them, leading to confusion and shame in the more hardy and terrifying sensations of suffocation in the more sensitive. Agnes Moran, for one, turned terribly red. "I had these rushes of blood to my head," she later explained. "I felt as though if I only had some way to escape I certainly would but I had to stand my ground."[77] Another woman imagined herself squeezed in the room, "like a sardine packed in a box."[78] Emily Philpotts, thirty-five and single, was "very much upset" by the questions psychiatrists asked her, one going so far, her sister complained to Southard, "as to ask her if she ever got drunk."[79] And Mildred Brown, also thirty-five and single, recalled that she had been "stunned and wild by turns at their questions and treatment." She could not answer those men, she continued. "I know now that I answered many questions untruthfully. I just lost my head and said anything in the hope those men would go away from me. I didn't think men ought to question me." She claimed that their inquiries had harmed and insulted her. "Oh why didn't I speak then to some woman," she lamented, suggesting that it was not only the questions but also the gender of those who put them that offended.[80]

Psychiatrists knew full well that the disclosure they demanded of patients was extraordinary, even objectionable. They might reassure themselves with the fiction that patients were subjected to examination for their own good, simply to enable the psychiatrist to determine what was best to do, and they might, by familiarity, dull themselves to the examination's singularity, but their strained defense of its necessity—their insistence on its routine nature—was a measure of just how much it collided with the conventions of everyday life. "The whole modern trend," Southard argued, was toward venting publicly what had been private. From his perspective, the private self was an anachronism, a survival of the hated Victorian past—to be modern was to tell all. Though he admitted that in exceedingly intimate matters he sometimes resorted to the star chamber, which he tellingly associated not with coercion but with secrecy, he boldly, self-consciously pronounced that patients ought to be examined publicly —"in the presence of other patients and persons, non-patients."[81] And, in the case of a young woman, Herman Adler explicated the rationale behind public interrogation, arguing to his colleagues that although "some people may object that it does harm to a person" and "while a girl like this may be a little embarrassed by the sudden change of environment, it doesn't do any permanent harm." "It does one thing," he continued, "it brings her into a different environment which catches her more or less unprepared. The consequence is that she will be a little off guard and she will act in a way more natural." This was not, he argued, the "third degree": "We are simply trying to find out what is there."[82]

As Adler himself was aware, what was natural or there was not so simply determined. Psychiatrists might maintain that the procedure was uncontrived, structured merely to reproduce what already was, but they also knew that it unnerved patients, and they sometimes used this knowledge to augment their own advantage in an already unequal contest. Harmless "Socratic bantering" could, in these cases, take on a more sinister cast.[83] One psychiatrist announced to his colleagues as he was about to question Katherine Downey, a twenty-five-year-old trained nurse, who, in his estimation, "remembers more than she likes to admit," that his intention was "to upset her a little" in the hope that she would speak more freely about her suspected hallucinations and immoralities. He opened his questioning by asking her, "What is this young lady's name?" ("meaning the patient," the stenographer added), and he succeeded in ruffling her composure to the point where she felt compelled to assert her identity, exclaiming, in the midst of complaining about the lack of respect psychiatrists accorded her, "I think I am supposed to be a woman," her tentativeness a mark of their success.[84] Likewise, forty-seven-year-old William White told Southard, who had opened his questioning by stating "there seems to be some doubt as to what sort of person you are," that he had it exactly right: "To tell you the truth, from the raking over I have received since I have been here I am rather in doubt as to who I am, or what I am."[85]

In these instances the sensation of losing hold on one's sense of self, of not knowing exactly who one was, that was a common corollary of the imperative to disclose manifested itself in particularly dramatic form. Other patients experienced the same sensations less acutely. Some were instructed beforehand by their mates and, aware that the interrogation would culminate in a judgment of their sanity and alert to the possibilities for dissembling and prevarication it offered, were able to shield themselves against the full exposure psychiatrists desired and thus to preserve a measure of the self that Downey and White had lost. A nineteen-year-old male clerk, for example, who had overheard "emminent doctors" remark that he was "no good, and never would be," wrote that "when they asked me how I felt . . . I said I felt well, while in my heart, felt very sick." He had steeled himself for the ordeal, he later admitted, by repeating to himself, "now I must not let myself become a public charge. NO."[86]

But the less resolute were easily flustered by psychiatrists' probes. Sternly and crisply, with businesslike efficiency, psychiatrists could conduct an examination with dispatch, as they did in the case of George Henderson. Yet their questioning often took turns that puzzled, offended, or angered patients who could not understand where psychiatrists were leading them or why they asked such questions. Patients were affronted when challenged in what they considered inappropriate ways, such as when one psychiatrist asked a woman, in reference to her companions, "Aren't they sometimes queer, these musicians and artists?";[87] or when his colleague asked a man, "Do you think you are better than the average man?";[88] or when Southard asked a woman, "Do people laugh at you?"[89] Psychiatrists undoubtedly had reasons for posing these questions (they may, for example, have been trying to elicit delusional thinking), but it is also possible that they were merely bantering somewhat freely with patients, ignoring for the moment the unwritten rules that patients thought governed the encounter: that questioning should be directed toward some concrete aim, and that it should be for the patient's benefit. Aggressively posed challenges only underwrote the already unpredictable character of the examination.

So too did questions aimed less at assessing patients' feelings than at testing their composure. Responding to a series of arithmetic exercises— six times five equals? twelve times twelve equals? thirteen times fifteen equals?—one woman angrily exclaimed, "You don't ask people such question as these!" and demanded that the psychiatrists desist.[90] Psychiatrists proceeded similarly in their examination of a nineteen-year-old they deemed childish who had unaccountably aced the Binet test, asking her to name the presidents (who was the first assassinated? who had been assassinated since she had been born?) and, in quick succession, the country's major rivers, mountain ranges, and capital cities. Frustrated by her repeated claims that she could not remember, the psychiatrists first contradicted her—"Yes you do, don't get rattled. . . . You can answer those things"; then admonished her—"You made a good impression in the two months you have been here, don't spoil it at the end"; and finally put it to her straight—"Why is it you don't like to answer these questions? . . . Is it because you are embarrassed, or is it because it seems foolish to you?" She did not know why, she told the psychiatrists, but she simply did not want to answer them.[91]

Patients could go wrong in assuming that the rules governing ordinary social intercourse held sway in the psychiatric examination. From the patient's perspective, the small reciprocities and light humor that smoothed the edges of life had no place in the psychiatric examination; so essentially meaningless in everyday exchange, these could, in the hands of psychiatrists, assume a bewildering significance. Some patients later complained that psychiatrists' demeanors—too saucy, too fresh, inappropriately good-humored and genial in view of the gravity of the situation—in combination with their own nervousness had lulled them into forgetting the extraordinary nature of the situation and, in turn, to admitting to what they later protested had never been there. One woman, for example, had met psychiatrists' solicitude with politeness, not realizing at the time the former had been a ploy. Southard, she wrote, was "rather snappy in [his] Quizzes"; another psychiatrist was, by contrast, "rather Jolly in some of his remarks," so, she continued, "I thought I would be pleasant with him." But his disposition had only led her, she later realized, to admit under the pressure of his "persistent questioning" to delusions she did not experience.[92] Similarly, a seventeen-year-old had, with serious consequences, owned up to fainting spells he never had. "I didn't know what to say," he later wrote, "and I thought it would be best to say something."[93] And an apparently ridiculous question elicited from one man, Martin Frazer, a good-humored reply that he later realized had been a grave mistake. Frazer, a forty-nine-year-old Irish gardener who had been arrested as drunk and subsequently examined at the hospital, later wrote to the psychiatrist who had questioned him concerning certain of his replies. In the course of the events that had resulted in his arrest Frazer had gotten a black eye. The psychiatrist asked him which eye it was. Frazer wrote that he "wondered at this question," as would anyone who did not understand the conventions of the psychiatric examination. "I simply said through fun as much as anything else if you cannot see with your glasses on, you better take them off," a reply that he later realized had marked him as decidedly strange.[94]

Southard recognized that under questioning some patients tended to "admit too much as in a self depreciating [sic] manner,"[95] but the issue of determining what was real was deeper than this. What of shamming? Some patients appeared to adopt different poses intentionally, tussling wildly with attendants, say, then becoming quiet and tractable in the presence of a physician. Was shamming a symptom of mental disorder or a conscious strategy intended to subvert the diagnostic process? How would psychiatrists know?[96] "It is part of our duty to prove our patients normal, particularly, when such patients themselves claim they are diseased," Southard explained in a summary of a case he and his colleagues judged was "simulated," adding, "We always try to put faith in a patient's claims concerning himself."[97] This determination could have grave consequences in the disposition of military cases, which came before psychiatrists from late 1917 through 1918 in increasing numbers. How could psychiatrists determine whether the soldier Albert Henry was suffering from dementia praecox or merely seeking an exemption? Henry, a twenty-nine-year-old single man of Irish descent, explained to psychiatrists that he had started out "in good condition," but that at boot camp he had "commenced to wander about as if I was in a trance." Complaining of not feeling right, he immediately consulted a doctor, who sent him to the Psychopathic Hospital for observation with the notation that Henry had delusions. "Was that so?" Southard asked. "I guessed it must have been when he said so," replied Henry. When asked to specify the content of the delusion, Henry had to admit ignorance. What of the headaches of which he had complained? Could he describe them? Henry hesitated. Southard pressed him: "You don't remember much about the headaches?" Was Henry shamming or simply unable to verbalize the sensations he had experienced?[98]

How were psychiatrists to determine whether what patients told them was "true"? Adler observed that some were "adepts at covering up their true minds";[99] how was the psychiatrist to know when he had reached the bedrock to which an individual's tales presumably could be traced?[100] Prompted by vanity, driven by spite, patients might cast themselves in spectacularly different roles—innocent ingenue one moment, jaded seductress the next. Was the capacity to do so a sign of hysteria or an enviable dramatic gift? Or was it simply, as psychiatrists hypothesized in the case of one young woman, the mark of adolescent lability?[101] And what of outright denial? Patients could exhibit a symptom or confess to a thought and later deny it entirely. Southard's concern that a young woman was "inventing a narrative and speaking it to" psychiatrists spoke to a larger difficulty: whether, in the absence of much hard knowledge, "anybody's fictions yet amount to the true story of psychopathology."[102]

The symptom itself, commonplace but unscrutinized, was hardly so simple as psychiatrists perforce treated it. In part, symptoms were fragments of behavior and experience that observers culled from a larger life and rendered in a concise medical idiom. Negativism, apathy, flight of ideas, press of activity—this, the language of symptomatology, constituted, Southard wrote, "the slang of the psychiatric clinics."[103] For the most part, psychiatrists questioned neither the terms' utility nor their referents' apprehensibility. But "accurate observation," the psychiatrist's, even the physician's, metier, was not so straightforward as it appeared.[104] Psychiatric symptoms lacked the appealing objectivity associated with medical symptoms—"the appearance and disappearance of edema of the ankles," for example—and could thus betoken quite different behaviors and thoughts.[105] Further, there was the routine problem of distinguishing between, say, a figurative phrase and a schizophrenic delusion (such as one patient's claim that his head was hollow, which he explained meant "when you don't agree with people and they think they are smarter than you"),[106] between a religious and a paranoid delusion.[107] The symptom, however much psychiatrists might treat it as "fact," could not stand alone; it demanded interpretation.

But the symptom also presented difficulties of another order. The symptom's referents were not only ascribed but also "real" to the patients who could experience them as disturbing sensations arising from within the body, unsettling its integrity. One elderly man, for example, testified that immoral spirits had haunted him, poisoning his food with a bitter, nasty substance. "I was frantic with myself . . . awful nervous, thinking I was going under any minute," he told psychiatrists, who had suggested that only someone crazy would see spirits. "It is up to them to think so," he replied; for his part, he knew what he had seen.[108] Other patients told of being hounded by voices, of seeing and speaking to long-dead relations, of feeling strangely different—rotten, dopey, stuporous. From this perspective, the patient was the only "true" observer.[109] That what another could observe was but a meager measure of what lay within was pointedly manifest in the case of Fernando Dias, a twenty-three-year-old leatherworker from the Azores. His "story," as psychiatrists pieced it together, was suggestive of dementia praecox: "He didn't care about his personal appearance or eating, he would get up and sit in one place by the window for a long while, apparently taking little interest in anything." But the torpor apparent to the observer masked a tumult of sensation and feeling. "There's a monster preying on my mind and gnawing at my heart," Dias, "on the verge of hysterics," wrote to a friend. He had indeed "crouched in a corner," forgoing speech, fixed in "a sort of stupor" that he could neither explain nor define. Only this behavior, not the gnawing at his heart, was apparent, yet they were equally real to him.[110]

Diagnosis, then, was highly imperfect, dependent on observation but also on knowledge extracted from embarrassed, recalcitrant, confused, and possibly deceptive patients. Diagnostic categories were useful but fictive, constituting a genre that stood in some uncertain relation to what was real and true. Only by appreciating psychiatrists' awareness—keenly felt, rarely articulated—of the contingent nature of psychiatric knowledge can one hope to account for their resort to menacing persuasion when confronted with stubborn patients. Psychiatrists sometimes allowed themselves to be annoyed, angered, and engaged by patients they could have dispensed with straightforwardly and punitively, as indeed they sometimes threatened to do. Examination was an arena, after all, in which psychiatrists set the rules, called the plays, and determined the outcome. Nowhere did patients feel their subjugation more acutely. But to rest with this analysis would be to present only the more familiar half of the disciplinary story. To psychiatrists, examination was not only an exercise in power and persuasion, but also the point at which they confronted most painfully the limits of their disciplinary knowledge, and thus the elusiveness of their quest for the certainty that they saw as a mark of medical science. If, as later critics would contend, diagnosis was the sum of progressive psychiatric science, then to fail in this endeavor was to admit defeat. Southard, for one, wrote that could he "not specify the form of psychopathology in each given case," he would count himself as failing in medical diagnosis. At the same time, he realized it was not "humanly possible" always to do so.[111] The tension Southard voiced, between what psychiatrists aspired to and what they could in fact achieve, tempered their otherwise blustery confidence and generated in them considerable anxiety.

Gendered Psychoses: Wild Women, Dour Men

The contingent character of their disciplinary knowledge was nowhere more painfully evident to psychiatrists than at the juncture where dementia praecox and manic-depressive insanity met. The impossibility of reliably distinguishing between the two entities was an "open secret," a constant irritant to psychiatrists who readily confessed to errors in the differential diagnosis—nearly all of them cases of manic-depressive insanity they argued were wrongly diagnosed as cases of dementia praecox—in the range of 10 to 25 percent.[112] They considered but uniformly dismissed the possibility that an *actual* variation in the nature of cases lay behind the fluctuating rates at which practitioners in different institutions conferred the two diagnoses. Rather, they hypothesized, the difficulty lay with the categories. The referents of the dementia praecox diagnosis were so imprecise, they argued, varying widely in accordance with the temperament and disposition of the one who was diagnosing, that the term rightly might be deployed only with great caution and with a healthy respect for its limitations. To do otherwise was, in the estimation of Lawson Lowrey, a chronicler of the problem, nothing less "than a scientific crime."[113]

That wrong diagnoses would "retard the progress of psychiatry" was Lowrey's chief concern, but the consequences of incorrectly distinguishing between the two entities went beyond psychiatrists' professional interests. Southard emphasized that nothing less than the fate of patients was at stake, for a diagnosis of manic-depressive insanity, although serious, promised a patient a hopeful future while "incurable dementia" awaited those unfortunate enough to receive a diagnosis of dementia praecox. Manic-depressive patients might more readily return to their families; dementia praecox consigned its victims to "some receptacle for the incurable insane."[114]

As psychiatrists saw it, the difficulty here was that symptoms—what patients did, thought, and attested to, and what psychiatrists could see— were deceptive. All the symptoms associated with manic-depressive insanity might appear in dementia praecox; excitement and depression, for example, were ubiquitous, and grandiosity, persecutory ideas, hallucinations, and delusions could appear, singly or in combination, in any number of diseases.[115] The problem, Southard argued, was that in psychiatry, unlike medicine, there were no "indicator" symptoms, symptoms pathognomic of a single, specific disease. To the medical man, the pock of smallpox, for example, always indicated smallpox, and the tubercle bacillus always pointed to the presence of tuberculosis. The psychiatrist's task was more difficult; he was forced to interpret arrangements of symptoms that stood in varying (and largely unknown) relations to the underlying disease processes of which they were at best "mere indicators"—not, Southard emphasized, the thing itself.[116]

The difficulties of psychiatric diagnosis prompted Southard, in the mid-teens, to adopt a posture on the issue that represented an extraordinary retreat from the scientific stance to which he had formerly devoted his energies. Personally he would prefer, he averred, that the psychiatrist "be a simple type of person . . . a rather naïve person," rather than a shrewd or keen person, that he be one who could make unprejudiced judgments of "his fellow man pretty well in accordance with what the Freudians conceal in their term *Unconscious*." The psychiatrist, that is, should chart his reactions to the patient in question. Could he identify with, see himself in, the patient? Or was the patient bizarre and different? What of the laboriously compiled anamnesis, the careful toting up of symptoms, the painstaking observations of behavior, the judiciously arrived at synthesis—the diagnosis as commonly understood? Should the psychiatrist not, Southard countered, "make some use of the off-hand and global view of a man which a reasonably normal fellow finds himself to possess?" In any attempt to fathom the essence of another the interrogator necessarily read himself into the object of his inquiry. This process of identification or empathy made social life possible, Southard argued; completion of the many acts that made up everyday life, from the most mundane (such as reading a newspaper) to the most singularly revealing (such as romantic entanglements), was predicated on this capacity to see oneself in another.[117]

Southard may have been merely posturing here, trying out a radical skepticism that he would reject in practice and from whose more extreme consequences he would retreat; he was not proposing that the man in the street make psychiatric assessments, only that the physician leaven his professional knowledge with the wisdom engendered by age and experience. Further, his relatively benign, even favorable invocation of Freud, usually so reviled, would seem to indicate he conceived the statement in a moment of whimsy. Yet however playfully subversive his intentions, Southard was proposing an alternative stance on diagnosis that incorporated what others were well aware of: that the psychiatrist knew very little. Lowrey underscored this point with his proposal that half of all psychiatric diagnoses delivered less than they promised, for while a diagnosis, in medical terms, implied that the nature of the disease had been determined, psychiatrists could only know what they could see. A modest "clinical description," not a diagnosis, was what psychiatrists in fact could offer.[118]

At no point was the psychiatrists' subjectivity more critical than in the differential diagnosis of the "sister" diseases of manic-depressive insanity and dementia praecox.[119] Psychiatrists were well aware that, especially in difficult cases, the diagnosis turned on the quality of their reaction to the patient—simply, how they felt about him or her. Their reaction to patients they diagnosed manic-depressive was largely favorable. As they told it, the story of the manic-depressive was lively, often raucously so, and entertaining. Such individuals engaged the world around them head-on, often wreaking havoc at home and driving their relations mad (one woman characteristically was, in the eyes of her disgusted mate, "a corker"),[120] but they did so with a verve that drew admiration. Their signal characteristics—loquacity, excitability, intense sociability, and mordant wit—differed from those of normal individuals only by virtue of their excess. Southard's supposition that "every one of us is of manic-depressive stripe" was a tellingly innocuous observation concerning what was, after all, one of the major psychoses.[121] Invited by his colleagues to imagine himself a layman and to divulge his reaction to a potentially manic young woman's flamboyant gaiety, one psychiatrist admitted that he laughed at it; he found her "bright and witty." Added another, "she is amusing, not cynical."[122]

Looking at the dementia praecox patient, psychiatrists did not like what they saw: stolidity, catatonia, stupidity, disfiguring stigmata, and, most damning, an overwhelming differentness. If the manic was an enticing, somewhat entertaining variation on the normal, the dementia praecox patient represented, in Southard's estimation, "the apex of strangeness." Such individuals, he went on, gave off "an impression of queerness that probably no other phenomena can give." Southard ventured that the psychiatrist could reliably diagnose dementia praecox based on the "general impression" the patient conveyed.[123]

In theory the distinction between the two types might seem clear, but the average clinical case was not so easily decided. In practice, potentially manic patients were not all so attractive as psychiatrists liked to imagine, nor were all potential dementia praecox patients so strange. If observation yielded only confusion, as it so often did in practice, psychiatrists resorted to the even less reliable criterion of the patient's expected future. If we think the case will get worse, psychiatrists would reason, we will call it dementia praecox, for "practical men," Southard ventured, know that dementia praecox deteriorated and that, if it did not, the diagnosis was wrong.[124] Yet the bleak future that psychiatrists saw when they looked at the dementia praecox patient—the patient concerning whom, they admitted, they could muster little emotion[125]—was only an imputed future. Further, cases could be observed only briefly (for, on average, ten days), while the diagnosis might turn on the illness's unknown future course and take neither ten days nor ten weeks, but a daunting ten years to determine.[126]

All diagnoses, once conferred, acted as templates for life stories that psychiatrists could apprehend only incompletely, filling in what was hidden in those stories' pasts and, more important, endowing them with a future. In no circumstance was this more critical, however, than in the differential diagnosis of the sister psychoses. The interpretive nature of the diagnostic endeavor was in this determination especially clear. How should this person's tale be told? We could build the case up this way, psychiatrists would say, or we could make out his character in that way.[127] In one particularly difficult case, in which psychiatrists admitted there was "nothing . . . to indicate praecox," Lowrey pointed out that "all you need to do to make this a praecox case is to claim that he says he is drunk when he has these [hallucinatory] experiences. We know praecox cases do that." Psychiatrists rejected this tack, finding the patient, a twenty-one-year-old Irish clerk, mentally deficient.[128] Similarly, Southard asked his colleagues, "What can we say for dementia praecox?" before examining a forty-seven-year-old drinking man, a self-confessed vagrant possessed of "wanderlust." His love for wandering, offered one; his mannerisms, his silliness, and his emotional tone, added others. Pointing out that the patient had no hallucinations, Southard argued that psychiatrists could still "build up quite a case for schizophrenia," although were they to do so, his doubts were sufficent that he "would not care to be registered as [the] diagnostician."[129] Psychiatrists found the man manic-depressive.

Despite the tenuous nature of the differential diagnosis between manic-depressive insanity and dementia praecox, psychiatrists decided it in a strikingly consistent manner. If, thinking the way psychiatrists claimed they did, one isolates for analytical purposes a group of psychotic patients, candidates for either diagnosis, one finds that the men in this group were twice as likely as the women to receive a diagnosis of dementia praecox, to be classed as incurable and destined to deteriorate (table 5.3).[130] Neither social class nor ethnicity came into play in this determination. Psychiatrists considered middle-class and working-class patients equally susceptible to both disorders; despite their attribution of characterological deficiencies to certain ethnic groups, in making this differential diagnosis these purported traits held little sway. For example, Jews (whom psychiatrists thought highly excitable) were not overrepresented in the manic-depressive group, nor were Irish (often considered constitutionally deficient) overrepresented

TABLE 5.3
Dementia Praecox and Manic-Depressive Insanity Patients, Classified by Gender
and Ethnicity (percent)

	Dementia Praecox	Manic-Depressive	(N)
Men			(179)
Irish	86	14	(42)
Jewish	80	20	(20)
WASP	56	44	(18)
Other native-born	82	18	(51)
Canadian, U.K.-born	70	30	(10)
Other foreign-born	84	16	(38)
Women			(226)
Irish	73	27	(77)
Jewish	55	45	(20)
WASP	52	48	(31)
Other native-born	66	44	(41)
Canadian, U.K.-born	55	45	(29)
Other foreign-born	68	32	(28)
Odds ratio for dementia praecox diagnosis: men compared to women[a]		2.11	

Note: From the log-linear model: {DG} {GE} (where D = diagnosis, G = gender, E = ethnicity); G^2 = 14.26, df = 10, p = .16. A model that also included the {ED} term did not differ in a statistically significant way from the one presented here.

[a]The ratio of the odds that men would be diagnosed dementia praecox compared to the odds that women would be diagnosed dementia praecox, controlling for ethnicity.

among those deemed to be suffering from dementia praecox.[131] The striking gender difference, so consistent over ethnic groups, suggests that psychiatrists perceived something essentially male or female in the diseases themselves. Kraepelin, who had first distinguished the disorders, reported finding that 70 percent of manic-depressive patients "belong to the female sex with its greater emotional excitability," suggesting that the gender difference was not just a matter of perception but was encoded into the very categories that ordered psychiatrists' observations.[132] From the start, manic-depressive insanity was interpreted as a peculiarly female malady.

In practice this encoding operated invisibly and efficiently, providing a criterion—so apparently natural that it occasioned little comment—by which psychiatrists might assess patients with symptoms that indicated either disorder. Thus, psychiatrists unwittingly but consistently brought considerations of gender and sexuality to the fore in their determination of hard cases, downplaying the significance of patients' other behaviors and symptoms. The most salient characteristics they saw in the manic patient were those associated in other contexts with an unbounded, out-of-control femininity that was at once frightening and alluring. In women this commonly took the form of an appealing "eroticism." The diagnosis of Winifred Reed, a "sporty [and] man crazy" young stenographer, endowed, by her own account, with an "excess of erotic passion," turned on her eroticism. Psychiatrists had first thought her a praecox patient, but as social workers provided them with reports of her sexual exploits, and as she divulged that her first experience of intercourse (at twenty-one) had stimulated an "intensity of passion" that she was helpless to control, they changed their diagnosis. "A fresh outburst of eroticism," nearly two years after the initial diagnosis was made, which, Southard argued, was "medically to be regarded as a form of attack in her disease," underscored to the psychiatrists how prescient their change of heart had been.[133]

Although in telling Reed's tale the psychiatrists may have privileged her eroticism over, say, her fits of depression or her excitability, it was not in this case simply a matter of their own perceptions. Reed's eroticism was, rather, a congeries of activities ("cohabitation," for example) and inclinations (her boldly proclaimed sportiness, her crazy passion) to which she could attest and in which she could delight. Yet psychiatrists asserted, then scrutinized, the purported eroticism of many potentially manic women for whom the term referred less to a woman's willfully chosen style of worldly engagement than to their own interpretation of qualities and behaviors that excited their interest. How much of one woman's "foolish" behavior —feigning faintness, throwing herself about on her bed—was, Lowrey asked his colleagues, "purely erotic"? How much, that is, attracted rather than repelled the observer?[134]

Southard proposed on one occasion that the manic's lack of the normal inhibitions rather than her eroticism could account for her "hypersexuality," but he continued to invoke the term as a useful diagnostic criterion.[135] Of the forty-year-old Marie Dubois, for example, a French Canadian woman whose live-in "paramour" had recently died and who had, presumably in consequence, become restless and distracted, Southard observed that although she sang and played about dramatically in her room, nude much of the time, it was a nudity bespeaking not eroticism but a temporary loss of delicacy.[136] The nudity of the middle-aged woman failed to attract.

The men psychiatrists diagnosed as manic-depressive appeared to their relatives and friends, as well as to psychiatrists, much like women. The manic man, as psychiatrists described him, like the normal woman, was excitable, distractable, and talkative, his conduct governed less by rational considerations than by plays of fancy.[137] His purportedly effeminate character was the subject of painful self-criticism and psychiatric speculation as well as of the unforgiving judgments of workmates, relatives, and friends. The mother-in-law of a middle-aged elevator operator whose wife did not "care to have any more dealings with him" told psychiatrists that he was a very nice but very fastidious fellow, a "sissy" who had always been "somewhat effeminate." The man himself volunteered that he was depressed, that he cried easily, and that although he had twice "turned on the gas," he doubted he had the courage to commit suicide.[138] Alfred Stevens, although not in Southard's estimation a homosexual (he was married and disclaimed any interest in sex), was "a rather effeminate and timid man," like the elevator operator, "a regular sissy." Well positioned at a dry-goods firm, Stevens's proclivity for pilfering ribbons, laces, collars, and the like from his employer showed him to be damnably weak-willed, a most unmasculine trait. Further, like a woman, he was given to weeping and was "unduly finical about his clothing."[139] Another man, whom psychiatrists thought suffered from a mild form of the disease, had, they noted, "never been very strong" and "had never taken much part in games with other boys." Supersensitive, he was lacking in initiative and deficient in aggressiveness. After treatment, which was directed toward remedying his deficiencies and which was effected through the medium of the Men's Club, he was "doing a man's work and was filled with the idea of getting ahead in the world."[140]

While the manic's sexuality could entice and delight, there was nothing attractive about the sexuality of the praecox patient. Although psychiatrists sometimes questioned whether excessive self-abuse caused the disorder, for the most part they nervously skirted the issue of such patients' sexual feelings and practices. In the fulfillment of his desires, the praecox patient was exhibitionistic rather than properly furtive.[141] But his often self-directed, autistic sexuality fell outside the "social danger zone" and could be thought of, Southard proposed, as an annoyance much like "bad table manners and other impolitenesses," this uncharacteristically benign interpretation a measure of how much embarrassment the subject engendered.[142]

The characteristics attributed to the praecox patient—stolidity, stupidness, and catatonia—contrasted unfavorably with the excitability and suggestive elusiveness of the manic. Such characteristics were merely the extreme, pathological manifestations of men's naturally more stable nature, just as the periodicity that characterized the manic mimicked in a more marked form the natural periodicity of women. Some psychiatrists attempted to inscribe the salient gender differences between the two psychoses onto the body, hypothesizing, for example, that an attack of mania might be traceable to pelvic lesions (such as lacerations of the cervix and perineum), or that the pubic and mammary hair of female praecox patients was configured as if on a man.[143] But this was not necessary. From the psychiatric observer's viewpoint, the eroticism of the manic was visible, as real—and as much a sign of disease—as the neurosyphilitic's positive Wassermann reaction.

SIX

INSTITUTIONAL DISCIPLINE

A LIVELY CLINIC, a general hospital, a boarding school—the institutional culture of the Psychopathic Hospital was, in the estimation of its proponents, as eventful as the first, as salubrious as the second, and as benign as the third. In favorable contrast to the desolate asylum, the institution was in their view a whirl of scientific and therapeutic activity. Laboratory work, meetings, administrative duties, physical and mental examinations filled the psychiatrist's days; therapeutic baths, gossip, visitors, physical and mental examinations filled those of the patient. An ethos of openness and democracy reigned. Independent thinking was encouraged; science and common sense were esteemed in equal measure; "tug-of-war discussions" of abstract principles were forsworn in favor of concrete attacks on real problems. "Institution men"—those asylum physicians, noted for their nihilism, who, Southard emphasized, admitted to having "drifted into hospital work"—were nowhere in evidence. A staff composed of what Southard again and again called "higher types"— psychiatrists, psychologists, social workers, nurses, and attendants—so expertly managed patients, the abnormal and the normal, that the unwitting visitor was apt to wonder "where the really crazy ones are."[1]

Not only the crazy ones, to which any patient could have directed the caller, but also power as usually conceived was conspicuously absent from the psychiatrists' sanguine portrait of their institution. The execrable asylum never far from their minds, Southard and his colleagues repeatedly maintained that Psychopathic Hospital patients were handled in a modern manner, without coercion or restraint, much "like patients with physical diseases at general hospitals."[2] Restraint—actual and metaphorical— resonated with particular force through the story they told of their discipline's past. That asylum superintendents too often resorted to what was called mechanical restraint, employing various forms of apparatus to immobilize unruly patients, was, next to commitment, psychiatry's greatest shame. "In no other aspect," a chronicler of the profession's progress would later write, "were American institutions so backward as in this."[3] As moderns, psychiatrists would answer only to science. They framed their approach to institutional management, as they had their approach to commitment and diagnosis, in purposeful opposition to the ways of their disciplinary forebears.

Even as psychiatrists were renouncing the repressive power that their predecessors had wielded, they were delineating, in practice and in print, an alternative, disciplinary vision of power. In this vision, institutional power was not vested in the person of the superintendent but in the neutral machinery of administration—procedures and conventions indifferent to the vagaries of individual agency. Power was not to be exercised from the top down, by the psychiatrist over the patient, but, more subtly, by compliant patients over themselves. It was to work its effects not violently but unobjectionably, through bureaucratic—and thus innocuous—regulation of what Foucault has called the "little things." Psychiatrists chafed at the restrictions of practice behind "brick walls." Their ambitions larger, they attempted to create a space that was neither carceral nor altogether free, a space in which all individuals would regulate themselves in accordance with the tenets of psychiatry's "gospel of mind."[4] If psychiatrists could barely bring themselves to think of the institution as a space of confinement, this was but a corollary of their disciplinary perspective in the making.

Discipline in Practice

The Psychopathic Hospital was designed with what Southard referred to as the "modern handling" of the psychiatric patient in mind. The desirable private room was scarce; patients were housed in wards of four to six beds. Spaces in which patients could mingle—dayrooms, workrooms, gardens on the ground and on the roof—were scattered throughout the institution. Bathtubs for hydrotherapy were installed on two floors, six to a room. A spacious medical library and a number of laboratories were centrally located. Much of the four-story brick building, which to Southard's mind suggested "a school house," was given over to sleeping quarters and dining areas for staff—male physicians, female officers, nurses, attendants, and other help.[5] Throughout the day, patients moved from one sort of "standardized environment" to another. For most, privacy was out of the question; patients were purposely mixed together and kept busy. In all, a bustling atmosphere of normality prevailed.[6]

In providing so few places for solitary repose, the building's planners were guided not by considerations of "economy of management" but by the burdens of history. Patients and their friends might argue that solitude was necessary, but psychiatrists, mindful of their discipline's past, realized that in the public's eyes the *chambre séparée* was but a prison cell, privacy merely a cover for the secret machinations of asylum doctors bent on promoting their "professional metaphysics."[7] When psychiatrists trumpeted the virtues of publicity in the treatment of psychiatric patients and argued that such patients ideally should be granted no more privacy than "persons in general demand," they were offending common sense but, more importantly, making amends for their profession's past and responding obliquely to its critics.[8] Lay and medical critics argued that psychiatry's institutional practices, primarily restraint and seclusion, were barbaric relics of a bygone era.[9] From the fetters and chains of old, through the straitjackets and muffs of the mid-nineteenth century, to the gradual dawning of freedom, progress in psychiatry led from secrecy to openness, from restraint to freedom.[10]

A "regime of visibility" governed the day-to-day workings of the Psychopathic Hospital. Fashioned in contrast to the gothic asylum, the "darkened spaces" of which were widely thought to have sheltered corruption, brutality, and despotism from the "healthy breezes" of public sentiment, this regime was difficult but, from psychiatrists' perspective, necessary to maintain.[11] Psychiatrists professed to welcome the scrutiny of the same public that had condemned their predecessors. Visit our institution, Southard exhorted a gathering of charitable reformers, and "you will be struck by" this, "you will note" that, and, he said three times, "you will see"— patients, procedures, perhaps even a recovery or two.[12] We have nothing to hide, he was suggesting, and if "psychopathic matters" were discussed in the presence of patients, their friends, minor officials, and "sundry other bystanders and listeners," that was merely indicative of the "whole modern trend" against the secrecy that bred suspicion.[13]

Deployed rhetorically like this, visibility was provocative but ultimately unexceptionable; public visits were, after all, mandated by law. As what Foucault has called a strategy of power, however, compulsory visibility was double-edged. That patients should be subject to constant scrutiny had been an institutional imperative from the early years of the nineteenth century. That the psychiatrists who perpetuated this policy would find themselves subject to its strictures underscores the degree to which discipline could refer as much to self-discipline as it could to the control of others. In the asylum, typically staffed by two or three physicians, everyone was watched by everyone else: patient by alienist, patient by patient, alienist by patient. In the Psychopathic Hospital, employer of roughly three times as many medical workers as other contemporary state institutions, psychiatrist was also watched by psychiatrist, social worker by social worker, members of one profession by members of the other.[14] If among the objectives of discipline was that the patient become her own overseer, then among its unregistered effects was that the psychiatrist became his own as well.

The hospital psychiatrist's day began at eight o'clock with morning rounds. For an hour, he and his colleagues discussed the medical status of a portion of the institution's one hundred or so patients. Rounds served to keep psychiatrists au courant with the constantly changing case mix. The daily ritual also allowed them a well-defined arena in which to engage in a form of collective self-discipline, for the torpor of the fatigued and the partisanship of the prejudiced became apparent in psychiatrists' wide-ranging discussions. Rounds were "especially serviceable," Southard wrote, for bringing into line those physicians who were given to "carrying things in their heads"—a secretive habit he associated with asylum superintendents—instead of following the modern practice of "committing them to the records."[15] Instilled with a sense of common purpose, psychiatrists were prepared to weather the day's inevitable disagreements.

Psychiatrists spent the rest of the morning performing physical and mental examinations, administering treatments, admitting and processing the hospital's three to four new patients and discharging the same number. Every day at noon the staff again convened, with social workers and (on Wednesdays) practicing physicians from the community and other institutions in attendance, for the hour-long staff meeting. Like morning rounds, this convocation served both to inform psychiatrists and to socialize them into the hospital's ways; it was at these meetings, Southard wrote, that he was able to secure "the maximum effect upon the staff."[16] Other daily tasks drew the psychiatrists' collective attention. There was research to carry out and write up (many of the staff published regularly in medical journals); there were medical students to instruct and interns to supervise; there were visitors—friends and families of patients—to handle.[17] Some of these tasks evoked sentiments of professional beleaguerment. Southard was constantly supplicating a legislature that granted his institution too little money to retain experienced staff at all levels—assistant physicians, for example, earned twelve hundred dollars a year.[18] But psychiatrists also cemented their professional solidarity in the face of an imputed public skepticism. Aware that their findings in a case might sound "very suspicious to the layman however it sounds to us," Southard maintained that in general it was important "to omit minutiae of psychological, social and medical technique from reports to public agencies and the laity." Arguing that "the machinery of the law" was ill suited to handle many problems that they routinely confronted, he and his colleagues presented judges with carefully orchestrated reports, tactically suppressing their differences.[19] Still, it seemed to several psychiatrists that in forensic cases, influenced by "the clamor of the mob" that sought vengeance, they were underdiagnosing insanity.[20] Psychiatric reasoning, they realized, could appear merely soft, not reasonable.

"Medicine is an exigent mistress," wrote one hospital psychiatrist; "never satisfied, always with new tasks, the fulfillment of one task leading to the development of many others."[21] Indeed, psychiatrists were pulled in many directions—scientific, clinical, administrative. Although they sometimes complained of being overburdened, for the most part they reveled in their busyness, for it signaled their importance, to others and to themselves. Psychiatrists told of entertaining a steady stream of official visitors, from distant states and from abroad; of explaining, over and over again, the hospital's operation to delegates from various state commissions and heads of social bureaus; and of propagandizing tirelessly on behalf of what was becoming known as the psychopathic hospital idea. The better known among them regularly attended conferences and visited other institutions; in 1917, Southard crossed the continent, delivering addresses in ten cities.[22] From the start it was clear that administrative tasks, from filling out state-mandated accident reports to negotiating with public and private officials, were occupying too much of psychiatrists' time, a situation that was addressed by the appointment, in 1915, of Dr. Elisha Cohoon as full-time hospital administrator. Praised by Southard for ably smoothing "the plane of contact between the hospital and extramural world," Cohoon was succeeded in 1917 by A. P. Noyes. "Relieved of many uncongenial duties" by this unconventional arrangement, psychiatrists were better able to focus their attention where they desired, on research and clinical work.[23]

Southard's approach to institutional management was avowedly scientific but in fact quite bureaucratic. In contrast to the nineteenth-century asylum superintendents who had imagined themselves fathers of their patient-children, benevolent but imperious heads of households, he eschewed domestic imagery, instead speaking brusquely of handling, managing, and expeditiously processing patients or, less sentimentally still, "psychopathic material."[24] Contemporary superintendents might think it necessary to know the names of the six hundred to eight hundred patients under their control, but to Southard this was just one especially telling manifestation of their general tendency to "stuff their minds" with meaningless trivialities. And they might, he pointed out, "believe that what has been must be," the complacency of the one who had proclaimed "there is nothing new under the sun" surely in mind, but to him it was clear that the effective superintendent must be adaptable, willing to see his institution evolve as science dictated. Old-time superintendents might hold that they should be fully in charge of their institution's medical and business affairs, but to Southard it seemed that the diagnoses made by distraught superintendents were inferior to the democratically arrived at judgments of a modern medical staff. By his own lights more "human being" than despotic director, Southard happily heralded the end of the "one-man clinic."[25]

The social worker's day, like the psychiatrist's, began collectively, with a half-hour staff meeting at which current cases were discussed under Jarrett's direction. Much of the rest of the day she typically devoted to managing her "intensive" cases, the approximately 250 men and women whom the social service department fully investigated and treated each year. Such treatment was in Jarrett's estimation painstaking, demanding the social worker's "close application"; it entailed visiting, interviewing, assessing, and advising patients, their families, and their friends.[26] Friday afternoons were given over to social service clinics, at which special cases were presented in the presence of psychiatrists and social workers from the community. Her day occupied by meetings, administrative tasks, and supervision of her own cases, the psychiatric social worker traveled in as public an arena as the psychiatrist. Her competence, like his, was constantly on display. Because it was not propped up by what Jarrett described as "the funded knowledge tested and retested by generations of students," and because she was a woman, hers was even more open to question than his.[27] Still, the professional persona that the psychiatric social worker sought to project was, like the psychiatrist's, one of resolute service in the name of science.

The invigorating cover of this persona enabled social workers to venture confidently into uncharted disciplinary territory. Following patients "into the scenes of their daily lives" was risky from a professional point of view, for there, far beyond the hospital's legitimating walls, only their staid dress and serious demeanor distinguished them from mere women, only their scientific stance from mere friendly visitors.[28] They were sometimes taken for both, castigated as old maids or busybodies by those who objected to their presence. The paradox social workers confronted as they went about their daily visits was that while friendliness was more effective than a display of authority in securing cooperation, it was antithetical to the objectivity and impartiality celebrated by the professional ethos. The social worker navigating the streets of South Boston, calling on patients' neighbors and interviewing their relatives as she pieced together her "objective" assessments, might strategically downplay her professional identity and chat amiably and at length with a potential informant in hopes of eliciting a shred of useful information. On their citywide forays, social workers experienced the embarrassment of the occasional nasty rebuff and the frustrations of dealing with uncooperative informants, but, fashioning themselves students of the human personality, they could at least consider such encounters grist for their scientific mill.

Regular encounters with the psychiatrists who depended on but also denigrated their skills could be equally trying and less enlightening. The apportionment of tasks between psychiatrist and social worker in the work of aftercare is significant in this regard. Holding that aftercare was central to the hospital's mission, psychiatrists met with ex-patients during the day and after hours, singly and, under the aegis of the Men's Club (a loose association of former patients diagnosed as alcoholic), collectively. Psychiatrists delegated the task of enticing former patients back to the hospital to social workers, who each year sent out more than a thousand letters reminding them of the doctor's desire to see them. Typically, one "regulation printed" letter was sufficient, but in 20 percent of the cases a personal letter, a phone call, or a visit to the patient's home was necessary. "I wish [your son] would come to the Club Friday night. Won't you try to persuade him to come?" one letter to a discharged patient's mother read.[29] Aware that patients might be antagonized by their persistence, social workers used cheerfully firm language to persuade the hesitant. As less than 10 percent of ex-patients reported to the hospital without reminder, social workers rightly deemed their epistolary efforts an integral part of psychiatric treatment.[30]

To social workers it seemed that psychiatrists appreciated neither the effort nor the skill that such work—indeed, all social work—entailed. Jarrett maintained that investigations of patients' circumstances and history, undertaken at the behest of psychiatrists for the purpose of diagnosis, were especially irksome. The social worker charged with carrying out such an investigation, which typically took her away from her own cases for a full day, was, she wrote, "bound to feel a certain sense of interruption" and could not be expected to show great enthusiasm for the task. Psychiatrists might consider the making of such investigations the primary function of the social service, and Jarrett might agree that this was "in a sense" so, but she suggested that to conceive of social work in this way was to underestimate the social worker's true capabilities. As she told it, psychiatrists were apt to request a painstakingly compiled social history but then ignore it, arriving at a diagnosis on purely medical grounds.[31] Displaying the same disregard for the social worker's expertise, they were apt to discharge patients who needed supervision without alerting the social service, and they were several times taken in by steady drinkers' claims to be dry. Dorothy Hale, another worker, reported that the police returned one alcoholic man to the hospital, to which he was then committed, only days after psychiatrists had examined him and deemed him better. Calling into question psychiatrists' claims to diagnostic expertise, she pointedly suggested that had the man been under social work supervision the entire embarrassing sequence of events might have been averted.[32] Diplomatically, Jarrett maintained that "a certain amount of confusion" characterized the institution's division of labor, but her point, that the psychiatrist demanded the social worker's labor and respect but offered little in return, was clear.[33]

Although Jarrett and her staff cooperated day to day with psychiatrists, she repeatedly aired her grievances in print. She pointed out, for example, that the hospital's architect had, at the urging of several psychiatrists, drawn into the building's plans only two rooms for the social service, a small office and a larger waiting room. She bluntly insisted that the vision animating this gesture was flawed, "about as far as possible from a true picture of social work." Social workers, like other professionals, needed their own desks; they had no time to play hostess to patients and their friends. Jarrett grumbled that in general hospital administrators gave too little thought to the specifics of social work, assuming that as more workers were hired the work would "grow spontaneously." In social work as in other work, she maintained, it was not enough for individuals simply to make themselves useful. Rather, it was critical that every worker be a specialist, in charge of her own area of expertise.[34] And she countered Southard's admittedly prejudiced insistence that psychiatric social workers be "dominated" by physicians with a prediction that only a few "trained social worker[s] of the future," well-versed as a profession in the tenets of the social psychiatry that he thought beyond their capacities, would be content to "assist the psychiatrist."[35]

Psychiatrists might deem social workers incapable of exercising "executive authority," they might disparagingly characterize them as qualified "to arrange for food, shelter, vacations, crutches and the like," and they might warn them not to make even indirect "psychotherapeutic prescriptions," but in fact the press of daily activity in the hospital allowed social workers the latitude to set the parameters of their craft far more expansively than psychiatrists thought advisable.[36] Their specialty was new and, with psychiatrists out of the way, engaged much of the day by medical matters, its possibilities were in Jarrett's opinion boundless. On a paltry budget, two (later, in 1917, three) paid social workers, along with students, a few volunteers, and several privately funded workers, methodically charted new territory and developed new techniques. They defined the dimensions of their charge broadly. Verging closely on the psychiatrist's prerogative to diagnose, Jarrett argued that the psychiatric social worker must be able to recognize the signs of mental disorder and to investigate their ramifications. She must, like the psychiatrist but without duplicating his efforts, directly examine the patient, inquiring into his or her attitudes, tastes, and preferences.[37] She should objectively observe and study the patient, and question the accuracy of his or her account, a prerogative that Southard reserved explicitly for the psychiatrist.[38] Ideally, she was an expert on the human personality. In all, the purview of Jarrett's psychiatric social worker was more like that of the psychiatrist than that of the agency-type, non-psychiatric social worker. Jarrett deferentially allowed that her workers made do "without any exact knowledge of psychology and psychiatry," but she and her colleagues insisted they were made of more professional stuff than the agency workers from whom they carefully distinguished themselves. Jarrett chided agency workers for claiming to work only with "normal persons," pointing out out that the term had "no exact meaning" and proclaiming that perfection was in any case rare and uninteresting. Her associate Helen Wright maintained that psychiatric social workers resolutely and scientifically handled cases that agency workers considered "too sensitive" or too difficult. And Jarrett maintained that too many agency workers "censured and despised" problematic patients who deserved understanding and respect, precisely what the psychiatric social worker was prepared to offer them.[39]

In social work, as in psychiatry, discipline building demanded self-discipline. To fashion an alternative professional stance the psychiatric social worker had to discipline herself as much as her patients, to suppress the censorious judgments of the dissolute and feckless that her disciplinary forebear, the friendly visitor, had reflexively issued. Suppressing such judgments was hard enough; delineating an alternative was more difficult still. Through the first quarter of the century, psychiatric social workers explicitly attended to perfecting the mechanics of casework while, in their measured handling of actual cases, enlarging its scope and changing its meaning. Creatively exploiting new technologies—the typewriter, telephone, streetcar, and automobile—and embellishing older ones, hospital social workers pushed casework in a direction that was, if not scientific, at least bureaucratically efficient. The typewriter allowed them to amass patient files in which the minutiae of patients' lives were neatly recorded. The telephone enabled them to call patients at their homes and workplaces, some 10,839 times in 1918.[40] The trolley and the automobile allowed them expeditiously to visit patients' homes and communities. Refining and ordering older pen-and-paper techniques, they developed a complex bureaucratic apparatus to track the five hundred or so persons they typically investigated each year. On special calendars and appointment slips, in chronological and alphabetical files, and in quarterly reports, each patient's progress through the social service was scrupulously recorded and assessed.[41] These measures were substantial, enabling social workers to attain the "exact knowledge" they sought. But it was in their quiet, piecemeal, and often frustrating attempts to realize the vaguely defined "psychiatric point of view" that social workers fundamentally changed the nature of social work knowledge and practice.[42]

Social workers did this largely in their supervision of intensive cases. Thrusting themselves into the lives of patients, orchestrating the most minute aspects of their day-to-day existence, and attempting somehow to treat them, social workers were engaged in an experimental endeavor. With no "written down" science of personality to guide them, they were often forced to improvise, to abandon one strategy and adopt another on the spot, to formulate principles and then violate them. Your science "exists in lives," not in textbooks, the physician Richard C. Cabot told a gathering of social workers. The transition from life to science varied from case to case, he suggested; "balanced and cautious doctrine" was, in "real life," subject to "the 'bludgeonings of chance.'"[43] The twists and turns that social workers' handling of the case of Eliza Conway took underscores Cabot's point, in which, like so many others, doctrine and technique took shape fitfully, refracted unevenly through life.

An admittedly willful and difficult sixteen-year-old of Irish ancestry, Conway had twice attempted suicide by poison. She entered the hospital voluntarily, on the advice of an older friend, and was discharged after ten days with a diagnosis of psychopathic personality. Helen Anderson, the worker who took charge of her in October 1915, opened her investigation with a visit to the family home in Lynn. Seated in the front parlor of the freshly painted two-story structure, she cast a disapproving eye over the state of the "dusty and musty" interior, which she noted was "furnished in cheap pieces," unmatched, "upholstered and ugly." She questioned Conway's mother (whom she judged "a gross uneducated woman," affable but "without force or cleverness") on the family's income and expenses, when and what sort of food they ate, and the health and occupational histories of her eleven children. Anderson learned that the mother considered her daughter indolent and somewhat spoiled, a youngest child often subjected to the teasing of her older siblings, and that although she preferred having her at home, she would consent to her entering training to become a nurse. Before Anderson departed, she managed to peek into the kitchen, which she allowed was fairly clean, and she observed enough of one of the patient's brothers to deem him a courteous, "neatly dressed, brisk young man." Her stance censorious and superior, Anderson at this point sounded more like the reproachful social worker of old than the dispassionate, psychologically minded worker of Jarrett's imagining.

Anderson at first attempted to handle the case straightforwardly, as an agency worker might have, focusing not on Conway's personality but on her social circumstances, past and present.[44] She solicited information on Conway's habits from former employers, tracked down the nun who taught her in the sixth grade, quizzed other acquaintances about her past, and, turning to more immediate issues, tried to find her a job and a place away from home to live. She regularly spoke to her patient on the phone, and met with her at least six times in the space of several weeks, at the hospital and at her family's home (which continued to draw Anderson's censure, the food on one occasion having been "put on the table every which way"). After several weeks, Anderson treated Conway to a lunch at Filene's, during which Conway for the first time confided in her. By the end of the month, Anderson felt she had made some progress on the case. She noted that Conway had given "a good account of herself and her character," and had signaled a willingness to "make something of herself." Anderson found her "more open than ever before."

The case quickly began to push beyond the bounds within which Anderson had tried to manage it, however, and in the months that followed she would find her patience tried and her professionalism challenged. Conway began withholding information, promising but then failing to reveal secrets, staying in touch but refusing to say where she was. She then ran away from home, met up with another girl in the city, and, as Anderson would soon discover, began to get money not from working but, as she boldly claimed, by "going out with men." As the case took a more psychiatric turn, with Conway claiming not to care what became of her and flaunting a bottle that appeared to contain poison, Anderson was forced into making decisions ad hoc. Throwing off the cloak of condescension (and forswearing further commentary on domestic conditions), her engagement with Conway became scrappier and, from our contemporary perspective, more therapeutic. At the end of a particularly trying day, for example, Anderson agreed to meet with Conway in hopes of persuading her to stay off the streets. Anderson rushed downtown and found Conway on a street corner, outside the YWCA where she was staying, in the company of several men. From 8:30 to 11:30, she tangled with her, listening to Conway's gleeful tale of being pursued by police, unsuccessfully attempting to have her mother send for her, summoning an officer to escort her to Lynn, and, finally, after Conway, pills in hand, threatened to commit suicide, arranging for her admission to the hospital, to which she was committed for sixty days.

Anderson enjoyed something of a reprieve while Conway was confined to the hospital. She visited Conway frequently on the ward, finding her moody and sullen, provocative toward the attendants and flirtatious with the male patients. Anderson continued to inquire into her past and to speak with her about her family, but, with Conway's day-to-day care in the hands of others, she did so more calmly, on her own terms. At a remove from "life in the raw," in what the social worker Jessie Taft called the artificial, "false and misleading simplicity" of the hospital environment, psychiatrists dismissed Conway's "outer world difficulties" as sentimental and her suicide attempts as histrionic, and admonished her for "wander[ing] about and get[ting] into difficulties." As Southard aggressively put it to her, "Can't you straighten out—we are piling up reels of records, what boots it all?" The social worker had to be more circumspect, for she had to manage difficult patients "in real life," without the aid of keys, walls, and keepers. Her mandate was in Taft's words "complicated and experimental" —through a mix of friendliness and authority to win patients' confidence and secure their compliance.[45] Anderson tried to keep Conway under control for six months following her discharge from the hospital, meeting her at odd hours, accompanying her to the dentist, sending her candy, seeing her through several changes of residence and employment, and putting up with her insolent remarks and threats to run away to New York, all in the interest of reforming her character and keeping her out of the institution. In the end, however, Anderson was no match for the wily Conway, with whom psychiatrists dispensed by arranging for her commitment to Danvers State Hospital, even though several thought her "no more abnormal" than many others they let go free.

This case, like many, came to no neat resolution. Reflecting wearily on her lack of success in managing it, Anderson highlighted her patient's love of gaiety, her "inclination toward cafes and attention from men," and her aversion to work, as if to convince herself that Conway's troubles were deeply rooted in her character—"evasive, changeable and thoroughly unreliable"—and thus beyond her own imperfect reach. Whether they were or not, Anderson's efforts in this case bear examination, for they provide one instance of the more general phenomenon of social workers' search for knowledge through practice. Discussed with her colleagues, written down in the file, Anderson's tactics in this case and those of her colleagues in many others would eventually constitute the funded knowledge—the science of personality—for which psychiatric social workers were searching. In the meantime, acting as "working psychologist[s]," they honed their techniques and defined a particular field of expertise for themselves, spiritedly managing, even treating, cases for which psychiatrists had little time and few remedies.[46]

Routine Discipline

The men and women who entered the hospital were unequally endowed with social and emotional resources. They came from stations as different as those of lawyer and teamster, middle-class housewife and domestic servant. Some were perfectly lucid, others plagued by hallucinations and delusions. Yet once the hospital's "large swinging iron gate" had closed behind them, all were subjected to the same battery of procedures, which generated feelings of despair, shame, and confusion among patients who shared little else. Hustled into the bare, undecorated admissions office, where psychiatrists questioned them briefly before handing them over to waiting attendants, patients were initiated into the ways of the hospital as they were summarily stripped of all their belongings. Eyeglasses, false teeth, collars, hairpins, and watches were removed, and patients were issued identical hospital gowns. The transformation from person to patient, from admissions office to ward, took a mere thirty minutes. Psychiatrists applauded the efficiency of their procedures, likening them to those employed in general hospitals. Many patients suffered them with equanimity, but to others, like the twenty-five-year-old nurse who claimed she "went all to pieces" when she realized where she was, the experience of becoming a patient was deeply unsettling.[47]

The patients were shown to the ward, assigned a bed, and introduced to their fellows, separated, in the words of one woman, "from all they love, their native city, a lover, perhaps." Their days followed a routine alternately intrusive and monotonous.[48] Each was pulled off the ward at least five different times to be photographed, X-rayed, and examined mentally and physically. For some, especially women, the twenty-minute physical, which included an internal gynecological examination, held particular terrors; "You'll be lucky if you don't get killed," one young woman warned her terrified mates.[49] Unfamiliar with the examination's conventions, women could interpret the ordeal as so much insolent squeezing and unwarrantedly intimate touching.[50] Many patients, male and female, objected to the lumbar puncture, a painful procedure in which spinal fluid was drawn to be tested for the presence of syphilitic infection, but many underwent it, sometimes taking to bed for several days to recover.[51] More routinely, patients might pass their mornings on the roof garden, talking with others, and their afternoons on the ward, resting in bed. The more composed chatted amiably with attendants, telling them of their families and work lives. Women could busy themselves stitching sheets and aprons in the hospital's sewing room.[52] The young could jump rope, dance, and sing. Psychiatrists maintained that the institution's lively social regimen—the daily social hours, weekly teas, and dancing classes—contrasted distinctly with the isolation and inactivity of the asylum. Still, some patients complained of having inactivity forced on them. One said that he was "most always locked in the ward," another that "the confinement, the lack of work, and activities, my sedentary life," exacerbated his nervousness.[53]

From the patients' perspective, the hospital was a small world governed by rules and conventions that were both familiar—at least by virtue of the logic that informed them—and strange. Among the former was that as inmates they would be deprived of rights and subjected to privations, much as prisoners were. Familiar with the notion of imprisonment, some patients protested that their hospitalization was nothing less. Those who cast their institutional experience in terms of the patently carceral glossed over some important distinctions between their plight and the prisoner's, not the least of which was that many noninstitutionalized persons thought justice was on their side. But, invoking well-established and resonant antinomies— liberty and restraint, freedom and incarceration—allowed them not only to succinctly sum up their predicament but also to render it comprehensible. "You are not in jail," psychiatrists would challenge a patient who insisted he or she was, adducing as incontrovertible evidence thereof the locked doors and the rattling of keys.[54] So predictable were these exchanges that psychiatrist and patient often spoke as if their parts were scripted.

Many institutional procedures, especially those that took shape in accordance with the principle of visibility, could not be so easily subsumed within the familiar compass of rights and their lack. Such procedures did not so much anger as unsettle patients. It was sometimes difficult to name, even to register, their subtle effects, for next to the grand question of liberty and its lack they appeared trifling. The reading of patients' mail, the regulation of the men's shaves and the women's ironing, the bedside discussions of patients' difficulties conducted without regard to the audience thus created: these were among the "little things" through which psychiatrists expressed their disciplinary vision. Many of the rules that governed institutional life followed straightforwardly from the hospital's stated purpose of diagnosing and treating the mentally disturbed. Although patients often objected to examinations, psychiatrists could at least explain the purposes that informed them. By contrast, the rationale behind the formal and informal conventions, such as the reading of mail, that regulated the most minute and intimate of patients' daily activities was obscure, integral to the psychiatrists' disciplinary program but never explicitly articulated for the patients. Such conventions thus seemed to them especially arbitrary, and in their minds they assumed great—and to psychiatrists, unwarranted—significance. To psychiatrists, for example, the initial, ritualized defrocking was a practical measure, necessary to ensure efficiency and to prevent harm, but to a patient it could signify her changed fortunes. In the words of one patient's worried husband, for example, removing her wedding ring was "like stripping her of her last tie to the world."[55]

Many patients found the lack of privacy the most annoying and baffling aspect of their institutional experience. In the hospital, it seemed, every thought and every action was open to the scrutiny of others. Seasoned patients initiated newcomers into the ways of the hospital with incessant gossip, dissecting the personalities and habits of this or that psychiatrist, spinning scandalous tales about them and other patients, attempting to decipher the meanings of the many mysterious procedures and tests that psychiatrists never adequately explained. Gossip provided information and entertainment, but its ubiquity—"everyone hears what is said," one woman complained, "and it spreads like wild-fire"[56]—was annoying to the diffident. So, too, was the lack of decorum on the wards, which at least one woman thought "a terrible thing." A reclusive thirty-eight-year-old, this woman was shocked her first night in the hospital to see "all sorts of women in dishabille" come into her room, for she had never before seen "women going about in such a half-clad condition."[57] Similarly, an elderly Irish priest thought it "most disgusting and indecent" that an attendant, saying he was following orders, would allow him to use the toilet only with the door open wide.[58] Such offenses against common decency were routine but nonetheless disconcerting to those who entered the hospital expecting to find it a sanctuary from everyday concerns and pressures. The institution instead confronted them with unfamiliar routines and rules, noise and confusion. Patients found it hard to avoid the ravings of the demented, the cries of the depressed, the pacing of the restless, and the repetitive self-reproaches of the desperate. "The atmosphere of the place is so suggestive," Florence Edwards, claiming she was not "over suggestible," told psychiatrists.[59]

In the hospital, patients' words, bodies, even thoughts (if committed to paper) became common property. It was hospital practice to confiscate and scrutinize anything patients wrote, whether it was the note hastily scribbled on a scrap of paper filched from another patient or the lovingly composed missive to one's sweetheart penned on paper doled out by attendants. "Pardon Stationary," Henry Sanders, a paretic sales manager, wrote at the bottom of a long letter, written on small sheets of cheap, lined paper. "We have to swipe it." Patient files are thick with notes, letters, diaries, and other writings, either the originals, which never reached their destination, or copies meticulously transcribed by members of the hospital's clerical staff. Although they were to hand over outgoing mail open, for psychiatrists to censor, it is clear that patients had little idea how many of their letters went straight to their files, "case history" scrawled across the top. "Again another week passed and not a line from the little Girl that I love best," the unwitting Sanders opened a letter to his wife, this, like five others, destined only for his record. There it assumed the status of a damning symptom—"he wrote a letter to his wife which would indicate that at times he had delusions," psychiatrists noted—much like his positive Wassermann test and slight euphoria.[60] Content aside, the mere fact of excessive letter writing could signify mental disturbance; many manic patients, for example, produced thick piles of commentary, much of it unintelligible, on their experiences. The point here is not that psychiatrists' procedures were misguided, but that their ardent scrutiny, which only rarely yielded diagnostically useful information, became an end in itself, a small but significant ceremony of power.

It was difficult for patients to specify, let alone counter, the effects of this sort of disciplinary power. Representing power more conventionally—in juridical terms as punitive, forceful, and visible, exercised from the top down—made it possible for some to formulate strategies of resistance. Strategic submission was one choice. "Be obedient and submissive, and work with the doctors," a mother advised her hospitalized daughter; show self-control and submit "to the rules of the institution," one friend advised another.[61] In their dealings with particularly trying patients, psychiatrists could abandon their disciplinary perspective and dispense advice along similar lines. Instead of arguing with psychiatrists, "you should have catered to their wishes," a psychiatrist purportedly told one patient.[62] This sort of reasoning, however, was predicated on a calculus of right and wrong that psychiatrists, for the most part, did not honor. A middle-aged man sought his release from the institution, for example, emphasizing that he had been "a good patient" who had found the "best way is to keep quiet and try and behave," but to no avail, for the axis along which psychiatrists assessed his behavior was medical, not moral.[63]

Power exercised in a disciplinary mode was more difficult to represent and more difficult to strategize against. In the typical patient's hospital career, the workings of power were first apparent in the perception that it was the other patients who were insane. Any satisfaction patients might have derived from having decided that it was "these others [who] belong in safe-keeping" was invariably fleeting, however, for the commonality of their predicament nurtured uncertainty and, in the more insightful, fostered self-scrutiny.[64] "Of course I am classed amongst those I am placed with," wrote one woman in a supplicatory letter to psychiatrists, neatly expressing one of their guiding precepts.[65] Other patients told of feeling constantly caught off guard, not by anything in particular but by the hospital experience in general. In a few of those most receptive, by temperament or disposition, to the workings of discipline, the hospital experience was strangely salutary. In a juridical vein, they could condemn the hospital's overtly punitive practices, primarily commitment and detention. But they could also testify that the hospital had done them good. George Maguire, who complained as volubly as any, told psychiatrists that a month's rest in the hospital had built him up to the point where he felt "better physically and mentally" than he had in twenty years. A forty-two-year-old machinist who entered the hospital in hopes of "gain[ing] in nerve control" announced he had "gained considerable" and was "satisfied with the results." And an elderly Jewish baker said of his hospital experience: "Another thing it shows to me that with only a little will power I can keep away from tobacco, whiskey, anything I wish." These men—whom psychiatrists had diagnosed respectively as manic, paranoid, and psychoneurotic—represented perfect disciplinary subjects, for under psychiatrists' supervision they had learned to supervise themselves. If only all patients were as welcoming of discipline as was Maguire, who, outwardly resistant but inwardly compliant, proclaimed, "I have made a study of myself for years."[66]

Gendered Discipline

Their eyes trained on the big picture, Psychopathic Hospital psychiatrists managed at a remove, delegating the more literal, less pleasant aspects of handling patients to attendants, men and women (usually but not always referred to as nurses) whose lowly origins and rough behavior constantly threatened to undermine the distinction so carefully drawn between their institution and the asylum. Although psychiatrists could insist that their staff was of higher than average quality, all too often they found themselves engaged, like their predecessors, with the decidedly prosaic question of the help—how to secure, discipline, and retain it. In demonstrating the superiority of their modern methods, they were more dependent on the conduct of the attendants than they could comfortably admit. The prototypical attendant, in the estimation of asylum superintendents and inmates, was at best an uncultivated country boy, at worst a brute, a petty tyrant who daily slaked his thirst for violence by hitting, abusing, and restraining helpless patients. In asylums, "accidents" were rife, and superintendents admitted that overzealous or careless attendants were in most cases responsible. Southard and his colleagues insisted that asylum-type attendants were inadequate to the demands of Psychopathic Hospital work. A higher grade of help was needed.

From the start, however, psychiatrists' complaints concerning the staff echoed those of their asylum counterparts. One year after the hospital opened, Southard gloomily reported that its nursing service, provided by attendants "of asylum type," remained at the "custodial or vigilance" level. In a "stormy" second year of operation, fifty-seven accidents were recorded, leading to "wholesale discharges and unregretted resignations." A thorough reorganization ushered in a new regime. Nine graduate nurses, women who had completed a hospital-based course of study, were hired and a supervisory system to manage the approximately thirty attendants in the hospital's employ was established. Good management and good spirit prevailed until the wartime call to service drained the institution of its more reliable workers.[67] Plans for training courses and the like were shelved. In 1922, a hospital trustee wrote that a decade's worth of earnest planning had resulted in a nursing service as mediocre as ever.[68] The problem of the help, which so concerned asylum superintendents, would prove as insoluble at the Psychopathic Hospital as anywhere else.

Asylum and hospital administrators collectively proposed several strategies to compensate for what one called the "poor material" with which they perforce dealt. "Proper training and discipline" was one solution. The superintendents from across the state who gathered to confer on the issue in 1909 told of employing policies of surveillance and coercion of attendants, arguing that only their own "unremitting watchfulness," "constant supervision," "judicious discipline," and "eternal vigilance" could ensure that patients would be handled properly. One physician cautioned his colleagues that many persons, seeking a laxly supervised, easy job, "will resent disciplinary measures"; they will "object to necessary features of hospital life, trump up trivial complaints, [and] misrepresent the facts regarding their past history." They would use profane language, contributed another; still others added that they would lose their tempers, act dictatorially, and nag patients. Short of securing a better class of employee, the superintendent could, one suggested, make unscheduled visits to the wards, taking a different route each time. He could "instruct and admonish" the troublesome, advised another, and keep a meticulous record of all disciplinary infractions. One superintendent's view that the attendants "should be treated with as much consideration as the patient" unintentionally pointed to the rationale implicit in these disciplinary measures: that the help, in Foucault's words subjected "to the same coercions as the inmates themselves," would learn something of "the art of power relations."[69]

On other occasions, administrators focused their attentions on the carrot of better conditions rather than the stick of relentless discipline. In general, they agreed that the attractions of the position were few. The work was irksome and monotonous; the hours were long (at minimum, sixty hours per week); the food was of poor quality; and the pay was low (for men, in the range of twenty-five dollars monthly, equal to what a teamster or farmhand might earn; for women, five dollars less). Rates of turnover were high; men stayed an average of four months, women six. Living beside their charges in poor accommodations, in many institutions attendants took their meals with patients, spent their evenings with them, and cleaned up after them. Although the superintendents bemoaned the presence of timeservers, they had to admit that most attendants worked not because they were inspired to serve but because they had to. One superintendent's suggestion that his colleagues continually emphasize to attendants that their work was important, dignified, and valued was ignored. Most knew that only the endlessly discussed higher wage could keep attendants from fleeing to other jobs in times of relative prosperity.[70]

Neither carrot nor stick addressed the fundamental issue—that the attendant's job, in practice and as formally defined, was shot through with contradictions. Denied recourse to mechanical restraints, attendants were to manage patients by exercising heroic self-restraint.[71] They were to persuade, not command, to practice forbearance, not humiliation, while their superiors' denigration of their characters and habits denied them the moral authority on which such tactics were premised. They were to be masters of patients one moment, servants the next. Responsible for maintaining order on the wards, they were also obliged to perform a variety of menial tasks. The Psychopathic Hospital employed several maids, but attendants, too, spent their days sweeping hallways, polishing floors, cleaning toilets, making beds, tidying rooms, and seeing to patients' many requests for newspapers, books, and writing paper.[72] Although some patients complained that attendants ignored them, played favorites, told lies, and read the newspapers for which they themselves had paid, the more sociologically inclined took note of the attendants' lowly position in the hospital hierarchy and excused their lapses. They "were as kind as they were allowed to be," wrote a middle-aged man, for "they have to do as they are told." A young woman maintained in a similar vein that "they have a lot to try their patience and have all kinds to deal with."[73]

The attendant's job demanded a mix of strikingly incongruous qualities and behaviors. Patients expected attendants to be polite, solicitous, and even tempered, and complained when they were not.[74] Psychiatrists expected them to be firm, vigilant, and imperturbable, and disciplined them when they acted otherwise. To satisfy both doctor and patient, the attendant needed a psychologist's sensibility, a pugilist's reflexes, a martyr's resolve, and, as many pointed out, a man's strength as well as a woman's patience, tact, and sympathy.[75] It was hospital practice to discharge immediately those who abused patients outright, striking, punching, or kicking them, or those under whose care patients hurt themselves, attempting suicide with knives carelessly left out or by jumping from open windows. But the distinction between proper handling and abuse was ambiguous. In the course of an investigation of an accident in 1916, for example, the attendant John McElroy said that in his opinion the patients were "used very nicely." Yet, he explained, simply getting a recalcitrant patient into his room—not pulling but "just walking him along"—could take a bit of force. He had seen some roughness, but stonewalled his psychiatrist-inquisitor on the particulars, offering only that it happened "at times when a man gets a little too discouraged with a patient—when the patients curse him or anything like that." Yet, he testified, "great violence"—choking and the like—was rare, resorted to only in desperation, for example to keep one patient from hurting another. McElroy's coworker Frank Higgins, asked to define what "very rough" treatment was, explained that "sometimes you have to set patients down to keep them from striking others, and you have to use a little force sometimes." He argued that if disturbed and excited patients were running around, it showed better judgment "to use a little force, not too much, and make them sit down and behave."[76]

Attendants maintained that, for the most part, they did not mind patients calling them names, cursing them, or grabbing them. Although they preferred obedient patients, they claimed to know how to handle those who were not. They distracted the troublesome, busying them with mindless tasks; they subtly coerced the intractable, leading them firmly by the wrists; they meted out small punishments to the deliberately provocative, putting them to bed or surreptitiously roughing them up. Patients who fabricated charges of abuse, like the one who was "always telling the Attendants and nurses they pushed or struck him, and is going to tell his {Lawyer} about the cruel treatment he undergoes," were especially irksome, because psychiatrists usually took the patient's word over the attendant's and fired the latter.[77] It is significant, however, that attendants felt they were at their most violent not when keeping order on the wards but when administering treatments at the behest of psychiatrists—specifically, putting patients in packs. Psychiatrists maintained that the pack—a procedure in which patients were wrapped tightly, mummylike, in water-soaked sheets—was not a restraining device but an enlightened form of treatment.[78] Patients argued otherwise. One woman claimed to have been so tightly wrapped that she was "all in ridges" when the sheets were removed after eight hours; another "could hardly breathe, just pant," and protested that her hands and arms emerged from the sheets "numb and dead and blue."[79] Attendants regularly resorted to force in administering this therapy, leading fearful patients roughly, pinning their hands behind their backs, and holding them down in order to wrap them up. Attendant McElroy's declaration that "putting a patient in a pack" was the "most violent thing" he had done in the hospital stands as a rebuke to the psychiatrists who would class the pack as treatment, not abuse, while daring to impugn his character and credibility.[80]

The point here is not that abuse did not occur, for it did. Various patients reported that they or others had been struck, kicked, or punched, that their hair had been pulled, or that—a more common complaint—attendants had not treated them in, as one put it, "a human way."[81] Others admitted that they had provoked attendants, purposely or not, wrongly accusing them, making nasty remarks, swinging and lunging at them. Two weeks after George Maguire was admitted, for example, he reflected on his conduct, telling psychiatrists "I knew what I was doing." Acting the part of a lunatic, he said, he had come "in with a big noise and it was all a bluff . . . four people had to hold me and I wanted bottles of champagne and glasses of ale, and then I slammed around a few chairs when they did not move fast enough . . . and it took three of them some time and exercise on the floor but I went in and went to bed."[82] Taking stock of his ill-tempered behavior, another man offered his "most sincere apologies" to the nurses who, despite his insults, had gone "about their work with the spirit of a 'Good Samaritan.'"[83] Much of the violence that sporadically punctuated the hospital routine can be traced to the inescapably volatile nature of the give-and-take between attendant and patient, both of whom were enmeshed in webs of disciplinary practices and coercions.

Psychiatrists deplored attendants' rough manners while exploiting them to the full. They saw violence as characterological, not structural, and repeatedly assailed the motivations, integrity, and characters of the men and, to a lesser extent, the women who worked as attendants. They considered them guilty of abuse until proven innocent. They grilled them concerning their workmates' behavior. They faulted their attitudes and gruff manners. And, in 1916, they tested the intelligence of a series of candidates for the position and found barely 60 percent normal, which only seemed to underscore what superintendents had been saying in different words for years—that the ranks of attendants were thick with "defective and otherwise mentally incompetent individuals."[84] Both the patient George Maguire, who observed of the attendants that "here they don't care about the patients, they must get the beds made and clean the floors," and the supervisor L. B. Ricketson, who contended that the attendants did not speak frankly with patients but instead told them "anything to smooth them down for a while," understood better than psychiatrists how constrained attendants were by the formal requirements of the job: on the one hand menial servants, on the other masters by word alone.

Asylum superintendents and hospital psychiatrists, concerned with staffing their institutions, had neither the time nor the desire to confront the many contradictions of the attendant's lot. Instead, they approached the issue obliquely, through the lens of gender, resolving it by proposing simply that male attendants be replaced by women. The administrators' argument, simply put, was that whereas men, by nature brutish and rough, had been well fitted to serve in the prisonlike asylums of the nineteenth century, only women were innately disposed to diligently serve and cheerfully master patients.[85] Naturally skilled in the domestic arts, women kept hospital wards tidier, made rooms more homelike, and saw to the finer details of housekeeping, arranging flowers and making up wrinkle-free beds. As important, they managed not by force but by force of character. In the estimation of one superintendent, a woman's mere presence was enough to put an end to the profanity and racy stories with which male patients habitually entertained themselves. Another agreed, arguing that a woman's soft voice and natural reserve rendered her nursing more effective than that of a man.[86] To the many asylum and hospital administrators vexed by the help problem and concerned with their profession's marginal status, the strategy of replacing men with women was compelling in its simplicity.

It was not without its problems, however. To put women in charge of men, whether patients or fellow attendants, was to upset the supposedly natural order of gender that informed this strategy. Everyone agreed that it was possible, citing as precedent general hospital practice, in which it was standard for head nurses to direct subordinates and report to physicians. In mental hospitals, too, argued proponents of this strategy, women should manage the wards. Male attendants would still be required to bathe and shave male patients, and to meet the occasional emergency, but only the woman placed "in the superior position" by hospital administrators could assuredly exercise her greater natural talents.[87] The prospect of women disciplining men raised the hackles of male workers and patients alike. At McLean Hospital, for example, a private institution just outside the city, psychiatrists appeased the male attendants who saw their female counterparts as impediments to their own authority and prospects for promotion by limiting the women's work on male wards to caring for the linen and entertaining the patients.[88] At the Psychopathic, some male patients, invoking a suppressed dimension of the gender stereotype at work in this discussion, complained of being insulted and annoyed by bossy, loud-mouthed, swaggering women. George Maguire, for example, objected to one nurse's "all the time hen-pecking them poor men," the male attendants, whom she had hard at work "sweeping before breakfast." "Her mouth is going all the time, if I was her husband I would have her in one of these places," he blustered, exercising an imagined patriarchal prerogative.[89]

Sex presented difficulties of a different order. The specter of women intimately tending to men roused visions of sexual anarchy in the more cautious among superintendents. Female nurses would "sexually excite" male patients, they cautioned; they would incite what one referred to as the slumbering passions of the reticent and would, others warned, encourage the indiscretions of the salacious. Those who allied themselves with the hospital ideal demurred, arguing that erotically disposed male patients could simply be isolated from women nurses.[90] Sex between male and female attendants was also a concern; at least one patient, commenting on the behavior of the nighttime staff, remarked that he "would not be surprised to hear of an elopement" of two attendants, one of whom was "a married man."[91] Progressively minded superintendents dismissed this concern as well, proposing that the benefits of hiring the "right kind" of women outweighed the dangers.

When it came to specifying what kind of woman was right, however, proponents of women nurses were divided. Some argued that the nurse, like the physician, was ideally a trained and specialized expert; others that, in effect, "every woman is a nurse."[92] Hospital schools had been graduating nurses of the former sort, specially trained to care for the insane, since the 1880s. Psychopathic Hospital administrators, chiefly Southard and Adler, several times attempted to set up postgraduate courses for nurses, but their efforts were stymied by the war, which stimulated a demand for nurses overseas, and by bureaucratic wrangling over costs and organization between the hospital and the state.[93] Invoking women's "nursing instinct," others maintained that because the essence of nursing was service, not science, disposition was the proper criterion of fitness. Training schools, expensive to operate, were overtraining nurses, they argued, turning out high-grade professionals little interested in performing the housekeeping chores that fell to the asylum-type nurse.[94] Qualities, not qualifications, were needed; good women, sensible, tactful, and resolute, could ably nurse the insane.

"Nurse" was an ambiguous occupational designation. The term usefully but spuriously set the untrained female attendant apart from her male counterparts, allowing institutional administrators to imagine that in hiring more women—who were in any case cheaper—they had resolved the attendant problem. The term's ambiguity could also be exploited to bring the trained nurse down a notch; in times of labor shortage, for example, administrators charged her with doing domestic work alongside her un-trained namesake. However much the trained nurse might insist she was not a mere woman but a woman of science, she would find herself con-stantly cast as the former by the patients who called her "dear" and the physicians who sentimentally summed her up as, in the estimation of one, the embodiment of "all that we mean by the word[s] 'womanly' and 'moth-erly.'"[95] Tactful, patient, sympathetic, adaptable, good-natured, conscien-tious, and given to self-sacrifice: the nurse as woman-mother. Not surpris-ingly, the psychiatrists and superintendents who addressed "the burning question" of the attendant-nurse's gender traded in the most venerable of stereotypes.[96]

Yet they did so with a significant twist. In the context of the help prob-lem, woman signified progress, not, as was usual, backwardness. A politics of class was implicit in this inversion of the usual story, for the man in question here was at the bottom of the occupational hierarchy. Any man worthy of the designation, given the opportunity, would abandon the posi-tion for something better. Even as they decried the lack of satisfactory men, administrators came close to admitting that nursing was no career for a man, for what sort of man would sign up for "life-long employment" in a woman's job? The job offered no prospects for advancement; more impor-tant, only what one called a "nonentity" would submit to the discipline of a woman in charge.[97]

Domesticity arose in any discussion of the problem of the help, unset-tling once again psychiatrists' bid for modernity. Two conflicting institu-tional visions informed this discussion: one, of the asylum as a homelike enclave of privacy, without, in Adolf Meyer's words, the family's "petty and irritating features"; the other of the hospital as a site for the advancement of science.[98] One superintendent's pronouncement, that "people want nurses for acceptable personal service, and do not care so much about a liberal education," was expressive of the first; the commitment of Southard and his colleagues to the education of nurses reflected the second. The character of the nurse came under sustained scrutiny. A woman who worked for a wage and traveled in the semipublic arena of the institution, she was at the same time a mother in uniform, a domestic drudge who tended tirelessly and intimately to the needs of others. In the many discus-sions, articles, and conferences devoted to the nurse question, it was never entirely clear whether she was a woman of superior virtue who needed shielding from the male patients' language and rough manners, or a woman of questionable morals from whom the male patients needed protection. Psychopathic Hospital psychiatrists tried to skirt the issue of the nurse's character by focusing on her qualifications, but the contradictions, which were the contradictions of womanhood itself, would not so easily be resolved. What psychiatrists were seeking, in their advocacy of the female nurse, was harder discipline in a softer voice, a point that Charles Eliot, the president of Harvard, suggested obliquely when speaking, at a hospital-sponsored gathering, of lessons he had learned while convalescing in Ceylon after a serious operation. Eliot observed that women, unlike men, cannot rely on sheer strength to control dangerous and violent patients. Rather, he maintained, they must rule by "personal influence," by exhibiting "the courage that is visibly associated with tenderness and bodily weakness," courage of a sort that men found "peculiarly fascinating." Unintentionally revealing his own inner demons, Eliot's statement speaks to the sexual currents that coursed through institutions that housed both men and women as well as to the peculiar pleasures of discipline—or, at least, of what men could imagine of the pleasures of being subjected to the discipline of tender little women.[99]

Persuasive Discipline

For Psychopathic Hospital psychiatrists, the question of treatment was fraught with difficulties, many of their own making. Treatment was among the diciest aspects of their bold professional program, the issue concerning which they promised the most and delivered the least. On the one hand, they held out the promise of a scientific psychiatry, casting themselves as scientists, arguing that their institution was more akin to the general hospital than the asylum, and, with the paradigm of general paresis in mind, defining mental disorders as mental diseases. On the other hand, they eschewed drugs, which were widely used in other settings and seen by many as synonymous with medical treatment, and instead adopted measures—baths, packs, and talk—that many patients thought were at best unscientific, at worst counterproductive. They abjured the term "cure," preferring the more equivocal "recovery," although, Southard reported, the more eager among them often unthinkingly used it.[100] And they stressed that, contrary to public expectations, their institution was not a "marvellous curatorium," Southard going so far as to suggest that the "semi-public high-priced hospital[s]" that were supposedly so marvellous had carefully selected their patients with an eye to their curability.[101] Not surprisingly, patients entered the hospital expecting that psychiatrists would cure them, aggressively employing efficacious treatments; otherwise, several asked, why were they there? But with respect to treatment as with other matters, psychiatrists were guided as much by the burdens of the past as by the demands of the present, and they decided they could accomplish more by doing less.[102] They set a strict standard for themselves. If restraint—mechanical or chemical—was the mark of the old psychiatry, self-restraint, on the part of attendant and psychiatrist alike, would serve as the guiding principle for the new.

The psychiatrists' stance with regard to drugs is particularly instructive. "Deep-rooted in most human minds," wrote one, was the idea "that for every disease there is some curative drug."[103] Indeed, many patients expected as much, and voiced annoyance that they were, as George Maguire complained, "not given any medicine here."[104] Psychiatrists did administer Salvarsan, a specific, to paretics, but they dispensed the stimulants and depressants in common use at asylums and general hospitals only stingily, to one patient a day on average. In even the best of general hospitals, they charged, overmedication, especially of unruly, delirious persons, was common. In such hospitals, one-quarter of all delirium tremens patients were "discharged dead," their demise hastened by the enormous quantities of drugs they ingested—one woman reportedly received seventy-five doses in three days—and the immobilizing physical restraint to which they were subjected. At the Psychopathic Hospital, where delirious patients were immersed in baths and given only eliminatives to speed the passage of toxic substances through their bodies, the corresponding mortality rate for such patients was near zero. The therapeutic bath was a treatment of at least thirty years' standing, but it drew censure because it was both labor-intensive, a procedure that occupied an attendant for a period of up to eight hours, and, for drunken patients, insufficiently punitive, for during it the patient merely lay motionless in the tub. Southard reported that "hospital men," although aware of their institutions' high mortality rates, voiced skepticism concerning Psychopathic Hospital practices, which he deemed "modern" but which they thought too expensive and, probably, too lax.[105] Psychiatrists held that although the interests of efficiency and order might argue for restraining, drugging, and secluding delirious patients, science was better served by honoring their obstreperousness, allowing them to rave and move about in a controlled setting.

From a professional perspective, however, the parsimonious use of drugs was risky, for it undercut the psychiatrists' contention that they were meeting the mental maladies more aggressively than their do-nothing predecessors. One young cocaine user's challenge to psychiatrists—"I don't see how I have been treated in any way," he said—appears to have unsettled them, for in the course of the ensuing give-and-take they proposed one way after another in which he had been helped, only to have him reject them all. In exasperation, the psychiatrist Harriet Gervais asked him, "What sort of treatment did you expect here?" to which he replied several times that he did not know, finally bursting out, "What are you trying to get out of me?" In this discussion, psychiatrist and patient talked past one another, for he scorned the baths, the trips to the roof garden, and the lectures on changing his ways that she classified as treatment. To him these practices seemed not treatment but at best of no consequence, at worst a form of punishment.[106] Patients tended to conceive of treatment narrowly, using the term to refer to discrete measures and interventions—drugs, baths, special conversations— that they saw as somewhat independent of (and, rightly or wrongly, more efficacious than) much of what they were subjected to daily in the hospital. By contrast, psychiatrists defined treatment broadly to encompass the institutional experience as a whole, from the most general, the conditions on the ward that Southard argued offered patients "a species of schooling or training," to the most specific, the baths, packs, and eliminatives for which they wrote specific orders.[107]

That talk might function as a form of treatment was difficult for patients to comprehend and for psychiatrists to conceptualize. For all their stress on the novelty of baths and packs, it was in their tentative explorations of the power of talk that psychiatrists broke new therapeutic ground. As patients (and later commentators) pointed out, baths and packs were variations on psychiatry's well-established tradition of restraint.[108] Talk was by contrast a relatively new, untheorized form of treatment. Many patients did not recognize it as such. Florence Edwards's response to one psychiatrist's inquiry about whether she felt he and his colleagues were trying to help her expressed sentiments that were likely typical: "I cannot truthfully say that I feel that as yet, because all that you have done with me so far, as you know, has been to question me very closely, which," she concluded, "does not help me."[109] Close questioning, however, was only one among several forms talk assumed. Talk was everywhere in the institution: hectoring, inquisitive, casual, gossiping, confidential, even, at times, what we might recognize as therapeutic.

Psychiatrists, social workers, nurses, and attendants talked to patients in passing, on the ward, and in formal settings, such as the staff meeting and the social work interview. Nurses and attendants, who spent long days with patients, sometimes acted as confessors and amateur therapists. They listened to patients' woes and constantly assessed their moods, dispensing advice and commonsense reassurance. Patients could reject what was offered them, as did an elderly widower, convinced he was soon to die, who brushed aside an attendant's reassurances that he was in no danger by saying, "There is no use to tell me that."[110] But they could also take the assurances to heart, as did a young woman, torn apart by her worries about sex, who was told by a kindly nurse that "if any girl had fallen she could start anew and everything would be all right," unconventional advice that made her feel "much better."[111] Although most of the patient commentary on attendants that has survived is negative, scattered throughout the records is evidence that relations between patients and attendants were not uniformly bad. The reaction of the girl who cried when her favorite nurse left, saying "it was always thus, as soon as she grew fond of someone they were always taken away," was likely singular, but it is clear that patients could feel enough of a connection with attendants, especially women attendants, to confide in them concerning their work lives and family troubles.[112]

Attendants did not probe into patients' affairs; consequently, when patients spoke with them they did so of their own volition. Psychiatrists, by contrast, did probe, in structured encounters that patients found quite trying. Although aware of the new technique of psychoanalysis, Southard and most of his colleagues were skeptical of Freudian claims, considering them fanciful, teleological, and exaggerated. Still, careless of technique, they spoke at length and in private with some patients, encouraging them to review the past for clues to the present. One psychiatrist's four visits, at weekly intervals, to the bedside of twenty-two-year-old Dennis Walsh, an Irish-born bronzer plagued by fears he could not explain, were typical of the unstructured encounters that commonly took place. The psychiatrist listened to Walsh, recorded in ever-greater detail what he said, and refrained from offering advice. It is possible that Walsh, like several other patients, found such talks unsettling, for while at the outset he claimed he was cheerful and much improved, six weeks later he was pouring out his many fears, hallucinations, and delusions to the psychiatrist, who recorded them in painful detail.[113] Thirty-five-year-old Charlotte Page was similarly unsettled, telling psychiatrists at her staff meeting that after talking one-on-one "with the doctor about experiences that happened to me in the past, things that troubled me in the last two years," she felt worse than she had formerly. "It would have been better" had they not talked, she maintained, for "rehearsing it brought back to me the feeling in connection with them." Page assured psychiatrists she had "not read any Freudian literature."[114] To another patient, a clerk in his late twenties who felt like killing himself after every time he met with Myerson, talk was a poor substitute for action. "I feel that not one of them Doctors know anything," he wrote, demanding to know why he was not cured. "Them Doctors Cure men who go around and Lead Sinful Lives with Sinful women," he complained, "they Cure them of Terrible Diseases. . . . Talking dont do me any good."[115]

In the end, however, talk worked its effects even on this recalcitrant man, whose diagnosis psychiatrists recorded as unclassified, but it did so through the medium of the social worker, not the psychiatrist. Where psychiatrists were often abrupt and distracted in their relations with patients, social workers attended closely to the particulars of their lives. They aimed for a professional constancy, meeting patients' rebuffs with renewed solicitude, anger with friendliness, hopelessness with cheer. Although they could not always maintain this stance of strict but concerned neutrality, over the course of months-long supervision they managed to convince a number of their patients that they cared for them. Some patients, the clerk among them, reciprocated with secrets, trust, and the sorts of worries that one might today class as neurotic—How much do you care for me? Why have you taken an interest in me? More common and more problematic when the patient, like the social worker, was a woman, these worries testified to the rudimentarily psychotherapeutic nature of much social work practice.

Psychiatrists had neither the time nor the inclination to foster such therapeutic relationships.[116] Psychotherapy demanded a level of professional self-restraint far beyond what they could muster, a point dramatically underscored by Solomon's declaration in one case that if none of his colleagues objected he was "going to try the bullying method" with a patient, a young hysteric, and made more prosaically by their advocacy in various other cases of arguing patients "out of their resentment," "conversation[s] of a persuasive nature," influence "along some 'big brother' or ecclesiastical line," and "re-education and strict discipline."[117] When psychiatrists used the term *psychotherapy*, they usually meant by it persuasive talk, from what Southard and Jarrett called the "simple 'Cheer up' or 'Forget it' kind" to the more subtle sorts that worked by means of suggestion.[118] Although prepared to engage only in the former but not the latter, psychiatrists were at the same time unwilling to cede the field of psychotherapy entirely to social workers. Surveying this uncharted professional turf, Southard and Jarrett struck a bargain, writing that neither the psychiatrist, with his faith in his "arm-chair methods," nor the social worker, disposed to see deepset social problems, would have the last word. Principles of psychotherapy, they both agreed, were in flux.

Psychiatrists skirted the professional issues at stake here by hiring a Freudian psychologist, L. Eugene Emerson, to conduct psychotherapy. Although, Southard reported, Emerson's assumption that "Freudism" was "a solid doctrine" provoked some amusement, he and his colleagues had had to put aside their reservations, for no one could dispute "that an extremely severe case of hysterical paralysis has recovered under his ministrations."[119] Emerson was among the earliest practitioners of Freudian analysis in the United States. A native of Maine, he was graduated from Harvard College and, influenced by the work of William James, went on to earn a Harvard Ph.D. in philosophy in 1909. After a brief stint in Ann Arbor, where he saw his first clinical patients, Emerson returned to Boston, first to the Massachusetts General Hospital, then, in 1912, to the Psychopathic Hospital.[120] There he had his own office, where he saw a number of hospital patients for analyses.

"Psychoanalysis is just *beginning* to be respectable," Emerson maintained in an address to his fellow psychoanalysts the following year.[121] Among his hospital colleagues, he felt it necessary, on occasion, to explain why his psychoanalytic endeavors ought to be tolerated. The intensely secret nature of his dealings with patients—"I cannot do it in conjunction with anybody else who is observing it, observing it auditorily, at any rate," he commented—aroused their suspicions, for it contrasted sharply with the public character of their own dealings.[122] And the indulgence he displayed in listening to patients' long, fantastic tales rather than judging them poor stuff or their strange symptoms "a matter of will" also puzzled and irritated some members of the hospital staff.[123] Still, despite his and his specialty's only qualified acceptance, Emerson was allowed a good deal of latitude in shaping the nature of his practice. He had his pick of the hospital's patients, and he treated them without charge for as long as he thought necessary. He attempted, with mixed success, to subject sixteen persons to psychoanalysis in his first six months at the hospital, but he thought only four of these merited intensive treatment. All four were women who manifested hysterical symptoms of varying severity; he judged two of them recovered.[124] Explaining to his colleagues why he chose to treat cases of hysteria, a relatively uncommon malady, rather than, say, dementia praecox, which afflicted a quarter of all patients, Emerson contended that while the former responded to questions "to a certain degree as normal people do," the latter were "covered with a shell of resistance that I never touch." Such patients were unsuitable candidates for psychoanalysis, for they evinced no personal reactions and offered the doctor only "words and answers." He could "not lay a finger upon" them, he explained: "I could not bring them into proper relationship."[125]

"A case you are interested in is a case that you can make well"—so Southard summed up Emerson's criterion of therapeutic suitability. Emerson objected to the director's choice of the word "make," preferring instead "assist" and going on to explain that he tried to help patients reorganize "certain of their psychic material so that they can take hold of life again and meet it." Had he been less skeptical of Emerson's enterprise, Southard might have seen in his demurrals echoes of more orthodox thinking on dementia praecox—the psychiatrist's intuitive "praecox feeling," for example. In truth, Southard's taunting statement was directed as much at his medical colleagues as it was at Emerson, for it expressed a sentiment that psychiatrists both silently adhered to and more openly struggled against. In another context, Southard scorned those hospital physicians who would object to psychiatrists lavishing attention and care on drunken, delirious patients, while arguing that such patients were "unworthy persons to start with and liable to immediate relapse." Apart from the "moral intolerability" of this position, its scientific shortsightedness drew his ire. "Even if these patients were as comparatively worthless as so many apes," he wrote, treating them in line with principles advanced the interests of science, generating information that might be used in handling "more worthy subjects."[126] Southard was here suggesting that it was the psychiatrist's duty to serve science, not conventional morality. It was only natural that the psychiatrist or psychologist should prefer patients he could cure, patients with whom he could feel some connection. Given the state of psychiatric knowledge, however, this was an unattainable luxury.

The "talking cure," or what Southard insisted on calling "persuasive psychotherapy," in time would be classed among the "medical measures" central to the psychiatrist's armamentarium.[127] Southard's designation, strange to our ears, aptly characterized Psychopathic Hospital practice, in which persuasion predominated over psychotherapy, Emerson's novel efforts notwithstanding. Indeed, having consigned mechanical and chemical restraint to their discipline's past, psychiatrists were left with little else but persuasion. Especially in cases that were "almost entirely disciplinary," they—or their deputies, the attendants—wielded it firmly, compelling patients to do what they did not want to do.[128] It was the psychiatrists' hope, however, that "by appealing to the reason" innate to patients who were troubled, alcoholic, or psychopathic but not insane, patients might become their own and others' persuaders. In instances of intrapsychic difficulty, where patients' problems were neither material nor medical but "sexual or related to personal ambition," the psychiatrist's role was limited to helping them solve the problem, by means of "intimate examination" that verged on the confessional.[129] In instances of "self-inflicted disease," where exhortations and punishments had failed, self-supervision and mutual supervision might succeed. Coercions would fade away as patients, seeing "the true state of their affairs," decided "to cure themselves" by means of endless "talk[ing] it over among themselves" and meetings with psychiatrists and their fellow sufferers.[130] The psychiatrists' goal was not so much to cure—for they knew that in many cases they could not—as it was to instill in patients a desire for self-control, a desire to discipline themselves. If this much could be accomplished, the psychiatrist, freed from the punitive, supervisory role that his predecessors had filled, could turn his attention to science.

1. E. E. Southard, director of the
Boston Psychopathic Hospital.

2. Mary C. Jarrett, director
of the social service, Boston
Psychopathic Hospital.

3. Boston Psychopathic Hospital medical staff, 1918. From left: Richard H. Price, Karl A. Menninger, Abraham Myerson, James V. May, Annette M. McIntire, E. E. Southard, Esther S. B. Woodward, Lawson G. Lowrey, Edwin R. Smith, Clifford G. Rounsefell.

4. Boston Psychopathic Hospital social service, 1916. Jarrett is at front left;
Maida H. Solomon, rear middle; and Helen Anderson, rear right.

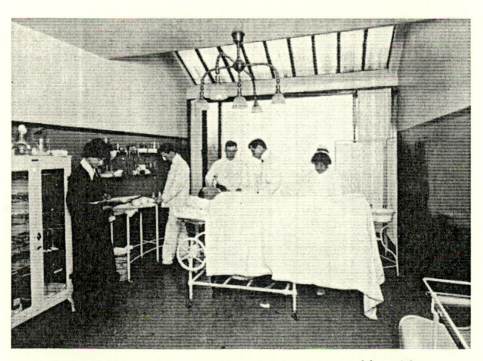

5. Treating neurosyphilis, 1916. Harry C. Solomon is second from right;
Maida H. Solomon is at left, in her words, "checking the follow-up."

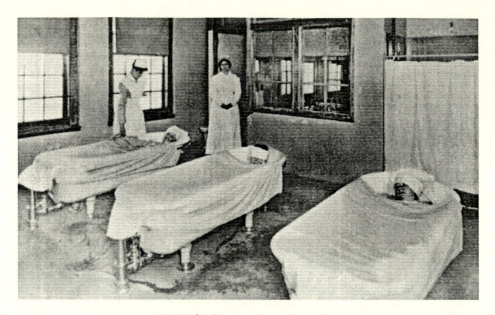

6. Hydrotherapy, women's ward.

7. The daily staff meeting, during which psychiatrists questioned and diagnosed patients. Southard presides; Maida H. Solomon is at right front.

8. The laboratory.

9. Social worker interviewing a relative of a patient, circa 1916.

10. Social worker Helen Anderson with a family.

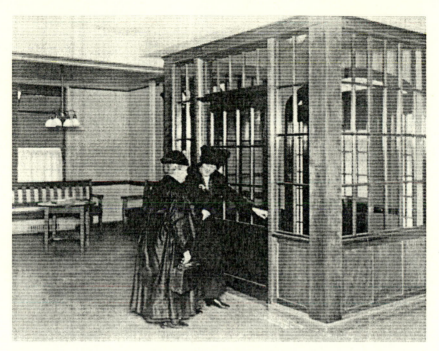

11. Going home, circa 1914.

12. Social worker handing slip with date of next appointment to patient, circa 1916. Note the telephone and the two sets of files.

13. Meeting of the Men's Club for discharged patients with
alcohol-related diagnoses.

PART THREE

PSYCHOPATHOLOGIES OF

EVERYDAY LIFE

SEVEN

WOMAN AS HYPERSEXUAL

THE HYPERSEXUAL FEMALE, the willfully passionate woman who could not control her desire for sexual pleasure, quickly emerged as a central player in Psychopathic Hospital psychiatrists' drama of the everyday. Attractive, high-spirited, and in many respects "perfectly normal," this woman was in fact a psychopath, psychiatrists insisted, a grave but unrecognized threat to the social order. The stock psychopath of the psychiatric literature was a man, his characterological and vocational failings manifest in behaviors ranging from the kiting of checks to the fomenting of revolution. The psychopaths who actually came to psychiatrists' attention were, by contrast, overwhelmingly female, their telltale deficiencies narrowly sexual. Psychiatrists first outlined a specifically female psychopathy around the enticing but much-maligned figure of the prostitute, who in the nineteenth century had embodied all that was base in woman's nature, but few actual prostitutes came under their scrutiny. In practice they elaborated the category's particulars in confrontations with a panoply of lesser offenders against prevailing conceptions of proper womanly deportment: juvenile delinquents (most of whom were labeled so on account of immoral behavior), sexually assertive young women, and defiantly single women in their twenties and thirties. Some of them young and impulsive, others self-styled "New Women," these putative psychopaths were united, in psychiatrists' eyes, not only by their immorality but also by their near-normality. Both drew psychiatrists' interest.

Although Psychopathic Hospital psychiatrists diagnosed a mere 5 percent of all patients psychopathic, none of the many rubrics they deployed in their program to bring aspects of everyday life into science was as emblematic of the new psychiatry (or as internally contested) as female psychopathy. It was, in their hands, a wholly metric category, signifying deviation from an ill-defined normality that they claimed to be able to recognize—as one said, "I know that the girl is not normal"—but that they could not consistently specify.[1] It encapsulated a culturally resonant narrative of decline—of women, newly freed from familial obligations, corrupting innocent men and compromising the city's morality—that they construed as license to enter a discussion, in which sociologists, social workers, and criminologists were already engaged, concerning the nature and future of womanhood. And in it, the many items on their domestic agenda, from the hypocrisy of Victorianism to the family's failures, found equivocal expression. In short, psychopathy, in Lawson Lowrey's estimation an "enormously interesting field," brought the psychiatrist precisely where he wanted to be, "nearer to everyday life."[2]

Although psychiatrists exploited the opportunities this privileged position presented, they also succumbed to some of its dangers. Brandishing the threat of the hypersexual psychopath, they proclaimed themselves arbiters of rapidly changing sexual mores. Confronted by an apparent revolution in sexual behavior among the youth of the working class, psychiatrists, like other social investigators, constructed the issue in highly gendered terms as one of female immorality, ascribing the lax sexual etiquette of the time to the deterioration of women's standards and exempting men from blame. Adding a medical gloss to what was becoming a well-established line of argument, psychiatrists explained that hypersexual women, constitutionally unable to restrain their boundless sexual desires, were to blame for slack sexual mores. That families, police, and social workers were bringing immoral young women to their attention, seeking their explanations and remedies, enhanced psychiatrists' sense of self-importance and suggested to them how pivotal a role they might play in the regulation of everyday concerns.

At the same time, however, presented with patients who manifested none of the usual symptoms of mental disease, who were in their collective estimation attractive, pleasant, and even alluring, psychiatrists found themselves constantly struggling to keep the diagnostic entity of psychopathy clearly in view. Even as they diagnosed one woman after another psychopathic, they conceded that the term might refer to a conduct disorder, not a disease, and among themselves they voiced grave doubts concerning its ontological status. Still, on territory as fraught with sex and laden with power as this, they were unwilling to allow women, whether patients or social workers, the upper hand by admitting to uncertainty. Standing on new disciplinary terrain, bereft of the authority conferred by tradition, the psychiatrist's own subjectivity—his desires, his identity as a man—sometimes came to the fore, and he could issue statements that drew more on his own everyday experience as a gendered being than on any theoretical position he might have advanced in other contexts. Perhaps aware of this, one of the hospital's psychiatrists attempted to shore up the boundary between science and life, psychiatrist and patient, relating the tale of a lively young psychopath who was given to prattling on about the "double moral standard, duties of a wife, obligations of motherhood, venereal disease," and so on. The psychiatrist commended her for evincing interest in such topics, but faulted her for speaking "as though dealing with a detached problem such as philosophy or politics," the scientist's domain, "rather than something quite vitally personal."[3]

For all their posturing concerning the dimensions of the psychopathic threat, psychiatrists equivocated when others presented them the opportunity of doing something to counter it. They knew they had no remedies for the condition, and, arguing that psychopaths were too normal to be committed long-term to psychiatric institutions, they willingly ceded supervision of the women they diagnosed to hospital and state social workers, who were far more censorious of the young women's behaviors than were they.[4] Any satisfactions psychiatrists might have derived from conferring this sexually and morally charged diagnosis were undercut by recurrent doubts concerning its applicability, even its existence. In consequence, the diagnosis was important to psychiatrists less for any control it brought them than for the discursive field they were able to define around it. Here, they could with justification question young women on their sexual activities and desires, passions and proclivities. Holding up the psychopath as case in point, they could declaim authoritatively on the normality and abnormality of behaviors and issues that were the focus of popular debate, bringing the behaviors into their science and themselves into the ongoing discussion.

The Gender Politics of Adolescence

Early-twentieth-century psychiatrists argued that the sexual natures and needs of young women and men differed fundamentally. A woman, they held, was by nature wholly sexual, her life colored by barely controllable sexual impulses that surfaced in adolescence. Adolescence was a time of rapid physical and mental growth, of strong, conflicting emotions and stress for both sexes; if difficult for boys, it was treacherous for girls. Subject to the caprice of her developing physique, a growing girl was ever in danger of straying from the narrow path of respectability into promiscuity; indeed, the slightest sign of interest in boys or sex might set her on the road to ruin. The growing boy's course was less hazardous. Not burdened like a girl by the efflorescence of strong sexual impulses, he could celebrate their acquisition with ardor and evoke only the amused tolerance of psychiatrists; the curiosity, experimentation, and satiation of desire that were symptomatic of gross defect in a girl they interpreted as the commendable manifestations of the boy's natural drive for self-expression and mastery. Psychiatrists held that social convention, which tolerated and even encouraged the fulfillment of male desire, only mirrored the immutable dictates of human nature. For a girl it was "once soiled, forever spoiled," but a boy could "sow an unusually large crop of wild oats," straighten up, and become a good citizen thereafter. Psychiatrists agreed that men, unlike women, could weather a phase of intense sexual activity without breaking down under it; indeed, on the authority of experience they observed that such activity "was quite common among the freshmen and sophomores at college." Among men, they maintained, "a separate standard of moral and sexual life" could and did prevail.[5]

Psychiatrists positioned themselves as pragmatic moderns here, for the double standard that they were championing, in its recognition of female desire, differed from its previous Victorian incarnation. Middle-class Victorian sexual ideology had set the passionlessness of women against the lustfulness of men, elevating the former and excusing the latter, tacitly tolerating prostitution as a necessary social evil.[6] Alhough they paid a high price in their renunciation of passion, middle-class Victorian women managed to turn this ideology to their advantage; trapped in a society that offered them little outside marriage, they fell back on their supposed passionlessness to gain a measure of control over sexual relations with their husbands and thus over the timing and number of their pregnancies.[7] Progressive psychiatrists, as they ceded some ground to women by recognizing their capacity for passion, stripped away from them the protections this ideology had offered. They not only overturned sexual Victorianism, but also reversed its equation of desire, casting women as sexual predators, men as sexual victims. If women wanted passion, they would give it to them with a vengeance.

Psychiatrists' recasting of the Victorian sexual drama is most starkly evident in their elaboration of the category of the hypersexual. Hypersexuality, like its elusive counterpoint, normal sexuality, first became apparent in adolescence. It was then that, according to psychiatrists, overdeveloped girls, who prematurely developed the womanly contours—the enlarged "hips and bust, and general rounding of the figure"—that so enfeebled male resolve, first began to be seen as a real social menace.[8] Upstanding men were thought to be unable to resist these young women. As psychiatrists and social workers related it, particularly attractive young women seduced many a hapless man over telephone lines, in automobiles, on public conveyances, and even in church; young temptresses led countless sailors astray. The city's abundant public places teemed with hypersexuals, ready to lure unsuspecting men into questionable establishments, to hire rooms for immoral purposes, to plague men with the demands of their insatiable immorality.

Psychiatrists elaborated this theory of female desire as they confronted the sexual mores of a generation of working-class "New Women." These women—"a new generation of women," in the characterization of one of them—were born between 1890 and 1905.[9] They were among the first to achieve for themselves some freedom from family obligations and some freedom to earn and spend and to associate with whom they pleased—all freedoms now seen as the prerogatives of late adolescence. Experts on juveniles, the psychologist G. Stanley Hall and the physician William

Healy foremost among them, had only recently delineated adolescence as a socially and biologically constructed interlude between childhood and adulthood. Working-class boys, however, had been enjoying the privileges of adolescence for decades. For them, adolescence was a time to taste the pleasures of adulthood—independence, mastery, sexuality—without having to assume all its burdens. Parents who loosed boys from the bonds of the family economy as soon as they entered the workplace, together with juvenile authorities who tolerated the lapses of boys who went too far— who smoke, drank, or associated with "fast" companions—on the conviction that they could later go straight, smoothed the way for widespread acceptance of adolescent boyhood as an admittedly difficult but indisputably normal stage of life.[10] Adolescent girlhood was, by contrast, nearly unthinkable, the very phrase so oxymoronic in its coupling of the female sex with what was essentially male that expert commentators could barely imagine its contours. Female adolescence appears only fitfully in Hall's works, the psychologist on the one hand arguing that women were by nature forever adolescent—dependent, childish, without ambition—and on the other advocating, in prose thick with sexual innuendo, that they forever teeter on the brink of knowledge and sexual maturity. In many other works, including Healy's, considerations of what might have been the pleasures of adolescent girlhood—growing independence, pride in a maturing body—are so conflated with the problem of juvenile delinquency as to make them one and the same; indeed, the girl who sought the independence that was a boy's by birthright was by her very desire delinquent. As parents and juvenile authorities conceived it, the years of a girl's life that corresponded to those of the boy's adolescence were filled with danger, not possibility. They were years in which she was to submerge, rather than free, her yearnings for independence, years in which she was to reconcile herself to her dependence on men and the inevitability of marriage. They were years best avoided altogether; ideally, a girl would progress from childhood directly to the exalted state of motherhood.[11]

These young women of the early twentieth century were the first to live in large numbers on their own in cities. They challenged, if only for a few precious years, the familiar, patriarchal paradigm that saw them moving from their fathers' to their husbands' homes. The rapid entrance of young women into the urban work force—into the new pink-collar clerical occupations; into factory work like candy making, in which they had long predominated; and, to a lesser extent, into occupations like printing that had been the exclusive preserve of men—provided the context in which some of them staked their claim to a rightful adolescence. Living alone or in boardinghouses with others like themselves, working for meager wages, skimping on food to buy the fine clothing that conferred status and an air of sophistication, these young women, many of them country-bred, chose to participate fully in the life of the city. With little cash, without family obligations, and with few concerns for the future, they worked by day and pursued pleasure by night in the exciting world of commercial amusements —movies, dance halls, and theaters—that was just appearing on the urban scene. In these public, anonymous establishments, young women and their men, as they carried on the courtships formerly overseen by watchful parental and neighborly eyes, rewrote the code that governed their mutual relations. This code had long sanctioned sexual play—passionate kissing, petting, even intercourse—between young women and men who intended to marry.[12] After the turn of the century, some young women sought, with varying degrees of self-consciousness, to engage in the same sorts of intimacies with men they had no intention of marrying.

Participating in the sexual sphere was no easy task. With no construction of respectability available to her, the working girl struggling to define a morality that would enable her to do more than sit alone in her room at night was frustrated at every turn by the seemingly timeless equation of the working girl and the prostitute. Codified in countless late-nineteenth- and early-twentieth-century investigations that found her virtue wanting, this equation was assuming new and damning resonances as reformers campaigning to eradicate the necessary evil once and for all transformed the prostitute from a pitiable yet redeemable fallen woman into a hardened predator, a spreader of vicious disease.[13] It was also an equation to whose strictures she might be subject in her day-to-day dealings with men. Too often the working girl was taken for an easy mark, complained one woman who, because she had worn silk stockings to work one day, had been taunted by her male workmates. Surely only a kept woman could afford such luxuries, they teased. "No one has anything on me," she shot back.[14]

The working girl seeking a good time and respectability was frustrated, too, by the restrictions of poverty. Many girls worked long hours to earn between six and eight dollars a week, barely enough to cover room, board, and carfare. To participate in the social scene, some of them who claimed respectable status—who did not, that is, consider themselves prostitutes— chose to bargain with sexual favors, ranging from flirtation to sexual intercourse, exchanged for men's "treats" to entertainments. Others thought such exchanges unworthy of a self-respecting young woman. Yet the urban working-class view of sex as a commodity shaped the heterosexual relations of even those working girls who thought "treating" beneath them.[15] The woman who did not want to give herself to a man knew she must refuse any favors or money he might proffer; as one woman, pregnant, out of work, and desperate, explained, "I never approved of taking money from men. It places you in their obligations."[16] The nature of those obligations was understood by all; they were nakedly manifest in the many cases where men paid women one or two dollars in exchange for intercourse. The implicit bargain that structured such exchanges—that sex came at a price, for men as well as for women—allowed women some leverage in their dealings with the opposite sex, enabling them to extract something of value in return for their favors. But the bargain also put the working girl at a disadvantage in her relations with men, for men knew women had little in the way of capital besides sex and taunted them with this knowledge. As one young woman, desperate for money, told hospital social workers: "Time and time again I have had chances to go astray, large sums of money and flattering remarks." As an example she offered the fellow who wanted to give her fifteen dollars "to go to a room with him, but I told him money could not buy me, he had the wrong girl." She continued: "Then he asked me, 'would I go as a gift,' and I said no and not for charity either."[17]

If sex, or its promise, was the working girl's capital, to middle-class eyes it was capital she too readily squandered. It is hardly surprising that middle-class observers of the working-class sexual economy saw girls' behavior as promiscuous. Nor is it surprising that they focused on the dangers to which the young working woman was daily exposed: On her own in the anonymous metropolis, bereft of male protection, underpaid and overworked, the working girl was easy prey for male seducers, schemers, and white slavers. There was much that was true in this construction. Among the women who came to psychiatrists' attention were several who told of having been subjected to exploitation at the hands of dishonest men. At least one was raped, by a man claiming to be an employment agent, as she looked for work in the city, and women regularly complained of having to rebuff unwanted advances.

Yet the psychiatrists, hospital social workers, and state visitors who examined these young women absolved men of blame, casting women as the predators in the stories of sexual danger they spun. Why did the sexual prowess of the young woman on her own assume such mythic proportions in their eyes? When state visitors reported that young women hauled men through windows, waylaid grocery boys, and tried to force unwilling, respectable young men "to sexual connection," they may have been reporting the facts. It is more likely, however, that attraction, seduction, and conquest were reciprocal, if not, as some young women insisted, solely the work of men. The evolving conventions of working-class courtship celebrated easy familiarity between the sexes on the streets and in theaters and dance halls. The sexual behavior of working-class men was of little concern to social workers, who saw that women bore the untoward consequences of their new sexual freedom. Ignorant of any means of birth control other than abortion (to which some of them claimed to have resorted), women faced the prospect of pregnancy with each encounter. Additionally, a man, free of the constraints of custom, family, and neighborhood, might renege on his promises, explicit or not, to support or marry a woman he impregnated. As one pregnant twenty-one-year-old domestic servant, abandoned by the man she had hoped would marry her, put it: "It is pretty mean of a fellow to get a girl into trouble and not to stand by her." Her only recourse her vow "to make it hard for him," uttered "rather vindictively" in the estimation of a hospital social worker, this woman's predicament pointedly illustrates that the turn-of-the-century revolution in sexual mores rendered women, in many cases, vulnerable to new forms of exploitation.[18]

Still, this concern for young women's vulnerability does not fully explain why psychiatrists and social workers blamed girls, not boys; women, not men. Nor does it explain why they cast the problem in terms of the "uncontrolled sex impulses" of one sex and not the other.[19] Psychiatrists claimed to understand the girl from a bad home who got into trouble. Her upbringing poor and her material pleasures few, this girl—the "classic delinquent," to their minds—traded favors for money. Material need, not passion, motivated her. Most likely, they hypothesized, she felt no passion at all, like the sexually active young woman whom psychiatrists judged merely delinquent, not psychopathic, because, as she told them, she was "entirely without sexual feeling." By contrast, psychiatrists were at a loss to explain the woman who did not receive money in exchange for her favors, who was "attracted to such acts by sexual passion alone."[20] As psychiatrists and social workers understood it, men were expected to seek sexual pleasure; indeed, a man's failure to do so might earn him the designation psychopathic. It was, on the other hand, unseemly but increasingly all too common for a woman forthrightly to pursue sexual fulfillment. Women, according to conventional wisdom, properly relied on intrigue and feminine wiles to attain their ends; men followed a "direct and open procedure."[21] It was expected that women would be sly and devious, that they would seduce and tease. A woman who openly avowed passion, who could observe of her sexual exploits, like one putative psychopath, that "life is too short to worry. If you don't enjoy this life you might as well be dead," was, in psychiatrists' eyes, inexplicable, altogether without moral sensibility.[22]

The psychopath's forthright sexuality was the most visible and disturbing manifestation of the social autonomy that drew psychiatric censure. The right to seek sexual fulfillment was only the most salient of male prerogatives she assumed. She wanted the freedom to earn and spend, like a man, free of supervision; she wanted to enjoy the pleasures of the city without having her character impugned; she wanted to make her own choices and live independently. Her independence of what many held were the proper and fitting constraints of family and home was nearly as troubling to middle-class professionals as her hypersexuality. Many putative hypersexuals had nothing to do with their families. Employed in factories or as domestic servants, they enjoyed a freedom from adult supervision that, many social commentators agreed, was the source of their troubles. Others, in their twenties or thirties, eschewed marriage and chose instead to work and to live singly or with other women. To be sure, some of the young women whom psychiatrists diagnosed psychopathic looked forward to becoming respectable wives and mothers. One unmarried mother, for example, told psychiatrists she was "not worried about the morality of her act as many other young women have gotten into the same trouble and they have turned out alright and later established good homes."[23] But others rejected the conventional female life pattern that saw a woman passing from her father to her husband.

The concern over female autonomy implicit in the category of hypersexuality helps explain why psychiatrists considered a woman's failure to engage in heterosexual courtship—whether expressed as simple lack of interest or as overtly lesbian behavior—just as psychopathic as too vigorous an exercise of her seductive powers. The "spark of womanliness," for example, glowed "but feebly" in the prattling psychopath described above. So deficient was she in "ordinary feminine charm and appeal," wrote her chronicler, that "it would be difficult to imagine . . . even the most accomplished Lothario successfully drawing her into a flirtation or being able to keep a sustained interest in the pursuit."[24] A more explicit rejection of heterosexuality, like that of a woman who lived with a female companion and questioned the institution of marriage, could mark a woman psychopathic as well. One twenty-year-old, who claimed she had "never cared for boys" and had "never had anything to do with them," informed psychiatrists she did not intend to marry. Asked to account for this, she explained: "You don't know what you are getting into. It is just as well to live single and be happy. From what I have seen, they don't always get along in marriage."[25] Twenty-eight-year-old Rose Butler, too, preferred what she called "single blessedness." She did not lack offers; indeed, it seemed to her that men were "like flies around a sugar bowl, when they see a girl." A psychiatrist confronted her: "On the whole you have not much use for men?" She replied: "As much as I have for women." Butler turned the tables on psychiatrists, asserting that "Adam made woman sin. They say it was Eve who gave him the apple, but he did not have to bite into it."[26]

The psychopath's disturbing assumption of male prerogative was carried to its extreme in the case of Julia Brown, alias Alfred Mansfield, a lesbian cross-dresser who for twelve years before she came to psychiatric attention had lived as a man—smoking a pipe, drinking whiskey regularly, sporting men's suits, working as a printer, and, most puzzling to psychiatrists, escorting young women to dances, suppers, and shows. Brown said she had originally adopted male attire expecting "to find it easier to get work and better pay as a man." But she admitted to hospital social workers she had "always enjoyed the company of girls more than that of men," telling them that she had flirted with young women just as her male associates had. To their puzzled query as to how she avoided the problem of matrimony, she voiced their worst fears, averring that "all women cared for was a good time, they did not want to get married."[27] The sexual activities of these women who refused to seduce men was of little interest to psychiatrists, who focused instead on their gender-inappropriate independence. Before the mid-twenties, psychiatrists focused on the lesbian's supposed masculinity, not her choice of sexual object; the lesbian's refusal to court men, not her preference for women, marked her as a sexual deviant.

A Psychiatric Diagnosis for Immorality

It was in this context of growing concern over female independence and sexual deviance that psychiatrists settled on psychopathic personality as an explanation for female immorality. Many correctional and psychiatric experts had assumed that defective intelligence would prove responsible for immorality. Psychiatrists first considered a diagnosis of feebleminded, which could be established with certainty and precision, when faced with immoral behavior, and reformers cited feeblemindedness as the cause of prostitution until it became clear that the mental tests that were to have proven prostitutes defective instead demonstrated they were normal. Many sexual delinquents, like prostitutes, scored too high on mental tests to be diagnosed feebleminded, and they rarely manifested any of the usual signs of mental disease.[28] Psychiatrists observed that in contrast to the many feebleminded persons they saw, most of the girls they considered psychopathic "rate very high from the intellectual point of view."[29] But if immoral women were too intelligent to be feebleminded, psychiatrists still considered them too defective to be normal, maintaining that they belonged to a group of subnormal individuals that intelligence tests could not identify. The diagnosis of psychopathic personality satisfied, at least for a time, their search for a medical diagnosis for immorality.

The women whom Psychopathic Hospital psychiatrists diagnosed as psychopaths were overwhelmingly young (75 percent were younger than twenty-one), single, native-born whites. Half were Protestant, a third were Catholic, and the rest were Jewish. Although a few worked at middle-class occupations, such as teaching or office work, most, if employed at all, worked in factories or as domestic servants. Families, police, or courts committed half of them to the hospital for a variety of reasons; state social workers, also known as visitors, committed the rest.

Twenty-two-year-old Lillian Turner's background, sexual behavior, and path to the hospital were similar to those of the many young women committed to the hospital by families or courts. Turner lived on her own in a home for young working women. Her ties to her family had long been severed; at the age of ten she had come under the care of the city as a neglected child. Court workers placed her with a woman who, she told the psychiatrist who questioned her upon her arrival at the hospital, "looked after her very carefully and would not allow young men to call on her regularly." When she turned eighteen, Turner began living on her own, working as a waitress and "discouraging advances from young men for fear they might lead her into temptations." Within the year, however, she fell in love with a man she judged honorable and twice agreed to what she called "illicit relations" with him. Finding herself pregnant, she considered his proposal of marriage. But she discovered he drank and, she told the psychiatrist, she "preferred the alternative of living single and fighting out her own battle rather than being the wife of a drunkard." Turner entered a home for expectant single women; one month after her boy's birth the matron of the home had her committed to the hospital to determine whether she was capable of caring for him. Having made inquiries of her associates, hospital social workers made note of her several "redeeming qualities," but they concluded that her reputation was less than exemplary. As evidence, they detailed the seamy character of her "relations with men": at her previous lodgings she had been accused of entertaining men in her room at night; she "went often to dances and came home very late"; one man told them that she "could make up to men quicker than any girl he ever knew"; and, they recorded portentously, "it is said she was discharged from one restaurant for underchecking accounts to men."[30]

Turner was a single working woman who adhered to a standard of sexual morality that many working-class women and men lived by, a standard that sanctioned sexual relations between those who intended to marry. Her only mistake—the only evidence of her hypersexuality, for she told psychiatrists that she had "no sexual inclinations apart from this young man"— lay in her withdrawal from the impending compact. Many of the other women committed to the hospital by their families, police, or courts had, like Turner, long been on their own. Some had run away from intolerable family situations, others had been orphaned, and still others, in their late twenties and early thirties, had chosen not to marry. Many lived in boardinghouses; in some cases the matrons of these homes, observing behavior they judged either bizarre or promiscuous, petitioned to have the women committed to the hospital. The failed suicide attempts of lonely and despondent young women brought a few others under psychiatrists' scrutiny; family members, deeming the behavior of a daughter or sister inappropriate, committed still more.

The other young women diagnosed as psychopathic were "state

charges" sent to the hospital for observation. Courts had already found these girls delinquent, primarily on the basis of their sexual behavior, and had committed them to the State Industrial School at Lancaster. Many of their parents, underemployed and alcoholic, burdened with large families they could barely support (many of these girls had six or seven siblings), had originally petitioned for their commitment, claiming that they could not control the girls. The mothers typically complained that their daughters went with undesirable companions, were on the streets at all hours, had immoral relations with boys, and in general ran wild. Some of this behavior, like taking to the streets, was a form of protest against overly strict parental control. Many widowed fathers, for example, expected their young daughters to keep house for them, prepare their meals, and wait on them as their wives had. Many mothers expected their daughters would perform heavy household labor—laundry, scrubbing, cleaning—as well as care for younger siblings. Some of it, too, was textbook delinquent behavior; more than a few girls had consented to intercourse in exchange for various sums of cash, ranging from twenty-five cents for sex among the barrels at a beach resort to fifteen dollars—a substantial sum—for six episodes in a cheap hotel. But the relatively innocuous driving in automobiles with immoral persons; the frequenting of poolrooms, dance halls, and saloons; the carousing with evil-minded girls and boys; and the casual sexual play that figured so prominently in parental and professional accounts of girls gone wrong point to the larger battle being waged between parents and daughters, between middle-class professionals and working-class girls, over the nature of working-class adolescent girlhood. Could a girl make her own life, as a boy could? To parents who expected their adolescent daughters to refrain from sexual activity, to hand over their wages without protest, and to assume the household duties of a wife, the straying girl undermined not only her own reputation but also the fragile family economy.

Committed to reform school, these delinquent girls were subjected to a heavy dose of domestic service—cooking, cleaning, sewing—designed to inculcate industrious habits in the slack and shiftless while exposing them to the pleasures of true domesticity. These pleasures, though, remained beyond the reach of girls for whom domesticity was, and would always be, drudgery. Further, the conditions under which they were paroled from Lancaster, as domestic servants in private homes, were loathsome enough to quell even the strongest domestic yearnings. State social workers justified the placement of girls as domestic servants by arguing that only in private homes could troublesome girls be constantly supervised. Occupations other than housework were too fraught with peril for young women already convicted of immorality, they maintained; such occupations as waitressing or factory work afforded too many enticing opportunities. As a visitor said authoritatively, discussing one girl's placement: "I do not think she should wait on table. It would lead to prostitution."[31]

As domestics, many girls began anew with their employers the sorts of battles that had landed them in reform school in the first place. The city's pleasure palaces beckoned, and lonely, underpaid, and overworked girls saw little reason to resist their allure. Many ran away from their employers for short periods, during which they roamed the streets and indulged their cravings for music, dancing, and male companionship. The private homes in which they were placed could themselves be problematic, for they offered ample opportunities for secret assignations with employers' husbands and sons. The matron of one home, for example, found her nineteen-year-old domestic servant, clad only in a kimono, perched on the lap of her son, a Harvard student.[32] Another woman dismissed her state charge after she overheard her husband suggest they have sex.[33] And the girl who became pregnant after two years of frequent sexual relations—in the "hall, pantry or anywhere"—with her employer's widowed thirty-five-year-old son was one of many young women whose behavior mocked social workers' earnest efforts.[34]

The state social workers who committed these "Burleigh girls"—girls supervised by Edith Burleigh, superintendent of the Girls' Parole Department, and her staff of twelve visitors—invariably deemed them bad tempered, irritable, untruthful, and saucy, and complained of their waywardness and petty thievery.[35] Psychiatrists, by contrast, were charmed yet baffled by what they agreed were the girls' good-natured, pleasant, and essentially normal dispositions, and they admitted to finding nothing remarkable in the mental examinations of most of them. As a psychiatrist observed in one case, "the contrast between the impression gained by the examination of the girl, and the report as given by the Parole Department, is rather striking."[36] Remarked another: "It doesn't seem possible that everyone who goes to Lancaster can be surly, sullen, have outbursts of temper, etc. etc. Certainly we never see a case whose description doesn't have nearly all those adjectives. On the whole when they come here they behave pretty well."[37] "It is always the same thing," observed still another; the report portrays her as saucy and feebleminded, yet she "appears sweet" and proves intelligent.[38] Similarly, Myerson, after questioning another suspected psychopath, said to his colleagues, "if we want to catalogue her, we can say she is psychopathic personality; that will not explain the very favorable impression she makes on me."[39] In the end, psychiatrists diagnosed this girl and nearly all of the state charges sent to them psychopathic, on the one hand judging them "perfectly attractive sorts of girls" and on the other reminding themselves that this was "the group to which all Miss Burleigh's girls belong."[40]

The history that state visitors prepared upon committing eighteen-year-old Gertrude Blackstone to the hospital tells a story of familial failure and adolescent rebellion that was replicated many times over. Noting that from earliest childhood Blackstone had been a persistent liar who stole repeatedly, went with bad companions, and in general ran wild, the visitors retrospectively judged her "a stubborn, disobedient child." When she was fourteen, her widowed father, claiming he was unable to control her, placed her in the care of an organization that sent her to one private home after another. She proved unsatisfactory in each. "Lazy, slack and shiftless about her work," she was accused of telling vulgar stories to young children and of continuing to steal. After confessing to immoral relations with two men, Blackstone was committed to Lancaster, where, although "bad tempered and saucy at times," she proved "not a difficult girl." She was paroled at home, and allowed to study shorthand and typewriting. But she soon became "saucy, lazy and independent" and was placed out to do housework. At this point Blackstone's real trouble began. She paid visits to disreputable families, was immoral on several occasions, and stole from her employer. After visitors discovered the extent of her immorality, she fled and married a man whom they judged "poor stuff," quickly left him, and began to work as a waitress and go out with other men. Eventually she was returned to reform school. Noting that she was "good-natured, pleasant company, but deceitful and unreliable," Burleigh had her committed to the Psychopathic Hospital for observation. "Seems very much fascinated by the life of prostitutes," Burleigh noted of her charge. "Enjoys and seeks the attention of men whom she knows to be not good and voluntarily talks about 'white slave traffic.'" Burleigh closed her report with the observation that Blackstone "says she cannot see the use of living unless you can live as you wish."41

For girls like Gertrude Blackstone, the widely shared desire to live life as they wished was well-nigh unattainable. Once identified as delinquent and enmeshed in the state's agencies of social and moral reform, they enjoyed few opportunities and had few choices. Confronted with the bleak reality of these girls' lives—the isolation, the low wages, the endless round of domestic duties—psychiatrists voiced their concern that "a great many of these people don't have enough decent amusement." But the "sport, basketball and such things" that they hoped to substitute for the moving pictures, automobiles, and dance halls that the visitors saw as sources of girls' immorality would hardly have appealed to those they deemed psychopathic, like one Violet, whose recreational tastes ran to "noisy, frolicking times with jazz music, dancing and loud laughter," or to girls like the fifteen-year-old who preferred "dancing and nice clothes and amusements of rather low character" to what social workers primly referred to as "interest in the healthy pursuits of life."42 The wholesome entertainments that social workers advocated—church concerts, choir rehearsals, chaperoned dances—elicited only the disdain of girls who frequented dance halls and moving-picture shows. The much-vaunted young man of good reputation, who would carry on a courtship "by bi-weekly letters and semi-yearly visits," stood little chance of engaging their interest.[43]

Competing Immoralities

Psychiatrists, social workers, and state visitors did not distinguish among the many varieties of female sexual activity they subsumed under the rubric of immorality. In relating the histories of women whose behavior appeared to violate accepted moral standards—girls who merely rode unchaperoned in automobiles with young men, as well as those who accepted money in exchange for intercourse—social workers pointed to the prostitute, the archetypal sexually active woman, with whose sordid activities and fallen state they identified all sexual activity outside marriage. So resonant with associations of voracious sexuality and irredeemable immorality was the prostitute that they had only to invoke her for a young woman's sexual expression to be transformed into hypersexuality and thus psychopathy. To social workers, the distinction between the young woman who received indecent letters from men and the prostitute who received money was of little consequence, for they assumed that reception of the former led inexorably to reception of the latter.

The women who readily admitted to their uncontrollable sexual desires conformed to the psychiatric notion of hypersexuality. Theresa Beauvais, for example, confessed "that she could not control herself with respect to sexual relations."[44] Bessie Dunston "seemed thoroughly ashamed" of the activities that had resulted in her pregnancy, but told visitors that "she could not seem to help it, the desire was so strong."[45] Other young women admitted variously that "the temptations [were] too much" for them, that they "did not have the strength to decline," and that they were "powerless to resist."[46] One girl's declaration that she would choose to be shut up in an institution could she not "live the life" exemplified the defiantly immoral sexuality psychiatrists considered psychopathic.[47]

These women, however emblematic their declarations, were in the minority. More commonly, women argued that they were not hypersexual, objecting that the psychiatrists and social workers who claimed they were assumed only the worst. Reflecting on the ups and downs of her four-year entanglement with social workers, nineteen-year-old Eliza Conway, Helen Anderson's charge, admitted to Jarrett that she had "acted very foolish" but maintained that she had "not gone to the extremes as perhaps you and a good many others think." She protested that she had never been "so overwhelming with joy to devote my time to such indiscriminate lewdness," adding, "I am no ——, for if I had ever been why should I ever be in want of money? I would have lots of clothes and an apartment." Instead, she was a girl having difficulty finding work.[48] Psychiatrists explained to nineteen-year-old Alice Lawson that her difficulties resulted from her bad temper and sexual activities. She disagreed, telling them, "all my troubles started with the social workers. . . . They imagine a whole lot." "They say you are fond of boys," a psychiatrist challenged her. "I like boys but I am not crazy about them," she replied.[49] "Are you very fond of men?" Lowrey asked a twenty-year-old. "Well, naturally, it is only nature," she contended. "Are you so very fond of them so that you cannot get along without them?" he asked. "No," she conceded, "I could get along without them."[50] These women maintained that their activities were normal. A young woman naturally would want, as one said, "to be on the go, to see life, movies, young men and dances."[51] But in girls' activities, however limited, psychiatrists and social workers saw only nascent immorality.

Psychiatrists' and social workers' conceptions of respectable, moral behavior rigidly divided good from bad women. The specter of the prostitute informed their prescriptions about girls' proper dress and deportment. To social workers, working girls who spent their meager incomes on frivolous ribbons and silk stockings and who purchased clothing on installment plans were no better than the "dolled-up" psychopathic prostitutes who found satisfaction in lavish personal adornment, plucking and penciling their eyebrows and flaunting their wares as they strutted about in striking, "cheap-rich" styles of dress.[52] But flashy dress, so tellingly tawdry to middle-class eyes, was the norm among working girls. Fine clothing compensated for the daily drudgery of work. It could bolster self-esteem flagging under the double burden of overwork and low pay, and it could also enhance a young woman's desirability in the marketplace of pleasure. Social workers held that the working girl's meager wages were best allotted to the necessities, not the frivolities, of life; the claim of room and board on a young woman's wages, according to their calculus of economic rationality, was prior to that of clothing. Social workers might complain that working girls had "no idea of the value of money," but from the working girl's perspective, money invested in clothing was money well spent, capable of yielding ample returns.[53]

Many observers agreed that girls' sartorial desires and recreational tastes exposed them to moral dangers. Young women may have made light of these concerns, but they were not necessarily inappropriate. As young women moved more visibly into the public sphere, they confronted new dangers as well as new opportunities. Many knew nothing of sex—its mechanics, its pleasures—until knowledge was forced on them. As one twenty-five-year-old woman who became pregnant after her first experience with men, automobiles, and drink ruefully noted, "I thought a few cigarettes, one or two cocktails were harmless, that a girl could always take care of herself, and there I was mistaken." Women did, however, object to the narrow construction of respectability that rigidly separated good from bad women, that blurred the distinction between prostitution and sexual activity outside marriage, and that saw in this woman's pregnancy, even though, as she emphasized, "I never had anything to do with men except that once," the start of "a new career."[54]

It was the readiness of professionals to consign them, on the thinnest of evidence, to the ranks of the promiscuous that young women found so irksome. Psychiatrists and social workers measured them against a middle-class moral standard, a code that ensured that the middle-class woman would not squander her virtue, her most marketable asset. But the strict morality they advocated held little appeal for working girls for whom a willingness to play fast was worth as much as the middle-class girl's chastity. A number of putative psychopaths struggled to define standards of sexual morality appropriate to their lives. Psychiatrists were puzzled that they could entertain any real self-respect—testified to in some cases by the girls' refusal to accept any money for their irregularities—while engaging in relations the psychiatrists judged promiscuous.[55]

Yet this distinction was central to these women, who were trying to forge another standard of sexual morality. They objected to the double standard that marked them defective. "A new generation of women has arrived, and the wrong of Grandma's day is the right of today," proclaimed Ethel Hancock, a twenty-one-year-old waitress. "Do you think there will ever be equality of sex, one moral standard for both?" she demanded of Jarrett. "If so, I hope it comes in my day, I would be as good as a bad man, which is twice as good as a virtuous woman. Wouldn't it be great to do just as one pleased?"[56] In response, psychiatrists and social workers proclaimed that for women "a little knowledge is a dangerous thing" and urged them not to question the dictates of conventional morality.[57] Jarrett warned Hancock not to "read or discuss on any subject, especially sex, that [she] did not understand and had not the education and intelligence to grasp in just the manner the author intended."[58] Yet young women did think about sex in spite of experts' warnings. Hancock's declaration that she herself would "love it, simply revel in it" could she indulge her desires and maintain respectability at the same time only highlighted how weakened were the foundations of conventional morality. And Rose Talbot's admission that she had "read Casqueline's (I think it is spelled) *Truth about Woman* and Havelock Ellis' *Psychology of Sex* which," she wrote, "quite knocked all my good resolutions to smash," only underlined the dangers of free thinking. "So you see it is not wicked to have sexual intercourse with other men than your husband. It is merely not the fashion."[59]

Even as they decried the injustices of the double standard, these women fell back on its distinctions as they assessed their own behavior. The hyper-sexual of psychiatric imagination—the woman who, were it "possible for her to get the sexual indulgence she wants," would—shamelessly pursued her desires.[60] Many of the actual women psychiatrists diagnosed hypersexual, however, lived by moral codes structured, like those of social workers, around considerations of good and bad. They merely defined good behavior far more broadly than social workers did, and their respectability was a complex thing that turned not on chastity but on self-respect. Social workers and their charges, for example, agreed that a woman could "go wrong" or "to the bad." But while to social workers these phrases signified a debased state from which a girl could never recover, to the young women they denoted a process that could be reversed at any point. A girl could start to go to the bad and stop; Rose Butler, for example, jilted by the lover whom she had hoped to marry, thought of herself as a now-respectable woman who had once "started to go wrong."[61] "Going wrong" had as much to do with a woman's attitude as with her activities. It was not the social fact of her surrender to temptation, whether occasioned by need or by passion, that signified a woman's debasement but, rather, the discouraged state of mind that often preceded it. Although she might stray, a respectable young woman only became truly bad, in the idiom of the working class, when she succumbed to despondency and thought of herself as bad.

From this female working-class perspective, material need was a familiar culprit. Young women implored hospital social workers to confront this, but the latter were indifferent to economic arguments. Rose Butler emphasized that she was not fast, nor did she wish to be. She pointed out, however, that need could sorely tempt a girl: "Why is it girls get discouraged? Why do girls get tired of trying? Why should a girl be befriended and then scorned and snubbed and squashed when she does try? I have come to the point where I don't blame a girl to get discouraged."[62] Similarly, a twenty-year-old tried to impress upon social workers that desperate circumstances like hers—for two years she had owned barely any clothes—"would drive anyone to the bad, no work, no money, and nothing to wear." She was getting to the point, she wrote, where she did not care what anyone thought of her.[63] In cases like these, the road to ruin could begin with discouragement and end with a lost reputation.

Still, a woman could salvage her wavering self-respect by dint of determined hard work, and reclaim respectability, which pulled powerfully even on those women who most brazenly flouted its strictures. Eliza Conway, whose nonchalance appeared the embodiment of the hypersexual's disdain for morality, sporadically responded to its call. By her own choice still under social work supervision five years after her initial commitment to the hospital, Conway delighted in casually telling social workers of her exploits, on one occasion informing them that she had "learned a great deal in the past few days," and on another announcing her intention to secure an abortion, claiming "quite calmly" that "lots of girls get in the same box and take the same way out." Yet for all her bravado, Conway could admit something was wrong. "I can't control myself when I am once started," she wrote. "I do my self really know there is something the matter with me and I do want to grow and be a respectful young woman."[64] Ethel Hancock, too, sought respectability. Sexual relations with her first husband disgusted her, she confided to Jarrett; it was only with her next husband, with whom she was not much in love, that she had experienced "strong sexual desires." Separated from him by a bitter quarrel, Hancock began living as a single woman, working as a waitress in a restaurant with a crowd of young women she judged fast. She quickly and deliberately went to the bad, she told social workers; on one occasion she went with her workmates to a sporty place but left, intoxicated and disgusted, when their unspecified sexual debauches began, and on another she was found with a man in her room in the early hours of the morning by the matron of the home in which she lived. It seemed to social workers that Hancock did not take her many transgressions seriously. But over the course of her five-year epistolary relationship with Jarrett, Hancock struggled to make good. "It seems as if I'm always doing some fool thing and the harder I try the more of a muddle I get in," she observed. "I have not yet learned self control, not even a wee bit. Goodness knows I try hard enough." She wrote triumphantly to another social worker: "Oh, my dear, you can't imagine how proud I am to be able to write that I've actually been good for two whole weeks." Hancock desperately sought respectability. Her lament—"I've been so dreadfully bad and I will truly do something big if I can make something to be proud of out of my comparatively wretched life"—was echoed in those of the otherwise confident young women who found it difficult to manage the psychic conflicts their unconventional behavior engendered.[65]

Hancock did make good, although, as she put it, only "by force of circumstance." Working as a telegrapher at Western Union, she could find "no time at all for mere masculine sex." She derived some satisfaction from the knowledge, gained through experience, that she could "start out at any time and make a good living" for herself. Yet she still wished—"when I am up to devilry," she added, "mischief is too mild"—she could "give rein to all [her] evil desires" without incurring social workers' wrath.[66] Hancock's repentance redeemed her in social workers' eyes. As they told her tale—her fall, her struggle, her triumph—they cast her as both offender and victim. Both were familiar roles; the prostitute had played the two well. Need, bad fortune, poor company: all led women astray, all fit neatly with social workers' moral universe. True, this construction of Hancock's story overlooked her willful sexual experimentation, her professions of desire, and her own interpretation of her successful struggle for respectability as one in which she had paid an almost unacceptably high price; but the final, favorable outcome allowed social workers to mold it to fit the conventions of a familiar genre, that of the fallen woman redeemed through the timely, though lengthy, intervention of middle-class female rescuers. In casting hypersexuals as prostitutes, then, social workers were not just relegating them to the bottom of the moral spectrum, but rendering them familiar as well.

The prostitute, though deplorable, was at least a known quantity. The young women who celebrated the pleasures of sex free of the moderating influence of moral concerns or social context—who, that is, perfectly exemplified the psychiatric notion of the hypersexual—were, by contrast, women wholly outside the social workers' and psychiatrists' moral universe. Simple declarations of erotic desire unmediated by morality stunned them into silence. Prudence Walker, for example, a nineteen-year-old with a long history of sexual exploits, followed her desires even as they led her into trouble. "I must have someone all the time to love me," she told social workers. Sometimes, she confessed, "I get so excited that I don't know what I do—and it's then I consent to do the things I do and have done." She had no excuse to offer "except the old one—that we don't know what we do—in that condition."[67] In a similar vein, eighteen-year-old Helen Skinner wrote to a friend of her latest adventure: "The old saying is go as far as you like the Sky is the limit But Jee I think we have gone our limit. don't you?" She had "fallen in love" with a man who had come to repair her home's furnace. "Of course you know what that means. I was so God Dam hot that I didn't know weather I was going home or to hell. I suppose you got yours from Fred," she added generously. "I hope so anyway."[68] Psychiatrists and social workers focused on practice, not pleasure. They were uncharacteristically reticent when confronted with evidence of the latter, tacit recognition, perhaps, that these declarations of female desire were, indeed, altogether new.

Although psychiatrists considered the immorality of white girls a sign of disease, they deemed that of black girls entirely normal. The dangerous psychopathy that psychiatrists so confidently perceived in the immorality of white girls became, at worst, a conduct disorder—a manifestation of conduct that did not match the conduct prescribed by society—and at best a manifestation of normality when the girl in question was black. "On the whole I have been very chary in making the diagnosis of psychopathic personality in these colored girls," Lowrey—"knowing the race well"—explained to his colleagues. "The level of the negro regarding conduct, using that term in the broad sense, is decidedly different from the conduct of the white." In their discussions concerning the young black women committed to the hospital from the Girls' Parole Department, psychiatrists consistently interpreted the promiscuous sexual activity that was highlighted in visitors' reports not as symptomatic of disease but as the natural, expected expression of the immorality of the race. A "normal negress" was, in their estimation, unintelligent but high-spirited, and her immorality, like that of one twenty-year-old who admitted to exchanging sex for money with three men, could be shrugged off with the assurance that there was "nothing abnormal about her delinquencies. Some of us get caught, some do not."[69]

Adding a psychiatric twist to an old set of beliefs concerning the sexual nature of black women, psychiatrists diagnosed those with histories every bit as flamboyant as those of whites as normal—"not insane, not feeble-minded." Psychiatrists diagnosed as psychopathic only the few black women whose immorality was of such proportions that it offended even the purportedly low standards of their race. Psychiatrists agreed that they had first to determine whether a woman was "normal for her race," taking into account, for example, that—as their superficial sociology had it—the marriage conventions of blacks "for thousands of years have been other and peculiar," calling into question whether they could "get on under the marriage conventions of the Aryan race."[70] Disorderly sexual conduct was, in psychiatrists' estimation, "presumably extremely common among the negroes, without attracting any particular notice."[71] Southard's cautionary admonition that immoderate sexual behavior could not be "merely racial" because "not every member of the race does this sort of thing" fell on deaf ears.[72] It was a singular disease indeed that so respected social convention.

Yet back on familiar territory, diagnosing white girls, psychiatrists were firm in their conviction that psychopathic personality was an inborn and incurable condition. Unlike "simple" delinquents, who psychiatrists hypothesized were "perfectly able to do otherwise if they wish" and who could learn from experience, the psychopath had inborn defects that rendered her unable to refrain from misdeeds.[73] Some putative psychopaths thought differently, acknowledging their delinquent behavior but attributing it to poor upbringing, not constitutional makeup. Several girls told psychiatrists that their mothers had been unable to care for them properly, that no one had taught them right living. Others insisted there was nothing at all wrong with them. As Alice Lawson spelled it out for psychiatrists: "There is not a thing the matter with me. I eat and sleep well. I am perfectly normal. I have no hallucinations, illusions or delusions."[74]

Some young women rejected not only psychiatrists' etiologies but also their pessimistic prognoses, promising they would make good if psychiatrists would only give them their freedom. But the policies of the parole department and social workers' distrust of the world of work ensured that they would be trained for little. "There are a number of things I should like to do," one young woman told psychiatrists, "but there is only one thing I will be able to do, and that is to go back to housework. I am very fond of study, and I should like to study more."[75] Another said that she "wanted to do something different from housework, such as in an office of some kind," but added, "I don't think I am educated enough."[76] Still another wanted "to try factory work with other women."[77] Alice Lawson, too, did not want to do housework. "What else can you do?" one psychiatrist queried. "There are lots of things a girl can do besides housework," Lawson countered, but to the psychiatrist's challenge, "What else can you do?" she could only reply, "Can't I wait on table?" "What else?" he demanded. "I have not thought of anything else," she replied.[78]

Psychiatrists and other professionals ridiculed these women's aspirations and made light of their resolve to go straight. Yvette Gagnon, a newspaper editor, was sent to the institution by a physician who warned the psychiatrists that she entertained "many extreme ideas as to women's rights," adducing as evidence that she was writing a book entitled *Daughters of Tomorrow*. This testified, he wrote, to "her delusional insanity re her mental genius in the art of book writing."[80] A Psychopathic Hospital psychiatrist, commenting on the prospect of Alice Lawson's release (which he favored), quipped that "the worst thing that would happen would be an outburst of temper and an increase in the population."[79] In still other cases, psychiatrists predicted that psychopaths would later prove paranoid, feebleminded, or simply burdensome.[80] Psychiatrists consigned these women, endowed with boundless sexual desire and limited occupational skills, to futures circumscribed by their sexuality. As a psychiatrist confidently predicted of one young woman, "I can see her becoming a manic depressive or a prostitute."[81]

The proposal that all psychopaths be permanently segregated in rural colonies surfaced frequently in the literature of psychopathy, but in practice psychiatrists betrayed an awareness that this solution was not only impracticable but draconian. On the one hand, they noted with frustration that they would never be able to ensnare the many psychopaths running wild in their communities. That large numbers of defectives, "stunningly asocial in conduct," would "never see an institution" was a measure of the public's complacency and, more important, of their own marginality.[82] One psychiatrist's lament, that "we have no way of solving the problem of psychopathic personality unless they do things that break laws and get into trouble with the police," directly spoke to psychiatrists' sense that they were subordinate to the law and its regulatory mechanisms, a situation that the malleable category of psychopathy in part was intended to remedy.[83] On the other hand, when it came to actually deciding the psychopaths' fate, psychiatrists recoiled from the literature's dire warnings and from the state visitors' harsh appraisals. They recommended that the girls be set free, for they had trouble seeing evidence of civilization's demise in the spirited, attractive young women they diagnosed psychopathic. Miss Burleigh's girls were returned to her, labeled psychopathic but sane; most of them continued to labor as domestic servants under state supervision until age twenty-one. The rest gained their freedom immediately.

In the twenties, as the sexual revolution reached the ranks of the middle class, and as behavior that psychiatrists labeled hypersexual became more prevalent and less easily ascribed to a deviant working-class minority, psychiatrists' interest in hypersexuality flagged. The sexual psychopath of the late twenties and beyond was male and most often homosexual; rapists, child molesters, and other sex offenders displaced working-class women as objects of psychiatric attention.[84] As psychiatrists adjusted their theories to new sexual mores, they championed a sanitized heterosexuality that could be safely contained within marriage, transforming the passion that had been such a mark of deviance into the criterion of normality. Frigidity, not its obverse, marked the deviant woman; the lesbian, the all-too-independent woman who rejected men and patriarchy altogether, inherited the mantle of sexual deviance from the hypersexual, who, however worthy of contempt, at least had played the game. As the hypersexual faded, the lesbian became the exemplar of female sexuality gone awry.[85]

It is possible to see in psychiatrists' rendering of the hypersexual an exemplary instance of Foucault's suggestive observation that the science of sexuality has functioned as the *ars erotica* of the Western world. In the guise of a decent positivism, Foucault argues, the late-nineteenth-century sexologists such as Krafft-Ebing, Tardieu, and Havelock Ellis, who recorded and classified the manifold forms human sexual desire assumed, inadvertently created "a great archive of the pleasures of sex." There was pleasure to be derived from the very creation of this archive, Foucault goes on; the "obligatory and exhaustive confessions" psychiatrists elicited, and, one might add, the subjects from whom they were drawn, could themselves stimulate and titillate.[86] The confrontations between psychiatrists and the young women they deemed hypersexual partook, at times, of the erotic. One psychiatrist, watching his colleagues succumb to Alice Lawson's blandishments, dismayed at seeing the very scenario of female seductiveness and male helplessness that the category of female psychopathy encapsulated played out before him, burst out: "You all say give her a chance. To say 'Give her a chance' is an emotional way of putting it. The question," he reminded them, "is whether this girl is hypersexual." An attractive girl who assumed the pose of injured innocence, she was, he argued, all the more dangerous in her ability to "get the sympathy of men."[87] Uncomfortable with their own vulnerability to young women's charms, and eager, perhaps, to establish the collective innocence of men, psychiatrists fell to blaming women for seducing them. The overdrawn sexuality of the adolescent girl is in part, by this interpretation, the projection of these psychiatrists' own barely acknowledged desires.

But there was more to the hypersexual than this. Proclaiming women wholly sexual creatures, psychiatrists fixed on their sexuality in attempting to comprehend a larger process of social change that saw women moving out of the home and more visibly into the public sphere. The psychopathic hypersexual was in part a product of the psychiatric imagination; the confident hedonist who seduced men left and right was the working-class new woman, the woman with a little cash and a lot of savvy, seen through middle-class, mostly male, eyes. But the sexually assertive woman, the woman endowed with passion equal to that of a man, was by her own account real, and psychiatrists (however exaggerated their notions of her sexual prowess) were alone in recognizing her passion as dangerous. They neither reduced it to its exchange value, as did those who held that a woman's passion was but an ephemeral manifestation of her natural desire for status or fine clothing, nor did they strip it of its equivocal qualities by situating it within marriage. For the moment, they stood back, a bit awed perhaps, and attempted to comprehend this new phenomenon, the passionate woman. Reflexively, they turned to the familiar categories of the pure woman and the prostitute, at the same time recognizing that this old dichotomy would not do. The uneasiness of the construct of the female hypersexual expressed their confusion and ambivalence toward women. With it they enjoined women to be chaste and seductive, to tease but not to conquer. In their discourse, the psychopathic hypersexual was at times a pathological deviant. More often, however, she was Everywoman. If, as one authority proposed, "a clean and protected moron [was] not far from corresponding to the ideal woman of the Victorian age," the psychopathic hypersexual was her redoubtable twentieth-century counterpart.[88]

EIGHT

HYSTERIA

THE REVOLT OF THE "GOOD GIRL"

IN HYSTERIA, as psychiatrists conceived of it and as the young women whom psychiatrists diagnosed as hysterics experienced it, the broad-based early-twentieth-century sexualization of womanhood that was manifest in the category of female psychopathy reached its apogee: In hysteria, every thought, every symptom was linked to sex. The flamboyant eroticism of the hysteric had a long and distinguished history; psychiatrists fascinated with Freud and emboldened by his frankly sexual discourse could even propose that the hysteric's convulsions were "equivalent to a sexual climax" and were "of the nature of an orgasm."[1] Although this rather indelicate formulation enjoyed only fleeting currency, Freud's positing of an entirely sexual etiology for hysteria—his conceiving of hysterical symptoms as expressions of repressed sexual conflicts—gave early-twentieth-century psychiatrists license further to eroticize this female malady. It served, too, to reinforce its deep-rooted and multifaceted association with women and the worst of womanliness, an association manifest most literally in the term's etymology (from the Greek *hysterikos*, or womb) and more metaphorically and powerfully in the many damning resonances the term's use as an epithet evoked. To act hysterically had long meant to act as a woman.[2] What it meant to act as a woman was now, however, up for grabs, and the confrontation between psychiatrists and the women they diagnosed as hysterics was correspondingly confused.

The hysteric's tale, as she told it and as psychiatric theory constructed it, was a narrative of seduction. This seduction was from the start double-edged, the question of who was seducing whom implicitly posed but never addressed. The coquettish, swooning young woman was central to the iconography of hysteria as the Parisian physician Jean-Martin Charcot, working in the 1870s, constructed it. Charcot embellished the overtly erotic photographs he took of the fifteen-year-old hysteric Augustine, who had been raped by her father's employer, with such suggestive titles as "Extase" and "Erotisme."[3] In Freud's writings, too, seduction was ambiguous. Although, as he told it, his "discovery" of psychoanalysis—of the unconscious, the repressive mechanisms, and the transference—was predicated on his interpretation of the hysteric's account as one of infantile sexual trauma, of unwanted seduction,[4] and although he would later envision this seduction more equivocally, substituting a universally desired, fantastic coupling with the parent of the opposite sex for the actual seduction he had earlier hypothesized lay at the root of hysteria, the ambivalence of seduction was there from the beginning. From the mutually imagined seduction of Anna O. and Freud's early collaborator Josef Breuer, which culminated in her hysterical pregnancy and his fleeing the scene of the imagined crime, through Freud's seduction at the hands of Dora, who was at once antagonist and object of desire, the sexuality of the seduced—the hysteric—was never so passive as the manifest tale would have it. Yet so subversive was the sexual subjectivity of the hysteric that Freud could never directly confront it.

This sexual subjectivity—this desire to act rather than be acted upon— was evident in the tales the young women themselves told, though here, as in Freudian theory, it was subsumed within a sexual drama more compelling (because more orthodox) in both professional and popular estimation. This was the Victorian sexual drama, of which the hysterical girls and women who came to the attention of the Psychopathic Hospital psychiatrists were, for the most part, captives, engaged in debilitating struggles to establish their status as "good girls." This drama's stark casting of womanhood in terms of female virtue and female ruination appeared especially compelling to them, and they struggled mightily, against men and against their own desires, to maintain their virtue. Many of them wanted to participate in the sexual sphere, but found themselves—by reason of sexual abuse, traumatic heterosexual experience, or delicate temperament—psychically, and sometimes even physically, paralyzed and unable to act. These hysterics were self-described good girls in an increasingly sexualized world, girls suffering, in the words of one, from their modesty.[5]

Just as hypersexuality was the bad girl's ailment, hysteria was the good girl's. And just as psychiatrists worried that the former were too active sexually, they were concerned that hysterical women would withdraw from heterosexuality altogether. To psychiatrists, the hypersexual and the hysteric were two sides of the same coin of female desire. They confronted both on the uncertain terrain of female subjectivity. Around both they spun cautionary tales of feminine deceitfulness and tried out various visions of modern womanhood. And in both, the normal and the pathological were mixed. In the end, however, psychiatrists found the hypersexual—that cunning ruiner of innocent men—far more palatable than the hysteric, even though the hypersexual not only rejected the diagnosis but also impertinently questioned their authority. The hysteric, by contrast, not only acquiesced in the diagnosis of hysteria, she invited it. In the psychiatric encounter, the hypersexual's malady—attested to by advance reports detailing her every transgression—was in danger of simply disappearing, eclipsed by the normality psychiatrists were disposed to see in her. The hysteric resisted normalization. She came to psychiatrists having already constituted herself, through her symptoms, as a hysteric, and in the encounter, as she detailed the sordid transgressions of others and enacted her symptomological responses thereto, her malady appeared more, not less, substantive. Indeed, the validation that psychoanalysis offered is precisely what she sought.

The diagnosis of hysteria was singular in several respects. An ancient entity, it had been reconstructed relatively recently by Charcot, endowed with, in Jan Goldstein's words, "a coherent and conceptually elegant array" of symptoms, and given new, more psychological interest by Freud.[6] The "aristocrat" of functional disorders, it was, until the war, almost entirely associated with women—patently unreliable women whom many accused of lying and simulating.[7] A bizarre, foreign disease, thought by many Americans "peculiar perhaps to Paris or Berlin, but not to Boston or New York," hysteria was at the same time intensely familiar, bringing the psychiatrist directly into the most private recesses of the self, laying bare the family's sordid secrets.[8] To no other psychiatric category was the distinction between truth and reality on the one hand, lies and simulation on the other so critical but so impossible to determine. No other category— and no other group of patients—so stirred psychiatrists' anxiety and so unsettled their professional equanimity.

Psychopathic Hospital psychiatrists professed only disdain for sexual Victorianism and urged on hysterical women a modern, rationalist sexual ethos structured not around the polarities of good and bad (which were, to their minds, ideological remnants from the past), but on the supposed sexual equality of women and men. But these women, even as they elicited from psychiatrists a vision of the battle of the sexes as fair, balanced, and straightforward, posed a serious challenge to that vision. Although she sometimes envisioned it otherwise, the hysteric told a tale that was a narrative of seduction at the hands of men, and the psychiatrists, although fierce proponents of modern sexual ethics, unwittingly adopted that narrative's conventions. The pleasing complementarity of male aggression and female passivity structured this narrative, in which the man, possessed of an uncontrollable sexual appetite, used the passionless woman for his pleasure while she, feigning indifference, coyly teased him. This scenario was so deeply culturally embedded that both the psychiatrists and the women who endeavored to envision an alternative sexual politics found themselves constrained by its terms. Psychiatrists could condemn the stratagems of "old-fashioned" courtship, which depended on a sort of male libertinism and female artifice that was anathema to them. But the best they could propose as an alternative was that women become as sexually knowledgeable, assertive, and even as aggressive as men. As psychiatrists conceived it, the rules of the marketplace (or, in a more pointed formulation, of the battlefield)[9] governed heterosexual relations; equally endowed men and women should be left the freedom to resolve their differences, to fashion mutually pleasing accommodations. Psychiatrists thus committed themselves to the aim of achieving a parity of sexual power between men and women. They would educate women in the ways of sex and attempt to curb the worst of male sex abuses—incest, rape, assault. Paradoxically, however, as psychiatrists began to define these relatively common acts of aggression against women as beyond the range of the "normal," they incorporated within that range a level of male sexual aggression that many women found vexatious, a level that gave the lie to their conception of the battle of the sexes as a contest of equals. Male sexual aggression was so deeply ingrained in the culture of heterosexuality that only at its worst was it available for inspection as pathology. To psychiatrists, then, hysteria was a malady suffered by undersexed prudes in a sexualized world. To "hysterics" themselves it represented a dramatic protest against the general cultural precept that the woman's body was fair game.

Sex, Lies, and Claims of Rape

Although Psychopathic Hospital psychiatrists made the diagnosis of hysteria infrequently, conferring it on fewer than 1 percent of their female patients, hysterical girls and women constituted perhaps one-quarter of the patients of the hospital's Freudian, L. E. Emerson, and occupied a disproportionate amount of his time and interest. Most of the women who were diagnosed as hysterics considered here were institutionalized at least once, for from one week to several months. Emerson later treated a number of them, as well as some who were never hospitalized, as outpatients, seeing them several times a week. Nearly all were registered as voluntary patients, and although some were brought to psychiatrists' attention by their mothers or fathers, there is little evidence that any objected to the diagnosis or the treatment. By contrast, several told Emerson that they found the treatment helpful; "This is just want I wanted—I've never talked things over with anyone," said one.[10]

The typical woman manifesting hysterical symptoms was young, single, native-born, and white. Most were between the ages of eighteen and twenty-three, although some were in their mid-thirties and even early forties; their median age was twenty-one. Although psychiatrists diagnosed a few married women as hysterical, the group was overwhelmingly single, in part because it was so youthful but also in part because many of the older women diagnosed as hysterics had purposely avoided men and marriage. Approximately half of those for whom occupational information is available labored at working-class occupations, in factories, as domestic servants, or as cooks or hospital attendants; 40 percent held low-level white-collar women's jobs as clerks in stores or as office workers; several were teachers.[11] These women suffered from a range of psychic and bodily ailments. Spells of depression and crying temporarily incapacitated some; severe, inexplicable pains plagued others; vertigo, fainting spells, temporary paraplegias, twitching, tremors, and convulsions beset the most severely afflicted.

Most of these women told psychiatrists tales of sexual contest and conquest.[12] Their tales fall into into three groups of equal size that can be arrayed along a spectrum of sexual activity, ranging from outright sexual abuse at the one extreme, through active but vexed engagement in the middle, to almost entire withdrawal from heterosexuality at the other extreme. Into the first group fell young women who told of being sexually assaulted, subjected to incest at the hands of brothers or fathers, or raped by strangers. The middle group encompassed women who told of experiencing what men, and their culture, considered "normal" heterosexuality—whether it was the boss's hand surreptitiously slipped up the leg or the boyfriend's acting on his assumed right to her body—as unwanted aggression. The third group was composed of women, by the time they came to psychiatric attention, who had experienced the terrors of womanhood—from the facts of life to the ethics of courtship—so acutely that they had withdrawn almost entirely from the field of heterosexual play in which most of them wanted desperately to be engaged.

These women, however diverse their experience, shared a language with each other and with psychiatrists. So compelling, and so common, was the drama of seduction, so familiar were its players, that these women unwittingly adopted its terms even as they protested against it. The woman "gave way" to the man in the traditional sexual scenario, the language casting her as passive; at the same time all felt she was likely responsible for inciting his passions to a level that would demand her submission. One of Emerson's patients, for example, who complained of being constantly apprehensive, plagued by pains in her heart and weakness in her knees, and so afraid she would commit suicide that she had her mother put the kitchen knives out of reach, told him that prior to her first "breakdown" she "gave way" to a man and engaged in regular coitus interruptus with him for a year. Even though he sometimes prevailed upon her to have sex when she was less than willing, she worried that she had "led him on, more or less, teased him, etc.," and thought of him as "a good fellow" because he was prepared to marry her should she become pregnant.[13] This woman experienced heterosexuality as aggression. Others told of interpreting aggression as normal, routine heterosexuality. For example, a woman who came to Emerson suffering from throbbing head pain told him, through her tears, that she thought she had been indiscreet in accepting a man's offer to escort her home late at night and that she had led him to do "something wrong with her"—he had raped her, her first brush with sex.[14] Another, a forty-four-year-old businesswoman who had turned down many proposals of marriage, was haunted by memories of a "compromising drive" she had taken at age nineteen.[15] And twenty-year-old Laura Jean Harper described being raped by an acquaintance in terms of "submission to sexual intercourse." As she recounted it, the "man drew her into a room and she lay down and prepared herself." That she could comment that at the time she felt, as sexual Victorianism prescribed, "little pleasure, some pain," is tellingly indicative of just how conflated were heterosexuality and male sexual aggression, for some women could neither envision nor experience them as discrete phenomena.[16]

Psychiatrists were only beginning to conceive of the male sexual aggression expressed in such acts as rape, incest, and forceful attack as apart from the ordinary, intermittently classing as instances of sexual assault what their culture comprehended in terms of seduction.[17] Rape and assault were, to be sure, recognized by the law as crimes, but physicians and other authorities met women's claims of violation with immense skepticism. That men actually assaulted women was given short shrift in the scant medico-legal literature on the subject, which focused instead on women's ruinous lies—their misstatements, untruths, staged accusations, and simulated hysterical attacks—and upon, in the rare instances where rape was determined to have occurred, their acquiescence. Do not believe a woman who cries rape, the authorities roundly warned, for more likely than not she was oversensitive and hysterical, making of "innocent playfulness" a serious offense, like the girl "roughly handled by some young man of the neighborhood, although with no evil intent," who falsely accuses him of assault.[18] "Truth is told about once in thirteen cases," maintained one self-proclaimed expert; the prisons are filled with innocent men falsely accused of rape, declared another.[19] That "the mere crossing of the knees absolutely prevents penetration" was apparently common belief among physicians, for, as one wrote, "every competent physician knows" that "sexual assault is physically impossible without consent."[20] In this literature, the paradigmatic case of "rape"—wrongly labeled as such, of course—involved two intimates engaged in heated "amorous sport." The *via voluptatis* pleasurably and mutually traversed; the man ready to claim what was naturally his; the girl—ignorant, like most, of male physiology and suddenly aware of "adverse considerations"—suddenly, inexplicably indignant, said no. "In a state of sexual hyperexcitability," the man pressed on, unfairly bringing on himself the charge of rape.[21]

The sexual politics that structured this and the other scenarios that enliven the literature of assault are the same as those within which hysterical women attempted to negotiate daily. A number of them told Emerson of informing their mothers that they had been assaulted, only to have the mothers doubt and scorn their claims. Under no obligation to come to any legal determinations in any of the cases of hysteria they treated, Emerson and his psychiatric colleagues were somewhat more inclined, in general, than their forensically minded brethren to believe the stories their female patients told.[22] But there were differences between psychiatrists and the psychoanalyst. Psychiatrists focused for the most part on symptoms, not stories, in staff meetings questioning patients more about what had happened since they had entered the hospital than about what had led them to the institution in the first place. Thus, psychiatrists asked young women to elaborate on their "spells," demanded to know why they refused food, berated them for not talking, and elicited from them promises they could not possibly keep—"I know I shan't bite myself again and I shan't have another convulsion," one, under intensive scrutiny, told Southard.[23] Much of the give-and-take between hysteric and psychiatrist yielded nothing that the latter considered diagnostically useful. "Why did you get that spell?" one asked a girl who could only answer, "Because." "Because what?" he demanded. "I don't know myself, hardly," she replied. Neither did the psychiatrists, but that did not stop them from characterizing her as stubborn and silly.[24]

To Emerson, the hysteric's symptoms were of interest not in themselves, but for the stories they encoded. He spent little time quizzing hysterics about the particulars of their symptoms, and he rarely, if ever, asked them to explain or account for their convulsions, tics, and twitching. Instead, he encouraged patients to dredge their pasts for incidents that might bear on their present distress. "Do for yourself just what you have learned to do with me," he wrote to one young woman. "Just sit in your chair and close your eyes and think, and look to see what you see."[25] Much of what Emerson elicited from patients had to do with sex. This is what he, as a Freudian, expected, and although it is impossible to reconstruct the mix of subtle suggestion and emotional incentives that in nearly every case yielded the information he sought, it is clear that, in theory at least, he maintained that it was "bad to work up a whole lot of theories in your own mind and then try to inject them into the patient." Still, on occasion he admitted to impatience.[26] Barely three weeks into the treatment of a woman suffering from blurred vision who thought analysis was "silly," he noted that he could "get no sign of any consciousness of any sexual experience or thought sufficiently adequate to explain trouble." "Chews the rag," he noted during one session in which, like many others, she produced little with which he could work.[27]

Bluntly asserting that "all hysterics tell untruths; some hysterics lie," Emerson argued that it was up to the psychoanalyst to discriminate truth from fiction. He was confident he could do so. Yet philosophically a prag-

matist, he held that truth was neither final nor absolute, always representing a compromise. Truth, he maintained, "means the agreement of our
ideas with reality," which was not to be opposed to unreality but considered as "a matter of immediate experience."[28] What he called the "subjective truth" of the hysteric's account, which the analyst could glean from her
"manner and attitude," was to his mind of greater psychological consequence than any impossible-to-corroborate "objective truth."[29] Philosophy aside, it is clear that, in practice, Emerson believed much of what his
hysterical patients told him (and he sometimes excoriated others who did
not believe the stories). That the hysteric's symptoms waxed and waned
in concert with the narratives of assault and trauma that she painfully
patched together in analysis was evidence enough for him of her essential
truthfulness. Still, he was well aware that Freud no longer maintained that
actual assaults were implicated in the etiology of hysteria. Although social
workers did corroborate several accounts of assault (and police several
others), and although several men told of visiting upon their sisters the
sorts of sexual abuses of which some of these young women complained,
the historian of hysteria has no choice but to adopt Emerson's stance vis-
à-vis the truth of the hysteric's account.[30] "The patient herself fully believed what she said"; lacking evidence to the contrary, so might we.[31]

Good Girls, All

The consequences of sexual assault for many of the one-third of hysterical
women who claimed to be its victims was hysteria in its most severe,
debilitating, and classic form.[32] Theresa Cellini, for example, a twenty-
one-year-old office worker of Italian descent who was brought to the Psychopathic Hospital by her parents in 1912, complained of twice-weekly
attacks of dizziness, shooting abdominal pain, headaches, nausea, blurred
vision, and transient paraplegia. Although she appeared to be a normal girl
who could hold a job and who took flight, like others, into the pulp fiction
"world of fancy and romance," she was in fact deeply troubled by the
sexual abuse to which she tearfully told Emerson she had been subjected
since an early age. Her great-grandfather had "monkied" with her—put
his penis in her, fingered her, urinated on her—from childhood until she
was seventeen; a man had attempted, unsuccessfully, to penetrate her at
age thirteen (she had been left to cry while he then "sat on a lounge and
worked himself off by masturbation"); and she had had a series of sexual
encounters with men she had pleased, but she had been left unsatisfied. It is
hardly surprising that Cellini thought of intercourse a lot, or that she was
overcome with "a queer sensation" as she dreamed of a man giving her
plenty of money, taking it back, and then "fooling" with her as they argued.

Like many girls subject to sexual abuse she had turned to promiscuous, passionless sexual activity, making her body available to men and getting her own satisfaction only solitarily—she could "get the thrills" if she dwelt on the subject of sex.[33]

Cellini was in this respect more fortunate than the other women who told of being so traumatized by sexual violation that they spurned sexuality altogether. Thirty-six-year-old Margaret Knight, for example, a self-described Catholic "good girl" who had been "running away from marriage" all her life and who suffered from what she called nervous prostration, told Emerson of a man hugging her several times when she was ten years old, of another exposing himself to her and a friend when she was fourteen, and of being traumatized, at age thirty-two, after she had allowed a man to fondle her breasts, having stopped him when he wanted more. "There is no such thing as love," she observed to Emerson, turning over the possibility of entering the convent.[34] And forty-year-old Emily Patton, who opened her first session with Emerson by disclosing that at age fourteen she had been drugged and raped by an elderly neighborhood man, an experience she felt "had ruined her life," told of keeping company in her youth with a man she loved, who wanted her to submit to him, but of being unable to act: "I was burning all over, I wanted to give in to him, but I couldn't." Her life "gone for nothing," she mused that she could have "got married, and brought great children in the world."[35] These and several other sexually traumatized women who repudiated sexuality altogether found themselves, in middle age, still plagued by ambivalence and unresolved desires. A number of them considered entering the convent, which held the promise of psychic and social salvation, representing the obliteration of sex conflict and offering community to women on their own. "To live in a convent is grand—they have good food," Knight exclaimed to Emerson, but she and all the others decided against it. One woman's explanation that as a girl she had thought "there were only three vocations: marriage, single, and convent life," and her admission that she had not known exactly where she fit in, only underscored how paltry yet how full of significance were the good girl's choices.[36]

The many ways in which sexual abuse could confound a girl's progress toward social and sexual maturity are manifest in the case of eighteen-year-old Dorothy Mather, who, several months into her two-year psychoanalysis with Emerson, told of having been traumatized by her uncle (who lived with the family) when she was eleven. In 1911, Mather entered the Massachusetts General Hospital (which employed Emerson at the time), suffering from twitching and inexplicable pains; one year later, having developed temporary paralysis of her arms and legs, she entered the Psychopathic Hospital for an eight-week stay. Her symptoms, which were near-literal expressions of the sexual traumas she had experienced and repressed, faded as she first remembered and then worked through what she had struggled to forget. She agreed, for example, with Emerson's surmise that the twitching of the head from which she suffered was "a symbolic representation of the 'no-no'" no one had allowed her to utter. When she had told her mother that her uncle had attacked her on the cellar stairs, grabbed her leg and rammed his fingers up her vagina, the mother, although she summoned a physician, could only reflect that "if she was so weak as to let her uncle do what he did she would let others do more"; her sister could only offer that it "would count against her when she came to marry"; and she, not surprisingly, blamed herself for the incident, wondering what she had ever done to her uncle "that he would treat me like that." "Dorothy Mather is a bad girl," she wrote on the psychologist's papers when left alone, in the midst of a session, for fifteen minutes.[37]

As severe as were the manifest consequences of Mather's uncle's abuse and her mother's reaction thereto, worse yet, because more insidious, were the many subtle but powerful ways in which both underscored her position as the family's dutiful daughter, suffused her every heterosexual encounter with an aura of danger, and nurtured in her a debilitating psychic struggle between good and bad. The mother who had failed her so miserably died when she was sixteen; Mather left school to care for the family household, which consisted of her four younger siblings (one of whom, her sister, blamed her for killing their mother), her eighty-four-year-old grandmother, and her bereaved father, who spent every Sunday afternoon in tears. Although Mather saw to the work of running the household, her grandmother (who could not die soon enough to suit Mather) ruled it with an iron hand, keeping her at home when she wanted to go to moving pictures (which the grandmother dismissed as being for those who had nothing else to do) with the girlfriends who already called her an old maid. Robbed of her childhood by her uncle, Mather found herself at her mother's death robbed of her adolescence by her grandmother.

Mather described her three-year courtship with her boyfriend "Dutchy" to Emerson in terms of his pursuit of her, and was troubled by recurrent dreams of him getting into bed and having sex with her. So vivid were the dreams that Mather could barely distinguish them from reality: Had she in fact slept with him? So unable was she to accept, let alone act on, her desires, that sixteen months into the treatment she began to stick pins into herself whenever the feeling of being "hot" and sexually excited came on.[38] Mather wanted desperately to be like other girls: to have chums, to work, to go with boys. Released from the hospital, she first secured a job as a salesgirl in F. W. Woolworth's store, earning five dollars a week, made some new girlfriends there, and wrote enthusiastically to Emerson that she was "getting along fine." But within three months she was writing that the work was "getting the best of" her. Her feet and back ached; more significantly, exposure to the working girl's easy morality made pointedly clear how much the struggle to be good was exacting. "I am not going to be good any more," she proclaimed, adding "I dont give a —— for to be good it's mor fun to be bad now." It was hard to be good, she went on, for "whear I work are girls' that go on good times' but they are more happie than I am when it comes to a fine point." Her sister and father, she declared, "can all go to hell," excusing her strong language with the observation that she had lately been saying much worse.

Within yet another three months, in January 1914, Mather seemed to have reached a satisfactory resolution of her struggle. Although still bothered by bad dreams, she wrote to Emerson that she understood why she had them and that she knew there was no longer any need for her to be sick. "I am out all the time," she reported. "Father think's I am terrible now." Still, she had gained his grudging respect in giving up her position as the family's dutiful daughter: "Well for a wonder my father thinks I am some girl but he dont like to see boy's calling for me." The debilitating battle between good and evil apparently behind her, Mather was free now to enjoy the prerogatives of adolescence to the full. "I am full of the devil now," she went on. "Gee, but it [is] great to be working." She had gotten a raise, had three dollars a week for herself, went to dances and the theater, and was "happy as a lord." Too busy to write a proper letter, she scribbled Emerson a note of appreciation. "For you are the one that had made a girl out of me," she explained, expressing succinctly her view of her struggle as one for normality. Mather was eager to shed the persona of "insane girl" and to become just a girl, and although the path she followed from dutiful daughter to bad girl to normal girl was treacherous and possibly never complete, it was, in its painful, episodic manner and in its stark casting of good and bad, paradigmatic of the paths followed by a number of hysterics subject to sexual abuse.[39]

In a culture that nurtured male sexual aggressiveness and in which even heterosexual couplings that had been openly entered into were suffused with this aggression, it was sometimes difficult for women to draw a firm line between abuse on the one hand and consensual sexual activity on the other. Sexual mores were in flux, and this only blurred the already tenuous distinction. One-third of the women who manifested the symptoms of hysteria told of being subjected to unwanted male sexual aggression that fell just short of outright rape or assault. Yet so powerful was the paradigm of seduction that even as these women conveyed to Emerson and to psychiatrists that what they were experiencing was aggression, they could not articulate it as such. The language of seduction—of feminine wiles masquerading as feminine submission—sustained the widely accepted fiction that women had the upper hand in the negotiations of heterosexuality, and it imputed an aura of contingency to those negotiations that veiled only imperfectly their inevitability: if in social fiction women directed them, in social fact women were relatively powerless.

The saga of twenty-eight-year-old Sally Hollis, who came to psychiatric attention complaining of a fear of crowds, shows how debilitating the consequences of "normal" heterosexuality could be. Hollis had been working since the age of seventeen, living on her own at the Frances Willard Settlement. She told Emerson, who quickly took charge of her case, of being irritated all the time and of suffering from "an awful feeling at the pit of [her] stomach"—"my breath is tied up and my stomach is sick." Years before she had been going with a young man, Walter, who worked in the the same shop as she; from the beginning of their relations, she said, "I was working against my own feelings." Very quickly he began to get "fresh"; he kissed her within a month, within two he was feeling up her legs, within three, taking off her garter, and on one occasion he ripped her drawers in "trying to get at her." "Before I marry a girl I'm going to find out what she's made of, how she's built," he boasted to her as he forced her to have intercourse. Hollis thought of herself as "queer" and felt unable to resist this man's advances; the only protest she could mount was symptomological—she began to vomit. Hollis paid a high price for her desire to participate in the world of heterosexuality. After Walter left the scene, having impregnated another young woman and been forced into marriage, she took up with another young man. Although he was less of a sexual bully, she still felt deeply torn. For several years, during which he masturbated her twice weekly, their relations were pleasant and uneventful. She was terribly shaken, however, one morning after he had almost "seduced" her, and could only try to put the memory out of her mind. This man, like the first, eventually left her, informing her by letter that he was going with another girl he liked better.[40]

Hollis knew she had been wronged, subjected to unwanted male sexual aggression, but she could only cast the issue in terms of her own reticence, not men's bullying. The materials from which she might have constructed an alternative sexual politics were not at hand; the sexual aggression of courtship was not a pressing social issue in the way that female aggression was. Her illness—her hysteria—testified to the psychic toll this ideological inversion of the actual power relations of heterosexuality between the sexes could exact. Psychoanalytic treatment only reinforced the power of this inversion. On one occasion, for example, she dreamed she had been in a hammock when, she related to Emerson, "some fellow came alongside of me and put his arm around me and kissed me." "Then I thought of you," she told Emerson. "Then I thought you said 'you shouldn't allow a person to kiss you. It was encouraging them.' But I couldn't help it," she protested, "it was he that kissed me!"

As they delimited a range of unacceptable male aggression, psychiatrists tacitly sanctioned a broad range of male aggression the psychic sequelae of which could be especially vexing—because so "normal"—to women. Even girls and women who openly struggled against male aggression, like one fifteen-year-old who was referred to Emerson by another physician because of the cutting abdominal pain from which she suffered, could pay a high price for that struggle. This girl told of fighting until she was "exhausted" with the boy she had been seeing for three years the first two or three times they had had intercourse. After that, she claimed, she "didn't care," even "rather enjoyed it." Still, when he forced himself on her when she was unwilling, she fought back by calling him "son of a bitch" and "bastard." She knew she had been wronged. Men "shouldn't have to fight to do it," she claimed authoritatively. But Emerson could only engage with her failings, not his; she, after all, was the patient. He assessed her as "*very repressed*"—this, concerning a girl who told him she was "dreaming of intercourse all the time"—and homed in on the conflict between her conscious and unconscious desires.[41]

That the ethic of seduction was as pervasive in the workplace as in courtship was especially confusing, even galling, to women. A colleague of one twenty-eight-year-old teacher, for example, told her over lunch that she "needed to be waked up" and invited her to meet him in a hotel.[42] Another woman, who began to work at age thirteen, told Emerson of a man hugging and squeezing her at work, and "going through coitus-like movements," a traumatic experience she kept to herself.[43] And forty-four-year-old Ada Buxton, who had worked as a proofreader when younger, related to Emerson that an older man in her office "had put his arms around her waist several times." She was mortified and was still ashamed of the incident; the man was let go for unrelated reasons but the one who replaced him, she felt, always "looked at her as if he thought there might have been something wrong going on." "I was so afraid someone would think I was immoral," she admitted.[44] Whether occasioned by her own heightened sensitivity or by the man's leering glances, Buxton's fears are indicative both of how hysterical women tended to fault themselves—not the men whose advances they rebuffed—in sexual negotiations, and of how little the sexual ethics of the business world differed from those of courtship: the paradigm of seduction was as compelling in the former as in the latter context. Seduction, which encoded the male belief that women wanted sex whether they admitted to it or not, and which cast a woman's hauteur as but one pose in her repertory of come-ons, gave men license to grope and fondle. An aloof manner and professional bearing offered women little protection against predatory workmates and employers. Harriet Andrews, a stenographer, described herself as "very ambitious": "I have plenty of ability, I am very able." But Andrews did not "take well with men in business. They like my work but they don't like me." Andrews displayed an unusual, even unseemly, degree of self-confidence for a working woman. She had nevertheless several times been subjected to unwanted sexual advances—hugs, kisses, leering looks, and groping hands—from the men who spurned her as too professional. Her employer proclaimed that "girls were likely to go astray if they didn't have work," but men acted as though the reverse was just as true, interpreting a woman's working as a sure sign of her desire to be led astray.[45]

The one-third of women diagnosed as hysterics who had little or no experience with boys and men provide evidence that the struggle to be a good girl could be waged on an entirely psychic front. Twenty-four-year-old Ethel Bowen, for example, dated her "awful dread of men" to age six or seven when she used to make the rounds with her father, who had a milk cart. Even now she was extremely sensitive to the presence of boys. Sometimes she could "meet them all right," but at other times she was too self-conscious. It worried her that she was unable, like other girls, to go out and feel free to talk to boys.[46] Likewise, eighteen-year-old Helen Haley, who characterized herself as sensitive and shy, wanted to go with boys but could not talk to anyone outside her family without becoming "terribly nervous and sick in every fibre of her being."[47] And twenty-five-year-old Clara Hill, a mill worker raised by her maternal grandmother who had told her "never to marry and [that] girls are happier single," dreamed of dancing and of boys talking to her, but admitted to never having had a lover and never having kissed, except at a game of post office.[48] These young women had suffered the terrors of womanhood so acutely that they had withdrawn entirely from the field of heterosexual play.

Those terrors were legion. From the biological facts of womanhood—menstruation, pregnancy, childbirth—to the social strategies of heterosexuality, many young women's minds were filled with frightening misinformation that cohered into a great cautionary tale concerning the dangers of sex. Because many knew nothing of menstruation, the first sight of blood was terrifying; one fifteen-year-old, for example, thought she was bleeding to death, and another was "shocked and horrified beyond measure," thinking, until convinced otherwise by a schoolmate, that it could only have been "a horrible peculiarity of her family."[49] Pregnancy, which only some knew resulted from what one called "badness between man and wife," was an even greater source of terror and mystery.[50] One girl thought a man "touched" a woman to impregnate her; what Emerson called the family fiction of another was that Indians brought babies; and yet another, whose father was "violently opposed to sex knowledge," thought a girl could become pregnant by being kissed or hugged or by sitting on a man's lap. Schoolgirls regaled each other with shocking tales—of "little girls who died from relating to boys," of neighborhood women who succumbed in childbirth, of babies being pulled out of mothers split open "from the navel down."[51] The truth offered little solace. "I don't see how they can get out unless they cut through at the sides," a puzzled seventeen-year-old put it to Emerson. "Told her," the psychologist tersely noted. "I should think it would hurt," she responded.[52]

To the psychoanalytically inclined, it was an article of faith that sexual ignorance was harmful, knowledge beneficial. "It is the function of the analysis to show," wrote Emerson, "that virtue consists in virtuous acts, and not in barren purity of thought," such as that revealed in an exchange with a twenty-four-year-old who, when asked "what do you know about sex," could only reply she did not "know what the word means."[53] This woman's seemingly willful ignorance troubled Emerson, who, when confronted with the extent of girls' sexual ignorance and with the psychic distortions such ignorance wrought, felt compelled to enlighten them. "Sex knowledge almost nil," he wrote of one; "has no knowledge of meaning of menstruation or sex matters at all," he noted of another, a seventeen-year-old who "denied all curiosity," saying she "believed her mother would tell her all she needed to know."[54] A good Freudian, Emerson maintained that there was "sex running through everything," and to woman after woman he explained the facts of sex.[55] "Told her facts"; "talked with her and told her about sex, etc."; "told her of possible sex connection"; "explained the sex act somewhat"—scattered through Emerson's notes is evidence of his pedagogical project.[56] At least some women knew what they were facing. A woman friend of Ada Buxton's, for example, cautioned her that if she was to continue seeing Emerson, "the sex question would have to be met."[57]

Emerson's zealotry on the sex question stemmed in part from the psychoanalyst's conviction that the roots of hysteria lay in sexual conflict. He urged women to sift through their memories of the past for the unpleasant sexual experiences that might help explain their ailments, and he expected women would find, then divulge, these memories quickly. If they failed to do so, he was likely to judge them repressed, as he did one twenty-one-year-old Scotswoman who, to his mind, exhibited characteristic Scottish reserve because she had not told all within an hour of meeting him. "Told her the necessity of thinking all things," Emerson noted to himself; "trying to persuade her to look consciously at sex ideas." This woman—the perfect pupil—complied, and within a week she was reporting that she felt, somewhat improbably, "no repulsion to sexual understanding" and "wondered how she could have been so unobservant before."[58] But other women were less complaisant. Prompted by Emerson, one twenty-four-year-old asked her mother, from whom she had earlier tried to pry information, "about the difference between men and women," but her mother only upbraided her, telling her it was not nice to ask such questions and that she would know the answers soon enough.[59]

Emerson's zealousness on the subject of sex was a reflection not only of his educational mission but also of how eroticized the hysteric had become in psychiatric discourse. The psychiatrist diagnosed hysteria on the basis of patients' convulsions and their erotic conduct, Southard observed to his colleagues, invoking not Freud but the unassailable authority of Kraepelin to support this conflation of observed and imputed behavior.[60] The eroticism of the hysteric likely took shape most clearly in the eyes of her beholder, and the very technique of psychoanalysis—the intimate revelation of sexual secrets and misdeeds—intensified her sexualization. Emerson characterized several hysterical girls as erotic: just after he finished explaining the "facts" of sex to a fifteen-year-old who "seemed a little disinclined to believe them," he characterized her as "highly erotic";[61] and after listening to a seventeen-year-old recount the many reasons she did not want to marry, including her fear of poverty and of "His"—the generic male's—temper, Emerson paused to assess her as "highly erotic" and noted that "as she lies on the couch, is apt to expose a part of her legs."[62] The milieu psychoanalysis fostered likely evoked these assessments that, apart from their context, appear in large part the fanciful projections of Emerson's own desires, sparked by hearing of girls' lack of heterosexual interest. Situating them makes the sexual tension of the psychoanalytic encounter more palpable. Sally Hollis, the woman who fought with her boyfriend Walter, told Emerson she wondered both whether he was a married man and how he had the nerve to ask the questions he did. "Your questions rouse one's passions," she told him. "I was wondering if your passions were roused and how you could control them."[63]

The eroticization that psychoanalysis fostered sometimes went the other way. Several of Emerson's married women patients eroticized *him*, telling of their desires and fantasies revolving around him. One, married to an unfaithful man, told Emerson that she had often wished her husband was like him; "transference talked out," he recorded.[64] Another, after an explicit discussion of her sexual practices, related that she had "had the feeling in her vagina" that accompanied a desire for sex—*Übertragung*, the transference, he scribbled in his notes.[65] Calling on the transference, Emerson quickly mastered these situations. By contrast, he was clearly unsettled by what developed in the course of his treatment of a sixty-year-old woman, a widowed grandmother whom he saw at her home. Within the first month, this woman was confessing that her mind was filled with thoughts of sex, that she craved intercourse, and that she liked to imagine herself a romantic heroine in tales "which always ended in the sexual act." On one occasion, dressed only in a negligee, she wanted Emerson to "hold her hand tight." "I refused," he wrote. "She kept putting her hand on my knee, until I told her not to touch me, and when I drew back she wanted me to come nearer." The next day, after telling him "I would like to pound you black and blue, throw you out of the window, and jump on you," Emerson wrote that "it came out that she had a craving, for me." "I told her she must sublimate it; and suggested that she make a basket for my daughter," the young analyst told her.[66]

It was the Freudian's flouting of sexual proprieties that evoked the greatest hostility from the more traditionally minded psychiatrist. If hysterical women could only be cured "by dragging out all the disgusting details"— masturbation, incest, dreams charged with erotic symbolism—"for my part," one psychiatrist declared, "if a patient tries to tell me that, I say— 'Let up on that, I don't want to hear about it.'"[67] A dangerous compound of sex and lies, psychoanalysis stirred the psychiatrists' professional passions. Discussing one particularly charged case involving masturbation, sexual assault, and incestuous sex play, they fell, quite uncharacteristically, to squabbling among themselves in the presence of the patient (who provocatively claimed that no one but Emerson had helped her), making sport of his handling of the case and ruffling his composure to the point where he briefly joined them in deriding his own expertise.[68] Concerning another seamy case, one that turned on a father's "Saturday night debauches" involving his daughter, Southard and Jarrett maintained that "it is to be pointed out that" routine social work would have unearthed the information just as promptly as had the psychoanalyst, with his talk of "infantile sex experience," "buried memories," and Freudian mechanisms.[69] Emerson's psychiatrist colleagues were skeptical of the indulgence he showed in tolerating, not condemning, his patients' weirdly suggestive symptoms, for they were more inclined to evaluate the hysteric's behaviors as matters of discipline and will. Dorothy Mather told Emerson of several psychiatrists' threats that she would be "sent away" after they had heard of her calling out in her sleep for the pins and needles she used to stick herself when sexually excited; and Dr. Myerson, she told Emerson, was talking of doing something "to see if it wouldn't stir me up."[70] To psychiatrists, Mather's illness, like that of many of the other hysterical girls, was a matter of obstinacy.

Psychiatrists could complain that hysterics dragged them into the sordid morass of sexuality, but they were already there. Hysterical girls, like hypersexual girls, piqued their prurient curiosities. "I just want to know if she has been immoral," demanded Southard in the case of a sixteen-year-old factory worker who suffered from intermittent attacks of acute pain. Hysteric or hypersexual? The case "could be converted into a Freudian case," suggested Adler, opting for the first diagnosis. Southard demurred, hoping "the whole thing could be managed without resort to buried complexes" —a vote for the second. He suggested psychiatrists could trick the girl—

who claimed she had neither boyfriends nor girlfriends—into admitting she had been immoral by telling her they had discovered a physical disease in her that indicated she had been immoral but that could be cured, putting an end to her painful attacks, if she would only confess. Southard's colleagues rejected this tack and diagnosed the girl, who was by all accounts rather sad and lonely, as a hysteric.[71]

Some women objected to the psychiatric casting of them as wholly erotic. One felt Emerson was mistaken in characterizing her as passionate, preferring the less equivocal "strong-minded."[72] Another told Emerson she was sick of talking about sex all the time.[73] "The male, specialist or other, does not understand the true nature of the sexual life of the hysteric," wrote a female physician.[74] Few, however, could mount as explicit an attack on the assumptions that underlay psychoanalytic modernism as did Julia M. Dutton, who had attended Charcot's lectures at the Salpêtrière and who ran a sanitarium for neurasthenics. "I do not accept Freud's opinions as far as women are concerned," she wrote. "About men I do not know. Their minds are an unknown land to me." Dutton objected to the assumption that the source of one girl's maladies lay in sexual immorality. "Men do not realize women are receptive," she explained. "They have no sexual emotions till they are roused—I mean the vast majority of women."[75] Dutton's protest, although impassioned, was couched in the language of seduction (she defended the girl in question as clean-minded), showing how paltry were the resources women could call upon to counter the sexualization that psychiatry and psychoanalysis were proposing, and how hard it was to get beyond the terms of sexual Victorianism to fashion some sort of subjectivity for women.

A Female Malady

Nearly all of the women diagnosed as hysterics by Emerson and at the Psychopathic Hospital conformed to the classic picture of the disease, suffering from some sort of bodily malady—convulsions, tics, spells, and so on. But so deep and feminine were the cultural resonances of hysteria, and so underscored were these in practice by identification with a demographically quite homogeneous group of single women, that psychiatrists at times used the diagnosis less as a proxy for symptoms than as an epithet expressive of their disdain for troubling aspects of womanhood.[76] The hysteric was for the most part compliant, willing to be tutored by psychiatrists in the ways of womanhood. Several, however, expressed nothing but contempt for psychiatric authority. Psychopathic Hospital nurses judged one, a sixteen-year-old, rude and impetuous. The only symptoms of hysteria she displayed—and these, the nurses were careful to note, only when a psychiatrist was present—were crying, shaking, and constant movement of her arms and legs. Always attracting attention to herself, she warned the other girls not to consent to gynecological examinations and made loud, disparaging comments about the nurses and psychiatrists—"Half the doctors here don't know what they are doing. They ought to be in an insane asylum themselves." Yet in the presence of the male authorities she was so quick to malign, she transformed herself, much to the disgust of the nurses, into a seductress—giggling, flirting, sulking, and, they noted, speaking pettishly. By the end of her short hospital stay she was buoyantly happy, walking arm-in-arm with other girls on the ward, talking, and singing ragtime music.[77]

It was this young woman's seemingly calculated obtuseness that evoked such a passionate response and fed the fears of those physicians to whom hysteria was no more than a weapon women deployed, willfully and unfairly, in the battle of the sexes. Hysteria appeared, in this formulation, as the ultimate expression of feminine wiles; the hysteric's symptoms— her "spells," paralysis, loss of speech—the modern substitute for the tears women had proverbially wielded in marital combat.[78] Psychiatrists were fascinated with hysterics on the one hand, contemptuous of them on the other. They found their youthful enthusiasm endearing. "The hysteric reacts in a lively manner to the events of life," Southard noted, the stolidity of the praecox patient, the torpor of the depressed, the wild mania of the manic-depressive serving as a flattering foil for her antics.[79] But the hysteric could also elicit psychiatrists' hostility. Her silence could be maddening; "I suppose it takes psychoanalysis to find out whether she has eaten anything," Adler acidly observed of one. Her fantastic tales—tales that sometimes indicted fathers—about delicate matters could madden too: "I believe hysterics are liars myself," Myerson said of the same woman. "I wouldn't take her story about her."[80] Her symptoms could appear to be willful expressions of feminine obstinacy; a physician told one young woman suffering from hysterical paraplegia, "If you had any *spunk* you would get up and walk," and admitted to thinking that the same woman, whose claim to having been abused he believed, was "suffering as much from lack of sexual intercourse as she [was] from thinking over what happened to her." This physician's surmise, which he admitted was perhaps "gross and all wrong," was but a medicalized variation on the time-honored adage, current among men, that the penis could see to any of a woman's problems while fastening her firmly in her place.[81]

The hysteric evoked hostility in part because the psychiatric debate on hysteria was a debate on the worthiness of psychoanalysis itself. That most hysterics were single women both stirred up psychiatrists' anxiety and allowed them to trivialize the issues arrayed about the disorder. The women whom psychiatrists diagnosed as hysterics were neither so willful nor so resourceful as they imagined them. Nor were they so heroic as a strain of feminist thinking has considered them.[82] They were, rather, a sad lot, and their collective experience was one of thwarted ambition, lonely passion, and psychic misery. A number of them told of feeling acutely that they were queer and different. One described herself as "the most miserable girl in the world";[83] another confessed that she felt she was "not like other girls—I don't feel myself, just what I'd like to be";[84] still another said she felt "like two persons, and the one cannot control the other."[85] None of these women made a name for herself in the public world, like Bertha Pappenheim (Anna O.) so successfully did in the world of reform and feminist activism. They were, by contrast, ordinary women, women who wished more than anything else to be normal, an aim as ambiguous as the term itself.

In psychiatrists' evolving discourse, the hypersexual and the hysteric served as emblematic representations of modern womanhood and its possibilities gone awry. Attempting to consign the frigid, prudish Victorian woman to the past, psychiatrists found it difficult to portray her successor along consistent lines, at least in part because the program she was meant to project was itself contradictory and not yet fully worked out. Psychiatrists' writings attest to their desire to normalize female sexuality, but in practice they located it in the hypersexual one moment, in the hysteric the next. Each could serve reflexively as foil to the other, obscuring any middle ground, as they did in Emerson's short treatment of the hypersexual Prudence Walker. Emerson was uncharacteristically censorious of Walker. He quickly summed her up as sentimental, a "mental light-weight," warned "her not to 'flirt,'" and laid out for her what he called the "possibilities of lack of self-control." "Syphilis, illegitimate baby or abortion, nervousness, or insanity"—Emerson's catalogue of horrors was *echt* Victorian, straight out of the textbooks he and his colleagues had long ago discarded, a stark contrast to the program of sexual modernity he pressed on the patients he deemed hysterics.[86] Hypersexual and hysteric: psychiatrists might have located normal womanhood somewhere between the two categories. They did not, falling back on the language of pathology as they went about charting the new territory of female desire that sustained both.

NINE

MODERN MANHOOD, DISSOLUTE

AND RESPECTABLE

I N THE EARLY YEARS of the century, a lively debate concerning woman's nature raged in the public arena of politics and print and in the private realm of the home and individual heart. The many referents of the hotly contested "woman question" were clear; in an atmosphere of heightened awareness of sexual difference, few were without opinion with respect to woman's real nature, proper role, and corresponding rights. There was, by contrast, no discretely defined "man question" to inflame passions and fuel debate, for everyone could agree, it seemed, on what made a man. Manhood, in contrast to womanhood, appeared unproblematic; concerning it there seemed few questions to ask.

The apparent silence on the question of man is, however, but an artifact of its subsumption within a number of other wide-ranging debates over the state of society in general. Threaded through discussions of issues ranging from the future of work to the future of drink was a discussion of the parameters of manliness. Yet, manhood was rarely conceptualized—as was womanhood—as a discrete phenomenon. Rather, a man's class, ethnicity, and race defined him in the public eye; his gender was rendered invisible by reason of its seeming naturalness. In common parlance and in social fact man's relation to the generic Man was synecdochic, while woman's was at best qualified, at worst nonexistent.

Until quite recently, historical accounts of manhood replicated their subject's paradoxical universality and invisibility. Such accounts have, on the one hand, conflated masculinity with such abstractions as the national temper or the progressive character and, on the other, located its essence in the hortatory rhetoric of advice literature or in the rarefied masculinity of the Boy Scouts or the military.[1] Early-twentieth-century masculine identity has been rendered along two lines. One has posited a manhood under siege from the combined forces of an industrial capitalist economy becoming ever more rationalized and bureaucratic, denying men access to "manly" work, and of reforming women who would make society over in their own images, denying men access to drink and sexual dalliances. The other puts forth a manhood that is bloodless, a congeries of qualities—aggressiveness, self-control, honor, integrity—with which few would take issue, but with which only the middle-class intellect could have been fully engaged. In addition, many of those who have attempted to examine masculinity as a construction akin to femininity have chronicled its woes—the scarcity of manly work, the feminization of society—and slighted its privileges.[2] The history of manhood as men lived it day to day, with its peculiar mix of vulnerabilities and prerogatives, has only begun to be written.

This chapter addresses that historiographical void, attempting to tease the gendered man out of the universal Man. Drawing on the approximately 10 percent of all male patients who came to psychiatrists' scrutiny suffering not from well-defined mental disease but from difficulties they experienced in everyday life, as well as on the men who sought Emerson's advice, it addresses the gendered thinking that informed psychiatric and popular pronouncements on a range of apparently gender-neutral issues.[3] It problematizes the manhood that in common parlance needed no explication: an effeminate man's worry that "he could not make a man out of himself,"[4] a mother's certitude that a good woman would "make a man" of her son,[5] or a social worker's admonishment to one, "see if you are man enough to get a hold on yourself."[6] These commonly voiced sentiments invoked a rarely examined realm of thinking about what constituted a man. Two constructions of manhood emerged from confrontations between psychiatrists (and the psychologist Emerson) and their patients. One cast the bachelor, untrammeled by home and family, as the most manly among men; the other cast the breadwinner, happily beholden to the same, in his place. The masculinity of the one was separatist and, in the minds of its adherents, oppositional. Rejecting home and family as emasculating, this was the masculinity of the gang member, the saloon-goer, the latter-day rake who appreciated feminine company but could only envision it in the context of "wine, women, and song." A construction of masculinity few women could embrace, it contrasted sharply with the respectable masculinity of the breadwinner, who supported his family in comfortable style, working for a good wage at a manly trade or profession. Eschewing the pleasures of dissipation, the respectable man—whether working-class or middle-class—was faithful to and solicitous of his wife, and was forceful and in command of his home.

The first construction of manhood was that of youth, the second of adulthood. Men, it was assumed, would outgrow the dissolute masculinity of youth and embrace the respectable masculinity of adulthood. Yet few men entirely relinquished the enjoyments of the first as they entered marriage; the grown man's jealously guarded right to drink with his mates was the most common and most contested adult holdover from the youthful masculinist ethos. And although the masculinity of the married state appeared straightforwardly respectable, in practice it was shaded by men's darker desires and ambitions. The two paradigms of masculinity fit sequentially into the model of a man's progression from adolescence to adulthood, but each had its adult adherents and, more confusingly, one man could respond to the pulls exerted by both. Psychiatrists, although for the most part proponents of respectable masculinity, were unwilling, when pressed, to condemn outright the masculinity of dissoluteness, for they recognized in the overzealous condemnations of women threats to masculine prerogative.

Forging Masculine Identities

Because boys were, for the most part, raised by mothers, and thus subject daily to what they would come to perceive as an untoward degree of feminine influence, many set about fashioning an aggressively masculine identity from an early age. Fathers and peers aided them in this endeavor, outlining for them manhood's first lessons. A mother might teach her son it was permissible to cry and wicked to fight, but boys early learned otherwise. A boy was not to cry; a boy, when provoked, fought back; a boy knew it was better to be somewhat rough than to risk the appearance of femininity. Young boys subjected insufficiently aggressive schoolmates to merciless teasing, hurling at them such gender-laden epithets as "sissy girl," "girl-sucker," or "molly-coddle," the last especially, with its damning association of effeminacy and maternal overprotection, underscoring how little feminine leaven the aggressive masculinity of youth could withstand.[7] A preadolescent, ten- or eleven-year-old boy might privately seek his mother's arms for solace but he knew that to admit to the same was to invite the taunts of his mates.

The onset of adolescence only intensified the boy's desire to distance himself from feminine influence. The early adolescence of many boys was spent largely in the male company offered by neighborhood clubs and gangs. Several mothers complained to psychiatrists and social workers that at about age fourteen, their once-normal boys had undergone changes of character that the mothers attributed to the boys' having fallen under the influence of older, evil boys, invariably gang members. This assessment was sometimes correct. Twenty-one-year-old Patrick Collins, for example, an apparently well-brought-up young man whose character had changed, in his mother's estimation, much for the worse at about age fourteen, admitted to psychiatrists that before that time he had been very good to his mother, but that he had gotten "into the habit of going around with bum companions" who had encouraged him to be mean to her.[8] At about age fourteen, nineteen-year-old Elliot Newman admitted, he had, with the encouragement of the older men with whom he had begun to consort nightly, turned against the grandmother and oversolicitous aunt who had raised him.[9] By the time Collins and Newman came to psychiatric attention, both had settled comfortably into loafing. Neither worked regularly, preferring to while away the hours in the poolroom, and neither showed any evidence of what psychiatrists held was the proper sort of interest in women. Collins had recently taken up with a married woman ten years his senior and Newman, they noted, had never had any "love affairs." Collins, like others, could only account for his attraction to gang life in the vaguest of terms; other fellows hung about poolrooms and he, like they, got accustomed to the life. But his admission that his mother regularly got on him, talking to him "about what other boys are doing, and why I didn't amount to something, if I was getting work and so on," suggests that the laconic indifference of the poolroom habitué was a carefully cultivated position in a long-standing struggle to distance himself from his mother.

The dissolute life that these young men embraced—and showed no intention of giving up—was the outcome of adolescence gone wrong. For boys adolescence constituted an extended reprieve from female supervision. Loosed from his mother's exacting oversight, the adolescent boy was free to sow his wild oats on the understanding that in his early twenties he would again submit to the influence and authority of a woman, this time in marriage. The gang member's preference for male over respectable female companionship and his insouciant embrace of the dissolute life marked him as an eternal adolescent. Psychiatrists, like the psychologists of adolescence G. Stanley Hall and William Healy, on whose work they drew, condemned the adolescent boy's excesses—smoking, drinking, gambling, running with gangs, and petty criminal activity. Yet, aware of how precarious the boy's right to freedom from supervision was, they were quick to defend that right against the influence of meddlesome women. Psychiatrists helped nineteen-year-old John Butler, in the estimation of the police one of the worst gang members in Charlestown, shape his account of his conduct into a tale of abuse at the hands of women. Butler, like Collins, told of having drifted into the habit of going with "bum companions," a crowd of about fifty that was known in the neighborhood for drinking and "going to the devil"—getting into unspecified "girl scrapes"—and although he admitted he had not done as he ought to have, he complained that his mother and the neighborhood gossips had (and here psychiatrists prompted him) "laid it on a bit thick." They had said his character had changed at age seventeen, but to Butler it seemed only natural that "of course, there would be a change in anybody's character from the age of seventeen on." They accused him of being a dope fiend, but Butler claimed that none of his crowd used dope. Butler's recounting of the slanders neighborhood women had heaped on him evoked from Southard a time-honored maxim: "Women are the cause of more or less difficulty in the world," Southard declared, asking sympathetically, man to man, "were they the cause of yours?" Butler replied in the negative, stating that he did not believe they were. "Perhaps if it is not women it is wine?" Southard suggested.[10]

In the end, psychiatrists warmed to Butler. Several thought him delinquent, a victim of circumstance; others judged him a psychopath. But yet another analysis located his narrative in a field of sexual antagonism, assessing the sum of his depredations as a somewhat disreputable variant on the boy's necessary pathway to independence and manhood, and seeing in his account a tale much like "the old story of the boy who begins to go wrong, and gives his mother and sister a pretty bad time, and then straightens up and is a good citizen thereafter."[11] The old story was a loose, pleasingly familiar, and commonsense amalgam of social practice and everyday ideology on which psychologists and psychiatrists built their theories of adolescence. In it, and in the theories of adolescence to which it lent support, the boy was allowed a good deal more latitude than the girl.

The boy's masculine identity thus took shape partly as he distanced himself from his mother and his home and partly as he immersed himself in a male peer culture. Sexual knowledge and experimentation were central to boys' culture from early adolescence on; a boy's, later a man's, gender identity was thus inextricable from his sexual identity from an early age. Many men told of learning about sex from other boys at age ten or eleven, when they had then begun masturbating, by themselves or in groups with other boys, and said they kept up the practice through adolescence. Twenty-eight-year-old Harold Stewart, who consulted with Emerson about his nervousness, learned about masturbation when he was eight or nine years old. While in the toilet, he explained, "one of the boys started doing it to me," and although he was not sure whether he finished it that time, "it started the ball rolling."[12] And Ralph Calderwood, a married, forty-two-year-old scientist, told Emerson he had started the practice at age ten with his twin and another boy.[13] Although their parents had told them fearsome accounts of the consequences of masturbation—they would go insane, contract loathsome diseases, or do themselves irreparable harm—boys saw for themselves that masturbation led only to pleasure, and they paid little attention to their parents' interdictions. This was in part because evidence of parental duplicity on the subject of sex was in some cases close to hand. The father who punished a boy for exploring his sexuality might secretly harbor a collection of pictures of sexual activity and cheat on his wife, and the mother who punished a boy for the same might show herself to be less than wholly pure, caught by her son, as was one, staring at a man undressing before an open window.[14] But boys also ignored their parents on the subject of sex and masturbation because the boys were, from an early age, actively engaged by a male peer culture that taught them sex was pleasurable and had few negative consequences. Boys talked of sex incessantly—many men recalled that as youths they were obsessed with the subject—and they did so in their own idiom, which others considered dirty, that served both to set them apart from girls and to celebrate their masculinity.[15]

Many boys first experienced the pleasures of masculine prerogative in the sexual sphere. From their mates and from willing girls—such as those who entreated them to expose their privates, or allowed them some fondling—they learned that girls were fair game, an attitude many of them carried to adulthood. Young boys, flush with newly acquired sexual knowledge, taunted schoolgirls. Two women, for example, told of eight-year-olds writing "Will you give me a fuck?" on their slates and shoving it before their eyes.[16] Another, who said she had been pudgy as an adolescent, told of boys teasing her by calling her pregnant—"I didn't know you were married," said one to her on the telephone. Several others reported that they had first become aware of sexual difference after seeing boys expose themselves. Older boys, flaunting their greater experience and sophistication, used bullying lines to get unwilling girls to agree to sex. "Every girl ought to know about that"—meaning sex—"before she got married," proclaimed one to his reticent girlfriend.[17]

By early adolescence many men had learned to distinguish between what they called good and bad girls, and to treat the two sorts differently. A twenty-year-old factory worker who said he had first had sex at fifteen, for example, told of giving up trying to "seduce" a girl—making "a few moves to see if she would let him have intercourse"—when he found "she was a good girl." He was willing to have sex with "Damaged Goods," however, the last time having been a passionate experience, for which he paid a dollar, in a doorway on a major thoroughfare.[18] And a medical student described his current girlfriend—a nurse, "a woman I'm enjoying sex with"—as "light," associating her with wine, dissipation, and other men.[19] Many men's cavalier stance toward "bad" women developed early, when they learned of the easy availability of commercial sex. One, for example, had turned, when fifteen, from masturbating with a group of boys to visiting, again with a group, a woman "who would give them all a go for fifty cents" or a night for five dollars.[20] And a twenty-two-year-old dentist told of visiting, at age thirteen, a couple of prostitutes who masturbated him and a friend; by age fourteen or fifteen he was "fooling with girls freely."[21] The lasting allure of bad women was confusing to men who envisioned their tastes as above reproach. Harold Stewart, for example, who had recently stopped having sex with a "common woman," told of his youthful attraction to a teacher he characterized as "something of a flirt." She was, he explained to Emerson, "a little bit suggestive in sexual things, not bad" but passionate. He enjoyed dallying with her on sexual subjects, but "didn't want to think her bad."[22] And Joseph Scott, married six years, still pined for his former sweetheart, whom he had left after quarreling over her morals. Explaining that "she went with other men and had connection with them," he claimed to have seen her enter a hotel with another man and register as his wife. Still, he chastised himself for "not recognizing her readiness for sex relations."[23]

At some point in adolescence the connection between sex and reproduction —or pregnancy, more directly—dawned on the sexually active boy. This, and the harrowing but distant specter of venereal disease, dampened the sexual ardor of some. Thirty-three-year-old Timothy Nolan, a Catholic of Irish descent who claimed to have had an active heterosexual life since the age of eleven or twelve, told Emerson, whom he had consulted because of a constant nervous twitching, that although he usually felt ashamed after intercourse, the fear "lest the girl get pregnant," which came on him around age fifteen, was what slowed him down. He then went with fewer girls until he began, at seventeen, to go with girls he described as fast.[24] The seeming-reflexive ease with which Nolan spoke of and engaged in sex was characteristic of the many men to whom sex was unproblematic. These men recounted their sexual experience straightforwardly, admitted to sexual fantasies and thoughts unashamedly, and appeared, as youths, never to have wanted for partners. This is not to say they were oblivious; Nolan, for example, was in some respects a sexual gentleman, withholding, he claimed, "until the girl had 'come through.'"[25] But their sensibility was peculiarly male.

Sex was central to a man's life in a way it was not to the life of a woman. Many men said they thought of sex constantly. One confessed that he could not think three thoughts before thinking of sex.[26] They dreamed of sex, whether of pretty girls they had seen the previous day, or of naked women, or of meeting women on the street and "having them." And they saw sexual opportunity in everyday exchanges, like the dentist who reported that he "had the shivers go through him" while talking to a married woman who, he claimed, approached him suggestively in his office.[27] Although psychiatrists would have it that excessive sexual impulses could lead even a man astray, the retort of one man to another who tried to convince him that too much sex could be harmful—"What's getting you? I'm no worse for it, am I?"—speaks to a widespread acceptance of male sexual expression as normal and even necessary.[28]

Prevailing sexual mores thus allowed men a far greater sexual latitude than women. But the price of male sexual privilege—paid, to be sure, only by some—was the far more disabling toll sexual deficit could exact. With respect to women sexual deficit was still a nebulous, even contested concept, encompassing for some failure to marry, for others failure to entice, and, for the most advanced, failure to respond (frigidity). For men, by contrast, sexual deficit was at once singularly specific—denoting failure of the sexual apparatus, impotence most commonly—and overwhelmingly inclusive, undermining the whole of a man's masculine identity.[29] The grown man's sensitivity to sexual slight was conditioned by his early experience of sex, power, and manliness as one and the same. The brother-in-law of a childless, married thirty-eight-year-old artist, for example, jested to the man's wife that she ought to "call in the neighbors," a vulgar but essentially innocent remark in the psychiatrists' estimation that, they noted, the artist "misinterpreted as a slur on his 'manhood.'"[30] Psychiatrists could judge the artist overly sensitive with respect to his manhood only because they had attended so little to the precise delineation of the term. In popular parlance, by contrast, in which manliness and virile sexuality were virtually synonymous, few would have thought the remark anything but a vicious insult.

One man boasted that it was difficult for him to think of any particular girl in whom he had been interested as a youth because there had been so many; the male sensibility that fostered this attitude could mask a real vulnerability. This man later admitted that he had been interested in "a pretty passionate little woman" but had been afraid to attempt sex with her: "I didn't have any experience," he explained, "and I didn't know how to go about it." Attempted sex with a "professional" was no better: "She lay stripped and seemed to say, 'here I am take it,'" but he did not know what to do. A young nurse finally showed him how to do it.[31] Manhood was neither so easily achieved nor so unproblematic as the culture suggested. Once achieved, however, it was far less problematic than womanhood.

Psychopaths

Although psychiatrists never approached masculinity head-on, in their elaboration of the psychopathic personality they revealed their concerns about its condition and fate. And although the psychopath of the psychiatric literature suffered from such a range of damning characterological deficits that he was basically unfit for civilized life, the few male psychopaths whom psychiatrists came upon in practice were a rather benign lot of misfits and eccentrics. The specter of unachieved manhood haunted many of these men. Solitary and introspective, they felt apart from the easy camaraderie of men, whether at work or play, that constituted for the adult man the equivalent of the boy's club or gang experience. As a boy, for example, fifty-year-old Henry Allen, an unmarried mechanical draftsman possessed of what he called an artistic temperament, had wanted to be but never was "one of the boys." Throughout his life he had never adapted well to the company of men and had never felt able "to talk freely and frankly to men of his own age." He had been made fun of and laughed at his whole life, he claimed, and related to psychiatrists how, more than fifteen years earlier, another man's taunts that he was a masturbator nearly drove him insane when the story circulated among people in his office. Psychiatrists thought Allen was "entirely too sensitive to 'attitudes,'" and conferred with a former employer about why he was so often the "butt of jokes." The employer speculated that it was "because he was so like an 'old woman.'"[32] This was a damning judgment indeed, indicative both of how narrowly men themselves set the parameters of manhood and of how limited were a man's occupational and sexual choices. A man who chose womanly over manly work (and artistic work was by definition suspect); who preferred being single to married life; or who manifested feminine traits (who cried or was of delicate temperament)—who was, in short, all that a man was not—was in the popular estimation "a regular sissy," in psychiatric estimation a likely psychopath.[33]

The insufficiently aggressive, emasculated male was the hyperaggressive, would-be masculine woman's psychopathic counterpart. While the new woman's occupational and sexual referents were clear, the subject of heated public and professional debate, the effeminate man's were obscured because they were more often discrete than of a piece. In the sexological literature the male homosexual had already emerged as a type, but in practice psychiatrists found it difficult to identify him. They diagnosed men who exhibited such traits as an "abnormal dread of dust and dirt,"[34] a finicky attention to clothing and personal appearance,[35] or an affinity for pretty things[36]—all in their judgment feminine proclivities—not homosexual but psychopathic. Only the man who presented himself as a homosexual was labeled one, such as the fifty-year-old, self-described effeminate man in whose case feminine traits were explicitly coupled with what he called perverted sex and deficient manliness. This man, who told psychiatrists he spent his money on flowers, candles, and silk shirts and that, desirous of "new sensations," he experimented with the sex perversions of which he had read in French books, summed up his inadequacies for psychiatrists by admitting he had "never been one who felt like taking a man's place among men."[37] More often, in hospital practice, the connections among effeminacy, homosexuality, and manliness remained inconclusive, as in the case of a "shy and retiring, queer and erratic" man who had no definite history of homosexuality but said "his feelings were those of a girl," or in the cases of "sissies" with homosexual interests.[38] Although alert to evidence of homosexual acts, hospital psychiatrists were concerned more with the feminine passivity they connoted than with their purportedly perverse nature.

Among heterosexually inclined men, homosexuality was understood less as effeminate behavior than as a perversion associated with bad men; one nineteen-year-old's accounting for his homosexuality by blaming "some 'street boys' who taught homosexual habits," whether accurate or not, spoke to this association of homosexuality with the demimonde.[39] Although the consequences of the youthful homosexual play in which many men had engaged are impossible to document, it is clear that to many heterosexual adult men homosexual feelings were anathema. Singular in his candor was the married man who struggled to reconcile his masculine and feminine tendencies—imagining, for example, "how it would feel to be the woman" in coitus—and who admitted to "responding sexually to a lot of men," especially young and fair ones who stimulated in him "sexual thoughts and phantasies."[40] The worries of the artist, his manhood impugned, that he might be a sexual pervert were likely more representative of those men who recognized feminine feelings in themselves. This man entered marriage fearing that his homosexual tendencies would get between him and his wife; after a frank discussion of "modern sexuality" with the psychoanalyst Lydiard Horton, he reported that "everything was lovely" with her.[41]

The homosexual, in the teens, was too innocuous a character around which to organize a successful campaign; not until the late twenties, when psychiatrists nationwide set about establishing connections among male homosexuality, child molestation, and rape, was he transformed from a perverse but for the most part harmless character into a dangerous monstrosity—the sexual psychopath.[42] For the moment, psychiatrists elaborated a psychopathy that was less specifically sexual but even more damning, because more prosaic, in its assessment of modern manhood. Although psychiatrists regularly invoked what became in the overwrought literature of psychopathy a familiar litany of life's failures—vagabonds and tramps, drifters and ne'er-do-wells, swindlers and liars, poets and sex perverts—to underscore precisely how dangerously, and contentedly, antisocial the psychopath was, the men they diagnosed psychopathic in practice were neither so singular as psychiatrists described them nor so unburdened by social opprobrium as they imagined them. Rather, it was the man who did not measure up as a man—with all that entailed—who became the stock male psychopath.

The contours of the diagnosis were as inexact as those of manhood itself. Men regularly invoked this ideal of manliness as a standard against which to measure themselves. Few could aspire to manhood with as little guile as twenty-four-year-old Thomas Fuller, a purportedly feebleminded youth who was committed to the Psychopathic Hospital after he had been charged with setting fire to his room (in a boarding house) in a fit of despair over losing his job as an elevator operator. While hospitalized, Fuller befriended several social workers, to whom, for several years, he would refer as his best friends. Upon his discharge, Fuller set out to make good. He joined the marines, went to France to "fight in earnest for our belove and dear President Wilson, the man off the hour," and thought himself "a man with some experience." Reflecting upon having won out despite having had a hard life, Fuller wrote to Jarrett, "and I don't mind tell you that I am now 'some man.' And I feel like a man who has eaten a real dinner, very much satisfied and at peace with the world." Back in the United States two years later, earning a good wage, with three Liberty Bonds to his name, Fuller wanted to marry but was still looking for a "good loving girl."[43]

Whether Fuller's rather straightforward equation of manhood and respectability—a good woman, a good wage—resulted from his artless naïveté or from deep conviction, it highlights how ambiguous, how clouded with darker desires, was the manhood of many others. While Fuller could write of his desire to give his "heart to the girl I love," others confessed to struggling with their attraction to bad women while settling for good. And while he could be content with thirty-six dollars a month, they wanted much more.

Many of the men who consulted psychiatrists were plagued by the exactions of worldly ambition. A virtue, almost a necessity, ambition could also spawn the destructive vices of envy and greed. It might not be enough for a man, in everyday estimation, to be a steady worker; he should rather show some ambition, some desire to advance himself. One man's sister-in-law, for example, dismissed him as "rather a shiftless person," explaining that "his ambition is not of a very high order."[44] And the wife of another, a railway inspector whom psychiatrists diagnosed psychopathic, told psychiatrists that she was disappointed by her husband's inability to provide for even a meager standard of living.[45] But to psychiatrists it was better that a man should merely be a steady worker than that he not work at all. The ambition of which psychiatrists spoke with the men they diagnosed psychopathic was a narrowly specified quantity, signifying only that which would spark a man's desire to work. Ambition construed in this way was an unqualified necessity, the common coin of socialized man. It was distinctly absent from the psychopath's mental makeup. One out-of-work psychopath, for example, had no desire to get back.[46] Patrick Collins, the gangster, admitted he had no ambition and that he "just couldn't get right down to it and accomplish anything," explaining that he "had the 'don't care' feeling."[47] And another, a nineteen-year-old auto mechanic, told psychiatrists he felt dopey and had no ambition: "I feel as if I don't give a damn, how it goes." Psychiatrists noted that "he says he starts to do something, and something in his mind says, 'O to hell with it.'"[48] These men spoke of their slothfulness with an ease that was illustrative to psychiatrists of the general precept that the psychopath was one who chose to sit by the sidelines as others more manly than he participated in the struggle for existence. Yet even these men, so like the textbook psychopath in their disdain for the routines of the workaday world, were at times, unlike him, given to reflect painfully on their inadequacies.

The man vexed by his lassitude was at least playing the game, and psychiatrists were likely to diagnose him, at least in part by virtue of his purportedly greater insight, as nervous or neuropathic rather than psychopathic. Twenty-year-old Henry Perkins, for example, the son of a lawyer, sought psychiatric help with the complaint of feeling lazy, without energy or ambition; Emerson diagnosed him neuropathic.[49] But an excess of ambition could damn a man in psychiatrists' eyes as surely as a shortfall. Several men, ambitious beyond their capabilities, owned up to feeling envious of others more successful than they. A dentist who owned a moderately successful practice conceded to Emerson that he envied a fellow who had been in his class who was engaged to a wealthy girl.[50] And the scientist Calderwood, who claimed his career "had been hampered by his wife"— Emerson noted that the man "felt he had been taken in charge of by wife"—admitted to feeling envious of a better-endowed colleague's skill in testifying in a court case.[51] Even the outwardly successful could judge themselves failures. Joseph Scott, a twenty-six-year-old traveling salesman who earned a healthy thirty-five dollars a week and who felt "fairly sure of his job" because he was able to make the sales, let on that he was not making them "as skillfully as he would wish." He wanted a car and a motorboat but felt he did not earn enough to afford them.[52] And Daniel Madison, a university mathematician characterized by his wife as "intensely ambitious," felt bitter that he was not "doing something really worth while." His wife explained that he would compare himself and his accomplishments "with men of genius and then more modestly with men many years his senior" and would feel crushed.[53] The angst that these men's longings provoked could have served well as an object lesson concerning what psychiatrists considered the folly of excess ambition.

Psychiatrists assessed ambition equivocally. Too often even modest amounts were lacking; the outcome was the psychopath's languid indifference toward life's responsibilities. But the outcome of ambition wrongly directed could be just as problematic. In the scenario psychiatrists most often invoked, such ambition nurtured the psychopathic longing for escape from the monotony of everyday existence that led men into lives of antisocial deceit. The psychopath in this scenario was invariably a genius, not endowed, however, with the sort of intelligence the Binet tests measured— although psychopathic men, like their female counterparts, scored disconcertingly high on the tests—but rather with cunning interlaced with personal magnetism. His genius served him well, allowing him to prey on inoffensive, law-abiding citizens. "Clever, quick-witted, brilliant," he often made, one authority warned, "a far better impression upon the uncritical than [did] the more plodding, conservative, and reserved normal-minded individual."[54]

But the "normal" to which psychiatrists thought men should aspire existed only as a foil to the psychopathic. Drained of all that animated a man, the hypothetical normal man had appeal only as a rhetorical trope, a warning against the excesses of genius. Once specified, his characteristics proved vacuous, his personality nonexistent. Indeed, psychiatrists were reluctant to diagnose one man psychopathic, arguing he did not have "enough personality to come under" the rubric.[55] Yet psychiatrists consistently claimed to prefer plodding normality to the instability of genius. Normal personalities adjusted "fairly well to all situations," while psychopaths, "the least versatile of all people," adapted poorly "to changing conditions and environment."[56] Normal individuals, they explained, were willing to submerge their individuality to the "mode of behavior which best suits the community."[57] One psychopath's "self-willed, unplastic nature" and another's "self-important, self-sufficient, self-centered, and selfish" spirit contrasted sharply with the highly-touted malleability of the normal.[58]

Psychiatrists' preference for mediocrity over genius signaled their allegiance to the emerging psychology of adjustment, which celebrated conformity, placing the interests of society before those of the individual. But it was also a peculiarly psychiatric rendering of the long-standing American distrust of intellect to which theories of adjustment, in the course of the twentieth century, would lend steadily increasing weight. Psychiatrists who prided themselves on their courageously antidemocratic advocacy of intelligence tests were unlikely but nonetheless vigorous advocates of the culture of anti-intellectualism. One psychiatrist's warning that we "must cease to look upon intellect as the foundation of social conduct" and his insistence that "extreme dulness [sic] [was] compatible with a moral life" were medicalized variants of the American tendency that, according to Richard Hofstadter, pitted intellect against character in the belief "that intellect stands for mere cleverness," which too easily shades over into the sly and diabolical, and that, as William H. Whyte observed in the fifties, cast genius as suspect, coupling brilliant with such damning qualifiers as erratic, eccentric, and screwball—precisely those terms psychiatrists applied to the psychopath.[59]

That comfortable mediocrity fitted a man better than flighty genius for the demands of wage earning became axiomatic among the psychiatrists and social workers who preached the gospel of industrial psychiatry. Southard and Jarrett were central participants in the establishment of the discipline.[60] Its origins, late in the teens, lay in their (and others') conviction that the conflict between what Southard called the "over-conservatism of Capital" and the "over-radicalism of Labor" could be efficiently mediated, by the psychiatrist, psychologist, and the psychiatric social worker, so that "social justice" would prevail and "the industrial problem" would be resolved.[61] Maintaining that a high but unrecognized incidence of mental disease in the workplace undermined, invisibly and insidiously, what they argued were employment managers' well-intentioned strivings for efficiency, proponents of industrial psychiatry contended that both outcomes were at bottom a matter of worker psychology. To their minds, managers were well aware of the toll that physical disability—classed in the literature under occupational neuroses—exacted, but were remarkably, even willfully, ignorant of the even greater toll exacted by psychopathic, alcoholic, and otherwise mentally disturbed employees. Absent from, late to, and dissatisfied with their work, such employees contributed more than their share to the problems of industry. If advocates of industrial psychiatry could have their way and, by substituting the precision of psychiatric science for the managers' customary but inefficient "rough and ready" style, properly fit the worker to the job, then the "queer guys, eccentrics, disturbers, querulous persons, unreliable and unstable fellows" who sullenly roved from job to job, leaving behind them trails of unrest, would be transformed into the drones of modern industry.[62] It was well known, Southard wrote, "that many a psychopathic, cranky, grouchy, queer, or otherwise difficult person may be just the man wanted for a special task"; it was the task of industrial hygiene to match him to it.[63]

Social workers invested considerable energy in doing precisely that. Under the direction of Mary Jarrett, social workers identified a number of cases, primarily of men diagnosed psychopathic, that they followed aggressively, sometimes for several years.[64] Social workers found jobs for these men, intervened with employers when difficulties arose, and argued tirelessly on their behalf. They nurtured relationships with sympathetic employment managers who would tolerate troublesome employees; one of these, W. J. Rhodes of the Carter's Ink Company, saw a small troupe of putative psychopaths pass through his establishment. Social workers visited patients on the job, advised them concerning the ethics of the world of work, and chided them when their performance was less than satisfactory.

The case of Herman Blumberg, an out-of-work Jewish clothes-presser who came to psychiatric attention complaining of unbearable leg pains, is illustrative of how expansive the aims and techniques of industrial psychiatry could be. From the start, psychiatrists and social workers judged Blumberg hopelessly neurotic but intelligent. They quickly settled on a strategy to make him self-supporting: He would be set up in business, running a small store. Social workers wrote to a number of individuals known for their beneficence, endeavoring to raise funds for this somewhat extraordinary venture, characterizing Blumberg as a good man ("of the Jewish faith," in letters to prominent Jews) who "was suddenly struck down, without fault of his own." A good deal more than the requisite five hundred dollars was subscribed, and social workers set about trying to identify a suitable business. They failed to find one, however; more problematic, Blumberg's mental attitude, they came to realize, "unfits him at present for any business requiring initiative." Cranky and sullen, complaining that those who had subscribed sums in his name had done so to augment their own reputations as charitable individuals, Blumberg was finally set to work as a porter in a factory, at ten dollars a week, where, Jarrett noted, he "must be humored, for everyone near him must hold his opinion or none."[65] Still, Blumberg was one of social workers' favorites; it is likely that his very crankiness was part of what so endeared him to them.

Psychiatrists and social workers claimed to prefer malleability to opinionated individuality; indeed, strict adherence to the tenets of industrial psychiatry, which at its most utopian envisioned a society of selfless automatons who would happily submit to the general will as interpreted by experts, left them little choice. Yet Southard, for one, recoiled from this stark vision nearly as soon as he had outlined it. The vision contained a kernel of sociological truth; the opportunities for the play of individuality, at least in the world of work, were by all accounts diminishing. But the personality best suited to that world was one so passive and so acquiescent as to be unmanly. From this perspective, Blumberg's recalcitrance was preferable to acquiescent indifference.

The blanket indictment of manhood that psychiatrists—local and nationwide—drew up around the figure of the male psychopath would prove difficult to sustain in day-to-day practice. This difficulty inhered in the nature of that practice, in that the psychiatrist's own subjectivity—his sense of himself as a man—was constitutive of his practice. (Consider, for example, that Emerson, who nurtured intimate therapeutic relationships with many of his female patients, advised a striking freight-handler who was troubled by dreams of being a scab simply to "brace up," delivered "a talk in courage" to the envious dentist, and gave "a good scolding" to a neurasthenic man who wanted to enter a sanitarium, noting that he "sent him away with a little more back-bone."[66] Was the intimacy that psychoanalysis fostered simply too dangerous when both analyst and patient were men?) Under scrutiny, the psychopath's defects—isolated, attested to, repeated, and recorded—could assume damning proportions. But in the give-and-take of the staff meeting, a largely masculine conclave, his defects could also shade perilously close to what everyone thought normal—his "wild oats," for example, a sign of excess but hardly worth "wrestl[ing] with."[67] Psychiatrists, when pressed, were reluctant to throw their weight fully behind the prudish, bookish, pleasure-averse "normals" of the literature, and they could even offer psychopathic men opportunities to wipe their slates clean. "You will turn over a new leaf?" Southard asked one. "The Psychopathic Hospital is a sort of lesson?"[68] Only the offenses of the homosexually inclined were irredeemable. Narrowing in on these, psychiatrists in the late twenties would proffer the sexual psychopath as an icon of failed manhood, for his prerogatives could be safely limited without infringing on their own.

Alcohol

In the widespread turn-of-the-century discussion of drink one can see men poised precariously between the two competing conceptions of manhood —dissolute and respectable—that psychiatrists promoted. For the most part, the culture of drink promoted an especially aggressive variant of dissolute masculinity, an ideal world of pleasures men could celebrate free of feminine oversight. A separatist ethos structured the drinker's world. The saloon, its centerpiece, was an unregulated haven in an increasingly feminized world; alcohol, its medium, promoted male camaraderie as it loosed everyday inhibitions; the wife, its enemy, was by custom excluded. Thus, the culture of drink could reinforce masculinity. But drink could also bring men to ruin, and many drinkers were well aware of this long before their depredations brought them under psychiatric scrutiny. Still, that drinking was such a minefield of sexual politics kept many men, including psychiatrists, from accepting what they saw as the rather feminine equation of abstinence and respectability. According to its adherents, drink was part and parcel of manly respectability, providing occasions for celebration of the noble masculine virtues of honor, loyalty, and fellowship.

The drinker, as he took shape in public debate and popular discussion, defies categorization, his character almost wholly determined by the perspective of the one who would scrutinize him. As a long, impassioned, and partly feminist temperance tradition had it, he was a drunkard who squandered his wages, beat his wife, and ignored his wretched children. From what we might term a respectable masculinist perspective, however, he appears as a genial man who imbibes only moderately, and only for the pleasure of the company. Although each figure captured a piece of the complex reality of men's drinking, the pieces fit into wholly different stories. Of the two, the drunken brute was more clearly etched in popular consciousness; a staple of temperance propaganda from the early nineteenth century to the early twentieth, his specter animated early woman's rights activists' vivid evocations of the baneful consequences of unrestrained male tyranny and provided evidence to support their argument that male drunkenness lay at the root of many of their sex's afflictions.[69] "Drunkard" was no mere description but, rather, a heavily freighted image forged in the heat of public, politicized sexual antagonism.

In political discourse the figure of the gregarious and generous man who drank regularly but moderately with his mates was less sharply drawn but just as powerfully resonant as that of the drunkard. He and the saloon that hosted him bore diffuse but heavy political loads. For the man robbed of manhood by ever more meaningless and routinized work, the saloon was a democratic club, an arena for the play of the masculine egalitarianism that the market would increasingly deny him.[70] The drinker from this perspective was an avatar of reputable manliness. The pleasures of saloon-going spoke as much to his gender as to his political identity. From its decor, the walls typically graced with posters and photographs of sports figures and scantily clad women; to its customs, foremost among them treating, which was, in the words of one commentator, a "ritual of masculine renewal"; to its ethos, which was exclusively and aggressively masculine, the sensibility that the saloon nurtured and to which it catered was that of manliness.[71] That manliness, however, as it took shape in countless daily exchanges with wives who wanted their husbands home, was as embattled as the disreputable masculinity of the drunkard. Masculinity, once specified, was not some neutral congeries of uncontested virtues like honor, worthiness, and dependability. Rather, it was the outcome of a continual struggle, real and imagined, against woman. To drink in the company of men was to cement manly solidarity, but it was also to assert a glorious manhood unfettered by the nagging demands of women who would, had they their way, ensconce men at home, squander their wages, forbid them to drink—in short, emasculate them.

The masculinist ethos that emerged from the many debates about drink that divided households and legislatures alike was defensive, exaggerated, and bombastic. It held that a man's right to drink was inviolate, a woman's right to object nonexistent. Psychiatrists, some of them sympathetic to Prohibitionist aims, tried to temper this ethos, but their respect for the male prerogatives that the culture of the saloon flaunted so aggressively constrained them. They were far less condemnatory of drinking and drunkenness than their sternly unforgiving pronouncements on a range of other social problems might lead one to expect. This was in part because they, like other physicians, were attempting to transform drinking and alcoholism from moral into medical matters.[72] In the extended, not-yet-complete campaign to do so, they would relinquish the impassioned, inflammatory language, the starkly drawn choices, and the vividly cast villains of the temperance crusader and adopt instead the reasoned language of medicine and its measured respect for the sick and impaired. But psychiatrists were also unwilling fully to condemn drinkers because they saw that for many men drinking was not indicative of pathology, but woven into the fabric of everyday life, a sentiment expressed in Southard's observation that "what the alcoholic does is something like what any of us might do."[73] In addition, psychiatrists realized that a touch of dissipation might figure among the qualities that made a man's reputation.[74]

The case of James McGinley provides ample evidence to support the claims of woman's rights activists that male brutality resulted directly from drunkenness. On an April night in 1916 McGinley, a thirty-six-year-old machinist who had been a heavy drinker for eighteen years, took a quart of whiskey home and drank half of it. After an hour or so, he began to run about the rooms of his furnished apartment, jumping over tables, "showing how he would shoot the Mexicans," threatening his little boy, who begged him not to hurt him, chasing and sparring with his wife until she ran upstairs to another tenement from which she telephoned the police. Two officers soon arrived at McGinley's door. They informed him that his wife had called, told him to put on his clothes, and hauled him down to the station house. Soon committed to the Psychopathic Hospital, McGinley, who had, one day later, no memory of the evening's events, reluctantly admitted to psychiatrists that he "must have been drunk."

This bout of drinking was not the first to have landed McGinley in the arms of the law. His wife, Alice, had summoned officers three times previously, but he had never served any time. When sober, McGinley was kind and considerate, his wife told psychiatrists. Possessed of "fine feelings and sensibilities," he was "fond of music, good reading and nice people." He earned one hundred dollars a month and handed over seventeen or eighteen of it to her each week, enabling her to purchase plenty of wholesome food and to keep up a comfortably furnished home in a good Cambridge neighborhood. When drunk, however, McGinley was irritable, ugly, and abusive to his wife and their three children, and she never saw any of his wages. She had been afraid of him since the time three years before when he had "grabbed her and pulled her all over the house and tore her things." Two or three times she had gathered the children and left home, lured back only by his desperate entreaties.

McGinley told psychiatrists he drank not because of any particular fondness for liquor but to be sociable. Through his trade, he told psychiatrists, he came "in contact with a class of people that drink more or less"; a victim of treating, he could not say no to an invitation. McGinley equivocated on the question of whether his drinking was problematic. Only his reputation suffered, he maintained; he could stop any time he wished. Yet his admission that he had made up his mind to stay away from barrooms and to stop drinking altogether hinted at an awareness of his problem that he was unable to articulate fully; as psychiatrists put it to him, "Why should one stop if it doesn't do any harm?" Agreeing that McGinley's drinking was certain to cause him more trouble, psychiatrists diagnosed him a chronic alcoholic.[75]

Although drinking was neither an exclusively male nor an exclusively working-class nor, for that matter, an exclusively Irish vice, there were enough working men of Irish extraction whose drinking had serious consequences for themselves and their families to sustain the popular image of the drunk as an Irishman.[76] The outlines of the McGinley case—the prodigious intake, the consequent violence, the denial, the appeal to sociability —were replicated in many others. The amount of alcohol heavy drinkers like McGinley regularly ingested was impressive. On the day that the wife of Richard Byrne, the abusive thirty-four-year-old paper stock dealer, had him arrested, for example, he admitted to having started the day with two or three drinks and, he went on, "after dinner [midday] I had a Benedictine and about three o'clock I had a cocktail, and I had about four or five of that kind of drink and I had one whiskey."[77] And it was not unusual for thirty-nine-year-old Andrew McKeever, a chemist, to drink more than a quart of liquor a day; one morning between rising at five o'clock and leaving the house for work at half past eight, his wife (who had him arrested) told psychiatrists, he drank half a quart of whiskey and two bottles of beer.[78]

The diagnosis of alcoholic mental disease did not turn, however, on the straightforwardly ascertainable criterion of absolute intake, but on a more complex assessment of symptomatology—whether the patient had visual or auditory hallucinations; how much alcohol was necessary to bring them on (less in this instance signifying a more serious condition); whether he was deteriorating. In their questioning of patients, however, psychiatrists were as interested in drinkers' motives as in their overt symptoms. Accordingly, assessments of will and self-control figured in nearly every alcoholic's staff meeting. Popular lore at its most simple had it that men drank for companionship, and many men spoke to this understanding. One, for example, told psychiatrists he drank for the company: "I don't buy it and go behind the door to drink it," he explained.[79] When another man was among friends, he told psychiatrists, he was a "good fellow" and took many more drinks.[80] And another man, who came home drunk two or three times a week, blamed the friends who coaxed him into saloons after work. But men could also adopt the terms of the psychiatric theory that held that men drank to compensate for their failings. Thirty-year-old Charles Bristol, for example, at first could only say that he got into the habit of drinking when he was "a young feller." Was it that he was blue? psychiatrists asked. "I don't know," he replied, "I just drink from the habit; sometimes I drink a lot when I am blue." Psychiatrists pressed him further; was nothing causing his boozy spells? There was, he admitted: "Well, I think they come around once in a while because I never made a success in life, I never learned a trade, or had any education."[81]

Bristol was single, and his reply, like those of the other single men psychiatrists diagnosed alcoholic, was relatively straightforward but halting. Single drinkers as a group answered to no one except, in a few cases, their mothers, and in consequence the reasons they submitted to account for their drinking were rather artless. Married men, by contrast, could typically call up any number of elaborate scenarios to account for their drinking, for years of answering to suspicious wives had left them with stores of excuses. They could deny outright that they drank or, when pressed, admit that they did but insist that it had no effect on them. Forty-three-year-old Michael Fitzpatrick, for example, a bookkeeper of Irish descent, first claimed he had quit drinking—he could specify the exact day, 27 July, that he had stopped—then boasted that alcohol did not affect him in any case: "I don't think I have drank enough to affect me in any way that I can see." Yet his wife had repeatedly summoned police to the house because of his violent, drunken threats.[82] Men could also admit they drank but claim they had done so in the interests of their families. Andrew McKeever, for example, wrote to his wife that she should remember that "if I worked myself into a nervous breakdown my ambition was to benefit you and the children more than myself."[83]

But many of the married men who told psychiatrists of their alcoholic revels and debauches and then attempted to provide reasonable accounts for their behavior quickly tossed aside their more carefully crafted excuses and adopted the blustery language of men's rights. They brashly asserted that drinking was a man's activity and that their wives drove them to drink in any case. A fifty-two-year-old Irish butcher drank because his family bossed him around too much ("He thinks anyone would drink if they had the family he has," social workers sardonically noted);[84] Edward McBurney, a thirty-four-year-old Irishman, told social workers that if his "wife would not jump on him when he takes one drink everything would be all right, but she gets him so nerved up that he gets drunk" ("I am tired of trying to impress on everybodys mind that I am through with booze for life," he complained);[85] Richard Byrne, pointing out that his wife did not go to church, claimed that if he could see her say her prayers, "that would make me a better man" and, presumably, provide sufficient reason for him to stop drinking;[86] and William Burke, an Irish coal-heaver who had been arrested several times for drunkenness, blamed his wife entirely for his drinking, closing his conference with psychiatrists by claiming, "I would never drink a drop if it was not for her."[87]

In Ireland, to drink was to affirm masculinity and male privilege. Drink provided the Irish men who imbibed communally an escape from the womanly strictures that governed the home. The Irish drinker's raunchy stance toward sex was a consequence of his culture's constraining sexual puritanism; traces of the barroom's ribald sexual joking and habitual denigration of marriage and women are evident in the excuses of the men quoted above, all of whom had emigrated from Ireland.[88] Sexual antagonism was part and parcel of Irish drinking. Mixed with the Irishman's legendary wit, an almost comically exaggerated masculinism emerges.[89] Charles Connelly, for example, took on not only his wife but also his neighbors. He regularly insulted one, Mrs. McCarty, by referring to her as "The

Chicken," and he called another woman a grass widow and still another a suffragette. "To hell with your wife and my wife," he would yell, wandering drunkenly up and down his street in South Boston.[90]

These men were skilled at presenting themselves as victims of their wives' desires for control. William Burke, who admitted he had been in the House of Correction eight or nine times and had been arrested six times in the past fourteen months, laid it all at the feet of his wife: "All a woman has to do in South Boston now is to call an officer—she has done all the bellowing."[91] And Richard Byrne claimed that his troubles with drink had begun when his wife had decided to stop fixing his dinners. "I would have to go to my room all by my lonesome and I suppose I got to drinking more than usual and staying out nights," he explained, confident he would elicit psychiatrists' sympathy.[92] Although these men could pose as powerless, they could just as easily assume the prerogatives of their sex. When trying to convince the wives who had committed them to argue for their release, they cast themselves as responsible patriarchs who could provide handsomely for their families. From the House of Correction, to which he had been sentenced for six months, Edward McBurney expressed a concern for his family's welfare that years of freedom had never elicited. "There is a hard winter ahead for her now," he wrote of his wife to a social worker. "You know I could make big money this fall and winter and they will all be taken care of."[93] If he were only to be given one more chance, another man wrote to his wife, he would make good. "I have a plan that will benefit us all and I am sure you will agree when you hear it," he wrote.[94]

The competing pulls of respectable and dissolute masculinity are evident in the three-year saga of Joseph O'Meara, a twenty-nine-year-old who voluntarily sought psychiatric attention complaining of a "tight feeling" around his heart, vertigo, and an inability to breathe. O'Meara lived with his mother, his alcoholic father, and five or six of his seven siblings, all of whom worked and contributed to the family finances, in a clean, large house in a good area of Roxbury. The family was financially secure but emotionally perched somewhere between respectability and despair. Although the father earned a good wage as a clerk in the city waterworks, he regularly went off on three-week sprees during which, knowing better than to come home, he would find lodgings in a hospital.[95] Social workers quickly ascertained that the family's home life had never been happy on account of the father's drinking and his abusiveness to his wife who, for her part, testified that she loathed the sight of him but, explaining that the family was proud, felt it necessary to keep up appearances. Like his father but unlike any of his siblings, O'Meara was a heavy drinker. He had held perhaps twenty jobs from the time he had first worked at age fifteen, had been fired from nearly all of them because of drink, and had spent much of the previous six years loafing. He had been hospitalized six times for drink and he claimed to be lazy, with no tastes in particular for anything excepting alcohol and cigarettes.

Psychiatrists quickly determined that alcohol lay at the root of O'Meara's troubles and set about trying to wean him from it. The battle for O'Meara's soul was thus entered. On the one side stood psychiatrists, social workers, and his mother, all of whom tried to impress on O'Meara the virtues of sober respectability. On the other stood drink and loose women—the classic tempters of men—and O'Meara's friends and workmates, participants in a culture of rough sociability. For three years O'Meara vacillated between the two sides. When abstemious he could earn good wages and was in his mother's estimation clever, cheery, and properly domestic, an excellent cook and wonderfully useful handyman who made repairs and painted about the house. When O'Meara drank, however, he sank very low indeed. "I am damn down and out," he telephoned to social workers from a hotel barroom at the end of one three-day spree; shabbily dressed in a torn coat, his shoes unbuttoned and his trousers practically falling off, he visited social workers at the hospital several days later in hopes of being committed.

Accounting for his drinking, O'Meara—like psychiatrists, social workers, his mother, and his employer—moved easily between two explanatory paradigms, one moral, the other medical. The first cast drinking as a struggle between good and bad and the drinker as responsible for his conduct. When O'Meara explained with a touch of bravado that he occasionally found it necessary to brace himself up for work with a drink or contritely promised he would make good and never touch a drop again, he was assuming the poses of willful obstinacy and then abject piety that were characteristic of the drinker as the moralist saw him. Likewise, when psychiatrists implored O'Meara to show some backbone and stop drinking; when social workers pointed out to him that drinking was a matter of self-control; when his mother played on his guilt by signing off a letter to him, "Your crippled mother," and taking to her bed for six months, they were speaking to deeply resonant matters of virtue. But when O'Meara long-windedly explained after a year under social work supervision that "he felt he had gained in some respects even if he had not gained in fighting alcohol, that he had some confidence in himself and was beginning to meet people and enjoy people, once more," he was working within the medical paradigm. And when social workers deemed his lack of self-confidence "the only significant and real reason" for his drinking, and when his employer refused to censure him after an incident when he had "caused quite a little disturbance playing the piano" after he had been found "hitting it up with alcohol" by saying "we must not be too hard, we do not know what tempted him," they all showed evidence that they had adopted the therapeutic stance toward alcohol, which absolved the drinker of responsibility for his actions.

Although O'Meara could fashion himself the impotent victim of drink and circumstance, he managed to direct the drama that his life under social work supervision became, and this showed him to be possessed of a remarkable force of will. His capacity to engage everyone's sympathies, which irked at least one psychiatrist, while orchestrating events to his own immediate advantage was manifest in the handling of one incident especially, a party five months after the advent of Prohibition. Just prior to the gathering, O'Meara had begun a clerical job at the Schrafft's Paper Box Factory, in an office with six women and one man. It seems that the group had obtained some liquor and had organized a lively party—which was, O'Meara claimed, "perfectly legitimate"—to which he had gone proclaiming he was on the "water wagon" but from which he had emerged drunk. O'Meara explained that the others had "kidded" him and he had taken a little for sociability's sake. He stayed out all night, spent the next day groaning in bed, missed several days' work, and on his return was so nervous that he mixed up his candy accounts.

His mother, social workers, and employer were distressed at O'Meara's behavior, but he, acting the part of an ashamed "whipped cur," managed to escape their censure. As social workers investigated the incident, they pieced it together along familiar lines. A woman some suspected was of questionable character—a new telephone operator in the office who, although formerly married, posed as single—was at fault. She had invited O'Meara to the party and although no one knew "how far things had gone that night," plans to fire *her* were made, even though it was O'Meara, not she, who had missed work in the party's aftermath. And although several psychiatrists felt strongly that O'Meara should be committed as a chronic alcoholic, everyone involved was willing to let him try yet again to reform himself. His employer was loath to dismiss him, explaining that it was "when everybody else [was] down on a fellow" that he felt most interested; his parents did not want him committed because the Thanksgiving and Christmas holidays were approaching and they thought he could make good; and even the physicians who might have committed him were willing to give him another chance to prove himself sober.

The play of masculinity in O'Meara's case was subtle. This was in part because, as a single man who answered not to a wife but to a mother and as one who never went with gangs, he was not so well versed as many other men in the language of sexual antagonism, which cast drinking as a male prerogative and was alert to any feminine enchroachment on it. Further, as a drinker who was likely severely alcoholic—a physician at the Washingtonian Home, who had also treated his father, deemed his "one of the most stubborn of cases" he had ever treated· –the pleasures of dissoluteness were fleeting: O'Meara could indulge in a three-week "glorious celebration" of "wine, women, and song," but he would emerge from it a physical and mental wreck. O'Meara was more aware than many drinkers of how debilitating drink could be and, the incident of the office party notwithstanding, he was less inclined than many other men to cast blame for his drinking onto another.

Yet O'Meara needed a masculine identity as much as any other man, and social workers were willing to help him fashion it.[96] Because O'Meara had on many occasions proved himself susceptible to the temptations of modern, urban living, social workers tried to press on him a manliness that was both markedly anachronistic in its celebration of the virtues of rural life and markedly bourgeois in its celebration of the virtues of self-control. While claiming to prefer work at which he could use his "bean," O'Meara moved to Maine—a dry state—for a short time in 1918 to work on a farm. "I really feel ashamed not to be doing something more substantial," he wrote to his social worker soon after he had moved; she replied that to her mind there was "no more noble work than farming." As she put it to O'Meara, the choice was between being "a man who is a mere machine and works eight, ten and thirteen hours a day and makes big money" and being an individual living among people who could broaden and educate him. "Do not let the miserable dollar interfere," she admonished him. No one "will think less of you as a man and most will think more of you as a man if you stick to the job." O'Meara rejected this construction of manhood and returned to the city to seek office work. But he could not evade social workers' regular lectures on the necessity of forgoing excess, which they presented as a measure of manliness. Was he man enough to get hold of himself? Had he enough backbone to leave alcohol alone?

In the end, some four years after he had originally been committed to the hospital, O'Meara adopted the respectable identity that social workers had worked so diligently to press upon him. This identity did not take shape around the manly independence—so difficult for a wage earner to achieve—that social workers had earlier advocated, but around a congeries of slightly feminized practices and pursuits. The worker who visited him at home, for example, in February 1920, was treated to some of his "daintily served" sponge cake, which, his mother proudly announced, he had baked that morning between washing and ironing his shirts. The worker also ascertained that O'Meara had recently spent a day baking apple pies with his mother (noting that he aspired to making a crust as good as hers), and that he no longer went out with other men, preferring instead to read in his room or to attend the theater. Working hard at the candy factory, O'Meara was "radiantly happy," according to his employer "a clean straight fellow" who never swore or said "anything out of the way." When social workers closed his case, O'Meara had been on the wagon for more than a year.

O'Meara's transformation from drunken rake to respectable homebody underscored the general precept, to which psychiatrists and patients alike subscribed, that a man gave up something of his manhood in becoming a patient. Patienthood involved a submission to authority, a resignation of will, and an acquiesence to emotion that many deemed unmanly. The Men's Club, organized in 1915 as an association of discharged alcoholics, served to counter this perception, to remind its members that manhood and patienthood were not altogether incompatible. The formal structure of the club—its proceedings governed by a constitution, bylaws, and elected officers—allowed them a say in its operation and usefully clothed its therapeutic aims in the garb of participatory democracy. Within the club's safe confines, a man could feel that he was, as one said, "one of the boys."[97]

War and Gender Confusion

For psychiatrists, American and European, the war yielded large numbers of men who acted like women. Hundreds of case reports detailing the strangely hysterical behavior—paralyses, convulsions, paraplegias, tics, and tremors—of battle-weary (and battle-shy) soldiers began to flood medical and psychiatric journals in 1915 and 1916, prompting psychiatrists nationwide to reexamine the commonly accepted characterization of hysteria as a peculiarly female malady.[98] "Shell shock," a term—resonant with military associations—coined during the war, quickly came to denote hysteria in what Southard referred to as "the rougher sex." Afflicted from without by cataclysms equal to those that tormented the hysteric from within, the victims of shell shock that peopled the literature were cast variously as subnormals, psychic weaklings, malingerers, and draft evaders. Still, military physicians stressed that in civilian life many had been and would be "perfectly normal men,"[99] and they boldly asserted what few would say when the hysteric was a woman—that "everyone has hysterical small coin in the bank of his personality," that the hysterical tendency "shades off toward normal constitution by gradual transition."[100] Thus, medical authorities normalized the male hysteric even as they excoriated him.

Few victims of shell shock passed through the Psychopathic Hospital; the military men who came to psychiatrists' attention were for the most part psychopaths, men whose failings became manifest long before they could be shipped off to Europe. Psychiatrists warned that the unfit and unstable were often the first to enlist (Stearns, a wartime Navy surgeon, admonished his correctional colleagues for encouraging their charges to sign up for service, using the armed forces "as a sanitarium or reform school"),[101] and maintained that military life—the excitement, intensity, and male companionship it offered—first attracted, then repelled psychopathic men who could not adjust to its strictures. Official estimates put the psychopathic proportion of enlisted men at less than 1 percent, but psychiatrists were as drawn to them as the men themselves purportedly were to the services.[102] Many of these men presented straightforward scenarios of what psychiatrists could easily classify under the rubric of malingering. The man who claimed he was a conscientious objector and said he was courageous but would only "do some praying" if someone aimed a pistol at his mother; and the man who, three weeks after he had been called up by the Naval Reserve, in which he had enlisted in order to avoid the draft, was sent to the hospital complaining that the other men "were making disparaging remarks about his appearance and behavior" and promising that if he were discharged "he will be all right," a telltale sign of simulation —psychiatrists quickly summed these men up as inadequate, queer, and psychopathic.[103]

But malingering could take more subtle forms. What of the man, a former hospital attendant familiar with the signs of mental disorder, who was sent to the hospital from camp for observation because of the hallucinations and delusions he claimed to psychiatrists he had faked? He wanted "to give the doctors a run for their money," he maintained, sure that they would find him sane even as he was trying to convince others he was not. But psychiatrists judged him a malingerer *and* a victim of mental disease, thus fusing what the received wisdom on malingering so carefully distinguished.[104] The issues around malingering—truth, facts, the reality of "merely" mental disease—were situated at the center of psychiatrists' evolving science, determinants, as they saw it, of their own standing in medicine's hierarchy of specialties. The specter of large numbers of disabled, hysterical men forced a reexamination not only of the gender specificity but also of the metaphysics of hysteria, and thus of functional— merely mental—disease in general. During the war, as the casualties piled up and as various authorities attempted to distinguish between the malingerer and the hysteric, they proposed a reordering of what many had maintained before, asserting now that the hysteric's symptoms were real *because* not under his conscious governance. Many psychiatrists were skeptical of Charcot's early observations on hysteria, Southard wrote in 1918, but "the Shell-shock data of this war" proved that his observations were right. "I feel that physicians will have to brush up their ontology to the extent of conceding that a symptom may be in a sense imaginary and yet not in any sense non-existent," he wrote, admonishing those physicians who would scoff at the distinction.[105] In other words, when men became hysterics, hysteria became real.

That early-twentieth-century psychiatrists never elaborated a program for manhood is not altogether surprising. If it is a mark of the human sciences that their object is, to paraphrase Foucault, of a type to which the scientist himself belongs, that difficulty was all the more pertinent when the object was the gendered dimension of man.[106] Psychiatrists were never able to identify the concepts through which they might have apprehended the "man" in the men who came before them; psychopathic personality, the closest they came to doing so, was too broadly construed a category, too mired in pathology to be put to general use. The models of manliness that psychiatrists put forth—in confrontations with individual patients, in the collective arena of the Men's Club, and in their professional literature— were contradictory and largely untheorized, patched together in practice, informed by their own largely unexamined experiences as men. In contrast to their emphatic, certain pronouncements concerning women—who were, for the most part, defined by their gendered qualities—their dicta concerning men were undisciplined and inconsistent. The legacy of their efforts was confused. The war over, for example, Karl Menninger outlined the case of a male hysteric as a "male analogue" to Myerson's willful female hysteric, a man who was as susceptible to the vagaries of domestic life as any woman. In this instance, the pathological (hysteria, the man's twitching) was normalized, brought within the familiar domestic compass.[107] Another strand of psychiatric thinking about men pathologized what was normal; this was manifest, for example, in the psychiatrist Martin Peck's conclusion (to a study of Harvard students) that large numbers of college men suffered from "personality disorders and functional nervous illness"—a damning, expansive judgment that many would come to see as characteristically psychiatric.[108]

Was manhood, in psychiatrists' hands, normal or pathological? Let us allow the artistically inclined mechanical draftsman Henry Allen the last word on this. Declining a "group examination," which he submitted was "suggestive of an abnormal mentality," but agreeing to submit to a "private, personal interview," he grasped quite clearly the psychiatric propensity to render the normal abnormal. "I am trying to live a normal life amid normal surroundings and to gain a normal mental outlook," he politely but firmly wrote to the social worker whose task it was to entice him back to the institution for further scrutiny. The examination, he maintained, "would not be helpful, but the reverse, in my gaining the normal state of mind which I hope to achieve."[109] Perhaps sensing that he was right, the social worker let the matter drop.

TEN

THE SEXUAL POLITICS OF MARRIAGE

VARIOUS HISTORIANS have provided us the rough outlines of a history of marriage in the early years of the century, moving from the tightly regulated confines of Victorian marriage, based on separate spheres, control of male sexuality, and repression of female sexuality, to the supposed triumph, in the twenties, of companionate marriage, which celebrated heterosexual mutuality. We have some understanding of what women gained and lost in the transition from one form of marriage to the other: Women, or so the synthesis goes, gave up the right to say no, which they had exercised—if not enjoyed—in the Victorian period, and, as psychiatrists, sexologists, and social commentators elaborated a new ideal of sexualized womanhood, gained the right to say yes. This transition took place in the context of popular and professional concern about the future of marriage as an institution—a generally acknowledged "marriage crisis." As the nation's divorce rate more than doubled from 1890 through 1920, many were left to wonder why what some referred to as the new type of woman seemed not so well fitted for marriage as her forebears had been. Education, feminism, the world of work: all, it seemed, lured women away from marriage with the promise of an independent and fulfilling life.[1]

Psychopathic Hospital psychiatrists were eager participants in this turn-of-the-century recasting of marriage, for it allowed them ample opportunity to display the fiercely anti-Victorian modernism of which they were such vocal proponents. As they scrutinized the hundreds of domestic dramas that unfolded before them, they developed a pragmatic position on marriage. They had little patience with much of the sentimental discourse that, to their minds, obscured the real nature of the marriage bond. Marriage to them was a matter not of romance, for romance was inevitably ephemeral, or even obligation, for obligation as traditionally conceived wrongly bound incompatible men and women. Marriage was rather an imperfect, constantly evolving enterprise that united men and women endowed with fundamentally different natures and interests. Harmony, not ecstasy, was the most to be hoped for from an institution that opened each spouse, and his or her most objectionable habits, entirely to the other's view; familiarity dulled passion and often bred contempt. It was no wonder to psychiatrists that men and women were constantly at odds.

The many women and men who, voluntarily or involuntarily, subjected themselves and their marriages to psychiatric scrutiny have left a rich record of their everyday lives and domestic disputes.[2] In this record one can trace the particulars of what Karl Menninger, writing from the Psychopathic Hospital, characterized as "the complex intricacies of the relation between domesticity and psychiatry."[3] In practice, for a number of reasons, this relation was often reduced to the relation between women and psychiatry. Women appear to have initiated the majority of cases of marital dispute. The husband in an unhappy marriage could flee every morning into the world of work, while the wife had no choice but to spend her days at home, surrounded by the wreckage of her failed relations. Women consulted the lawyers, clergymen, and family doctors who advised them to put their troubles in psychiatrists' hands; they initiated the court proceedings that culminated in the commitment of their mates; some, worn down by constant marital conflict, even signed themselves into the institution under the provisions of the voluntary statute. Further, in many cases of marital dissension, psychiatrists and social workers focused their attentions on the wife, who was more available and thought to be more compliant than her husband. Finally, women appear to have been better versed in the conventions of self-disclosure on which the psychiatric analysis of marriage depended, more willing to engage with professionals in a dialogue about their emotional needs and desires. Some men, by contrast, objected vehemently to the scrutiny that their wives had set in motion. "I didn't like to get up and make those statements that should be kept in a home," explained one, committed by his wife; "She has made a show of the house by having all kinds of agents come to see her and also a show of me," wrote another.[4]

The cavils of these patriarchs notwithstanding, men were often drawn into the dialectic of marital scrutiny and intimate disclosure. From the give-and-take between them and their wives, among both parties and psychiatrists, and among all three groups and social workers, we can glean the makings of a prosaic but popular sensibility on marriage, a sensibility whose outlines writers on the battle of the sexes were in the process of sketching. In this sensibility, the stark oppositions between female dependency and male responsibility, between female virtue and male vice, so central to middle-class campaigns for social purity and the end of the double standard, played little part. Rather, both sexes had their faults. It was expected that in marriage men, though professing otherwise, would be unfaithful, unreliable, and selfish with their earnings; that women, though possessed of strong desires, would become undesirable household drudges; and that each sex would struggle incessantly and bitterly against the other. Some expected no more from marriage or, indeed, from life. But many, especially women, whose testimony on this point was especially voluble, sought more and, against the foil of this grimly realistic sexual politics, their dreams of finding affection, love, and intimacy flourished. For the most part quietly resigned to what they had learned was the natural order of things, they could still rail against what they saw as men's deficiencies and marriage's injustices with impassioned conviction.[5]

Great Love, Profound Misery

On a March day in 1914, Frank Kinney, a skilled engraver of Irish descent who lived in South Boston with his twenty-four-year-old wife Barbara, decided to put an end to the week-long quarrel in which the two had been engaged by taking the matter to the police. His demand, to which she would not accede, that they break up housekeeping and board out their baby set in motion a fight that rapidly escalated. He took the baby to her mother's house; she followed, "made a scene, during which a police officer was called in," and decided to stay there for a few days. Then because, by her own admission, she "hated her husband so that she felt impelled to bother him," she began to hang around outside the shop where he worked, periodically looking in the window to annoy him. When he emerged at the end of one day's work, she took hold of his arm, followed him into a store, and tried to get him to buy her some candy, which he refused to do. Angered, he marched her "to a police station and told the captain that she was following him about and that he could not get rid of her." She made another scene, during which he walked out; she sat on the floor and demanded to be taken to the Psychopathic Hospital.

Barbara Kinney told hospital psychiatrists she was determined to be through with her husband, with whom she was no longer in love. They had been fairly happy until recently. She then had been hospitalized for several months with rheumatic fever, during which time he had gone to live with his mother, who had taken the opportunity to set him against her, bending his ear about her extravagance and begging him not to give her any money. Since then he had refused to give her enough to run the household properly. He took his meals in restaurants while she had barely enough to eat. He had, she maintained, even struck her on the head with a shoe. She had consulted a lawyer but claimed not to care what became of her. The tale as Frank Kinney told it was much the same. The two had been happy until Barbara had fallen ill. He admitted he had given her no money, but maintained he brought home plenty of food that she had refused to cook. He countered her charge of abuse with a like charge of his own, testifying that she had struck him with a tin pan and had thrown a teapot and other dishes at him. He, too, had engaged a lawyer and claimed to care little of what became of her.

A week later Barbara Kinney was ready to go home and do housework, "to sew buttons on [her] man's clothes." She now was sorry that she had caused so much trouble, and she admitted she had not done right by her husband. "To tell the truth," she confessed to psychiatrists, "I didn't even cook his meals for him for three weeks before I left home. I didn't even wash a handkerchief for him." She had been "sore on him" on account of the alliance she suspected he had forged with his mother in her absence; she was sure he missed her now and would want her back.

He did, and the two set up housekeeping again. This reconciliation, however, like several subsequent ones, lasted only a few months. Old resentments and familiar complaints came inexorably to blight the initial period of cooperation and mutual appreciation that social workers in each case carefully orchestrated, the cheery domestic scenes in which the worker was treated to ice cream, cake, and tea giving way to spectacles of filth, disorder, and neglect from which one or the other of the drama's protagonists had fled.[6] The Kinneys' case was unique in its particulars but typical in the patterns of domestic arrangements and resentments it displayed. Many of the women and men who came to psychiatrists' attention squared off against each other dramatically and publicly, engaging relatives, police, and lawyers in support of their causes; they sometimes then sought to undo some, if not all, of whatever familial, legal, or social service agitation they had set in motion against their partners. Fighting couples moved only hesitantly toward divorce; many who would never divorce (and who thus never appear in any official compilations of statistics of marital disputes) took a number of intermediate steps, such as separations, both legal and extralegal, that they often reversed. In such volatile unions it was thus difficult to distinguish between the everyday, expected trials of married life and the stuff of a more serious breach.

Married working-class and middle-class women and men of modest means lived in separate worlds. Men moved in the public domain of workplace and saloon by day and evening, returning to the women's world of home and neighborhood by night. A strict division of labor that cast men as providers and women as household managers structured the sexes' day-to-day relations. Because it was only the fortunate working-class man who was regularly employed at a good wage, the bargain ensured that spouses would constantly be at odds. A man was obligated to hand over some if not all of his weekly pay packet to his wife, the exact amount a matter of negotiation. She was to provide the family with regular meals and clothing in return. Many men saw it in their interest to conceal the amount they earned and to withhold as much as possible from their wives, who, by their accounts, wasted money in buying and preparing food and in furnishing their households. A wife might lay claim to nine or ten of the typical husband's weekly fifteen to eighteen dollars, the rest his own for drink and sociability with his mates. If her husband was unemployed or prone to loafing, it was up to a woman to piece together a family wage, taking in sewing, letting out rooms, begging small amounts from relatives and charitable agencies, and, in the hardest times, dipping into the savings she had carefully accumulated by scrimping and saving on an already impossibly tight budget.

The prodigal wife who squanders her weekly household allotment appeared with impressive frequency in the accounts of men who landed under psychiatric scrutiny, testifying to their near-total ignorance of what it took to make a home. Alec Bundy, for example, could not understand why his forty-year-old wife, a mother of seven, could not do all of the housework and washing herself; he accused her of "sitting around and eating all the time."[7] Another man, committed at his wife's behest, complained to psychiatrists that he had no idea what his wife had done with the money he had given her: "God bless my soul! What did she do with the $2092?" he exclaimed. Psychiatrists elicited his admission that he had handed over not a lump sum but his weekly wages for three years. He wondered yet what she had done with it. "She fed you and took care of you," the psychiatrist explained.[8]

If making a home in straitened circumstances was difficult, making a common emotional life was even harder. Although many of the men and women who came to psychiatrists' attention shared a diffusely romantic vision of marital happiness, they differed sharply on the nature of the marriage compact. To many of the women it was affection and love, not law and authority, that bound the sexes in marriage. Each spouse's love for the other obscured the inequalities of marriage and made its many annoyances palatable. A wife's obligations to her husband were contingent on his providing not only financial support but love as well. As one woman accounted for the timing of her decision finally to divorce her husband of more than forty-five years, a man with whom she had quarreled often and heatedly: "My complaint against him is that he does not love me any longer."[9] From the man's point of view, there was no need to camouflage the inequalities of marriage; they were fixed, right, and natural. A man "should run the house and family," boasted one, "and his wife should have nothing whatever to say about it."[10] Added another, driven to distraction by his wife's desire to "boss the house the same as her mother": "It is a woman's duty to give in to her husband."[11] These men's casting of their particular grievances as general laws (a man's rights, a woman's duties) was no doubt prompted in part by the psychiatric encounter itself, for in the process of constructing one's case—telling one's story, answering psychiatrists' questions, assigning blame for one's faults—dimly felt grievances could come into sharp focus.[12] But men also brought the makings of this stance with them. As such, it must also be seen as a measure of their self-importance and of the distance and deep distrust that separated the sexes and nurtured one's hostility to the other.

Neither women nor men imagined that marriage would be so difficult. Those who had married for love told psychiatrists of watching defenselessly as the aggravations of married life came to outweigh its pleasures. Sometimes disenchantment came swiftly. Thirty-four-year-old Nellie Byrne, for example, had been shattered to discover on her honeymoon that the teetotaler she had happily courted for two years was in fact a regular drinker. She had "almost died of fright" watching him confidently order a drink at a celebratory dinner; gravely wounded by his deception, she claimed she had not known happiness with him in the nine years since.[13] More commonly, however, the first flush of marital bliss faded slowly, falling victim to tensions and acrimonies generated in the grubby, day-to-day business of making a common life. Quarrels over food, money, sex, children, and relatives dampened the ardor of even those who had entered marriage the most romantic and devoted of spouses. When sixty-one-year-old Minnie Nelson married her husband Frederick she had loved him so much, she wrote, "that if I could say now that I loved God as well as I did [him] in 1870 I should be sure of a bright place in heaven." Forty-six years later the best she could muster was that her "married life was made up of spaces of 'the greatest love' and 'the most profound misery.'"[14] The many who had drifted into rather than chosen marriage had little romantic capital on which to draw as times became harder. Some women and men told of engaging in nonprocreative sex, kissing, fondling, and masturbating each other before eventually engaging in intercourse, all the while recklessly avoiding the issue of marriage until pregnancy forced it. A sexually active but semihonorable man hoping to evade marriage could try to secure an abortion for a woman he impregnated; before they married, for example, Frank Kinney had directed his several-months-pregnant lover first to a pharmacist who supplied her with black pills—abortifacients—that failed to do the job, then to a physician who refused to perform an abortion.[15] Others told of feeling honor-bound to marry women with whom they had been sleeping. Long-accumulated resentments, on both sides, fueled hostility in cases where pregnancy precipitated marriage. Margaret Smith, for one, liked intercourse but not William Kelly particularly; yet she slept with him often for a year and a half on the assumption that he would marry her should she get pregnant. He, on the other hand, made the equally improbable assumption that his simultaneous relations, which he dismissed as so many "summer flirtations," with several other women would relieve him of any responsibility for her condition. In the event, her assumptions proved more durable and the two married, only to separate later when she became pregnant by another man.[16]

Many wondered why marriage was so difficult. Psychiatrists wondered why anyone would have imagined it otherwise. Psychiatrists saw conflict in marriage as commonplace, the outcome of men's and women's different natures and needs. A man by nature bridled against the restraint marriage demanded of him. It diminished sharply the freedom he had learned in adolescence was his as a man, subjecting him to control that was doubly odious because exercised by a woman; in marriage, his earnings, his sexuality, his time—all that had been his alone—became matters for negotiation with his wife. In the best of cases a man would willingly relinquish the immediate but ephemeral pleasures of late adolescence for married manhood's more durable gratifications; responsibility for home and family would nurture in him a pleasing sense of contentment and accomplishment, tempering his more selfish desires. The problem for most working-class and some middle-class men was that the pleasures of proper manhood, which depended on a level and consistency of earnings far beyond their reach, were as oblique as they were unattainable. Indeed, it was not so much the responsibility for family that men found so pleasing but rather the power attendant upon it; the pleasures of manhood as psychiatrists saw them were the pleasures of the patriarch, who exercised control over his family as a prerogative of providing for them. For the majority of men, by contrast, marriage was a poor bargain, burdening them with responsibility as it robbed them of their freedom.

If men could not be patriarchs, they could imagine themselves as such. Their actual power within the family contingent on decent behavior and regular provisioning, men, even the most dissipated among them—like one Henry Loyal, a drunken, surly loafer with a history of engaging in "all manner of unspeakable sex practices"—could be made to feel, through psychiatric intervention, more manly.[17] Some men, however, needed little prompting in this campaign to substitute imagined for real manhood, for they were already taking refuge in elaborate fantasies of domestic felicity in which they, as real men, exercised total control over their wives and households. Some knew well—or learned from psychiatrists and social workers —that a wife, a few children, and a home were the accoutrements of proper manhood. After five months of social work supervision, for example, thirty-nine-year-old Frank Grant, who had been brought to the hospital by two officers and his disgusted wife (who had had him arrested for drunkenness and nonsupport three times previously), plaintively wrote to his social worker of his desire for "the pleasure of a home[,] wife and babies," the having of which "will mean the making of a new man."[18] Grant and others like him imagined themselves absolutely devoted to the wives they engaged in daily combat. As one maintained concerning his wife, whom he had committed with the complaint of being unable "to hold and control her": "I feel that I would have devoted my life to making [her] a happy and contented little wife"—this, from a man who had thrown his wife against the wall in anger.[19] This man's use of the subjunctive is telling, a measure of how easily noble intentions could outdistance behavior. Many of the men whose marriages foundered were unable to distinguish love from obedience and submission, unable to imagine love unlinked to patriarchal authority.

That a man's prerogatives were not what they had been generated some confusion. Richard Byrne, for example, who opened his conference with psychiatrists by explaining that he had "a sort of an independent girl for a wife," told them that he had seen his father strike his mother. Although, he boasted, he had never struck his wife, he claimed it was her duty to give in (maintaining that "if she only had just cried, we would have patched things up"), just as his mother always had after a row with her husband, coming to him with a cup of soup and making up. The authority Byrne sought here to exercise—a "real man," to his mind, answered to no one, least of all his wife—was of a sort to which many women, by their own accounts, were no longer willing to submit.

Their households riven by constant, acrimonious quarreling, a number of men entertained visions, which they eagerly shared with psychiatrists, of genteel domesticity, the particulars of which had little to do with the circumstances of their lives. Their wives, in these idylls, commanded the labor of a bevy of servants and were thus free to attend only to them. Their homes were not the cramped and dirty quarters in which they actually lived, but the quiet, private residences of bourgeois patriarchs. A thirty-nine-year-old chemist, the would-be paterfamilias par excellence, expected his wife, weary from the day's round of domestic drudgery, to stay up late with him and sit silently by the fire, poised and ready to fill his pipe, take off his shoes, and fetch his slippers, while he read the day's paper.[20]

This sort of mise-en-scène drew psychiatrists' censure. Their tolerance for the shenanigans of such miserable men was limited, and they regularly expressed disbelief when men laid before them their conceptions of their rights vis-à-vis their wives. Richard Byrne, for example, unashamedly told psychiatrists that "little things that would annoy her I tried to do." He regularly hid his wife's glasses and refused to tell her where he had put them; on one occasion, intending "to get her a little mite angry," he took off for New York, mailing back pictures of himself sitting in an automobile. Frank Kinney tried to frighten his wife with mice;[21] another man cut his wife's clothesline, ordering her to return, unwashed, the laundry she had taken in to earn a few extra dollars;[22] Frank Grant tussled over baby clothes with his pregnant wife and, according to her sister, engaged in many similarly mean and trifling acts.[23] Such pettiness was in part the isolated teasing of a few quirky men, but it was also one small part of a larger pattern of men's hostility to women. Men voiced this hostility with a forced jocularity that betrayed their anxiety. Among men it was waggishly understood that authorities who usurped men's rights were in fact women, the gender inversion at once diminishing the stature of these resented authorities and endowing them with devious, controlling desires. As noted above, the judges who committed men at women's behest were, according to police lore, "a lot of old women in men's clothes" and "the hospital people" could be ridiculed as "fools because they are all women."[24]

Psychiatrists who tried to undermine men's conceptions of their prerogatives precisely fit this characterization. One faulted Charles Connelly, for example, who complained that his wife—a mother of ten—bossed him around too much, for lacking a "serious and sober view of [her] as working hard all these years," admonishing him, "I don't see as you give her quite credit for that. . . . She had a hard time bearing the children." Connelly lightheartedly replied that it had been hard for him too.[25] And toward Richard Byrne, who complained that "a woman's word is always taken before a man's" and that it was not a square deal for psychiatrists to listen to his wife's rendition of their marital woes—"for I have said a lot of things to be nasty, and it sounds bad to have them repeated"—psychiatrists adopted a punitive stance. How long would it be before he got out of the hospital, he asked them. "I don't know. I can't foretell that any more than the weather," replied one disingenuously, adding, "This place is going to be mighty good for you."[26]

Many of the women whom psychiatrists saw were deeply disappointed in their spouses as men. They learned in marriage that men were not all they were cracked up to be. Too often they were insipid when they should have been forceful, coarse when tenderness was called for, secretive without apparent reason, unfaithful even as they fathered children they held dear. It was not the authoritarian patriarch of male fantasy for whom women yearned, but rather the man who had been domesticated but not emasculated by his experience of family life. A home and children should instill refinement and respect in a man, women maintained; immersion in domesticity should give him the strength to "rise to the occasion and be a man" when this was called for, one woman explained.[27] For many women marriage entailed constantly adjusting their visions of "men" to accord with the reality of "a man." Some of their complaints were economic; Agnes Blair, a black woman, told social workers that her husband had never shown any inclination "to build up their home" or to improve their economic situation.[28] But other grievances had more to do with men's emotional shortcomings. Nellie Byrne complained that her husband had never been "kind and sympathetic as I supposed a married man would be," that he had always been unenthusiastic about sex with her, so that "it always seemed . . . as if he always had somebody, or else he must have been an abnormal man. He didn't seem to me natural," she explained, "as I would think a man would be."[29] And Jean Swift, a thirty-seven-year-old housewife and mother of two, was satisfied with her husband as a provider but unhappy with him as a mate; "he has never given me his entire confidence," she explained to the psychiatrists who wanted to hear her story and invited her "to speak freely."[30] Other women remarked that their husbands were similarly aloof. Eleanor Herbert wrote to a social worker that her husband had never given her love and kindness, had never made her feel as if she were somebody. Rather, she averred, "he fairly kills the spirit in me."[31] And Helen Mellars, a thirty-two-year-old Irish-American housekeeper whose husband, convalescing in England during the war, had become engaged to marry another woman (European women, he wrote, excusing his behavior, "are fairly throwing their selfs at any man that comes along"), wrote to her employer that she had "appealed to his manhood to try and be what I always thought him to be but," she confessed, "I guess I have lost all hope over him."[32] Women's expectations of men were perhaps unrealistic —they wanted them strong yet tender, passionate yet domestic, and this in a culture in which the markers for proper manhood were confused indeed—but their disappointments were real. It was painful for women to confront their spouses' shortcomings. "I try to fool myself that he is the finest specimen of manhood," Eleanor Herbert wrote of her husband. But, she added wistfully, "we grow wise as we grow older."[33] And Mary O'Brien's lawyer, she told psychiatrists, "has told me lots of times that I expected too much from him [her husband], that he was just like the average man"—just that for which many women claimed they were no longer willing to settle.[34]

Women elaborated their critique of men collectively. In the women's world of the neighborhood, emptied of men by day, they enjoyed a rich sociability, meeting in the streets and gathering in each other's kitchens to share information, confidences, and gossip as they went about the business of making a home. Through talk women defined themselves, their work, and their worldview. A woman's everyday chores assumed substance and worthiness as the subject of neighborly conjecture; speculation on the morals, marriage, and housekeeping of another tinged ordinary concerns with an edge of excitement. Women could judge each other harshly; the woman who wrote, unsolicited, to social workers of her sister-in-law's housekeeping—"all who live in this neighborhood cannot help but see and hear how things go"—articulated the regulatory spirit that informed much neighborhood talk.[35] Several of Agnes Blair's Roxbury neighbors were certain that she and her husband were not in fact married but only posing as such; they were, one wrote, "annoyed to death with her."[36] Questioned by social workers, the elderly Irish woman who lived next door to Alice McGinley in a nice Cambridge neighborhood deemed her "rather peculiar" and said she showed "very little energy to live with a man who treats her so badly." Likewise, McGinley's upstairs neighbor thought her "mentally deficient," noting that she wore "old, disreputable clothing" and confessing to being "ashamed of the things she put on her line." This neighbor's observation that "she should do better with her income" was a mark of just how much of a woman's life was subject to scrutiny and of just how catty that scrutiny could be.[37] But women could also offer one another support. One might take refuge in another's house when her husband was drinking. Friends might inform a woman of her husband's straying; less dramatically, they might keep her abreast of his more prosaic doings. Alice McGinley relied on her neighbor, the wife of her husband's foreman, for information concerning his whereabouts, earnings, and affairs in general, even though he came home every night.[38]

It was the rare man who could survey this scene—a tableau of feminine solidarity—with equanimity. Many simply could not abide their wives' associations with other women, demanding that their wives eschew female friendship and instead devote themselves entirely to them. It was little wonder that Charles Connelly did not want his wife friendly with her South Boston neighbors; every time he said a word, he complained to psychiatrists, "they will stick their heads out of the windows and say 'there is a murder here.'"[39] Ernst Kaiser was outraged to find his wife entertaining her downstairs neighbor with beer and gossip in his kitchen. He claimed the woman was immoral—he had heard (was this not gossip?) that she and her husband had visited a house of ill repute together—and in any case everyone knew idle women could only be up to no good.[40] For women, unlike men, advertised their troubles widely and shared what men considered private business with nosy neighbors. Women would ideally confine themselves and their interests to the home and it would be better, in the words of one gruff man, if "they kept their mouths shut."[41]

Men rightly perceived women's talk as a challenge to the undisputed authority they imagined themselves commanding within their families. Through gossip women exercised some small measure of regulation over men's behavior. Women were quick to assess—too harshly, to men's minds—the merits of another's husband. Mary O'Brien told psychiatrists it had taken her years to decide to leave her husband although, she noted ruefully, people had been telling her to do so for years.[42] This sort of advice, its power reinforced through countless daily exchanges, was galling evidence that men's much-vaunted privacy and highly prized control was illusory.

But it was not just that gossiping women were likely to judge them unfavorably—for women were just as harsh in their assessments of each other as they were of men—that men found so objectionable. It was also that as women collectively appraised the state of their world they formulated a cynical sexual politics, grounded in bitter experience, that contrasted sharply with men's loftier and more theoretical views. Many of the men who came to psychiatrists, their marriages unraveling, were nonetheless unreconstructed romantics. They wrote tenderly and lovingly to the wives who had committed them in disgust, proffering hugs and kisses and expressing hopes for reconciliation. "Life will be one long sweet dream," promised thirty-four-year-old Edward McBurney, arrested for the third time at his wife's behest. "I have no doubt but everything will end like the fairy tales. '*Lived happily ever after.*' "[43] Few of the wives could have mustered such sanguine sentiments. Mary O'Brien, eighteen years of marital experience behind her, spoke for many when she told psychiatrists it seemed to her that "men are funny animals, some of them"—unpredictable, easily ruffled, their emotional lives unfathomable.[44] Maude Porter voiced similar sentiments in a discussion of male nature with psychiatrists. "Are all men alike?" asked one, parodying her position. "They are all the same," she replied, to which he responded, "You don't care much for them?" Sure, she attested, "I love them all."[45] The cynicism Porter voiced lay at the bottom of many women's view of men and marriage. Married life from this female perspective was not even potentially idyllic; the most a woman could hope for was that her husband would bring home regular wages and not beat her. Men were inherently unreliable. Constantly seeking ways to evade familial responsibilities, they had to be watched with circumspection; a too-romantic spouse, for example, was likely plotting new escapades with either a woman or his mates. Finally, the conviction that men had it better was central to this female worldview. As one woman put it: "It seems the way of this world when a man does anything no matter how he has wronged a woman he can receive gifts, sympathetic letters, while the woman always gets trodden down. Suppose I played the same game as he did," she speculated. "I would be perhaps now at the Reform school or probably Deer Island or Sherburne"—nearby penal institutions.[46]

Women's proclivity for talk—gossiping or nagging—was the subject of heated commentary.[47] Psychiatrists colluded with working-class men in constructing the gossip as the archetype of the married woman. The nagging shrew, who constantly has her husband walking the line; the gossiping slattern, who entertains women with her slanderous tales and men with her dubious favors; the lecturing, straitlaced prude, who treats her husband to regular lectures on reform—all were stock characters in the domestic drama as psychiatrists saw it. If she did not exist, psychiatrists would assist in her creation. "Why does she pick on you so?" they asked one man who complained that his wife "was telling [him] such stories."[48] "Did you ever nag your husband?" they asked one woman, who assured them she did not. Disbelieving, they pressed her: "You never started in to give him a course in discipline?" "Never," she said.[49] Their assessment of Jean Swift, distressed by the latest of her husband's long string of public sexual escapades, was characteristically severe. Psychiatrists first faulted her for "talking to"—nagging—her husband and thereby causing him to stray, then for "talking"—gossiping—with her friends about her troubles. "Why not hold your peace and let him go to the devil? . . . Wasn't it a bit irrational on your part not to go to law, to talk to a lot of people that could do nothing but spread the hearsay evidence?" demanded one. "Haven't you talked pretty freely?" Inquired another, "Didn't you discuss these things rather excitedly in public?" Swift dissented; she had only spoken of her husband's affairs with one friend and the others, she averred, knew nothing at all. The psychiatrists judged her reaction to her trouble excessive, psychopathic, paranoid, and rather pointless, although they allowed that the trouble "seems to be real."[50]

The vehemence of men's objections to women's talk points to its deeper resonances. The man who imagined his wife whiling away her days, squandering her time as well as her money, was invariably the one to accuse her of infidelity, often in the most improbable circumstances. Several men spied on their wives. One, for example, admitted to lurking on street corners, expecting to watch a parade of men into his wife's bedroom; another told psychiatrists he had seen a man standing suspiciously outside his house; still another, a Russian-born Jewish physician, rousted his wife from her bed one night, accusing her of intimacy with a neighborhood priest. One man, in a striking reversal of the conventional wisdom, wanted his wife to have a job so she could not be with other men during the day.[51]

Why were men so quick to imagine themselves cuckolded? The husband who strayed was in fact more common than the wife who did; indeed, many men saw sex outside marriage as a man's prerogative. Among psychiatrists, it was common knowledge that men, especially alcoholic men, were sometimes prone to delusional thinking regarding their wives' infidelities, and Southard went so far as to propose that there were men "who think their wives are going to be unfaithful even before they have wives."[52] Still, the issue was bigger than this. Woman's nature, not infidelity per se, was the subject of this discussion. Neither psychiatrists nor the men with whom they consulted had yet settled upon a satisfactory conception of married womanhood. Images of women as sexual or matronly, as permissive or severe, as whores or prudes played in the collective male unconscious, a realm, like many others, in which a woman's sexuality was the measure of her character. When a woman acted as a *woman*, whether she was irrational, gossipy, or in concert with others, she evoked this panoply of warring associations in men's minds, becoming at once object of desire and enforcer of morality. The balance often tipped toward the latter. In the heated discussion of gossip, then, and in its sexual subtext, one can glimpse a collective male protest against the harrowing specter of a society subject to the irrational, immoral, and extralegal control of women.

Psychiatric Feminism

Psychiatrists' position on marriage was pragmatic, their relation to conventional morality complex. Although at times they could color the scheming and betrayal to which they were privy with the grand passion of the Russian novel, and see Balzacian overtones in their patients' struggles for control of petty sums of money, psychiatrists for the most part were content to see marriage, and their own role in mediating its conflicts, rather prosaically. Conflict in marriage was commonplace, they argued, in many apparently peaceful homes. Psychiatrists generally looked on the marital battles enacted before them with detached amusement, seeing them as so many inconsequential engagements in the age-old battle of the sexes. At times, however, they saw deeper forces at work, hypothesizing that the balance of power was shifting subtly in women's favor. In Myerson's analysis, for example, men, in times past, had ruled their homes as sovereigns, and any power a woman exercised was hers by privilege, not by right. Women were now beginning to press their claims. Some feminists were addressing the inequalities of marriage directly; other women, who married later, practiced birth control, and sought divorce, did so more quietly but with no less determination. Public opinion, still mired in the patriarchal ways of the past, had not yet recognized the inexorable trend toward egalitarianism in marriage.[53]

Psychiatrists were proud that they had. They saw that women's dissatisfactions with marriage were beginning to outweigh those of men. From their perspective, marriage had always offered men a fair deal. Although it had asked an unnatural fidelity from them, it was doubtful they had ever honored the ideal, and although marriage had demanded that they support their families, in a world where honorable and dignified work was widely available, this was a pleasure, not a burden, endowing them with all manner of prerogatives. For women, however, marriage as traditionally conceived was becoming ever more problematic. Marriage cruelly and unnecessarily isolated a woman from the larger world in which men traveled, immuring her in a home to whose defects many social commentators were calling attention. Individual housekeeping—shopping, cooking, cleaning —entailed enormous waste and inefficiency that communal arrangements could eliminate; "the home," shrouded with the aura of piety, bred pettiness where a largeness of spirit was to be desired.

Assessing failed marriages allowed psychiatrists an arena for the display of their modernity. More often than not they judged the woman's plight in a marital dispute more vexed than the man's, and they regularly rendered judgments of male inadequacy quite pleasing to women. Yet psychiatrists could more easily sympathize with women unhappy with the particulars of their own marriages—their mates, their circumstances—than with those who questioned the foundations of the institution itself. Thus the woman, overburdened with housework, say, or ignored by her pleasure-seeking husband, who claimed that her marriage was intolerable elicited psychiatrists' sympathy, while the woman who claimed that marriage itself was intolerable only raised their ire. Psychiatrists "worked up a good deal of sympathy" for Eleanor Herbert, who complained that her husband hit her and refused to give her money for food and clothing; any feminist implications of her complaint that "he had to have his fun but I had to stay home because I had Babies" were muted by his character as a playboy (she had once, she told psychiatrists, found him with some actresses on a yacht).[54] Thirty-four-year-old Caroline Gage's claim that marriage had thwarted her ambitions presented an altogether different scenario. "I think I have worked too hard for one thing and I haven't been out enough, haven't had enough interests outside my home," she told psychiatrists. One tried to trace her discontent to her lack of amusements, but she corrected him, stating it was not a matter of recreation, though if she had had some help about the house she would have done better, but of her larger ambition to go to college. "You don't think marriage has interfered with your ambitions," asked one psychiatrist, incredulous. "Of course it has," she replied. "I think it would have been better to have had an education." Psychiatrists commented on her "emptyheadedness and the poverty of her thoughts" and trivialized her desire for an education, seeing it as a manifestation of her jealousy toward her husband.[55]

Psychiatrists were feminist by intellect but not temperament. They expressed only contempt for convention and sentiment, only disdain for "old-fashioned" marriage. Yet even as they imagined themselves iconoclastic moderns, their essentially conservative sensibilities constrained them. They could imagine what form modern marriage might assume; they did not, however, want women to spell it out for them.

Marital and Extramarital Sex

No issue elicited psychiatrists' ambivalent modernism more reliably than sex. In advancing the notion that women, like men, had sexual desires and needs, they broke decisively with the Victorian sexual system that was premised on women's and men's different capacities for sexual pleasure. Further, although they did not endow the married woman with desires of hypersexual proportions, they did argue it was normal for her to want regular sexual relations with her husband, and the woman who did so appears with some frequency in case records. As advocates of moderation in all things, psychiatrists worried about women who seemed promiscuous, asserting that excessive sexual desires led many astray. They could, however, envision circumstances in which a woman justifiably might sleep with a man other than her husband. Myerson held that the infidelity of a bored or neglected wife might be tolerated just as for centuries those of men had been; the psychiatrist beholden to the best interests of the patient might find himself in the position of advising "what runs counter to the present-day code of morals."[56]

Psychiatrists thus adopted a stance of tolerant open-mindedness on the issue of marital sex. Compounded of fierce anti-Victorianism and contempt for convention and sentiment, their position crumbled in practice as they alternated between propounding positions of extreme iconoclasm on the one hand and upholding the most conventional morality on the other. They could assume insouciance regarding morality, as expressive of their contempt for women as of their modernity, as one did when questioning a forty-four-year-old woman distressed by her daughter's open liaison with a married man: "And you don't approve of this?" one psychiatrist demanded. This woman, who reported that she had been told by the city doctors she had consulted that her daughter "could do as she wants to do—that she could marry a married man if she wants to," replied, "No, Doctor, I don't."[57] Another asked Jean Swift, concerning her philandering husband, "What do you care of men gone wrong?" "I care of a man, not men," she tersely reminded him.[58] But psychiatrists could also be shocked when women owned up to their infidelities. Thirty-year-old Maude Porter's admission that she had conducted perhaps five affairs while still married to the husband upon whom she had stumbled in flagrante delicto, hooking up the gaiters of another woman in the kitchen, baffled and annoyed them. Were her own "improper relations" not simply the consequence of a hurt and jealous mind? psychiatrists wondered. Was it not all just a spell to be gotten through? No, she told them, her mind was perfectly clear, and their analysis was entirely wrong. She slept with other men because she needed to be loved. Was it not adultery to go with a married man? they asked. Not if she was not coveting his wife, she replied; the Bible said nothing of coveting husbands. Taken aback, one pressed her: "Do you mean to say the Bible allows women to sleep with other people's husbands?" "If they want to," she replied, adding, "the Bible tells us to love one another." The psychiatrist now wanted only the facts: "Do I understand that you did, or did not go to bed with them?" "I did," she said.[59]

Psychiatrists were more conventional on the subject of sex than they liked to imagine. Like the women and men they advised, they wavered between the sexual Victorianism they held in contempt and a still unformed modern outlook. Was marital sex for women duty or pleasure, burden or right? Did men desire and women reluctantly yield to sex, or did both parties actively seek it? Psychiatrists wanted to believe the latter, but their disdain for women patients brought out contrary sentiments. They were almost brutally literal, for example, in their questioning of Charlotte Page, a thirty-five-year-old woman who proclaimed that her sexual feelings had lately "grown more and more intense" and that consequently men had shown more interest in her. "How do you know men are attracted to you?" one psychiatrist asked. She replied haltingly, "Why, because, I . . . because they have acted so." The psychiatrist pressed her: "How did they act when they were sexually attracted to you? Do they follow you with their glances? Do they make love to you?" "Came pretty near to it," she contended. "I met a couple this summer. I had no intention of attracting them." "What else?" her interrogator demanded. "You know as well as I do," she responded. Puzzled by the late efflorescence of her sexual feelings, "expressing the exact opposite of normal development of life," psychiatrists were at a loss to interpret her condition. One suggested that she was a psychopath; another, "an unsophisticated lover."[60]

Men and women grew up and entered marriage with strikingly different sexual sensibilities. The grown man's sexual ease and confidence was the product of years of relatively straightforward, worry-free experience. In some marriages, to be sure, men and women subjected their sexual relations to complex negotiation, "talking naturally about sex" and seeking a fair distribution of pleasures. But many men, even in marriage, could think of sex only in terms of their own pleasure; one, married eleven years, could admit to Emerson that he had "never thought of his sexual life as having any more meaning than [as] a source of sexual satisfaction." Under his wife's careful tutelage, reinforced by psychiatric authority, he learned of the act's higher meanings.[61]

Few women could have seen sex so simply. Many women, like men, told of early sexual experiences, in many cases with other girls. Yet it is clear that the sexual experience of boys outweighed that of girls, and that it usually took place at an earlier age. Further, what was for boys relatively unproblematic was for girls fraught with difficulties. For adult women sex was rarely free of the terrors of unwanted pregnancy; for girls, sexual knowledge and activity was hedged about by secrecy and an aura of the illicit from the start. Even the most innocent of childhood sex play was for girls never free of coercion; as women recalled their youthful escapades, they told of girls coercing each other, boys coercing girls, brothers coercing their sisters. Many mothers refused to tell their daughters anything about sex, or so filled them with loathing for the whole enterprise that, years later, their daughters felt themselves permanently scarred. What girls heard from their friends or at school was not much better; one girl, for instance, left school for a year after she was told of intercourse, which she judged disgusting.[62] Further, many girls told of boys taunting them and bullying them to have sex before they were ready or willing.

Despite such a profusion of negative experience, a number of women managed to envision sex beyond the matrix of duty and obligation. From sex they derived both physical pleasure and some of the makings of an identity as a modern woman. Charlotte Page, who openly testified to her sexual feelings; the divorced woman who claimed she "always lost consciousness in a sort of ecstasy when she had coitus";[63] the woman who, speaking of her satisfying weekly relations with her husband, said she "could not live with him without it";[64] and Maude Porter, who took up with another man as she was divorcing her unfaithful husband, establishing her modernity as she quipped, "They say without love you have nothing"[65]—these married women, like their single counterparts, were charting new erotic territory for women both within and beyond marriage. That women could complain of their husbands' lack of interest in them— deeming the husbands abnormal, speculating that they must have been sleeping with other women—was evidence that a number of them thought regular marital sex normal.[66]

For some women, however, sex was simply another of marriage's many burdens. For every woman who enjoyed ecstatic relations with her husband, there was likely another to whom sex was, as one put it, a source of "pain and disgust,"[67] or, as another proclaimed, "a regular nuisance," something "like having a tooth filled."[68] Although these women experienced and complained to psychiatrists of the many inequalities associated with sex, they did not have the materials at hand from which to fashion a coherent, critical position. Psychiatrists' confident coupling of sex and pleasure lay beyond their experience, as did feminists' impassioned critique of marital sexual slavery. Yet they knew that in sex, as in marriage, men were free, women bound. To these womens' minds, men's nearly certain pleasure contrasted cruelly with their more contingent fulfillment. The man's constant desire, his appetite for unnatural and perverted acts, and his roughness offended their sensibilities. It is clear that some women advised others on the pleasures of sex; but, as the instance of the woman who told Emerson that her husband's mother had advised her "never to let him know she had no thrills" suggests, women could also participate in perpetuating their gender's ignorance. Many couples practiced coitus interruptus, which satisfied neither party, as a means of birth control, and a number of men consulted Emerson to discuss the unfavorable consequences of the practice—"morbid anxiety due to c.i." read the short records of several.[69] In other marriages wives shouldered all the responsibility for contraception. Several complained bitterly of having to get up on cold nights to douche after intercourse while their husbands slept contentedly. Some Catholic women had to fight their husbands for even this meager right. Mary McBurney's husband, for example, who wanted sex but no more children, would not allow her to douche, arguing that if he knew of it *he* would have to confess it.[70] Under circumstances like these, sex could be no more than a grudgingly fulfilled duty, a service traded for monetary support.

Psychiatrists offered women a self-consciously modern sexual scenario as a middle ground between sexual repression on the one hand and sexual license on the other. Myerson, for example, proposed that sex cemented the marital bond while prudery and ignorance weakened it; that women's fulfillment was uncommon but absolutely essential to marriage; and that it was a man's duty to see to his wife's fulfillment. He railed against the duplicity of the "ministers, rabbis, editors, and lawmakers" who warned of race suicide and publicly stood against birth control—in the methods of which it was illegal for a physician or anyone else to instruct women— while, in the space of one generation, drastically reducing the sizes of their own families. "Most of the advice and injunctions in the past seem to have come from the sexually abnormal," he maintained: "It is time that this was changed."[71]

Myerson and his colleagues, Emerson foremost among them, set out to do precisely that, advancing, in print and practice, their program of moderation and frankness, and pleasurable, healthy sex.[72] But the psychiatrist more easily maintained his equanimity in articles and books than in the conference room; he could become embarrassed, ruffled, and even bullying in his dealings with the actual women who offered up their marital woes for his scrutiny. Emerson, by contrast, allied himself with the married women (much as he was doing with hysterical women) who told him of their marital and sexual troubles, and whether it was due to his conviction that the "fundamental family relationship [was], of course, sexual" or to the exceptional intimacy of the psychoanalytic encounter itself, in his presence woman after woman unburdened herself of her most tightly held sexual experiences and fears.[73] A widowed Irish woman, for example, a longtime resident of South Boston, told Emerson within minutes of meeting him— she had consulted him on account of weakness and depression—that she had "never had orgasm," but that she knew that, as she put it, "the body craves something." The third time she saw him, she said someone once had told her husband "that if he would try it backward it would be better," going on to say that he did and it was—"I liked it." Psychoanalyst and patient discussed her peculiar vaginal feelings, and within several more visits she was telling him of realizing that she had been fighting her sexual feelings and cravings and that, as he hurriedly scribbled in his notes, she could now make "her body 'go'—orgasm—*never had such feelings in life, before.*" This woman's treatment ended with her telling Emerson that she, a good Catholic, was now convinced that sex was not a sin.[74]

This case, like several others, ended with the patient well and happy, testimony to the efficacy of Emerson's efforts. By the early teens, then, psychiatrists had embarked on the great campaign to domesticate sexuality that the major sexologists of the twentieth century—from Katherine Bement Davis in the twenties through Alfred Kinsey in the forties and fifties and Masters and Johnson in the sixties—would avidly carry on.[75] Among the aims of this campaign were the undoing of the Victorian sexual system's worst injustices toward women and the normalizing of its worst perversions. That by 1931 two authorities could isolate abstinence as "the only distressing perversion" in the modern sexologists' lexicon was evidence of that campaign's at least partial success.[76]

But sex would not be so easily tamed. Alongside the psychiatric discussion, arrayed along an axis spanning from pleasure to duty, raged another controversy, far more lively, focused on the opposition of sexual vice and sexual virtue. The ostensible topic of this debate was marital fidelity, and as it developed each sex accused the other of adulterous acts both plausible and implausible. Women accused men of desiring "bad women," of seducing servants, of cavorting with actresses, of seeking out immoral women to perform on them the "indecent acts" that they themselves would not; men accused women of walking the streets, of entertaining dandies, of aborting suspicious pregnancies, of enticing men to meet the demands of their perverse appetites. In this debate the changing nature of men's and women's extramarital liaisons and their perceptions of their rights to the same were overlaid with a fantasy of rampant illicit sexuality, entertained by men and women alike, that rendered the sexual politics of adultery particularly volatile.

Sex outside marriage had long been a man's prerogative. Indeed, the Victorian sexual system had tolerated, even encouraged, male infidelity as the guarantor of female purity. Writing that monogamous marriage was based on the assumption that each mate's loyalty to the other was moral and possible, Myerson soberly maintained that it was "probable that in no age [had] this agreement been loyally carried out by the husbands."[77] This, he noted in 1920, was changing, as women were beginning to hold men to the standard of faithfulness that governed their own lives. In many of the cases of marital dissension that came to psychiatrists' attention, it was the male's seemingly insatiable appetite for extramarital sex that elicited women's most bitter commentary. If their response to issues arrayed along the pleasure-duty axis was muted, on this issue it was voluble and impassioned. Men who supported other women while keeping their families in penury; men who posed as single to venture alone into the demimonde of cafés, theaters, and hotels; men who took up with other women while their wives were sick or confined—these men incited women's passions in a way that psychiatrists' more subtle discussions did not. Although it is likely that

some of the many derelictions of which women complained were the products of fantasy, there is no doubt that many men saw sex outside marriage
as a man's right. In the accounts of men and women alike one can see men
conducting affairs openly and with practiced ease, often at home, accosting
and seducing their domestic servants, oblivious to their wives' displeasure
and their own unseemliness.[78] Many women told psychiatrists and social
workers of their husbands' having left evidence of philandering where they
could not help discovering it. William Kelly's wife found in his coat pocket
letters, typed on business stationery, in which the arrangements for an
assignation were detailed; she tracked down the woman involved, who
admitted to the affair but claimed not to know she was consorting with a
married man.[79] Jean Swift, suspicious because her husband came home
from business trips "looking like a wreck," with "no sexual feelings for
her," found among his things first a postcard "with a picture of a man and
two ladies and with some insinuation about him," then a partially used
box of protectors.[80] Other men were more brazen still. One middle-aged
man invited an eighteen-year-old stenographer to his house, telling her his
wife was away and promising he "would give her a good time."[81] Another,
a recently widowed man, on one occasion assaulted his wife's cousin,
inviting her into his bedroom to see his new bed, and on many others
attempted to talk her into becoming his mistress, promising not to impregnate her and offering her money if she would have sex with him.[82] A
middle-aged woman told of several times stumbling on her husband with
their maid, dressed only in her corset, drawers, and stockings, in his bedroom; of hearing him begging the maid for sex; and of seeing the two
"having connection standing up" in the chicken coop behind their house.
She eventually divorced her husband, but only after he had invited the
maid to move in with him and put his wife out.[83] It was not that men were
without sensibility on the issue of extramarital sex; a number developed
positions that accommodated, at least to their minds, the demands of
conventional morality and their own desires. One young husband, for
example, excused his extramarital liaison on the grounds that "sex was not
the predominant thing in their relationship"—the psychiatrist listening to
his story wrote that "he was with her every night, but they had sexual
relations seldom more than once a week"—and that his companion in any
case "knew exactly what kind of goods she was buying."[84] Another man, a
traveling salesman who admitted to going with women a good many times
since he had married, justified his behavior with the twin claims that he
only strayed if he had been drinking and that he always employed a
"safe."[85] Yet another, a well-situated middle-class man claiming he would
not be disloyal to his wife, let women, as Emerson wrote in his notes,
" 'massage' 'it' " but refused to have intercourse with them.[86]

In complaining of men's philandering, women were protesting marriage's inequalities in as direct a way as they could. Those inequalities were here starkly evident, and although it is likely that some of their charges grew more weighty in the realm of fantasy—like those of the woman who claimed her husband rode streetcars in order to meet girls, or of the woman who swore her husband was going with a number of women whom he had impregnated—women expected that few would question their status as wronged women. The psychiatrists, however, did. Although professing sympathy for wronged women, they judged them harshly. Helen Mellars, who would not give up on her philandering husband, was in the estimation of one a "fussy, psychoneurotic," emotionally unstable, and intellectually deficient woman possessed of "a peculiar attitude toward life." She poured out her marital woes, another noted, in a "meek and mildly complaining, high pitched tone of voice," going on to fault her for seldom allowing her thoughts "to wander from her own trials and tribulations." As the first psychiatrist summed her up, "she is certainly an inadequate person all around."[87] Psychiatrists were just as contemptuous of forty-four-year-old Molly Ryan and her troubles. Ryan told them that her husband, who had had her committed to the institution, had been attending to other women since they had married. His recent flirtations with the servant girl he had hired had pushed her to the edge; on her arrival the girl had "put her arms around [his] neck and kissed him" and often they "would be in the den with the door shut." One evening, in response to Ryan's entreaty, "Pa, give me a kiss," he had instead kissed the girl before her eyes. Molly Ryan maintained she was a good woman who did not deserve such treatment. Her desires were simple; she wanted to move in with her sisters and earn her own living. What if she were to return home and her husband began to flirt again? one psychiatrist asked. He continued, "I should think your husband would want to keep you here. He could go with that girl. Isn't it strange?" After dismissing her, psychiatrists concluded that Ryan had "definite ideas of jealousy and of being the butt of fate." They agreed that she was feebleminded—"she must be feeble-minded to put up with that sort of thing"—and that "she should have left him long ago."[88]

In practice, psychiatrists' stance on the issue of male philandering was cavalier. A man who engaged in extramarital sex could be characterized as a "sort of flirt," a "busy man who probably wanted a little fun on the side."[89] A woman who stayed with such a man was digging her own grave. And a woman who complained too much about such a man was questioning sacrosanct male prerogative. The only prudent thing for a woman to do was to leave the marriage quietly, sparing her own and her husband's honor and dignity.

Men's complaints of their wives' adulterous behavior were premised on a hefty dose of fantasy. Some women did admit to extramarital liaisons, especially those women whose husbands had affairs themselves, but the woman who admitted to entertaining fantasies of other men was more common. One thirty-three-year-old, who had discovered that her husband was planning a rendezvous on Martha's Vineyard with another woman, told of imagining herself "lying in the arms" of a hospital orderly who had once tried to kiss her, but said she would not let herself "think any further than this."[90] A thirty-five-year-old woman, who said that her husband left her cold, admitted to being really tempted by a doctor to whom she had first been attracted "as if he were a snake." As Emerson noted, she told him that the physician "made a sort of love to her"—he would look at her and say, speaking of her husband, "I don't see how he can fail to be thrilled." Telling Emerson what she admitted she "couldn't hardly acknowledge to myself," she confessed, "I didn't know how far I could go and be safe."[91] And Alma Wilcox, separated from the husband she suspected was unfaithful, was completely taken with another man, a physician who massaged her neck and chest, asking Emerson whether she could "play with fire and not get burned."[92] That not one of these women acted on her fantasies, although all were willing to engage in extended flirtations, only underlines how differently women and men assessed the risks of marital infidelity, and how hedged about with guilt sex for women remained. The soon-to-be-divorced woman who consulted Emerson, telling of her intense love for a married man and of her "strong craving for sexual intercourse," was singular, for not only had she "gone the limit" with several men before marriage, but she was also prepared, as she said, to "give myself, body and soul, to anybody I loved," polite conventions notwithstanding.[93]

The women who came under psychiatrists' scrutiny were, on the whole, true to their husbands.[94] The regularity with which their husbands leveled charges of adultery against them, and the implausibility of many of those charges, suggests that they were drawing on more than meager reality in formulating them. The discussion of women's fidelity, like that of gossip, contained within it a debate over the nature of married womanhood. Was the married woman sexual or matronly, whore or prude? What had become of the hypersexual girl, with whom so many men had engaged in illicit sex—in hotels, in parks—premaritally? If in the discussion of gossip the scale had tipped toward women's prudish side, in this debate men righted it with a vengeance.

The married woman was the embodiment of license in men's collective fantasy. Sexuality suffused her life. The men who accused their wives of secretly signaling their desires to men on the streets; those who accused them of hiring plumbers, handymen, delivery men, or male nurses to do their immoral bidding; those who monitored their wives' incoming telephone calls; and those who accosted men on the street and accused them of making advances to their wives—all these men had so eroticized their wives they could barely distinguish what was sexual from what was not. Nellie Byrne told psychiatrists that her husband had "almost killed" her after a young man had approached her at a whist party they attended together, and he was quick to anger whenever a man acted too familiar toward her. Her husband's suspicions were entirely unfounded, she claimed; with two children to care for she did not have "very much time to fool around."[95] William Burke claimed he was a much-abused man; his wife, he claimed, had slept with a neighbor, and the man was now hanging about their house. Psychiatrists, though they professed sympathy for him—asking how he had "stood this woman all these years"—deemed his charges delusional. "There is nothing in any reports," they concluded, "that would lead one to believe his wife is untrue."[96]

Psychiatrists were struck by the regularity with which men expressed jealousy toward their wives, and they speculated that imagined competitors served to heighten desire.[97] This was in part the case. In eroticizing their wives men were endowing them with the licentiousness that ten or twenty years of marriage, motherhood, and family life had dampened; if a woman was cold with her husband, to many men's minds, she was likely hot with another. But in sexualizing married womanhood men were also demeaning it. A man could allege he had no use for women of low moral character; he could then turn around and tell his wife to earn her living on the streets.[98] To many men women were erotic creatures, as desirable but as debased as courtesans.

Social Workers' Domestic Agenda

However intolerable her circumstances, it was still a big step for a woman to leave a man. Women who for years had endured economic deprivation and verbal (and even physical) abuse found it difficult to initiate separation or divorce proceedings. Many found it easier to confront each crisis as it arose, fleeing to a mother's or sister's house for a few days and returning home when the worst had blown over, than to engage lawyers, social workers, and other officials in support of their cause. Even women who were determined to be through with their mates moved hesitantly. To leave, women had to relinquish whatever hopes they had invested in their marriages. Many were well aware that their material prospects as single women were meager. Finally, a concern for propriety bound many women to husbands they could barely tolerate. In a letter to one of the social workers who had taken charge of her case, Eleanor Herbert summed up the unhappily married woman's dilemma: "If I do go . . . the world will say, I deserted my children. If I stay, and things keep on as they are, I'll lose my mind."[99]

Psychiatrists had little conception of how hard it was for a woman to leave a man. They could muster little sympathy for women who stayed too long in bad marriages and they expressed contempt for those who professed to mixed feelings toward their husbands. Because they saw marriage as a practical arrangement rather than as a matter of romance, they could not fathom why any woman would stay with a man when those arrangements broke down—when men, for example, because of drink or simple disinclination, no longer supported their families. When it came to managing marital disputes, they proffered implausibly simple solutions, showing little appreciation for the complexities and ambiguities of many of the situations women and men offered up for their scrutiny. One asked Jean Swift, for example, a woman whose husband had been involved in a scandalous affair with two women, why she could not just keep her peace and "let him go to the devil?" "What shall I tell his children?" she replied. "They will ask, where is my father."[100] In their ardor to open women's eyes to what they took to be their real circumstances, psychiatrists sometimes overlooked how convention could bind. One asked May Stockwell, whom he characterized—in her presence—as "a rather happy old maid" who had gotten into difficulties when she had married in her late forties, "Why do you live with your husband if he treats you so badly?" "When you marry a man you marry to live with him," she tersely reminded him.[101]

In practice, Psychopathic Hospital psychiatrists exhibited little commitment to the family as such. Southard doubted the heuristic value of the very construct in the realm of psychopathology, and, day to day, he and his colleagues focused only intermittently on "the family." The sharp critique of the home and its effects, which Myerson articulated and to which many of them subscribed, served to underwrite the rather dismissive stance they adopted vis-à-vis the family in their confrontations with patients. To the psychiatrist, Southard maintained, many "so-called 'family cases'" were in fact cases compounded of difficulties traceable to the peculiarities or deficiencies of one of its members. Speaking for his professional brethren, Southard submitted that "time forbids the psychiatrist himself to indulge overmuch in the domestic details of family adjustment," which routinely engaged hundreds of "social-worker hours."[102]

Not only time but also professional temperament and traditions distinguished the psychiatrist from the social worker on the question of the family. Psychiatrists saw patients, on the wards and in the conference room, as individuals, apart from the family members with whom they were in many instances at odds, who had, in many cases, committed them, and who could in consequence be easily caricatured, sided with, argued against, and summarily dismissed. Social workers, by contrast, ventured into patients' homes; interviewed their spouses, friends, and neighbors; commented on their housekeeping; brought them small gifts; and helped them with their shopping. The nature of their practice yielded them a sometimes inadvertent but often useful familiarity with the particulars of patients' emotional, social, and material circumstances, particulars on which they could draw in putting together the stories they told about them. Their stories, unlike those of psychiatrists, which tended to focus on the patient, encompassed large casts of colorful characters, most of whom they had met. They could hardly be so quick to dismiss them as were psychiatrists. Consider, for example, one psychiatrist's summary of a case of marital discord: "This is an absolutely concrete thing—absolute incompatibility between husband and wife, they are different by age and habit and everything."[103] Compare his statement with the social worker's description of her charge to the husband of a patient: "Our efforts and interest have been for the family as a whole, and we would do anything possible to help adjust their difficulties."[104]

Yet however troubling one might find psychiatrists' cavalier advice to women, the advice that social workers dispensed was in many respects more problematic still. Social workers, unlike psychiatrists, were ideologically committed to the survival of the family unit, and for that reason they invariably emphasized to women contemplating separations how difficult it would be for them to manage their families without a husband's support and protection. Many of them single, social workers were doubtless aware of how difficult it was for a woman, especially a poor woman, to make it on her own. The thrust of their advice to such women was that men, however deficient, were necessary to a proper family and that wives should do all they could to retain them, even at the expense of their own pride and well-being. Thus, they routinely advised women to "be nice" to abusive husbands. They told Mary McBurney, whose husband was often drunk and violent, that scolding him did no good; she was instead to be cheerful around him, to prepare him "plenty of hearty food, sweets and coffee," and to make the house as pleasant as possible for his sake, and they presented her with "two alternatives"—"normal sexual relations" with her husband, or his drinking.[105] They advised the wife of Michael Piso, a drinker who had twice choked her when she had refused his excessive sexual demands, to coddle her husband, specifically "to 'dress up' Saturdays for the purpose of taking [him] shopping," and they noted with approval that she had allowed him to buy a derby hat, telling the workers, "You have to let them have something when they work so hard."[106] And the social worker who in May 1917 visited Alice McGinley, a mother of three, eight months pregnant, whose husband had been arrested a week earlier after violently attacking a policeman, wrote later in her notes that she had extended her sympathy to McGinley before delivering a lecture on "how difficult it would be to bring family up without husband's support and protection." The worker advised McGinley, whom she judged "stupid and inert," to make her husband "feel that she trusts in his efforts," to make their home as attractive as possible, and "to tempt him with good food."[107]

How could social workers have gotten it so wrong? In these cases it was the woman who was threatening to leave, the woman whom the men should have been entreating to stay. As a result of their extensive investigations, social workers knew that these men were poor providers, some of them long enmeshed in the legal system's regulatory mechanisms. In advising women to coddle and humor such men, social workers were colluding in the psychiatric construction of the working-class man as so stupid, weak, and pitiable that he would be unable to distinguish between real and feigned affection. This man was best gotten into line and then used for his breadwinning ability. His bombast, his threats, his delusions were not worth getting wrought up about. "You must try not to take your husband too seriously," a social worker advised Eleanor Herbert. "Joke things off a little more. I am sure that will make it better for you."[108]

Social workers urged upon the married women under their supervision a vision of domesticity toward which they, as single career women, could only have felt ambivalence. Their unrelenting advocacy of domesticity— good food, pleasant surroundings—as a salve for all manner of marital woes was an expression of their desire to find common ground on which to meet women with whom they otherwise shared little. Though their advocacy was not insincere, it was yet a strategy, and consequently tinged at times with condescension. "I am rather envious of the people who take [your] rooms for the summer," one social worker who would never have considered living in those rooms wrote to Herbert, referring to her plans to earn some extra income. This in itself was nothing new; one more manifestation of the middle-class reforming woman's long-standing hauteur toward her less fortunate sisters, it could easily be ignored. More problematic, however, were the terms in which social workers constructed their domestic vision. Even as they compiled voluminous accounts of their patients' daily lives and travails, preferences and desires, they were unable to interpret the tales these records told. The social workers' commitment to an exaggerated ideal of domesticity, which they may have experienced when young but which only a few of them were living out, stood between them and the bleak reality of their married patients' lives.

A well-ordered home lay at the center of the social worker's domestic vision. The worker making a home visit thus surveyed the scene with an unforgiving eye, dutifully assessing (and recording in minute detail) the condition of the home's furnishings (whether cheap and gaudy or cheap but in good taste), the children (whether wild and dirty or well mannered and thoroughly scrubbed), and the housewife's clothing (whether old, dirty, and rumpled, or old but cleaned and pressed). They held women to exacting standards of cleanliness. Evidence of housekeeping properly executed cheered them immensely, and women labored mightily to gain social workers' favor. They swept, scrubbed, polished, and dusted; they mended worn clothing, purchased new tablecloths, tried new recipes. Social workers rewarded such industriousness with small gifts and lavish compliments, encouraging women to strive for ever-higher levels of domestic accomplishment. The condition of the home, to social workers' minds, mirrored the condition of the marriage. Domesticity was, to be sure, a not altogether inaccurate barometer of marital tensions. During each of Barbara and Frank Kinney's several reconciliations, for example, their household was clean and cheerful; as their relations soured, recriminations and dirty laundry alike testified to that breakdown.[109] In many other cases, too, a poorly kept home was the consequence not only of inadequate means but also of incessant marital battling.

But social workers used domesticity not only as a measure but also as a strategy, and as such it was even more fraught with difficulties. To social workers unsure of their craft, domesticity held out the promise of a simple, straightforward approach to human happiness, and they employed it enthusiastically in many cases. Their tendentious advocacy in the case of Eleanor Herbert was typical. Herbert, a thirty-eight-year-old Catholic mother of two married to a man with whom she had never been happy, made it clear to social workers and psychiatrists that she wanted to separate from her husband. The tale she told was grim indeed. Her husband had been carrying on an active extramarital sex life for years; since the early days of their marriage he had forced her to perform unnatural sex acts, which she, even though repelled and disgusted, had agreed to do in the hope her compliance would secure his fidelity; he had infected her with syphilis, for which she was undergoing painful treatment; and he regularly fought with and even struck her, several times so hard that she had seen a physician. "He doesn't care for me really," Herbert told psychiatrists and social workers. "He seems to be trying to make me mad. I don't think the man wants me." From the start, social workers questioned her portrayal. "Is this all supposed to be fact? Do you think she is not exaggerating her husband's treatment?" Jarrett asked. Southard defended her account, asserting that to him it appeared "a pretty concrete story." Another social worker objected; the husband had issued only denials, and it seemed to her as if more investigations were in order. "It strikes me that the data are not equivocal," Southard firmly declared.[110]

This exchange was a minor skirmish in psychiatrists' and social workers' ongoing battle for professional turf, social workers proposing that what was manifest was neither necessarily true nor complete and thereby arguing for their own intervention in a case that, like so many others, psychiatrists seemed to be deciding precipitously. But the exchange also offered an inauspicious foreshadowing of the strategy on which social workers settled, a strategy in which Eleanor Herbert's cooperation was to be engaged, her family preserved, and her faults, not her husband's, scrutinized. Social workers began admonishing Herbert to "wipe the slate clean," to put behind her the abuses she had suffered at her husband's hands. They arranged several family conferences in which they hoped "to have all sides of the question presented impartially and thrashed out" in order "to prompt a more friendly family relationship." And they interviewed her children, her priest, her mother; her husband's employer, best friend, and sister; her friends, cousins, and lodgers—all in order to determine what exactly "the question" was.

The possibility that the question might have been John Herbert's abusiveness (or even simple incompatibility) lay beyond social workers' imagining. Two weeks of dogged shuttling between the parties—dispensing advice and encouragement in equal doses to each, eliciting gripes, complaints, and secrets in return—had yielded more evidence of John Herbert's brutishness (he admitted to beating her, blaming her "constant nagging") but not, to the social workers' minds, an unmistakable culprit. Unable to maintain for much longer their neutral stance, the social workers quickly fixed on what seemed to them the real problem: Eleanor Herbert's wastefulness.

Food accordingly assumed center stage in the drama as the social workers began confidently to direct it. Family conferences were arranged; Eleanor Herbert's daily expenditures tallied (amounting to an average of two dollars a day), scrutinized, and declared extravagant (surely a dollar and a half was adequate to feed a family of four); recipes and tips for pennywise purchasing proffered. Pessimistic and discouraged, protesting all the while, Eleanor Herbert promised to read the booklet "Food for Workers," a grim compendium "of properly planned menus with their caloric value" that social workers pressed on her, and to try to spend less. The social workers' strategy, however, only heightened familial tensions and diminished what little leverage she had enjoyed within the family by virtue of her household manager's role, for they had given John Herbert the new ax of wastefulness to grind. He immediately cut his wife's daily allowance from a few dollars to the requisite dollar and a half and began delivering lectures on economical purchasing. "The subject of cutting down expenses here is getting a little too strong," Herbert reported, as she dutifully added up expenses, tried new recipes, and bought less and cheaper food. But the children, hearty eaters accustomed to several servings each meal, and Mr. Herbert, used to the best, complained and raided the pantry. "I notice no one here but I cut down on their expenses," she observed ruefully after three weeks on the new regimen; she had given up magazines and candy but her husband was still buying cigars and tobacco.

More galling still, he was regularly insulting her, charging "that all I think of is my stomach and self." Sardonically, she observed, "It is not a happy life for a Woman."

Social workers followed Eleanor Herbert aggressively for one year and with less attention for another. Throughout, she insisted that she and her husband would separate, which they eventually did. When heard from last, Herbert was living in New York, working in a publishing house for good money. Fights over food had gradually given way to fights pure and simple; the social workers' efforts to orchestrate this marital battle proved inadequate.

The tenacity with which social workers had adhered to their domestic agenda, even though they had materials before them from which they might have fashioned an entirely different account, is the most striking aspect of this case. From the start they judged Herbert a tastefully dressed, attractive, and refined woman married to an inferior man. Psychiatrists, within a week, had judged him "a typical rounder" and categorized him as a sex delinquent (an especially damning characterization for a man); the social workers themselves had observed that "her home was quite a difficult one" and that her husband was unkind to her; and at least one psychiatrist was of the opinion that, as "the case hinge[d] on the type of man the husband" was, and as the facts Herbert had presented characterized him well, she should be set up in a home with her children so that she could enjoy "an interesting life." Finally, Eleanor Herbert had warned social workers from the outset that the tactics of food would fail; "I have tried to make him better suppers to make him better tempered," she told them, "but he never gives me credit, and he never gives me sympathy." In the last letter she wrote to the social workers, Eleanor Herbert, away now from her husband, informed them, "I am less nervous and feel fine." The terms on which the social workers had engaged her prevented them from ever suspecting that this might have been so.

Social workers saw family life as a drama for which domesticity provided the script. Thus it was enough for them if a husband or wife acted his or her part: if the husband brought home a regular, decent wage, if the wife played the proper housewife. Never mind if she were unhappy; like psychiatrists, social workers assumed that in marriage many women and men would be. Social workers could authoritatively, straightforwardly, and sympathetically address the stuctural problems that married women confronted: poverty, deserting husbands, single motherhood. They could offer practical advice on finding inexpensive food and lodging, and they could even advise women on the legal intricacies of support payments and child custody. But on the new terrain of marital discontent, where the issues, centered on questions of compatibility, were less clear, their footing was less sure. Professionally beholden to the best interests of the family, not of the patient, they ignored women's subjective demands and desires, seeing in them threats to the family's survival.

For this reason social workers, like psychiatrists, simply did not see much of the abuse men dealt their wives. They seriously misjudged the balance of power in many marriages, for a woman's nagging, however irksome, was no match for a man's blows. Advising women to humor verbally and physically abusive husbands only reinforced the widespread conception that it was the nagging wife who invited the abuse. Two months after Eleanor Herbert left the hospital she reported to her social worker that her husband had "threatened her with his fist and said that she needed a good beating." The social worker "reassured" her. A week later, when questioned about this "alleged threat," the social worker reported, Herbert stated that her husband "became exasperated and shook his fist at her," but that she now thought it "quite probable that she more or less misunderstood his intention of actually giving her a beating." The beating dispensed with, the social worker steered the conversation where she wanted it—toward food, carefully itemizing in the case record three days' worth of expenditures on tuna fish (thirty-eight cents), hamburg steak (one and a half pounds at forty cents), potatoes (half a peck for twenty-eight cents), and cupcakes (four for four cents).[111]

Woman's Character

Social workers were able to engage their male charges more directly than they could the women whom they supervised. Clear of the troubled domestic nexus, they could settle on the issues in a man's case straightforwardly. Drink, inadequate income, unemployment—these, the man's customary failings, appeared the stuff of objective social fact next to women's more nebulous domestic deficits, indicative of more troubling characterological deficiencies. Social workers rarely engaged married men on the issue of character. Their reluctance to do so was due in part to their uncertainty on the question of married manhood; the thicket of sexuality into which an examination of the subject would inevitably lead was enough to account for their reticence. Thus, although they could forthrightly, efficiently, and even cheerfully handle the requests and attend to the needs of married men sure of what they wanted, such as those who wanted to divorce their wives but who were willing to make support payments, for the most part in dealing with men, many of them from the working class, social workers maintained an aura of imperiousness meant to kindle fear in the otherwise dauntless. They gently but firmly chided abusive men for ill-treating their wives; they made it clear to those who had deserted their families that they had to make support payments; they advised men in no uncertain terms when their actions were grounds for arrest and incarceration. Grateful wives reported to social workers that their visits had served the useful function of "frighten[ing] the life out of" husbands, and some entreated social workers "to try and scare" their wayward men. The social workers' imperiousness made it possible for them to handle hostile men who would denounce them as "a bunch of women,"[112] and their craft as "a bluff," or those who would make, as one fifty-year-old Irishman did, unseemly sexual advances. This man, inappropriately attired in his shirtsleeves, had stood "disagreeably near" to a social worker and, she noted, "asked if I would rather go up stairs to his room to talk"—he lived in a lodging house—an invitation she refused. Her conviction that the man was a low type, worthy of her contempt, enabled her to maintain her professional bearing through this trying encounter and others like it in which men attempted to discredit social work by demeaning its practitioners as mere women. This man's lawyer, for example, demanded an interview with the social worker, during which he questioned her competence and intentions. Clearly rattled by the experience, she summed him up as an "uneducated, unmannerly man. . . . Determined and conceited, rather shrewd but also stupid." The lawyer had written Southard to protest the propriety of the actions of "the two ladies in the Social Service Department of [the] Institution," which had been to his mind in the nature of an "unparalleled impertinence"; he backed off from his threat of taking legal action only when a psychiatrist rose to the ladies' defense.[113]

If social workers could steer clear of the morass of character when dealing with men, with women they could not avoid it. Even in cases where the man was the identified patient, they drew in and set to work on the woman.[114] In part this was because women, at home by day, were more accessible than men. In part, too, it was that working-class men could be physically and sexually intimidating to the single young women who labored as social workers. But the social workers' proclivity for making the woman the patient had deeper roots. In the case of the boorish man above, social workers decided that as the wife, although not a patient, was "generally considered 'peculiar'" she ought to be kept under observation.[115] In several other cases, social workers' charts listed the suspicious, tactless, or "irritating wife" under the rubric "unfavorable conditions," among such other items as "change of jobs," "arrest," and "prison sentence" (figure 10.1). What else but social workers' presumption that the trouble lay with the wife could account for their extraordinary misreading of the plight of Emma Marburg, a twenty-six-year-old mother of five, whose poorly paid Austrian-born husband held her to account for their household's disorder and blamed the large size of their family on "her laziness," as a case of "an untrained woman with an income insufficient for the needs of her family"

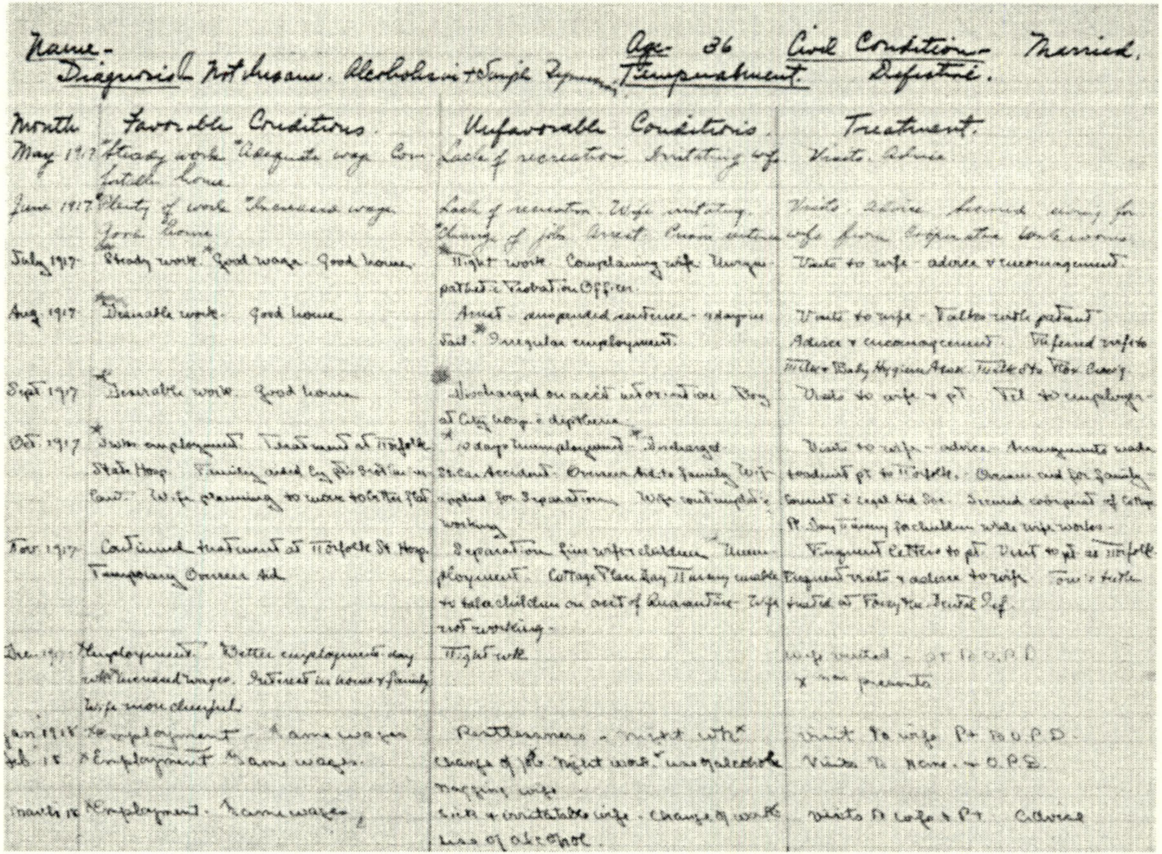

Fig. 10.1. Chart, prepared by social workers, in which the irritating, complaining, sick, and nagging wife is listed among the "unfavorable conditions" that characterized the patient's life (case 6682, 1917).

rather than of, say, a selfish, "peculiar" man (the only well-fed member of his family, social workers noted) possessed of wildly unrealistic notions of cleanliness? He, like his brother, was disappointed in the poor housekeeping of American women; the social work task, in this case, was to educate the wife in the hope that "the marital dissension would subside to a normal level." Though social workers cheered Mrs. Marburg with gifts of household goods and clothing and sent her to a convalescent home for four weeks' rest, these were panaceas that diverted attention from her fundamental complaints—"the poverty of her relations with her husband" and that she had stayed with him only on account of the children. Social workers judged this case a moderate success because by its close, pregnant yet again, Emma Marburg had become somewhat happier and more reconciled to her husband: the household was preserved, domesticity triumphant.[116]

Domesticity provided social workers with not only a measure and a strategy, but also a language with which to explore the murky realm of women's character. In social work, as in gossip, character was at issue. In both, accusations of poor housekeeping bore connotations of the greater crime of sexual license. As one peeved social worker wrote in the record of Margaret Kelly, a woman she had been unable to track down, and who was already suspect on account of her claim that she "liked intercourse": "Little can be learned of how she spent her time. She was out a great deal." This observation merely anticipated her judgment that Kelly "never took any interest in her housework and seldom had meals ready for her husband."[117] Likewise, a neighborhood gossip, claiming she did not intend to interfere, reported to social workers that Alice Bundy's home was "neglected, the meals seldom prepared," further damning in social workers' eyes this woman they had already determined was immoral.[118] Slack housekeeping, to social workers, connoted slack morals.

Social workers went door-to-door trying to assess women's morals. They called on neighbors, friends, landladies, relatives, and employers, eliciting information, trading one bit of gossip for another, in some cases sowing suspicion where there had been none. A social worker spoke with Margaret Kelly's sister-in-law, for example, and in the process managed to inform her of Kelly's "present delinquency"—she was pregnant, but not by her husband. The sister-in-law was surprised to hear of this, the social worker noted, for "she had not heard of her being out with men." Not all potential informants were so cooperative. A distant cousin did not care to comment at all on the marriage, maintaining she was not "either one's keeper." And Kelly's former landlady, interviewed one week later, claimed to know "nothing of patient's men friends, said none ever came to her house that she knew of." Several times she repeated, "All I can say is that she was a fine, straight girl." The social worker made it clear she did not believe her, for while she judged the sister-in-law who had volunteered information about the patient's shady past an intelligent "person of character," she condemned the landlady, who, she wrote reproachfully, "said she went to bed and 'paid no attention to the doings of her lodgers,'" as a "slack, toothless, loud voiced Irish woman." Although social workers saw their interviewing as a necessary part of the process of arriving at the truth of a case, it would be hard to fault Margaret Kelly for protesting to her social worker that she "would do me a great favor by stop going around to friends of mine inquiring about me, as it only keeps them guessing and also looks bad chasing me around like a policeman."[119]

Not all social work was police work. Women in social workers' favor considered them friends, and social workers could be quite generous with women they deemed worthy. The social worker who deviled eggs (going out to buy pepper, mustard, and other essentials) and hemmed curtains for Barbara Kinney was rewarding her—not atypically—for a domestic job well done; Kinney's home was for this visit especially clean and the worker had come upon her scrubbing the front hall. But the substance and methods of social work appeared, at times, dangerously close to those of gossip. A social worker on her way to visit Mary McBurney noted that among her objectives was encouraging McBurney to divulge the contents of a letter, marked "private," that she knew her husband had written her; the social worker was successful in convincing McBurney to divulge the particulars of her troubled sex life that the letter detailed.[120] And only a thin veneer of professionalism distinguished one social worker's observation that Eleanor Herbert was, on one occasion, "exceedingly well, even expensively, dressed," from Charles Connelly's sister's surmise that his wife "tried to live on too high a scale for his income";[121] or Alice Bundy's sister-in-law's confidential testimony that Bundy was "quite a wild girl and was spoken of as a 'dirty little slut,'" from a social worker's candid admission that she had, "without much evidence," wondered whether Margaret Fitzpatrick, who had testified that her husband had repeatedly threatened to kill her and her children, was "a straight, moral woman."[122] The interpretation of a case could thus turn on a woman's character.

The social workers' focus on women's character is clearer when seen in the context of the nature of their practice. The social worker who placed herself between the warring parties in a failed marriage must have felt herself, at times, on treacherous professional terrain. Emotions ran high, recriminations piled up, threats were exchanged. Intervening in these already charged situations, she was apt to become an actor in the drama she was trying to direct. A friend of James McGinley, for example, reported that the man and his wife usually had a row after the social worker's visits, because the wife would then taunt the patient;[123] and Eleanor Herbert's husband, she told her social worker, constantly "throws it up at her" that she was under their supervision, "saying she must be queer" on that account.[124] Formally neutral by conviction and by professional training, the social worker shuttling between spouses could find herself unable to determine "which party was telling the truth."[125] Much of what she had, after all, consisted of the many elaborate stories that each party—in conjunction with friends, relatives, employers, and others—spun out. Constructing her own story, the social worker cast about for truth-laden clues, seeking to square what she heard with what she could see. Thus, it might matter whether an informant was intelligent or stupid; whether she spoke frankly or was "a little on her guard"; or whether her overall appearance was refined and artistic or cheap and gaudy, like one patient's landlady, who, the social worker interviewing her noted, wore pearl earrings and sported "hair that seemed to be artificially colored."[126] Social workers were not alone in seeing in a woman's dress and deportment clues to her nature, details that carried far less significance in a man. Still, a consequence of their doing so was that women—patients, wives of patients, and informants of all kinds—were subjected to harsher social work scrutiny than were men.

Psychiatric social workers searched through the first quarter of the century for firm ground on which to base their claims for professional expertise. "Character"—the social worker's stock-in-trade—was insufficiently scientific for their purposes; only adoption of "defined and systemized principles" would secure for them a status approaching that of psychiatrists. In the twenties, social workers would look to psychotherapy to give them the theoretical consistency, a necessary basis for professional autonomy, that simple casework could not provide. In the meantime, however, they dealt in morals, bandying about such terms as feebleminded, immoral, and slovenly on the one hand and intelligent, upright, and refined on the other, evoking with each use a range of associations they only rarely felt compelled to spell out. Social workers—like psychiatrists, working-class men, and perhaps even working-class women—had not yet settled on the nature of married womanhood, but in character, and its auxiliary, domesticity, they had a sure measure of it.

The advice psychiatrists and social workers purveyed and the interventions they made did, in sum, offer more to women than the Victorian conventions they were so ardently attempting to unseat. To be sure, psychiatrists, with their self-consciously modern stance on sexuality, underestimated the practical difficulties that kept women from simply abandoning their marriages and mates, and social workers, more realistic in this regard, too eagerly counseled appeasement. In many cases, however, they did manage to alter the marital balance of power, often in a woman's favor; by the very fact of their scrutiny some men felt themselves under regulation and altered their behavior accordingly. Still, the marriage problem was, at the end of this period, still evolving. Speaking as a psychiatrist but also as a man, Myerson put the difficulty succinctly, writing that it was "comparatively easy to deal with" what he characterized as "the ancient woman," but that "it is very much more difficult to deal with her modern sister."[127]

ELEVEN

WOMEN, ALONE AND TOGETHER

FEMINIST HISTORICAL WISDOM has it that in the last years of the nineteenth century, as psychiatrists and sexologists—the "medical profession," in the historian's shorthand—turned to scrutinizing female friendships, they began to cast the intensely emotional and richly sensual relationships middle-class Victorian women enjoyed with each other in a sexual light. By the 1920s, when lesbianism had taken shape in medical discourse as a well-defined, pathological phenomenon, the innocence of the nineteenth-century female world was but a memory, the world itself narrowed and pinched, tainted by pathology. Psychiatrists' and sexologists' construction of the lesbian persona as distinct was predicated in part on the turn-of-the-century increased visibility, especially in urban areas, of women without men. Some educated, many gainfully employed, these women could not so readily be cast as the sexless spinsters their numerous forebears had been; their choice to remain single—and it was interpreted as precisely that—took on a more sinister shading against the backdrop, on the one hand, of the crisis in heterosexual relations to which the marriage crisis and feminism pointed and, on the other, of the establishment of women's capacity for sexual aggressiveness. As women showed they could live on their own, and as reformers redefined marriage less as a legally binding relationship than as an emotionally binding one, the institution's very rationale seemed undercut. For what did women now need men if not for sex and companionship, some wondered, and what if they chose to get those from each other?

This interpretation of the emergence of lesbianism is, for the most part, plausible, persuasive, and well established.[1] Yet it wrongly envisions the broadly based twentieth-century attack on lesbianism solely as the work of sexologists and, in implying that the medical profession was unreservedly hostile to evidence of female friendship and female homosexuality, it slights a small but significant alternative tradition within sexology—ranging from Katherine Bement Davis's work in the twenties to Alfred Kinsey's in the forties and fifties—that looked less with alarm than with self-conscious benignity on lesbianism.[2] Psychopathic Hospital psychiatrists and social workers fell somewhere between this tradition and the conservative popular tradition—which condemned lesbianism as perverted, lesbians as would-be men—that it opposed. Even into the 1920s, by which time, the synthesis goes, the medical profession had constructed the lesbian as a distinct

type—masculine, aggressive, and sexually perverted—psychiatrists' and
social workers' stance on the issue of sex between women was ambiguous,
alternately alarmed and benign, and their conception of the lesbian equivocal, alternately distinct and confused.

This was in part because, to their minds, the dangers of heterosexuality
—unwanted pregnancy, ruination—were more pressing than those of
homosexuality. But it was also because in observing and classifying sexual
behavior, they took their cues as much from the culture in which they lived
as from medical traditions. Like many other commentators, they expected
that girls would—as in fact girls did—develop "crushes" on one another,
and attributed no special significance to their doing so; too, like many
others, they reflexively cast the mature lesbian as a frustrated man, and
when homosexually active women did not fit that popular stereotype, they
retreated in confusion. Further, psychoanalysis, with its positing of a fundamentally bisexual human nature, provided them with a theoretical
framework within which to interpret the widely observed phenomenon of
the crush as developmentally normal.[3] Psychiatrists and social workers
expected that girls would tire of each other and turn their attention to men;
when women failed to do so, or when their attractions to women took
sexual form, psychiatrists condemned their behavior as perverted and
wrong, but their condemnation was no more—at times even less—
vehement than that of popular opinion.

The standard interpretation of the emergence of lesbianism is even more
problematic in its envisioning of a sexually innocent nineteenth-century
woman's world, which accepted, even ennobled, female love, spoiled by
twentieth-century psychiatrists and sexologists who would see perverted
sex in every form of female association. This is the story implicit in the
history of sexology: As experts constituted "the lesbian" out of the richness
of woman's culture they sowed fear and suspicion where there had been
none.[4] While there can be no doubt that the sexological construction of the
lesbian represented a narrowing of the female sphere, historians have only
recently registered that in constituting the lesbian sexologists were also, for
the first time, attributing to her sexual—not just sensual—desires and
aims.[5] Although this sexualization of lesbianism, like that of womanhood
in general, was shaped to a large degree by patriarchal conventions—
casting the lesbian as a would-be man, the lesbian couple as a heterosexual pair—and thus double-edged and often hostile, in its recognition of
women's sexual needs and capacities it did represent a significant step in
constituting modern womanhood.

The standard interpretation is problematic as well in its implicit casting
of the language of woman's sphere as transparent. Although the issue is
perhaps best avoided, it is undeniable that it is, in large part, on this
language's rich texture and erotic tenor that our picture of—and fascina-

tion with—this world's sensuousness is based.[6] But, as Christine Stansell has provocatively argued, the conventions of literary sentimentalism structured the language of love and affection in the Victorian woman's sphere; an image of womanly virtue—as constricting as it was uplifting, deeply embedded in the patriarchal relations to which it promised an alternative —was at work in this woman's world of "trembling, delicately-put emotion," of harmonious female community.[7] We will never know to what exactly women's language referred; indeed, the sexual ambiguity, the sensuous physicality, of women's language reflected, to some extent, the irreducible sexual ambiguity of womanhood, an ambiguity that sexologists were only beginning to explore. But what scant evidence exists of sexual relations between adult women in the same period suggests that when it came to sex—mutual masturbation and "imitative coitus," in the sexologists' inimitably dry language—women were not always so entirely innocent as our portrait of their world would have it. Women may have enjoyed sex with other women, but those who did were careful not to flaunt their relations, and spoke of them only uneasily.[8] It is among these women's early-twentieth-century descendants—women who rejected men and with varying degrees of defiance chose women for companionship and sex— that the shadowy outlines of an urban lesbian subculture can be glimpsed. This chapter explores the nature of psychiatrists' and, especially, social workers' confrontation with that world in turn-of-the-century Boston.

Female Friendship and Lesbianism

Among psychiatrists, through the early twenties, female friendships sparked little interest. Lesbianism was not a well-defined phenomenon, the lesbian not a fully elaborated persona to the psychiatric mind. Still, much evidence of girls' youthful homosexual play came to their attention. Many poor and working-class girls grew up in homes and neighborhoods in which evidence of youthful and adult sexual activity was all about. Young girls and boys in cramped households often slept together until eight or nine years of age; more than a few adult women recalled first becoming aware of sexual difference and sexual feelings as they tussled with their brothers. And some boys and girls, when not subject to the scrutiny of adults, engaged in a range of sexual play, from the relatively common entreaties of one sex to the other to remove all clothing to boys' relatively infrequent attempts to coerce girls into trying intercourse with them. Sexologists estimated that perhaps a quarter of all preadolescent girls engaged in various forms of sex play with boys and other girls in this period.[9] For the majority of girls who engaged in homosexual play, this was only one expression of the polymorphous sexuality of the young.[10] Edith Miller, for example, a former teacher who lived on her own in a boardinghouse, told of masturbating with girls as a child of nine; Alice Moore, a thirty-seven-year-old married woman, told of dressing up as men with her girl cousin and masturbating—of rigging up "pillows to look like men and do[ing] something with them"; and Harriet Waters told of licking the genitals of another girl.[11] Neither psychiatrists nor these women themselves attributed any special significance to early homosexual experiences like these. Although she never married, Miller was heterosexually inclined, engaged at the time in a flirtation with a friend's husband. Moore had shown no further sexual interest in women, having "let boys play with her" before she married, and she was torn, in 1912, when she consulted psychiatrists, over her passion for another man. The claim of one thirty-seven-year-old woman, who recalled in 1914 that as a girl of twelve she had let another girl masturbate her about once a month for a few years, that only in retrospect did the experience seem odd—she knew as a girl never to let a boy touch her, "but she did not think it was wrong to let a girl masturbate her"— testifies to how innocent and uncomplicated such play could seem to the girls involved.[12]

The relatively unreflective, preadolescent sex play in which these and many other girls engaged was sometimes superseded by the "crush."[13] In the crush the widely recognized intimate and even passionate feelings that adolescent girls developed for one another assumed a highly stylized form. "Smashing" girls acted out with each other the familiar rituals of middle-class heterosexual courtship, fashioning themselves a "couple," rejecting other lovers, exchanging lovers' tokens, and avowing passionate and everlasting love—replicating, even, that courtship's sexually charged play of desire. In the crush, desire was ambiguous. It could be of an ethereal sort, like that twenty-five-year-old Marguerite Jacobs told of experiencing when she "fell in love" with a nun—"a sweet, beautiful soul"—at the convent school she had attended. "I breathed but for her," she wrote. "I followed her like a dog follows his master." Although their relationship had never been physical, Jacobs had been so passionately devoted to "her dear little nun" that she had ignored men altogether until she turned twenty-three.[14]

Psychiatrists saw the crush as a normal phase of girlhood, and they were taken aback, at times, by girls' claims they had not had any. "Isn't it unusual that you didn't have a 'crush'?" one psychiatrist asked thirty-three-year-old Grace Wilkins. "I thought all girls had those."[15] In this and other cases psychiatrists skeptically noted that they had uncovered no history of "so-called crushes" or "flames," testifying to their generally benign stance on the phenomenon.

But such passions of the mind as Jacobs experienced, in addition to keeping women's attention directed at each other rather than at men, could, many knew, incite the more dangerous passions of the flesh. The baleful effects of such incitements were all too evident in institutions—reformatories, training schools, hospitals—that housed poor and working-class women. Just as the relatively chaste crush was the secret embarrassment of the middle-class woman's colleges, rampant and overt homosexuality was, to many reformers' minds, the scourge of the poor woman's institutions. Troubling reports of homosexual activity, often interracial, among institutionalized girls began to appear in the psychiatric literature in the teens, and although enlightened penologists could dismiss the kissing, petting, mutual masturbation, and oral sex in which institutionalized girls engaged as the desperate stratagems of sexually experienced but otherwise normal girls denied access to men, the intense rivalries and jealousies —"even more real than the husband-wife jealousies of the everyday world," in one commentator's estimation—that these relationships spawned provided evidence of the practice's darker side.[16]

The desire that the middle-class girl's crush parodied and inflamed was, in the accounts of poor and working girls, rendered in a harsher idiom. Power, coercion, and a harder-edged sex diluted, even negated, the practice's aura of sentimentality. The working girl's crush was less a playful parody of middle-class heterosexuality than a same-sex reenactment of its real inequalities and pleasures.[17] Describing the modus operandi of one particularly successful "crush"—the term referred both to the relationship and to the woman directing it—at the nursing school she attended, twenty-eight-year-old Henrietta Clark stressed the crush's near-ruthless exercise of her seductive powers. She would go after two or three girls in each class, "just like a man would if he wanted to seduce a girl," drawing them in, eliciting gifts from them, and exciting them sexually to the point where she would get "her solid work in" on them. As passion cooled, she would drop one, badly hurt, and move on to another. Clark could see no difference between the crush and a prostitute—"they both work in the same manner . . . for what they can get"—and judged the whole business disgusting. Clark was no prude; she spoke openly of her sexual passions and desires for women and men. It was the crush's tactics, not her sexuality, to which she took exception.[18]

The unflattering light in which Clark cast her crush was perhaps singular, but the predatory sexuality of which she wrote was not an isolated phenomenon. Other women told of girls having talked them into relations as adolescents. Some rebuffed their advances; one mentioned several girls trying to get her to join in masturbation when she was seven, and another told Emerson of letting a girl masturbate her, but only after the second girl convinced her by warning that "she would be regarded as queer if she didn't as other girls did it and liked it."[19] And twenty-year-old Carrie Campbell learned of "abnormal practices" from a girl known as "a bad one" while working as a hospital maid; dismissed because of their mutual relations, she seduced an initially unwilling girl, Eliza Paxton, at her next place of employment and the two had regular relations that ended in Campbell "faint[ing] away." The fact that some of Campbell's workmates had warned her about the girl who had first taught her homosexual practices points to an awareness of lesbianism, whether fearful or intrigued, among at least some working girls. Campbell's claim to innocence, that she knew nothing of the abnormality of her relations with Paxton until she confessed the matter to a priest, fared poorly under psychiatric scrutiny. "You confessed the matter to the priest?" asked one. "Then it must have dawned upon you as a sin." Campbell admitted it did: "It is a sin, I can't deny that." This established, psychiatrists were yet unsure whether, as one put it, "the homosexuality is the important thing" in the case. Campbell claimed she had found a sister in Paxton, and though psychiatrists thought the "sistership" had gone rather too far, they could take the repentant Campbell's word that her experiences had left "no permanent trace upon [her] character" and judge her "all right."[20] Psychiatrists could look on even explicitly sexual relations between girls rather unexcitedly, seeing in them evidence of youthful passion gone wrong but not necessarily of permanent defect.

The girl's homosexual enthusiasms could be judged a passing perversion; the mature woman's were potentially more troubling. Psychiatrists began tentatively to sketch the contours of a perverted female homosexuality as they caught glimpses of the distinct lesbian identity that was beginning to take shape in some urban areas in these years. This identity was mostly hidden but sometimes open to public view. When thirty-three-year-old Grace Wilkins took up with a new lover, a "coarse, mannish woman" known about the neighborhood as a homosexual "sport," she began to fashion such a persona for herself. This persona conformed in part to psychiatric and popular notions of the "mannish lesbian"; Wilkins began to smoke and drink publicly and, to many minds, excessively. But this identity was also ultrafeminine, for the normally untidy Wilkins began to pay particular attention to her toilette before going out with her lover, to wear fancy lingerie, to shave her pubic hair, all likely private signs of her newly public lesbian identity. She and her lover, to whom she had been first drawn on overhearing her say "damn," consorted openly, much like a high-spirited heterosexual couple, drinking cocktails and dining in disreputable hotels, attending the theater, and driving recklessly through the city. It is hardly surprising that their fast behavior drew neighborly and psychiatric censure (it is worth noting that neighbors, many of whom were interviewed by social workers, were even quicker than psychiatrists to condemn such actions); what is remarkable is how slow psychiatrists were to fill in the outlines of the lesbian persona with the rich details that cases such as this presented. Wilkins's ultrafeminine lesbian style squared poorly with their conception of the female homosexual as a frustrated would-be man; psychiatrists in the late teens were still casting lesbianism in terms more of gender identity than of sexual orientation.[21]

Just how fixed gender identity could be is evident in psychiatrists' and social workers' treatment of Julia Brown, alias Alfred Mansfield, the lesbian cross-dresser. The forty-three-year-old Brown had been living quite comfortably as a man for twelve years when she came to psychiatric attention. Dressed, as always, as a man, she had one night after an evening of drinking in a saloon turned on the gas in her room—claiming to have no memory of doing so, and vigorously contesting psychiatrists' contention that she must have been trying to commit suicide—and had woken up undeniably a woman at the Boston City Hospital to face the questions of puzzled physicians who deemed her a "man-woman" and sent her forthwith to the Psychopathic Hospital. She told psychiatrists there she was happy living as a man. Like many single men, she lived in a boardinghouse and took all her meals in restaurants; she smoked, drank—mostly in saloons—and sang regularly in a barbershop quartet; she enjoyed an active public life, and was known about the neighborhood as a gentleman. Brown's choice of male attire was in part instrumental; as a masculine-looking girl, she told psychiatrists, she had been tormented by children on the street calling out, "Look at the boy"; in addition, she said that she found it easier to get well-paid work as a man. But, she admitted to social workers, "I think I really did it because I was so crazy about the girls," telling them that she "got more pleasure in making love to women than she ever did in having men make love to her." She had lived with one woman for a year and a half, had escorted many others on dates, and was currently going with a twenty-two-year-old woman who worked at Filene's. If ever there was a woman who should have fit sexological and popular conceptions of the homosexual woman, Brown was she. In handling her case, however, psychiatrists and social workers focused entirely on altering her gender identity, and ignored her sexual orientation. They tried, that is, to make her over as a woman, but not to wean her from women or interest her in men.

Brown halfheartedly agreed to try life as a woman, and social workers enthusiastically began to refashion her identity. They pressed on her the uncomfortable women's clothing—proper suits, waists, shirts, and most loathsome of all, corsets—whose strictures she had spent a lifetime avoiding; they worked on her personal hygiene, urging her to bathe regularly, to use mouthwash, and to fix her hair with fancy combs; and they tried to nurture in her an appetite for life's finer pleasures, taking her to shows and concerts and lending her respectable novels from the Boston Public Library in the hope this would divert her from her usual fare of dime novels. Although Brown hated the clothes, she wore them, and social workers were cheered by her general progress toward womanhood: her formerly untidy room was now immaculate, her drinking had tapered off, and she had even had sex with a man in her room. All the while, Brown tried to impress on social workers that she knew she was meant to be a man and that she was attracted to pretty girls and women. Yet so unsuspecting were they that they encouraged Brown to live with a woman companion rather than by herself. Ignoring their advice, Brown continued to live on her own until she met a woman—to whom she referred as her "wife"—and the two made plans to move in together. Social workers were strangely silent on the matter. Brown's landlady, by contrast, was quite agitated over the plan. She would not "have any queer goings on in her house," she proclaimed; should the girlfriend move in, she would "bore a hole in the door and the moment she sees anything 'out they both go.'"

Brown's case, which spanned the years 1915 through 1919, underscores just how tentative a construct the lesbian remained, how psychiatrists' and social workers' concern with the lesbian's gender-inappropriate behavior outweighed their interest in her sexual activities. Brown's gender identity— her presentation of self—was a public, even legal, matter. City newspapers ran short, titillating stories about the "man-woman" or "girl-man" when her identity was first revealed. In addition, she could have been prosecuted for disorderly conduct for wearing men's clothing. So fixed was her identity as a man that social workers unwittingly treated her as one even as they were making her over as a woman. In conversations with the startled neighbors and acquaintances—all of whom characterized Brown as "gentlemanly"— to whom they revealed Brown's true identity, they slipped confusedly between the masculine and feminine pronoun in reference to her, or him; they respected her desires for independence and autonomy, at one point noting without condemnation that she was "really happiest sitting in her room smoking a pipe and reading"; and they never questioned her morals, only those of her female lovers. Social workers were, for the most part, uninterested in Brown's sexual activities.[22]

Therapeutic Woman's Culture

Brown's case highlights the ambiguous relationship between woman's culture and lesbianism that has so intrigued and frustrated historians. Social workers—young, single, college-educated women—pressed on their female patients a therapeutic variant of the nineteenth-century bourgeois woman's culture that ennobled the domestic world, encouraged passionate (if chaste) friendships among women, and looked rather disdainfully on men. Intimately involved in the lives of some of their single women patients, social workers awakened in them passionate longings, not unlike those at play in the crush, that they could neither comprehend nor reciprocate. The psychic territory social workers and patients explored in these relationships was uncharted and unpredictable. A later generation of psychiatric social workers, schooled in Freudian psychology, would see in patients' longings the makings of the transference; largely ignorant of Freud and of psychoanalytic technique, these social workers struggled vainly to account for them.

Thirty-two percent of the women between the ages of twenty-five and forty-five who lived in Boston were single in 1910. Nearly all of them worked for wages. A number lived in female communities: working women's homes, boardinghouses, apartments, the YWCA. In these small and heterogeneous institutions, far distant from the middle-class woman's colleges and sitting rooms, they created a working women's world, a world in which the bonds of womanhood were less tightly woven, the feminine solidarities less self-consciously elaborated, the sensibility less stylized than in the middle-class woman's world.[23] The sentimental tradition that shaped the middle-class woman's voice had little impact here; absent it, women's dealings with one another were direct, their disappointments raw, their celebration of female friendship equivocal. There was much misery in this women's world—loneliness, hunger, poverty. But the many small pleasures of everyday life—a kind word, a shared meal, a fierce hug—could bring great comfort. Women's consciousness in this world took less the shape of an ideology than of an uneasy accommodation to the difficult task of surviving as a single woman.[24]

However meager the middle-class single woman's portion, that of her working-class sister was even more so. Her institutions were poor and dirty; in them she was served inadequate food and watched over by gratuitously mean matrons. Even the best among them, like the YWCA, could seem like prisons, their inhabitants—many of whom had landed in them less by choice than by unfortunate circumstance—like inmates.[25] Yet in these institutions women created a lively culture for themselves. Sleeping two or three to a room, women quickly became acquainted with each other. They shared confidences, telling their life tales, arguing about men and marriage, gossiping about others in similar circumstances; they planned outings to theaters and shows, cooked grand suppers, and hosted parties in their rooms. At bedtime, there was much tucking-in to do, and women particularly fond of each other occasionally shared beds. "Such fun . . . we do have," wrote one woman to another of her stay at the YWCA.[26]

Shared experience cemented bonds among these women; jealousies and differences just as often divided them. The women sometimes ennobled female friendship; one wrote of the virtues of "standing by and helping" a girl in trouble. But they could also disappoint a particularly valued friend by gossiping about her with others. They could roundly condemn men as unreliable and untrue; but they could also go out with them and, in some cases, decide to marry them. These women were as aware as any of woman's lesser lot, but they voiced their consciousness of themselves as women only fitfully, pausing to comment, say, on the perfidy of men, like one who complained bitterly that "it was a man who signed paper to send me to an Insane Asylum it was a man that ruined me and I have had to pay the penalty of it all," but going out with yet another man the next week.[27]

By example and precept, social workers nurtured these women's fledgling gender consciousness. They encouraged them to associate only with women and to avoid men altogether. Although these single women appear to have agreed with social workers that men were inherently unreliable and sexually too aggressive, the former were more willing than the latter to venture into the heterosexual world. Rose Butler wrote to Helen Anderson that if she "knew what fun dancing is," she too might try it. "Don't worry about me being in the company of men," she wrote on another occasion. "I am *very very* careful. One needs to be," she added, establishing thereby common ground on the subject of male nature. Butler spent most of her time with women and claimed to "hate men"; she was too tired, after a day at work, "to pose for men, as their sweethearts etc." Yet she liked to go out, and she liked the fellows with whom she worked ("don't go to war yet," she wrote to Jarrett as she informed her of this).[28] Social workers envisioned independent lives for these women, and independence, to their minds, was most easily achieved in an environment free of the frivolous distractions of heterosexuality. Women too alert to the presence of men would be unlikely, for example, to stay home evenings to read the high-minded books social workers pressed on them or, if they went out, to attend the evening classes to which they directed them. Social workers' advocacy of female over male companionship was not only expressive of the deep distrust with which they looked on men; it was also indicative of their larger strategy of making these single women over in their own, middle-class image.

Social workers pursued this strategy aggressively. They arranged for some women who still lived with their families to live independently. They saw to the women's material needs, buying them clothing, taking them shopping, lending them small sums of cash, and helping them find jobs. They introduced some of them to a world of pleasures they had not known, treating them to lunches in restaurants, going with them to lectures and shows, and arranging for vacations in the country.[29] They visited them at home, met with them at the hospital, and corresponded with them regularly, even voluminously, on subjects ranging from the difficulty of finding work to the unfairness of prevailing sexual ethics. Social workers bestowed love and affection on women who had known neither, becoming no less than mothers to women whose biological mothers had been—by reason of death, desertion, or inclination—inadequate.

In this woman's world, the mother who had never shown her daughter any affection was not uncommon. Rose Butler told social workers that "when she would put her arms around her mother she would be cast off," although her sister "could do as much caressing as she wanted to."[30] Ethel Hancock could not "remember having ever kissed or caressed any member of the family, except the baby, or they me."[31] Bertha Greenwood, "hungry for love" on one occasion, threw her arms around her mother's neck and "was going to kiss her," but her mother rebuffed her, saying she had "never kissed me when I was a baby and she wouldn't kiss me then."[32] And Carrie Campbell's mother, whom she had wanted to kiss "about every five minutes," often discouraged her shows of affection with slaps, telling her "she wanted to be loved too much."[33] Other women told of growing up with mean mothers, like Alice Moore's, who, when her daughter told her she might be pregnant, remarked, "Nobody would care enough for you to get you that way."[34] Mothers like these haunted women through adulthood. Some women managed to dull painful memories of rejection by turning to fantasy, imagining their mothers transformed into loving, nurturing, perfect mothers. As Rose Butler, pushed away by her own mother, put it: "What is there more comforting to a girl after her days work, than to go to a bright home with a mother to fondle and caress."[35] Mothers sometimes fed those fantasies by temporarily acting the part of the "normal" mother. On Christmas in 1916, for example, twenty-seven-year-old Katherine Warner was delighted to get "the nicest letter from Mother I ever received in my life," a letter that encouraged her to hope the two might "talk to each other as Mother and daughter instead of like strangers."[36] But the letter, like the other conciliatory gestures these unreliable mothers made, proved an aberration, and Warner tried to convince herself she did not care so much about her mother anyway.

But the legacy of maternal disappointment was not so easily overcome. These unmothered women, offered the opportunity, invariably but unwittingly began to cast "their" social workers as surrogate perfect mothers, seeking from them the approval, encouragement, and affection their own mothers had been unwilling or unable to give. This they often secured; but what some of them desired most, the mother's—now the social worker's—exclusive love, proved frustratingly elusive. Even as social workers decried women's "excessive attachments" to individual workers, maintaining that several different workers could treat one case successfully, even profitably, and that the advantage of gaining a friend in a new worker would offset the loss a patient might feel in losing a treasured one,[37] with their generous solicitude—the essence of their craft, but a mark of their empathy as well—they unwittingly invited the longings they condemned. These longings were intense, passionate, homoerotic, and ambiguously sexual, dangerously like those at work in the crush. Ellen Knox, for example, took comfort in the "loving seemingly cheerful and winning way" of her social worker, Helen Anderson, whom she loved as a mother; "There are those I love and those I l-o-v-e!!!!!!!!!!" she enthusiastically wrote to her.[38] Rose Butler was taken with Anderson, too, especially her "soft refined voice and eloquent flow of language," which, she wrote, "seemed to win my affections. (Lucky I am not a man) ah, ah," her nervous invocation of heterosexuality highlighting the ambiguity of her desire. Anderson became Katherine Warner's "mother," too; deeply upset on one occasion, she wanted to rest her head on Anderson's shoulder and "cry it all out," and on another, surrounded by "4 couples spooning," she exclaimed, "I feel I better stop short before I try to embrace you for you know spooning in cozy nooks is very contagious."[39] And Ethel Hancock, seeing Jarrett as her "mother confessor and advisor," delighted in her "magnetizing" personality and regularly sent her "bushels of love." "You I like in and out and around and about and especially that little crinkle in your forehead," she wrote on one occasion, adding, "I'm simply crazy about you."[40] Social workers recoiled from declarations like this. Jarrett regularly upbraided Hancock for voicing her desires, and for more than a year the two tangled over the rules of their relationship, Hancock expressing her love, Jarrett rebuffing her, Hancock agreeing she only "liked" Jarrett—sending her "bushels of 'like' (how's that)"—and thereby regaining her favor, only to lose it again as she began the cycle anew.

Social workers did not warm to all of their women patients. They could be harsh and censorious of those they deemed feckless, as was Jarrett in her management of a twenty-three-year-old woman whom psychiatrists had diagnosed psychopathic. Jarrett wrote this woman, who staged a widely reported "drowning" in the Charles River that resulted in her removal to the institution, a long, hectoring letter, two years after her discharge from the hospital, in which she branded her silly, lambasted her for not being "sensible for once"—the young woman wanted to give up her job—and excoriated her for attempting to escape the reputation her actions had earned her. "Of course I know you won't take my advice," Jarrett ended her letter. "The reason you have had so much trouble is that you never do the sensible thing. I wish you could grow up and learn to live right, and be happy."[41] It is likely that Jarrett and her colleagues often experienced the frustrations so manifestly on display here. What is remarkable is how self-restrained they were in their handling of their effusive female patients.

For the most part unfamiliar with the Freudian psychology that would have helped them interpret their patients' longings as possibly having to do with the transference, social workers responded to their patients' effusions with anxious firmness, warning them to dampen their feelings even as they continued to elicit them. Jarrett cast Hancock's unwillingness or inability to temper her outbursts as an issue of self-control, and dismissed her longings as imaginary. This only angered and confused Hancock, who complained with some justification that Jarrett did "not credit [her] with *honest* and *truly* feelings"; she did not feel free, she wrote, "to say, I love you. . . . I wish you were my 'society lady' and then I'd have a ghost of a right."[42] Many of these women's stylized declarations of love and ritual profferings of hugs and kisses fit comfortably within the discourse of woman's culture, in which social workers were well versed. But others expressed an urgency that frightened social workers, who sometimes responded by replacing a particularly beloved social worker with an unknown, often unacceptable, other. Jarrett eventually assigned Hancock to a new worker; Hancock, deeply hurt, grudgingly accepted that Jarrett liked her—"of course you like everybody"—but she hated "like the dickens," she wrote to her new worker, "to be ousted out of my place but then I must so as to make room for new comers. Please tell Miss Jarrett I'm a wee bit sore at being ousted out of first place."[43] And Rose Butler, temporarily assigned a new worker to replace her beloved Helen Anderson, admitted that the new one was lovely, but, she added, "you can only have one Miss Anderson."[44]

Through the teens, leaders in psychiatric social work were well aware that if social work were ever to achieve the status of a profession, the discipline would have to be based less on the personal qualities of its practitioners and more on "defined and systemized principles." In the twenties, social workers would adopt psychotherapy as a technique, establishing thereby a more theoretically consistent and scientifically derived conception of casework as well as a stronger basis for professional autonomy. The resentment and anger that grew out of social workers' constant skirmishes with psychiatrists who would dismiss them as so many nurses and their craft as the handmaiden to medicine fueled, in part, their quest for a more systematic technique. So, too, did the tensions generated by the intimate relationships they developed with a number of single women. These women and their longings pushed the social work of everyday life to its limits, and they made manifest how inadequate was Jarrett's advocacy of "impersonal friendliness" as a technique when the friendliness was that of a woman.[45] The therapeutic woman's world replicated and then threw in sharp relief the many sexual ambiguities of woman's sphere; women's maternal fantasies freighted their relationships with social workers with dimensions the latter could barely understand. It is hardly surprising that social workers staved off, sometimes gently, sometimes firmly, women's longings, all the while throwing down the gauntlet of professionalism.

CONCLUSION

IN THE CONTEMPORANEOUS estimation of one prominent practitioner, psychiatry in the late twenties was still the "Cinderella of medicine," a characterization suggestive—especially in its gender imagery—of just how marginal psychiatrists could feel themselves.[1] Still, one should not allow this and other psychiatrists' intermittently expressed sense of professional inferiority to obscure the many conceptual and concrete accomplishments to which the psychiatry of the century's first two decades could rightfully lay claim. If knowledge in the guise of science had not yet effected the discipline's transformation from stepsister to princess of the medical specialties, much else *had* changed.

Most significant was psychiatry's abandonment of the distinction between sane and insane that had structured nineteenth-century practice, and its concomitant reorganization around a metric concept of the normal. By the 1920s, the metric mode of thinking that psychiatrists first elaborated around psychopathy would be dominant within, and beyond, the discipline. The psychiatric point of view no longer dichotomously classed individuals as sane or insane but arrayed them on a scale, assessing their variations from what was thought normal. The degenerate was displaced by the deviate; even the most severe psychopathologies would come to be evaluated not against a fixed standard but, in the words of one authority, "in terms of how it deviates from the norms and expectancies of society in general."[2] That psychiatrists could specify the parameters, even the ontological status, of normality in only the most general terms would become a staple of professional self-criticism.[3] Still, despite intraprofessional disagreement over the question of whether normal individuals were common or rare, and over whether the term could be stripped of its evaluative dimension, the existence and attainability of normality—broadly conceived and ambiguously defined—would serve as psychiatry's ruling fiction for much of this century.[4] One psychiatrist was not far off the mark when he saw the makings of "a new era in the history of psychiatry" in the discipline's turn-of-the-century reorientation toward normal minds and persons.[5]

Equally important was psychiatrists' corollary project of defining what one prominent authority, following Freud, would call "the psychopathology of everyday life."[6] Focusing not on the symptom or even the disease, psychiatrists in the thirties and forties would claim that their science was one of the whole person and his or her fit to the environment. How "normal" persons thought, felt, and behaved: this, not merely insanity, was the modern psychiatrist's province. No human activity, however prosaic, lay beyond his ken; individuals' doubts and worries, passions and desires, aggressions and hates, assets and liabilities were the stuff from which he fashioned a portrait of the total personality, his unit of interest. Establishing the conceptual and material foundations for a psychiatry of the everyday, a discipline to whose practices everyone might be subjected, was among early-twentieth-century psychiatrists' signal achievements. "Even though we regard ourselves as 'normal,'" William C. Menninger would explain to the laity in the late forties, "all of us need some help every now and then"[7]—a formulation that succinctly captured the new psychiatry's orientation and ambitions. To be sure, psychoanalysis, with its positing of mental mechanisms common to all and its bestowal of significance on the routine practices of everyday life, would figure importantly in psychiatry's reorientation. But it would not do so until the late teens at the earliest, by which time psychiatrists positioned within institutional psychiatry had already established their discipline's new foundations.

The Psychopathic Hospital psychiatrists' practices—based in the hospital, not the asylum—presaged their discipline's extra-institutional future in two salient respects. In the course of the century, American psychiatrists would abandon the mental hospital in favor of the outpatient clinic, the general hospital, and the private office. The late-nineteenth-century alienist typically practiced in an asylum; by 1960, less than 20 percent of psychiatrists practiced in state hospitals.[8] The psychiatrists, in Boston and nationwide, who lobbied for new laws that would bring not only the insane but the nearly normal under their scrutiny; who established new forms of institutional discipline, more persuasive than punitive; and who fashioned a new professional persona for the psychiatrist as a man of science, not a keeper of the insane, were instrumental to the process that saw psychiatry's locus of practice shift so dramatically. The psychiatrist's professional status rose as the sites in which he practiced multiplied. Purveyors of a discipline with applicability to everyone, not only the patently insane, psychiatrists defined and assessed maladjustment, and even ordinary unhappiness, in the home and the family as well as in education, industry, and criminology, enhancing their own standing within and beyond medicine. Reflecting on nearly seventy years of hospital practice, Harry C. Solomon told two interviewers in 1980 that in the teens "the average physician just couldn't understand why anybody would want to work in a mental hospital. It was inconceivable to most of them. There was something odd about the guy that did it." Now it was different. "The prestige of the psychiatrist today is enormous. He's a big-shot guy."[9]

This book has traced, locally and intensively, the genesis of a psychiatric point of view that would take firmer shape in the course of the century. From the twenties on, a significant portion of the profession would turn to

Freud, assimilating and—as they blunted the many aspects of his theory they deemed unpalatable—domesticating him to create a distinctively American psychiatry, the so-called dynamic psychiatry or adjustment psychiatry. The conceptual labors of institutionally based, non-psychoanalytically oriented early-twentieth-century psychiatrists were critical to the appeal and success of the dynamicists' project, for not only did they effect the turn to the personality but they also were among the first to articulate the rationale that informed a critical aspect of dynamic psychiatry—the imperative to disclose, to offer up for the psychiatrist's analysis what was private and closely held. Psychopathic Hospital practice, in which this imperative was adumbrated, yielded a congeries of normative gender discourses. Some, encoded in patently gender-neutral categories like manic-depressive insanity, operated invisibly. Others took shape in the narratives that animated psychiatric textbooks. Still others, like those that underwrote the category of female psychopathy, informed the policies of the professionals from other disciplines that pressed them into service.

The historical fate of psychiatrists' categories and practices proved various. The hypersexual was normalized as the flapper. The hysteric, harking back to a Victorianism that nearly everyone agreed was dead, largely faded from psychiatrists' view. The male psychopath was more narrowly delineated as a distinctly criminal type, the sociopath. And the issues arrayed around marriage, the family, and sex would figure at the center of the mid-twentieth-century psychiatrists' practice, especially as the Freudianism that psychiatrists brought to their science highlighted the significance of the child's early experiences. The project of modernity and limited gender equality that Psychopathic Hospital psychiatrists so avidly promoted would be largely forgotten as a new gender synthesis gained ascendancy within the larger culture and as organized feminism faded from view. In this new synthesis, the essentials of the Victorian gender system were modernized but not fundamentally displaced: men and women were still assigned different natures and capacities, and men were—as in Victorianism—granted dominion of the public sphere, women of the home. The sharpest contrast between the old and new gender systems lay in the degree to which woman's nature was thoroughly sexualized in the new, a circumstance that the category of the hypersexual had enabled and that the lives of the young women suffering from hysteria had so painfully reflected. In the thirties and forties, psychoanalytically informed psychiatry would promote a neo-Victorian conception of woman's nature and limited capacities that gained popular and professional currency, coming under Betty Friedan's outraged scrutiny in her 1963 classic, *The Feminine Mystique*.

If the particular orientation of psychiatrists' everyday psychiatry met an uneven fate, its formal aspects proved enduring. It is significant in this respect that nearly half of those who seek psychotherapeutic treatment today do not meet the diagnostic criteria for any defined mental disorder and that a portion of them suffer only from "problems in living"—the annoyances and anxieties thrown up by day-to-day life over which Psychopathic Hospital psychiatrists had attempted to assert their disciplinary authority.[10] The conceptual dimension of psychiatrists' everyday project, their delineating of normality, proved no less enduring but perhaps more equivocal. It sustained the pathologizing sensibility that would prompt one psychiatrist to respond to his own rhetorically put question, "Who of us, then, is normal?" with the damning but untenable verdict that "none of us" is, a sensibility that would invite public censure and nurture popular skepticism of psychiatry's aims and outlooks.[11] But the project also sustained a countercritique that would question the concept itself, not the capabilities of those who were presumed not to measure up to its strictures. The issue, never adequately resolved, is perhaps best left with the protest of a patient, a woman diagnosed as manic who regularly questioned the institution's procedures and rationales: "If normal means ordinary, I don't want to be normal, do you!!"[12]

APPENDIX

Demographic Characteristics of the
Boston Psychopathic Hospital Patient Population

Race and Ethnicity

Psychopathic Hospital patients were drawn from Boston's racial and ethnic groups in proportions roughly equivalent to their representation in the city's population.[1] This is true (with the exception of the Irish, who were slightly overrepresented among patients) irrespective of the lines along which racial and ethnic categories are drawn. If we simply divide the general and hospital populations between foreign-born and native-born whites (and add a category for native-born African-Americans, who did not figure in contemporary calculations), we find that, among patients, both groups were represented proportionally to their representation in the city's population (table A.1). Foreign-born whites made up 46 percent of the Boston population and 49 percent of the hospital population; there are no statistically significant differences between the two populations. If we classify patients by country of origin, we find that no national group, with the exception of those born in Ireland, was overrepresented in the institutional population (table A.2); it is likely—although impossible to establish definitively, due to the way in which national origins were reported in the census—that the different age distributions of the general and institutionalized populations account for some of this difference. Finally, if we group patients into ethnic categories contemporaries would have found meaningful, we again find that the racial and ethnic composition of the city and the patient population was, with the exception of the Irish, quite similar (table A.3).

Contemporary commentators—psychiatrists, eugenic propagandists, and legislators—were certain that the foreign-born and their children were more prone to insanity than Americans of old stock. Many commentators marshaled figures that purported to show the former disproportionately represented in institutional populations. As early as 1903, it was pointed out that because both immigrants and the insane were concentrated in the older portions of the population (those who entered the country as immigrants tended to be older than the native-born population, and few young people were committed to institutions), population figures should be corrected for age (as I have done in table A.1), but the practice of doing so did not become standard until much later. More significant, in their equation of immigration and insanity psychiatrists and other propagandists glossed over the critical fact that their figures measured not the overall incidence or

TABLE A.1
Nativity of Boston and Hospital Populations, Age 15+ (percent)

	Boston[a]	Hospital[b]
Native-born white	51	46
Foreign-born white	46	49
Native-born African-American	3	4

[a] 1920 census year.

[b] $N = 581$. No proportion in this column is significantly different from the corresponding proportion in the Boston population ($p < .05$).

prevalence of insanity but, rather, hospitalizations or commitments for insanity. Thus, researchers could not know whether they were measuring the real distribution of mental disease (as many claimed to be doing) or the effects of other unknown factors determining who was actually hospitalized or committed. Early-twentieth-century data are further skewed because both immigrants and those most likely to be hospitalized clustered in urban areas where they were more likely to come to the attention of authorities and where there were facilities—hospitals, asylums, almshouses—to hold them.

The significance of these data lies simply in their support for the contentions of neither the contemporary commentators nor the historians and sociologists writing later who have collectively advanced, for different rhetorical purposes, the argument that immigrants were overrepresented in turn-of-the-century institutions. Although it is possible that other Bostonians were committed to institutions without first being brought to the

TABLE A.2
Selected National Origins of Boston
and Hospital Populations (percent)

	Boston[a]	Hospital[b]
U.S., black	2	5
Canada	6	8
England	2	3
Ireland	8	13
Italy	5	3
Russia	5	6

[a] 1920 census year.

[b] $N = 703$.

[*] Significantly different from the proportion in the Boston population ($p < .05$).

TABLE A.3
Ethnicity of Boston and Hospital Populations (percent)

	Boston[a]	Hospital[b]
African-American	3	4
Irish	26	30[*]
Italian	7	5
Jewish[c]	10	9

[a] 1910 census year.
[b] N = 710.
[c] The proportion of Jews in Boston is assumed to equal the proportion of the Russian-born enumerated in the census.
[*] Significantly different from the proportion in the Boston population (p < .05).

Psychopathic Hospital, it is likely that their numbers were small. Boston families, police, and courts—those who usually petitioned for commitment for the insane—were encouraged, and in the case of the police mandated, to bring the suspected insane to the hospital for observation rather than to petition courts for their commitment. In many cases, and probably in all cases where the patient had not formerly been committed or hospitalized, Boston residents who were committed through regular court processes spent time in the Psychopathic Hospital before entering asylums. Thus, although the data presented here capture neither the incidence nor the prevalence of mental disorder in Boston, nor the total population of Boston residents committed for insanity, they come close to measuring the last. And although the Psychopathic Hospital population was in some respects singular, it was in others quite similar to the population of persons committed for insanity in San Francisco in the same period; it is likely that other institutional populations did not differ significantly from it.[2]

Occupation and Class

The material circumstances from which patients came were of little concern to contemporary commentators, who for the most part simply assumed that all institutional inmates composed an undifferentiated pauper class. Only in the late thirties would psychiatrists and sociologists begin to examine the class composition of institutional populations; they would find the prevalence of serious mental disease disproportionately high among the poor and argue that the environment was at fault.[3] Many of the historians and sociologists who more recently have analyzed institutional populations have accounted for the preponderance of poor persons in them by pointing not to illness per se but to the practices of authorities who, they argue, have interpreted the behavior of those lowest in the class hierarchy harshly, labeling them insane in larger-than-warranted numbers. Overshadowed in the early years of the century by polemicists' fixation on race, class has since figured centrally in discussions of psychiatric epidemiology and institutional practices.

Although class as an analytic category presents fewer difficulties than race, it is far from perfect. Historians have commonly interpreted a man's occupation as a rough measure of his material circumstances and position in the social hierarchy. Determined in this way, class is at best a descriptive measure, one that tells us nothing of persons' consciousness of their own and others' class identifications and interests; more problematic, it is an imperfect measure of wealth and, by extension, social power. Hospital psychiatrists recorded the occupations of nearly all entering patients, and in many cases they made note of other factors that, together with occupation, convey something of the patients' means: employment histories, wages, educational attainments. Social workers not only commented on the dress, language, and comportment of the patients they investigated and supervised but also described and evaluated their neighborhoods and homes. Still, none of this information, which conveys a much richer and more nuanced sense of patients' circumstances—if not their class—than a straightforward occupational designation, appeared consistently enough in the case records to be put to use quantitatively.[4]

Male patients, considered collectively, were slightly less well positioned in the city's class and occupational hierarchy than the general population from which they were drawn (table A.4). Between 32 and 35 percent of men in Boston worked at middle-class occupations, but only 25 percent of patients did. Conversely, while between 65 and 68 percent of male Bostonians labored at skilled, semiskilled, and menial blue-collar jobs, 75 percent of the hospital population came from this stratum of the city's population. Men who worked at the most menial of occupations were the most disproportionately represented of all; teamsters and those whom psychiatrists classed simply as laborers made up 23 percent of all male patients. These findings are skewed toward the bottom of the occupational hierarchy, yet this should not obscure what is surely most striking about them: that men who worked at middle-class occupations—dentists, engineers, businessmen, small proprietors, agents, clerks, and salesmen—made up as large a part of the institutional population as they did.

An imperfect measure in the case of men, occupation as a proxy for social position and economic power is even more problematic in the case of women. First, the extent to which a married woman's occupation measured her social position is unclear; in nearly all of the cases in which a woman and her husband both worked for wages, his occupational ranking

TABLE A.4

Occupational Distribution of Boston and Hospital Populations:
Men, Age 15+ (percent)

	Boston[a]		
	1910	1920	Hospital[a]
White-collar			
Professionals, high-white-collar workers	5	5	3
Proprietors, managers, and low-white-collar workers	30	27	22[b]
Total	35	32	25[c]
Blue-collar			
Skilled workers	22	27	28
Semiskilled workers	32	31	24
Unskilled and menial workers	11	10	23
Total	65	68	75[c]

Source: Boston figures from Stephan Thernstrom, *The Other Bostonians: Poverty and Progress in an American Metropolis, 1880–1970* (Cambridge, Mass., 1973), p. 50; hospital figures from hospital sample.

[a] $N = 304$.

[b] One-third proprietors and managers, two-thirds low-white-collar workers.

[c] Significantly different from the proportion in the Boston population ($p < .05$).

was higher than hers. Thus, although a married woman's occupation may be easily ascertained, the relation between it and her class position often remains unclear.[5] Second, because standard occupational scales were formulated with reference to male occupations, what we might consider the "real" ranking of men's and women's occupations differs within the same occupational category. The difference is most marked in the white-collar strata; in 1920, for example, 50 percent of Boston's working women were classed as white collar, while only 32 percent of male Bostonians were in the same stratum. Yet it would be absurd to claim that a higher proportion of women than men worked at jobs that were prestigious and that offered high wages and opportunities for advancement and exercise of authority over others.[6] Thus, the income, status, and education of a teacher or nurse (typical women's occupations) were not equal to those of a physician or engineer, although all four occupations appear at the top of the occupational hierarchy. The skilled stratum of the bottom half of the occupational hierarchy is similarly misleading in the case of women, for while many of the men classed in this category were highly paid machinists and mechanics, many of the women were poorly paid dressmakers or seamstresses who did piecework at home.

TABLE A.5
Occupational Distribution of Boston and Hospital Populations: Single,
Divorced, and Widowed Women, Age 15+ (percent)

	Boston[a]	Hospital[b]
White-collar		
Professionals, high-white-collar workers	11	10
Proprietors, managers	4	2
Low-white-collar workers	40	13
Total	55	25[*]
Blue-collar		
Skilled workers	3	2
Semiskilled workers	29	40
Unskilled and menial workers	13	34
Total	45	76[*c]

[a]1910 census year.
[b]$N = 229$; "housewives" and students ($N = 174$) excluded.
[c]Does not sum to 100 due to rounding error.
*Significantly different from the proportion in the Boston population (p < .05).

Approximately a third of all women resident in Boston aged fifteen and over worked for wages. Eighty-seven percent of these women were single, widowed, or divorced; married women made up only 13 percent of the female work force. Conversely, 89 percent of single women worked for wages, while only 11 percent of married women did.

Because so few of Boston's wage-earning women—and, in consequence, so few wage-earning female patients ($N = 21$)—were married, it is most useful to focus comparison of the occupational distributions of women who lived in the city and of female patients on single, divorced, and widowed women. These distributions differed substantially (see table A.5). Patients were drawn disproportionately from the lower half of the occupational hierarchy; 76 percent of patients, as opposed to 45 percent of Boston's single working women, were employed in blue-collar jobs. The age and marital structure of the female work force can account for some of this discrepancy, for while the office workers—bookkeepers, accountants, clerks, stenographers, and typists—and saleswomen who amounted to nearly three-quarters of the city's single white-collar workers were as a group younger than all single working women, single patients were older. A disproportionately large number of them were widowed and divorced, and a correspondingly small number were never married. Single women patients labored in candy and shoe factories, laundered, stitched, scrubbed, cooked, and waited tables in small establishments and private homes for sums—six, seven, eight dollars a week—whose meagerness drew reformers' outrage. By reason of their age, they were largely shut out of the new pink-collar office jobs for which employers were loath to hire any but the most attractive, youthful, and ethnically "American" women.

In short, single female patients were older than single female Bostonians in general, and this accounts for some of the discrepancy between the proportions of white-collar workers in the patient and Boston populations. The remaining difference between the two proportions is possibly larger than the corresponding difference for men. In the absence of firm evidence to the contrary, however, it is most prudent to assume that the material circumstances and social positions of single and married women patients bore the same relationship to Boston's population as male patients did to the city's population; in other words, working-class and poor women were slightly overrepresented among patients.

Marital Status

It has become popular wisdom that, with respect to mental health, marriage is good for men, bad for women. Analyzing nationwide admissions figures from 1919, a female statistician observed that the numbers appeared "to indicate that, from a mental-hygiene point of view, marriage is beneficial to men, but detrimental to women."[7] Admissions figures from the Psychopathic Hospital are equivocal on this score. Men and women entered the hospital in roughly equal numbers: the proportions of men and women hospitalized—49 percent men, 51 percent women— matched those of the city's population. But the relationship between marital status and hospitalization followed no simple pattern (table A.6). Married

TABLE A.6
Age and Marital Status of Boston and Hospital Populations (percent)

	Single		Married		Other		
	Boston[a]	Hospital	Boston[a]	Hospital	Boston[a]	Hospital	(N)[b]
Men							(334)
15–24	91	96	8	3	1	2	(67)
25–44	36	60	61	31*	3	10	(148)
45+	14	25	71	52*	14	23	(119)
Women							(355)
15–24	81	83	19	12	—	5	(99)
25–44	32	39	62	43*	6	19	(155)
45+	17	24	49	41	34	36	(101)

[a]1910 census year.
[b]Hospital sample.
*Significantly different from the proportion in the Boston population (p < .05).

women twenty-five through forty-four years old are underrepresented in the hospital population, as are married men over the age of twenty-four. Within the other age strata the distributions are similar; single men and women were not overrepresented among patients. Most surprising, women patients over the age of forty-four were drawn proportionately from the single, married, and divorced, separated, and widowed portions of the population; older women on their own were not overrepresented, common wisdom notwithstanding.

Patterns of Commitment

Police Patients

Because, due to the way census data were compiled, there is no way to recover the cross-tabulated ethnic-by-occupational breakdown of the Boston population from which patients were drawn, the question of whether patients' class or ethnic backgrounds were related to the likelihood of their being apprehended by the police on suspicion of insanity cannot be addressed directly. We can determine that the occupational distribution of police patients differed from that of the Boston population, and that the ethnic distribution differed as well. We do know that occupational distributions (and thus class identifications) differed across ethnic groups, with some clustered more heavily in the lower-level occupational groups. The question I would like to be able to answer but cannot is, controlling for the relationship between class and ethnicity, was either factor, or both, related to the likelihood of being picked up by the police on suspicion of insanity?

A somewhat differently framed issue—who, of all patients, was most likely to have been brought to the hospital by police rather than other means—can be addressed. This analysis will not answer whether it was the class or ethnicity of certain persons that accounted for their apprehension as police patients. Rather, it assumes that there existed a group of potential patients who would have been institutionalized in one of any number of ways, and asks, of all these potential patients, whom did police commit and whom did families, friends, and neighbors commit. This analysis cannot address whether, for example, the police were more likely to suspect working-class Italians than middle-class Irish of being insane. Instead, it considers only the patient population and asks whether the working-class Italians it encompassed were more likely than the middle-class Irish to have been committed by the police. Historians and sociologists have tended to conflate the two questions.[8] The way I put the question here compares the ethnic, occupational, and gender breakdown of police patients to the rest of the hospital population and asks how they differ, allowing us to use multivariate (specifically, log-linear) analysis to address a multivariate

TABLE A.7
Male Patients Brought by Police, Classified by Ethnicity and Occupation

	Occupation	Percent	(N)
African-American	white-collar	—	(0)
	blue-collar	53	(17)
Irish	white-collar	22	(27)
	blue-collar	46	(118)
Italian	white-collar	33	(3)
	blue-collar	64	(22)
Jewish	white-collar	6	(16)
	blue-collar	29	(28)
WASP	white-collar	21	(29)
	blue-collar	28	(25)
Other native-born	white-collar	40	(35)
	blue-collar	43	(81)
Other foreign-born	white-collar	30	(10)
	blue-collar	38	(102)

Odds ratio for police pathway:		
by occupation (controlling for ethnicity): blue-collar compared to white-collar[a]	1.77	
by ethnicity (controlling for occupation): each group compared to WASP		
African-American	—[b]	
Irish	1.77	
Italian	3.64	
Jewish	0.76	
Other native-born	1.98	
Other foreign-born	1.43	

Note: From the log-linear model: {PO} {PE} {OE} (where P = pathway [police/other], O = occupation [white-collar/blue-collar], E = ethnicity); $G^2 = 3.63$, df = 6, p = .73.

[a]The ratio of the odds that male blue-collar patients would have been police patients compared to the odds that male white-collar patients would have been police patients, controlling for ethnicity.

[b]No odds calculated, due to small cell size.

question; the advantages of doing so outweigh the conceptual difficulties involved.[9]

Patients' gender, class backgrounds, and ethnic identities were all related to the pathways they traveled to the institution. Not surprisingly, men were twice as likely as women to have been police patients. (The number of women police patients is small, and the data concerning them inconclusive and not presented here.)

A greater proportion of working-class than middle-class men ended up in the hospital as a result of being brought by the police (see table A.7). The proportions varied across ethnic and racial groups: police brought 46 percent of the working-class but only 22 percent of the middle-class Irish male patients to the hospital, for example, and 29 percent of the working-class but only 6 percent of the middle-class Jews. These are simply observed proportions; table A.7 gives the odds of being brought to the hospital by the police rather than by other means generated by the model that best describes the relationships inherent in the data. This model—{PO} {PE} {OE}, where P = pathway (police/other), O = occupation (white-collar/blue-collar), and E = ethnicity—indicates that, controlling for the relationship between occupation and ethnicity, both are linked to the pathway patients followed to the institution. Across all ethnic groups, working-class men were 1.77 times as likely to have been police patients as middle-class men. With the exception of working-class Italians, men of all sorts were less likely to have been police patients than to have been committed by other means. The table gives each ethnic group's odds of following a police pathway compared to that of WASPs, a low proportion of whom were police patients. An odds ratio of 1.00 would indicate that the group in question was as unlikely as WASPs to have been committed by the police; the ratios shown indicate that only Jews were less likely than WASPs to have been committed by the police, and that Italians, of all other groups, were most likely. Irish, other native-born, and other foreign-born patients were nearly twice as likely as WASPs to have been committed after falling into police hands. Still, such patients were more likely to have been committed by other means.

These findings suggest, but cannot definitely establish, that the police did in fact deal more harshly with persons who were poor or who appeared to be of foreign extraction, but this tells us more about the police than about psychiatric assessments of deviance. A social control argument based on the character of police patients could not be specific to psychiatry, but rather would consider these patients within the larger context of police work.

Pathways from the Institution

Contemporaries, social psychiatrists, sociologists, and historians have argued that gender, class, ethnicity, and marital status have some bearing on the likelihood of persons being committed for insanity. This proposition was examined above, and the conclusion was reached that Psychopathic Hospital patients followed a number of routes to the institution in proportions similar to their representation in Boston's population. None of the demographic characteristics I considered distinguished between persons who were committed and those who were not. Examination of police patients suggested that the pathways patients followed to the institution varied with their ethnicity, but the rather untenable assumption on which this finding was premised, that a group of potential patients existed who would have been committed in any one of several ways, limited the sorts of conclusions that could be drawn from this data.

Comparing patients who were committed and patients who were released at the end of their Psychopathic Hospital stays (two to three weeks long, on average) allows us to examine the multivariate problem of the relationships among demographic characteristics and patterns of commitment using multivariate techniques. This approach offers several other advantages. We can reduce the undesired distortions that patients' different mental statuses introduce into models of commitment by limiting analyses to patients with the same diagnosis. Because we look for differences within a group of already hospitalized patients, the problem of adjusting for the different pathways patients traveled to the hospital is circumvented. And, because equal amounts of data exist for both groups (we need not rely on census tabulations for a social portrait of those who were not committed), both groups can be compared on a wider range of characteristics.

At the end of the hospital stays, 43 percent of all patients were committed to asylums; 38 percent were discharged in care of themselves; and 10 percent were discharged to the officials—police, probation officers, state visitors, and judges—who had first brought them to the institution. An additional 3 percent died while in the hospital; 5 percent entered asylums voluntarily; and psychiatrists did not record the fates of 5 percent of those they discharged.

Commitment to one of the state's many asylums or state hospitals was a procedurally formal matter. Psychopathic Hospital psychiatrists, in order to commit, had to provide evidence to two physicians in the employ of the state that the patient in question was legally insane and thus committable. Analysis of patients who were committed and those who were discharged in care of themselves shows that a patient's mental status was the most important determinant of the likelihood of his or her commitment to a state institution (table A.8); gender and social class were unrelated to patterns of commitment.

Although dementia praecox patients were committed to asylums at a rate higher than that of any other group of patients (with the exception of patients deemed senile), 40 percent were released, and 28 percent of those psychiatrists judged unimproved were not committed. The proportions of such patients committed varied across ethnic groups (table A.9). Persons from all ethnic groups were more likely to have been committed than released (with the exception of Jews, who were more likely to have been returned to their families than committed). The table gives each group's odds of commitment compared to that of native-born Protestants; the ratios indicate that non-Irish Catholics were most likely to have been committed, followed by foreign-born Protestants and the Irish.

TABLE A.8
Patients Committed to Asylums, Classified by Diagnosis

	Percent	(N)[a]
Dementia praecox	65	(286)
Manic-depressive insanity	55	(116)
Alcoholic psychoses	31	(107)
Syphilitic psychoses	50	(87)
Other psychoses[b]	48	(182)
Feeblemindedness	17[c]	(92)
Psychopathic personality	6[c]	(52)
Psychoneurosis	5	(41)

[a] $N = 963$. Excludes patients diagnosed "sane" ($N = 47$) and "other" ($N = 82$). Patients returned to officials (10% of total) and patients who died in the hospital (3% of total) are not included in total N.

[b] Includes senile and epileptic patients.

[c] 42% returned to officials.

TABLE A.9
Final Disposition of "Unimproved" Dementia Praecox Patients, Classified by Ethnicity and Living Situation

	Lives	Percent Committed	(N)
Catholic (non-Irish)	alone	85	(26)
	with others	83	(35)
Irish	alone	72	(32)
	with others	77	(44)
Jewish	alone	71	(7)
	with others	25	(16)
Native-born Protestant	alone	50	(12)
	with others	62	(21)
Foreign-born Protestant	alone	89	(18)
	with others	71	(17)

Odds ratio for commitment:
ethnicity, each group compared to native-born Protestants[a]

Catholic (non-Irish)	3.56
Irish	2.18
Jewish	0.49
Foreign-born Protestant	2.70

Note: From the log-linear model: {CE} {L} (where C = final disposition [committed/not committed], E = ethnicity, L = lives [alone/with others]); $G^2 = 9.22$, df = 9, p = .41.

[a] The ratio of the odds that persons diagnosed "dementia praecox" from each ethnic group would be committed compared to the odds that native-born Protestants diagnosed "dementia praecox" would be committed. (I regrouped ethnicity in this table and in table A.10 to better capture the effect of religion without losing ethnicity or nativity entirely.)

TABLE A.10
Patients Removed against Psychiatrists' Advice, Classified
by Ethnicity and Living Situation

	Lives	Percent Removed	(N)
Catholic (non-Irish)	alone	7	(55)
	with others	21	(100)
Irish	alone	11	(62)
	with others	20	(115)
Jewish	alone	31	(13)
	with others	60	(35)
Native-born Protestant	alone	17	(58)
	with others	15	(73)
Foreign-born Protestant	alone	11	(37)
	with others	26	(47)

Odds ratio for removal against advice:	
lives alone compared to lives with others (controlling for ethnicity)[a]	0.50
ethnicity (controlling for living situation), each group compared to native-born Protestant	
Catholic (non-Irish)	1.00
Irish	1.04
Jewish	5.56
Foreign-born Protestant	1.23

Note: From the log-linear model: {CL}{CE} (where C = commitment [committed/removed against advice], L = lives [alone/with others], E = ethnicity); G^2 = 9.90, df = 8, p = .27.
[a]The ratio of the odds that patients living alone would have been removed against advice compared to the odds that patients living with others would have been removed (controlling for ethnicity).

Examination of patients removed against the advice of psychiatrists provides another way of looking at the issue of ethnic variations in patterns of commitment. Family members and friends could remove a patient from the institution against psychiatrists' advice upon signing a paper assuming responsibility for him or her. Ten percent of all patients were discharged from the hospital under this provision. If such patients are classified by ethnicity and social resources (measured by whether they lived alone or with others), it becomes clear that Jews were far more likely to remove patients against psychiatrists' advice than were members of any other ethnic group (table A.10). Relatives would not allow 60 percent of Jewish patients who lived with others to be committed, and they removed 30 percent of Jews who lived alone from the hospital, a proportion higher than that of any other ethnic group.

NOTE ON SOURCES

Boston Psychopathic Hospital case records form the most important source for this study. The records, which include psychiatrists' notes, typewritten transcripts of staff meetings, ward notes, letters written by and to patients and, in many instances, extensive social service notes, vary in bulk and usefulness; some are sketchy while others amount to over one hundred pages of dense documentation. Several typical social service records are reproduced in E. E. Southard and Mary C. Jarrett, *The Kingdom of Evils: Psychiatric Social Work Presented in One Hundred Case Histories Together with a Classification of Social Divisions of Evil* (New York, 1922), pp. 571–670; something of the character of psychiatric and social work practice can be gleaned from them and from the other cases, presented in narrative form, that make up this wonderfully rich book.

I subjected approximately eight hundred cases pulled from the first twelve thousand admissions to the hospital to intense scrutiny. In addition, for the purposes of quantitative analysis, I drew a random sample of cases admitted from 1912 to 1921 (see Appendix).

The psychoanalyst Louville Eugene Emerson left approximately one hundred case records, spanning the early years of his practice, from 1911 to about 1916, among his papers. A number of the men and women he treated were also patients at the Psychopathic Hospital; I made use of their records as well as of records of the other Bostonians he saw.

I consulted the following manuscript sources: at the Countway Library of Medicine, Boston, the E. E. Southard Papers, L. E. Emerson Papers, and A. Warren Stearns Papers; at the Schlesinger Library, Radcliffe College, the Maida Herman Solomon Papers, Jessie Donaldson Hodder Papers, and Molly Dewson Papers; at the Harvard Law School Library, the Roscoe Pound Papers; and the Harvard University Archives.

NOTES

Cases from the Boston Psychopathic Hospital are cited as "case," followed by the case number, the date of first admission (or sometimes the year in which the material cited was produced), and, in most instances, the part of the record from which the material was drawn. Hospital cases are under the control of the Superintendent of the Massachusetts Mental Health Center, Boston. Cases drawn from the practice of L. E. Emerson are cited as "LEE case," followed by the case number and the date treatment began. Emerson's cases are at the Countway Library of Medicine, Boston.

Patients' names and identifying characteristics have been changed; I have systematically altered Psychopathic Hospital case numbers (researchers with permission to use the records may obtain original numbers from me). I have retained the original spelling, capitalization, and punctuation in quotations from hospital staff meetings, correspondence, Emerson's notes, and published material.

INTRODUCTION

1. S. H. Kohs, "'We've Gone Psychiatric,'" *Survey* 64 (1930): 188–90.

2. Michel Foucault, *Discipline and Punish: The Birth of the Prison*, trans. Alan Sheridan (New York, 1979), p. 191.

3. I refer here to the large antipsychiatry and social control literatures. Antipsychiatry, associated with the writings of Thomas Szasz and R. D. Laing, enjoyed popular currency in the 1970s and 1980s. Among the best-known historical works on social control are David J. Rothman, *The Discovery of the Asylum: Social Order and Disorder in the New Republic* (Boston, 1971); Andrew Scull, *Museums of Madness: The Social Organization of Insanity in Nineteenth-Century England* (New York, 1979); and, on the period this book covers, Rothman, *Conscience and Convenience: The Asylum and Its Alternatives in Progressive America* (Boston, 1980).

4. Quotation from Nikolas Rose, "Engineering the Human Soul: Analyzing Psychological Expertise," *Science in Context* 5 (1992): 354. Tracing the discipline's roots to Freud (and, by extension, to the concept of neurosis, identified in the American context with George Beard) is standard in the literature. For a popular rendering of this genealogy, see William C. Menninger, *Psychiatry: Its Evolution and Present Status* (Ithaca, N.Y., 1948), pp. 50ff. Writers proposing this disciplinary lineage tend to conflate a focus on neurosis (one effected by neurologists, which took place outside asylum psychiatry, in which neurosis never played a significant role) with psychiatry's focus on the normal; I see them as separate projects. The public-health-oriented mental hygiene movement, which took formal organizational shape in 1909, promoted a notion of positive mental health. Herman Adler's succinct contemporaneous formulation—"the term psychopathic lays the emphasis upon the variation from normality, whereas the term mental hygiene empha-

sizes the maintenance of mental health"—captures the difference in orientation between it and the psychiatric project I chronicle. There were, to be sure, some overlaps in personnel and organization, but I have downplayed them. Barbara Sicherman, *The Quest for Mental Health in America, 1880–1917* (1967; reprint, New York, 1980), remains the classic work on mental hygiene. Many works focus on the therapeutic ethos; see, for example, Philip Rieff, *The Triumph of the Therapeutic: Uses of Faith after Freud* (New York, 1968); and Christopher Lasch, *Haven in a Heartless World: The Family Besieged* (New York, 1979).

5. I am indebted to Kurt Danziger, *Constructing the Subject: Historical Origins of Psychological Research* (Cambridge, 1990), pp. 13–14, 204, for the notion of reflections on practice.

6. Case 4339, 1915, staff meeting.

7. Foucault, *Discipline and Punish*, pp. 170–94, lucidly lays out the essentials of the disciplinary perspective. See also Foucault, *Power/Knowledge: Selected Interviews and Other Writings, 1972–1977*, ed. Colin Gordon, trans. Gordon et al. (New York, 1980). On normalized subjects, see p. 255.

8. Quotations from C. Macfie Campbell, "History of Insanity during the Past Century with Special Reference to the McLean Hospital," *Boston Medical and Surgical Journal* 185 (1921): 543; Thomas W. Salmon cited without reference in Albert Deutsch, *The Mentally Ill in America: A History of Their Care and Treatment from Colonial Times* (Garden City, N.Y., 1938), p. 272 (the quotation dates from the late twenties); and Menninger (citing a colleague, Galdston), *Psychiatry*, p. 17. I have used the masculine pronoun throughout in reference to psychiatrists (the presence of female psychiatrists notwithstanding), both to distinguish them from social workers and to highlight the gender ideology their practice encoded.

9. For instances of this, see, for example, Milton Greenblatt, Richard H. York, and Esther Lucile Brown, in collaboration with Robert W. Hyde, *From Custodial to Therapeutic Patient Care in Mental Hospitals: Explorations in Social Treatment* (New York, 1955), pp. 37–245, on the Boston Psychopathic Hospital; for self-criticism, see Karl Menninger with Martin Mayman and Paul Pruyser, *The Vital Balance: The Life Process in Mental Health and Illness* (New York, 1979), which opens with Menninger's (faulty) memories of Psychopathic Hospital diagnostic practices; and the interview with Harry C. Solomon, conducted by Evelyn Stone and J. Sanborn Bachoven, September 1980, in the Solomon Papers, Countway Library of Medicine, in which he subjects the Psychopathic Hospital's early practices to sharp scrutiny.

10. Campbell, "History of Insanity," p. 543. Thomas Osborne, "Medicine and Epistemology: Michel Foucault and the Liberality of Clinical Reason," *History of the Human Sciences* 5 (1992): 63–93, offers a persuasive reading of Foucault.

ONE: PSYCHIATRY BETWEEN OLD AND NEW

1. William A. White, "The Origin, Growth, and Significance of the Mental Hygiene Movement," in *Proceedings of the First International Congress on Mental Hygiene, Washington, D.C., 1930*, ed. Frankwood E. Williams, vol. 1 (New York, 1932), cited in Richard W. Fox, *So Far Disordered in Mind: Insanity in California, 1870–1930* (Berkeley and Los Angeles, 1978), p. 184.

2. The assessment of Boston is common; for one example, see John C. Burnham, "Boston Psychiatry in the 1920s—Looking Forward," in *Psychoanalysis, Psychotherapy, and the New England Medical Scene, 1894–1944*, ed. George E. Gifford, Jr. (New York, 1978), p. 196. Many contemporary and later observers placed the Boston Psychopathic Hospital at the center of the profession in this period; in Alfred Deutsch's classic account of psychiatry's history, the establishment of psychopathic hospitals was one of several signs of psychiatry's emergence from professional and social isolation (*Mentally Ill in America*, chap. 14). Gerald N. Grob, *The State and the Mentally Ill: A History of Worcester State Hospital in Massachusetts, 1830–1920* (Chapel Hill, N.C., 1966), p. 334, writes that under Elmer Ernest Southard, the first director of the Boston Psychopathic Hospital, "it became the leading mental hospital in the United States." Among similar institutions were the Henry Phipps Psychiatric Clinic, which opened in 1913 in connection with the Johns Hopkins Hospital under the direction of Adolf Meyer, and the State Psychopathic Hospital at the University of Michigan, the first American psychopathic ward attached to a general hospital, which opened in 1906 and assumed the above name in 1907.

3. Quotation from Eva Whiting White, "Social Welfare: Social Agencies in Boston, 1880–1930," in *Fifty Years of Boston: A Memorial Volume*, ed. Elisabeth M. Herlihy (Boston, 1932), p. 553.

4. Charles Dickens, *American Notes and Pictures from Italy* (London, 1926), p. 34; also cited by Martin Green, *The Problem of Boston: Some Readings in Cultural History* (New York, 1966), p. 47. L. Vernon Briggs et al., *History of the Psychopathic Hospital, Boston, Massachusetts* (1922; reprint, New York, 1973), pp. xi–xii, reproduced a long excerpt from *American Notes*, a favorable account of the State Hospital in South Boston.

5. George Silsbee Hale, "The Charities of Boston and Contributions to the Distressed of Other Parts," in *The Memorial History of Boston, Including Suffolk County, Massachusetts, 1630–1880*, ed. Justin Winsor, 4 vols. (Boston, 1880–1881), 4, pp. 672–74. Hale wrote that a catalogue of persons associated with charitable endeavors, such as had appeared in a recently published directory of charitable organizations, "shows, like Homer's catalogue of the Grecian ships gathered for another warfare, how heartily and readily the men and women of Boston have joined with each other in the great siege, which has been bequeathed from sire to son, of the fortresses of poverty, ignorance, and crime" (p. 659).

6. White, "Social Welfare," p. 528. The author compiled a list of Massachusetts "firsts," from "First State to have statutory probation for criminal offenders" (1880) to "First State Cancer Hospital" (1926) (p. 559).

7. Grob, *State and Mentally Ill*, p. xii, terms Worcester prototypical. On early trends in state care, see Grob, *Mental Institutions in America: Social Policy to 1875* (New York, 1973). Nathan Irvin Huggins, *Protestants against Poverty: Boston's Charities, 1870–1900* (Westport, Conn., 1971), argues that, with respect to charitable reform, "Boston's experience was national in that it served the national movement by its example, leadership, and experimentation" (p. 13).

8. The state's high rate, calculated on the basis of data from 1919, was a measure of "first admissions per 100,000 of population" (Edith M. Furbush, "Social Facts Relative to Patients with Mental Diseases," *Mental Hygiene* 5 [1921]: 589). Massa-

chusetts State Board of Insanity, *Annual Report* 1, 1900, pp. 9–12, lists the state's institutions, and presents data throughout pertaining to numbers of inmates.

9. On the social landscape of turn-of-the-century Boston, see Robert A. Woods, ed., *The City Wilderness: A Settlement Study* (Boston, 1898), a study of the South End, and Woods, ed., *Americans in Process: A Settlement Study* (Boston, 1902), on the North and West Ends; Winsor, *Memorial History*, vol. 4; Herlihy, *Fifty Years of Boston*; and more recent works, among them Arthur Mann, *Yankee Reformers in the Urban Age* (Cambridge, Mass., 1954), esp. chap. 1. Geoffrey Blodgett, "Yankee Leadership in a Divided City: Boston, 1860–1910," in *Boston, 1700–1980: The Evolution of Urban Politics*, ed. Ronald P. Formisano and Constance K. Burns (Westport, Conn., 1984), pp. 87–110, esp. pp. 88–89, provides an astute, nuanced account of the city's political fortunes. On the Brahmins, see Frederic Cople Jaher, "Nineteenth-Century Elites in Boston and New York," *Journal of Social History* 6 (Fall 1972): 32–77, and Jaher, *The Urban Establishment: Upper Strata in Boston, New York, Charleston, Chicago, and Los Angeles* (Urbana, Ill., 1982), esp. chap. 2. Frederick A. Bushee, "Ethnic Factors in the Population of Boston," *Publications of the American Economic Association*, 3d ser., 4 (1903): 299–477, is one example among many alarmist accounts of the baleful effects of immigration. On the racial physiognomy of city dwellers, see Willard De Lue, "The Contribution of the Newer Races," in Herlihy, *Fifty Years of Boston*, p. 73; the "three out of four faces" found its way into Lucius Beebe, *Boston and the Boston Legend* (New York, 1935), p. 243.

10. Henry Cabot Lodge, *Boston* (New York, 1902); and M. A. DeWolfe Howe, *Boston: The Place and the People* (New York, 1903). The former is patently nativist (see pp. 198 ff.), while the tone of the latter is reserved and cautiously inconclusive.

11. For the first, see Walter Blackburn Harte, "The Back Bay: Boston's Throne of Wealth," *Arena* 10 (June 1894): 1–22; and Benjamin O. Flower, *Civilization's Inferno; or, Studies in the Social Cellar* (Boston, 1893) (both cited in Mann, *Yankee Reformers*, pp. 9–10). For the second, see, among others, Harold K. Estabrook, *Some Slums of Boston* (Boston, 1898); Woods, *City Wilderness* and *Americans in Process*; and Albert Benedict Wolfe, *The Lodging House Problem in Boston* (Boston, 1906).

12. On the city, see Barbara Miller Solomon, *Ancestors and Immigrants: A Changing New England Tradition* (Chicago, 1972), and Green, *Problem of Boston*. The theme of inevitable, divisive, and leveling modernity runs through many contemporary works. The first pages of DeWolfe Howe's *Boston* calmly assess the issue.

13. Woods, *City Wilderness*, p. 9.

14. On street noises and lights, see Arthur A. Shurcliff, "Everyday Life in Boston: Its Changing Aspects," in Herlihy, *Fifty Years of Boston*, pp. 690–91. According to Boston, *Municipal Register for 1912*, City Document no. 41 (Boston, 1912), gas streetlights still outnumbered electric lamps 11,800 to 6,100 (p. 88). And, according to Boston Statistics Department, *Boston Year Book, 1923–1924* (Boston, 1924), in 1924, "horse-drawn vehicles [were] still prevalent in the down-town section" (p. 198). On streetcars, see Sam B. Warner, Jr., *Streetcar Suburbs: The Process of Growth in Boston, 1870–1900* (Cambridge, Mass., 1962). The author of the chapter on industry and manufactures in the Herlihy volume writes that there

were 2,000 telephones in Boston in 1880; 70,467 in 1905; and 445,594 in 1930 (figures are for the metropolitan Boston area; figures for the city alone are not available) (Thomas F. Anderson, "Boston—The Industrial Heart of New England," p. 174). The first electric streetcars appeared in 1889; automobiles around 1895; electric lights around 1880; and telephones after 1876.

15. Shurcliff, "Everyday Life," pp. 699–700.

16. Ibid., p. 699; see also the various reports on noise in Women's Municipal League of Boston, *Bulletin 5*, March–April 1914, pp. 51–53, and *Bulletin 6*, May 1915, pp. 51–52, among others. The Committee on Abatement of Noise closely monitored and complained of noises of all sorts—automobile horns, horses trotting at high speeds over cobblestones, streetcars screeching as they rounded corners, and, especially, milk bottles jangling as the milkmen made their early morning rounds in wealthy neighborhoods (most of the complaints concerned Beacon Hill and the Back Bay).

17. The city assessor counted some thirty cows in the area in 1911 (Boston, *Municipal Register for 1912*, p. 249).

18. Anderson, "Boston," p. 175.

19. Mary Antin, *The Promised Land* (Boston, 1912), p. 279; see also Woods, *Americans in Process*, pp. 97–98.

20. See, for example, the report submitted by the Department of Streets and Alleys, Women's Municipal League, concerning refuse collection in the Back Bay: Women's Muncipal League of Boston, *Bulletin* 4, January 1913, p. 22.

21. Shurcliff, "Everyday Life," p. 700, and the many complaints to be found in the *Bulletin* of the Women's Municipal League of Boston.

22. Women's Municipal League of Boston, *Bulletin 5*, December 1913, p. 27.

23. Jaher, *Urban Establishment*, pp. 25–26.

24. Edward Stanwood, "Topography and Landmarks of the Last Hundred Years," in Winsor, *Memorial History*, 4, pp. 33–38.

25. The first building of the Museum of Fine Arts, incorporated in 1870, was erected in Copley Square in 1876; it was moved to Huntington Avenue in 1909. The Boston Public Library, founded in 1848, moved to Copley Square in 1895. On Brahmin stewardship, see E. Digby Baltzell, *Puritan Boston and Quaker Philadelphia: Two Protestant Ethics and the Spirit of Class Authority and Leadership* (New York, 1979).

26. Quotation from a physician, secretary of the State Board of Health, writing in 1881; Samuel A. Green, "Medicine in Boston," in Winsor, *Memorial History*, 4, p. 550. On ward-by-ward death rates, see John S. Billings, *Vital Statistics of Boston and Philadelphia, Covering a Period of Six Years Ending May 31, 1890*, U.S. Department of the Interior, Census Office (Washington, D.C., 1895).

27. Wolfe, *Lodging House Problem*, pp. 13, 14. On the character of the South End and the movement of the city's elite from the area to the Back Bay, see also Stanwood, "Topography and Landmarks," pp. 63–64; Woods, *City Wilderness*, pp. 29–32; Warner, *Streetcar Suburbs*, esp. pp. 57, 134–35; and Matthew Edel, Elliott D. Sclar, and Daniel Luria, *Shaky Palaces: Homeownership and Social Mobility in Boston's Suburbanization* (New York, 1984), pp. 82–84.

28. Wolfe, *Lodging House Problem*, pp. 20–24.

29. Antin, *Promised Land*, p. 272.

30. Ibid., chaps. 14, 16; quotation from p. 266. On clothing, see Woods, *City Wilderness*, p. 107. The author applauded the taste of the young, noting that there was "comparatively little vulgar finery to be seen on the thoroughfares."

31. Antin, *Promised Land*, p. 295.

32. See Woods, *Americans in Process*, chap. 1, for an expression of the area's foreignness.

33. Stanwood, "Topography and Landmarks," p. 53.

34. Ibid. Chapters 2 and 3 of Woods, *Americans in Process*, are titled "Before the Invasion" and "The Invading Host" (the latter by Frederick A. Bushee).

35. Billings, *Vital Statistics*, pp. 67–68.

36. Woods, *Americans in Process*, chap. 5; quotation from p. 127. Around 1900, 128 liquor licenses were held in the area (pp. 200–201).

37. On African-Americans in Boston, see Elizabeth Hafkin Pleck, *Black Migration and Poverty: Boston 1865–1900* (New York, 1979); on pushcarts, Woods, *Americans in Process*, p. 108; on hawkers, Philip Davis, *And Crown Thy Good* (New York, 1952), excerpted in *The Many Voices of Boston: A Historical Anthology, 1630–1975*, ed. Howard Mumford Jones and Bessie Zaban Jones (Boston, 1975), p. 336; on street scenes and gaming, Woods, *Americans in Process*, pp. 225, 202–6; on girls and the background of brothels, Isaac Goldberg, "A Boston Boyhood," *American Mercury* 17 (July 1929): 354–61, excerpted in Jones and Jones, *Many Voices of Boston*, pp. 345–55; on safety, Woods, *Americans in Process*, pp. 222–23. As of 1911, the concentration of shops in the North End (ward 6) was second only to that of the central business district (ward 7): 1,100 to 1,300. No other district had more than 225 stores (Boston, *Municipal Register for 1912*, p. 249). (Note that Boston's ward boundaries were frequently redrawn.)

38. See Woods, *Americans in Process*, chap. 8, "Life's Amenities," which is a paean to the glories of immigrant family life, and Women's Municipal League of Boston, *Bulletin* 10, February 1919, for another account of the Brahmin ladies' enthusiasm for the "delightful old traditions and customs" of immigrants (p. 18). Reference to cake, Woods, *Americans in Process*, p. 246; quotation from p. 356.

39. The Census of 1900 showed that another quarter of the keepers of lodging houses were single. Native-born landladies predominated (34 percent); landladies of Irish extraction constituted another 28 percent; and 55 black women ran houses catering to blacks (Wolfe, *Lodging House Problem*, pp. 52–54). See also Woods, *Americans in Process*, pp. 36–39, on the late-nineteenth-century appearance of lodging houses in the West End, run by widows and spinsters "thankful for this new means of bread-winning at a time when needlework and teaching were the only occupations for American women." The lodging-house population in 1900 amounted to approximately forty thousand, 10 percent of the city's population.

40. Wolfe, *Lodging House Problem*, chaps. 6–12. The author estimated that the lodging-house population was evenly divided between men and women, although the way in which the census figures were tabulated makes this impossible to verify (p. 82).

41. The sociologist Wolfe termed the lodgers a *population nomade* (ibid., p. 82). The author of the introduction to Woods, *City Wilderness*, saw a "weird fascination" in the area's "garish picturesqueness . . . set against a mixed background of poverty and moral tragedy" (p. 3).

42. Woods, *City Wilderness*, p. 169. For maps showing the South End's places of commercial amusement, see pp. 176ff., and Wolfe, *Lodging House Problem*, pp. 28ff.

43. Wolfe, *Lodging House Problem*, p. 137; Woods, *City Wilderness*, pp. 148–49; quotation from p. 153.

44. Wolfe, *Lodging House Problem*, pp. 136–65 (quotations from pp. 154, 138). Woods, *City Wilderness*, p. 199, noted the tenement dweller's familial contentment.

45. Joanne J. Meyerowitz, *Women Adrift: Independent Wage Earners in Chicago, 1880–1930* (Chicago, 1988), skillfully chronicles the fortunes of the single wage-earning woman in reform, popular, and academic discourse. Quotations from Robert A. Woods and Albert J. Kennedy, *Young Working Girls: A Summary of Evidence from Two Thousand Social Workers* (Boston, 1913), pp. 6, 1. Commenting on the dangers men encountered in the lodging houses, Wolfe writes of the "woman of immoral type [who] happens to take a room next to the young country lad on the third floor rear" (*Lodging House Problem*, p. 112).

46. Ednah D. Cheney, "The Women of Boston," in Winsor, *Memorial History*, 4, 331–56. Quotations from pp. 331–32, 350.

47. Frances G. Curtis, "Woman's Widening Sphere," in Herlihy, *Fifty Years of Boston*, pp. 626–35. Quotations from pp. 626, 634–35.

48. Quotation from Jacques Donzelot, *The Policing of Families*, trans. Robert Hurley (New York, 1979), p. 8.

49. See E. E. Southard and Mary C. Jarrett, *The Kingdom of Evils: Psychiatric Social Work Presented in One Hundred Case Histories Together with a Classification of Social Divisions of Evil* (New York, 1922), p. 395.

50. In suggesting that psychiatrists' everyday program has been hidden from historical view, I am not saying that it was in any sense premised on covert intentions, but rather that it took shape in practice in ways that psychiatrists could not predict. Psychiatrists pursued this agenda while at the same time outlining their formal institutional and political program, a program that has drawn historians' exclusive, and largely censorious, attention. Chroniclers of the profession's history have focused too narrowly on psychiatrists' stated aims and on their conception of the discipline's progress, overlooking what was articulated piecemeal and imparting a specious tidiness to developments that were contested and not at all obvious.

51. Southard and Jarrett, *Kingdom of Evils*, pp. 373–75.

52. E. E. Southard, "Contributions from the Psychopathic Hospital, Boston, Massachusetts: Introductory Note," in Boston Psychopathic Hospital, *Collected Contributions*, no. 1 (Boston, 1913), pp. 1–26. Quotations from throughout the article.

53. Ibid. Quotations from throughout article. Emphasis in original.

54. Something of the ferocity with which psychiatrists took up the cause of progress can be gleaned from Southard and Jarrett, *Kingdom of Evils*, p. 248: "No matter what the cake of custom fixates in the minds of uncivilized communities, the Psychopathic Hospital movement must and will irresistibly go forward, and perchance engulf those very superconservatives that everywhere block progress." Much discussion of the psychopathic hospital ideal appears in the contemporary literature; see, for example, Albert M. Barrett, "Hospitals for the Acute and

Recoverable Insane," in National Conference of Charities and Correction, *Proceedings* 34, 1907, p. 398, where the author (the director of the State Psychopathic Hospital at the University of Michigan) asserts that psychiatry is in "a sort of renaissance period"; Albert Warren Ferris, "Psychopathic Wards in General Hospitals," in National Conference of Charities and Correction, *Proceedings* 37, 1910, pp. 264–75; and E. E. Southard, "The Psychopathic Hospital Idea," *Journal of the American Medical Association* 61 (1913): 1972, referring to psychiatrists "preaching the gospel of psychopathic hospitals." Quotation in text from a Dr. Thomson, comment following an address by A. R. Turnbull, "Female Nursing of Male Patients in Asylums," *Journal of Mental Science* 49 (1903): 639.

55. Gerald N. Grob, *The Inner World of American Psychiatry, 1890–1940: Selected Correspondence* (New Brunswick, N.J., 1985), p. 11. Grob notes that by 1956, only 17 percent of the American Psychiatric Association's ten thousand members were practicing in state hospitals or Veterans Administration hospitals.

56. Adolf Meyer, "Thirty-Five Years of Psychiatry in the United States and Our Present Outlook" (1928–1929), in *The Collected Papers of Adolf Meyer*, ed. Eunice E. Winters, 4 vols. (Baltimore, 1950–1952), 2, p. 10. Meyer was, in the estimation of Karl A. Menninger, "Southard's greatest academic foe" (Menninger to Frederick P. Gay, 23 February 1937, Southard Papers, Countway Library of Medicine).

57. Michael Donnelly, *Managing the Mind: A Study of Medical Psychology in Early Nineteenth-Century Britain* (London, 1983), p. xii. On the social, see also Denise Riley, *"Am I That Name?": Feminism and the Category of "Women" in History* (Minneapolis, 1988), chap. 3; Donzelot, *Policing of Families*.

58. Herman M. Adler, "The Broader Psychiatry and the War," *Mental Hygiene* 1 (1917): 365.

59. See, for example, Barbara Sicherman, "Isador H. Coriat: The Making of an American Psychoanalyst," in Gifford, *Psychoanalysis*, pp. 163–80.

60. E. E. Southard, "Neuropathology and the Emotions," MS, Southard Papers.

61. Sigmund Freud, "Analysis Terminable and Interminable," in *The Standard Edition of the Complete Psychological Works of Sigmund Freud*, 24 vols., ed. and trans. by James Strachey (London, 1953–1974), 23, p. 235, cited in Melvin Sabshin, "Psychiatric Perspectives on Normality," *Archives of General Psychiatry* 17 (1967): 260.

62. Juliet Mitchell, "Introduction—I," in *Feminine Sexuality: Jacques Lacan and the École Freudienne*, ed. Juliet Mitchell and Jacqueline Rose, trans. Jacqueline Rose (New York, 1985), p. 11.

63. A fuller consideration of Freud and psychoanalysis is beyond the scope of this book. On Freud in the American context, see John Chynoweth Burnham, *Psychoanalysis and American Medicine, 1894–1918: Medicine, Science, and Culture* (New York, 1967); and Nathan G. Hale, Jr., *Freud and the Americans: The Beginnings of Psychoanalysis in the United States, 1876–1917* (New York, 1971). For one expression of the degree to which psychiatrists would come to see dynamic psychiatry and psychoanalysis as one and the same, see Menninger, *Psychiatry*, pp. 50ff.

64. See, for example, Menninger, *Psychiatry*: psychoanalytic psychiatry's "fund of knowledge dates from the truly great discoveries of Freud, which began in 1890" (p. 50). See also J. K. Hall, ed., *One Hundred Years of American Psychiatry* (New

York, 1944), the profession's centennial history, in which individual authors trace a variety of disciplinary trajectories.

65. Quotations from Herman M. Adler, "Unemployment and Personality—A Study of Psychopathic Cases," *Mental Hygiene* 1 (1917): 17, and Adler, "Broader Psychiatry," p. 365.

TWO: PROFESSING GENDER

1. Abraham Flexner, "Is Social Work a Profession?" *School and Society* 1 (1915): 904, an address delivered at the National Conference of Charities and Correction in 1915, also published in the organization's *Proceedings* of 1915. Flexner, educated at Johns Hopkins, is best known for the Flexner Report (1910), which documented the execrable state of the nation's medical schools and argued for higher, "professional" standards.

2. John Ayto, *The Longman Register of New Words* (London, 1989), 2, p. 241, defines "masculinism" as "advocacy of a dominant role for men in society, and of qualities traditionally thought of as characteristically male." I use the terms *masculinism* and *masculinist* to refer to the complex of gender-specific interests that men historically have pursued. Marilyn Lake, "The Politics of Respectability: Identifying the Masculinist Context," *Historical Studies* 22 (April 1986): 116–31, uses the terms similarly.

3. Barbara Melosh, *"The Physician's Hand": Work Culture and Conflict in American Nursing* (Philadelphia, 1982), p. 17, makes a similar point; I have been guided by her incisive analysis of gender and professional ideologies throughout this chapter. I also found especially useful Joan Wallach Scott's essay, "American Women Historians, 1884–1984," in her *Gender and the Politics of History* (New York, 1988), pp. 178–98, which charts the workings of gender in the historical profession. The literature on the professions is voluminous. Andrew Abbott, *The System of Professions: An Essay on the Division of Expert Labor* (Chicago, 1988), surveys the literature and contains an up-to-date bibliography.

4. Robert H. Wiebe, *The Search for Order, 1877–1929* (New York, 1967), p. 112. Wiebe's concise, deceptively breezy, and finely nuanced rendering of the turn-of-the-century professional ethic conveys better than any other work its satisfactions and contradictions.

5. Nelson W. Aldrich, Jr., *Old Money: The Mythology of America's Upper Class* (New York, 1988), p. 41.

6. Wiebe, *Search for Order*, p. 131, makes this point, arguing that "transmutation" rather than "emancipation" best characterizes the fate of old values and feelings—concerning, for example, ethnicity and wealth—in the hands of the new middle class.

7. Chapter 3 of this work examines a third dimension, looking at psychiatry's knowledge or "science."

8. Throughout this work I use the term "science" much as those about whom I write did, intending to imply nothing of whether such science was true or false, sound or unsound, from our own, purportedly more enlightened, perspective. Science could not, however, refer to just anything; it referred to a network of meanings and practices distinguishable from the general culture.

I have relied heavily here on Paul Starr's skillful account of medicine's fortunes in this period: *The Social Transformation of American Medicine* (New York, 1982), chap. 3. For an account of public enthusiasm for science, see John D. Buenker, John C. Burnham, and Robert M. Crunden, *Progressivism* (Cambridge, Mass., 1977), pp. 19–20.

Historians have seen the Flexner Report as critical—if not causally then symbolically—to medicine's emergence in its current form. The report argued that doctors should be trained as scientists, that medical schools should support laboratories and value research, that most schools should be closed, and that training at the remaining top-rank institutions should be oriented equally to the laboratory and the hospital. Medicine was already headed in the direction Flexner proposed: proprietary schools were closing for lack of funds, and elite institutions were following the lead of the Johns Hopkins Medical School, established (in 1893) as a scientific institution that would also teach students in the clinical setting of the hospital. But Flexner's recommendations, adopted by the American Medical Association, accelerated the demise of the institutions. In the period from 1890 to 1920, the profession became more homogeneous as the numbers of black men and black and white women entering it were limited by quotas and exclusionary practices. On women in medicine, see Regina Markell Morantz-Sanchez, *Sympathy and Science: Women Physicians in American Medicine* (New York, 1985).

9. Tracing the complicated relations between psychiatry and neurology is beyond the scope of this book. See Bonnie Ellen Blustein, "'A Hollow Square of Psychological Science': American Neurologists and Psychiatrists in Conflict," in *Madhouses, Mad-Doctors, and Madmen: The Social History of Psychiatry in the Victorian Era,* ed. Andrew Scull (Philadelphia, 1981), pp. 241–70, and, on the specialty of neurology, her excellent *Preserve Your Love for Science: Life of William A. Hammond, American Neurologist* (Cambridge, 1991). Gerald N. Grob, *Mental Illness and American Society: 1875–1940* (Princeton, 1983), pp. 50–55, highlights some of the differences between the two groups. To simplify: the practice of neurologists was office-based, urban, and Eastern; their clientele affluent; their purview the "nervous" diseases. The practice of the alienists was institutionally based, their patients on the whole poorer, their purview broader. Until World War I, when psychiatrists and neurologists made common cause under the rubric "neuropsychiatry," many psychiatrists were careful to distinguish themselves from neurologists. Concerning the latter, for example, Southard, at a state-sponsored conference, offered a characteristically sharp taunt—"some of the professional neurologists, of whom it may truly be said that their little knowledge is a dangerous thing" (Massachusetts State Board of Insanity, *Annual Report* 12, 1911, p. 269). Others allied with psychiatry attacked the neurologists' diagnoses as insufficiently scientific. Stanley Cobb, "Applications of Psychiatry to Industrial Hygiene," *Journal of Industrial Hygiene* 1 (1919): 344, complained that hospital wards were "full of patients to whom the doctors apply long meaningless labels—'neurasthenia,' 'psychasthenia,' 'psychoneurosis.'" Mary C. Jarrett wrote that "the old idea of 'nervousness' . . . has become meaningless" ("Nervous Women in Industry," *Industrial Psychology* 1 [1926]: 271). Psychopathic Hospital psychiatrists rarely used the diagnosis; Barbara Sicherman explores its early deployment in "The Uses of a Diagnosis: Doctors, Patients, and Neurasthenia," *Journal of the History of Medi-*

cine 32 (1977): 33–54. Abbott, *System of Professions*, chap. 10, skillfully examines what he calls neurology's "ramshackle system of knowledge."

10. S. Weir Mitchell, "Address before the Fiftieth Annual Meeting of the American Medico-Psychological Association, Held in Philadelphia, May 16th, 1894," *Journal of Nervous and Mental Disease* 21 (1894): 413–37. Grob, *Mental Illness*, chaps. 2 and 3, ably characterizes nineteenth-century psychiatry's relationship to medicine.

11. E. E. Southard, "Cross-Sections of Mental Hygiene, 1844, 1869, 1894," *American Journal of Insanity* 76 (1919–1920): 110–11; excerpted as "The Individual as Social Unit," *Mental Hygiene* 4 (1920): 760.

12. Herman Adler's father emigrated from Germany in 1857, returned there to earn a medical degree, and became a professor of clinical pathology at the New York Polyclinic Medical School (*National Cyclopaedia of American Biography*, s.v. "Adler, Isaac"). Adler (d. 1935) was Southard's age, born in 1876; so was Robert M. Yerkes (d. 1956). Harry Solomon's father, also a German immigrant, had mined coal and sold spectacles before going into medicine (interview with Solomon, September 1980). Information on Lawson Lowrey from *Who Was Who In America*, s.v. "Lowrey, Lawson Gentry" (1890–1959).

13. Lawson Lowrey hailed from Centralia, Missouri, and Arthur Noyes from Enfield, New Hampshire.

14. Biographical information from *National Cyclopaedia of American Biography*, s.v. "Adler, Herman Morris"; *Who Was Who in America*, s.v. "Lowrey, Lawson Gentry," "Noyes, Arthur Perry" (1880–1963), and "Stearns, Albert Warren" (1885–1959); and the Harvard University Archives. A number of Psychopathic Hospital psychiatrists were graduated from Harvard College: Adler (A.B. 1897), George E. Eversole (1907), Thomas H. Haines (1898), Clifton G. Rounsefell (1907), and Southard (1897), as were the Psychopathic Hospital psychologists L. Eugene Emerson (1907) and Robert M. Yerkes (1898).

15. Frederick P. Gay, *The Open Mind: Elmer Ernest Southard, 1876–1920* ([New York], 1938), pp. 13, 79, 93. A boyhood friend of Southard's, Gay was a professor of bacteriology at Columbia University College of Physicians and Surgeons.

16. Quotations from E. E. Southard, "All through my youth," handwritten autobiographical fragment, dated "Spring of 1914," Southard Papers (hereafter, Autobiographical Fragment). The Southard family lived at 268 Gold Street, then at 66 G Street: Gay, *Open Mind*, pp. 6–7. For photographs of South Boston's housing, see Warner, *Streetcar Suburbs*, figs. 4 and 5. Substantial single-family homes lined the main streets, wooden row houses the back alleys. Fig. 5 depicts Silver Street, two blocks from Southard's first home.

17. Gay, *Open Mind*, p. 30.

18. Jaher, *Urban Establishment*, p. 104, terms Eliot a "progressive Brahmin." On Eliot, see also Bruce Kuklick, *The Rise of American Philosophy: Cambridge, Massachusetts, 1860–1930* (New Haven, 1977), pp. 129–33.

19. Quotation from Porter Sargent to Gay, 13 November 1937, Southard Papers.

20. Quotation from Gay, *Open Mind*, p. 65. In Saul Benison, A. Clifford Barger, and Elin L. Wolfe, *Walter B. Cannon: The Life and Times of a Young Scientist*

(Cambridge, Mass., 1987), pp. 147–48, Southard is pictured among Cannon's Cambridge friends, not his Boston (that is, medical) friends.

21. On Southard's club membership, Ralph Barton Perry to Gay, 16 February 1935; on the St. Botolph Club, see Jaher, *Urban Establishment*, pp. 109–10. Kuklick mentions the Wicht Club, a "small social group" that he suggests met its members' needs for masculine companionship and stimulation (*American Philosophy*, p. 421). Gay wrote that "rehearsal of the names of the ten or eleven 'Wichts' who composed this informal assemblage, suffices to indicate how men of genius or near genius, tend to foregather even in the early stages of their careers," and lists the Harvard psychologists Edwin B. Holt and Robert Yerkes, the philosopher Ralph Barton Perry, and the physiologist Walter B. Cannon among its members (*Open Mind*, p. 75; quotations in text from p. 76).

22. Aldrich, *Old Money*, chap. 2, brilliantly analyzes the Old Money obsession with genealogy. He reports that in the late nineteenth century, Tiffany set up a genealogical service for its customers (p. 58).

23. Southard, Autobiographical Fragment; Southard to Richard C. Cabot, "Dr. Southard's Plans," 28 August 1919, Southard Papers.

24. Flexner, "Social Work," pp. 904ff.

25. Aldrich, *Old Money*, chap. 3, examines Old Money's sensibility concerning money.

26. Following an informally arranged internship under Southard at the Psychopathic Hospital, Solomon joined the hospital staff, remaining there his entire professional life (interview with Solomon, September 1980). His life was highlighted in Robert C. Cowen, "Commissioner of Calm: Dr. Harry Solomon," *Saturday Review* (4 June 1960): 46–47.

On Brahmin domination in Boston medicine, see Jaher, *Urban Establishment*, pp. 30–31, 100. Jaher writes that Brahmin preeminence, declining in other areas by the turn of the century, "was best preserved in medicine," attested to in part by "charges of nepotistic staff appointments . . . made in the 1920s." Green, *Problem of Boston*, p. 49, notes that "five families, the Warrens, the Jacksons, the Bigelows, the Shattucks, and the Cabots, had supplied the majority of the physicians and surgeons" at the Massachusetts General Hospital, a Harvard-affiliated hospital, since its founding in 1821, a record unmatched by any other major hospital. Solomon considered certain positions at the medical school "hereditary," a charge supported by the historical record. Charles W. Eliot oversaw the medical school's reorganization. For him, Bruce Kuklick observed, "a man's education, personal qualities, and scholarly work . . . were secondary. What counted was that a man and his family were known" (*American Philosophy*, p. 414).

27. On Abraham Myerson (1881–1948), see his daughter-in-law Mildred Ann Myerson's "Biographical Note" in Myerson's *Speaking of Man* (New York, 1950); his son Paul's tribute, "Abraham Myerson," in Gifford, *Psychoanalysis*, pp. 242–50; and *Dictionary of American Biography*, supp. 4, s.v. "Myerson, Abraham." Quotation from P. Myerson, "Abraham Myerson," p. 243.

28. Among Abraham Myerson's writings on the private sphere are *The Nervous Housewife* (1920; reprint, New York, 1972); "The Nervous Husband," *Ladies' Home Journal* 38 (September 1921); and "Hysteria as a Weapon in Marital Conflicts," *Journal of Abnormal Psychology* 10 (1915–1916): 1–10.

29. Abraham Myerson and Rosalie D. Boyle, "The Incidence of Manic-Depressive Psychosis in Certain Socially Important Families," *American Journal of Psychiatry* 98 (1941–1942): 11–21. In *The Foundations of Personality* (Boston, 1927), p. 32, Myerson argued that much of character was better attributed to environment than to heredity; how else could the rise of the Jewish prizefighter, "a divergence from tradition that mocks at theories of inborn racial characteristics," be explained? With Maurice B. Hexter, executive director of the Federated Jewish Charities of Boston, he attacked the methods and conclusions of Carl Brigham: "13.77 versus 12.05; A Study in Probable Error: A Critical Discussion of Brigham's 'American Intelligence,' " *Mental Hygiene* 8 (1924): 69–82. In 1922, he attacked Henry Ford's anti-Semitic ravings in his short book, *The Terrible Jews, By One of Them* (Boston, 1922).

30. Yerkes, in *A History of Psychology in Autobiography*, ed. Carl Murchison (Worcester, Mass., 1932), 2, pp. 381–84, 407. Hamilton Cravens makes the point about the scientist's journey from religion to science: *Dictionary of American Biography*, supp. 6, s.v. "Yerkes, Robert Mearns." On Yerkes and psychology at Harvard, see Kuklick, *American Philosophy*, esp. pp. 418–20. See also Ernest R. Hilgard, "Robert Mearns Yerkes," in National Academy of Sciences, *Biographical Memoirs* (New York, 1965), 38, pp. 385–425; Donna Haraway, *Primate Visions: Gender, Race, and Nature in the World of Modern Science* (New York, 1989), pp. 59–83; and James Reed, "Robert M. Yerkes and the Mental Testing Movement," in *Psychological Testing and American Society, 1890–1930*, ed. Michael M. Sokal (New Brunswick, N.J., 1987), pp. 75–94.

31. In a similar vein, Thomas W. Salmon, "Some New Fields in Neurology and Psychiatry," *Journal of Nervous and Mental Disease* 46 (1917): 99, issued a call for "frontiersmen"—"men with sound scientific training, energy, tact and vision"—to extend psychiatry's frontiers. The cultural association of psychiatric knowledge and practice with femininity has continued; consider, for example, that one characteristic that the *New York Times* (8 June 1992) listed, half in jest, as a criterion by which to assess the claims of the presidential candidates to a Texan lineage (which the article conflated with manliness) was their stance toward psychiatry. George Bush, the article reported, "does not like to 'get on the couch,' " a mark of his manliness.

Quotations from Southard, "Contributions," p. 12; E. E. Southard, "The Modern Specialist in Unrest: A Place for the Psychiatrist in Industry," *Mental Hygiene* 4 (1920): 562; and Douglas A. Thom, "The Out-Patient Department," in Briggs et al., *Psychopathic Hospital*, p. 162.

32. Solomon was married to Maida Herman (Solomon), a Smith College graduate with whom he worked in close collaboration and with whom he wrote many articles and several books, among them *Syphilis of the Innocent: A Study of the Social Effects of Syphilis on the Family and the Community* (Washington, D.C., 1922). On nights working at the hospital, see oral memoir of Maida H. Solomon in the Maida Herman Solomon Papers, Schlesinger Library, Radcliffe College.

Southard was married in 1906 to Mabel Fletcher Austin, daughter of Horace Austin, governor of Minnesota; she was a graduate of the Johns Hopkins Medical School (*National Cyclopaedia of American Biograpy*, s.v. "Southard, Elmer Ernest"). The couple had three children, and she was, at the time of her marriage, an associate professor of hygiene at Wellesley College. "Mabel is her own cook, maid, and bath steward," Southard wrote to his friend and future biographer; "as for her being a wife, I have little or no time to be a husband" (Southard to Gay, 11 August 1917, Southard Papers). Many of Southard's medical friends would later comment that the marriage was not entirely successful, and that Southard spent little time at home.

Yerkes was married to Ada Watterson (Yerkes), with whom he wrote *The Great Apes: A Study of Anthropoid Life* (New Haven, 1929); he wrote that the union "perfectly blended our lives and incalculably increased our professional and social usefulness," and added that his professional autobiography from the time of his marriage "is no longer mine alone." Yet Yerkes mentions her only once in his twenty-five-page autobiography (Yerkes in Murchison, *Psychology in Autobiography*, p. 391). (Margaret W. Rossiter, *Women Scientists in America: Struggles and Strategies to 1940* [Baltimore, 1982], comments on this tendency, pp. 208–9.)

In the course of a six-month residency at the Psychopathic Hospital (in 1918), Karl A. Menninger, by his own account, "spent every available moment with" Southard, whom he regarded as his mentor. Like Southard, Menninger was unhappily married (to a woman discontented with her domestic lot); the two often dined at restaurants and clubs, afterwards playing chess or walking Boston's streets, and they traveled together to professional meetings. It pleased Menninger that Southard was "more intimate" with him than with the other young residents (Lawrence J. Friedman, *Menninger: The Family and the Clinic* [New York, 1990], pp. 30–31; and Menninger to Gay, 21 January 1935, Southard Papers).

33. Menninger to Gay, 21 January 1935, Southard Papers (Menninger was married at the time); and Norman Fenton to Gay, 6 February 1935, Southard Papers. The "girl" in question was the poet Louise T. Nicholl, who would later claim that their "friendship" was "no mature, adult, serious 'affair' at all. It was a divine kind of playtime for us both." (Nicholl to Gay [n.d. (1934?); "Friday morning"], Southard Papers). Southard and Nicholl corresponded fervently and met at other professional meetings. Southard described her as "my wonderful girl of Atlantic City provenience [*sic*]" (Southard to Gay, 5 February 1920; Atlantic City was the site of a professional meeting).

34. Yerkes, like Southard, was a member of the Wicht Club: Kuklick, *American Philosophy*, p. 421. Kuklick captures the intertwining of social and intellectual life in Cambridge at the time, as do Benison, Barger, and Wolfe, *Walter B. Cannon*.

35. Yerkes in Murchison, *Psychology in Autobiography*, p. 402; P. Myerson, "Abraham Myerson," p. 244.

36. In the period from 1872 to 1900, as many as two hundred women physicians worked in asylums nationwide (Constance M. McGovern, "Doctors or Ladies? Women Physicians in Psychiatric Institutions, 1872–1900," *Bulletin of the History of Medicine* 55 [1981]: 88).

37. Interview with Solomon, September 1980. Many of the doctors who would come to call themselves psychiatrists had trained as pathologists, and a number of women physicians worked in laboratories scattered about the state. Gay writes that "these laboratories were staffed by men with ideas"—four pages after a photograph of "Pathologists to the Massachusetts State Hospitals" that included Canavan (*Open Mind*, p. 100).

38. Christine Stansell, *City of Women: Sex and Class in New York, 1789–1860*

(New York, 1986), esp. chap. 4. Quotation from Associated Charities of Boston, *Annual Report* 7, 1886, p. 9, cited in Roy Lubove, *The Professional Altruist: The Emergence of Social Work as a Career, 1880–1930* (Cambridge, Mass., 1965), p. 13. Lubove's perceptive analysis of social work's ideology and fortunes has been supplemented but not superseded.

39. Melosh, *Physician's Hand*, p. 25; Lubove, *Professional Altruist*, pp. 22–24.

40. I am here relying on and paraphrasing Melosh's incisive analysis of medicine's domination of nursing: *Physician's Hand*, p. 19.

41. Southard, "Psychopathic Hospital," MS, Southard Papers; E. E. Southard, "Remarks on Advanced Training for Social Workers: A Physician's Point of View," *Radcliffe Quarterly* 1 (February 1917): 35, text of an address delivered at a meeting of the Radcliffe Union.

42. Southard, "Modern Specialist in Unrest," p. 551 (text of his presidential address to the Boston Society of Psychiatry and Neurology).

43. Among the most pointed of the journal articles in which the dispute was carried out is Jessie Taft, "The Limitations of the Psychiatrist," *Medicine and Surgery* 2 (1918): 365–69.

44. Southard, "Psychopathic Hospital."

45. Excerpt from an unpublished paper by Southard, cited in Mary C. Jarrett, "The Social Service, 1913 to 1918," in Briggs et al., *Psychopathic Hospital*, p. 173. In "Psychiatric Social Work," *Mental Hygiene* 2 (1918): 286, Jarrett referred to "the friction commonly known to occur between physicians and social workers."

46. *Notable American Women*, vol. 4, s.v. "Jarrett, Mary Cromwell."

47. Southard and Jarrett, *Kingdom of Evils*. Southard died unexpectedly in New York City on 8 February 1920, of a staphylococcus infection to the brain, his resistance weakened by an attack of influenza; Jarrett, in collaboration with Harry C. Solomon, readied the nearly finished manuscript for publication. Jarrett and Southard collaborated on a study of psychopathic employees in industry, financed by the Engineering Foundation of New York. Only portions of the study were published. Penina Migdal Glazer and Miriam Slater chronicle Jarrett's critical role in setting up the training course and, later, the School for Social Work in *Unequal Colleagues: The Entrance of Women into the Professions, 1890–1940* (New Brunswick, N.J., 1987), chap. 5. Their assessment of Jarrett's relationship with Southard is more sanguine than mine.

48. E. E. Southard, "Mental Hygiene and Social Work: Notes on a Course in Social Psychiatry for Social Workers," *Mental Hygiene* 2 (1918): 391–92.

49. Quotations from E. E. Southard, "The Individual versus the Family as the Unit of Interest in Social Work," *Mental Hygiene* 3 (1919): 437–38 (emphasis in original) and "Mental Hygiene and Social Work," pp. 389–90.

50. Southard and Jarrett, *Kingdom of Evils*, p. 107.

51. Quotations from Jarrett, "Psychiatric Social Work," pp. 285–87. Jarrett argued that official discomfort "should be distinguished from personal social relations with associates, as it is quite a different matter."

52. Mary C. Jarrett, "The Need for Research in Social Case Work by the Method of Study and Experimentation by Experienced Social Workers Who Are Themselves Doing the Case Work," MS, Roscoe Pound Papers, Harvard Law School Library.

53. Ibid.; Jarrett, "Proposed Plan for Research in Social Case Work if Under-

taken by the Commonwealth Fund under the Auspices of the American Association of Social Workers," MS, Pound Papers; Jarrett, "Memorandum on Study of Social Case Work," MS, Pound Papers. Jarrett sent the last to Pound in January 1923.

54. As Southard wrote, "the technique of an art can profitably be examined in the type of its personnel" ("Individual versus the Family," p. 438); Jarrett, "Psychiatric Social Work," p. 287.

55. Jarrett, "Psychiatric Social Work," p. 287.

56. Abraham Myerson did allow that social workers were building up "an independent social science," in "The Psychiatric Social Worker," *Journal of Abnormal Psychology* 13 (1918–1919): 225–29. Female relatives of several psychiatrists worked as psychiatric social workers: Myerson's daughter Anne, born in 1925 (his two sons became psychiatrists; Myerson, *Speaking of Man*, p. 257); and Maida Herman Solomon, who met Harry C. Solomon at the Psychopathic Hospital, married him, and enjoyed an extraordinarily long and distinguished career of her own. Adolf Meyer, claiming that his "heart [had] been with the movement from the beginning" of his career, dated his involvement to 1904, when "Mrs. Meyer began to give me volunteer help by visiting my patients" ("Historical Sketch and Outlook of Psychiatric and Social Work," *Hospital Social Service* 5 [1922]: 222).

57. Jarrett, "Psychiatric Social Work," p. 287. My analysis of Jarrett's stance differs somewhat from that of Glazer and Slater (*Unequal Colleagues*, esp. pp. 202–3), who suggest that Jarrett's work expressed her integration of social work's older, friendly visiting tradition and its newly articulated professionalism. In my reading, Jarrett was much more firm in her rejection of the older, "womanly" position. Regina G. Kunzel, "The Professionalization of Benevolence: Evangelicals and Social Workers in the Florence Crittenton Homes, 1915 to 1945," *Journal of Social History* 22 (Fall 1988): 21–43, shows how social workers used the language of science to underwrite their professionalism, arguing that "social work leaders denigrated the values associated with benevolent femininity as overly sentimental, embarassingly anachronistic, and suggestive of professional immaturity" (p. 25).

58. Glazer and Slater, *Unequal Colleagues*, pp. 187–88, 192; Maida H. Solomon, "1st Draft of Hist. of P.S.W.[,] 8/11/72," MS, Maida Herman Solomon Papers.

59. E. E. Southard, "A Lay Reaction to Psychiatry," part of a symposium, "The Training School of Psychiatric Social Work at Smith College," *Mental Hygiene* 2 (1918): 584–85.

60. Stuart Chapin, "A Scientific Basis for Training Social Workers," in "Training School," p. 591. Edith R. Spaulding, a physician, director of the Psychopathic Hospital (for delinquent girls) at the Reformatory, Bedford Hills, New York, and a participant in the course, noted that "in spite of the fact that lecturer after lecturer looked for symptoms of mental indigestion they found only unflagging enthusiasm and a high pitch of interested attention" ("The Course in Social Psychiatry," in "Training School," p. 586).

61. Myerson, "Psychiatric Social Worker," p. 228.

62. Southard, "Lay Reaction," p. 585.

63. Edith Spaulding, "The Training School of Psychiatric Social Work at Smith College," *Modern Medicine* 1 (1919): 720.

64. Southard and Jarrett, *Kingdom of Evils*, p. 388. From the context it seems

this section was written by Southard; he makes the same point in other writings, among them "Suggestions in the Nomenclature of Feeblemindedness," p. 3. Mary Richmond, *Social Diagnosis* (New York, 1917), p. 216, explicitly warned social workers against making medical diagnoses, arguing that nothing was more likely to antagonize physicians.

65. Southard and Jarrett, *Kingdom of Evils*, p. 389.

66. Lubove, *Professional Altruist*, chap. 3.

67. Jarrett, "Psychiatric Social Work," p. 288.

68. Mary C. Jarrett, "The Psychiatric Thread Running through All Social Case Work," National Conference of Social Work, *Proceedings* 46, 1919, p. 592. Scattered through Jarrett's works are comments indicative of professional frustration and fatigue. She complained, for example, that few persons appreciated the nature of social work; one's "able-minded friends" were apt to ask, she wrote, " 'Why do you think it is worthwhile?' 'Do you get anywhere?' " while the more emotional among them were given to exclaiming, " 'How happy you must be, doing so much good!' " ("Social Work as War Service," *Journal of the Association of Collegiate Alumnae* [1917]: 87). In a different vein, she observed (concerning patients whose ailments appeared less than serious) that "it is not easy to be patient with a person who complains constantly of feelings that we all have sometimes and do not make much of" ("Shell-Shock Analogues: Neuroses in Civil Life Having a Sudden or Critical Origin," *Medicine and Surgery* 2 [1918]: 269).

69. Maida H. Solomon, "Regular Day's Work—Sophie" (mid-1920s) and "How I Combined Career and Marriage and Childrearing," Maida Herman Solomon Papers. See Pnina G. Abir-Am and Dorinda Outram, introduction to Abir-Am and Outram, eds., *Uneasy Careers and Intimate Lives: Women in Science, 1789–1979* (New Brunswick, N.J., 1987), for a discussion of the material circumstances in which women scientists historically have worked.

70. Mary C. Jarrett, "The Educational Value of Psychiatric Social Work," *Mental Hygiene* 5 (1921): 510.

71. E. E. Southard, in Massachusetts State Board of Insanity, *Annual Report* 14, 1913, p. 29, noted the tendency of some workers to *"inspire patients, prospective patients, and relatives with fear of State institutions"* (emphasis in original). Quotations from Southard, "Mental Hygiene and Social Work," p. 393.

72. Myerson, *Speaking of Man*, pp. 84–86.

THREE: THE PSYCHIATRY OF EVERYDAY LIFE

1. Comment of E. Stanley Abbot of McLean Hospital, in response to E. E. Southard, "The Range of the General Practitioner in Psychiatric Diagnosis," *Journal of the American Medical Association* 73 (1919): 1256.

2. For an account of the nineteenth-century constitution of "the insane," see Donnelly, *Managing the Mind*. Quotations from Southard and Jarrett, *Kingdom of Evils*, pp. 373–75.

3. Stewart Paton, "Mobilizing the Brains of the Nation," *Mental Hygiene* 1 (1917): 342; Southard and Jarrett, *Kingdom of Evils*, p. 379.

4. Foucault, *Power/Knowledge*, p. 116.

5. Adolf Meyer, for example, wrote that "where the passing generation vainly

sought for exclusive salvation in the urine and faeces, and in the sham comforts of neurologizing tautologies," psychiatrists of his generation were finding "many common links with the normal" ("The Aims and Meaning of Psychiatric Diagnosis," *American Journal of Insanity* 74 [1917–1918]: 165); he later identified the distinctiveness of American psychiatry in its attempt to understand "mental disorders in terms of *life problems*" ("Historical Sketch," p. 223 [emphasis in original]). Several historians and sociologists have noted the shift from insanity to normality. John Chynoweth Burnham, "The New Psychology: From Narcissism to Social Control," in *Change and Continuity in Twentieth-Century America: The 1920's,* ed. John Braeman, Robert H. Bremner, and David Brody (Columbus, Ohio, 1968), pp. 383–84, registers but does not discuss what he calls "the common concern of the time about 'normality'"; Fox, *So Far Disordered in Mind,* chap. 7, chronicles the appearance of "the normal" in psychiatrists' professional program; and Abbott, *System of Professions,* chap. 10, offers an account of the profession's successful assertion of its jurisdiction over what he calls "personal problems" or "everyday life problems," a process he characterizes as "an intellectual invasion of areas of social control adjacent to that of the insane" (p. 295). Abbott historicizes psychiatrists' "invasion," but he locates it in a very different impulse than I do.

6. For a statement from within the discipline, indicative of its optimistic midcentury scientism, see Gregory Zilboorg in collaboration with George W. Henry, *A History of Medical Psychology* (New York, 1941), pp. 479ff. The authors locate what they call "the second psychiatric revolution" in the early years of the twentieth century, when psychiatrists abandoned the "formal descriptive psychiatry" of the nineteenth century and embraced empiricism, eventually creating what they celebrated as a scientific psychology. Fox, *So Far Disordered in Mind,* esp. chap. 7, interprets the same transformation in terms of the discipline's interest in social control.

7. Nineteenth-century psychiatric knowledge was organized around the distinction between insanity and sanity; symptoms were discrete and delimited, and diagnoses were premised on individuals exhibiting symptoms and behaviors that, psychiatrists hypothesized, differed qualitatively from those displayed by persons not afflicted. Only in the twentieth century would psychiatrists cast as symptoms behaviors that differed only quantitatively from traits anyone might exhibit—too much of this (abnormal selfishness, for instance), too little of that (insufficient willpower)—and only then would they reject the term *insanity* as too rigid and posit that the abnormal was but a variation on the normal. Donnelly, *Managing the Mind,* esp. chap. 7, charts the displacement, with the rise of the human sciences, of Enlightenment conceptions of "universal reason" by notions of individual variation; but note that "the mad," while a rich source of data for various nineteenth-century ideologues of difference, constituted a species apart from the not-mad. See Menninger, *Vital Balance,* appendix, for a survey of psychiatric nosologies from ancient times to the near-present.

Quotation in text from Foucault, *Discipline and Punish,* p. 183; for the argument, see pp. 170–84. Foucault locates the normalizing process—the establishment of "the Norm" as "the new law of modern society"—in the disciplinary institutions of the nineteenth century; I locate it, for psychiatry, later. Many of the normalizing judgments Foucault cites are perhaps better characterized as practices.

Drawn largely from the penal realm, they have more to do with economies of punishment than with hierarchically scaled conceptions of human nature. That Foucault could fail fully to historicize the normalizing imperative is a measure of how successful turn-of-the-century psychiatrists were in making it an aspect of the psychiatric agenda, where it now "naturally" appears.

8. William C. Menninger's observation that the psychiatrist did not limit his use of the word *normal* "to the opposite of sickness or pathology" but used it rather to talk about "our reactions, the outcome of our struggles, our work, our loves, and our hates"—in short, routine, everyday concerns—accurately if awkwardly captures both dimensions of the psychiatrists' project (*Psychiatry*, p. 4).

9. Michel Foucault, introduction to Georges Canguilhem, *The Normal and the Pathological*, trans. Carolyn R. Fawcett (New York, 1989), pp. 14–15, argues that "the historical tie which the different moments of science can have with one another necessarily" takes the form of discontinuity, which he defines as "constituted by the alterations, reshapings, elucidations of new foundations, changes in scale, the transition to a new kind of object" that results in "a new way of 'speaking true.'" This position challenges the usual tendency to posit continuity and development. It was widely articulated within early-twentieth-century psychiatry; for example, consider the proclamation of a Dr. Williams that "the subject of mental disease has emerged from its slough of superstition and stands removed from the murk of things weird and the supernatural" (comment made following an address by E. E. Southard, "The Causes of Feeble-Mindedness," *Proceedings of the Annual Congress of the American Prison Association* [1916]: 195). Although we need accept neither psychiatrists' claims to have severed their discipline from its nineteenth-century past nor their scientific claims as true, the effort to ground psychiatry in science must be registered, for it does distinguish between the two psychiatries even as it obscures continuities. In addition, to dismiss psychiatrists' scientific ambitions as wrongheaded (because "wrong") or to ridicule psychiatrists as stupid or duplicitous (which many historians and sociologists have done) is easy from our supposedly more enlightened perspective, but such dismissals also assume that "truth"—the right science, the right answers—exists, merely awaiting discovery. With respect to psychiatry it may prove more prudent to assume that truth is of this world. Quotation from Southard and Jarrett, *Kingdom of Evils*, p. 375.

10. I am here working with a variation on Foucault's explication of biological concepts. Arguing that "there is no object pertinent to biological science unless it has been 'conceived,'" Foucault maintains that the role of such a concept "is to cut out from the ensemble of the phenomena 'of life' those which allow one, without reducing, to analyze the processes proper to living beings." Further, he argues that "the moment that counts in a history of the biological sciences [which one might take to include psychiatry, as a science that takes for its object a type to which the scientist belongs—i.e., a human being] is that of the constitution of the object and the formation of the concept" (Foucault, introduction to Canguilhem, *Normal and the Pathological*, pp. 19–20). Southard maintained, in a similar spirit, that psychiatrists "must now wait for science to *make for us* new practical issues, real problems" (emphasis added) ("Feeble-Mindedness as a Leading Social Problem," *Boston Medical and Surgical Journal* 170 [1914]: 781). Attempting to describe the process of concept-formation, in another context he borrowed the language of the

laboratory, defining "social" issues as "those interests which concern society . . . outside the realm of government—social mechanisms not as crystallized from history but social tendencies as they seem about to precipitate out in organized form" ("The Psychopathic Hospital," MS of address delivered at the Fourth Annual Conference, Boston Psychopathic Hospital, Southard Papers).

11. Mary P. Ryan, *Cradle of the Middle Class: The Family in Oneida County, New York, 1790–1865* (New York, 1981), p. 15, uses the term "social reproduction." See also Jan Lewis, "Mother's Love: The Construction of an Emotion in Nineteenth-Century America," in *Social History and Issues in Human Consciousness*, ed. Andrew E. Barnes and Peter N. Stearns (New York, 1989), pp. 209–29.

12. Abraham Myerson, *The Psychology of Mental Disorders* (New York, 1927), pp. 100–101.

13. Quotation from Benedictus Rinius, *De morbo Gallico, tractatus*, cited in Ludwik Fleck, *Genesis and Development of a Scientific Fact*, ed. Thaddeus J. Trenn and Robert K. Merton, trans. Fred Bradley and Trenn (Chicago, 1979), p. 2.

14. For concise accounts of developments in syphilology, see Allan M. Brandt, *No Magic Bullet: A Social History of Venereal Disease in the United States since 1880*, expanded ed. (New York, 1987), chap. 1; and Fleck, *Scientific Fact*, chap. 1. See also John Thorne Crissey and Lawrence Charles Parish, *The Dermatology and Syphilology of the Nineteenth Century* (New York, 1981); and Claude Quétel, *The History of Syphilis*, trans. Judith Braddock and Brian Pike (Cambridge, 1990). The landmark paper by Hideyo Noguchi and J. W. Moore, "Demonstration of *Treponema pallidum* in the Brain in Cases of General Paralysis," originally published in 1913, appears, with concise commentary by Denis Leigh, in *The Origins of Modern Psychiatry* , ed. C. Thompson (Chichester, Eng., 1987), pp. 211–24.

15. T. S. Clouston, *Unsoundness of Mind* (London, 1911), cited in Thompson, *Origins of Modern Psychiatry*, pp. 217–18.

16. Quotation in preface, by Southard, to E. E. Southard and Harry C. Solomon, *Neurosyphilis: Modern Systematic Diagnosis and Treatment Presented in One Hundred and Thirty-Seven Case Histories* (1917; reprint, New York, 1973), p. 8.

17. Denis Leigh, in Thompson, *Origins of Modern Psychiatry*, p. 219, cites as examples of the absurdities that resulted from ignorance Henry Maudsley's condemnation of "that quiet, steady continuance of excess for months or years by married people which was apt to be thought no vice or harm at all," and other prominent physicians' warnings that excessive tobacco smoking might also result in syphilis. As the current furor over AIDS demonstrates, it has proven difficult, if not impossible, to extricate sexually transmitted diseases from a moral nexus. See Brandt, *No Magic Bullet*, chap. 6.

18. Southard, "Feeble-Mindedness as a Leading Social Problem," p. 781.

19. In *Kingdom of Evils*, Southard and Jarrett chastised the "sundry physicians" who had ignored one patient's many syphilitic symptoms, "which should have attracted medical attention" (pp. 203–4).

20. Fleck, *Scientific Fact*, p. 17, argues that as physicians elucidated the causes of syphilis, "the connection with the sex act was translated from the mystical-ethical domain into straightforward physical terms," which aptly characterizes the trajectory psychiatrists' thinking followed.

21. European sexologists had been classifying sex and treating it as fact since the

1870s, but psychiatrists made no reference to this tradition in their elaboration of an investigatory strategy. Rather, they premised their strategy—apprehending sex as fact—wholly on what they argued was the science of syphilis.

Nineteenth-century syphilologists knew that syphilis could be transmitted to the innocent—wives and children of profligate men. But regulation of prostitution (in the proclaimed interest of protecting men as well as the innocent from disease), in which prostitutes were subjected to registration and regular medical inspections at the hands of public health officials, did not catch on in the United States to the extent it did in Europe. On regulation, see David J. Pivar, *Purity Crusade: Sexual Morality and Social Control, 1868–1900* (Westport, Conn., 1973); Brandt, *No Magic Bullet*, pp. 31–37; and John D'Emilio and Estelle B. Freedman, *Intimate Matters: A History of Sexuality in America* (New York, 1988), pp. 139–50. Judith R. Walkowitz, *Prostitution and Victorian Society: Women, Class, and the State* (Cambridge, 1980), is the classic work on regulation.

22. Quotation from Prince A. Morrow, *Social Diseases and Marriage* (New York, 1904), cited in Brandt, *No Magic Bullet*, p. 18. Even as they were attacking the medical secret in the name of modernity, psychiatrists were conspiring to protect Southard's wife from knowledge of his extramarital activities. Myerson, for one, was willing to allow women their own secrets, writing that he advised one woman who had been unfaithful to her husband not to tell him of her affair (*Nervous Housewife*, p. 224).

23. Quotations from Maida H. Solomon, "Social Work with Syphilitics and Their Families," MS, Maida Herman Solomon Papers; another version appears in Boston State Hospital, *Annual Report* 9, 1918, pp. 57–63. On reticence in the press, see Brandt, *No Magic Bullet*, pp. 23–24. On the gender dimensions of the tradition of deception, see Brandt, *No Magic Bullet*, pp. 17–19, and Jill Harsin, "Syphilis, Wives, and Physicians: Medical Ethics and the Family in Late Nineteenth-Century France," *French Historical Studies* 16 (1989): 72–95.

24. Southard and Jarrett, *Kingdom of Evils*, pp. 211–15.

25. Ibid., p. 110.

26. Ibid.

27. Southard and Solomon, *Neurosyphilis*, p. 457.

28. Southard and Jarrett, *Kingdom of Evils*, p. 213.

29. Maida Solomon, "One Day's Spirit," MS, Maida Herman Solomon Papers. On momentousness, cf. Foucault, *The History of Sexuality*, vol. 1, *An Introduction*, trans. Robert Hurley (New York, 1978), p. 64.

30. Southard and Jarrett, *Kingdom of Evils*, pp. 571–81, contains a transcript of the record social workers compiled in Gordon's case.

31. Southard, "Feeble-Mindedness as a Leading Social Problem," pp. 781–82.

32. I thank Lorraine Daston for advice on this issue. Quotations from Maida Solomon, "One Day's Spirit." With respect to the self-discipline social work demanded, consider one social worker's observation (concerning an "ex-service man suffering from a mental and nervous disorder that is yet in a border-line stage"): "To the lay person, this type of individual seems merely irritable, suspicious, depressed, or stupid." The social worker had to be more circumspect in her judgments (Lila Kline, "The Personal Psychiatric History," *Mental Hygiene* 6 [1922]: 95).

33. Throughout this section, adopting psychiatrists' shorthand, I refer to mental

tests as "Binet tests" in order to convey that psychiatrists were as attracted by the principle as by the specific form of Binet's test. (Southard, for example, consistently referred to the "Binet grade" when, in fact, the grade in question most often resulted from the Point Scale developed by Robert M. Yerkes in collaboration with several other psychologists at the Boston Psychopathic Hospital: Yerkes, James W. Bridges, and Rose S. Hardwick, *A Point Scale for Measuring Mental Ability* [Baltimore, 1915].) I also want to avoid cluttering the text with distinctions not important to my argument. In addition, in this section I focus on how *psychiatrists*, not psychologists (about whom there is a large literature), viewed the tests. The essays in Sokal, *Psychological Testing*, cover many of the major figures and controversies in early American testing; the references cited are a useful guide to the literature from the perspective of the profession of psychology.

34. Alfred Binet and his collaborator Théodore Simon published a number of articles concerning their scale in *L'année psychologique* between 1905 and 1911, five of which appear in their work, *The Development of Intelligence in Children*, trans. Elizabeth S. Kite (Baltimore, 1916). Theta H. Wolf, *Alfred Binet* (Chicago, 1973), contains a full bibliography of Binet's works.

35. Lewis M. Terman, *Genius and Stupidity* (1906; reprint, New York, 1975), p. 311. (This work is Terman's 1906 Clark University Ph.D. thesis, subtitled "A Study of the Intellectual Processes of Seven 'Bright' and Seven 'Stupid' Boys.") Southard voiced the same sentiment, arguing that the Binet-Simon tests allowed an inexperienced examiner to assess a child's capabilities, the measure of which had "formerly depended on the teacher's trial and error" ("Feeble-Mindedness as a Leading Social Problem," p. 782).

36. On science as measurement, see Robert K. Merton, David L. Sills, and Stephen M. Stigler, "The Kelvin Dictum and Social Science: An Excursion into the History of an Idea," *Journal of the History of the Behavioral Sciences* 20 (1984): 319–31. One version of the Kelvin dictum goes as follows: "When you can measure what you are speaking about, and express it in numbers, you know something about it; but when you cannot measure it, when you cannot express it in numbers, your knowledge is of a meagre and unsatisfactory kind: it may be the beginning of knowledge, but you have scarcely, in your thoughts, advanced to the stage of *science*, whatever the matter may be" (p. 327). Southard, who observed, with respect to the tests, that "the fortunate thing for the science of the situation is that the Binet grade is something concrete," subscribed to the dictum; E. E. Southard, "The Promise of Research in the Anatomy of Feeblemindedness," MS, Southard Papers. Quotation in text from Terman, *Genius and Stupidity*, p. 311.

37. Terman, for example, in his 1906 investigation of bright and stupid boys, writes "we do not define 'brightness' or 'dullness' any more definitely than does the world in general" (*Genius and Stupidity*, p. 316).

38. Southard, "Causes of Feeble-Mindedness," pp. 192, 191.

39. E. E. Southard, "Psychological Wants of Psychiatrists: A Psychopathic Hospital Point of View," typescript of address delivered at the annual meeting of the American Psychological Association, 1917, Southard Papers.

40. Southard and Jarrett, *Kingdom of Evils*, pp. 463–64.

41. For example, Southard sharply questioned his colleagues concerning the disposition of one case, a twenty-six-year-old man diagnosed feebleminded, asking

"why he was brought into the hospital at all?" "Couldn't this case have been handled in the O.P.D. [Out-Patient Department]? Diagnosis rendered and enough done to solve all problems?" Case 7820, 1916, staff meeting.

42. Case 10263, 1918. As Southard summed up the case of a woman whom he termed a "motiveless" kleptomaniac: "If she did not happen to be measurably feebleminded we would be at a loss." The woman was diagnosed as "Not Insane (Moron)": case 9577, 1917.

43. C. Spearman, "Normality," in *Psychologies of 1930*, ed. Carl Murchison (Worcester, Mass., 1930), p. 445. The physician Richard C. Cabot argued that "we do not know what the normal is. Our conception of normal may mean 'average' or the 'ideal'—what we would like it to be. The conception of normal depends upon one's personality and cannot be scientifically stated" (Comment in response to Mary C. Jarrett, "Psychiatric Thread," p. 593). Cabot's observation was echoed some twenty-five years later in F. J. Hacker, "The Concept of Normality and Its Practical Significance," *American Journal of Orthopsychiatry* 15 (1945): 47–48: "The concept of normality is of central importance . . . for the theoretical foundation of psychiatry. . . . [yet] numerous authors try to show how certain types of behavior, ideas, or actions deviate from something that is called normal, without ever defining what they mean by this term."

44. Stephen Jay Gould, *The Mismeasure of Man* (New York, 1981), p. 149, makes this point.

45. James Reed, "Robert M. Yerkes," p. 76.

46. This was a refinement made in 1912 by the German psychologist W. Stern (Gould, *Mismeasure of Man*, p. 150) but apparently not adopted until after 1920. (At the Psychopathic Hospital, scores were reported as absolute numbers, not IQs.)

47. The outcome of the Binet test, and of Robert M. Yerkes' revision of it, the widely used Point Scale, which he developed and employed at the Psychopathic Hospital, was a number—9, for example, or 11.5—that purported to indicate the subject's mental age. On the Point Scale, an individual score was first totaled, based on the number of correct answers given, and then compared to the norms (average scores) calculated by Yerkes, who with his colleagues administered thousands of tests. The procedure, described by Yerkes, Bridges, and Hardwick, in chapter 5 of *Point Scale*, was cumbersome and rather roundabout. Terman, an advocate of universal testing who developed the Stanford-Binet intelligence test, a revision of Binet's test that could be admininstered in thirty minutes' time, addressed this problem by "standardizing" the test. (This, Gould stresses, was "not finagling, but a valid statistical procedure for establishing uniformity of average score and variance across age levels" [*Mismeasure of Man*, p. 177]. R. C. Lewontin, Steven Rose, and Leon J. Kamin dissent, linking standardization to tinkering [*Not In Our Genes: Biology, Ideology, and Human Nature* (New York, 1984), p. 89]. In part, the two positions reflect different assessments of the validity of statistical reasoning.) The "average" person at each age would score 100; setting the standard deviation at 15, Terman ensured that two-thirds of scores would fall between 85 and 115 (100, plus or minus one standard deviation) (Gould, *Mismeasure of Man*, pp. 174–77).

Many of the statistical issues that lie behind what follows are beyond the scope of this book. Both Stephen M. Stigler, *The History of Statistics: The Measurement of*

Uncertainty before 1900 (Cambridge, Mass., 1986), and Theodore M. Porter, *The Rise of Statistical Thinking, 1820–1900* (Princeton, 1986), cover them in great detail, the first more mathematically than the second. Few popular works on mental testing exhibit any appreciation for the technical issues involved (Gould's *Mismeasure of Man* is an exception); then again, the scholarly works restrict themselves largely to technical issues, and do not sufficiently acknowledge that the innovations that brought statistical thinking into the social sciences were made, from around 1880 on, by those (Francis Galton, most notably) set on establishing differences among men.

48. The distinction between average and most common is that the statistical mean need not be a real observation (Stigler, *History of Statistics*, p. 309). Canguilhem has brilliantly explicated the dual meaning of the normal in medical thinking and has explored the etymology and meanings of concepts related to it— abnormal, anomaly, pathological (*Normal and the Pathological*). See also Ian Hacking, *The Taming of Chance* (Cambridge, 1990), chap. 19. The *Oxford English Dictionary* notes that normal, meaning "constituting, conforming to, not deviating or differing from, the common type or standard; regular, usual," entered common English usage in the 1840s: s.v. "normal." Concerning abnormal, the *OED* (s.v. "abnormal") notes that "few words show such a series of pseudo-etymological perversions," a point that Canguilhem underscores (pp. 131–32).

49. On the army tests, see Gould, *Mismeasure of Man*, pp. 193–233; Daniel J. Kevles, "Testing the Army's Intelligence: Psychologists and the Military in World War I," *Journal of American History* 55 (1968): 565–81; and Yerkes' account of the testing (*Memoirs of the National Academy of Sciences*, vol. 15, *Psychological Examining in the United States Army*, ed. Robert M. Yerkes [Washington, D.C., 1921]).

50. Stigler, *History of Statistics*, p. 261. The testers' circular thinking is evident in, for example, the ardent eugenicist Henry H. Goddard's assertion that the reliability of the Binet scale is proved because the results of some 1,547 administrations can be distributed on the normal curve: "To a person familiar with statistical methods the foregoing curve of itself, amounts to practically a mathematical demonstration of the accuracy of the tests" ("Two Thousand Normal Children Measured by the Binet Measuring Scale of Intelligence," *Pedagogical Seminary* 18 [1911]: 236). The issue *was* addressed by the noted psychologist Edwin G. Boring, "The Logic of the Normal Law of Error in Mental Measurement," *American Journal of Psychology* 31 (1920): 1–33.

51. Edwin G. Boring, "Intelligence as the Tests Test It," *New Republic* 35 (6 June 1923): 35. Further, as many critics pointed out, the tests measured not the innate general intelligence that their proponents claimed they did but class-biased cultural knowledge (for example, rewarding subjects for choosing "pretty," delicate Anglo-Saxon physiognomies over "ugly," simian-featured Others). More recently, Gould, *Mismeasure of Man*, and Lewontin, Rose, and Kamin, *Not in Our Genes* (all citing Boring), have argued the case concerning reification powerfully.

52. Charles Spearman, as quoted by Terman, *Genius and Stupidity*, p. 311.

53. Francis Galton, *Memories of My Life* (London, 1909), pp. 315–16, also cited in Gould, *Mismeasure of Man*, p. 75.

54. My analysis here owes much to the insights offered by Porter, *Rise of Statisti-*

cal Thinking, pp. 141–43, which points to the issue of measurement, and Stigler, *History of Statistics*, chap. 8, esp. pp. 267–72, a more technical account. Stigler terms Galton (1822–1911) "perhaps the last of the gentleman scientists" (p. 266), and clearly explains the weakness of the analogous reasoning on which Galton's scale—and, indeed, all subsequent psychometric scales—rests. For a recent, non-technical, and pointed critique of scaling as "the grand illusion of psychometry," see Lewontin, Rose, and Kamin, *Not in Our Genes*, pp. 91–93.

55. Stigler, *History of Statistics*, p. 300, sums up Galton's achievements.

56. Terman, *Genius and Stupidity*, p. 312.

57. As an object of inquiry, intelligence was less amorphous than efficiency in part for historical reasons (by the second decade of the century, the conventions by which intelligence was measured were well established and for that reason apparently natural) but also because, as Kurt Danziger has suggested, intelligence tests comprised "tasks with answers that were unambiguously right or wrong. Performance on such tasks could be readily arithmetized by counting right and wrong answers" (*Constructing the Subject*, p. 156). Efficiency did not conform to the model suggested by intelligence; in social workers' hands, it was a purely subjective assessment with no numerical referents.

58. See Donnelly, *Managing the Mind*, chap. 7, for a brief discussion of the shift from the late-eighteenth-century emphasis on universal reason to the nineteenth century's stress on human variation, which the new sciences of man amply documented.

59. Southard, Autobiographical Fragment.

60. Herbert Croly, *The Promise of American Life* (New York, 1909), p. 138.

61. Mary C. Jarrett, "The Function of the Social Service of the Psychopathic Hospital, Boston," Boston Psychopathic Hospital, *Collected Contributions* , no. 5 (Boston, 1914), p. 19.

62. On environmentalism, see Paul Boyer, *Urban Masses and Moral Order in America, 1820–1920* (Cambridge, Mass., 1978), chaps. 13–19, and Merle Curti, *Human Nature in American Thought* (Madison, Wis., 1980), esp. chap. 7.

63. Southard, "Psychological Wants of Psychiatrists."

64. E. E. Southard, *The Mental Hygiene of Industry* (New York, 1920), p. 21; Southard, "The Movement for a Mental Hygiene of Industry," *Mental Hygiene* 4 (1920): 61. On eugenics, see Daniel J. Kevles, *In the Name of Eugenics: Genetics and the Uses of Human Heredity* (New York, 1985).

65. Southard and Jarrett, *Kingdom of Evils*, pp. 376–77; Porter, *Rise of Statistical Thinking*, p. 101; Stigler, *History of Statistics*, pp. 170–71.

66. Southard, "The Empathic Index in the Diagnosis of Mental Disease," *Journal of Abnormal Psychology* 13 (1918–1919): 199; Southard and Jarrett, *Kingdom of Evils*, p. 377.

67. Pearce Bailey, "Efficiency and Inefficiency—A Problem in Medicine," *Mental Hygiene* 1 (1917): 200. Writing that liberty and equality constituted "an agreeable delusion," Bailey argued that the individual's right to "dispose of himself as he pleases" resulted in "substandard men," criminals and delinquents that he called "waste products" (pp. 201, 205). E. E. Southard, "coldly speaking," assessed the feebleminded in similar terms: "it becomes a question with us, what to do with these waste materials. Now the modern doctrine of efficiency in economics and

other divisions of practical service is to make use of all such waste materials" ("The Feeble-Minded as Subjects of Research in Efficiency," National Conference of Charities and Correction, *Proceedings* 42, 1915, p. 316).

68. Henry Herbert Goddard, *Human Efficiency and Levels of Intelligence* (Princeton, 1920), p. 101.

69. Robert M. Yerkes, "How May We Discover the Children Who Need Special Care?" *Mental Hygiene* 1 (1917): 252.

70. Southard, "The Feeble-Minded as Subjects of Research in Efficiency," p. 316.

71. E. E. Southard referred to "metric psychiatry" as a new and promising psychiatric specialty in an article published in 1917, defining it as "psychological psychiatry, *i.e.*, a psychiatry that uses methods developed by psychologists, commonly called 'mental tests,' for the purpose of the psychiatrist's diagnosis not merely in the study of feeblemindedness but broadly in the field of deterioration" ("Alienists and Psychiatrists: Notes on Divisions and Nomenclature of Mental Hygiene," *Mental Hygiene* 1 [1917]: 569). I have not found any other references to metric psychiatry in Southard's published works.

72. Bernard Glueck articulated the limitations of psychometric methods in a review of Karl Birnbaum's *Psychopathic Criminal* in *Psychiatric Bulletin* 2 (1917): 544, noting, for example, that "the psychopath may not, and actually does not in many instances, demonstrate any such deviation from normality as might be defined by means of the various psychometric methods." Psychopaths, that is, scored quite high on the mental tests, a surprising and widely noted outcome that fueled psychiatrists' search for another way to account for psychopaths' obvious defectiveness.

73. Assessing the history of relations between psychiatry and psychology, Karl Menninger, David Rapaport, and Roy Schafer observed that in the late nineteenth century "the ways of the two disciplines, once so closely linked, parted," but that psychological testing "served as a temporary liaison" between them, a reading with which I am in agreement ("The New Rôle of Psychological Testing in Psychiatry," *American Journal of Psychiatry* 103 [1946–1947]: 474).

74. The meanings of the terms *psychopathy* and *psychopathic* were in flux through the first decades of the twentieth century. In 1900, psychopathy still retained "its original meaning of psychic ailment in general"—from the Greek *psyche* (soul) and *pathos* (suffering). Used in the compound terms *psychopathic inferiority*, *psychopathic constitution*, and *psychopathic personality*, its meaning shifted such that by the 1910s, in the German literature, it became synonymous with psychopathic personality. In the United States, for a short time, *psychopathic* was used as an antonym to *neuropathic*, to denote mental disease without neurological basis (Henry Werlinder, *Psychopathy: A History of the Concepts: Analysis of the Origin and Development of a Family of Concepts in Psychopathology* [Uppsala, Sweden, 1978], pp. 86–87). Southard used the term in this way in "A Series of Normal Looking Brains in Psychopathic Subjects," *American Journal of Insanity* 69 (1912–1913): 689–704, in which he pointed to the existence of normal brains in patients with dementia praecox and senile dementia. Early in the century Adolf Meyer introduced into American psychiatry the concept of psychopathy or constitutional inferiority as a designation for psychiatric conditions that fit none of the

established categories of mental disease; "Psychopathic" in the hospital's name referred to this dimension of the term's many meanings. Although American usage quickly fell in line with German usage (the psychopathy discussed in the text), the term was confusing to those outside (even, sometimes, within) the discipline. The psychiatrist Anna C. Wellington, under cross-examination in a trial concerning the Psychopathic Hospital's diagnosis of a wealthy patient as a psychopathic personality, was asked to state "the meaning of the word 'psychopathic.'" "I am not a Greek scholar," she said. "You are the administrator of a psychopathic hospital—can't you define it?" the lawyer challenged her. Wellington replied that she knew what a "psychopathic personality" was ("a person of more or less deviation from the normal"), but she could not say whether the word was of Latin or Greek derivation: "I think it is taken from the word—I am not a philologist, though" (case of M—— S——, Southard Papers).

75. Quotation from Editorial, "Psychopathic Constitution of Radical Individuals," *New York Medical Journal* 107 (1918): 800.

76. C. C. Wholey, "Cases of Insanity Arising from Inherent Moral Defectiveness," *Journal of the American Medical Association* 62 (1914): 926.

77. The literature on psychopathy proliferated with uncommon speed. For a bibliography, see Werlinder, *Psychopathy*.

78. Southard was fond of pointing out that fully half of the cases in Mary Richmond's casebook of social work practice, *Social Diagnosis*, had a strong "psychiatric flavor" (*Kingdom of Evils*, p. 375).

79. Glueck, review of Birnbaum, p. 546.

80. Salmon's testimony to Congress was reported in Massachusetts State Board of Insanity, *Bulletin* 9 (May 1915): 8–10.

81. Werlinder, *Psychopathy*, pp. 86ff.

82. Comment of A. A. Brill, in response to R. H. Bryant, "The Constitutional Psychopathic Inferior: A Menace to Society and a Suggestion for the Disposition of Such Individuals," *American Journal of Psychiatry* 83 (1926–1927): 687.

83. Case 9642, 1917, staff meeting. The term "rag-bag" came up repeatedly in the literature of psychopathy. William A. White, "On the Etiology of Psychopathic States," in "The Psychopathic Individual: A Symposium," ed. Ben Karpman, *Mental Hygiene* 8 (1924): 175, referred to the term as a wastebasket.

84. Case 9642, 1917, staff meeting.

86. G. E. Partridge, "Psychotic Reaction in the Psychopath," *American Journal of Psychiatry* 85 (1928–1929): 502; Southard and Jarrett, *Kingdom of Evils*, p. 347.

87. Comment of Theodore Diller, following James H. Huddleson, "Connotation of Constitutional Psychopathic Inferiority without Psychosis: A Study of Five Hundred Diagnoses," *Journal of the American Medical Association* 86 (1926): 1963. Invoking the authority of his colleague, Myerson subversively wrote, with respect to psychopathic personality: "[A. Warren] Stearns states that psychiatric ignorance of any subject can be measured by the number of names it has acquired" (*Psychology of Mental Disorders*, p. 102).

88. Southard and Jarrett, *Kingdom of Evils*, p. 445. A long review article by G. E. Partridge, "Current Conceptions of Psychopathic Personality," *American Journal of Psychiatry* 87 (1930–1931): 53–99, esp. pp. 97–99, which summarizes the

perspectives of many authorities, conveys some of the confusion surrounding the epistemological status of the category.

89. In this regard, it is suggestive that an early observer commented that successful transference with the psychopath was impossible to establish because such patients were so egocentric, narcissistic, and satisfied with themselves that, although gratified by the analyst's attention, they resisted analysis, preferring instead to hold on to their symptoms and taking refuge in self-love (Mary O'Malley, "Psychoanalytic Treatment of Psychopathic Personalities," in Karpman, "Psychopathic Individual," p. 201).

90. Editorial, "Psychopathic Personalities," *Journal of Neurology and Psychopathology* 5 (1924–1925): 241. For expressions of similar sentiments, see Karl Birnbaum, abstract of Fritz Fränkel, "The Psychopathic Constitution in Relation to War Neuroses," *Archives of Neurology and Psychiatry* 5 (1921): 82; and Johnson, "Constitutional Psychopathic Inferior," p. 467. Explaining to a general audience why the term *insanity* was no longer wholly serviceable, a psychologist wrote that "the dividing area between the normal and abnormal loses its sharp boundaries; the clues to the abnormal are often found within the normal, and the variations within the normal range find their interpretation in the more pronounced issues of the abnormal." He suggested that the transition from the old to the new conception of the psychologists' and psychiatrists' domain took place around psychopathy (Joseph Jastrow, "What Is Insanity?" *Current History* 29 [1928]: 406; also cited in Fox, *So Far Disordered in Mind*, pp. 172–73).

91. Quotation from Jastrow, "What Is Insanity?" p. 407; cf. Foucault, *Discipline and Punish*, p. 181, in reference to the "penal accountancy" evident in the administration of justice at a school, writes of "the play of this quantification, this circulation of awards and debits, . . . the continuous calculation of plus and minus points," which also characterizes the way in which Jastrow (and many psychiatrists) wrote of psychopathy.

92. James Cowles Prichard, *A Treatise on Insanity and Other Disorders Affecting the Mind* (Philadelphia, 1837), p. 20. In positing that psychopathy was not merely an elaboration of Prichard's "moral insanity" but a fundamentally new category premised on new conceptual foundations, I am in agreement with the assessments of Werlinder, *Psychopathy*, pp. 39–40, and of Roger Smith, *Trial by Medicine: Insanity and Responsibility in Victorian Trials* (Edinburgh, 1981), p. 114.

93. Raymond Williams, *Keywords: A Vocabulary of Culture and Society* (New York, 1976), pp. 194–97. In psychiatry, the definition of the personality remained somewhat vague. In 1919, for example, Richard C. Cabot argued that "the study of personality does not exist, either as a science or an art, written down. . . . The study of personality is not yet developed" (Comment, in response to Jarrett, "Psychiatric Thread," p. 593). In 1927, Myerson could refer to "that conglomeration of things called personality" (*Psychology of Mental Disorders*, pp. 6–7). And, in 1948, William C. Menninger wrote that "the psychiatric use of 'personality' covers all that a person has been, all that he is, and all that he is trying to become" (*Psychiatry*, p. 4). Danziger writes that "of all the slippery terms that define modern psychological discourse [personality] is perhaps the most slippery" (*Constructing the Subject*, p. 239, n. 17). See also John Chynoweth Burnham, "Historical Back-

ground for the Study of Personality," in *Handbook of Personality Theory and Research*, ed. Edgar F. Borgatta and William W. Lambert (Chicago, 1968), pp. 3–81.

94. Warren I. Susman, "'Personality' and the Making of Twentieth-Century Culture," in his *Culture as History: The Transformation of American Society in the Twentieth Century* (New York, 1984), pp. 273–74 and 279.

95. Susman provides evidence of but does not register the gender specificity of character as nineteenth-century Americans used it, for example citing (without comment) a popular authority's injunction to one interested in developing character: "Let him first be a Man" ("'Personality' and Twentieth-Century Culture," p. 279). Williams cites Alexander Pope, 1735: "most Women have no Characters at all," noting that this usage engages the dimension of character indicative of "a strong or striking quality." But compare an early attribution of personality to a woman, 1795: "even a French girl of sixteen, if she has but a little personality, is a Machiavel" (Williams, *Keywords*, pp. 195–96). Stefan Collini, in an otherwise nuanced and insightful exposition of the meanings of "character," argues that manliness, which Victorian Britons consistently opposed to sentimentality, was one of the staples of the language of character, but he—like Susman—does not register its gender specificity. With reference to personality, he cites another's reference to "the alleged usage of Hollywood press agents . . . : 'this girl has a terrific personality' being a euphemistic formula for conveying the fact that she had large and well-shaped breasts" ("The Idea of 'Character' in Victorian Political Thought," *Transactions of the Royal Historical Society* 5th ser., 35 [1985]: 29–50). These admittedly stray examples all testify to the two terms' gendered natures.

96. Susman, "'Personality' and Twentieth-Century Culture," p. 277.

97. Hacker, "Concept of Normality," p. 49. Danziger, *Constructing the Subject*, chap. 10, examines psychologists' attempts to bring personality under analysis (and notes the term's new prominence in psychiatric discourse [p. 164]). The two disciplines constructed the personality somewhat differently: while psychologists developed personality tests, modeled on intelligence tests, that relied on "an additive model of the human person" (p. 159), psychiatrists tended to conceive of the personality in global terms, attending to its overall adjustment or lack thereof. "'Personality' as a constructed object of [psychological] investigations never had anything in common with traditional concepts of the human person as a social agent" (p. 165). The reverse could be said of psychiatrists' use of the term.

On the personality's separability from the self, see the suggestive remarks of Ruth Leys, "Adolf Meyer: A Biographical Note," in *Defining American Psychology: The Correspondence between Adolf Meyer and Edward Bradford Titchener*, ed. Leys and Rand B. Evans (Baltimore, 1990), pp. 99–101; Nathaniel Cantor, "What Is a Normal Mind?" *American Journal of Orthopsychiatry* 11 (1941): 677: "The demands or wishes of others become incorporated in one's own personality. . . . The incorporation of other selves into one's own personality brings exceedingly painful experiences. Individuals fight to be 'themselves,' that is, to express their own unique differences"; and the comment of one psychiatrist concerning a young female patient: "She is too bright for the rest of her" (case 10032, 1918, staff meeting).

98. Collini, "Idea of 'Character,'" esp. pp. 38ff., suggests something similar to this.

99. See, for example, "Psychopathic Constitution of Radical Individuals," p. 800, which refers derisively to the "inordinate conceit" of the "self styled genius," the self-absorption of radical individuals interested only in the public impression they make, and the egotism and purposeful eccentricity of such individuals.

100. Williams, *Keywords,* p. 197. See also Donnelly, *Managing the Mind,* esp. pp. xi–xii, for a brief but suggestive analysis of the creation of freestanding individuals. Cf. Alain Corbin's discussion of the late-nineteenth-century "democratization of the portrait" and the enhancement of individuality ("Back Stage", in *A History of Private Life,* vol. 4, *From the Fires of Revolution to the Great War,* ed. Michelle Perrot, trans. Arthur Goldhammer [Cambridge, Mass., 1990], pp. 460–66). Although psychiatrists did not define personality, they tended to use the term in contexts emphasizing the importance of attending to the individual. Jarrett, for example, argued that the psychiatric point of view resulted in "greater respect" for individuals' personalities ("Psychiatric Thread," p. 592), and Herman Adler wrote that "the general problem of human personality has come to be one of the important issues of social organization," going on to argue for attention to the "individual case" and to "individual problems" ("Broader Psychiatry," p. 365).

101. For example, Huddleson, "Connotation," p. 1962, defined a psychopath as "one that does not possess and display the amount of kindliness, honesty, reliability, loyalty, independence, persistence, emotional control, and resistance to the development of psychotic episodes, average for his race and intelligence level; he need not be deficient in all these qualities, but his deviation from the normal is permanent." And H. W. Wright wrote that the condition's etiological elements were "exaggerations of normal, universally constitutional tendencies" ("A Consideration of Constitutional Inferiority," *New York Medical Journal* 88 [1908]: 1219).

102. Ben Karpman, in Karpman, "Psychopathic Individual," p. 174.

103. E. E. Southard, "Psychopathic Delinquents," National Conference of Charities and Correction, *Proceedings* 43, 1916, p. 535.

104. Wright, "Consideration of Constitutional Inferiority," p. 1217. Bernard Glueck, "Special Preparation of the Psychiatric Social Worker," *Mental Hygiene* 3 (1919): 417, expressed a similar sentiment somewhat differently: "How normal, after all, the abnormal are." Myerson accounted for psychiatrists' tendency to pathologize the normal, explaining that "we, as doctors, have constructed the normal from the hints and clues of disease. . . . Men have seized upon the abnormal as a basis for that experimentation and study which leads to the knowledge of the normal" (*Speaking of Man,* p. 193).

105. Explaining for a popular audience the psychiatric attitude toward the normal, Myerson wrote: "Are not the normal, if there exist any such . . ." (*Psychology of Mental Disorders,* p. 100).

106. Bryant, "Constitutional Psychopathic Inferior," p. 672; Partridge, "Current Conceptions of Psychopathic Personality," p. 60; and many other authorities.

107. Henry Herd, "The Diagnosis of Moral Imbecility," *Lancet* 207 (1922): 742. "Moral imbecility" in British usage referred to a complex of behaviors similar to that to which "psychopathy" referred in American usage.

108. Birnbaum, abstract of Fränkel, p. 82. See also Partridge, "Current Conceptions of Psychopathic Personality," p. 57: "In psychopathology we are always dealing with extremes of a series, and can only arbitrarily assign a line of cleavage

between the normal and abnormal"—a statement that few, if any, nineteenth-century American psychiatrists could have made; it nicely illustrates how quickly metric thinking became "natural."

109. On the rejection of norms, see Southard and Jarrett, *Kingdom of Evils*, p. 377; Southard, "Mental Hygiene and Social Work," p. 400 (sociology "too readily entertains the thought that norms exist"); and Southard, "Psychopathic Delinquents," p. 534 ("ever since Quetelet, with his *Physique Sociale*, we have been ever attempting to establish norms for men, at times forgetting the individual men within their skins"). On psychiatrists and subjectivity, see Glueck, review of Birnbaum, p. 546.

110. Quotations from Corbin, "Backstage," p. 468; and Southard, "Mental Hygiene and Social Work," p. 398.

111. Foucault, *History of Sexuality*, 1, p. 53; Southard and Jarrett, *Kingdom of Evils*, p. 393.

112. Foucault, *Power/Knowledge*, p. 125.

113. On apparent naturalness, see Andrew Ross, "The Everyday Life of Lou Andreas-Salomé: Making Video History," in *Feminism and Psychoanalysis*, ed. Richard Feldstein and Judith Roof (Ithaca, N.Y., 1989), p. 143.

114. Myerson, *Psychology of Mental Disorders*, p. 56.

115. In this they differed significantly from both the nineteenth-century classifiers of sexuality of whom Foucault writes and their contemporary colleagues in frankness, the social hygienists, who were "fundamentally conservative," committed to the preservation of the family (Foucault, *History of Sexuality*, and John C. Burnham, "The Progressive Era Revolution in American Attitudes toward Sex," *Journal of American History* 59 [1972–1973]: 907). See, for example, Myerson, *Psychology of Mental Disorders*, p. 132: "While the home is the keystone of our modern society, and unquestionably operates for good, it also does immeasurable harm to some personalities."

116. This stance of frankness informed the writings of a range of contemporary psychiatrists. For one example, on an apparently unrelated topic, see Michael Osnato, "A Critical Review of the Pathogenesis of Dementia Precox in Its Relation to the Borderline Psychoses," *Neurological Bulletin* 1 (1918): 106–18, which unexcitedly presents an extended case study shot through with sexual shenanigans.

117. Myerson, "Nervous Husband," p. 11. On the drudgery of housewifery, see Myerson, *Nervous Housewife*, chap. 4, and Myerson, *Speaking of Man*, chap. 5.

118. Myerson, *Nervous Housewife*, p. 126; Myerson, "Nervous Husband," p. 11.

119. Myerson, *Nervous Housewife*, pp. 10–13.

120. Myerson, "Nervous Husband," p. 120.

121. On woman's "freedom," see Myerson, *Nervous Housewife*, esp. pp. 11–16; for a nasty tale, see Myerson, *Speaking of Man*, pp. 84–86.

122. Southard, "Individual versus the Family," p. 442; and Southard, "Cross-Sections," p. 108: "Personally I hold, and I think every physician and especially every psychiatrist must hold, that the individual is not only the unit of the physician's interest, but also . . . the unit of the sociologist's interest. This we ought to maintain, I think, against the supposed sociological improvement [that holds] that the family is the social unit."

123. Harry C. Solomon and Maida H. Solomon, "The Family of the Neuro-syphilitic," *Mental Hygiene* 2 (1918): 76.

124. Southard, "Lay Reaction," p. 585.

125. Southard, "Individual versus the Family," p. 443.

126. On iteration as method, see Richard C. Cabot, introduction to Southard and Jarrett, *Kingdom of Evils*, p. xii; quotation from p. 369.

127. Southard and Jarrett, *Kingdom of Evils*, pp. 373, 385–87.

128. Ibid., p. 387. For discussions of the self in the liberal tradition, see Seyla Benhabib and Drucilla Cornell, eds., *Feminism as Critique: On the Politics of Gender* (Minneapolis, 1987).

129. The same might be said regarding the fashionable assertion, current in the history of sexuality, that psychiatrists "invented" the private, which relies on a common (mis)reading of Foucault's argument in *History of Sexuality*, vol. 1. There and elsewhere Foucault focuses on the process by which psychiatrists (and physicians and sexologists—the disciplinary divisions were inexact) constituted "lived experience as evidence" (p. 64) in the service of the human sciences. He details the procedures they employed, considering at length the examination, in which the "inducement to speak" was codified (*Discipline and Punish*, esp. pp. 184–94). But he does not claim that "experience" or "real lives" (p. 192) had no existence. His concern is rather to show how they were fashioned into a form science could apprehend, quite a different project. Barbara Duden, *The Woman beneath the Skin: A Doctor's Patients in Eighteenth-Century Germany*, trans. Thomas Dunlap (Cambridge, Mass., 1991), offers a sophisticated reading of the relationship between experience and science.

130. Lasch, *Haven in a Heartless World*, p. 18: "With the rise of the 'helping professions' in the first three decades of the twentieth century, society in the guise of a 'nurturing mother' invaded the family." I am not quarreling here with the broad outlines of Lasch's argument, but with his portrayal of the family.

131. On men's and women's separate spheres and divergent interests, see, for the middle class, Ryan, *Cradle of the Middle Class*; for the poor and working class, Stansell, *City of Women*. On the violence that the family often sheltered, see Elizabeth H. Pleck, *Domestic Tyranny: The Making of Social Policy against Family Violence from Colonial Times to the Present* (New York, 1987); Linda Gordon, *Heroes of Their Own Lives: The Politics and History of Family Violence, Boston, 1880–1960* (New York, 1988); and Benhabib and Cornell, "Introduction: Beyond the Politics of Gender," in Benhabib and Cornell, *Feminism as Critique*, esp. pp. 10–13.

132. Ryan, *Cradle of the Middle Class*, p. 159. Dorinda Outram, *The Body and the French Revolution: Sex, Class, and Political Culture* (New Haven, 1989), endorsing the argument of Norbert Elias (*The Court Society* [Oxford, 1983]) that in the late eighteenth century the family took over from court society the role of drive and affect control, terms the family coercive and, in a wonderfully suggestive passage, chronicles the travails Mme Roland experienced in breast-feeding her infant, a struggle in which, Outram observes, breast-feeding emerged "as an instrument of emotional domination" (pp. 140–46), a struggle that highlighted the contradictions between the "natural" and the coercive aspects of child-rearing. Kerreen M. Reiger, *The Disenchantment of the Home: Modernizing the Austra-*

lian Family, 1880–1940 (Melbourne, 1985), explores the same contradictions in the context of the efforts of various experts to rationalize the home while at the same time proclaiming certain of its aspects—sex, child-rearing—natural.

133. See, for example, Rieff, *Triumph of the Therapeutic*. Abbott, *System of Professions*, chap. 10, argues a variant of this position, and advances a number of contradictory claims, on the one hand arguing that in the nineteenth century, "angst and maladjustment [were not] subjectively real categories of experience" and that "general unhappiness was a new and newly important cultural fact" (pp. 281, 285), and, on the other, writing as if "personal problems" always existed, arguing that in the wake of the clergy's failure to conceptualize such problems, neurologists and later psychiatrists "invaded" the area (pp. 285ff.). Regarding the psychiatrist's function as cleric, Southard wrote: "Sometimes the physician engaged in such work [handling 'nonmedical' cases] feels as if he were performing the duties of the confessional. Such is not always, or often, the case. If the problem is a confessional problem, the case is forthwith handed to the proper religious authority" ("The Psychopathic Hospital's Function of Early Intensive Service for Persons Not Legally Insane," National Conference of Charities and Correction, *Proceedings* 43, 1916, p. 279).

134. Ellen Ross, *Love and Toil: Motherhood in Outcast London, 1870–1918* (New York, 1993); Stansell, *City of Women*. Cf. Foucault, *History of Sexuality*, 1, p. 111: "The family broadcast the long complaint of its sexual suffering to doctors, educators, psychiatrists, priests, and pastors, to all the 'experts' who would listen"—an overly formal reading that reifies the family's interests.

135. Southard and Jarrett, *Kingdom of Evils*, p. 450.

136. Southard, "Psychopathic Delinquents," p. 531; Southard and Jarrett, *Kingdom of Evils*, p. 375.

137. D. A. Miller, *The Novel and the Police* (Berkeley and Los Angeles, 1988), pp. 17–18.

FOUR: PATHWAYS TO PSYCHIATRIC SCRUTINY

1. Southard and Jarrett, *Kingdom of Evils*, p. 193.

2. Boston State Hospital, *Annual Report* 9, 1918, p. 34.

3. Adolf Meyer emphasized the benefits of liberal admissions policies "towards the normal side" of the patient population and excoriated the "complaining families" of patients as a "real poison militating against . . . early treatment" ("The Wisdom of Endowment of Well-Organized Psychiatric Work" [1913], in *Collected Papers*, 4, pp. 75–76).

4. In 1921, James V. May, superintendent of the Boston State Hospital, noted that twenty-nine states had enacted voluntary laws and fifteen (and the District of Columbia) had enacted temporary care and observation laws ("Laws Controlling Commitments to State Hospitals for Mental Diseases," *Mental Hygiene* 5 [1921]: 540–41). The distinction between the two sorts of statutes is explored below.

5. Adolf Meyer, "The Relation of Psychiatry to Psychology and to Practice" (1938), in *Collected Papers*, 4, p. 497.

6. Massachusetts State Board of Insanity, *Annual Report* 15, 1914, p. 39. For

one among many references to the stigma of insanity and formal commitment, see W. L. Worcester, "What Is Insanity?" *American Journal of Insanity* 52 (1895–1896): 604.

7. Persons were admitted or committed to the institution under a number of statutes, including the voluntary, temporary care, and police laws. The law under which an individual entered the hospital, however, did not always adequately reflect his or her status, nor was it a reliable measure of the reason for hospitalization. The figures presented in the text are derived from assessments I made, after reading entire cases, of what I coded as a "reason for hospitalization" (choosing from among a possible forty reasons). On the hospital sample, see Appendix.

8. Foucault, *History of Sexuality*, 1, p. 86; D. A. Miller, *Novel and the Police*, p. 75.

9. The Massachusetts voluntary admission statute (Chapter 272, Acts of 1881; revised as Chapter 432, Acts of 1905) held that the prospective patient was to sign an application for admission, was to be able to understand the nature of the request, and was to be released within three days of giving written notice of his or her desire to leave. Voluntary admission figures and the text of the law appear in Southard, "Notes on Public Institutional Work in Mental Prophylaxis, with Particular Reference to the Voluntary and 'Temporary Care' Admissions and the 'Not-Insane' Discharges at the Psychopathic Hospital, Boston, 1912–1913," in Massachusetts State Board of Insanity, *Collected Contributions*, no. 2 (Boston, 1914), pp. 1–3. Yearly admissions figures also appear in the board's annual reports.

10. Winfred Overholser, "The Voluntary Admission Law: Certain Legal and Psychiatric Aspects," *American Journal of Psychiatry* 80 (1923–1924): 476, lists the states that had passed voluntary admission laws, and accounted for their numbers by reference to the influence of the American Psychiatric Association. See also John Koren, *Summaries of State Laws Relating to the Insane*, rev. S. W. Hamilton and Roy Haver (1917; reprint, New York, 1980). Richard W. Fox assesses the history of the movement for voluntary admissions in California in *So Far Disordered in Mind*, pp. 56ff. Adolf Meyer was a vocal proponent of voluntary admissions. See, for example, "Reception Hospitals, Psychopathic Wards, and Psychopathic Hospitals" (1907), in *Collected Papers*, 4, pp. 17–23; and "Wisdom of Endowment of Well-Organized Psychiatric Work," pp. 70–77. Richard Dewey, "Commitment to Psychopathic Hospital as Related to Question of Personal Liberty: Advantages of a Proposed Law for Detention Instead of Present Law for Commitment," *Journal of Nervous and Mental Disease* 46 (1917): 279–81, an edited transcript of an address delivered at a meeting of the American Neurological Association and the discussion following, testifies to the popularity of the views advanced by Southard and his colleagues.

11. In fact, laws varied from state to state; see Koren, *Summaries of State Laws*. Gerald Grob categorizes the states' commitment provisions as of 1892: in five states justices of the peace could commit persons; in eighteen judges could; eight states provided for jury trials; five states called on commissions or asylum boards; and nine states "required merely a medical certificate" (*Mental Illness*, p. 10).

12. Overholser, "Voluntary Admission Law," p. 476. The historian Albert Deutsch also referred to the legal "red tape" that regular commitments entailed (*Mentally Ill in America*, p. 431), as did the state-hospital physician C. Floyd

Haviland, citing a colleague who had not followed the letter of the law ("The Commitment of the Insane: Points of Interest to Medical Practitioners," *Long Island Medical Journal* 9 [1915]: 329).

13. E. E. Southard, "Progress of the Psychopathic Hospital on the Prophylactic Side of Mental Hygiene," in Boston Psychopathic Hospital, *Collected Contributions*, no. 18 (Boston, 1914), p. 16.

14. Deutsch, *Mentally Ill in America*, p. 437.

15. See any of the sources cited in this chapter on the question of voluntary admissions; see also Ferris, "Psychopathic Wards," pp. 264–75, which includes a transcript of the discussion following his presentation. Meyer was especially fond of the barbaric-humane distinction; see, for example, "The Problem of the Public Care of the Insane" (1908), in *Collected Papers*, 4, p. 26. Quotations from Frederick A. Fenning, "Voluntary Submission to Treatment and Custody in Hospitals for the Insane," *Journal of the American Medical Association* 58 (1912): 1104–5.

16. The trope of civilization recurs throughout Southard's published and unpublished works. See, for example, "Notes on Public Institutional Work" and "Progress of the Psychopathic Hospital." Quotation from p. 11.

17. Dr. [William A.?] White, recorded in Dewey, "Commitment to Psychopathic Hospital," p. 280.

18. Frankwood E. Williams, "Legislation in Relation to Mental Disease," in Southard and Jarrett, *Kingdom of Evils*, pp. 677–79.

19. Comment of Samuel W. Hamilton, in response to Overholser, "Voluntary Admission Law," pp. 488–89. The complaint that, with respect to administering treatment, psychiatrists were held to a stricter standard than other physicians was common.

20. Massachusetts Senate, *Special Report of the State Board of Insanity to the Massachusetts General Court as to the Best Method of Providing for the Insane*, document no. 358 (Boston, 1908), pp. 28, 7.

21. May, "Laws Controlling Commitments," p. 537; Julian S. Jones, "The Legal Aspect of the Commitment and Detention of the Insane," *Maryland Psychiatric Quarterly* 7 (1917–1918): 70–73.

22. See, for example, Nancy Tomes, *A Generous Confidence: Thomas Story Kirkbride and the Art of Asylum Keeping, 1840–1883* (Cambridge, 1984), pp. 118–28; and Ellen Dwyer, *Homes for the Mad: Life inside Two Nineteenth-Century Asylums* (New Brunswick, N.J., 1987), chap. 3. See also Fox, *So Far Disordered in Mind*, pp. 37–74, for a deft treatment of the medical profession's successful campaign to establish control of the commitment process.

23. Quotation from the text of the 1851 Illinois statute, in Deutsch, *Mentally Ill in America*, p. 423. Elizabeth Packard published several books detailing her misfortunes (among them *The Prisoner's Hidden Life, or Insane Asylums Unveiled* [Chicago, 1868]) and successfully lobbied state legislatures concerning the necessity of instituting procedural safeguards to spare the sane her fate. Historians have judged her efforts effective; Deutsch was careful to note that her books "enjoyed huge sales from which she cleared many thousands of dollars" (*Mentally Ill in America*, p. 424). See also Grob, *Mental Institutions in America*, pp. 263–65. Hendrik Hartog, "Mrs. Packard on Dependency," *Yale Journal of Law and the Humanities* 1 (1988): 79–103, offers a highly original reading of the case.

24. Gerald Grob notes that Massachusetts and New York were the first states to address the issue of the insane with "administrative and bureaucratic" measures (*Mental Illness*, p. 82). Massachusetts established the first Board of State Charities, in 1863, a precursor to the State Board of Health, Lunacy, and Charity, set up in 1879; an autonomous State Board of Insanity was established in 1898. On New York's somewhat different bureaucratic path, and for a discussion of the evolution of states' policies concerning the insane, see Grob, *Mental Illness*, chap. 4.

25. Quotation from Tomes, *Generous Confidence*, p. 118, citing Thomas Story Kirkbride, chief physician of the Pennsylvania Hospital for the Insane from 1841 to 1883, in response to the hospital attorney's suggestion in 1867 that the institution obtain two doctors' certificates (instead of one, which was the current practice) for each patient. Drawing on admittedly inaccurate and incomplete census figures, Grob notes that there were approximately 41,000 institutionalized insane in 1880 (*Mental Illness*, pp. 4, 8). The corresponding figure for 1904 was 150,000 (Bureau of the Census, *Insane and Feeble-Minded in Hospitals and Institutions, 1904* [Washington, D.C., 1906], p. 15). Grob writes that in these years most families "did not find commitment a difficult undertaking or one that involved lawyers and protracted conflict" (pp. 10–11). Frankwood E. Williams, "Legislation for the Insane in Massachusetts, with Particular Reference to the Voluntary Admission and Temporary Care Laws," *Boston Medical and Surgical Journal* 173 (1915): 723–34, sketches, from a contemporary medical perspective, a short history of commitment practices in Massachusetts.

26. On this and other matters, psychiatrists' historical vision was strangely foreshortened. Meyer, for example, wrote that the notion that there should be "special insanity commissions is a residue of an antiquated period" (cited in Grob, *Inner World*, p. 82). And L. Vernon Briggs characterized treatment of the insane in turn-of-the-century Massachusetts as reminiscent of "the dark ages" (Briggs et al., *Psychopathic Hospital*, p. xii).

27. Overholser, "Voluntary Admission Law," p. 475.

28. Quotation from Meyer, "Reception Hospitals," p. 21. Persuasion and inducement are threaded through much of the discussion of voluntary admissions.

29. Overholser, "Voluntary Admission Law," p. 479.

30. Foucault explicates his notion of disciplinary society in *Discipline and Punish*, pp. 195–228 (quotation from p. 209). D. A. Miller succinctly summarizes Foucault's argument in *Novel and the Police*, pp. 16–18. Miller writes that "discipline attenuates the role of actual supervisors by enlisting the consciousness of its subjects in the work of supervision" (p. 18).

31. Case 6327, 1916, case history.

32. Southard, "Progress of the Psychopathic Hospital," p. 12.

33. Case 5008, 1916, letter to psychiatrists.

34. Case 4465, 1915, letter to Dr. Wellington.

35. Overholser, "Voluntary Admission Law," for example, obliquely raised but could not resolve this issue. The patient who was of entirely sound mind hardly needed psychiatric care, and the person of wholly unsound mind could be committed in the "regular" way.

36. Fox argues that awareness of "the fact that commitment was indeed a deprivation of liberty" was suppressed "within the medical profession after 1900" (*So Far Disordered in Mind*, p. 73). I would argue that the issue comes up too often in

psychiatrists' professional writings to support Fox's contention. See, for example, the wide-ranging discussion regarding personal liberty in Dewey, "Commitment to Psychopathic Hospital," a compilation of many psychiatrists' views. Quotation from Adolf Meyer, "Modern Views and Propositions on Enforced Treatment for Mental Diseases" (1917), in *Collected Papers*, 4, p. 129.

37. Southard, "Progress of the Psychopathic Hospital," p. 12.

38. Overholser, "Voluntary Admission Law," p. 479.

39. Case 1586, 1913, letter to psychiatrists. The Massachusetts voluntary statute allowed psychiatrists thirty days in which to decide whether to commit or release a patient.

40. Adolf Meyer, "The Extra-Institutional Responsibilities of State Hospitals for Mental Diseases" (1916), in *Collected Papers*, 4, p. 231. The superintendent of the Westboro Insane Hospital (a Massachusetts institution), George S. Adams, with reasoning similar to Meyer's, explained how he persuaded those voluntary patients who were "undoubtedly insane" not to leave the hospital: "As most of these patients know that if they go away they will be committed, they prefer to remain with the feeling that they are voluntary" ("Voluntary Patients in an Insane Hospital," National Conference of Charities and Correction, *Proceedings* 34, 1907, p. 437).

41. Quotation from Meyer, in Grob, *Inner World*, p. 82.

42. Southard wrote that "every person admitted under the voluntary law is entitled to consider himself in one [unspecified] sense a free man" ("Notes on Public Institutional Work," p. 6).

43. Southard, "Progress of the Psychopathic Hospital," p. 9.

44. Southard, "Notes on Public Institutional Work," p. 3.

45. The woman, who worked in a watch factory, replied that it was "indeed some comfort to know 'Not Insane' stands with my name and I will try to overcome my feeling about it and try to take it as a step up not down" (case 1556, 1915, letter to Southard).

46. Massachusetts Senate, *Best Method of Providing for the Insane*, p. 28.

47. Southard, "Progress of the Psychopathic Hospital," p. 11.

48. Case 12960, 1919, staff meeting.

49. In a discussion of the Thomas case, for example, one psychiatrist told his colleagues that he thought she could be committed but that she should not be "if anyone is willing to take care of her"—the proposal Thomas herself had made, and that had drawn psychiatrists' censure.

50. Litigation psychosis is referred to in Southard and Jarrett, *Kingdom of Evils*, p. 486.

51. Case 3721, 1914, staff meeting.

52. As Southard said to his colleagues in the discussion of Philpott's case, "There is quite a dispute, I see looking over the book, whether all of the litigants are sane really, and the decision seems to be that they are not all" (case 3721, 1914).

53. I located sixteen cases in which patients explicitly raised the issue of their rights in a democratic society.

54. Case 4342, 1916, patient writings.

55. Case 3759, 1914, patient's account and exchange between lawyer and Southard.

56. Boston State Hospital, *Annual Report* 10, 1919, p. 71.

57. Ibid., p. 70.

58. Ibid., p. 89.

59. Southard continually stressed that the Psychopathic Hospital was intended for the treatment of "acute, special, difficult and dubious cases," arguing that "its province is largely distinct from treatment of obviously committable cases" ("Psychopathic Hospital"). Still, approximately half of all patients admitted were committed to other state hospitals (or asylums) upon discharge from the Psychopathic Hospital. Quotation from discussion of case 7820, 1916, staff meeting.

60. Case 3804, 1914, letter to Adler.

61. Quotation from White, recorded in Dewey, "Commitment to Psychopathic Hospital," p. 280.

62. Constitutional provisions that protected persons from deprivation of liberty, Meyer wrote, were often interpreted too narrowly, "without due regard for the existence and nature of police power" of the sort mandated by "legislation on quarantine and health matters" ("Modern Views and Propositions," p. 128). Discussing voluntary admissions, and the need to detain patients "even if they want to go," Meyer wrote that "ours is the rule of the police authority of the health officer" ("Relation of Psychiatry to Psychology," p. 498).

63. Cf. Foucault's suggestion, among a number of hypotheses "which will need exploring," that "relations of power are interwoven with other kinds of relations (production, kinship, family, sexuality)": Foucault, *Power/Knowledge*, p. 142.

64. Case 9817, 1917, patient's mother to psychiatrists.

65. Miller, *Novel and the Police*, pp. 58–60. On intrafamily regulation, see the account of the supervision "Madame B." exercised over her children in Bonnie G. Smith, *Ladies of the Leisure Class: The Bourgeoises of Northern France in the Nineteenth Century* (Princeton, 1981), p. 64: "She kept a notebook on the strengths and weaknesses of each, wrung from them their most intimate thoughts, heard their lessons, rewarded and punished their actions. . . . To 'purge them of all evil thoughts and actions,' she rewarded the obedient at the end of each week and punished the disobedient by withholding her love in the form of a goodnight kiss." The kiss excepted and the identities altered, the account could have come from Foucault's *Discipline and Punish*.

66. Case 5306, 1915, letter from patient's sister-in-law to psychiatrists.

67. Case 8043, 1916, case record.

68. Examples from case 5879, 1916, various neighbors speaking of other neighbors (not necessarily with reference to patient).

69. Case 6595, 1916, letters to H. C. Solomon and M. Solomon.

70. Case 7794, 1914, statement of wife.

71. Case 830, 1913, case history.

72. "Family patients" were drawn from all of the city's ethnic and racial groups in proportions equal to their representation in its population, and they came from the working and middle classes in proportions similar to those of Boston's population: 32 percent of the men brought by families worked at white-collar occupations, for example; between 32 (in 1910) and 35 percent (in 1920) of Boston's male population was white-collar. Fox, *So Far Disordered in Mind*, pp. 83–85, also found that relatives predominated (57 percent of cases) among those who petitioned for others' commitment for insanity.

73. This finding is based primarily on quantitative results presented in the Appendix, but also on readings of cases and of a scant secondary literature. With respect to patterns of commitment, I have drawn tentative conclusions about the importance of class, race, ethnicity, and behavior by examining the characteristics of patients who were committed. But because I cannot perform multivariate analyses on these data (due to the way in which census figures for the population from which patients were drawn were tabulated, and because I have no way of controlling for "behavior" in the population from which they were drawn), I cannot determine which of these factors, if any, was most important and which, if any, were of little consequence. In this section, I have relied on results of multivariate analyses of the patient population at the moment of discharge (when patients were either sent home or committed to asylums); these show definitively that the attitudes of Jews differed from those of everyone else, regardless of class and the patient's behavior.

74. Mark Zborowski and Elizabeth Herzog, *Life Is with People: The Culture of the Shtetl* (New York, 1952), p. 356 (findings echoed in Jacob Jay Lindenthal, "*Abi Gesunt*: Health and the East European Jewish Immigrant," *American Jewish History* 70 [1981]: 420–21); Southard and Jarrett, *Kingdom of Evils*, p. 328; H. Oppenheim, "Zur Psychopathologie und Nosologie der russisch-jüdischen Bevölkerung," *Journal für Psychologie und Neurologie* 13 (1908): 4.

75. Case 6776, 1916, case record. Removing a patient against advice was a formal, regulated procedure (see Appendix).

76. Charlotte Adland, "Attitudes of Eastern European Jews Toward Mental Disease: A Cultural Interpretation," *Smith College Studies in Social Work* 8 (1937): 85–116.

77. Case 7013, 1916, social service record.

78. Case 6902, 1917, staff meeting. Pleck, *Black Migration and Poverty*, observes that "the Irish poor tended . . . to rely on state institutions to aid their needy" (p. 196).

79. For his part, Farrell, who had worked as an elevator operator at the courthouse, told social workers that he had "political friends"—among them John Fitzgerald, senator-elect of Ward 8 (John F. Kennedy's maternal grandfather)—who would secure him a job once he stopped drinking. Case 7064, 1916, letters from mother to social worker Warren, social service record.

80. Case 5937, 1915, Anna C. Wellington (Psychopathic Hospital executive assistant) to E. H. Cohoon (administrator), on the interventions of one senator; she listed six "political pressure cases," all with Irish names. In a report (marked "confidential") prepared for hospital trustees and members of the State Board of Insanity, Southard noted that in October 1914, seven cases came before the board "because various friends, relatives and legislators said they should be at Psychopathic Hospital when medically they did not belong there. Considerable complaint; little or no basis therefor." In addition, he noted, "there are almost weekly complaints from friends and relatives who wish to have cases retained at the Psychopathic Hospital on account of its supposed superior treatment." Relatives, Southard wrote, regularly enlisted "members of the legislature in their behalf. . . . There are from 2 to 8 or 10 cases in the Psychopathic Hospital at any time which do not medically belong there" ("Extract from Report of Director of Psycho-

pathic Hospital to the Trustees of Boston State Hospital, February 1915," in "Notes to Trustees," Boston Psychopathic Hospital, bound volumes in Countway Library of Medicine).

81. Zborowski and Herzog, *Life Is with People*, p. 356.

82. Case 1282, 1913, patient writings.

83. For example, case 5805, 1915.

84. Case 3424, 1913, letter to psychiatrists.

85. Case 5172, 1915, letter from niece to social worker.

86. Case 4798, 1915, letter from sister of patient to social workers.

87. Case 7064, 1917, letter from patient's brother to social workers.

88. Cases 7555, 1916, social service record; 8797, 1917, letter from patient's husband to patient's brother; 5441, 1915, letter from stepfather to psychiatrists.

89. Cases 9112, 1917, case history; 3127, 1914, letter from patient's cousins to social workers; 6789, 1916, letter from patient's aunts to Southard.

90. Case 10248, 1919, letter from patient's niece to psychiatrists.

91. I rely here on the argument advanced by Wendy Brown, "Finding the Man in the State," *Feminist Studies* 18 (1992): 7–34 (quotation from p. 20); and Gordon, *Heroes of Their Own Lives*, p. 256. I am especially indebted to Gordon's insightful treatment of wife-beating. On liberalism and the family, see also Benhabib and Cornell, introduction to *Feminism as Critique*, esp. pp. 10–13.

92. Case 2579, 1914, case history.

93. Cases 1111, 1913; 1279, 1913; 11691, 1918.

94. Myerson, *Nervous Housewife*, pp. 130–31.

95. Case 1111, 1913, staff meeting.

96. Southard and Jarrett, *Kingdom of Evils*, p. 194.

97. Case 1111, 1913, staff meeting and case history.

98. Ibid. On not having done anything, cf. psychiatrists' discussion in the case of another man, which revolved around whether he could be committed as a pest and a nuisance and for "making life miserable for everybody," even though he had not done anything: case 8851, 1917, staff meeting.

99. Case 1111, 1913.

100. Gordon, *Heroes of Their Own Lives*, chap. 8, makes this point.

101. Case 4198, 1914, examining physician's report, commitment papers, staff meeting. Fitzpatrick was committed under the Emergency Law (Section 42, Chapter 504, Acts 1909), which provided for the temporary detention (for up to five days without a court order) of persons certified as violently and dangerously insane by two physicians. The law allowed the police to bring such persons to the hospital without having to arrest or jail them while seeking a formal commitment. After several days in the institution, Fitzpatrick was committed for an additional sixty days.

102. Case 4916, 1916, letter to psychiatrists.

103. Case 9759, 1917, letter to husband.

104. Case 6595, 1916, letter to social worker Maida Solomon.

105. Southard and Jarrett, *Kingdom of Evils*, pp. 386–87.

106. Myerson, "Nervous Husband," p. 123.

107. Case 1282, 1913, case history, staff meeting, letters to lawyer and Adler, newspaper clipping.

108. Ibid., case report, letters from patient to lawyer, newspaper clipping.

109. Ten percent turned themselves over to police, and 10 percent were cases in which a family turned one of its own over to police. The number of patients admitted under the provision of the police law is not an accurate measure of the number of patients police actually brought to the hospital, for they registered some of those they apprehended under the provisions of the temporary care law.

110. Case 5879, 1915, social service record. For suggestive commentary on popular justice and the significance of "delivering up," see Michael Ignatieff, "Total Institutions and Working Classes: A Review Essay," *History Workshop* 15 (Spring 1983): 170–71.

111. Case 12993, 1919, case history.

112. Case 4284, 1915, social service record.

113. Case 8851, 1917, staff meeting.

114. Case 1111, 1913, staff meeting.

115. Case 6682, 1916, social service record.

116. Case 3212, 1914, staff meeting.

117. Police brought one-quarter of all patients to the hospital; 470 is approximately one-quarter of each year's admissions from 1913 through 1920. Neither this estimate nor this discussion includes the (relatively few) persons charged with serious crimes—murder, sexual offenses, larceny, and fraud—whom judges sent to the hospital for observation under indictment. Police department *Annual Reports* indicate that the police took 400 insane "in charge" annually. The overlap among these 400 insane, the 470 police patients, and the hundreds arrested for "nuisance" crimes is impossible to determine.

118. In 1910, the population of Boston was 670,585; by 1920 it had grown to 748,060. Approximately a third of those arrested were not residents of Boston, and nearly half of those arrested for drunkenness were nonresidents. Police arrested men ten times as frequently as women; the gender ratio of those arrested for drunkenness was ten to one as well. "Foreigners" constituted approximately 40 percent of all arrests, a proportion roughly equal to their representation in the adult population. Although only 10 percent of those arrested were minors, approximately 35 percent were nonresidents. Therefore, the relationship between the nativity of the population and that of those arrested can only be estimated. For a discussion of the problem of drunkenness in Boston and Massachusetts, see Maurice Farr Parmelee, *Inebriety in Boston* (New York, 1909). Leonard V. Harrison, *Police Administration in Boston* (Cambridge, Mass., 1934), p. 14, argues that police policy on the question of arrests for drunkenness remained essentially the same from 1910 to 1925. The rate of arrest for drunkenness proportional to the total population grew steadily from 1900 to a peak in 1915; from 1915 to 1920 the rate fell sharply.

119. *Rules and Regulations for the Government of the Police Department of the City of Boston* (Boston, 1909), pp. 252–53.

120. Boston Police Law (Chapter 307, Acts 1910).

121. Due to the way demographic data were tabulated in census reports, there is no way to address directly whether the police held the foreign-born or the poor to a more exacting behavioral standard than they exercised in dealing with "respectable," native-born Americans, more often deeming the behavior of the former

strange and irrational, indicative of insanity. See Appendix for statistics regarding police patients.

122. Boston State Hospital, *Annual Report* 8, 1917, p. 36.

123. Boston State Hospital, *Annual Report* 10, 1919, p. 70.

124. See Grob, *Mental Illness*, pp. 195–98, on the changing nature of institutional populations.

125. Southard, "Progress of the Psychopathic Hospital," p. 15.

126. In many respects the hospital's population closely resembled the population of persons committed for insanity, under the provision of similar laws, in San Francisco in roughly the same period; in both cities, the relationship between the institutionalized population and the city population from which it was drawn is similar. Compare, for example, Fox, *So Far Disordered in Mind*, table 9, p. 115, to table A.4 below; in both cities, approximately 25 percent of institutionalized men were middle-class, drawn from a population in which approximately 33 percent of all men were middle-class.

127. Grob, *Mental Illness*, pp. 236–43, discusses the evolution of psychiatric practice in a noninstitutional direction.

FIVE: CLASSIFICATION

1. Case 1494, 1913, letter to governor of Massachusetts.

2. Southard's use of philosophical language and terms of his own invention sparked some commentary among his contemporaries. Following an address in which he had used, inter alia, the terms *eudemics* and *euthenics*, Katherine Bement Davis—holder of a University of Chicago Ph.D., at the time chairperson of the Parole Commission of New York City—commented, "I believe I understand what he was talking about. . . . Unfortunately, I never have been able to learn big words, and I cannot remember the ones he has used" ("Discussion," following Southard, "Social Research in Public Institutions," National Conference of Charities and Correction, *Proceedings* 43, 1916, p. 386). Likewise, at a conference sponsored by the Massachusetts State Board of Insanity, one lay institutional trustee complained of having to listen to superintendents "making remarks . . . very far over our heads; that is, such that we as ordinary laymen have no mental comprehension of what is being talked about, and, with all deference to Dr. Southard, I feel that his paper, with my mental comprehension, was of that character." Identifying himself as "a country boy," another layman added his assent, saying he suspected that when his associates "want to put anything over on me they use the same terms that Dr. Southard does" (Massachusetts State Board of Insanity, *Annual Report* 16, 1915, pp. 236–38).

3. Karl Menninger, for example, wrote of classification, "Someone has suggested that this is almost an avocation—a veritable addiction—of psychiatrists, this defining new syndromes and reordering them" (*Vital Balance*, p. 11). Menninger, who received his M.D. from Harvard Medical School in 1917 and did postgraduate work (a six-month stint) at the Boston Psychopathic Hospital, founded one of the nation's best-known psychiatric institutions, the Menninger Clinic in Topeka, Kansas, and became one of twentieth-century psychiatry's great popularizers. He considered Southard his mentor, by his own account "spent every

available moment with him" (Friedman, *Menninger*, p. 31), and wrote in defense of his classificatory enthusiasms (see, for example, *Vital Balance*, pp. 470–72). He also, however, deemed Southard a "superficialist," writing that Southard depended "upon deductive logic and philosophical extensions" rather than "deep subsurface analysis," Freud's metier (Bernard H. Hall, ed., *A Psychiatrist's World: The Selected Papers of Karl Menninger, M.D.* [New York, 1959], p. 815, also cited in Friedman, *Menninger,* p. 30). On Menninger, see, in addition to Friedman's study, Howard J. Faulkner and Virginia D. Pruitt, introduction to *The Selected Correspondence of Karl A. Menninger, 1919–1945,* ed. Faulkner and Pruitt (New Haven, 1988).

4. See Michel Foucault, *The Birth of the Clinic: An Archaelogy of Medical Perception*, trans. A. M. Sheridan Smith (New York, 1975), chap. 1, and Jan Goldstein, *Console and Classify: The French Psychiatric Profession in the Nineteenth Century* (Cambridge, 1987), p. 5. On the germ theory, see Lester S. King, *Medical Thinking: A Historical Preface* (Princeton, 1982), p. 297, where he asserts that "the great progress in bacteriology probably did more to underscore the importance of science in medicine than did any other single advance."

5. In proposing this reading I take my cues, in part, from Foucault and from Jan Goldstein's brilliant explication: "Foucault among the Sociologists: The 'Disciplines' and the History of the Professions," *History and Theory* 23 (1984): 170–92.

6. Quotation above from E. E. Southard, "Recent American Classifications of Mental Diseases," *American Journal of Insanity* 75 (1918–1919): 339.

7. Adolf Meyer, "A Few Trends in Modern Psychiatry" (1904), in *Collected Papers,* 2, p. 397.

8. Emil Kraepelin, *Manic-Depressive Insanity and Paranoia,* trans. R. Mary Barclay, ed. George M. Robertson (1921; reprint, New York, 1976).

9. Several short excerpts from the Kraepelinian corpus have recently appeared, some newly translated. See, for example, "Patterns of Mental Disorder," which appeared in 1920, in *Themes and Variations in European Psychiatry: An Anthology,* ed. Steven R. Hirsch and Michael Shepherd (Charlottesville, Va., 1974), pp. 7–30; and the several selections on dementia praecox and manic-depressive insanity in Thompson, *Origins of Modern Psychiatry,* pp. 225–58. Kraepelin's *Lebenserinnerungen* have recently been translated and published: *Memoirs,* trans. Cheryl Wooding-Deane (Berlin, 1987). See Roger K. Blashfield, *The Classification of Psychopathology: Neo-Kraepelinian and Quantitative Approaches* (New York, 1984), for a discussion of the current revival of interest in Kraepelin.

10. See Meyer, "Trends in Modern Psychiatry," for a discussion of this.

11. In "Dementia Praecox," a translation of pp. 426–41 of the fifth edition of *Psychiatrie* (Leipzig, 1896), in *The Clinical Roots of the Schizophrenia Concept,* ed. John Cutting and M. Shepherd (Cambridge, 1987), Kraepelin noted that although he thought it likely a "tangible morbid process occurring in the brain" lay at the root of the changes characteristic of dementia praecox, it was "true that morbid anatomy has so far been quite unable to help us here" (p. 23). Better methods, he speculated, would possibly enable researchers to identify morbid changes.

12. Menninger, *Vital Balance,* p. 457. Southard, who would come under the dynamicists' unfavorable scrutiny, participated in forging the critique of the Ger-

man tradition. "Early in this century a flood of Teutonic verbiage overflowed the field," he wrote in 1918 ("Insanity versus Mental Diseases," p. 1259); the next year he wrote that psychiatrists' "own obscurantism has blocked progress" ("Range of the General Practitioner," p. 1253).

13. Hall, *Psychiatrist's World*, p. 678.

14. See Blashfield, *Classification of Psychopathology*, pp. 1–83, for a discussion of recent diagnostic controversies.

15. In, say, 1910, the "science" of medicine and the "science" of psychiatry were not qualitatively much different.

16. See King, *Medical Thinking*, pp. 73–89, for a discussion of the historically important distinction between signs and symptoms.

17. Southard, "Recent American Classifications," p. 338.

18. E. E. Southard, "A Key to the Practical Grouping of Mental Diseases," *Journal of Nervous and Mental Disease* 47 (1918): 2. See also Southard, "Applications of the Pragmatic Method to Psychiatry," *Journal of Laboratory and Clinical Medicine* 5 (1919): 139–45.

19. E. E. Southard, "Diagnosis per Exclusionem in Ordine: General and Psychiatric Remarks," *Journal of Laboratory and Clinical Medicine* 4 (1918): 33. Lowrey expanded on this article: "A Note on Southard's Order of Exclusion in Psychiatric Diagnosis," *Boston Medical and Surgical Journal* 180 (1919): 515–19.

20. Southard, "The Psychopathic Hospital."

21. William A. White, "The Geographical Distribution of Insanity in the United States," *Journal of Nervous and Mental Disease* 30 (1903): 279. The contemporary literature on immigration and insanity was voluminous; Örnulv Ödegaard, "Emigration and Insanity: A Study of Mental Disease among the Norwegianborn Population of Minnesota," *Acta Psychiatrica et Neurologica*, supp. 4 (1932), is an early literature review. Ödegaard notes that the first article to frame the problem of insane foreigners appeared in 1850; nothing appeared between then and 1880, when a number of articles that analyzed asylum admission figures across national groups appeared in professional journals. After several more years, the issue died again, reappearing only after the turn of the century, when eugenically minded articles flooded the journals.

22. Figure from John Higham, *Strangers in the Land: Patterns of American Nativism, 1860–1925* (New York, 1975), p. 159. Higham's classic work, originally published in 1963, has not been superseded; I have relied on its insights, but have not been able to convey its subtleties, in this and the following paragraphs.

23. Quotations from Harry H. Laughlin, "Analysis of the Metal and the Dross in America's Modern Melting Pot," in U.S. Congress, House Committee on Immigration and Naturalization, *Hearings*, 67th Cong., 3d sess., Nov. 1922. Laughlin was superintendent of the Eugenics Record Office in Cold Spring Harbor. John Higham points out that the House Committee on Immigration and Naturalization (the Johnson Committee) appointed Laughlin its "expert eugenics agent" after he first testified before the committee. In 1923, Albert Johnson was elected president of the Eugenics Research Association at Cold Spring Harbor (*Strangers in the Land*, p. 314). Oscar Handlin, *Race and Nationality in American Life* (New York, 1957), chap. 5, analyzes Laughlin's distortions. Laughlin failed to correct his figures for the age distribution of the immigrant population and he used population

figures from the 1910 rather than the 192J census; consequently, his estimates of the immigrant insane were too high. More important, his flawed statistical method rendered his figures meaningless.

24. From the hospital Patelsky wrote to his lawyer, who had an Irish name, that he would describe the place to him "and you will be able to say that you had for once one Jew client who wrote you a brief letter from the Boston State Hospital for the feeble minded" (case 1282, 1913). Geary: case 1515, 1913.

25. In this and the following paragraphs, I have capitalized terms in accordance with psychiatrists' usage.

26. The new form was adopted around March 1916.

27. The system of racial classification in use at the Psychopathic Hospital was not unique. Charles W. Burr explained the system used at the Philadelphia General Hospital, in which "only the country of birth is recorded, not the race. Hebrews are not recorded as such. . . . [but] credited to the lands in which they were born" ("The Foreign-Born Insane: A Racial Study of the Patients Admitted to the Insane Department of the Philadelphia General Hospital in Ten Years [1903–1912]," *Journal of the American Medical Association* 62 [1914]: 25).

28. Case 7441, 1916, staff meeting. The psychiatrist who referred to his "racial characteristics" was himself Jewish. On the purported Jewishness of neurosis, Southard and Jarrett wrote that "in one of the great Atlantic seaboard hospitals (which shall be nameless) there used to be an out-patient department diagnosis *Judaism.*" Although noting that "there is some basis for the idea of a preponderance of psychoneurotics amongst Jews," they attributed it to the Jews' "excellent habit . . . of very speedily resorting to physicians for their ills" and concluded that "it would be difficult to point out anything really differential in the psychology of the Jew" (*Kingdom of Evils*, p. 328). There is a large literature on the subject of Jewish nervousness; see, for example, *The Jewish Encyclopedia*, s.v. "Nervous Diseases." Among other instances of psychiatrists and psychologists classing Jews as neurotic are G. E. Partridge, "Psychopathic Personalities among Boys in a Training School for Delinquents," *American Journal of Psychiatry* 85 (1928–1929): 177 (reference to an overindulged boy having a "Jew complex"); case 10131, 1918, staff meeting (the overexcitability of a woman attributed to her "race").

29. Case 9134, 1917, staff meeting. Of another man, classed as racially Irish, Myerson noted, "The wit and humor are likely for his race" (case 11691, 1918, staff meeting).

30. Case 10032, 1918, staff meeting. For contemporary commentary on the racial character of African-Americans, see Mary O'Malley, "Psychoses in the Colored Race: A Study in Comparative Psychiatry," *American Journal of Insanity* 71 (1914–1915): 309–37; John E. Lind, "Diagnostic Pitfalls in the Examinations of Negroes," *New York Medical Journal* 89 (1914): 1286–87; and W. M. Bevis, "Psychological Traits of the Southern Negro with Observations as to Some of His Psychoses," *American Journal of Psychiatry* 78 (1921–1922): 69–78.

31. This is not to absolve psychiatrists of racism. Rather, these sorts of determinations often resulted from comparisons between two groups, unfavorable to both. As one physician explained: "The stolidity and indifference of the Slav would suggest melancholia if presented by the Hebrew. The sanity of an Englishman would be questioned if on slight provocation he evinced the external manifestation

of emotion that would occur in the Sicilian. . . . Some races are extremely emotional, others slow; and unless the normal is known it is impossible to pick the abnormal" (A. J. Nute, "Medical Inspection of Immigrants at the Port of Boston," *Boston Medical and Surgical Journal* 170 [1914]: 645).

32. Alcoholic disorders are discussed in chapter 9; feeblemindedness in chapter 3; the psychoneuroses in chapters 8 (female patients, many of them hysterics) and 9 (male patients); and psychopathic personality in chapters 3, 7 (female), and 9 (male).

33. Southard and Jarrett, *Kingdom of Evils*, p. 458. A specimen of blood was taken from every patient; if a positive result was obtained, the patient's cerebrospinal fluid was examined (E. E. Southard, "The Internal Organization of the Psychopathic Hospital," MS, Southard Papers). The term *neurosyphilis* encompassed six different forms of disease.

34. The male to female ratio of neurosyphilitic patients was 5:1.

35. Case 8773, 1917, letters from patient to Lowrey.

36. Case 7418, 1916, letter from sister to psychiatrists.

37. Lawson G. Lowrey noted that the diagnoses dementia praecox and manic-depressive insanity were first used at Danvers State Hospital in 1903 ("Notes on the Psychiatry of 1895 and of 1915," *Journal of Nervous and Mental Disease* 54 [1921]: 97–106). Southard, "The Psychopathic Hospital," referred to dementia praecox and manic-depressive insanity as diseases "young in science," and elsewhere noted that Kraepelin had introduced the term *dementia praecox* as recently as 1899 ("Non-Dementia Non-Praecox: Note on the Advantages to Mental Hygiene of Extirpating a Term," MS, Southard Papers; the French alienist Bénédict-Augustin Morel had used the similar term *demence precoce* as early as 1858, but Kraepelin was the first to use it to refer to a distinct clinical entity). Menninger, recalling nearly fifty years after his Psychopathic Hospital experience that nearly all patients were diagnosed "dementia praecox" (his memory was faulty—the proportion was in fact 26 percent), wrote, "We dutifully employed historic designations and historic concepts associated with them" (*Vital Balance*, pp. 1–2)—an example of psychiatrists' tendency to foreshorten their own history.

38. Southard, "Non-Dementia Non-Praecox." In "Shell Shock and After," *Boston Medical and Surgical Journal* 174 (1918): 83, Southard noted that he intended "to write a paper entitled '*Non-dementia, Non-praecox*,'" which he did, but he never published it.

39. Case 7518, 1916, staff meeting.

40. Case 9949, 1917, letter to attorney general of Massachusetts.

41. Southard, "Non-Dementia Non-Praecox" (emphasis in original); case 6693, 1916, staff meeting. See also Southard and Jarrett, *Kingdom of Evils*, pp. 298–99: "perhaps no more unfortunate term than dementia praecox has yet been devised."

42. Southard defended Kraepelin against the attacks of dynamic psychiatrists like Adolf Meyer, writing that Kraepelin had "virtually given up on the Dementia Praecox idea in its original form" ("Non-Dementia Non-Praecox"). Helm Stierlin, "Bleuler's Concept of Schizophrenia: A Confusing Heritage," *American Journal of Psychiatry* 123 (1966–1967): 996–1001, summarizes Bleuler's work, highlights his differences with Kraepelin, and chronicles his brief advocacy of a Freudian perspective.

43. Case 12066, 1919. This was the first case I found that was diagnosed with the term "schizophrenia." Southard canvassed his colleagues nationwide on the suitability of the new term; August Hoch wrote that he was "not specially pleased with schizophrenia. It is a rather uncouth term, and I remember, when it first came out, how I balked at it and how, . . . at the New York Psychiatrical Society, all of them made a lot of fun of the term" ("Dr. August Hoch writes me . . . ," MS, Southard Papers).

44. Case 7628, 1918, letters and staff meeting.

45. Case 7523, 1916, case report.

46. Southard and Jarrett, *Kingdom of Evils*, p. 423.

47. H. Douglas Singer, "A Case of Ambulatory Automatism," in *Archives of Neurology and Psychiatry* 9 (1923): 347–57, an account of case 11676 from the Psychopathic Hospital.

48. See Foucault, *Discipline and Punish*, pp. 190–94, a particularly lucid and incisive passage that sums up, improves on, and slightly alters the interpretation put forth in *Birth of the Clinic*. Goldstein, "Foucault among the Sociologists," offers a reading of this.

49. Methods of record keeping varied widely from one institution to another; McLean Hospital, for example, was known for its long records (Massachusetts State Board of Insanity, *Annual Report* 14, 1913, p. 35).

50. This view was expressed in Massachusetts State Board of Insanity, *Annual Report* 16, 1915, pp. 201–41, transcript of a state-sponsored conference on "uniformity of hospital records and better classification of patients." On the transition from casebooks to files in medicine, see discussion in Massachusetts State Board of Insanity, *Annual Report* 11, 1910, pp. 182–203, transcript of a state-sponsored conference on "clerical medical work in State hospitals"; Stanley Joel Reiser, "Creating Form out of Mass: The Development of the Medical Record," in *Transformation and Tradition in the Sciences: Essays in Honor of I. Bernard Cohen*, ed. Everett Mendelsohn (Cambridge, 1984), pp. 307ff.; and Barbara L. Craig, "The Role of Records and of Record-Keeping in the Development of the Modern Hospital in London, England, and Ontario, Canada, c. 1890–c. 1940," *Bulletin of the History of Medicine* 65 (1991): 376–97. Ruth Leys, "Types of One: Adolf Meyer's Life Chart and the Representation of Individuality," *Representations* 34 (Spring 1991): 1–28, discusses technologies in the context of Meyer's record keeping conventions.

51. Massachusetts State Board of Insanity, *Annual Report* 11, 1910, p. 191.

52. On the dictating machine, see ibid., pp. 193–202 (quotation of Southard from p. 193). The all-female stenographic staff of the Psychopathic Hospital earned between $480 (for the three who lived in the institution) and $660 yearly ("Classification of Stenographers and Typewriters," in "Notes to Trustees").

53. Craig, "Role of Records," p. 394.

54. Southard to Henry Lefavour, 11 January 1915, in "Notes to Trustees."

55. Foucault, *Discipline and Punish*, p. 191.

56. E. E. Southard, "Notes on James," MS, Southard Papers.

57. E. E. Southard, "Possible Sources for 'Psychiatry of the Individual' or 'Personal Psychiatry,'" MS, Southard Papers.

58. Southard, "Psychological Wants of Psychiatrists."

59. E. E. Southard, "Individual Psychiatry," MS, Southard Papers.

60. E. E. Southard, "Mental Hygiene," MS, Southard Papers; Massachusetts State Board of Insanity, *Annual Report* 11, 1910, p. 46.

61. E. E. Southard, "Dementia Praecox Brain Material," MS, Southard Papers.

62. E. E. Southard to Frederick Parker Gay, 20 March 1919 and 10 April 1919, Southard Papers.

63. Southard, "Individual Psychiatry."

64. E. E. Southard, "Individual Disposition," MS, Southard Papers; Southard, "Usages of the Term *Person*," MS, Southard Papers.

65. E. E. Southard, "Jean-Martin Charcot," MS, Southard Papers.

66. E. E. Southard, "Charcot as Casuist," MS, Southard Papers. For an exemplary statement of the psychiatrist's allegiance to "facts," see Meyer, "Trends in Modern Psychiatry."

67. Foucault, *Discipline and Punish*, p. 187. Foucault writes, "It is the fact of being constantly seen, of being able always to be seen, that maintains the disciplined individual in his subjugation."

68. Ibid., pp. 184–89.

69. Case 7504, 1916, autobiographical account. "I hope some day to copy this over in decent writing," Moran wrote, in a very precise hand, at the end of her account.

70. Ibid.

71. Southard located the staff meeting in the history of psychiatry's progress, contrasting the "extreme democracy and freedom" that he argued characterized it to the autocratic ways of the alienists, with their "*ex parte* opinions" (Boston State Hospital, *Annual Report* 8, 1917, pp. 45, 70). Various psychiatrists—among them Adolf Meyer, Edward Cowles, and Southard—claimed credit for (or were credited with) establishing the staff meeting or conference method in psychiatry.

72. Case 770, 1913, staff meeting.

73. Case 8498, 1917, staff meeting.

74. Case 1546, 1913, staff meeting.

75. Case 8498, 1917, staff meeting.

76. Case 13058, 1919, staff meeting.

77. Case 7504, 1916, autobiographical account.

78. Case 6964, 1916, letter to social worker.

79. Case 4568, 1915, letter from sister of patient to Southard.

80. Case 3748, 1914, letter to unspecified physician.

81. E. E. Southard, "The Atmosphere of Psychopathic Hospitals and the Question of Terms Taboo *Coram Publico Psychopathico*," MS, Southard Papers.

82. Case 4339, 1914, staff meeting.

83. E. E. Southard, "Jean-Martin Charcot."

84. Case 11077, 1918, staff meeting.

85. "There are lots of ways that you big clever fellows can turn me over, and I would not know it at all," White told the psychiatrists, and suggested therefore that since he was trying to get himself "out of this thing the easiest way possible," they ask him as few and as simple questions as they could. "I don't like to be considered something that is peculiar when I tried to be my natural best, to be a man amongst men." Case 9300, 1917, staff meeting.

86. Case 9006, 1917, letter to psychiatrists.

87. Case 9658, 1917, staff meeting. "Everybody is a little queer," she replied. Lowrey asked her, "Are you?" "Certainly," she answered. "So are you."

88. "Everyone has a right to think it," he replied. "It is not a sin, is it?" Case 8851, 1917, staff meeting.

89. "That is the most absurd thing," was her answer. Case 12960, 1919, staff meeting.

90. Case 2363, 1913, staff meeting.

91. Case 8300, 1918, staff meeting.

92. She explained that he "persuaded" her to say she heard voices; in fact, she protested, she meant to say she heard *his* voice, but "did not want to be impudent in saying to leave off the S." In addition, a "Visiting Italian Jew Doctor, Dr. Lodgeni," also mistakenly noted that she had delusions. She explained how the misunderstanding arose, and added that in light of her "perfectly clear memory she found it surprising that a question of doubt would not arise among a body of professional men on such a *thing* as a delusion." "It is no wonder," she added, "that the public loses confidence in many physicians." Case 5280, 1915, letter to Southard.

93. Case 921, 1913, letter to Dr. Frost.

94. Case 2320, 1914, letter to psychiatrists.

95. Case 3862, 1914, letter from Southard to a professor at Harvard University discussing the case of a young woman who had under questioning admitted to "illicit intercourse," an admission that S ʌuthard thought "was based on facts" though he clearly had some doubts about it.

96. Case 1258, 1913, staff meeting, contains an extended discussion of "shamming" or "putting on."

97. Case 691, 1912, prepared statement for the press. Underscoring psychiatrists' neutrality, Southard went on to say that "the extent of the boy's simulation goes far to prove that his personality is in many respects exceptional and of decidedly scientific interest." He added, "We were in no wise deceived as to his symptoms, feigned or otherwise."

98. Case 10031, 1917, staff meeting.

99. Case 4339, 1915, staff meeting.

100. The historian has no choice but to accept each of an individual's tales as in some sense "true," while reserving the right to weigh their various claims.

101. Case 4339, 1915, staff meeting.

102. Case 7798, 1916, staff meeting; and E. E. Southard, "Structure vs. Function in Psychopathology," MS, paper read at the 1912 meeting of the American Psychological Association, Southard Papers.

103. Southard, "Range of the General Practitioner," p. 1255.

104. Southard commented at length on the medical commonplace that diagnosis (even, by some accounts, the whole of medicine) was constituted solely of observation ("Diagnosis per Exclusionem in Ordine," pp. 31ff.).

105. Southard, "Range of the General Practitioner," p. 1255.

106. Case 9296, 1917, staff meeting.

107. Southard remarked of one man, "I am rather impressed that the hallucinations are within the range of a Roman Catholic—one brought up on holy pictures and the like has these devils so in the mind's eye" (case 7518, 1916, staff meeting).

108. Case 11199, 1918, staff meeting.

109. E. E. Southard, "The Nature of Delusions," MS, Southard Papers. The historian might venture, alternatively, that many "truths" made up the case.

110. Case 4131, 1915, staff meeting and letter to friend.

111. Southard, "What Is a Psychopathic Hospital?" MS, address delivered at Springfield State Hospital, 1915, Southard Papers.

112. Quotation from Southard and Jarrett, *Kingdom of Evils*, p. 295. Well aware that the issue of "error" was highly charged, likely to redound to their detriment if publicized, psychiatrists proffered different error rates to different audiences. In the professional literature, they placed the rate in the 20 to 25 percent range. To a patient's insurance company, however, Southard suggested that the rate was a far more acceptable 10 percent (case 4878, 1916).

113. Quotation from Lawson G. Lowrey, "Differential Diagnosis in Psychiatry: A Comparison of Symptoms in Various Disease States," *Boston Medical and Surgical Journal* 178 (1918): 703. Southard admitted that "our staff has been inclined . . . to call cases dementia praecox a bit too freely," and added that he felt "extreme dogmatism . . . unwise in the differential diagnosis of dementia praecox and manic-depressive psychosis" ("The Psychopathic Hospital"). Other discussions of the issue include Lowrey, "An Analysis of the Accuracy of Psychopathic Hospital Diagnoses," *American Journal of Insanity* 75 (1918–1919): 351–70; Lowrey, "A Study of the Diagnoses in Cases Seen at the Psychopathic Department and Hospital Department of the Boston State Hospital," *American Journal of Insanity* 77 (1920–1921): 437–49; and Lowrey, "Variations in the Diagnosis of Dementia Precox and Manic Depressive Psychosis," *Journal of Nervous and Mental Disease* 58 (1923): 33–39.

114. Southard and Jarrett, *Kingdom of Evils*, pp. 312–14.

115. Myerson voiced this worry: How was the psychiatrist to distinguish the "negativism" of the dementia praecox patient from the "impertinence" of the manic? (case 7764, 1916, staff meeting). Further, how was he to differentiate between the mania associated with manic-depressive insanity and the mania that might occur in dementia praecox? (case 7798, 1916, staff meeting).

116. Southard and Jarrett, *Kingdom of Evils*, p. 452.

117. Southard, "Empathic Index," pp. 206–7.

118. Lowrey, "Psychiatry of 1895 and of 1915," p. 105.

119. Southard and Jarrett, *Kingdom of Evils*, p. 447.

120. Case 2597, 1914, staff meeting.

121. Case 2262, 1914, staff meeting, and Southard and Jarrett, *Kingdom of Evils*, p. 477, where the authors argue that the manic-depressive group "offers more of interest to the psychiatrist and psychiatric social worker than any other group of cases."

122. Case 7798, 1916, staff meeting.

123. Southard, "Empathic Index," p. 211. This "praecox feeling" would become a well-established diagnostic criterion. See, for example, H. H. Drysdale, "The Manic-Depressive and Dementia Praecox Psychoses: Their Differential Symptomatology," *American Journal of Insanity* 73 (1916–1917): 637: "There is invariably something in the makeup of persons afflicted with dementia praecox which the experienced observer has intuitively learned and which serves him in good stead even when distinctive symptoms are absent." Sander L. Gilman, "Why

Is Schizophrenia 'Bizarre': An Historical Essay in the Vocabulary of Psychiatry," *Journal of the History of the Behavioral Sciences* 19 (1983): 129–30, credits H. C. Rümke with coining the term "praecox feeling," to refer to the diagnostician's experience of the dementia praecox patient.

124. Southard, "Practical Grouping of Mental Diseases," p. 14.

125. Case 6745, 1916, staff meeting, and many other cases.

126. Case 8124, 1917, staff meeting, is one among many in which psychiatrists voiced doubt and frustration. Southard, invoking the authority of Kraepelin, argued for ten years of observation (case 7764, 1916, staff meeting).

127. Four examples among many appear in staff meetings in cases 7764, 1916; 9296, 1917; 9923, 1917; and 10031, 1917.

128. Case 12481, 1918, staff meeting.

129. Case 9300, 1917, staff meeting. In discussing one case, a psychiatrist observed that diagnoses were "largely matters of interpretation" (case 8466, 1917, staff meeting).

130. Table 5.3 may be read as showing that diagnosis (D) is related to gender (G) but only indirectly to ethnicity (E); thus, if attention is restricted to male patients (or to female patients), ethnicity and diagnosis are not related in a statistically significant way in the sample. The odds ratio of 2.11 indicates that on average the men in the sample were 2.11 times as likely as the women to receive a diagnosis of dementia praecox.

131. The group of potential manic-depressive and dementia praecox patients may be distinguished from the rest of the hospital population by the presence of psychosis (that is, patients psychiatrists considered at least temporarily insane) and the absence of alcoholic, syphilitic, or organic conditions. The thinking behind the isolation in table 5.3 of dementia praecox and manic-depressive patients from the rest of the hospital population thus replicates psychiatrists' own thinking.

132. The possibility that women *were* in fact more often manic—excited and uncontrollable—than men when psychiatrists diagnosed them can neither be substantiated nor wholly ruled out. Yet this matters little, for I am here examining how psychiatrists *represented* the two entities and how those representations in turn structured their perceptions of patients. Quotation from Kraepelin, *Manic-Depressive Insanity and Paranoia*, p. 174.

133. Southard and Jarrett, *Kingdom of Evils*, pp. 312–17.

134. Case 11077, 1918, staff meeting.

135. Case 2363, 1913, staff meeting.

136. Southard and Jarrett, *Kingdom of Evils*, pp. 319–21.

137. Case 10131, 1917, staff meeting.

138. Case 8873, 1917, letter from wife's friend to psychiatrists, interview with mother-in-law of patient, and patient's statement on voluntary application for admission to hospital.

139. Southard and Jarrett, *Kingdom of Evils*, pp. 142–46.

140. Ibid., pp. 317–19.

141. On such patients' "autistic" sexuality, see, for example, case 10221, 1918, staff meeting; and case 7518, 1916, staff meeting. On autoeroticism, see, for example, James C. Hassall, "The Role of the Sexual Complex in Dementia Precox," *Psychoanalytic Review* 2 (1915): 260–76; and Karl Abraham, "Die psychosex-

uellen Differenzen der Hysterie und der Dementia praecox," *Zentralblatt für Psychoanalyse und Psychotherapie* 1 (1910): 127.

142. Southard and Jarrett, *Kingdom of Evils*, p. 286.

143. Gordon Gibson, "The Relationship between Pelvic Disease and Manic-Depressive Insanity," *American Journal of Obstetrics and Diseases of Women and Children* 74 (1916): 439–44; and Charles E. Gibbs, "Sexual Behavior and Secondary Sexual Hair in Female Patients with Manic-Depressive Psychoses, and the Relation of These Factors to Dementia Praecox," *State Hospital Quarterly* 9 (1923–1924): 526–43.

SIX: INSTITUTIONAL DISCIPLINE

1. Quotations from Southard, "Mental Hygiene"; Southard, "The Psychopathic Hospital"; Massachusetts State Board of Insanity, *Annual Report* 14, 1913, p. 28; Southard, "Psychopathic Hospital"; Southard, "Atmosphere of Psychopathic Hospitals."

2. Southard, "Atmosphere of Psychopathic Hospitals."

3. Deutsch, *Mentally Ill in America*, p. 217.

4. Southard and Jarrett, *Kingdom of Evils*, pp. 373–74.

5. Southard, "Psychopathic Hospital."

6. Quotation from Southard, "Atmosphere of Psychopathic Hospitals." On the hospital atmosphere, see Helen B. Hopkins, "Nursing and Occupational Departments," in Briggs et al., *Psychopathic Hospital*, p. 204.

7. Quotation and "chambre séparée" from Southard, "Atmosphere of Psychopathic Hospitals." Second quotation from Dorman B. Eaton, "Despotism in Lunatic Asylums," *North American Review* 132 (1881): 264. Gerald N. Grob discusses the article in *Mental Illness*, p. 58.

8. Quotation from Southard, "Atmosphere of Psychopathic Hospitals."

9. Deutsch, *Mentally Ill in America*, pp. 213–28; Grob, *Mental Illness*, pp. 17–19; and Grob, *Inner World*, pp. 71–74, 150–52, present and discuss contemporary debates concerning restraint. Tomes, *Generous Confidence*, and Dwyer, *Homes for the Mad*, cover the issue in depth from the perspective of the nineteenth-century institution.

10. Eaton, "Despotism in Lunatic Asylums," p. 265.

11. Foucault, *Power/Knowledge*, p. 153; Eaton, "Despotism in Lunatic Asylums," p. 266. In a wide-ranging assessment of the state of psychiatric knowledge and practice, Thomas W. Salmon referred to the "dark places of neglect into which the light of humanity and science must be brought" ("Some New Fields," p. 93).

12. E. E. Southard, "The Purposes of the New State Psychopathic Hospital at Boston, Massachusetts," MS, Southard Papers.

13. Southard, "Atmosphere of Psychopathic Hospitals." Southard wrote that the hospital welcomed visits by "the medical and general public" as a matter of policy, "on the ground that there has been in the past too much concealment of hospital conditions" (Briggs et al., *Psychopathic Hospital*, p. 136).

14. In 1917, for example, thirteen physicians were listed as resident officers of the much larger Boston State Hospital, while its Psychopathic Department boasted thirty-four physicians (Boston State Hospital, *Annual Report* 9, 1918, pp. 6–7).

15. Massachusetts State Board of Insanity, *Annual Report* 15, 1914, p. 98. At a state-sponsored conference on the issue of record keeping, Southard gently chided the unnamed superintendent who often told him "that his men are doing so much work that they have no time to record it," suggesting that unrecorded work was work lost to science (Massachusetts State Board of Insanity, *Annual Report* 16, 1915, p. 232).

16. Massachusetts State Board of Insanity, *Annual Report* 15, 1914, p. 99.

17. From 1913 through 1915, the hospital staff collectively published 132 articles in professional journals ("The Boston Psychopathic Hospital," Southard Papers).

18. For the year 1912–1913, salaries were as follows: director, $3,000; first assistant physician, $1,200–$1,500; assistant physician, $800–$1,200; junior assistant physician, $600–$800; social worker, $720–$900 ("Schedule of Salaries, Psychopathic Department," in "Notes to Trustees"). Interns were not paid; they were either undergraduates who worked full or half time in exchange for hospital room and board, or students drawn from the city's medical schools.

19. Case 6916, 1916, staff meeting; Boston State Hospital, *Annual Report* 8, 1917, p. 37.

20. Myerson, *Psychology of Mental Disorders*, p. 105, adding his assent to an observation made by his colleague A. Warren Stearns.

21. Campbell, "History of Insanity," p. 543. Campbell succeeded Southard as director of the Psychopathic Hospital in 1920.

22. Commenting on his policy of dispensing "*admonitions to attend more meetings*," Southard wrote: "We cannot safely murmur at the unscientific programs and nonprogressive attitude of certain . . . national associations without assuming a portion of responsibility therefor. It is more than a matter of pride for Massachusetts to be in evidence at these national meetings" (Massachusetts State Board of Insanity, *Annual Report* 14, 1913, p. 28; emphasis in original). On his travels, see Boston State Hospital, *Annual Report* 9, 1918, p. 65. In 1915, Southard wrote that "hardly a week passes in which letters and visitors fail to arrive" at the hospital, asking questions "on behalf of some local movement to [*sic*] the establishment of a new hospital" ("What Is a Psychopathic Hospital?").

23. Elisha H. Cohoon, "The Administration Problem," in Briggs et al., *Psychopathic Hospital*, p. 149.

24. On the "family metaphor" in the nineteenth-century asylum, see Dwyer, *Homes for the Mad*, pp. 4–5, 125–27. Southard, "Cross-Sections," p. 92, suggested that just as society had passed through a kinship stage in its emergence from barbarism, psychiatric institutions had evolved from "the simple institution where all were but one really almost happy family" to the specialized institution. Southard, "The Psychopathic Hospital," contains one of several references to patients as "material." Several others can be found in Southard, "Contributions," p. 3 (patients as "living material") and p. 4 ("clinical material"). Katherine Bement Davis expressed a common sentiment in a discussion following a presentation by Southard: "We are come [*sic*] to recognize our great state institutions as human laboratories," she argued, going on to refer to "the study which can be made of this human material" (Southard, "Social Research in Public Institutions," p. 387).

25. Massachusetts State Board of Insanity, *Annual Report* 16, 1915, pp. 194,

197, 187, 193, 232 (transcript of a conference on hospital organization). See also Williams, "Legislation for the Insane": "The superintendents in the early days were autocrats" (p. 727); Henry Stafford Whisman, "Commitment Procedure and the State Hospital," *Mental Hygiene* 7 (1923): 358: "Superintendants [*sic*] of hospitals in those days were autocratic"; and Southard, "Cross-Sections," p. 91, speaking to his colleagues as president of the American Medico-Psychological Association: "Many of us must have thought of our superintendents as *despots*—benevolent despots, if you will, but still as despots" (emphasis in original). Myrtelle M. Canavan, a pathologist, assessed Southard's role much as he might have, writing, for example, that he "felt that if each worker had an aroused conscience regarding the work, rule and methods were unnecessary; the consequences of the work were reviewable at staff meetings and subjected to logical analysis, suggestions made and knots untangled, but the individuality of the worker was preserved and indirectly trained" ("Survey of the Work of the Director," in Briggs et al., *Psychopathic Hospital*, p. 188).

26. Mary C. Jarrett, in Boston State Hospital, *Annual Report* 9, 1918, p. 50.

27. Jarrett, "Psychiatric Social Work," p. 285.

28. Mary C. Jarrett, "Applications of Sociology in Psychiatry," in *Manual of Psychiatry*, ed. Aaron J. Rosanoff (New York, 1927), p. 420.

29. Dorothy Q. Hale, in Boston State Hospital, *Annual Report* 9, 1918, p. 55; case 1607, 1914, Jarrett to patient's mother.

30. Stearns wrote that in the three months before the social service department was established, only seven ex-patients reported back to the hospital ("The After-Care Program and Results of the Psychopathic Hospital, Boston, 1913–1914," Boston Psychopathic Hospital, *Collected Contributions*, no. 19 [Boston, 1914], p. 19). On aftercare, see also Stearns, "The Value of Out-Patient Work among the Insane," *American Journal of Insanity* 74 (1917–1918): 595–602; and Stearns, "Out-Patient Work in the Massachusetts State Hospitals for the Insane," Massachusetts State Board of Insanity, *Collected Contributions*, no. 14 (Boston, 1914), pp. 1–8.

31. Jarrett and Hale, Boston State Hospital, *Annual Report* 9, 1918, pp. 50–51.

32. Hale, in ibid., p. 54.

33. Jarrett, in ibid.

34. Jarrett, "Social Service," pp. 172–75.

35. Southard, excerpt from MS, quoted by Jarrett, "Social Service," p. 173; Jarrett, "Psychiatric Thread," p. 219.

36. Southard, in Boston State Hospital, *Annual Report* 8, 1917, p. 39.

37. Jarrett, "Applications of Sociology in Psychiatry," p. 422. Writing in 1929, one clinician recalled that at Psychopathic Hospital lectures, he "frequently heard the professors of psychiatry and members of the staff caution the social workers at this institution not to make diagnoses of mental cases when they were compiling or reading their sociological reports. On many occasions I have heard social workers making diagnoses of psychiatric cases in other institutions and at various clinics" (Paul E. Bowers, cited in Burnham, "Boston Psychiatry," p. 202).

38. Jarrett, "Psychiatric Thread," p. 217; Southard quoted in Jarrett, "Social Service," p. 173.

39. Jarrett, "Psychiatric Thread," pp. 217, 212, 214 (Jarrett citing Wright, 218).

Southard and Jarrett outlined their understanding of the relationship of psychiatric social work to other types of social work in *Kingdom of Evils*, pp. 381–82 (see also p. 53). For the agency workers' assessment of the psychiatric social worker, see Ellen Fitzpatrick, *Endless Crusade: Women Social Scientists and Progressive Reform* (New York, 1990), p. 213. Concerning the Smith School, considered the best school of psychiatric social work, Edith Abbott wrote (in the early forties): "Therefore, since it can never be made into anything good, I would say the sooner it is given up the better . . . it is not for me to 'attack' another School, but I do want you to know that many of us think this School does more harm than good."

40. Boston State Hospital, *Annual Report* 10, 1919, p. 83.

41. Linda Gordon, "Social Insurance and Public Assistance: The Influence of Gender in Welfare Thought in the United States, 1890–1935," *American Historical Review* 97 (1992): 19–54, perceptively explores some of these same issues in another context. She suggests that "the very premise of casework was anti-bureaucratic . . . since it insisted on the worker's discretion" (p. 44); Psychopathic Hospital social workers cast casework in a bureaucratic mode, and, in yearly summaries of their work, focused more on enumerating the interventions they had made than on the results they had achieved.

42. Jarrett, "Psychiatric Thread," pp. 219, 217.

43. The social worker Jessie Taft termed social work "experimental" ("Limitations of the Psychiatrist," p. 368). Quotations from Richard C. Cabot, "Informal Discussion" following Jarrett, "Psychiatric Thread," p. 593; Cabot, introduction to Southard and Jarrett, *Kingdom of Evils*, p. xii.

44. Case 5612 (readmitted as case 6964, 1915–1916).

45. Taft, "Limitations of the Psychiatrist," pp. 367–68.

46. Taft, "Qualifications of the Psychiatric Social Worker," *Mental Hygiene* 4 (1920): 428.

47. Case 11077, 1918, staff meeting. Greenblatt, York, and Brown, *From Custodial to Therapeutic Patient Care*, pp. 45–46, would later describe the admissions procedure at the Psychopathic Hospital, arguing that "the admission of patients was a classic example of man's insensitivity to man" (quotation from p. 45). Harry C. Solomon, in an interview conducted in 1980, was equally critical of past practices. "There was the feeling . . . of great progress—the fact that handcuffs and so on were removed. But this was only a fictitious change in a way because they were at once grabbed by a couple of attendants. After a few papers had been done, the attendants rushed them to the ward, stripped them, took away dentures, glasses, every possession, shoved them under a shower, and the battle began at that point" (interview with Solomon, September 1980).

48. Case 955, 1913, staff meeting.

49. Case 7858, 1916, case report. The embarrassment, crying, and refusals of some are understandable because many had never before been examined by a physician.

50. Case 4342, 1916, letter to Southard.

51. In July 1915, for example, 134 Wassermann tests and 61 lumbar punctures were performed ("Report of Operating-room, July 1915," in "Notes to Trustees").

52. Case 3800, 1914, letter.

53. Case 8636, 1917, letter from sister of patient to social worker; case 1844, 1913, letter to Adler.

54. The staff meetings in cases 6902, 1916; 6954, 1914 (patient was readmitted); 5521, 1915; and 5112, 1915, contain discussions of this issue.

55. Case 9347, 1917, letter to supervisor of women's ward. Foucault discusses the significance of the "little things" within a disciplinary framework in *Discipline and Punish*, pp. 139–41.

56. Case 402, 1912, letter to Dr. Vosburgh. *"Hospital walls have ears,"* Southard wrote ("Atmosphere of Psychopathic Hospitals"; emphasis in original).

57. Case 8049, 1915, case history.

58. Case 3804, 1914, letter to superintendent of nurses.

59. Case 13058, 1919, staff meeting.

60. Case 3932, 1914, letter to wife, case history.

61. Cases 505, 1912, letter from mother; 9923, 1917, letter to Cohoon, recounting the advice he gave the patient.

62. Case 3180, 1913, diary.

63. Case 5112, 1915, letter to Southard.

64. Quotation from Southard, "Atmosphere of Psychopathic Hospitals."

65. Case 5172, 1915, letter to Wellington.

66. Quotations from staff meetings in cases 6954, 1914; 8867, 1917; and 11199, 1918.

67. Quotations from Southard in Hopkins, "Nursing and Occupational Departments," pp. 194–96. See also Mary L. Gerrin, "Impressions of a General Hospital Nurse Beginning Work in the Psychopathic Hospital (Boston, Massachusetts)," *Boston Medical and Surgical Journal* 171 (1914): 483–85.

68. Hopkins, "Nursing and Occupational Departments," p. 194.

69. Foucault, *Discipline and Punish*, p. 295; all other quotations from Massachusetts State Board of Insanity, *Annual Report* 11, 1910, pp. 162–82 (transcript of a conference on "precautions against illtreatment of patients in institutions"). Southard's comment that "it would be well to have psychologicals done on all of the public service group" is suggestive in this regard (case 8242, 1917, staff meeting). Elaborate rules governed the lives of attendants and nurses. Among the strictures to which nurses were subject were that "loud laughing, talking or conversation in corridors and on stairs" was forbidden and that their "quarters must be open to inspection at all times." They were "to exercise self-denial, forbearance and good temper at all times," were "to cultivate a gentle voice and dignified manner," and were not "to have too much or expensive clothing." The personal bearing of male attendants occasioned no comment ("Rules for Nurses, Psychopathic Hospital," MS, Southard Papers).

70. See, for example, Massachusetts State Board of Insanity, *Annual Report* 13, 1912, pp. 179–99 (transcript of a conference on "improving the condition and promoting the efficiency of nurses in our State institutions"); Massachusetts State Board of Insanity, *Annual Report* 12, 1911, pp. 273–91 (conference on "vacations, sick leave, hours of duty and relief from duty" for institutional employees); Massachusetts State Board of Insanity, *Annual Report* 15, 1914, pp. 190–227 (conference on "training schools for nurses").

71. The notion of self-restraint is threaded through the discussion in Massachusetts State Board of Insanity, *Annual Report* 11, 1910, pp. 162–82. The superintendent Charles W. Page, for example, lauded the self-abnegation and self-restraint exhibited by "intelligent, kindly disposed employees" (p. 168).

72. Gerrin, "Nurse Beginning Work," p. 485, cites "a careful statistical study," carried out in the hospital's first year of operation, before maids were hired, which showed that nurses and attendants spent nearly as many hours each week on domestic tasks (twenty-three) as they did on nursing duties (twenty-four) (they also devoted twelve hours to unspecified "executive tasks"). "The night or day man will get me or any one what they want and I want to buy some fruit," one man, requesting five dollars, wrote to his wife (case 1452, 1913).

73. Cases 9617, 1918, letter to social worker; and 2588, 1914, letter to social worker Wright.

74. Complained one woman, "One day they call me 'sweet-heart' and the next they are saucy and look cross at me." Case 3180, 1913, letter to Southard.

75. On gendered qualities, see Gerrin, "Nurse Beginning Work," pp. 483–84, and Henry R. Stedman, "The Art of Companionship in Mental Nursing," in Boston Psychopathic Hospital, *Collected Contributions*, no. 3 (Boston, 1914).

76. Case 1728, 1913, inquiry concerning injury to patient.

77. Case 3474, 1914, petition signed by three attendants, addressed to Adler (braces in original).

78. Harry C. Solomon, reflecting in 1980 on nearly seventy years of Psychopathic Hospital practice, had this to say of the pack: "Now this was not restraint. This was a therapeutic method of calming. If the pack had been dry, it would be restraint; wet, it was therapy [laughter]." He continued: "It is said that this was the only restraint that Houdini was unable to get out of" (interview with Solomon, September 1980).

79. Case 2318, 1914, letter to psychiatrists; case 3180, 1914, patient writings.

80. Case 1728, 1913, inquiry concerning injury to patient.

81. Case 11077, 1918, staff meeting.

82. Case 6954, 1914, staff meeting.

83. Case 9006, 1917, letter to psychiatrists.

84. Briggs et al., *Psychopathic Hospital*, pp. 132–35.

85. Referring to nursing standards current in the second half of the nineteenth century, one physician, Barbara T. Ring, wrote that "asylums were little more than prisons, and the nurses merely keepers; now, physicians attending mental and nervous patients feel the necessity of employing women especially trained for this work" ("Psychopathic Nursing," *Boston Medical and Surgical Journal* 166 [1912]: 484).

86. Charles R. Bancroft, "Women Nurses on Wards for Men in Hospitals for the Insane," *American Journal of Insanity* 62 (1906–1907): 182–83; Thomas J. Moher, "Employment of Women Nurses on the Men's Wards in a Hospital for the Insane," *American Medico-Psychological Association Proceedings* 16 (1909): 483–84. Superintendents also discussed the issue at many of the state-sponsored conferences cited above.

87. Bancroft, "Women Nurses," pp. 180–81.

88. Massachusetts State Board of Insanity, *Annual Report* 11, 1910, pp. 177–78.

89. Case 6954, 1914, staff meeting. Another man referred to a nurse as a "bossy, domineering, coarse, vulgar Virago" (case 3804, 1914, letter to psychiatrists).

90. Views expressed in Bancroft, "Women Nurses," pp. 184, 186–87 (citing the views of his "Scotch brethren," among them Turnbull, "Female Nursing,"

pp. 629–40), and Moher, "Employment of Women Nurses," p. 486 (citing common wisdom).

91. Case 3804, 1914, letter to Dr. Wellington.

92. The phrase is Florence Nightingale's; see Melosh, *Physician's Hand*, p. 3. For an argument in support of specialization and science, see M. Adelaide Nutting, "The Training of the Psychopathic Nurse," Boston Psychopathic Hospital, *Collected Contributions*, no. 11 (Boston, 1914).

93. Hopkins, "Nursing and Occupational Departments," pp. 194–201.

94. Positions articulated in Massachusetts State Board of Insanity, *Annual Report* 15, 1914, pp. 190–227 (conference on "training schools for nurses").

95. Ring, "Psychopathic Nursing," p. 485.

96. The quoted phrase came up repeatedly; for one example, see Massachuseetts State Board of Insanity, *Annual Report* 15, 1914, p. 215.

97. Ibid.; Bancroft, "Women Nurses," pp. 186, 181.

98. Adolf Meyer, "Kankakee: The Treatment of the Insane" (1894), in *Collected Papers*, 2, p. 45.

99. Charles William Eliot, "Remarks at Conference on Modern Developments in Mental Nursing, February 16, 1914," *Boston Medical and Surgical Journal* 171 (1914): 477 (the conference was held at the Psychopathic Hospital). Eliot referred to the particularly adept movements of "a little Danish nurse" in this talk. Albert Warren Ferris, president of the New York State Commission in Lunacy, also made reference to the persuasive powers of the "little nurse," although he imagined her handling a particularly violent woman ("Psychopathic Wards," p. 275).

100. E. E. Southard, "Analysis of Recoveries at the Psychopathic Hospital, Boston: I, One Hundred Cases, 1912–1913, Considered Especially from the Standpoint of Nursing," Boston Psychopathic Hospital, *Collected Contributions*, no. 14 (Boston, 1914), p. 2. Southard wrote that in psychiatry, "as in medicine at large, the *vis medicatrix naturae* is often more in evidence than the *vis ipsius medici*." Commenting on psychiatry's progress, the physician George S. Sprauge wrote: "Many people have a regrettable way of thinking too highly of the hospital that cures, in contrast to those other institutions whose function it is to maintain whatever level of adaptation is possible" ("The Rôle of the Psychiatric Hospital," *Mental Hygiene* 21 [1937]: 570).

101. Southard, "The Psychopathic Hospital."

102. As Harry C. Solomon would later say, "the less you do, the greater your chance of success" (interview with Solomon, September 1980).

103. Donald Gregg, "A Comparison of the Drugs Used in General and Mental Hospitals," *Boston Medical and Surgical Journal* 171 (1914): 476.

104. Case 6954, 1914, staff meeting.

105. Quotations from Donald Gregg, "Treatment of Deliria in General and in Mental Hospitals," in Boston Psychopathic Hospital, *Collected Contributions*, no. 7 (Boston, 1914), p. 4; E. E. Southard, "On Institutional Requirements for Acute Alcoholic Mental Disease in the Metropolitan District of Massachusetts in the Light of Experiences at the Psychopathic Hospital," in Boston Psychopathic Hospital, *Collected Contributions*, no. 34 (Boston, 1913), p. 165. Herman Adler, "Report of Clinical Demonstration of Alcoholic Mental Diseases, with Remarks on Current Practice at the Psychopathic Hospital, Boston, Massachusetts," in Boston

Psychopathic Hospital, *Collected Contributions*, no. 30 (Boston, 1913), pp. 142–46, is a general statement on the virtues of nonrestraint. Tomes found that morphine was prescibed for between 75 and 88 percent of patients at the Pennsylvania Hospital for the Insane (based on records from the years 1841–1842 and 1876–1877) (*Generous Confidence*, pp. 194–95). Charles L. Dana, *Text-Book of Nervous Diseases and Psychiatry* (New York, 1906), pp. 591–94, describes hydrotherapeutic techniques as practiced at the time.

106. Case 5110, 1914, staff meeting.

107. Quotation from Southard, "Atmosphere of Psychopathic Hospitals."

108. To an early sociologist of the mental hospital, there was no question that the pack was a form of restraint. "The packroom is the true bedlam of modern psychiatry," he observed (Howard Rowland, "Interaction Processes in the State Mental Hospital," *Psychiatry* 1 [1938]: 333).

109. Case 13058, 1919, staff meeting.

110. Case 5985, 1915, ward notes.

111. Case 1103, 1913, staff meeting (this case is also LEE case 48).

112. Case 3800, 1914, ward notes. Ward notes in case 3932, 1914, record that the patient, "when ward was unusually quiet, talks pleasantly about his work and etc." to attendants.

113. Case 7518, 1916, ward notes. Psychiatrists never settled on a diagnosis for Walsh, whom they thought to be suffering from either psychoneurosis, manic-depressive insanity, or dementia praecox. They discharged him "slightly improved."

114. Case 9658, 1917, staff meeting.

115. Case 10005, 1918, letters to social worker. The sinful men this patient was referring to were presumably syphilitics.

116. This point was made by Southard and Jarrett, *Kingdom of Evils*, p. 331.

117. Staff meetings from cases 7455, 1916; 4568, 1915; 10165, 1918; 6916, 1916; and 6432, 1916.

118. Southard and Jarrett, *Kingdom of Evils*, p. 330.

119. Southard, "Mental Hygiene."

120. Eugene Taylor, "Louville Eugene Emerson: Psychotherapy, Harvard, and the Early Boston Scene," *Harvard Medical Alumni Bulletin* 56 (Spring 1982): 42–48. Burnham, *Psychoanalysis*, p. 29, cites the observation of Freud's biographer Ernest Jones that as of 1909 no American psychoanalyses had been reported.

121. L. E. Emerson, "Psychoanalysis and Hospitals," paper read at the annual meeting of the American Psychoanalytic Association, 1913, Emerson Papers, Countway Library of Medicine.

122. Case 1002, 1913, staff meeting.

123. Case 1158, 1914, staff meeting.

124. L. E. Emerson, "Summary of Four Cases," MS, Emerson Papers.

125. Case 1158, 1914, staff meeting.

126. Southard, "Institutional Requirements," p. 170.

127. Southard and Jarrett, *Kingdom of Evils*, p. 331.

128. A. Warren Stearns, "The Alcohol Club," in Briggs et al., *Psychopathic Hospital*, p. 186.

129. Southard, "Psychopathic Hospital's Function," pp. 278–79.

130. A. Warren Stearns and Mary C. Jarrett, "Notes on After-Care and Moral

Suasion Work with Alcoholics in the Out-Patient Department of the Psychopathic Hospital," in Boston Psychopathic Hospital, *Collected Contributions*, no. 33 (Boston, 1913), pp. 156–59.

SEVEN: WOMAN AS HYPERSEXUAL

1. Case 8155, 1917, staff meeting.
2. Lowrey, "Psychiatry of 1895 and of 1915," p. 105.
3. Martin W. Peck, "Psychopathic Personality: Report of a Case," *Journal of Abnormal and Social Psychology* 17 (1922–1923): 188. The case was from the Psychopathic Hospital.
4. Turn-of-the-century female reformers produced a large literature on female psychopathy and delinquency. Among the most significant are Edith R. Spaulding [M.D.], *An Experimental Study of Psychopathic Delinquent Women* (New York, 1923); Spaulding, "Emotional Episodes among Psychopathic Delinquent Women," *Journal of Nervous and Mental Disease* 54 (1921): 298–323; Spaulding, "An Emotional Crisis: A Description and Analysis of an Episode that Occurred among Psychopathic Women," *Mental Hygiene* 5 (1921): 266–82; Jessie D. Hodder, "Disciplinary Measures in the Management of the Psychopathic Delinquent Woman," *Mental Hygiene* 4 (1920): 611–25; and Hodder, "The Problems of Discipline of the Troublesome and Disorderly Prisoner," speech delivered before the American Prison Association at Columbus, Ohio (1920), pamphlet in Jessie Donaldson Hodder Papers, Schlesinger Library, Radcliffe College. Hodder, discussing the case of a "feebleminded, psychopathic woman," suggested that reformatories were for "the reformation of the normal woman" and offered this: "Frankly, I think execution is the only effective disciplinary measure if discipline is to continue to be our focus for these persons" (p. 11)—a sentiment that should put to rest any notion of an undifferentiatedly sympathetic stance toward their charges on the part of women reformers. On women penologists, see Estelle B. Freedman, *Their Sisters' Keepers: Women's Prison Reform in America, 1830–1930* (Ann Arbor, Mich., 1981).
5. Cases 6693, 1916; and 1040, 1913, staff meetings. On adolescent male sexuality, see William Healy, *The Individual Delinquent: A Text-Book of Diagnosis and Prognosis for All Concerned in Understanding Offenders* (Boston, 1915), esp. pp. 255–56, 588–89.
6. The nature of Victorian female sexuality—passionate or passionless—has generated much debate; the interpretation of Clelia Duel Mosher, *The Mosher Survey: Sexual Attitudes of Forty-Five Victorian Women*, ed. James Mahood and Kristine Wenburg (New York, 1980), defines the divide. On the passionate side, see Carl Degler, "What Ought to Be and What Was: Women's Sexuality in the Nineteenth Century," *American Historical Review* 79 (1974): 1467–90, and Peter Gay, *Education of the Senses*, vol. 1, *The Bourgeois Experience, Victoria to Freud* (New York, 1984). For critiques of these attempts to rehabilitate Victorian sexuality, see Carol Zisowitz Stearns and Peter N. Stearns, "Victorian Sexuality: Can Historians Do It Better?" *Journal of Social History* 18 (Summer 1985): 625–34, and Steven Seidman, "Sexual Attitudes of Victorian and Post-Victorian Women: Another Look at the Mosher Survey," *Journal of American Studies* 23 (1989): 68–72.

7. Daniel Scott Smith, "Family Limitation, Sexual Control, and Domestic Feminism in Victorian America," *Feminist Studies* 1 (1973): 40–57; reprinted in *A Heritage of Her Own: Toward a New Social History of American Women*, ed. Nancy F. Cott and Elizabeth H. Pleck (New York, 1979), pp. 222–45.

8. On the relationship between overdevelopment and sexual precocity, see Healy, *Individual Delinquent*, pp. 244–54, 402–4. The extraordinary nature of his claim that "the overwhelming attraction which negro men occasionally have for white girls and women . . . is to be explained by the hypersexualism of the female attracted" (p. 403) can best be appreciated when set against the racism that pervades the literature of the time. Quotation in text from p. 245.

9. Case 6535, 1917, letter to Jarrett.

10. See Leslie Woodcock Tentler, *Wage-Earning Women: Industrial Work and Family Life in the United States, 1900–1930* (New York, 1979), chap. 4, on the boy's relationship to the family economy. Both female and male criminologists considered the delinquencies of boys far less serious than those of girls. See, for one example among many, Mary W. Dewson, *Conditions that Make Wayward Girls: A Study Based on Last Year's Commitments to the Massachusetts State Industrial School for Girls* (Lancaster, Mass., 1910), pamphlet in Molly Dewson Papers, Schlesinger Library, Radcliffe College: "The boy often gets into trouble because of an excess of animal spirits, because of energy which, rightly utilized, should be his greatest asset" (p. 1).

11. In 1922, years after the appearance of his two-volume *Adolescence: Its Psychology and Its Relation to Physiology, Anthropology, Sociology, Sex, Crime, Religion, and Education* (New York, 1904), G. Stanley Hall noted that "of all the stages of human life, [the adolescent girl's] was *terra incognita*." The pubescent boy was, by contrast, an open book ("Flapper Americana Novissima," *Atlantic Monthly* 129 [June 1922]: 771). I found Carol Dyhouse's perceptive discussion of adolescent girlhood, although primarily concerned with middle-class girls, very useful in thinking about working-class adolescent girls. Dyhouse notes Hall's "leery" tone when writing of adolescent girls (*Girls Growing Up in Late Victorian and Edwardian England* [London, 1981], pp. 115–25). Dorothy Ross quotes Hall's assertion that "woman at her best never outgrows adolescence as man does" (*G. Stanley Hall: The Psychologist as Prophet* [Chicago, 1972], p. 339).

12. On the growth of commercial amusements, see Kathy Peiss, *Cheap Amusements: Working Women and Leisure in Turn-of-the-Century New York* (Philadelphia, 1986). Tentler, *Wage-Earning Women*, pp. 109–13, also discusses the appeal of commercial amusements. On small-town courtship, see Ernest W. Burgess, "Sociological Aspects of the Sex Life of the Unmarried Adult," in *The Sex Life of the Unmarried Adult: An Inquiry into and an Interpretation of Current Sex Practices*, ed. Ira S. Wile (New York, 1934), pp. 116–54.

13. Most noteworthy among the investigations are Carroll D. Wright, *The Working Girls of Boston* (Boston, 1889), pp. 118–26, especially where Wright attempts to counter what he considers the prevailing view that working girls are immoral; Woods and Kennedy, *Young Working Girls*, pp. 84–100; and William I. Thomas, *The Unadjusted Girl: With Cases and Standpoint for Behavior Analysis* (1923; reprint, Montclair, N.J., 1969), pp. 98–150. On changing views of the prostitute, see Ruth Rosen, *The Lost Sisterhood: Prostitution in America, 1900–1918* (Baltimore, 1982), and Brandt, *No Magic Bullet*.

14. Case 5830, 1917, letter to social worker.

15. Kathy Peiss, "'Charity Girls' and City Pleasures: Historical Notes on Working-Class Sexuality, 1880–1920," in *Powers of Desire: The Politics of Sexuality*, ed. Ann Snitow, Christine Stansell, and Sharon Thompson (New York, 1984), pp. 74–87, discusses "treating."

16. Case 10065, 1917, case history.

17. Case 5830, 1917, letter to social worker. My understanding of the working-class sexual milieu owes much to Stansell, *City of Women*, pp. 76–101, 171–92. See Thomas, *Unadjusted Girl*, pp. 98–150, for a contemporary analysis of the same milieu.

18. Case 8064, 1916, case record.

19. Elizabeth G. Evans and Mary W. Dewson, *Feeble-Mindedness and Juvenile Delinquency* (Boston, 1909), pamphlet in Dewson Papers, p. 1.

20. Case 7952, 1916, staff meeting.

21. William I. Thomas, *Sex and Society: Studies in the Social Psychology of Sex* (Chicago, 1907), p. 313.

22. Case 5370, 1915, letter to social worker.

23. Case 3403, 1914, case record.

24. Peck, "Psychopathic Personality," p. 192.

25. Case 5402, 1915, staff meeting.

26. Case 5830, 1915, staff meeting.

27. Case 5611, 1915, staff meeting. In their published account of the case, Southard and Jarrett wrote that they had "purposely laid little stress upon the sex delinquencies, heterosexual and homosexual, which are suspected or implicit" in it (*Kingdom of Evils*, p. 137). For an analysis of the stress on gender deviance, see George Chauncey, Jr., "From Sexual Inversion to Homosexuality: Medicine and the Changing Conceptualization of Female Deviance," *Salmagundi* 58–59 (Fall 1982-Winter 1983): 114–46.

28. Rosen, *Lost Sisterhood*, points out that prostitutes were among the first populations tested for feeblemindedness, citing contemporary investigations of prostitution that found high proportions—around 30 percent—of prostitutes feebleminded, and rightly concluding that the term "'explained' both 'inherited strains of degeneracy'—for which the prostitute could not really be blamed—and willful, immoral behavior" (pp. 21–22). But the majority of prostitutes proved *not* feebleminded, and this shocked and troubled reformers, who quickly turned to psychopathy to account for prostitutes' immorality. See, for example, Augusta Scott, "Three Hundred Psychiatric Examinations Made at the Women's Day Court, New York City," *Mental Hygiene* 6 (1922): 345–46, who reported that of 149 prostitutes—"not the old-timers or street-walkers, but younger women of the better type" (p. 351)—tested on the Terman intelligence test, 26 percent scored in the defective range (intelligence quotient below 70), 31 percent were of borderline intelligence (IQ between 70 and 79), and the rest scored 80 or higher, in the "normal" and "dull normal" range; Katherine Bement Davis, "A Study of Prostitutes Committed from New York City to the State Reformatory for Women at Bedford Hills," in George Kneeland's *Commercialized Prostitution in New York City* (New York, 1913), who found that only 30 percent of 193 prostitutes tested "decidedly mentally defective" (p. 188); and Edith Spaulding, "The Problem of a

Psychopathic Hospital Connected with a Reformatory Institution," *Medical Record* 99 (1921): 815, who noted that "when appropriation was made in the State of Massachusetts in 1911 for an institution for the defective delinquent, it was generally supposed that all those who had been misfits in . . . the mental hospitals, the schools for the feeble-minded, and the reformatories, would be found to be defective intellectually as well as emotionally and therefore would be fit subjects for permanent segregation," but that it was found that many "ranked high when psychometric tests were applied," making them not defective but psychopathic delinquents. Mabel Ruth Fernald, Mary Holmes Stevens Hayes, and Almena Dawley, *A Study of Women Delinquents in New York State* (New York, 1920), concluded that their data failed "absolutely to justify the view expressed recently by certain propagandists that delinquency and defective intelligence are practically synonymous, and that, accordingly, solving the problem of mental deficiency will solve the problem of delinquency" (p. 434). Steven Schlossman and Stephanie Wallach argue that progressive courts began to define female delinquency almost entirely in sexual terms ("The Crime of Precocious Sexuality: Female Juvenile Delinquency in the Progressive Era," *Harvard Educational Review* 48 [1978]: 65–94).

On Davis and other female criminologists, see Freedman, *Their Sisters' Keepers*, pp. 109–42; on Davis, see Fitzpatrick, *Endless Crusade*.

29. Case 8155, 1917, staff meeting.

30. Case 3403, 1914, case record.

31. Case 5855, 1915, staff meeting. The visitor may have been right. Frances Donovan, *The Woman Who Waits* (Boston, 1920), pp. 211–12, noted that the games waitresses played with men bordered "upon prostitution, although not actual prostitution because the waitresses earn the necessaries of life for themselves." See Barbara M. Brenzel, *Daughters of the State: A Social Portrait of the First Reform School for Girls in North America, 1856–1905* (Cambridge, Mass., 1983), for a history of the Lancaster state school. For accounts of the structure and work of the parole department, see Margaret Reeves, *Training Schools for Delinquent Girls* (New York, 1929), pp. 389–91; Edith N. Burleigh and Frances R. Harris, *The Delinquent Girl: A Study of the Girl on Parole in Massachusetts* (New York, 1923); Burleigh, "The Advantages of Parole under a Separate Superintendent," in *Proceedings of a National Conference on the Education of Backward, Truant, Delinquent and Dependent Children*, National Association of Training Schools and Juvenile Agencies (N.p., 1916), pp. 80–89; and Burleigh, "What Is Parole?" *Mental Hygiene* 8 (1924): 769–77. The overwork may have been intentional; Healy, *Individual Delinquent*, related the case of a sixteen-year-old girl who "finally showed that she never had done so well morally as when she had to do very hard work. . . . when she was working out in a place where she had to do big washings she controlled her sex tendencies much better than previously" (p. 193).

32. Case 6054, 1915, case record.

33. Case 10052, 1917, case record.

34. The state visitor handling her case faulted her for manifesting "no feeling of shame for her conduct and the betrayal of confidence which the family placed in her, nor contrition for the sorrow and disgrace her accusation brings upon them" (case 10213, 1918, state visitor's report).

35. One girl told psychiatrists "they call it saucy if you turn round up there" (case 10537, 1918, staff meeting).

36. Case 10032, 1918, staff meeting.

37. Case 10537, 1918, staff meeting.

38. Case 8231, 1917, staff meeting.

39. Case 9834, 1917, staff meeting.

40. Cases 7952, 1916, staff meeting; and 7431, 1916, staff meeting. Speaking of the "Burleigh girls," a member of the State Board of Insanity noted that they "appear perfectly normal under superficial examination" (Massachusetts State Board of Insanity, *Annual Report* 13, 1912, p. 220 [conference on "the relation of social service to our institutions"]).

41. Case 7521, 1916, vistor's report.

42. Case 7311, 1917, staff meeting; Peck, "Psychopathic Personality," p. 190; case 15552, n.d., case history.

43. Cases 4538, 1915, case history; and 10137, 1917, visitor's report.

44. Southard and Jarrett, *Kingdom of Evils*, p. 354.

45. Case 4538, 1915, visitor's report.

46. Cases 7361, 1916, case history; 7952, 1916, staff meeting; and 10537, 1918, staff meeting.

47. Case 5432, 1915, staff meeting.

48. Case 5612, 1915, letter to Jarrett.

49. Case 5855, 1915, staff meeting.

50. Case 10032, 1918, staff meeting.

51. Case 10409, 1919, staff meeting.

52. Scott, "Psychiatric Examinations," pp. 364–65.

53. Case 10814, 1918, visitor's report. Many contemporaries called attention to the working-class girl's near-obsession with clothes. Stansell, *City of Women*, pp. 92–101 and 187–88, and Peiss, *Cheap Amusements*, pp. 62–67, discuss the significance of clothing in working-class culture.

54. Case 10065, 1917, autobiography and case history.

55. Southard and Jarrett, *Kingdom of Evils*, pp. 60, 70.

56. Case 6535, 1917, letter to Jarrett.

57. Case 1040, 1913, staff meeting.

58. Case 6535, 1917, letter to Hancock.

59. Southard and Jarrett, *Kingdom of Evils*, p. 55. The book Talbot read was C. Gasquoine Hartley, *The Truth about Woman* (New York, 1914).

60. Case 1040, 1913, staff meeting.

61. Case 5830, 1916, letter to social worker.

62. Ibid.

63. Case 1970, 1916, letter to social worker.

64. Case 5612, 1915, letters and case history.

65. Case 6535, 1916–1917, letters to social workers.

66. Ibid.

67. Case 5370, 1915, letter to social worker.

68. Case 2234, 1913, letter to friend.

69. Case 10032, 1918, staff meeting.

70. Case 10776, 1918, staff meeting.

71. Case 10032, 1918, staff meeting.
72. Case 10434, 1918, staff meeting.
73. Case 7952, 1916, staff meeting.
74. Case 6397, 1915, staff meeting.
75. Case 7952, 1916, staff meeting.
76. Case 8231, 1917, staff meeting.
77. Case 7311, 1916, staff meeting. Scott, "Psychiatric Examinations," p. 355, remarked that "one very important stimulus to the younger girls is the sort of talk they hear in factories. Repeatedly, girls have said that they were innocent until they went to work; then the conversations that they overheard made them curious and lowered their standards of conduct." Several girls argued to psychiatrists that they had been exposed to more while under state supervision than ever before. "People do not realize what conditions are" at institutions like Lancaster, one young woman told psychiatrists; "the younger girls are allowed to associate with the older ones without proper supervision, and more immorality can be learned there than on the outside" (case 2134, 1913, case history). Still another told doctors she learned "more bad than good" at Lancaster, adding that she also "learned something about sewing and dressmaking" (case 6267, 1916, case history). Healy, *Individual Delinquent*, p. 313, noted that "many a girl has testified to us that she learned more in the first twenty-four hours under custody than she knew in all her life before."
78. Case 6397, 1915, staff meeting.
79. Case 10165, 1917, letter from physician, staff meeting.
80. Case 6397, 1915, staff meeting.
81. Case 1040, 1913, staff meeting.
82. Case 10032, 1918, staff meeting.
83. Case 6303, 1916, staff meeting.
84. Estelle B. Freedman, "'Uncontrolled Desires': The Response to the Sexual Psychopath, 1920–1960," *Journal of American History* 74 (1987): 83–106.
85. Christina Simmons, "Companionate Marriage and the Lesbian Threat," *Frontiers* 4 (Fall 1979): 54–59, and Michael Gordon, "From an Unfortunate Necessity to a Cult of Mutual Orgasm: Sex in American Marital Education Literature, 1830–1940," in *Studies in the Sociology of Sex*, ed. James M. Henslin (New York, 1971), pp. 53–77.
86. Foucault, *History of Sexuality*, 1, pp. 53–73.
87. Case 6397, 1915, staff meeting.
88. Thomas, *Unadjusted Girl*, p. 166.

EIGHT: HYSTERIA

1. Case 5426, 1915, staff meeting; L. E. Emerson, "The Psychoanalytic Treatment of Hystero-Epilepsy," *Journal of Abnormal Psychology* 10 (1915–1916): 327 (comment in reference to epileptiform seizures in a male hysteric).
2. Ilza Veith, *Hysteria: The History of a Disease* (Chicago, 1965), writes, "Throughout the tangled skein of its history runs the scarlet thread of sexuality" (p. viii). See also Elaine Showalter, *The Female Malady: Women, Madness, and English Culture, 1830–1980* (New York, 1985), chap. 6; and the classic treatment of nineteenth-century hysteria, Carroll Smith-Rosenberg, "The Hysterical Woman:

Sex Roles and Role Conflict in Nineteenth-Century America," in her *Disorderly Conduct: Visions of Gender in Victorian America* (New York, 1985), pp. 197–216.

3. Showalter, *Female Malady*, pp. 147–55.

4. James Strachey, introduction to Josef Breuer and Sigmund Freud, *Studies on Hysteria*, ed. and trans. Strachey (New York, n.d.), p. 20. I follow Strachey in seeing the basic mechanisms of psychoanalysis in these early studies, first published between 1893 and 1895.

5. LEE case 85, 1912. Citations to all of Emerson's numbered cases refer to handwritten—in a few cases typewritten—notes made on half sheets of paper during sessions with patients. Much of what he records appears to be verbatim transcriptions of patients' words—direct discourse; in several instances he incorporated grammatical errors, as in "Before that I never had no pain" (case 26).

6. Goldstein, *Console and Classify*, p. 326.

7. Southard and Jarrett, *Kingdom of Evils*, p. 335; Tom A. Williams, "The Simulation of Hysteria," *American Journal of Insanity* 67 (1910–1911): 287.

8. Emerson, "Psychoanalysis and Hospitals."

9. Myerson, "Hysteria as a Weapon," p. 1.

10. LEE case 240, 1914.

11. I culled sixteen cases of hysteria from Boston Psychopathic Hospital records, a small proportion of those so diagnosed. According to a document in the Southard Papers, "These lists include all cases." At least forty-four women under the age of twenty-one were diagnosed as hysterics in the years from 1912 through 1916. Of the cases I found, ten (63 percent) were from the working class; one (an adding-machine operator) was a pink-collar worker; one was the daughter of middle-class parents; and two were still in school. From Emerson's records, I drew an additional twenty-seven cases. Occupational information was available for only ten (40 percent) of these cases: two (20 percent) were from the working class; seven (70 percent) worked at low-level white-collar occupations in offices or stores or ran small (and not especially successful) businesses as milliners or dressmakers; one was training to be a teacher. This occupational breakdown should be interpreted cautiously, however, for it excludes the sixteen women (62 percent) for whom no occupation was listed. An undetermined number of these had not worked for many years. This chapter is based on these forty-three cases as well as on published case reports; although there is some overlap among the three groups, I have counted each case only once.

12. Seventy percent told such tales; I have excluded the others from my analysis here either because insufficient information concerning them was available or because they did not conform to the "classic" picture the other women presented.

13. LEE case 224, 1914.

14. LEE case 81, 1912.

15. LEE case 264, 1915.

16. LEE case 53, 1911–1915.

17. I found several uses of the term "sexual assault" in the records of women diagnosed as hysterics: case 5426, 1915, and LEE cases 70, 41, and 91 ("sexually assaulted by a boy when abt. 4 years").

18. F. R. Bronson, "False Accusations of Rape," *American Journal of Urology and Sexology* 14 (1918): 541.

19. Gurney Williams, "Rape in Children and in Young Girls," *International*

Clinics 23d ser., 2 (1913): 250; Charles C. Mapes, "Sexual Assault," *Urologic and Cutaneous Review* 21 (1917): 431.

20. Williams, "Rape in Children," p. 259; Mapes, "Sexual Assault," p. 430. Mapes cited another authority who wrote that "no woman in her senses can be entered without her consent; but with her ability to scream and her power to bring her thighs together unless there be semi-willingness on her part, be he never so strong and she never so small and delicate. . . . The man who enters into so hard a task will find that his penis will drop inevitably" (p. 434).

21. The physician who related this tale offered one rationale for men's behavior: "To quote a coarse but expressive Italian proverb, 'cazzo duro non ragiona'" (Bronson, "False Accusations," pp. 551–52). Some of Myerson's patients, by his account, were familiar with the expression, asking him "why has an erect penis no conscience if society is right?" (*Speaking of Man*, p. 86).

22. Southard and Jarrett's account of the case of nineteen-year-old Bessie Polski, a Polish immigrant, is telling in this regard. Polski was accosted and "raped by three men" while looking for work; "convulsions shortly ensued" and she was sent to the Psychopathic Hospital, where she was diagnosed as a hysteric. Southard and Jarrett's discussion focused on such issues as her probable feeblemindedness, economic difficulties, and language deficiencies, and they considered the possibility that she, by now "a probable victim of rape," was a sex delinquent. But they never made more than an implicit connection between the rape and her hysterical symptoms. They never overtly questioned the veracity of her account of the incident; rather, they obliterated its potential significance by burying it amid a host of other factors (*Kingdom of Evils*, pp. 105–7; case 5610, 1915, case history).

23. Case 1002, 1913, staff meeting.

24. Case 8498, 1917, staff meeting.

25. LEE case 50, 1912, letter to patient.

26. Case 1002, 1913, staff meeting.

27. LEE case 244, 1915.

28. L. E. Emerson, "A Psychoanalytic Study of a Severe Case of Hysteria," *Journal of Abnormal Psychology* 7 (1912–1913): 385–406; 8 (1913–1914): 44–56; 8 (1913–1914): 180–207 (quotation from p. 199); L. E. Emerson, "A Philosophy for Psychoanalysts," *Psychoanalytic Review* 2 (1915): 426–27.

29. L. E. Emerson, "The Case of Miss A: A Preliminary Report of a Psychoanalytic Study and Treatment of a Case of Self-Mutilation," *Psychoanalytic Review* 1 (1913–1914): 42.

30. LEE case 24, 1911, a man, told of having regularly masturbated his sister and of having pinched her genitals. He admitted to telling her that if she refused his attentions, "we'd have to cut her genitals out," and told Emerson that he "worked on her fears, that she mustn't ever do it to herself."

31. Emerson, "Case of Miss A," p. 42. John Forrester's observations that "the analyst behaves as an epistemological radical, by ignoring the difference between truth and lies, between truth and fiction," and that he or she "also behaves as a legal subversive in bypassing the distinction between rape and seduction," are pertinent here (*The Seductions of Psychoanalysis: Freud, Lacan, and Derrida* [Cambridge, 1990], p. 8). In the midst of one case, Emerson noted to himself, the patient "was so vehement in her denial of any possible intercourse, I suspect it" (LEE case 67, 1912)—the only instance I found of him turning a patient's words around.

32. Fifteen of the total forty-two cases (37 percent) make up this group of women subject to sexual assault; eleven (73 percent) of them had symptoms of severe hysteria. For the remaining four the consequences were medically less severe but socially quite marked; these women, who resolved their psychic traumas by taking flight from heterosexuality, are discussed below.

33. Case 677, 1912, case record, ward notes, patient's account of dream, and Emerson's notes of sessions with her. Emerson, "Summary of Four Cases," wrote that he had tried "psychoanalytic treatment for therapeutic purposes" with her (and, in his first months at the hospital, six others), but "without much success."

34. LEE case 83, 1912–1916.

35. LEE case 26, 1911–1912.

36. LEE cases 83, 1914; and 53, 1911. Other women also considered the option: one decided against it, saying "it is too strict, and you have to give up so many things" (LEE case 27, 1911); another thought about it for several years, because she "didn't care to go out much" (LEE case 219, 1914); yet another thought of becoming a nun but told Emerson that she "used to pray and [her] prayers used to turn into just the opposite" (LEE case 224, 1914).

37. LEE case 50, 1911–1913, Emerson's notes, his and patient's letters (note that the spelling and punctuation of the quoted material that follows is as in the original). Mather was not alone in confronting a skeptical mother; another told her mother of having been assaulted, to which the mother said, "people thought things so much they finally got to think so in reality. She wouldn't believe me." Emerson judged her "cowardice almost incredible" (Emerson, "Severe Case of Hysteria," pp. 404–5).

38. Emerson noted that he told her "that what she was doing was a sort of masturbation and it made her cross at first, but now she understands it."

39. Emerson saw Mather in August 1916, noting that she was "very well— married 1 1/2 years" to a mail-wagon driver. Among other cases of "classic" hysteria in which sexual assault or abuse was an etiological factor are that of a twenty-two-year-old woman (case 1002, 1913; LEE case 58), published by Emerson as "Severe Case of Hysteria," and that of the twenty-three-year-old "Miss A" (case 359, 1912), which appeared in print as Emerson, "Case of Miss A." Parts of this case appear in Martin Bauml Duberman, "'I Am Not Contented': Female Masochism and Lesbianism in Early Twentieth-Century New England," Signs 5, no. 4 (1980): 825–41.

40. LEE case 85, 1912, Emerson's notes and patient's letters. Another woman, an eighteen-year-old who was troubled by nausea and constant vomiting, told Emerson of being subjected to the same course of unwanted male bullying. Her boyfriend, telling her (as Emerson's notes read) that "every girl ought to know abt. that before she got married," progressed from kissing her to feeling her legs, then "fondled her—then had connection one night in a field near the edge of a wood" (LEE case 92, 1912).

41. LEE case 259, 1915.

42. Case 853, 1913, case history.

43. LEE case 256, 1915.

44. LEE case 264, 1915.

45. LEE case 45, 1911.

46. LEE case 78, 1912.

47. LEE case 242, 1914.

48. LEE case 27, 1911.

49. LEE cases 254, 1915, and 264, 1915.

50. Quotation from Emerson, "Severe Case of Hysteria," p. 388.

51. "Misinformation" from LEE cases 26, 85, 219, 236, and 244, among others.

52. LEE case 251, 1915.

53. Emerson, "Severe Case of Hysteria," p. 201; LEE case 263, 1915.

54. LEE cases 242, 1914, and 238, 1914.

55. Quotation from LEE case 48, 1912.

56. LEE cases 254, 81, 87, and 244. Emerson opened an unpublished paper, "Sublimation," Emerson Papers, with a long quotation from Freud: "One does as well as he can as an explainer where ignorance has produced timorousness, as a teacher, as a representative of a freer and superior world-conception, and as confessor, who through the continuance of his sympathy and his respect, imparts, so to say, absolution after the confession."

57. LEE case 264, 1915.

58. LEE case 255, 1915.

59. LEE case 263, 1915.

60. Case 1158, 1913, staff meeting.

61. LEE case 254, 1915.

62. LEE case 251, 1915.

63. LEE case 85, 1912.

64. LEE case 227, 1914.

65. LEE case 223, 1914.

66. LEE case 67, 1914.

67. "I will feel a great deal toward that subject as Huxley says about vivisection," the same psychiatrist added. "It is necessary, therefore, somebody must do it, but I can't do it" (case 1002, 1913, staff meeting).

68. "I think it is a little mistake to have her hear so much of the discussion," Adler admitted to his colleagues after the patient had left the room (ibid.).

69. Southard and Jarrett, *Kingdom of Evils*, pp. 335–37. Cf. Emerson's account of the same case in "Hystero-Epilepsy," pp. 318–19.

70. LEE case 50, 1912.

71. Case 3800, 1914, staff meeting.

72. LEE case 45, 1911.

73. LEE case 262, 1915.

74. Margarethe Kossak, "The Sexual Life of the Hysteric," *American Journal of Urology and Sexology* 11 (1915): 505. Kossak wrote from Vienna.

75. LEE case 244, 1915. Kossak, who stressed that it was "a *mistake* to assume that sexual desire arises spontaneously in the girl. . . . [Her] desire has always to be awakened," might have agreed with Dutton (ibid., pp. 505–6).

76. Consider Southard and Jarrett's conflation of diagnosis and epithet in this description of a "hysterical sex delinquent": "There was, as is frequent with hysterics, a good deal of the histrionic about her attitude" (*Kingdom of Evils*, p. 73).

77. Case 7858, 1916, case history, ward notes.

78. Myerson, "Hysteria as a Weapon."

79. Quotation from case 1158, 1913, staff meeting.

80. Case 1002, 1912, staff meeting.

81. LEE case 48, 1913, letter from a Dr. Smith to Emerson. Sigmund Freud related that as a young physician he had been told by an older colleague of a familiar "prescription," which the latter said he could not order, for a woman, married for eighteen years to an impotent man, suffering from severe anxiety: "Rx Penis normalis/dosim/repetatur!" ("On the History of the Psycho-Analytic Movement," in Freud, *Standard Edition*, 14, pp. 14–15). Neil Hertz, "Dora's Secrets, Freud's Techniques," in *In Dora's Case: Freud—Hysteria—Feminism*, ed. Charles Bernheimer and Claire Kahane (New York, 1990), pp. 221–42, discusses Freud's telling of this anecdote. Emerson concluded his article on "Miss A" by noting that "the assumption that what the patient was suffering from was lack of specific sexual satisfaction" was wrong (clearly, some readers might have thought it right), and that for that reason he had not advised "sexual relations or masturbation" ("Case of Miss A," p. 54).

The married uncle of one of Emerson's patients "told her he knew what the trouble was. He could make her well. She told him to go to hell" (LEE case 262).

82. Showalter, *Female Malady*, captures some of the confusion of feminists' positions, asking whether hysteria was "a mode of protest for women deprived of other social or intellectual outlets or expressive options" (p. 147)—a strain that runs through the literature concerning nineteenth-century hysteria—and then concluding that it "was· at best a private, ineffectual response to the frustrations of women's lives" (p. 161).

83. LEE case 85, 1912.

84. LEE case 53, 1911.

85. LEE case 48, 1912.

86. LEE case 247, 1915; see also case 5370.

NINE: MODERN MANHOOD, DISSOLUTE AND RESPECTABLE

1. On masculinity and the "national temper," see Joe L. Dubbert, "Progressivism and the Masculinity Crisis," in *The American Man*, ed. Elizabeth H. Pleck and Joseph H. Pleck (Englewood Cliffs, N.J., 1980), pp. 303–20. On the military, see Donald J. Mrozek, "The Habit of Victory: The American Military and the Cult of Manliness," in *Manliness and Morality: Middle-class Masculinity in Britain and America, 1800–1940*, ed. J. A. Mangan and James Walvin (Manchester, 1987), p. 234, where the author asserts that "the ultimate meaning of 'manliness' for the military—or of the concept altogether—may remain elusive, largely because its supposed attributes closely resemble those customarily related to the more general notion of 'character'"—a statement that should open up rather than end analysis. On scouting, see Jeffrey P. Hantover, "The Boy Scouts and the Validation of Masculinity," in Pleck and Pleck, *American Man*, pp. 285–301; and David I. Macleod, "Act Your Age: Boyhood, Adolescence, and the Rise of the Boy Scouts in America," *Journal of Social History* 16 (Winter 1982): 3–20.

2. Peter G. Filene, *Him/Her/Self: Sex Roles in Modern America*, 2d ed. (Baltimore, 1986), esp. chap. 3, treats manhood with sensitivity but does not ade-

quately account for male prerogative. Lake, "Politics of Respectability," which teases the turn-of-the-century Australian masculinist ethos out of the national culture and conceptualizes masculinity as a construct as interwoven into men's lives as femininity is into women's, is a brilliant forward step in the literature about men and manhood. Among more recent works on men are Mark C. Carnes and Clyde Griffen, eds., *Meanings for Manhood: Constructions of Masculinity in Victorian America* (Chicago, 1990), and Kevin White, *The First Sexual Revolution: The Emergence of Male Heterosexuality in Modern America* (New York, 1993).

3. Among these patients are men whom psychiatrists diagnosed as psychopathic, neurotic, or simply "sane" (most of those given the first two diagnoses were also deemed sane). Nearly all of these men were working-class; they were drawn from all of Boston's racial and ethnic groups.

4. Southard and Jarrett, *Kingdom of Evils*, p. 179.

5. Case 1607, 1913, letter to Jarrett.

6. Case 6984, 1916, social service record.

7. Quotations from Healy, *Individual Delinquent*, p. 585; and LEE cases 50, 1912, and 85, 1912.

8. Case 10070, 1918, staff meeting.

9. Case 10834, 1918, case history. J. Adams Puffer, *The Boy and His Gang* (Boston, 1912), provides a contemporary sociology of gang life in Boston.

10. Case 6693, 1916, staff meeting. "These adventures with literary women, don't they lead you to drink?" Southard asked another man, who said they did not (case 7489, 1916, staff meeting).

11. Case 7599, 1916, staff meeting.

12. LEE case 24, 1911.

13. LEE case 260, 1915. This man and LEE case 24 both told of engaging in oral sex with companions. M. W. Peck and F. L. Wells, both of the Psychopathic Hospital, reported in "Further Studies in the Psycho-Sexuality of College Graduate Men," *Mental Hygiene* 9 (1925): 512, that 34 percent of the men they had questioned learned of sex from companions. The behaviors cited in the text were not exceptional. M. J. Exner, *Problems and Principles of Sex Education: A Study of 948 College Men* (New York, 1914), p. 5, reported that 544 of 677 respondents first learned of sex from "boy associates," at an average age of 9.6 years. Alfred C. Kinsey, Wardell B. Pomeroy, and Clyde E. Martin, *Sexual Behavior in the Human Male* (Philadelphia, 1948), pp. 168–71, noted that about half the older males surveyed and nearly two-thirds of the preadolescent boys reported engaging in preadolescent homosexual activity. Two-thirds of this group engaged in mutual masturbation; in less than half of all cases preadolescent activity was continued through adolescence or into adulthood. Anecdotal evidence for the same can be found in Albert E. Stearne, "Effects of Lascivious Conversations, Books, and Companions in the Causation of Sexual Excess," *American Journal of Dermatology and Genito-Urinary Disease* 11 (1907): 323–34, and in the observations of one patient's worried mother, who wrote to psychiatrists that she had been informed "that the older boys in the class were undressing the youthful ones." She concluded: "A mother cannot be too watchful and observing in regard to the private life of her boys" (case 478, 1912, letter to psychiatrists).

14. LEE case 260, 1915. This man told of taking photographs of himself and his

wife in the nude, which, Emerson noted, he thought were "nice when he couldn't have intercourse." Another man told of seeing his father out with two women when he was eleven, and of informing his mother of his father's duplicity (LEE case 29, 1911). A twenty-three-year-old baker told of learning that his mother "went with other men" (LEE case 245, 1915).

15. Evidence suggests that psychiatrists considered youthful masturbation normal. M. W. Peck and F. L. Wells, "On the Psycho-Sexuality of College Graduate Men," *Mental Hygiene* 7 (1923): 702–5, reported the incidence of masturbation in a group of "normal" men (as opposed, in the authors' minds, to the heterogeneous abnormals of the sexologist Havelock Ellis's "histories"), finding that the majority had begun by age fourteen. In a story that perhaps reveals more about the masculine camaraderie that prevailed in the medical school lecture hall than about its purported subject, the authors wrote that "a certain medical professor used to ask those students, of a class of some hundred, who had not masturbated to raise their hands." Five would do so, and he would call them all liars.

16. LEE cases 50, 1912; and 85, 1912.

17. LEE case 92, 1912.

· 18. LEE case 226, 1914.

19. LEE case 185, 1913. He suspected the nurse was pregnant, and told Emerson he thought she would "be better for an abortion."

20. LEE case 232, 1914.

21. LEE case 29, 1911.

22. LEE case 24, 1911.

23. LEE case 228, 1915. Emerson reported the case in "Hystero-Epilepsy," pp. 324–27. He thought the man's reasons for breaking off "absolutely all relations with the girl" were "quite adequate." Peck and Wells, "College Graduate Men," p. 712, found that only 10 percent of their subjects reported that "mixing socially with better class of girls at dances, parties, etc." increased their sexual cravings; 54 percent reported that such mixing decreased their cravings. By contrast, "minor love making," reading "realistic love scenes" in modern fiction, and musical comedies increased desire for 60 to 84 percent of the men in the study. Clearly unsettled by this finding, the authors returned to it in their later study, writing that "if 'nice girls' did not afford erotic stimulation at least equal to their more liberal sisters, the whole social function of modesty would be called into grave question," and warning that "to give the devil a controlling interest in eroticism is unsound both as mental hygiene and technical psychology" (Peck and Wells, "Further Studies of College Graduate Men," pp. 513–14).

24. LEE case 35, 1911.

25. Ibid.

26. LEE case 260, 1915.

27. LEE case 29, 1911.

28. Ibid.

29. The medical literature on male sexual problems for the most part treated them in isolation from the social context in which discussions of women's sexual deficits were invariably located. See, for example, Eugene Fuller, "How to Diagnosticate Sexual Derangements in the Male," *American Medico-Surgical Bulletin* 8 (1895): 1156–59; Bukk G. Carleton, "The Cause and Treatment of the So-Called

Sexual Neuroses of the Male," *Medical Times* 25 (1897): 69–72; Albert J. Underhill, "Sexual Neurasthenia in Men," *Journal of the American Medical Association* 60 (1913): 1869–74.

30. Case 1258, 1913, case history. Abraham Myerson, "Anhedonia," *American Journal of Psychiatry* 79 (1922–1923), wrote that "there is widely diffused throughout every community a belief that potency is associated with the essential manhood of the individual" (p. 89).

31. LEE case 29, 1911.

32. Case 12266, 1919, case history; this case also appears in Southard and Jarrett, *Kingdom of Evils*, pp. 361–64.

33. Quotation from Southard and Jarrett, *Kingdom of Evils*, p. 144. One man characterized writing poetry among the "disreputable things" he had done in his life, telling Emerson he had had a "spark of poetry in him" that had been killed. "Father always hated two things, a fiddler, and poetry" (LEE case 267, 1915). Healy, *Individual Delinquent*, commented that one sixteen-year-old psychopath "has very few manly traits"—the boy was given to crying and petty thievery, he spoke in a high, childish voice, and he was helpful at school, attending to small duties—and that another, fourteen years old, was "an arrant coward" (pp. 578, 582).

34. Case 7794, 1916, wife's statement.

35. Southard and Jarrett, *Kingdom of Evils*, p. 144. Psychiatrists diagnosed this man a cyclothymic (manic-depressive), a diagnosis associated with femininity.

36. Case 4592, 1915, case history.

37. Case 10240, 1918, staff meeting. The man had entered the hospital voluntarily.

38. G. E. Partridge, "A Study of Fifty Cases of Psychopathic Personality," *American Journal of Psychiatry* 84 (1927–1928): 958; Loren B. T. Johnson, "Terminology," in Karpman, "Psychopathic Individual," p. 183.

39. Case 10140, 1918, case history.

40. LEE case 260, 1915.

41. Case 1258, 1913, transcripts of psychoanalytic treatment with Lydiard Horton, a psychoanalyst who practiced briefly at the Psychopathic Hospital. M. W. Peck, "The Sex Life of College Men," *Journal of Nervous and Mental Disease* 62 (1925): 31–43, written as a "preliminary contribution" to knowledge of the problem of homosexuality, presents the histories of nine homosexual men. Peck estimated that 10 percent of college men were homosexual; he noted that the "homosexual make-up" of most was unknown to their friends, although registering "the mysterious capacity which homosexuals had for recognizing each other."

42. Freedman, "Uncontrolled Desires," pp. 83–106.

43. Case 5085, 1917, letter to social worker. The case also appears in Southard and Jarrett, *Kingdom of Evils*, pp. 65–68.

44. Case 1624, 1913, social service record.

45. Case 10044, 1917, wife's statement.

46. Case 7366, 1916, case history.

47. Case 10070, 1918, staff meeting.

48. Case 11003, 1918, case history.

49. LEE case 226, 1914.

50. LEE case 29, 1911.

51. LEE case 260, 1915.

52. LEE case 228, 1914.

53. L. E. Emerson, "Case Report of a Mathematician," MS, Emerson Papers.

54. Mildred M. Scheetz, "The Psychopathic Judgment," in Karpman, "Psychopathic Individual," pp. 186–87.

55. Case 2754, 1914, staff meeting.

56. John W. Visher, "A Study in Constitutional Psychopathic Inferiority," *Mental Hygiene* 6 (1922): 744; James H. Huddleson, "Connotation," p. 1963, comment by a Dr. House.

57. Bryant, "Constitutional Psychopathic Inferior," p. 683, comment by a Dr. Hutchings.

58. Cases 10369, 1918, case history; and 10240, 1918, case history.

59. Ian D. Suttie, "Moral Imbecility," *Journal of Mental Science* 70 (1924): 367, 363; Richard Hofstadter, *Anti-Intellectualism in American Life* (New York, 1963), p. 46; William H. Whyte, Jr., *The Organization Man* (New York, 1956), p. 212 (also cited in Hofstadter, p. 264). Myrtelle M. Canavan, a Psychopathic Hospital pathologist, and Rosamond Clark wrote in "The Mental Health of 581 Offspring of Non-Psychotic Parents," *Mental Hygiene* 7 (1923): 777, that "from one point of view, a nation of moderate successes is superior to one of too perceptible differences, though historians might not find it so interesting."

60. Among the discipline's foundational texts are Herman M. Adler, "Unemoyment and Industry—A Study of Psychopathic Cases," *Mental Hygiene* 1 (1917): 16–24 (based on a study of one hundred unemployed men admitted to the Psychopathic Hospital); Cobb, "Applications of Psychiatry to Industrial Hygiene," pp. 343–47 (Cobb was a Massachusetts General Hospital neurologist); Mary C. Jarrett, "The Psychopathic Employee: A Problem of Industry," *Medicine and Surgery* 1 (1917): 727–41; Southard, "Movement for a Mental Hygiene of Industry," pp. 43–64; Southard, "Trade Unionism and Temperament: Notes Upon the Psychiatric Point of View in Industry," *Mental Hygiene* 4 (1920): 281–300 (in which Southard distinguished industrial psychiatry from Taylorism); Southard, "Modern Specialist in Unrest," pp. 550–63; and Southard, "The Mental Hygiene of Industry: A Movement that Particularly Concerns Employment Managers," *Industrial Management* 59 (1920): 100–106. Jarrett, "Nervous Women in Industry," is singular in its focus on women.

An early work, Southard and H. C. Solomon, "Occupation Neuroses," in *Diseases of Occupation and Vocational Hygiene*, ed. George M. Kober and William C. Hanson (Philadelphia, 1916), pp. 270–95, is essentially a review of the voluminous French and German literature of writer's cramp, the authors not even mentioning psychopathy, which would, in the space of a few years, dominate the literature of industrial psychiatry—testimony to how quickly the discipline cohered, and how significantly it differed from its predecessor. In 1917, Jarrett, "Psychopathic Employee," noted that only four articles culled from a recent forty-nine-page bibliography on the subject dealt with "psychopathic conditions" (p. 728). According to Southard, "Trade Unionism and Temperament," Irving Fisher, a Yale University political economist, coined the term "industrial psychiatry" (p. 282).

61. Quotations from Southard, "Trade Unionism and Temperament," pp. 284–85.

62. Quotations from Jarrett, "Psychopathic Employee," p. 727; Southard, "Mental Hygiene of Industry," p. 103.

63. Southard, "Movement for a Mental Hygiene of Industry," p. 51.

64. Southard and Jarrett stated that "men patients between the ages of twenty-five and fifty-five were selected" for a study of psychopathic employees in industry, funded by the Permanent Charity Fund, Inc., from 1914 through 1920. Industrial histories of 250 men were compiled, and an unrecorded number of cases, several of women among them, were assisted. See Southard and Jarrett, *Kingdom of Evils*, pp. 498–512, for a brief description of the work and a cursory evaluation of the cases.

65. Case 3868, 1914, case history, social service record; also presented in Jarrett, "Psychopathic Employee," pp. 732–33. In Blumberg's case, Jews and non-Jews alike contributed money. In other cases, however, non-Jews registered their objections. "You know it is proverbial that the Jews take care of their own," a Yankee Lady Bountiful wrote in response to social workers' request for money in another case, suggesting that they consult "one of the Rabbis in town. . . . I do not feel it demands my special attention" (case 8530, 1915, letter to social worker). Similarly, an annoyed New York social worker to whom a Jewish woman had been referred implored her fellow workers to "kindly mention that the family in whom you are interested is Jewish if such is the case" (case 10045, 1917, letter to social worker).

66. LEE cases 59, 1912; 29, 1911; 24, 1911.

67. Case 6693, 1916, staff meeting.

68. For "normals," see Partridge, "Psychopathic Personalities," pp. 179–80; case 10070, 1918, staff meeting.

69. See Pleck, *Domestic Tyranny*, pp. 49–66. Prohibition took effect 1 July 1919.

70. Roy Rosenzweig, *Eight Hours for What We Will: Workers and Leisure in an Industrial City, 1870–1920* (Cambridge, 1983), esp. pp. 57–64, makes this case most succinctly and powerfully.

71. Quotation from Richard Stivers, *A Hair of the Dog: Irish Drinking and American Stereotype* (University Park, Pa., 1976), p. 86, cited in Rosenzweig, *Eight Hours*, p. 63. On the saloon as workingman's club, on decor, and on the masculine ethos, see Jon M. Kingsdale, "The 'Poor Man's Club': Social Functions of the Urban Working-Class Saloon," in Pleck and Pleck, *American Man*, pp. 255–83. On treating, and on masculinity, see Rosenzweig, *Eight Hours*, pp. 59–63. See also Norman H. Clark, *Deliver Us from Evil: An Interpretation of American Prohibition* (New York, 1976), p. 1, which skillfully evokes, with the help of Jack London, the "finely masculine satisfactions" of the saloon.

72. Broadly speaking, Psychopathic Hospital psychiatrists did not consider "alcoholism" a psychiatric diagnosis, and were happy to leave the unraveling of its mysteries to other physicians; rather, they considered it a symptom of other, largely psychopathic, defects. They did consider alcoholic hallucinosis (a condition that was quite difficult to distinguish from delirium tremens) a species of mental disease, in which alcoholism was a predisposing but not sufficient cause. The various statutes governing involuntary commitment held that hospital authorities could refuse to admit persons suffering from delirium tremens or drunkenness; in practice, however, such persons were admitted and treated in the same manner as all others.

Further, because psychiatrists did not distinguish consistently among the many varieties of alcohol-related conditions, I have grouped them all under the rubric of alcoholism, a term used in practice to refer loosely to all the conditions among which theory distinguished. See Southard and Jarrett, *Kingdom of Evils*, pp. 244–61, for a discussion of alcoholism from a psychiatric point of view. Irwin H. Neff, superintendent of the Foxborough State Hospital in Massachusetts, in "Treatment of Inebriety," *Journal of Inebriety* 32 (1910): 133–44, forcefully argued the case for medical authority over alcoholism. William F. Bynum, "Chronic Alcoholism in the First Half of the Nineteenth Century," *Bulletin of the History of Medicine* 42 (1968): 160–85, provides an overview of nineteenth-century medical and psychiatric perspectives on drunkenness. See Parmelee, *Inebriety in Boston*, for a contemporary sociology of drinking.

73. Southard, "Empathic Index," p. 210.

74. One contemporary authority, a fervent proponent of the alcoholism-as-disease line, denounced his medical colleagues' tendency to proffer what he called "middle-of-the-road" positions, "trying to find a happy mean, between what they call the extreme of total abstinence on the one side, and the excessive use of spirits on the other" (T. D. Crothers, "A Review of the History and Literature of Inebriety: The First Journal and Its Work up to the Present Time," *Journal of Inebriety* 33 [1911–1912]: 148).

75. Case 6682, 1916, case history, staff meeting, and social service record.

76. Psychopathic Hospital psychiatrists diagnosed 18 percent of all male patients alcoholic. Of these, 35 percent were Irish (born in Ireland or parents born in Ireland). Twenty-three percent of all Irish males were found alcoholic.

77. Case 1111, 1913, staff meeting.

78. Case 3212, 1914, case history.

79. Case 4198, 1914, staff meeting.

80. Case 10274, 1918, case history.

81. Case 9779, 1917, staff meeting.

82. Case 4198, 1914, staff meeting.

83. Case 3212, 1914, letter to wife.

84. Case 5879, 1915, staff meeting and social service record.

85. Case 4284, 1917, social service record.

86. Case 1111, 1913, special interview with patient.

87. Case 8347, 1917, staff meeting. In another case, one psychiatrist commented that he thought it was "characteristic for alcoholics to throw responsibility for their condition on some outside person" (case 7441, 1916, staff meeting).

88. Stivers, *Hair of the Dog*, pp. 58–67.

89. As psychiatrists observed with respect to one Irishman, "The wit and humor are likely for his race." They had asked him how often he got drunk, and he replied, "About every time I drink." Remarking on his readmission to the hospital, a psychiatrist said, "Here you are back again." "Well, many a good man went back twice," he parried. Case 11691, 1918, staff meeting.

90. Case 5879, 1915, social service record.

91. Case 8347, 1917, staff meeting.

92. Case 1111, 1913, staff meeting.

93. Case 4284, 1917, letter to social worker.

94. Case 6682, 1916, letter to wife. Discussing another case, of a man whose wife had lost faith in his promises, a psychiatrist observed to his colleagues that "clinical experience teaches us that a patient of his present condition, the result of years of alcoholic excess, can be depended upon to make many promises to his family about drinking habits and to keep none of these promises" (case 7378, 1916, staff meeting).

95. Case 6874, 1916–1921, case history, social service record. Social workers judged the father "intelligent, but of the type frequently seen in City offices," a reference to his Irish ancestry.

96. He referred to social workers "making [him] over": O'Meara to social worker Warren, 1917.

97. Southard and Jarrett, *Kingdom of Evils*, p. 38. Jarrett described the first gathering of the club, on 17 October 1913: "We sat about in the waiting-room of the Out-Patient Department telling stories and jokes and a young man Dr. Stearns had brought played the piano. Gradually we all joined in singing college songs. Miss White and I made coffee, and we had some good buns made by the cook. Then we passed cigars, and they smoked and told more stories. Everybody wanted to come again" ("Notes to Trustees").

98. E. E. Southard, *Shell-Shock and Other Neuropsychiatric Problems: Presented in Five Hundred and Eighty-Nine Case Histories from the War Literature, 1914–1918* (1919; reprint, New York, 1973), presents excerpts from the wartime literature and contains a full bibliography. Showalter, *Female Malady*, chap. 7, perceptively examines shell shock in Britain. The author of an article published in 1903 complained that his medical colleagues underdiagnosed hysteria in men, noting that "in the female . . . we are always suspicious of hysteria" (Sheldon G. Evans, "Hysteria in the Male with Report of a Case," *Journal of the Association of Military Surgeons of the United States* 13 [1903]: 377); similarly, four years later another physician noted that hysteria was rare in men (Alexander W. Blain, "Hysteria in the Male," *Detroit Medical Journal* 7 [1907]: 96–97). Jan Goldstein, "The Uses of Male Hysteria: Medical and Literary Discourse in Nineteenth-Century France," *Representations* 34 (Spring 1991): 134–65, brilliantly examines the interplay of diagnosis and gender around male hysteria. Mark S. Micale, "Charcot and the Idea of Hysteria in the Male: Gender, Mental Science, and Medical Diagnosis in Late Nineteenth-Century France," *Medical History* 34 (1990): 363–411, persuasively documents Charcot's interest in male hysteria, but there is little awareness of this phenomenon in the American literature.

99. Southard, "Shell Shock and After," pp. 73–93, quotations from pp. 80, 79. Richard H. Hutchings, "Hysteria as Manifested in the Military Service," *State Hospital Quarterly* 4 (1918–1919): 300, also referred to wartime hysterics as "normal."

100. Hutchings, "Hysteria in Military Service," p. 297, citing the German neurologist Möbius; Aaron J. Rosanoff, "A Study of Hysteria, Based Mainly on Clinical Material Observed in the U.S. Army Hospital for War Neuroses at Plattsburgh Barracks, N.Y.," *Archives of Neurology and Psychiatry* 2 (1919): 422.

101. Albert Warren Stearns, "The Importance of a History as a Means of Detecting Psychopathic Recruits," *Military Surgeon* 43 (1918): 657–58.

102. For estimates, see Albert Warren Stearns, "The Psychiatric Examination of Recruits," *Journal of the American Medical Association* 70 (1918): 229–31.

103. Cases 10573, 1918, staff meeting; 10311, 1918, case history, social service record.

104. Case in Southard and Jarrett, *Kingdom of Evils*, pp. 308–9. See Rosanoff, "Study of Hysteria," for a contemporary statement of the received wisdom.

105. Southard, "Shell Shock and After," p. 77. Rosanoff, "Study of Hysteria," p. 443, chided the many authorities (whom he cites and excerpts) who made the distinction, claiming himself that hysteria was merely malingering in medical guise.

106. Foucault, introduction to Canguilhem, *Normal and the Pathological*, p. 20.

107. Karl A. Menninger, "Hysteria in a Male as a Defense Reaction: A Case Report," *Boston Medical and Surgical Journal* 180 (1919): 612–13 (the case was from the Psychopathic Hospital). Jarrett, "Shell-Shock Analogues," normalized male hysteria along the same lines.

108. Martin W. Peck, "Mental Examinations of College Men," *American Journal of Psychiatry* 81 (1924–1925): 621.

109. Case 12266, 1919, letter to social worker.

TEN: THE SEXUAL POLITICS OF MARRIAGE

1. Simmons, "Companionate Marriage," succinctly outlines the shift from Victorian to companionate marriage; see also Ben Lindsey and Wainwright Evans, *The Companionate Marriage* (New York, 1927). Lasch, *Haven in a Heartless World*, chaps. 1 and 2, briskly characterizes the turn-of-the-century crisis of the family and the medical response thereto. See Abraham Myerson, *Social Psychology* (New York, 1934), p. 568, on the divorce rate, which stood at 53 per 100,000 population in 1890, 139 in 1920. A social science literature on desertion obliquely addressed the question of marriage among the poor; see, for example, Zilpha D. Smith, *Deserted Wives and Deserting Husbands: A Study of 234 Families Based on the Experience of the District Committees and Agents of the Associated Charities of Boston* (Boston, 1901). On divorce, see Elaine Tyler May, *Great Expectations: Marriage and Divorce in Post-Victorian America* (Chicago, 1980), and Robert L. Griswold, *Family and Divorce in California, 1850–1890: Victorian Illusions and Everyday Realities* (Albany, N.Y., 1982). Karen Lystra, *Searching the Heart: Women, Men, and Romantic Love in Nineteenth-Century America* (New York, 1989), offers a revisionist interpretation of middle-class Victorian marriage.

2. This chapter is based primarily on the extensive psychiatric and social service records (many of them fifty to a hundred pages in length) of eighteen women and seventeen men, as well as on approximately fifteen other cases subjected to less intensive scrutiny. With respect to diagnosis, no clear pattern characterizes this group of patients: psychiatrists diagnosed some of them as sane; others sane but feebleminded; a number of the men alcoholic; and some of the men and women psychopathic. They thought a few others were victims of dementia praecox. The men in this group were divided evenly between the working class and the middle class; among the group were an attorney, several salesmen, a clerk, several skilled workers, and several laborers. Although occupational information concerning the

women is incomplete and inconclusive, it appears that they came from a range of material circumstances as well. None of the group was wealthy; most were of modest means, and a few were quite poor. With respect to ethnicity, 55 percent of the men in this group were of Irish descent, as were 25 percent of the women. On Irish-American marital relations, see Hasia R. Diner, *Erin's Daughters in America: Irish Immigrant Women in the Nineteenth Century* (Baltimore, 1983); on Irish marital relations, see David Fitzpatrick, "Divorce and Separation in Modern Irish History," *Past and Present* 114 (1987): 172–96.

3. Menninger, "Hysteria in a Male," p. 613.

4. Cases 1111, 1913, staff meeting; 8797, 1917, letter from husband of patient to brother-in-law.

5. For a sampling of the large popular literature of sexual antagonism, see Amanda Saepe Quaesita, "The Unattractiveness of American Men," *Independent* 67 (1909): 1065–67; Catherine D. Groth, "Man—The Timid Sex," *Harper's Weekly* 54 (19 March 1910): 17; Edward J. Ward, "Women Should Mind Their Own Business," *Independent* 70 (1911): 1370–71; "The Subjection of Man," *Living Age* 274 (1912): 765–66; Rose Young, "Men, Women, and Sex Antagonism," *Good Housekeeping* 58 (April 1914): 487–90; and Mary Heaton Vorse, "Is the American Man a Failure?" *Woman's Home Companion* 39 (12 January 1910): 10.

6. Case 2537, 1914, case history and social service record.

7. Case 5306, 1915, social service record.

8. Case 390, 1913, staff meeting.

9. Case 6613, 1916, letter to psychiatrists.

10. Case 5306, 1915, social service record.

11. Case 1111, 1913, staff meeting.

12. Cf. Hendrik Hartog, "Marital Exits and Marital Expectations in Nineteenth Century America," *Georgetown Law Journal* 80 (1991): "Husbands' marriage rights typically came into their full felt flowering only at the time of separation. During a 'working' marriage the social expectation (and often the reality) was of accommodation and restraint in the exercise of power" (p. 109).

13. Case 1111, 1913, staff meeting.

14. Case 6613, 1916, letter to psychiatrists.

15. Case 2537, 1914, case history.

16. Case 7889, 1916, social service record. In both the hospital records and in Emerson's cases, there is much evidence of youthful unmarried sex between partners who eventually married; some evidence that men forced themselves upon their less than wholly willing partners; and little evidence of concern—on the part of both psychiatrists and their women and men patients—with preserving women's virginity.

17. See Southard and Jarrett, *Kingdom of Evils*, pp. 22–29, for an account of the Loyal case.

18. Case 10471, 1918, letter to social worker.

19. Case 10369, 1918, letter to social worker.

20. Case 3212, 1914, case history.

21. Case 2537, 1914, case history.

22. Case 7781, 1916, social service record.

23. Case 10471, 1918, social service record.

24. Cases 8851, 1917, staff meeting; and 6862, 1916, social service record.

25. Case 5879, 1915, staff meeting. Psychiatrists did not maintain this stance for long. As soon as Connelly left the room, one launched an attack on his wife: "From what I saw of the wife, I do not think she had a very reasonable attitude about it."

26. Case 1111, 1913, staff meeting.

27. Case 830, 1913, case history.

28. Case 7781, 1916, social service record.

29. Case 1111, 1913, conference with patient's wife.

30. Case 830, 1913, staff meeting.

31. Case 9617, 1917, letter to social worker.

32. Case 10168, 1917, letter from patient to employer.

33. Case 9617, 1917, letter to social worker.

34. Case 9826, 1917, staff meeting.

35. Case 5306, 1915, letter to social workers.

36. Case 7781, 1916, letter to Southard from neighbor.

37. Case 6682, 1916, social service record.

38. Ibid.

39. Case 5879, 1915, social service record and case history. Other men voiced similar sentiments.

40. Case 8851, 1917, autobiographical statement.

41. Case 5879, 1915, case history.

42. Case 9826, 1917, staff meeting.

43. Case 4284, 1915, letter to wife.

44. Case 9826, 1917, staff meeting.

45. Case 12429, 1919, staff meeting.

46. Case 10168, 1918, letter to employer.

47. See, for example, Cyrus Edson, "Concerning Nagging Women," *North American Review* 160 (1895): 29–37, which purported to examine the "scientific aspect" of nagging, detailed cases of men driven insane by nagging wives; Lady Henry Somerset, Harriet Prescott Spofford, and Marion Harland, "Nagging Women: A Reply to Dr. Edson," *North American Review* 160 (1895): 311–17, an impassioned, witty feminist riposte; and Edson, "Nagging Women: A Reply," *North American Review* 160 (1895): 440–45, in which he claimed that the fate of children subjected to nagging mothers was worse than that of those terrorized by brutish fathers—some measure of how serious a threat the naggers posed.

48. Case 390, 1913, staff meeting.

49. Case 12960, 1919, staff meeting.

50. Case 830, 1913, staff meeting.

51. Cases 6813, 1916; 8347, 1917, staff meeting; 7378, 1916, case history.

52. On "jealousy psychosis," see Southard and Jarrett, *Kingdom of Evils,* pp. 262–63; and Myerson, *Psychology of Mental Disorders,* pp. 39–40. Quotation from case 6813, 1916, staff meeting. Nellie Byrne told psychiatrists that her husband had "frequently gone into shops and told strangers of [her] gallivanting and her being out looking for admiration" (case 1111, 1913, case history).

53. For Myerson's views, see his popular book, *The Nervous Housewife*; "Nervous Husband," pp. 11ff.; and *Social Psychology,* chaps. 16–20.

54. Case 9617, 1917, social service record. Social workers investigating the charge learned from the husband that he had indeed spent two weeks on his yacht with "some friends," but denied they were actresses.

55. Case 6303, 1916, staff meeting. Discussing whether or not she should have custody of her children, Adler said, "I don't know anything about [her husband], but assume he has better judgment than she has."

56. Myerson, *Nervous Housewife*, p. 220.

57. Case 6902, 1916, staff meeting.

58. Case 830, 1913, staff meeting.

59. Case 12429, 1919, staff meeting.

60. Case 9658, 1917, staff meeting, case history.

61. LEE case 232, 1914 (this man's wife was Emerson's patient; he agreed to meet with Emerson, who characterized him as a "slightly bulging-eyed sensualist"). Within a week, the wife was reporting to Emerson, as he wrote in his notes, that "she and her husband talked abt. it i.e. (sex) now and he was entirely changed. He said he used to think it was only just for pleasure."

62. Quotation from Emerson, "Severe Case of Hysteria," p. 388.

63. LEE case 87, 1912. The first time she had intercourse, she told Emerson, she "was in a state of sort of exaltation and knew nothing about it til it was all over."

64. Emerson, "Case Report of a Mathematician."

65. Case 12429, 1919, staff meeting.

66. Myerson, for example, recognized this in his comment on Jean Swift: "She is perhaps a woman who has more or less intense sexual feelings, and the husband has shown some reluctance to gratify them" (case 830, 1913, staff meeting).

67. LEE case 37, 1912.

68. LEE case 240, 1915. Emerson noted that this thirty-five-year-old woman, who had worked as a stenographer and a typewriter (as typists were sometimes called) and who had consulted him complaining of "painful coitus since marriage," looked "like [the] typical Boston blue-stocking." Other married women told Emerson of similar experiences with sex.

69. Emerson typically saw the men who consulted him solely to discuss coitus interruptus for one or two hours at most: LEE cases 28, 1912 ("wore a safe at first, till it was broken and got into trouble"—his wife became pregnant and had an abortion); 33, 1912 ("was told to sublimate his energies"); and several others. Some of these men were from the middle class (a bar owner, for example); others from the working class—a fireman. For a medical condemnation (and corresponding advocacy of "normal" sexual practices), see William J. Robinson, "Coitus Interruptus as a Cause of Impotence and Neurasthenia," *American Journal of Clinical Medicine* 19 (1912): 1180–82.

70. Case 4284, 1915, social service record. Cf. Eli Zaretsky, "Female Sexuality and the Catholic Confessional: Archives" *Signs* 6, no. 1 (1980): 176–84.

71. Myerson, *Nervous Housewife*, pp. 126–40; quotations from pp. 15, 140. On birth control, see Linda Gordon, *Woman's Body, Woman's Right: A Social History of Birth Control in America* (New York, 1976); James Reed, *The Birth Control Movement and American Society: From Private Vice to Public Virtue* (Princeton, 1984); and Wilson Yates, "Birth Control Literature and the Medical Profession in Nineteenth Century America," *Journal of the History of Medicine*

and Allied Sciences 31 (1976): 42–54. Myerson, *Social Psychology*, wrote that "while for an unreflective, egoistic male a satisfactory culmination of the sexual relationship for himself is all that he seeks, in a truly social sexual relationship a similar climax is sought by the male for the female" (p. 481).

72. Psychiatrists' thinking regarding sex appears to have been more liberal than that of their medical colleagues; see, for example, John B. Watson and K. S. Lashley, "A Consensus of Medical Opinion upon Questions Relating to Sex Education and Venereal Disease Campaigns," *Mental Hygiene* 4 (1920): 769–847, which contrasts the views of psychiatrists (a number of Psychopathic Hospital practitioners among them) to gynecologists and genito-urinary surgeons. A growing sexological literature promoted positions similar to those of psychiatrists, attacking sexual ignorance and advocating frankness and female fulfillment. For several examples among many, see Ralph St. J. Perry, "Sexual Hunger as a Factor in the Diseases of Women," *American Journal of Dermatology and Genito-Urinary Disease* 3 (1899): 5–8; J. A. DeArmand, "Women as Sexual Nondescripts," *St. Louis Medical Era* 12 (1902–1903): 152–57; C. W. Malchow, "Unequalized Sexual Sense and Development the Great Cause of Domestic Infelicity and Nervousness in Women," *Northwestern Lancet* 23 (1903): 64–68; and J. Rutgers, "Sexual Continence, with Special Reference to Sexual Continence in Women," *Journal of Sexology and Psychoanalysis* 1 (1923): 267–73. A large medical literature outlined the modern sexual problem; see, for example, Frederick R. Sturgis, "Sexual Incompetence: Causes and Treatment," *American Physician* 7 (1907): 61–63, 101–3; Sturgis, "Notes and Reflections on the Causes which Induce Marital Infelicity Due to the Relations of the Sexes," *American Physician* 7 (1907): 125–29, 163–65, 233–36, 269–71—a series of explicit articles, made available in pamphlet form for sale to physicians only ("Subscriptions from the laity are not received").

73. Emerson, "The Psychopathology of the Family," *Journal of Abnormal Psychology* 9 (1914–1915): 333.

74. LEE case 223, 1914. "Sexual thoughts at night of men etc.," the case ends.

75. Katherine Bement Davis, *Factors in the Sex Life of Twenty-Two Hundred Women* (New York, 1929); Alfred C. Kinsey, Wardell B. Pomeroy, Clyde E. Martin, and Paul H. Gebhard, *Sexual Behavior in the Human Female* (Philadelphia, 1953); William H. Masters and Virginia E. Johnson, *Human Sexual Response* (Boston, 1966). Among other important sexological works are G. V. Hamilton, *A Research in Marriage* (1929; reprint, New York, 1986); Robert Latou Dickinson and Lura Beam, *A Thousand Marriages: A Medical Study of Sex Adjustment* (Baltimore, 1931); and Dickinson and Beam, *The Single Woman: A Medical Study in Sex Education* (1934; reprint, New York, 1987).

76. Quotation from Dickinson and Beam, *Thousand Marriages*, p. 367.

77. Myerson, *Nervous Housewife*, p. 216.

78. Social workers were alert enough to the possibilities raised by this scenario to urge one man, who had taken custody of his children away from his wife and had hired a "young, American born, and attractive" housekeeper to care for them, to "have one less young just to avoid talk for the children's sakes." A week later, a social worker wrote to him, noting in his record that in the letter "the young attractive housekeeper is again alluded to" (case 6303, 1916, social service record).

79. Case 7889, 1916, social service record. The social worker wrote: "Patient

[Mrs. Kelly] did not care particularly for her husband but she did not like to be put in a position where people talked about her and sympathized with her on account of his going with other women."

80. Case 830, 1913, case history.

81. LEE case 92, 1912.

82. LEE case 225, 1914.

83. LEE case 87, 1912. Years after the incident, she told of a dream in which she "was chopping vegetables and unwittingly cut off the head of a meaty [?] green worm. The worm was not killed, however, and followed her about all the time." Emerson linked the worm to the woman, about whom she was thinking before retiring for the night.

84. Case 7489, 1916, case history.

85. LEE case 35, 1911.

86. LEE case 266, 1915.

87. Case 10168, 1918, case history, staff meeting.

88. Case 6902, 1916, staff meeting.

89. LEE case 253, 1915.

90. LEE case 227, 1914.

91. LEE case 240, 1914.

92. Emerson, "Case Report of a Female Patient" (1912), Emerson Papers (Wilcox was a patient at the Psychopathic Hospital). Six weeks later, Emerson wrote in his notes: "Wanted me to tell her she could go back to that doctor and not get sick from it [the woman manifested hysterical symptoms]. Thinks I have a great influence over her and if I tell her she could, she could. Übertragung [the transference] discussed some." Two days later: "Uebertragung discussed more."

93. LEE case 89, 1912.

94. Kinsey et al., Human Female, pp. 422–23, estimated that 22 percent of married women born before 1900 had engaged in extramarital sex by the time they were forty years of age. The hospital population was older than Kinsey's oldest population, and it is likely that the proportion of the former that engaged in extramarital sex was smaller than that of the latter. Kinsey estimated that approximately half of all married men had engaged in extramarital sex (Kinsey, Pomeroy, and Martin, Sexual Behavior in the Human Male, p. 585).

95. Case 1111, 1913, staff meeting.

96. Case 8347, 1917, staff meeting.

97. Case 6813, 1916, staff meeting.

98. Case 7489, 1916, social service record.

99. Case 9617, 1917, letter to social worker.

100. Case 830, 1913, staff meeting.

101. Case 12960, staff meeting.

102. Southard, "Individual versus the Family," p. 440.

103. Case 10369, 1918, staff meeting.

104. Case 3650, 1914, social service record.

105. Case 4284, 1915, social service record.

106. Southard and Jarrett, Kingdom of Evils, p. 266.

107. Case 6682, 1915 (case under supervision from 1915 until 1918), social service record.

108. Case 9617, 1917, letter from social worker.
109. Case 2537, 1914, social service record.
110. Case 9617, 1917, staff meeting, social service record.
111. Ibid.
112. Case 6682, 1916, social service record.
113. Case 3650, 1914, social service record, letter from lawyer to Southard.
114. Consider, for example, that in the case of Frank Grant, who had been arrested several times before going to the hospital, they wrote to another agency seeking "clues as to the wife's character" (case 10471, 1918, letter from social workers).
115. Case 3650, 1914.
116. Southard and Jarrett, *Kingdom of Evils*, pp. 161–64.
117. Case 7889, 1916, social service record.
118. Case 5306, 1915, social service record.
119. Case 7889, 1916, social service record.
120. Case 4284, 1915, social service record.
121. Cases 9617, 1917; and 5879, 1915, social service records.
122. Cases 5306, 1915, social service record; and 4198, 1914, staff meeting.
123. Case 6682, 1916, social service record.
124. Case 9617, 1917, social service record. "Whenever I receive letters from that Hospital my husband insults me," she wrote on another occasion. "It is very hard for me at my age."
125. Case 10471, 1918, letter from social worker to Associated Charities of Taunton, Mass.
126. Case 6153, 1915, social service record.
127. Myerson, *Nervous Housewife*, p. 131. I thank Christopher Lasch for helping me formulate the ideas in this paragraph.

ELEVEN: WOMEN, ALONE AND TOGETHER

1. See, for example, Nancy Sahli, "Smashing: Women's Relationships before the Fall," *Chrysalis* 8 (Summer 1979): 17–27; Simmons, "Companionate Marriage"; Lillian Faderman, *Surpassing the Love of Men: Romantic Friendship and Love between Women from the Renaissance to the Present* (New York, 1981), esp. pp. 297–331; and Chauncey, "Sexual Inversion to Homosexuality." John D'Emilio, "Capitalism and Gay Identity," in Snitow, Stansell, and Thompson, *Powers of Desire*, pp. 100–113, argues that the ability to live independently was a precondition for the formation of lesbian and gay identities.
2. Chauncey's invocation of "the nature and purposes of the medical profession" to account for the redefinition of female sexual deviance he outlines is representative of historians' tendency to cast the field of sexology—which included medical doctors, psychiatrists, and a number of Ph.D.-holding social scientists—as a unified whole ("Sexual Inversion to Homosexuality," p. 128). The medical doctors whose alarmist and hostile pronouncements historians have put to such good use— those quoted by Sahli, Simmons, and Chauncey, for example—were one part of the sexological tradition, but many of them were little more than cranks whose legacy within sexology was minimal (Carroll Smith-Rosenberg, "The New Woman as

Androgyne: Social Disorder and Gender Crisis, 1870–1936," in *Disorderly Conduct*, p. 283, characterizes them as "conservative popularizers of sexology"). The importance of these commentators lies in the uses to which their pronouncements were put by those who mounted a broad attack on lesbianism in the twenties; this hostile strain found continuing expression in such popular works as Frederick Lundberg and Marynia F. Farnham, *Modern Woman: The Lost Sex* (New York, 1947). Sexologists such as Katherine Bement Davis and Robert Latou Dickinson and Lura Beam were working *against* popular, hostile conceptions of lesbianism just as these were gaining ascendancy in the twenties. Within the sexological tradition, a tradition that historians have invoked but have neither explored nor specified adequately, these popularizers were invisible. The sexological mainstream can be traced from Richard von Krafft-Ebing and Havelock Ellis in the late nineteenth century, through the early Freudians on the one hand and the sociologists of sexual practice (G. V. Hamilton, Dickinson and Beam, and, most importantly, Katherine Bement Davis) on the other in the period from about 1900 through 1930, to Kinsey and his associates in the forties and fifties; it was as much the work of sociologists as of psychiatrists. There was much that was hostile to homosexuality in it (although it is worth noting that the *sexuality* of male homosexuality was always more vigorously condemned than the *sexuality* of lesbianism, the abhorrence of male abomination so historically ingrained that it continued to outweigh even the most conservative of moralists' abhorrence of female sex perversion); but there was much that was not. For the most part, historians have overlooked the alternative strain in this sexological tradition. Faderman, for example, discusses the studies of Davis and Dickinson and Beam, but she sees them as mere chroniclers outside the tradition, which is, to her mind, solely a medical one: *Surpassing*, pp. 325–27. Ronald Bayer, *Homosexuality and American Psychiatry: The Politics of Diagnosis* (Princeton, 1987), pp. 42–46, contrasts Alfred Kinsey's tolerant stance on homosexuality to the intolerance of the "psychiatric orthodoxy" but wholly overlooks—because he focuses on male homosexuality to the exclusion of lesbianism—the work of the 1920s sexologists, especially Davis, whose *Factors in the Sex Life* did for lesbianism what Kinsey did for male homosexuality: namely, demonstrate sociologically its prevalence and argue for its normality.

The story of female and male homosexuality is quite different, and the history of the former cannot be inferred from that of the latter; the lesbian remained more indistinct than the male homosexual throughout the period under consideration.

3. The legacy of Freud on bisexuality is mixed, leading on the one hand to condemnations of lesbianism as indicative of arrested development but justifying, on the other, tolerance of "youthful" (a category that sexologists would interpret quite broadly) lesbian interest and activity as within the broad range of the normal. Sexologists who looked without alarm on lesbianism would, throughout the twentieth century, invoke Freud in support of their stance.

4. Smith-Rosenberg has made this argument most recently: "New Woman as Androgyne," pp. 275 ff. Her classic essay "The Female World of Love and Ritual: Relations between Women in Nineteenth-Century America," which originally appeared in 1975 (*Signs*, vol. 1) and is reprinted in *Disorderly Conduct*, is the starting point for any discussion of woman's sphere.

5. For evidence of the narrowing, compare, for example, Davis's posing the issue

in terms of "strong emotional attraction" with Lewis M. Terman's interest in "overt homosexuality" (although he did attempt to measure "degree of homosexual feeling"): Terman, *Psychological Factors in Marital Happiness* (New York, 1938), pp. 342–43. But consider also Davis's attempt to differentiate between women's "intense emotional relations with women unassociated with consciousness of a sex experience" and involving only hugging or kissing and the same sort of relationships "accompanied by mutual masturbation, contact of genital organs, or other physical expressions recognized as sexual in character." Few nineteenth-century observers would have attempted such a distinction, for it was predicated on the establishment of women's capacity for sexual aggressiveness; the very conception of the second sort of lesbian relationship is significant (*Factors in the Sex Life*, p. 247, table 2).

6. Smith-Rosenberg cautions that the question of whether or not these women had genital contact anachronistically reads back into Victorian innocence a twentieth-century concern with identifying and classifying female homosexuality, but throughout "Female World" she stresses the "sensual and physical explicitness" of these women's writings (p. 59)—precisely what historians have found so vexedly compelling.

7. Christine Stansell, "Revisiting the Angel in the House: Revisions of Victorian Womanhood," *New England Quarterly* 60 (1987): 466–83.

8. Dickinson and Beam, *Single Woman*, pp. 203–22; quotation from p. 210. The cases on which the book is based are drawn from the first author's forty-year practice in gynecology, from 1880 to 1920; it is likely that the women were telling of late-nineteenth-century experience. Of approximately 350 single women for whom sexual histories were available, Beam judged 28 homosexual; in 18 of these cases, she found evidence of sexual activity (in contrast to the 10 cases in which she found evidence of companionship with women friends over a period of years).

9. This is a conservative estimate, derived from Davis's finding that 242 of 1,000 women she studied had engaged in youthful sex play (*Factors in the Sex Life*, pp. 56–58). Kinsey's estimates were higher. He reported that 30 percent of 8,000 women studied recalled engaging in preadolescent heterosexual play and 33 percent in preadolescent homosexual play. He stated that these estimates were in all likelihood low, adult women having recalled but a portion of their early sexual experience; he also noted that the percentages of women involved in any sort of preadolescent sex play had increased in the years covered by his sample, some 10 percent more of women born between 1910 and 1919 than those born before 1900 recalling such sex play (Kinsey et al., *Human Female*, pp. 107–10).

10. Kinsey reported that 61 percent of the women who had engaged in any preadolescent homosexual play did so for only a single year, and in many cases only once or twice (Kinsey et al., *Human Female*, p. 114).

11. LEE case 237, 1914; Emerson, "Case Report of a Female Patient"; case 577, 1912.

12. LEE case 232, 1914. Kinsey found that only 5 percent of girls who had engaged in preadolescent homosexual play continued this into adolescence (Kinsey et al., *Human Female*, pp. 113–15). Other cases of preadolescent sex play appear in the literature; see, for example, Dickinson and Beam, *Single Woman*, for the case of

an eighteen-year-old who told the physician that she and two playmates "used to fool with each other and massage each other, two fingers up each other's vagina" (pp. 215–16); and the case of a college woman who told of being aroused at twelve "by loving other girls, not sleeping together, but general caressing" (p. 216).

13. On the crush, see Sahli, "Smashing."

14. Case 10065, 1917, autobiographical account.

15. Case 8111, 1917, staff meeting.

16. Quotation from Charles A. Ford, "Homosexual Practices of Institutionalized Females," *Journal of Abnormal and Social Psychology* 23 (1928–1929): 446. Cf. also Davis, *Factors in the Sex Life,* p. 245, writing that she believed homosexual relations in educational and penal settings were "much more widespread than is generally suspected, or than most administrators are willing to admit"; Margaret Otis, "A Perversion Not Commonly Noted," *Journal of Abnormal Psychology* 8 (1913–1914): 113–16, which takes a darker view; and Spaulding, *Experimental Study.* One thirty-three-year-old woman, a patient of Emerson's, told him of her institutional experience: "One of the patients put her hand on her shoulder, saying, 'Oh, you are so sweet,' and caressed her down her breasts, last night in the spray bath, and it instantly sent her into an ecstatical thrill of bliss, as if she had risen into the seventh heaven of delight." "I never expected to have such feelings again," she told the psychoanalyst (LEE case 227, 1914).

17. Whereas middle-class schoolgirls and college students exchanged, in one classic account of the crush, bouquets, "tinted notes," packets of candies, and locks of hair (Sahli, "Smashing," p. 21), the institutionalized girls in another account exchanged heavily embroidered brassieres and wrote explicitly sexual notes to one another: "You can take my tie/You can take my coller/But I'll jazze you/'Till you holler," wrote one young black woman to her white friend, continuing, "Honey If you love me you will brake out your dam door and come an sleep with me and angle face if I could sleep with you I would not only hough and kiss you. But I will not take time to write it for I guess you can read between the lines" (Ford, "Homosexual Practices," p. 444).

18. Duberman, "'I Am Not Contented,'" pp. 831–33. The woman whom I call Clark was a patient at the Psychopathic Hospital; more information on her can be found in her hospital record and in Emerson's extensive notes on her case.

19. LEE case 38, 1912, and Emerson, "Hystero-Epilepsy," p. 320.

20. Case 5744, 1915, staff meeting.

21. Case 8111, 1917, case report and staff meeting. On the mannish lesbian, see Esther Newton, "The Mythic Mannish Lesbian: Radclyffe Hall and the New Woman," *Signs* 9, no. 4 (1984): 557–75. Kinsey et al., *Human Female,* p. 476, cite several references to turn-of-the-century lesbian clubs and bars. Evidence documenting these communities is scanty and incomplete; Vern Bullough and Bonnie Bullough found, for example, that Salt Lake City lesbians in the twenties and thirties kept their identities hidden and thought of themselves, for the most part, as respectable women. The larger society was, it seems, entirely unaware of the lesbians in its midst ("Lesbianism in the 1920s and 1930s: A Newfound Study," *Signs* 2, no. 4 [1977]: 895–904).

22. Case 6153, 1916, case history and social service record. W. J. Rhodes, who

oversaw Brown's temporary employment at the Carter's Ink factory, wrote to Helen Anderson that "the feminine in her needs very considerable tonic doses. . . . she is altogether an unprepossessing proposition. If there is any way you can revive the feminine pride in her you will do more good than can possibly be expressed." Anderson replied that she would do what she could to improve Brown's personal appearance (case 6153 [correspondence in case 3868], 1916).

23. See Martha Vicinus, *Independent Women: Work and Community for Single Women, 1850–1920* (Chicago, 1985), for a collective portrait of middle-class English single women.

24. Meyerowitz, *Women Adrift*, examines single working women's urban existence. My portrait here is based on 150 to 200 letters between social workers and single women patients, and approximately five hundred pages of social work documentation of their lives. Most attempts to chronicle the lives of adult single women have focused on the middle class, in part because middle-class women articulated and celebrated a vision of "single blessedness" and sisterhood that historians of women have put back into the historical record, but also in part because nineteenth-century contemporaries of these women, as they worried about the unmarried daughters of the middle class, linked being single—to them a sad fate—to autonomy, a more ambiguous lot that historians of women have rightly ennobled. See, for example, Lee Virginia Chambers-Schiller, *Liberty, A Better Husband: Single Women in America, the Generations of 1780–1840* (New Haven, 1984), and Vicinus, *Independent Women*. Cf. Stansell, "Revisiting the Angel," which recasts the lot of single middle-class women, bringing out just how unhappy a story Vicinus actually tells.

Historians' near-exclusive focus on middle-class women has led to something of a misreading of the connections among independence, autonomy, and the emergence of lesbianism in the early twentieth century. In the nineteenth century, these concerns were class-specific, the adult working-class single woman calling forth a different sort of critique. In the twentieth century, as it became possible for women with at least some high school education to enter white-collar occupations (but to retain at the same time their sense of themselves as working—not college—women), these same concerns about independence, autonomy, and sexuality (lesbian or heterosexual) focused on a more diverse group of women. A range of early-twentieth-century commentators discerned evidence of untoward female independence in heterosexual as well as homosexual activities. Historians writing from the perspective of the nineteenth century have missed this, and have cast the "New Woman"—who came to embody these concerns about autonomy and sexuality—as middle-class and lesbian. See, for example, Chambers-Schiller, who assumes that single women are lesbian, married women heterosexual (*Liberty*, pp. 190–204); and Smith-Rosenberg, "New Woman as Androgyne," which for the most part overlooks the heterosexual side of New Womanhood.

25. Rose Butler wrote to social worker Helen Anderson that upon nearing the YWCA, which was to be her home, she could think only of "State's Prison" (case 5380, 1915).

26. Case 8359, 1917, letter to social worker.

27. Case 6964, 1915, letter to social worker.

28. Case 5830, 1915, letters to social workers.

29. Anderson did this for a twenty-seven-year-old domestic worker whom she judged had not had enough "excitement or diversion" (case 7311, 1917, staff meeting).

30. Case 5830, 1915, social service record.

31. Case 6535, 1916, letter to social worker.

32. Southard and Jarrett, *Kingdom of Evils*, p. 77.

33. Case 5744, 1915, letter to social worker.

34. Emerson, "Case Report of a Female Patient."

35. Case 5830, 1915, letter to social worker.

36. Case 7311, 1916, letter to Anderson.

37. Southard and Jarrett, *Kingdom of Evils*, p. 548.

38. Case 8359, 1917, letters to social worker's assistant and to Helen Anderson.

39. Case 7311, 1916, letters to Anderson.

40. Case 6535, 1915, letter to social worker.

41. Case 7345, 1918.

42. Case 6535, 1916, letters to Jarrett.

43. Ibid., letters to Jarrett and social worker Hodge. Two years later Hancock was still struggling with the ambiguities of her relationship with Jarrett. "I love you dearly and sincerely, but, oh, I do so hate being a case," she wrote. "Please don't ask me to see another social worker, you know very well we can't be friends. That is as one considers friends, and I simply can't talk to a comparative stranger, even if she has, by reading, become familiar with my case."

44. Case 5830, 1915, letter to Jarrett.

45. Southard and Jarrett, *Kingdom of Evils*, p. 547.

CONCLUSION

1. Thomas W. Salmon, as quoted by Deutsch, *Mentally Ill in America*, p. 272; Deutsch did not cite his source for this comment, which apparently was, however, well known. Menninger, *Psychiatry*, p. 17, repeated it (again, without citation) with an interesting twist, writing that Salmon was "credited with having described World War I as playing Prince Charming to the medical Cinderella, psychiatry."

2. Rue L. Cromwell, "Attention and Information Processing: A Foundation for Understanding Schizophrenia?" in Lyman C. Wynne, Rue L. Cromwell, and Steven Matthysse, *The Nature of Schizophrenia: New Approaches to Research and Treatment* (New York, 1978), p. 219, cited in Sander L. Gilman, "Why Is Schizophrenia 'Bizarre,'" p. 135. Southard and Jarrett, *Kingdom of Evils*, pp. 392–93, registered and applauded the shift from degenerate to deviate.

3. Works falling under this rubric include L. Wallingford Darrah, "The Difficulties of Being 'Normal,'" *Journal of Nervous and Mental Disease* 90 (1939): 730–37; Cantor, "What Is a Normal Mind?"; Hacker, "Concept of Normality"; David Freides, "Toward the Elimination of the Concept of Normality," *Journal of Consulting Psychology* 24 (1960): 128–33; and Edmond A. Murphy, "The Epistemology of Normality," *Psychological Medicine* 9 (1979): 409–15.

4. Sabshin, "Psychiatric Perspectives," briefly outlines psychiatrists' divergent approaches; Murphy, "Epistemology of Normality," obliquely expresses his desire

for a unidimensional normality, complaining that too many had drawn from the Kinsey reports the conclusion "that such and such practices are not abnormal (despite the most explicit statement from the authors that they were attempting to make no normative inferences)" (p. 414). As this work has suggested, in the psychiatric domain the evaluative and descriptive dimensions of the normal were woven together from the start.

5. Hacker, "Concept of Normality," p. 48.

6. Menninger, *Psychiatry*, p. 3.

7. Ibid.; and William C. Menninger and Munro Leaf, *You and Psychiatry* (New York, 1948), p. viii.

8. Grob, *Inner World*, p. 11.

9. Interview with Solomon, September 1980.

10. See William E. Narrow et al., "Use of Services by Persons with Mental and Addictive Disorders: Findings from the National Institute of Mental Health Epidemiologic Catchment Area Program, " *Archives of General Psychiatry* 50 (1993): 95–107.

11. Cantor, "What Is a Normal Mind?" p. 682.

12. Case 4342, 1914, letter to Southard.

APPENDIX

1. All Boston population figures appearing in the text and tables of this book are derived from the *Population* volumes of the 1910 and 1920 federal decennial census; these data are presumably complete but their usefulness is limited by their presentation in two- and three-way cross-classified tables. All statistics concerning the hospital population are drawn from a simple random sample of 1,290 cases (from a total population of 17,000 admissions in the period from 1912 to 1921), yielding 1,130 first admissions that I coded on approximately fifty demographic, behavioral, procedural, and outcome variables. Comparison of sample and population proportions, estimated from figures published in the hospital's *Annual Reports*, demonstrated that the sample provided good estimates of population parameters. I have adjusted the hospital sample for each comparison to include only those patients resident in Boston or Suffolk County, depending on the corresponding census figures. Numbers in the hospital sample vary with the number of patients for whom information on the variable under consideration was available. In every instance I have compared the distribution of Boston and Suffolk County residents to that of the rest of the sample and have found that they do not differ, using chi-square tests of significance.

The classification of patients into historically and analytically meaningful racial, ethnic, and nativity categories was subject to several considerations. First, the need to keep up cell frequencies determined several choices. Because the sample yielded too few Italians ($N = 59$) and African-Americans ($N = 47$) to constitute discrete groups for multivariate analysis, in doing such analyses I classed both groups according to nativity. In addition, I deliberately conflated religion, ethnicity, and nativity to create categories contemporaries would have found meaningful. The categories employed throughout the book are as follows:

Irish ($N = 322$; 29 percent of all patients): persons either born in Ireland or with at least one parent born in Ireland; *Jewish* ($N = 97$; 9 percent): those for whom religion was recorded as "Jewish"; *WASP* (*N* = 135; 12 percent): native-born Protestants of native-born parents; *Other native-born* (*N* = 297; 26 percent): all others born in the United States (African-Americans make up 13 percent of this group); *Foreign-born, Canada, and the U.K.* (except Ireland) (*N* = 115; 10 percent); and *Other foreign-born* (*N* = 156; 14 percent): persons of Scandinavian, Russian, Polish, Italian, Greek, German, Austrian, and Asian origin.

2. Fox, *So Far Disordered in Mind*, chap. 5. Fox draws different conclusions from his data than I have from mine, but it is worth noting that the population of persons committed for insanity that he studied differs less (especially with respect to its occupational makeup) from the general population from which it was drawn when the effects of sampling are taken into account.

3. In the vast social-psychiatric literature dating from the late thirties, class was measured by occupational position, and mental disease by hospital admission or treatment by a psychiatrist. Among the most important of the standard works are Robert E. L. Faris and H. Warren Dunham, *Mental Disorders in Urban Areas: An Ecological Study of Schizophrenia and Other Psychoses* (Chicago, 1939); A. B. Hollingshead and F. C. Redlich, *Social Class and Mental Illness: A Community Study* (New York, 1958); and Leo Srole, T. S. Langer, S. T. Michael, M. K. Opler, and T. A. C. Rennie, *Mental Health in the Metropolis* (New York, 1962).

4. For this study, I developed a coding scheme with reference to Alba M. Edwards's 1930 occupational classification ("A Social Economic Grouping of the Gainful Workers of the United States," *Journal of the American Statistical Association* 28 [1933]: 377–87) and the modifications made by the Census Bureau and by Stephan Thernstrom (*The Other Bostonians: Poverty and Progress in an American Metropolis, 1880–1970* [Cambridge, Mass., 1973]). I used Edwards's six broad vertical categories (see table A.4); to these I added a seventh for housewives and for "housework, unspecified," and an eighth for such unclassifiable occupations as "wanderer," "poor," and "state charge." Following Thernstrom I merged the service groups that the Census Bureau had added to Edwards's original classifications back into their original vertical positions. On the classification of occupations, see also Joel Perlmann, *Ethnic Differences: Schooling and Social Structure among the Irish, Italians, Jews, and Blacks in an American City, 1880–1935* (Cambridge, 1988), pp. 13–42, 244–46.

5. In addition, census enumerators and psychiatrists did not consistently distinguish between housewives and women who did housework in others' homes. The hospital sample yielded 270 women who did not work for wages outside the home whom psychiatrists had classified variously as "housewife" (*N* = 137; 51 percent); "at home" (*N* = 23; 9 percent); "housework at home" (*N* = 1; 0.4 percent); "housework"—not specified but which I judged from the context was more likely in their own homes than for wages (*N* = 63; 24 percent); "none"—which in virtually all instances signified no wage-work but plenty of housework (*N* = 46; 17 percent). The compilers of the Fourteenth Census warned that so many servants and housewives were classed under the rubric "housekeepers" as to render their statistics inaccurate (U.S. Bureau of the Census, *Fourteenth Census of the United States*, vol. 1, *Population* [Washington, D.C., 1922], p. 17).

6. Thernstrom, *Other Bostonians*, pp. 293–94, lists the criteria sociologists have used to establish the relative rankings of occupations.

7. Furbush, "Social Facts," p. 594. Furbush hinted that her percentages over-

stated the causal role of marriage, suggesting that the proportion of male patients who were single was swelled by the large numbers of young (and overwhelmingly male) dementia praecox patients, and that the proportion of women who were married was similarly skewed because women marry earlier than men.

8. Fox, *So Far Disordered in Mind*, pp. 86–89, for example, writes as though he is comparing those persons the police committed to asylums to the general San Francisco population, when in fact he is looking within the group of those committed and asking who was more likely to have been committed by the police than by any other means. I have posed the question along the lines that Hollingshead and Redlich did, in *Social Class and Mental Illness*. They examined paths to the psychiatrist in New Haven, attempting to identify every city resident in treatment, whether public or private, and asking how routes to treatment varied with class and race. They found that lower-class persons were more likely than higher-class persons to have ended up in treatment as a result of police or other official action.

9. I used log-linear techniques to perform all the multivariate analyses in this book. Log-linear analysis provides a means for describing and testing the relationships among variables in multidimensional contingency tables. Chapter 5, note 130, explains how a typical table might be read; Yvonne M. M. Bishop, Stephen E. Fienberg, and Paul W. Holland, *Discrete Multivariate Analysis: Theory and Practice* (Cambridge, Mass., 1975), is a standard reference on log-linear techniques.

INDEX

References to figures and tables are printed in italic type.

Southard, Elmer Ernest (*cont.*)
347n.22; Karl Menninger and, 340n.32, 368–69n.3; on mental tests, 55, 348nn. 35, 36, 352n.71; Adolf Meyer and, 334n.56; on neurology, 336n.9; professional ambitions of, 28–32; on psychiatry of everyday life, 46, 81; on psychoanalysis, 178, 179, 180–81, 225; psychopathic hospital idea and, 94–95; on psychopathy, 66, 67; on racial morality, 205; on religious problems, 359n.133; on science of psychiatry, 345–46n.10; on self-disclosure, 138–39, 141; on social work, 38–40, 42, 159; on syphilis, 50, 52, 126, 346n.19; on temporary care patients, 90; time at Harvard, 30–31; on treatment, 176, 177; use of language, 368n.2; on voluntary admission, 81–82, 84, 86, 87; on women, 232–33
Spaulding, Edith R., 342n.60
staff meeting: description of, 135–36; establishment of, 374n.71; function of, 155
Stansell, Christine, 37, 295
State Industrial School at Lancaster, 196
Stearns, A. Warren, 20, 104, 136
stenography, case documentation and, 132
stillbirths, in turn-of-the-century Boston, 16
Susman, Warren, on character, 68–69
symptoms: interpretation of psychiatric, 142–43; medical vs. psychiatric, 118–19, 133, 145
syphilis: diagnosis of, 126–27; lumbar puncture and, 164; moral issues surrounding, 346–47nn. 17, 19, 20, 21. *See also* venereal disease
syphilology: disease paradigm and, 48; modern psychiatric science and, 49–54, 55, 116–17, 119; privacy and, 51–52, 106–7
Szasz, Thomas, 327n.3

Taft, Annie, 36
Taft, Jessie, 162
talk: as psychiatric treatment, 177–81; women and, 265–68
technology: effect on psychiatric casework, 160; in turn-of-the-century Boston, 330–31n.14

temporary care laws: police power and, 95–96; voluntary admission and, 89–90, 93
temporary patients: psychopathic hospital idea and, 94–95; voluntary patients vs., 89. *See also* patients
Terman, Lewis M.: on integration of life and science, 59; use of mental tests by, 54, 57
Textbook (Kraepelin), 118
therapeutic bath, 176
therapy. *See* psychotherapy
Thom, Douglas A., 20
Three Essays on the Theory of Sexuality (Freud), 24
transference: onto social workers, 300–305; psychoanalysis and, 224–25; psychopathy and, 354n.89
treatment, psychiatric, 171, 175–81
Tryon, Geneva, 36

venereal disease: male sexual development and, 235; morality and, 346n.17. *See also* syphilis
Victorianism: domestic violence and, 102; gender system of, 308; male infidelity and, 275; marital sex and, 270–71; marriage and, 256; psychiatric reversal of, 188; psychiatrists' critique of, 72–73, 75, 138, 211; sexual, 214; waning of, in turn-of-the-century Boston, 20; women's sexuality and, 293, 295
violence: domestic, 102–7, 245–46, 248; at Psychopathic Hospital, 170–71. *See also* sexual abuse
visibility, at Psychopathic Hospital, 154
voluntary admission: laws surrounding, 87–90, 360nn. 7, 9, 10, 11, 360–61 n.12; psychiatric commitment vs., 81–82, 84, 360n.7, 363nn. 40, 42; to psychiatric hospitals, 83–96, 359n.3. *See also* commitment
voluntary patients: early admission of, 83; legal rights of, 87–90; psychiatric commitment of, 363n.40; temporary patients vs., 89. *See also* patients

war: male psychopathy during, 253–55; psychiatric social work and, 42–43
Wassermann diagnostic test, 50, 55, 126–27, 151